Robert Wade

Douglas Smith is an award-winning historian and translator and the author of *Former People*, *Rasputin*, and other books
on Russia. Before becoming a historian, he worked for the
U.S. State Department in the Soviet Union and as a Russian
affairs analyst for Radio Free Europe/Radio Liberty in Munich.
He lives in Seattle with his wife and two children.

ALSO BY DOUGLAS SMITH

Former People:
The Final Days of the Russian Aristocracy

The Pearl:
A True Tale of Forbidden Love in Catherine the Great's Russia

Love and Conquest:
Personal Correspondence of Catherine the Great and Prince Grigory Potemkin
(editor and translator)

Working the Rough Stone:
Freemasonry and Society in Eighteenth-Century Russia

Additional Praise for *Rasputin*

"Douglas Smith has delivered the definitive biography [of Rasputin] that is brilliantly gripping, as hypnotic, wild, and erotic in its revelations as the Mad Monk himself, sensitive in its human portrait, astute in its political analysis, superbly researched with rich new material gathered in faraway archives, and populated with the zaniest cast of the deranged Romanovs, depraved bishops, whores, mountebanks, adventuresses, mystics, and murderers."
—Simon Sebag Montefiore,
London Evening Standard

"Powerful . . . [Douglas Smith] scoured diaries, letters, police files, and archives to create the definitive portrait of a man whose deeply held religious beliefs were often overshadowed by such debauchery and drunkenness that he's fixed in the popular imagination as the 'mad monk.' It is a masterful display of storytelling."
—Patricia Treble, *Maclean's* (Canada)

"Substantial, meticulously researched, and fluently written."
—Rodric Braithwaite, *The Observer* (UK)

"Superb and authoritative."   —Donald Rayfield, *Literary Review* (UK)

"[*Rasputin*] is by far the most comprehensive account of Rasputin to date, brimming with complexities and fascinating detail, and stands as an enlightening reevaluation of this crucial figure in Russian history."
—Helen Rappaport, *The Telegraph* (UK)

"How much does the mythology misrepresent [Rasputin]? Was everything he did bad for Russia? These are the two central questions Douglas Smith sets out to answer in this astounding biography. And he succeeds, eschewing the gossip and innuendo that have long surrounded his subject, to produce a well-rounded portrait of a complex individual."
—J. P. O'Malley, *The Mail on Sunday* (UK)

"The definitive account of Grigory Rasputin's life and times . . . Smith not only reinterprets the work of his predecessors but also provides a wealth of new information about Rasputin. . . . Far from uncovering banal reality behind Rasputin's supposed mystical talents, Smith instead explains how the man's forceful personality came to have such an impact on intelligent, learned people such as the Tsar and Tsarina. . . . Smith's book reads like a revelatory work of revisionist history, unearthing a flesh-and-blood person from a century's worth of lies and exaggerations." —Hank Stephenson, *Shelf Awareness*

"Gripping . . . A fascinating, often entertaining biography."
—Gerard DeGroot, *The Times Saturday Review* (UK)

"Utterly fascinating and forensically detailed . . . There are plenty of Rasputin biographies, but its superlative scholarship and attention to detail place this one in a class of its own." —Dominic Sandbrook, *The Sunday Times* (UK)

"[Smith] renders in great detail the ten years that Rasputin spent on the national stage, from 1906 until his murder in 1916. Sorting through the Rasputin mythology, Smith discards the apocryphal and weighs the plausible, balancing the extraordinary mix of mysticism and debauchery that made the peasant monk notorious. Digging through countless and often conflicting firsthand accounts and impressions, Smith gives Rasputin's mystique a depth and a fine edge missing from prior histories." —Robert Legvold, *Foreign Affairs*

"In this monumental and soul-shaking biography, historian and translator Douglas Smith demystifies the figure of Grigory Rasputin. . . . With a Dostoyevskian flair for noir and obsession, Smith exposes the base motivations behind Rasputin's enemies . . . [and] expertly handles the intricacies of the salacious scandals that enveloped the empire in anti-Rasputin hysteria and that eerily presaged the fall of the Romanovs in 1917. . . . Smith's depravity-laden history of turn-of-the-twentieth-century Russia hinges on his insightful readings of myth and motive, and their tragic consequences." —*Publishers Weekly* (starred review)

"[Smith] stuns with a scrupulously exhaustive biography of the monk's role in the Russian empire's fall and the rise of Bolshevism. . . . His dedication to extricating Rasputin's experience from newly available Soviet Union primary sources and international archives surpasses all previous academic works in breadth and scope. . . . Smith's study will surely be considered the seminal scholarly work on Rasputin, an essential read for students of Imperial Russia's downfall."

—Jessica Bushore, *Library Journal* (starred review)

"[An] amazingly detailed, deeply researched biography. [Douglas Smith] carefully lifts the myths away from the real story, which nevertheless is presented here as a greatly compelling picture of a figure who at the zenith of his influence was known all over Russia."

—*Booklist* (starred review)

"This brilliantly written, meticulously researched account of the life of Rasputin is the best, most complete and accurate I have ever read. Step by step, day by day, week by week, Douglas Smith tells the story from its humble beginnings, through its obscene sexual chapters, to its violent end. He describes how a peasant became 'our Friend' to the last emperor and empress of Russia. He explains why this dependency came at a terrible cost for the imperial couple, for their children, for Russia, and for the twentieth-century world. Readers will begin by saying that this is an impossible story to believe. They will read on because, in Douglas Smith's mesmerizing telling, it must be believed. And because it did happen."   —Robert K. Massie, author of *Catherine the Great*

"In his research, comprehensive to the nth degree, Douglas Smith has dug up previously unseen archives, followed previously unexplored leads, and connected the dots across the Russian landscape. They're dots of blood. Rasputin reveals the true character of the man without minimizing his malign hold on the feckless Romanovs."

—Ken Kalfus, author of *The Commissariat of Enlightenment*

"It is hard to imagine a historical figure more barnacled with myth than Rasputin. Douglas Smith unravels Rasputin's complex narrative in unprecedented detail, showing how he was a kind of chimera onto which could be hung all the ills of a disintegrating Russia. In the process, Smith vividly exposes the astonishing blindness of the ruling class that made its tragic end inevitable. A brilliant achievement."

—Rosemary Sullivan, author of *Stalin's Daughter:*
The Extraordinary and Tumultuous Life of Svetlana Alliluyeva

"In his magisterial, exhaustively researched work on Rasputin, Douglas Smith paints a rich, detailed portrait of one of history's most fascinating individuals while also chronicling the dramatic last days of the tsar. It's a wondrous read."   —Neal Bascomb, author of *The Winter Fortress: The Epic Mission to Sabotage Hitler's Atomic Bomb*

"A big book about a big figure in the demise of tsarism. Douglas Smith supplies chapter and verse on the extraordinary life of Grigory Rasputin, the éminence grise behind the Romanov throne. Without denying the salacious and corrupt ways of the 'holy man,' the book brilliantly and thoughtfully defends Rasputin against the worst of the myths that swirled around him. A tour de force."
                    —Robert Service, author of *The End of the Cold War: 1985–1991* and *Lenin: A Biography*

"The most complete and masterful study of Rasputin that I've read. Douglas Smith's work is not only extraordinarily readable, but rich in detail."   —Robert Alexander, author of *The Kitchen Boy: A Novel of the Last Tsar*

"Some years ago, when working on a historical novel, I had to read all the existing Rasputin biographies—and they do abound, in all literary styles and in many languages. What a pity that Douglas Smith's *Rasputin* had not yet been published; it would have saved me a lot of time. If you are interested in the story of the Romanovs' pet prophet, this is the book to read."   —Boris Akunin, author of *The Coronation*

"A prodigious piece of scholarship. Douglas Smith's exhaustive and forensic examination of a wealth of new and previously unseen evidence finally lays to rest the tired old myth of the 'mad monk' and rightly positions Rasputin as a crucial figure in late Imperial Russian history."
                    —Helen Rappaport, author of *The Romanov Sisters: The Lost Lives of the Daughters of Nicholas and Alexandra*

RASPUTIN

FAITH, POWER,

AND THE

TWILIGHT

OF THE

ROMANOVS

DOUGLAS SMITH

PICADOR   FARRAR, STRAUS AND GIROUX   NEW YORK

picadorusa.com • picadorbookroom.tumblr.com
twitter.com/picadorusa • facebook.com/picadorusa

Picador® is a U.S. registered trademark and is used by Macmillan Publishing Group, LLC, under license from Pan Books Limited.

For book club information, please visit facebook.com/picadorbookclub or email marketing@picadorusa.com.

Map artwork by ML Design

The Library of Congress has cataloged the Farrar, Straus and Giroux edition as follows:

Names: Smith, Douglas, 1962– author.
Title: Rasputin : faith, power, and the twilight of the Romanovs | Douglas Smith.
Description: First U.S. edition | New York: Farrar, Straus and Giroux, 2016. | Includes
   bibliographical references and index.
Identifiers: LCCN 2016027558 | ISBN 9780374240844 (hardcover) |
   ISBN 9780374711238 (ebook)
Subjects: LCSH: Rasputin, Grigoriæi Efimovich, 1869–1916. | Russia—Court and
   courtiers—Biography. | Russia—History—Nicholas II, 1894–1917. | Russia—Politics
   and government—1894–1917. | Romanov, House of. | BISAC: BIOGRAPHY &
   AUTOBIOGRAPHY / Historical. | HISTORY / Europe / Russia & the Former Soviet Union.
Classification: LCC DK254.R3 S66 2016 | DDC 947.08'3092 [B]—dc23
LC record available at https://lccn.loc.gov/2016027558

Picador Paperback ISBN 978-1-250-14126-2

Our books may be purchased in bulk for promotional, educational, or business use. Please contact your local bookseller or the Macmillan Corporate and Premium Sales Department at 1-800-221-7945, extension 5442, or by email at MacmillanSpecialMarkets@macmillan.com.

Originally published in Great Britain by Mantle, an imprint of Pan Macmillan

First published in the United States by Farrar, Straus and Giroux

First Picador Edition: November 2017

10 9 8 7 6 5 4 3 2 1

To Stephanie

And to the memory of my father,
D. William Smith
(1929–2013)

Auch behauptet man: die Tölpel,
Als sie an das Meer gelangten
Und gesehn, wie sich der Himmel
In der blauen Fluth gespiegelt,

Hätten sie geglaubt, das Meer
Sei der Himmel, und sie stürzten
Sich hinein mit Gottvertrauen;
Seien sämtlich dort ersoffen.

Heinrich Heine,
Atta Troll, Caput XII

It's also said that these fools,
Upon reaching the ocean-shore
And having seen how the sky
Was reflected in the blue tide below,

Believed that the sea
Must be Heaven, and in they plunged,
With faith in God,
And all were drowned.

Author translation, based on
Herman Scheffauer (1913)

Contents

Contents

Contents

Part Five

WAR: July 1914–1915

Part Six

THE FINAL YEAR: 1916

Contents

List of Illustrations

Maps

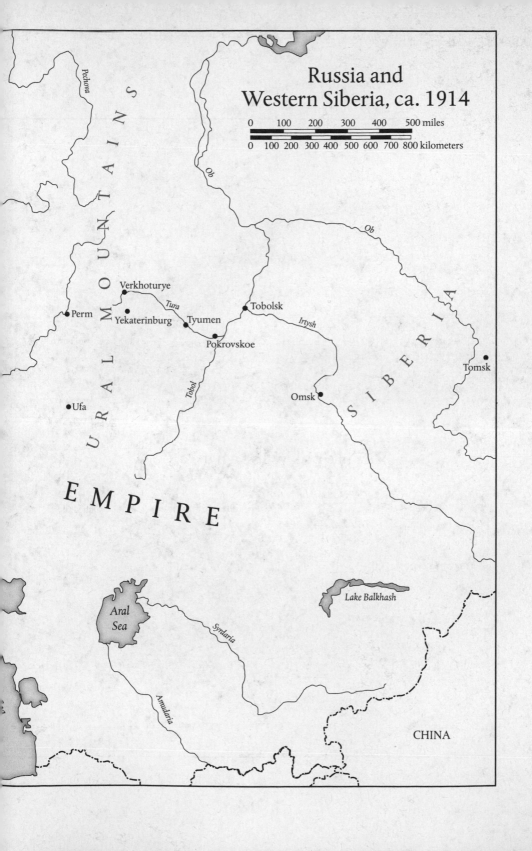

Russia and
Western Siberia, ca. 1914

0   100   200   300   400   500 miles

0   100 200 300 400 500 600 700 800 kilometers

Pechora

U R A L   M O U N T A I N S

Ob

Ob

Perm

Verkhoturye

Yekaterinburg   Tyumen

Tura

Pokrovskoe

Tobol

Tobolsk

Irtysh

S I B E R I A

Tomsk

Ufa

Omsk

E M P I R E

Aral
Sea

Syrdaria

Lake Balkhash

Amudaria

CHINA

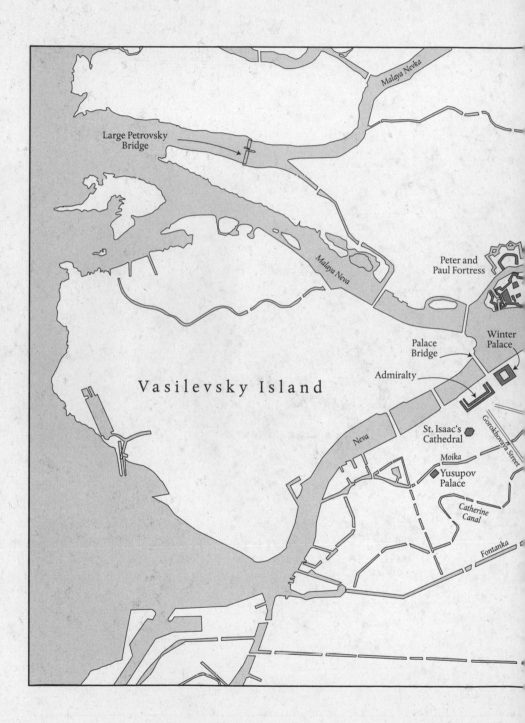

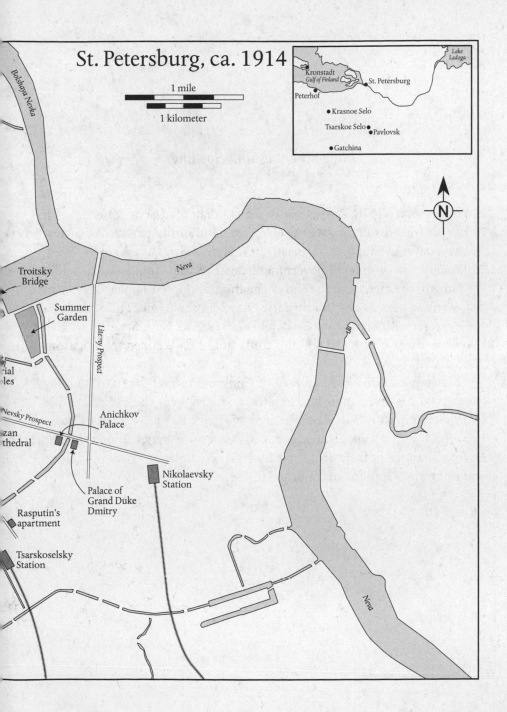

St. Petersburg, ca. 1914

1 mile

1 kilometer

Lake Ladoga

Kronstadt
Gulf of Finland
St. Petersburg
Peterhof

● Krasnoe Selo

Tsarskoe Selo ●
● Pavlovsk

● Gatchina

N

Bolshaya Nevka

Neva

Troitsky
Bridge

Summer
Garden

Literny Prospect

rial
les

Nevsky Prospect

Anichkov
Palace

zan
thedral

Palace of
Grand Duke
Dmitry

Nikolaevsky
Station

Rasputin's
apartment

Tsarskoselsky
Station

Neva

Note on Dates and Spelling

Before February 1918, Russia followed the Julian (Old Style) calendar that in the nineteenth century was twelve days (and in the twentieth century, thirteen days) behind the Gregorian (New Style) calendar used in the West. In January, the Bolshevik government decreed that Russia would adopt the Gregorian calendar at the end of the month, thus 31 January 1918 was followed the next day by 14 February. I have chosen to give Old Style dates for events in Russia before 31 January 1918 and New Style after that; wherever there is a chance for any confusion, I have added the notations "OS" or "NS."

I have used a modified Library of Congress format for transliterating Russian words and names into English and have kept the masculine and feminine endings of Russian surnames (Grigory Rasputin, Maria Rasputina, for example). In cases where individuals are better known by the English versions of their names, such as Tsar Nicholas II, I have used these and not transliterations of the original.

Introduction: The Holy Devil?

On a bright spring day in 1912 Sergei Prokudin-Gorsky carried his large tripod camera down to the banks of the Tura River in the remote Siberian village of Pokrovskoe. One of the great photographic innovators of the age, Prokudin-Gorsky had developed a technique for taking vivid color photographs, images that so impressed Emperor Nicholas II of Russia, he commissioned the photographer to record his empire in all its diverse splendor.

His camera captured a typical rural scene that day. The white village church, bleached in the sun, rises above the simple houses and barns, crude log structures, brown and gray, gathered around it. On one of the houses a window box cradles a plant with red flowers, geraniums perhaps, highlighted against the dark panes. A pair of cows graze casually on the green shoots released from the earth after another long Siberian winter. At the water's edge, two women in colored dresses have been caught in their daily chores. A solitary boat rests in the mud, ready for the next fishing trip out into the Tura. The image recalls so many similar anonymous villages that Prokudin-Gorsky photographed in the final years of tsarist Russia.

Yet this village was different from all the others, and Prokudin-Gorsky knew that the emperor and empress would expect him to include Pokrovskoe in his great survey. Pokrovskoe was the home of the most notorious Russian of the day, a man who in the spring of 1912 became the focus of a scandal that shook Nicholas's reign like nothing before. Rumors had been circulating about him for years, but it was then that the tsar's ministers and the politicians of the State Duma, Russia's legislative assembly, first dared to call him out by name and demand that the palace tell the country who precisely this man was and clarify his relationship to the throne. It was said that this man belonged to a bizarre religious sect that embraced the most wicked forms of sexual perversion, that he was a phony holy man who had duped the emperor and empress into embracing him as their spiritual leader, that he had taken over the Russian Orthodox Church and was bending it to his own immoral designs, that he was a filthy peasant who managed not only to worm his way into the palace, but through deceit and cunning was quickly becoming the true power behind the throne. This man, many were beginning to believe, presented a real danger to the church, to the monarchy, and even to Russia itself. This man was Grigory Yefimovich Rasputin.

All of this must have been on the mind of Prokudin-Gorsky that day. This was not just any village he was photographing, it was the home of Rasputin. Prokudin-Gorsky captured Pokrovskoe for the tsar, but, curiously, he was careful not to include in his image the house of its most infamous son, which he left outside the frame. Perhaps this was the great photographer's way of registering his own comment on the man Russia could not stop talking about.

The life of Rasputin is one of the most remarkable in modern history. It reads like a dark fairy tale. An obscure, uneducated peasant from the wilds of Siberia receives a calling from God and sets out in search of the true faith, a journey that leads him across the vast expanses of Russia for many years before finally bringing him to the palace of the tsar. The royal family takes him in and is bewitched by his piety, his unerring insights into the human soul, and his simple peasant ways. Miraculously, he saves the life of the heir to the throne, but the presence of this outsider, and the influence he wields with the tsar and tsaritsa, angers the great men of the realm and they lure him into a trap and kill him. Many believed that the holy peasant had foreseen his death and prophesied that should anything happen to him, the tsar would lose his throne. And so he does, and the kingdom he once ruled is plunged into unspeakable bloodletting and misery for years.

Even before his gruesome murder in a Petrograd cellar in the final days of 1916, Rasputin had become in the eyes of much of the world the personification of evil. His wickedness was said to recognize no bounds, just like his sexual drive that could never be sated no matter how many women he took to his bed. A brutish, drunken satyr with the manners of a barnyard animal, Rasputin had the inborn cunning of the Russian peasant and knew how to play the simple man of God when in front of the tsar and tsaritsa. He tricked them into believing he could save their son, the tsarevich Alexei, and with him the dynasty itself. They placed themselves, and the empire, in his hands, and he, through his greed and corruption, betrayed their trust, destroying the monarchy and bringing ruin to Russia.

Rasputin is possibly the most recognized name in Russian history. He has been the subject of dozens of biographies and novels, movies and documentaries, theatrical works, operas, and musicals. His exploits have been extolled in song, from The Three Keys' jazzy 1933 "Rasputin (The Highfalutin' Lovin' Man)" to Boney M's 1978 Euro-disco hit: "Ra Ra Rasputin, lover of the Russian queen . . . Ra Ra Rasputin, Russia's greatest love machine." There are countless Rasputin bars, restaurants, and nightclubs, there is Rasputin computer software (an acronym for **R**eal-Time **A**quisition **S**ystem **P**rograms for **U**nit **T**iming **i**n **N**euroscience), a comic book series, an action figure. He is the star of at least two video games (*Hot Rasputin* and *Shadow Hearts 2*) and features in Japanese manga and anime. There is an "Old Rasputin Russian Imperial Stout" and, not surprisingly, a Rasputin vodka. The life of Rasputin was even the basis for a 1991 ice-dancing performance by the Russian skaters Natalya Bestemyanova and Andrei Bukin. Popular culture is littered with Rasputin.

A century after his death, Rasputin remains fixed in the public imagination as "the mad monk" or "the holy devil," the oxymoronic yet evocative formulation created by the Russian priest Iliodor, one of his closest friends and, later, greatest enemies. With all that has been said about Rasputin over the past hundred years, it would seem there is nothing more to add. Or is there?

The collapse of the Soviet Union in 1991 accompanied an intense and at times tortured reexamination of Russia's past. The heroes of the old regime became villains, and the villains, heroes in one of the wild pendulum swings for which Russia is known. Nothing demonstrates the change better than the status of Tsar Nicholas II and his wife, Alexandra: despised as class enemies under the Soviets, they, along with their five children, were canonized as saints by the Russian Orthodox Church in 2000, their remains having already been interred with great ceremony alongside Russia's earlier tsarist rulers in St. Petersburg's Peter and Paul Cathedral.*

Rasputin has not been forgotten in this wholesale transvaluation of

---

* Except, that is, the remains of the tsarevich Alexei and his sister Grand Duchess Maria, still kept in a Russian archive at the insistence of the Russian Orthodox Church, which remains unconvinced of their authenticity.

Russian history. A new generation of historians has been at work reclaiming what they insist is the true Rasputin.[1] The stories told about him for the past century, they write, are nothing but a sea of lies, half-truths, and distortions constructed by his enemies. Rasputin, they contend, has been the object of the greatest calumny in history. He was a devoted husband and father, an honest man of God, a devout Orthodox Christian, a humble Russian peasant inspired by divine visions who placed his special gifts in the service of the royal family and his beloved Russia. The tales of his debauchery, his drinking, his corruption, and his interference in the affairs of state are nothing more than hearsay.

The campaign against Rasputin was part of a larger war against the monarchy waged by hostile forces intent on destroying not only the Romanov dynasty, but Holy Russia herself. The false image of Rasputin the devil was created to undermine the legitimacy and sacred aura of the throne and so foment a revolution that would bring to power a fanatical band of atheistic communists bent on wiping out Russian Orthodoxy and the country's sacred traditions. Rasputin, according to this interpretation, was the personification of true popular faith, a simple devout peasant who paid for his convictions with his life. The influential Orthodox priest Dmitry Dudko, harassed and imprisoned under the Soviets, said, "In the person of Rasputin I see the entire Russian people—beaten and executed, yet still preserving their faith, even when it means death. And with this faith they shall be victorious." The popular singer Zhanna Bichevskaya has gone further, calling Rasputin a great Russian martyr. In recent years icons bearing Rasputin's likeness, often depicted alongside members of the royal family, have appeared, and groups within the Russian Orthodox Church have demanded his canonization. The matter became serious enough to warrant convening a special synodical commission that after several years of investigation and debate eventually ruled in 2004 against conferring sainthood upon Rasputin. According to the opinion of Metropolitan Juvenaly on behalf of the commission, there was still too much doubt about Rasputin's possible connections to mystical sects, as well as his reputation for drunkenness and immoral conduct. A branch of the church, however, the Russian True Orthodox Church, self-proclaimed successor of the so-called Catacomb Church that broke off from the official Russian Orthodox Church in the 1920s, did recognize Rasputin as a saint in

1991. Russians, it seems, remain divided on the question of Rasputin's holiness.[2]

Along with an ugly anti-Semitism and paranoid xenophobia that pervade this new nationalist depiction of Rasputin is the larger problem of replacing one myth with another: Rasputin the devil becomes Rasputin the saint. The pendulum swings once more. Neither image is persuasive, and one is left with the question: Who, then, really was Rasputin?

I came to Rasputin while writing an earlier book on the fate of the nobility following the Russian revolutions of 1917. In researching the final years of the old regime I was repeatedly struck by Rasputin's omnipresence. No matter what sources I happened to be reading, whether personal correspondence, diaries, newspapers, memoirs, or political tracts, there was Rasputin. He was inescapable. As the Symbolist poet Alexander Blok remarked of the age, without exaggeration: "Rasputin is everything, Rasputin is everywhere."[3] Nothing in my decades of study and research of Russian history had prepared me for this. To a large degree this was due to the biases of the academic world in which I had been trained: to scholars of Russia, Rasputin did not exist as a worthy subject of study. He was simply too popular, too well known outside the university to be taken seriously. He had the whiff of the carnival about him, a figure better left to writers of fiction or pop history. It was a prejudice I too had come to share without realizing it. Nevertheless, I found I could not shake my growing curiosity about the man, and the more I read the more I realized just how important he had been to the history of the last Romanovs and the collapse of Imperial Russia. Once he had crawled inside my head, Rasputin refused to leave me alone.

After the fall of the Romanovs, on 11 March 1917 the Provisional Government established the Extraordinary Commission of Inquiry for the Investigation of Malfeasance in Office of Former Ministers, Chief Administrators, and other Persons in High Office of both the Civil, as well as Military and Naval Services.* Part of the Commission's remit was uncovering Rasputin's presumed nefarious influence on state affairs. Dozens of ministers, officials, courtiers, and friends of Rasputin, many of whom were being held prisoner by the new government, were

---

* Referred to hereafter as the Commission.

brought before the Commission for questioning. In an atmosphere of contemptuous hatred for the old regime, many witnesses tried to save themselves by depicting Rasputin in the worst possible light, arguing they had always been opposed to his influence and that he was chiefly responsible for the rot at the core of the tsar's reign that brought down the monarchy. Desperate to shift any blame from themselves onto Rasputin, they made him the scapegoat for Russia's misery. This strategy became the dominant trope for much of the literature on Rasputin, perhaps best exemplified by Prince Felix Yusupov's *Lost Splendor*, the memoir of Rasputin's murderer, in which his victim becomes Satan himself.

A century after his death Rasputin remains shrouded in myth, practically invisible underneath all the gossip, slander, and innuendo heaped upon him. Reading his biographies I could not shake the sense I was not seeing the man as he was, but others' projections, two-dimensional caricatures devoid of any depth, complexity, or beating heart. Part of the problem lay in the fact that for most of the twentieth century Rasputin's archives in the Soviet Union were closed to researchers, and this led to a situation in which the same limited number of published sources, with the same anecdotes and stories, were repeated again and again. This situation has changed only in recent years: Russia's archives have finally begun to give up their secrets.

I knew from the beginning that the only chance I had to get closer to the true Rasputin was to go back to the archives, to seek out the documents created during his lifetime before the myth of Rasputin had fully taken shape. It proved an unusually arduous undertaking. The trail led me to seven countries, from Siberia and Russia, across Europe, to Britain, and finally the United States. The first obligation of every biographer is to establish the objective, external facts of a life, something that has been lacking in our knowledge of Rasputin. And so I sought every bit of information that could place Rasputin squarely in his world: where he was on any given day, what he was doing, whom he met, what they discussed. I wanted to track Rasputin through time, to drag him out of the ether of myth and down into the banalities of daily life. This, it seemed to me, was the only way to extricate Rasputin the man from Rasputin the legend.

A curious thing happened, however, as I was following the footsteps of this elusive, real Rasputin. The deeper I went into my research, the more convinced I became that one of the most important *facts* about

Rasputin, the thing that made him such an extraordinary and powerful figure, was less *what* he was doing and more what everyone *thought* he was doing. No one could be certain about Rasputin's origins, about his sexual habits, about his possible connection to underground religious sects, and, most importantly, about the extent of his power at court and the nature of his relationship with the emperor and empress. The most important truth about Rasputin was the one Russians carried around in their heads.

Lev Tikhomirov, a radical revolutionary turned conservative monarchist in the final years of the nineteenth century, noted this crucial fact in his diary in early 1916:

> People say that the Emperor has been warned to his face that Rasputin is destroying the Dynasty. He replies: "Oh, that's silly nonsense; his importance is greatly exaggerated." An utterly incomprehensible point of view. For this is in fact where the destruction comes from, the wild exaggerations. What really matters is not what sort of influence Grishka has on the Emperor, but what sort of influence the people think he has. This is precisely what is undermining the authority of the Tsar and the Dynasty.[4]

To separate Rasputin from his mythology, I came to realize, was to completely misunderstand him. There is no Rasputin without the stories about Rasputin. And so I have been diligent in searching out all these stories, be it those whispered among the courtiers in the Romanovs' palaces, the salacious chatter wafting through the aristocratic salons of St. Petersburg, the titillating reports from the boulevard press, or the pornographic jokes exchanged among Russian merchants and soldiers. By following the talk about Rasputin I have been able to reconstruct how the myth of Rasputin was created, by whom, and why.

Rasputin's story is a tragedy, and not just that of one man but of an entire nation, for in his life—with its complicated struggles about faith and morality, about pleasure and sin, about tradition and change, about duty and power, and their limits—and in his bloody, violent end, we can discern the story of Russia itself in the early twentieth century. Rasputin was neither a devil nor a saint, but this made him no less remarkable and his life no less important to the twilight of tsarist Russia.

Part One

HOLY PILGRIM

1869–1904

1. Origins

Bordered on the north by the Arctic Ocean and on the south by the vast Central Asian steppe, Siberia stretches nearly three thousand miles from the Ural Mountains to the Pacific Ocean. The train from Moscow to the Urals travels roughly a day and a night and another five days from there to reach the Pacific. Were one to place the entire contiguous United States at the center of Siberia there would still be nearly 2 million square miles of extra space. It is a land of pine and birch forests, of lakes and marshes, drained by a series of powerful rivers flowing north to the Arctic. It is a land of extremes: temperatures can swing a staggering 188 degrees, from lows of −95 Fahrenheit (−71 Celsius) in the winter to 93 degrees (34 Celsius) in the summer. It is a severe, unforgiving place.

From earliest times, this vast, isolated land has conjured up fantastical images in the minds of outsiders. Parents were said to slaughter and eat their children. There were tales of Siberians dying when water trickling from their noses ran down their bodies and froze them to the ground. Some claimed the people of Siberia had no heads; their eyes were located on their chests, their mouths between their shoulders. Even as late as the eighteenth century, the manners and morals of Siberia were held in disregard by many. After his visit in 1761 to Tobolsk, Siberia's historic capital not far from the village of Rasputin's birth, the French astronomer Jean-Baptiste Chappe d'Auteroche wrote that, "Among the common people, men, women, and children lie together promiscuously, without any sense of shame. Hence their passions being excited by the objects they see, the two sexes give themselves up early to debauchery."[1] Siberia has long been synonymous with suffering owing to the untold thousands of prisoners sent there by the tsars and later commissars, whether into exile—*ssylka*—or the much harsher regime of *katorga*—penal servitude. For centuries common criminals, revolutionaries, and other subversives marched along the so-called "road of chains" that led from Russia over the Urals.

But not everyone who left Russia for Siberia went unwillingly. For many, Siberia meant a chance at a better life. Russian expansion into Siberia, begun in the sixteenth century, was driven by economic reasons, and by the hunger for "soft gold," animal furs, and particularly sable, which seemed as inexhaustible as it was profitable. The fur trade made many men fabulously wealthy and was the economic engine that drove expansion. Siberia, paradoxical though it might seem, also meant freedom, for there was no serfdom east of the Urals and the hand of the state was light, if not to say just. As the burdens on Russia's serfs increased during the seventeenth and eighteenth centuries, escaping to Siberia attracted ever increasing numbers of peasants. Between 1678 and 1710, the number of peasant households in Siberia grew by almost 50 percent, at the same time it dropped by over 25 percent in Russia. On the far side of the Urals, there were no lords to whom one owed the fruits of his labors. With freedom also came a wild, lawless nature to life on the Russian frontier. For centuries Siberia was the Russian empire's Wild East. The tsars' military governors were venal, corrupt, and violent, as were many of the traders and trappers. Not only was fur traded, so, too, were women and liquor. Violence was a common fact of life.[2]

The Russians who dared to escape to Siberia were among the country's most industrious subjects. Observing the local peasants, an English traveler crossing Siberia in 1861 on his way to China commented on an unmistakable "independence in their bearing." It was not like what he had seen in Russia, with its "poverty, negligence, and misery." He added that "The condition of their families evinces a certain amount of self-respect." Their villages had a "rude comfort," and one sensed these were people willing to take a risk in the hope of some better life.[3] They possessed a certain pride and dignity and a sense of responsibility for their lives lacking among the Russian peasant serfs west of the Urals.

Izosim, son of Fyodor, was one of the Russian pioneers who ventured into Siberia in the seventeenth century. A poor, landless peasant from the village of Palevitsy on the River Vychegda, a tributary of the Northern Dvina River, roughly eight hundred miles northeast of Moscow, Izosim, together with his wife and three sons—Semyon, Nason, and Yevsey—crossed the Urals and settled in the frontier outpost of Pokrovskoe around 1643.

Pokrovskoe had been founded a year earlier by order of the local archbishop, and by the time Izosim arrived it was home to some twenty peasant families. Pokrovskoe lay along the west bank of the undulating Tura River on the post road connecting the towns of Tobolsk and Tyumen and was used as a halting place where the coachmen could rest and change horses. The town took its name from the church of the Virgin Mary—consecrated on the holy day of the *Pokrov Presviatoi Bogoroditsy*—the villagers built there. The local peasants lived by hunting fox, bear, wolf, and badger in the surrounding woods and fishing the Tura and the area's many lakes for sterlet, pike, and sturgeon. They also farmed, raised livestock, and tanned leather. The people in this part of Siberia lived relatively well, in comfortable wooden homes—many of two stories. By 1860, around the time Rasputin was born, Pokrovskoe had roughly a thousand inhabitants living in some two hundred houses. It boasted a few dairies and stables, bakeries, taverns, inns, and markets, timber mills, a smithy and a small schoolhouse.[4]

The old village records do not list any surname for Izosim, but his son Nason had adopted "Rosputin" by 1650. The reason why he chose the name is not clear. Perhaps he had a second name or nickname of Rasputa (Rosputa) that gave way to Rasputin (as it came to be spelled in the nineteenth century), then a common surname in Siberia. Regardless, only some of Nason's descendants adopted and held the name Rasputin down through the generations.[5] It was from this Nason Rosputin that Grigory would descend, eight generations later.

Rasputin's name has been the subject of endless discussion, most of it ill-informed and incorrect. Many have tried to link it to the Russian word *rasputnik*, a reprobate, or *rasputnichat'*—to behave with wanton debauchery—as if Rasputin's name either derived from his moral depravity or was later given to him due to his wicked fame. The spurious assertions dogged him during his lifetime. The *Evening Times*, for example, published a story in December 1911 stating he had been given the nickname of "Rasputin" due to his immorality as a youth and it was then made official when it was written down in his passport. And even now, some historians continue to assert that Rasputin's name was meant to reflect the age-old depravity of his family.[6]

The origins of the name are obscure. If it indeed started with an ancestor who was a rasputnik, then Rasputin's family was far from unusual, given how many people in Siberia bore the name. But there are other more likely sources. *Rasputa* or *rasput'e* mean crossroads and long ago these places were seen as the haunt of evil spirits and, perhaps, the name was given to persons believed to be in contact with such forces. There is also the old Russian saying about the fool who was let go at the crossroads, meant to refer to an indecisive person. And then there is the untranslatable Russian word *rasputitsa* that refers to the wet, muddy, spring season when Russia's roads became unusable. It is possible a child born during this period might have been called Rasputa.[7] Whatever its origins, Rasputin was the surname Grigory, and the rest of his family, was born with, and it was never given as a signifier of his character.

Yefim Rasputin, Grigory's father, was born in Pokrovskoe in 1842. Sources describe him as "a thick, typical Siberian peasant", "chunky, unkempt and stooped," while a political exile who met Yefim around 1910 called him "a healthy, hardworking and sprightly old man."[8] He scraped by working at a number of things—fishing, farming, cutting hay. For a time he labored as a stevedore on the boats plying the Tura and Tobol rivers, and then he landed a job for the state conveying people and goods between Tobolsk and Tyumen. Money was usually tight; once Yefim was jailed for not paying his taxes. Sources as to his character are somewhat contradictory. He served as an elder in the village church, and one local spoke of Yefim's "learned conversations and wisdom," while others noted his fondness for "strong vodka."[9] Regardless of his drinking, Yefim slowly managed to rise up in the village. He acquired a plot of land and a dozen or so cows and almost twenty horses, not great wealth, but prosperous by the standards of the Russian peasantry.

Church records state Yefim married Anna Parshukova, from the village of Usalka, on 21 January 1862. She was two years his senior. The coming years saw several births and just as many deaths. Between 1863 and 1867, Anna bore four children—three girls and one boy—none of whom lived more than a few months. The first child to survive was a boy born on 9 January 1869, almost seven years to the day after their wedding. He was christened Grigory on the tenth in honor of St. Gregory of Nyssa, the fourth-century Christian mystic, whose feast was celebrated that day in the Russian Orthodox Church. At the church with Yefim and Anna and their baby boy were his godparents—Yefim's older brother Matvei and a woman by the name of Agafya Alemasova.[10]

Two or three more children followed. In 1874, Anna gave birth to twins, both of whom died within days of their birth, and then there was possibly a ninth child, a girl named Feodosiya, born in 1875, who did survive to adulthood. While the extant records are not clear whether she and Grigory were siblings, or more distant relations, they were, however, close. He acted as a witness at her wedding in 1895 and then later became the godfather to Feodosiya's two children. The oft-repeated story that Rasputin had a brother, or cousin, named Dmitry who drowned, and in whose death Rasputin foresaw his own demise is pure fabrication.[11]

Rasputin's entire youth, indeed the first thirty years or so of his life, is a black hole about which we know almost nothing, a fact that helped to make possible the invention of all sorts of tall tales. In 1910, at the height of one of the early scandals surrounding Rasputin, the newspaper *Morning of Russia* published a story claiming that researchers had uncovered shocking details about the life of Rasputin's parents. Yefim, so the article asserted, was a "very lecherous voluptuary" who insisted on having sex with his wife during her pregnancies. Once when Anna tried to resist, he screamed at her, "Push it out, hurry up and push it out!" And so the villagers came to call the little boy Pushed-Out Grishka.[12] Another story was told that toward the end of her pregnancy with Grigory when Anna's belly became quite enlarged, Yefim insisted she allow him to have anal sex with her, something purportedly witnessed by a man working in the home who told the story around the village.[13] Stories like these were fabricated to suggest sexual perversion was something that ran in the Rasputin family.

We do know Rasputin was never formally educated and remained illiterate into his early adulthood. This was not unusual. Most peasants who worked the land rarely attended school, and the literacy rate was about 4 percent in Siberia in 1900, and a mere 20 percent nationally. Nor had Rasputin's parents been schooled either. According to the 1897 census, no one in the Rasputin household was literate.[14] Little Grigory, like other boys in Pokrovskoe, helped his father as soon as he was able. He learned to fish, to care for the livestock, to work the fields. On Sundays, he attended church with his family. This was the life of the average peasant, and it does not seem that there was anything in his youth, from what the original sources tell us, to suggest Rasputin was bound for any other life than that of his forefathers.

It is in large part because so little is known about this period that others have been free to create their own versions of life in the Rasputin home. Typical is this description from the *Petrograd Leaflet* from December 1916:

> The holy man's village was poor and forsaken. Its inhabitants had a particularly bad reputation, even by Siberian standards. Do-nothings, crooks, horse-thieves. And the Rasputins were just like all the rest, and he would be the same once he grew up a bit.
>
> In his youth Rasputin was uncommonly hapless. With a foul mouth, inarticulate speech, driveling, dirty as can be, a thief and blasphemer, he was the fright of his native village.[15]

The *Petrograd Leaflet* called him a ne'er-do-well whose laziness provoked beatings at the hands of his father. The most serious charge, however, was that young Rasputin had been a thief and that the records of the local administration held the proof that he had been tried on charges of horse thieving and bearing false witness.

Pavel Raspopov of Pokrovskoe told the Commission in 1917 something similar about Rasputin's person and habits. They had fished together in their youth, he said, and none of the other young men wanted to even be close to Rasputin. Snot was forever running down his nose at meal time, and when he smoked his pipe, saliva dribbled from his mouth. Rasputin was eventually kicked out of the artel, so Raspopov stated, after he was caught stealing the group's vodka.[16] There are also reports of Rasputin's stealing hay and firewood, although most widespread was the claim of his stealing horses, a particularly grave offense in prerevolutionary Russia.[17] Like so much about Rasputin, the story grew with each retelling. If at first mention was made of Rasputin's stealing horses on one or two occasions, it later was said he came from a long line of horse rustlers. The Swedish composer Wilhelm Harteveld, who met Rasputin more than once, said after Rasputin's death that he had been born into a family of horse thieves. Yefim supposedly taught him the family business, as it were, and took great pride in his son when he became known by the age of sixteen as one of the best rustlers in the area. Prince Felix Yusupov made a similar comment in his influential memoirs.[18] Had any of these stories been true, they would have left some trace in the archives in Tobolsk or Tyumen, but despite historians' best efforts not a single reference to Rasputin having been brought up on any charges has ever been found.[19]

But there is evidence that proves Rasputin was an unruly youth. Details gathered from Pokrovskoe locals for a Tyumen gendarmes' report in 1909 confirm that Rasputin had "various vices," namely that he "liked to get drunk" and committed a number of "small thefts" before disappearing and returning a changed man.[20] The date of the document is important, for it comes well before Rasputin's notoriety took off and so is more likely to reflect the truth—or some aspect of it—and not villagers simply giving the gendarmes what they assumed the officials hoped to hear.

And then there is a series of documents that have languished unnoticed in the archives in Tobolsk until now. According to an official investigation, in late June 1914 a journalist and his secretary arrived from the capital at the district administration (*volostnoe pravlenie*) in Pokrovskoe claiming to be agents of the St. Petersburg governor-general sent to collect official proof of Rasputin's youthful horse thieving. The clerk, a man named Nalobin, too frightened to ask for proof of their identity, checked the village's "Book of Previous Convictions" and told them that Rasputin had never been caught or punished for any such crime. He did mention, however, that he had documents showing that in 1884 the district head (*volostnoy starshina*) had sentenced fifteen-year-old Rasputin to two days in jail for his "rude attitude" to him. This, he told them, was the only mention of Rasputin's criminal past. Nalobin asked the men to sign the log for receipt of the information, but they refused and hurried off.[21] When Rasputin learned of what Nalobin had done he was furious and insisted the governor of Tobolsk look into the matter. The investigation revealed that Nalobin had indeed shown the two men the village book with the incriminating details. For his failure to demand valid proof of the men's identities, Nalobin was fined five rubles.

It is a remarkable discovery, for it puts to rest the stories of Rasputin's horse thieving once and for all, as well as reports of other crimes. If there were "small thefts," as the villagers and Raspopov claimed, then they truly were "small," so small as not to warrant the attention of the village authorities. It is also remarkable for it offers the most irrefutable proof ever of the rebellious, and perhaps even wild, nature of Rasputin's youth, something that has long been surmised, and even vaguely hinted at by Rasputin himself, but never reliably documented. Of course, such youthful indiscretions are quite common, even among Christian holy men such as St. Augustine. Yet whereas Augustine stole and fornicated as a youth, he changed his ways for good after his conversion to Christianity. The same could not be said of Rasputin, who would struggle with his vices for the rest of his life, frequently failing and giving way to sin, something he himself, it ought to be noted, never denied.

About eighteen miles southeast of Tobolsk, the Holy Znamensky Monastery at Abalak sits high on a bluff overlooking the Irtysh River, built on the site where in 1636 an old peasant woman experienced a vision commanding her in the words of the Mother of God to build a church. The monastery became the home to a wonder-working icon of the Virgin Mary famous across Siberia for its remarkable healing powers. People from miles around traveled to Abalak to experience the holiness of the monastery and receive the blessings of its icon.

It was here at Abalak in the summer of 1886 that Rasputin met a peasant girl by the name of Praskovya Dubrovina. She was plump and blonde with dark eyes. She was more than three years Rasputin's senior, born on 25 October 1865, and so something of an old maid for a peasant girl.[22] She, like Rasputin, was there to celebrate the Feast of the Assumption that summer. They courted for several months and then wed soon after Rasputin's eighteenth birthday in February 1887.[23] Precious little is known about Praskovya. Everyone who knew her only had good things to say. She was a hard-working, loyal, dutiful (and even submissive) wife and daughter-in-law. As a spinster, Praskovya may have been grateful for Rasputin's proposal, which meant a home, family, and a measure of safety and stability. Peasant Russia was not a place for single women. Despite his womanizing and drinking and long absences, she remained devoted to him for the rest of his life, always there keeping home in Pokrovskoe patiently waiting for his return. For his part, Rasputin always made sure she had what she needed for herself and the house and hired young women to help Praskovya with her work and to keep her company while he was away.

After their wedding, they moved in with Grigory's parents, as custom demanded. Children soon followed. There would be seven in all, though most died young. Mikhail, born on 29 September 1889, died of scarlet fever before his fifth birthday. In May 1894, Praskovya gave birth to twins—Georgy and Anna. They succumbed to whooping cough two years later along with several others in the village. Dmitry, born 25 October 1895, was the first of their children to live to adulthood, followed by Matryona (better known as Maria), born 26 March 1898, and then Varvara, on 28 November 1900. A seventh child, Praskovya, born three years after Varvara, did not survive three months.[24]

According to the 1897 census, Grigory, by now twenty-eight, did not have his own household, but was still living with his father, then fifty-five, his mother, aged fifty-seven, his wife, and their one-year-old son Dmitry. Everyone in the household is listed as illiterate, the menfolk as state peasant farmers.[25] Up until then Rasputin's life appeared to be unfolding as it did for millions of Russian peasants: working the fields, attending church, saying one's prayers, obeying one's father, marrying, having children, and keeping the eternal rhythm of peasant life in motion. But then, everything changed.

2. The Pilgrim

In 1907, Rasputin spoke of his early life to one of his acolytes, a woman named Khionya Berladskaya, who wrote down his words and helped to have them published as a booklet under the title *The Life of an Experienced Pilgrim*. "When I first lived before the age of 28," Rasputin told Berladskaya,

> as they say, in the world, I lived in peace, that is, I loved the world and acted justly and looked for consolation from the secular point of view. I often joined baggage trains, I worked a great deal as a coachman, I fished and ploughed fields. All this is really good for a peasant!
>
> I had many sorrows, too: whatever mistake was made somewhere, I was blamed although I was not involved. Workmen from teams mocked me. I ploughed hard and slept little and I kept asking my heart how to find some way to be saved. I looked at priests as models but it was not exactly what I wanted. [...] So I started going on pilgrimages and I was quick-minded and observant, I was interested in everything, good and bad, I had questions but there was no one to ask what the answer was. I did a lot of traveling and searching and tried everything in life.[1]

The reasons behind the change in Rasputin's life that would eventually lead him from Pokrovskoe to the palace of the tsar have long been shrouded in legend. Nikolai Sokolov, head of the 1919 investigation into the murder of the Romanovs, claimed that Rasputin left Pokrovskoe not to seek God but to get out of hard work. Others have written that Rasputin's motivation was to avoid jail time or banishment for horse thieving. Rasputin supposedly proposed undertaking a pilgrimage to the St. Nicholas Monastery in Verkhoturye—over three hundred miles away—to atone for his sins.[2] Neither story is convincing. Dmitry Stryapchev, a long-time friend of Rasputin, told the press in 1914 that as a young man Rasputin had not had the best reputation in his village.

He had a weakness for the bottle, among other things. But then one night he had a dream. St. Simeon of Verkhoturye appeared before him, saying: "Give all that up and become a new man, and I will exalt you."[3] In his *Life*, Rasputin made reference to St. Simeon of Verkhoturye as well, noting how he had helped to cure him of insomnia and bed-wetting, a problem that carried on into his adulthood, and it was this miracle that sent his life in a new direction devoted to God.[4] Maria, Rasputin's daughter, who had not been born at the time of this transformation, wrote that her father had drunk, and smoked, and eaten meat just like other peasants, but then he suddenly changed. He gave all these things up and began to undertake pilgrimages to distant places. In one edition of her memoirs, Maria claimed that her father had had a vision: while out in the fields Holy Mary appeared in the sky and pointed toward the horizon. Rasputin felt that the Virgin was watching over him, directing him to wander as a holy seeker. He spent an entire night alone with an icon of Mary. The next morning he awoke to see tears streaming down her face. He heard a voice: "I am weeping for the sins of mankind, Grigory. Go, wander, and cleanse the people of their sins."[5]

Even if the story is true, it apparently took more than the encouragement of the Virgin to convince Rasputin to seek God beyond the horizon. Villagers told a visitor in 1910 that the sudden change in Rasputin's behavior was connected with a trip to Tyumen he had taken together with a young theological student named Melity Zaborovsky, who went on to become a monk and then rector of the Tomsk Theological Seminary. Maria also mentioned Zaborovsky, noting how her father had happened to meet him one day while returning from the mill. Rasputin began to tell Zaborovsky about his visions and asked for his advice, to which the student replied: "The Lord has called you and it is a sin not to heed."[6]

Almost as murky as the reasons for the change is the date it happened. Part of the problem lay with Rasputin himself. In 1908, for example, he stated that he had begun his pilgrimages around 1893, when he was twenty-four.[7] Here Rasputin appears mistaken. As he states in his *Life*, he first began to go on pilgrimages when he was twenty-eight, so in 1897, the same date he gave to Father Alexander Yurevsky in a conversation in Siberia in 1907.[8] That later date seems the more likely.

Rasputin was by the standards of the day a middle-aged peasant when he decided to leave his village and seek God. It was a radical decision and could only have been occasioned by some sort of emotional or spiritual crisis. Perhaps it was some form of mid-life crisis: he had been married for ten years, he had a little son and another child on the way, his life was one of toil without end. To get up and leave home was a form of escape, a chance at another life. Rasputin had already had a taste of this other life in his short pilgrimages to the Abalak Monastery and to Tobolsk's great cathedral, but now he wanted to go further and for longer. Rasputin had a restless nature. He could never stay in any one place for too long and would spend the rest of his life on the move. But there was more to Rasputin's decision than a wish to escape. The religious impulse expressed in the quote above was indeed sincere. He was restless in his religious searching as well, and his questions about the nature of God and religion had surpassed the (likely limited) capacity of the local priests.

There is no record of how the rest of the family reacted to his leaving home to seek God. Clearly, it must have been difficult. Grigory was Yefim's only son and he needed him at home to help with the work. He could not have been happy to see him go and there is evidence to suggest their relations suffered as a result.[9] Praskovya, too, could not have been pleased, but then in the patriarchal world of the peasantry, she had no choice but to go along. It is a largely overlooked fact that by the time Rasputin left home well over half his life was already behind him. He had only nineteen more years to live.

Stranniki, holy wanderers or religious pilgrims, were a common sight in old Russia. Throughout the eighteenth and nineteenth centuries, the idea of undertaking pilgrimages to holy places was widespread, among the rich and poor. If the rich could afford to travel by carriage, the poor had to make do with their own two feet, a knapsack in their hands. Wandering from village to village, the pilgrims relied on the generosity of strangers for food and a place to stay for the night. Often, however, they went hungry and slept out under the stars. They dressed in little more than rags and were typically barefoot. Many wore fetters. It was not an easy life. In 1900, there were about a million pilgrims in Russia, forever wandering from one holy place to the next in search of salvation and enlightenment. As they went the pilgrims would repeat the Jesus Prayer: "Lord Jesus Christ, Son of God, have mercy on me, a sinner."[10]

Many Russians held pilgrims in high regard. Fyodor Tyutchev, the great nineteenth-century poet, praised them in "The Wanderer": "He is by Zeus protected/Who plods the face of earth alone! . . . /Although by native hearths rejected, Among the gods he has his home."[11] To the authorities, however, pilgrims were far from innocent religious seekers. Alexei Vasilev, the last head of the tsarist police, wrote that these men and women "represent the out-and-out Anarchist element among the Russian peasants." Restless, aimless figures, they avoided all contact with the state chiefly so as to escape any and all social obligations. The stranniki, Vasilev was convinced, needed to be suppressed for the public good.[12]

"When I started doing pilgrimages," Rasputin recalled many years later, "I began to experience pleasure from being in a different world." He observed the different ways people served God and came to the realization that one could participate in His work while living in the world if one acted out of a profound sense of God's grace. Life as a pilgrim was hard. Rasputin walked thirty miles a day in all kinds of weather. He begged for alms or worked at odd jobs to earn a few kopecks. He was often set upon by brigands and chased by murderers. The Devil forever tempted him with "unholy desires." Rasputin humiliated himself to test his resolve. He would force himself to go without food or water for days, for six months he wandered without changing his underclothes or touching his body, for three years he traveled across Russia in fetters. In age-old Christian fashion, this mortification of the flesh brought him closer to the spirit of Christ. With time Rasputin gave up his metal chains for "the chains of love." He learned to read the Gospels, to contemplate their meaning, and to find God in all things, especially in the beauty of the Russian landscape. Christ's love filled his soul. "I loved everyone indiscriminately," he said. When bandits robbed him, he gave them everything he had, saying, "It's not mine, it's God," to their astonishment. What little food he had, he would share with his fellow stranniki, for it all came from God.[13]

Wonder at the beauty of nature. Conviction of the Devil's presence in the world around us. Struggle with the demands of the body. Disregard for money and material things. Awe at the power of love. Asceticism and unusual religious practices combined with an independent spirit. In these passages Rasputin revealed the themes that would dominate his life.

Verkhoturye, located in the Ural Mountains, is one of the holiest places in Russia, home to dozens of churches and the St. Nicholas Monastery.

It was an enormously popular destination for pilgrims, including Rasputin, and it was here that he met one of the day's most revered holy men. Makary, born Mikhail Polikarpov, was a *starets* or elder who lived in a small hut in the woods not far from the monastery. Margarita Sabashnikova, the first wife of the Symbolist poet Maximilian Voloshin, visited Makary in 1910 at his little hut surrounded by the chickens he loved to care for. "His face was outside time," she remarked. "The deep wrinkles testified to alarm, although not for himself but others." His eyes appeared not to have known sleep. He was dressed as a peasant and acted strangely, staring off into the sky and carrying on conversations with his chickens. Still, Makary exerted a mysterious power over her. "There was something captivating in his appearance, a sort of presence, the way our gazes met. He truly must be an elder, I thought, and sank to my knees before him."[14]

"An elder," Fyodor Dostoevsky wrote in *The Brothers Karamazov*,

> was one who took your soul, your will, into his soul and his will. When you choose an elder, you renounce your own will and yield it to him in complete submission, complete self-abnegation [. . .] this terrible school of abnegation is undertaken voluntarily in the hope of self-conquest, of self-mastery, in order, after a life of obedience, to attain perfect freedom, that is, from self; to escape the lot of those who have lived their life without finding their true selves in themselves.[15]

An elder possessed rare inner wisdom, a charisma inspired by God, that lent him the power to act as spiritual guide to persons seeking enlightenment. The first and most famous of all such elders was St. Antony of Egypt (251–356). He withdrew from the world to live in solitude in the desert for more than twenty years, and only after this intense period of isolation and contemplation did he begin to receive visitors in search of wisdom and faith. Central to Antony's life, which became the model for all future elders, is the idea of withdrawal before one's being ready to return to the world.

Russia's greatest national saint, Sergius of Radonezh (1314?–1392), lived the life of a starets, leaving the world behind for the lonely Russian forests where he founded a hermitage and lived a life of self-discipline and prayer. With time word of the hermitage and the saintly Sergius spread and people began to seek him out as a spiritual guide. As the numbers of his disciples grew, he founded a monastery north of

Moscow that became Muscovy's most sacred place. Yet Sergius never gave up the ways of the ascetic, and pilgrims were often shocked by what they encountered upon meeting him. Although born a nobleman, he still worked in the kitchen garden, dressed as a poor peasant, his clothes were dirty, and he seldom bathed. He looked like a beggar and had fled into the wilderness; nevertheless Sergius was a friend of the Grand Dukes of Muscovy and he did not eschew politics. In 1380, on the eve of the Battle of Kulikovo against the Tatars, Prince Dmitry Donskoy, the ruler of Moscow, sought out Sergius's blessing.

Although elders are a feature of the Orthodox Church in general, and have been found in various times, the greatest flowering of the phenomenon was in nineteenth-century Russia, what has been dubbed "the age of the *starets.*" Beginning with St. Seraphim of Sarov and then carrying on with the great *startsy* of the Optina Monastery (Leonid, Macarius, Ambrose), these charismatic figures had an enormous influence on Russian spiritual life, and not only among the common people, but writers and thinkers as well. The great starets of *The Brothers Karamazov*, Father Zosima, was in part inspired by the startsy of Optina.[16] Like so many others, Rasputin was profoundly moved by the starets Makary. This humble seeker had immersed himself in the Orthodox faith and had memorized a good deal of the Bible; his acolytes believed he could not only quote Scripture but live it, as if he were the personification of Jesus's teachings. The details of the two men's interaction are scant. It is possible Rasputin spent several months at the monastery at Verkhoturye and became something of a pupil of Makary. It was perhaps here, from the monks and not Makary, who was illiterate, that Rasputin began to learn to read and write, skills he did acquire although not at the highest level.[17]

Rasputin was impressed by Makary, but not by the monastery and its monks. He later told Maria that the "vice" that infected so many monasteries had also taken hold at Verkhoturye. The vice he had in mind was most likely homosexuality. He also felt there was an element of coercion in monastic life that repelled him. He once said, "Monastic life is not for me. One finds violence over people there." Rasputin insisted that the only true path as a Christian was to seek salvation in the world. Given Rasputin's restless nature, this was not surprising. He was never one to submit to routine or a higher authority, except God and the tsar. According to Maria, it was her father's visit to Makary that convinced him that the wandering life was the one for him.[18]

With time Rasputin journeyed ever farther from home. It is possible he traveled as far as Mt. Athos in 1900, the main center of Orthodox monasticism since the tenth century. On a rocky peninsula in Greece in the Aegean Sea rises up the so-called "Holy Mountain" of Athos, 6,670 feet high, and home to more than twenty monasteries, monastic settlements, and hermit cells. With Rasputin was Dmitry Pecherkin, a fellow pilgrim and possibly a relation, who was so moved by life on Athos that he chose to stay and enter the Panteleimonovsky Monastery and be tonsured as Daniil. Dmitry would remain at the monastery until it was engulfed in controversy in 1913, when he returned to Pokrovskoe.[19]

Such trips took Rasputin away from home for months and even years at a time. When he returned, he was not always recognized, even by his own family. Maria's earliest recollection of her father harked back to an autumn evening in 1903. She and Dmitry had been out playing with the other village children when their mother called them in for supper. A tall stranger, with a tired face, in a dusty sheepskin coat carrying a bag approached. He looked like so many other pilgrims they would see wandering through the village. Then Praskovya realized it was her husband and screamed out his name with joy. They had not seen each other for two years. Maria and her brother jumped into their father's arms and smothered him with kisses.

In her memoirs Maria quite accurately noted her father's love for his native village, a love he never lost. Nevertheless, every spring he would be overcome by an urge to leave. "Walks in the immediate neighbourhood," she commented, "no longer satisfied him. A wanderlust would suddenly seize him, and one fine morning, his wallet on his shoulder, he would set out, bent on some distant journey, either to a famous place of pilgrimage, or merely at random, trusting to the hospitality of the villages he would pass through and to his gifts as a preacher and teller of stories." Maria and Dmitry would beg their father to take them with him, mostly given their desire to escape the mean village priest in charge of their religious instruction, Father Pyotr Ostroumov, a man whom Rasputin apparently held in low regard.[20]

Holy pilgrims rarely kept a home, wife, and children that they would return to, and in so doing Rasputin distinguished himself from his fellow stranniki. Never one to recognize and submit to accepted norms, Rasputin sought out his own path, he defined what it meant to be a pilgrim as he saw it. His decision to give up wearing fetters offers one such example of his thinking. In 1907, Rasputin told Father Alexander Yurevsky how when he first began to wander he wore fetters. "But it is not good to wear them: you start to think only about yourself, that you are already a holy man. And so I took them off and began to wear one shirt for an entire year without taking it off. That is a better way to humble oneself."[21] Inquisitive, intelligent, and open-minded, yet at the same time independent and even rebellious, Rasputin took in all that the Russian religious world had to offer but kept only that which suited him, fashioning in the process his own version of peasant Orthodoxy.

The years spent wandering were Rasputin's university. Like the strannik Luka in Maxim Gorky's *The Lower Depths*, he had seen nearly all there was to behold in the sprawling empire of the tsars and had moved among all manner of people—hardworking peasants and laborers, crooks, thieves, and murderers, simple holy men and village priests (some moral, some not), venal officials, beggars and cripples, haughty nobles, penitent nuns, brutal police and hardened soldiers. His knowledge of the Russian social order was broad and his understanding of human psychology, deep. Rasputin developed through his travels a talent for reading people. He could meet someone for the first time and strangely see inside them—what was on their minds, what troubles they had experienced in the past, who they were as people. And he knew how to talk to them. He could speak freely about Holy Scripture and the meaning of God in a way unlike the priests with their book learning. His language was direct, personal, unmistakably alive, and earthy, filled with references to daily life and the beauty of the natural world.

"My father would often take us on his knees, my brother Mitia, my sister Varvara, and myself," Maria wrote of those times. "He would tell us wonderful stories with that tenderness he always showed and that absent look in which seemed to be mirrored the countries he had visited and the strange adventures he had met with on the road." He recounted the many wonders of the tsar's realm—the thousands of gold cupolas reaching to the sky, the sparkling riches of the Tatar bazaars, the mighty rivers, the holy silence of the Siberian forests, the wild beauty of the steppes. At times his voice would fall to a whisper as he told them of his visions. Maria never forgot how he told of a beautiful woman, "with the features of the Holy Virgin," who appeared before him and spoke of God. When he had finished, he reflexively made the sign of the cross over his children's heads. God was life's consolation, Rasputin told them, and he taught them how to pray. Not everyone could do it, he said, one had to believe in one's heart and banish all thoughts from one's mind, leaving nothing behind but God. He forced his children to fast as preparation for prayer. Rasputin instructed them that they did this not for their health, as educated Russians believed, "but for the salvation of our souls." Rasputin would pronounce the blessings at their meals and would hold a small service every evening. Out in the courtyard, he kept a lodging with icons as a shelter for pilgrims passing through Pokrovskoe.

But it was not all God and religion at home. Rasputin enjoyed laughing with his children, there were ball games, and rides in the wagon, Dmitry receiving instructions on how to control the horse from his father. In the fall, Rasputin loved the annual village festival with the music and dancing.[22]

Maria and her siblings gradually came to realize there was something special about their father. Visitors started coming to the house, local peasants and strangers from further away, wishing to open their hearts to Rasputin, to seek his guidance and counsel. Rasputin and Praskovya accepted them into their home, providing them with food and a place to stay along with Grigory's spiritual nourishment. Maria was proud when she heard talk that her father was seen by many in the area as a starets.

Rasputin by the early years of the century had attracted his own small group of acolytes, including Nikolai Raspopov, his brother-in-law; Nikolai Rasputin, his cousin (the son of Yefim's older brother Matvei); and Ilya Arapov, a Pokrovskoe peasant. Two women also joined their circle. Yevdokiya Pecherkina, a peasant from the Tobolsk district and Dmitry's sister, and Yevdokiya's niece, Yekaterina Pecherkina. The women—Dunya and Katya as they were called—moved into the Rasputin home sometime around 1906, initially to help Praskovya run the household although they soon became like family and would remain with the Rasputins until after Grigory's murder. Rasputin's followers would gather at the house on Sundays and religious holidays, or whenever they had free time, to sing religious songs and read the Bible, which Rasputin would then interpret for the others. Rasputin dug out a crude cave under the stables at his father's house, where he was still living at the time, that they used as a sort of chapel for their meetings. An air of secrecy surrounded these gatherings. The villagers grew suspicious and started to talk. Some said the Pecherkins would ceremoniously wash Rasputin in the bathhouse. Others claimed they had heard strange songs coming from the Rasputin home, not the accepted hymns sung on Sundays in the village church, and that he had been teaching his circle to practice mysterious rituals.[23]

Maria remembered that just as her father's popularity grew after each return home, so, too, did the suspicion and soon distrust of many of the villagers. There were reports Rasputin had been off on his wanderings with young women, something that required no commentary. In the case of Father Ostroumov, this manifested itself in the form of hostility. He, after all, was Pokrovskoe's religious head, not this jumped-up peasant now being sought out by ever greater numbers seeking spiritual guidance and miracle cures. Ostroumov became so upset he tried to break up Rasputin's circle and managed to talk Ilya Arapov into staying away from the Rasputin home.[24] But he was apparently the only one. Ostroumov was fighting a losing battle and word of the remarkable starets of Pokrovskoe began to spread across Siberia.

3. Nicholas and Alexandra

Nicholas Alexandrovich, the sixteen-year-old heir to the Russian throne, first laid eyes on her in June 1884. Princess Alix was then only twelve years old. She had come to Russia for the wedding of her older sister Elisabeth to Grand Duke Sergei Alexandrovich, the younger brother of the Russian Emperor Alexander III. As they stood in the chapel of the Winter Palace, Nicholas and Alix could not help stealing glances at each other. Before she returned home to Germany, Nicholas gave her a small brooch.

Alix was a granddaughter of Queen Victoria, born to Princess Alice and Prince Louis, heir to the Grand Duke of Hesse, in June 1872 in the quiet German town of Darmstadt. Alix, better known to history as Alexandra, the name she adopted upon converting to Russian Orthodoxy, was a pretty, happy child. The family called her Sunny, a nickname that would come to be cruelly at odds with her later personality. She was her grandmother Queen Victoria's favorite: "Too beautiful," she said of the little girl, "the handsomest child I ever saw."

It was five years after their first meeting that Alix and Nicholas met again, but Nicholas had not forgotten her, and when she next returned to Russia he set out to win her for his wife. They attended balls and suppers in the evening; during the day, Nicholas took her out skating. Alix, however, resisted, chiefly on religious grounds, for she was a devout Lutheran and would not consider giving up her faith for anyone.

There was talk of other suitors, including Prince George, the second son of Bertie, Prince of Wales. In 1889, she turned down a proposal from Eddy, Duke of Clarence, next in line to the British throne after his father, the Prince of Wales. Queen Victoria desperately wanted an English marriage for her beloved Alix, but Alix was not moved by the chance of becoming queen of England. Victoria grew increasingly worried about a Russian match for Alix. Such a marriage, she wrote, "would lead to no happiness [. . .] The state of Russia is so bad, so rotten that any moment something dreadful might happen."[1]

Nicholas next saw Alix at the wedding of her brother Ernst in Coburg in the spring of 1894. He was determined to win her over, but the decision was too difficult for her to make, and she broke down in tears. Ella, as Elisabeth was called, who had converted to Orthodoxy, spoke to her younger sister to calm her nerves. It worked, and Alix agreed to the proposal.

Tragedy, however, struck before they could be married. On 1 November 1894, Nicholas's father, Emperor Alexander III, died suddenly at the Livadia palace on the Crimean coast. Nicholas, who was there with Alix, was devastated. The burden that now shifted onto his shoulders was more than he could even contemplate. Crying, he turned to his brother-in-law, Grand Duke Alexander Mikhailovich (aka Sandro): "Sandro, what am I going to do? [. . .] What is going to happen to me, to you, to Xenia, to Alix, to mother, to all of Russia? I am not prepared to be a Tsar. I never wanted to become one. I know nothing of the business of ruling. I have no idea of even how to talk to the ministers." His words proved to be terribly prophetic.[2]

The next day Alix, under her new name of Alexandra Fyodorovna, took holy communion for the first time in the Orthodox Church. Not long thereafter, on 26 November, Nicholas and Alexandra were married in St. Petersburg's Winter Palace.

It was a happy marriage. Their love for each other was both profound and lasting and never deserted them up until their deaths. This is not to say their lives were easy, for from the start Alexandra chafed under the pressures of being the Russian tsaritsa. Oddly failing to recognize that her position made her a public figure with definite obligations to her new people, Alexandra insisted on living a quiet life, relentlessly guarding her family's privacy as if they were some minor German nobles rusticating in a provincial backwater. *Würde bringt Bürde*, the Germans say—with position come responsibilities. Alexandra, however, could only see the responsibilities her subjects owed the crown, not those she owed them. (Although, at the same time, Alexandra never once forgot the power of the Russian throne and refused to listen to even the slightest mention of political reform.) Yet the privacy she craved only made her feel isolated, alone, and unloved. She could not understand why even the members of the extended Romanov family started talking behind her back, even though most of this gossip was driven by their being shut out of the royals' lives. This would lead to tragic consequences. As for Nicholas, he was too blind and too weak either to realize the problem at hand or to make Alexandra change. He felt he needed her too much to impose. Alexandra's own brother once said, "The Tsar is an angel, but he doesn't know how to deal with her. What she needs is a superior will which can dominate and bridle her."[3]

Alexandra's chief duty was to produce an heir, and in this she was proving a terrible disappointment, one she was painfully aware of. In the span of six years, between 1895 and 1901, she gave birth to four daughters—Olga, Tatyana, Maria, and Anastasia—yet no son. The country was losing patience.

4. Monsieur Philippe

They were known by a number of names: The Black Ladies, The Black Peril, The Montenegrin Spiders, The Black Souls, The Black Crows, and The Black Princesses. Milica and Anastasia, born in 1866 and 1868 respectively in the Balkan city of Cetinje, were the daughters of the local reigning prince and later king of Montenegro ("Black Mountain"), Nicholas I Mirkov Petrovich-Nyegosh. While the two sisters were still girls, Tsar Alexander III invited them to Russia to attend the Smolny Institute of Noble Maidens and soon after they began to move in the capital's highest circles. In the summer of 1889, Princess Militsa (as her name is usually transliterated) married Grand Duke Pyotr Nikolaevich, a cousin of the future Nicholas II, and Anastasia—called Stana—married Prince (later Duke) George of Leuchtenberg, a member of the extended Romanov family. Stana's marriage proved an unhappy one, and George left her, and Russia, for his mistress in Biarritz. Stana, however, was not terribly upset, for she had found a lover of her own.

The two sisters were inseparable, and Stana spent most of her time at the homes of her sister and brother-in-law, whether their mansion on Petersburg's Galernaya Street or Znamenka, an immense palace on the Gulf of Finland near imperial Peterhof. It was at her sister's that Stana met and fell in love with Pyotr's older brother, Grand Duke Nikolai Nikolaevich, known in the family as Nikolasha. A giant of a man, with intense blue eyes and a stiff martial temperament, Nikolasha was a formidable figure, an army officer known for his love of dressing down his subordinates, whom he filled with terror. It was said he once sliced his own pet borzoi clean in half at a dinner party to prove to the shocked guests that his sword was indeed the finest in the entire Russian military. The "Evil One" some called him behind his back or, within the family, the "dread uncle." The Dowager Empress Maria Fyodorovna, mother of Nicholas II, said he was "sick with an incurable disease—he's a fool." One of Russia's greatest statesmen of the day said Nikolasha "was touched."[1] It took Stana several years but, finally, the tsar granted her a divorce in late 1906 and the following year she and Nikolasha wed. They made a formidable couple. She was one of Alexandra's closest friends, he was on the warmest of terms with Nicholas. To many in aristocratic society it seemed Stana and the grand duke would wield inordinate influence at court.

Both grand dukes deferred to their wives, and especially to the black-haired and strong-willed Militsa, a self-styled expert in the supernatural. She was undeniably well read, had studied Persian, and immersed herself deeply in all strains of mysticism and the occult, interests that she cultivated in her husband and Stana and Nikolasha. In September 1900, Militsa was awarded a diploma as a "Doctor of Hermeticism (ad honorem)" from the Advanced School of Hermetic Sciences in Paris. The school was run by the leading figure of the French occult, Gérard Encausse (1865–1916), best known as Papus. A trained medical doctor, Papus had steeped himself in ancient, esoteric knowledge that he believed had survived from the civilizations of Egypt, Babylon, and even Atlantis and was conveyed via various symbols and traditions, ideas that he explored in a number of extremely popular books. More than a teacher and writer, Papus was also a prominent Freemason and the head of France's L'Ordre du Martinisme and L'Ordre Kabbalistique de la Rose-Croix. Papus visited Russia several times around the turn of the century. In the winter of 1900–01 he gave private lectures to a number of grand dukes and duchesses, including the Black Princesses and their spouses, on various arcane subjects such as the archeometre. It is believed Papus established around this time a lodge of the Martinist Order (a branch of French Freemasonry with roots tracing back to the eighteenth century) in Petersburg whose members included Pyotr and Nikolasha. Some sources state Nikolasha introduced Papus to Nicholas and that he, too, joined the lodge. According to the later French ambassador to Russia, Maurice Paléologue, Papus held a séance at court during the Revolution of 1905 at which he summoned the spirit of Tsar Alexander III who instructed his son to remain strong and brave in the face of the danger and to resist the revolution at all costs. Papus told Nicholas that he, too, would use all his power to prevent revolution in Russia, but that this would only last during his lifetime. Papus died in late October 1916, four months before the collapse of the Romanov dynasty.[2]

Back in France Papus introduced Count Valerian Muravyov-Amursky, a Russian military agent, to a mysterious Frenchman by the name of Monsieur Philippe then taking high society by storm. "He is a sage," Papus exclaimed. "He speaks and the great secret of his power resides in his every word."[3] His full name was Philippe Nazier-Vachot (also given as Anthèlme Nizier Philippe or Nizier-Anthèlme Vachod). Born in Savoy in 1849 to a family of peasants, Philippe was apprenticed to his uncle's butcher shop and then moved to Lyon to study medicine as a young man. Whether he left the university willingly or was expelled, Philippe never did receive his medical degree, but this did little to stop his career. From the age of thirteen, so Philippe claimed, he had possessed rare healing powers, and after leaving university he dedicated himself to developing his gifts, delving deeply into the occult, hypnotism, and, some alleged, magic. In 1881, he set up his own laboratory and began accepting patients, treating them with a variety of techniques and substances, including what he called "psychic fluids and astral forces." No European institution would give him a diploma, but, according to one account, he did submit in 1884 a dissertation titled "Principles of Hygiene Applicable in Pregnancy, Childbirth, and Infancy" to the University of Cincinnati.[4] Diploma or not, Monsieur Philippe's fame quickly spread across France and he won a large number of followers among the elite. Although not much to look at—a thick figure of about average height with dark hair, an exaggerated mustache, and heavily lidded eyes—those who had seen him raved of "son charme." The press hailed him as the "Cagliostro of our age."[5]

One witness to a séance noted his great effect on women. He went about the room, his slippers embroidered with a dog smoking a pipe, to greet everyone by a gentle clasping of the hands. Next, each woman came up and whispered in his ear with "un air de confiance amoureuse." He told them he had little time to devote to each one of them, but that if they truly believed, they would all be healed. He then smiled at the women and they seemed to practically float off the floor under his spell. Next, he spoke to those gathered in vague terms about God and Magnetism and how he was a mere nothing, words which only seemed to convince his listeners even more firmly of his unique powers. Count Amursky attended one of Philippe's séances in Paris held on the anniversary of the execution of King Louis XVI. It was quite the event: Philippe called forth the king's spirit and to everyone's astonishment, a gruesome head dripping blood from its severed neck miraculously appeared in the air of the darkened room and then, before they knew it, vanished into darkness.[6]

It was perhaps through Count Amursky that the Black Princesses made Philippe's acquaintance in early 1900. Stana turned to him for help with her migraines and Militsa and Pyotr for treatment of their ill son Roman. They were all so impressed with Philippe that they invited him back to Russia with the thought of introducing him at court and particularly to the empress.[7] The sisters were among the few at court to open their arms to Alexandra upon her arrival in Russia. They went out of their way to make her feel loved and welcome and made certain to pay her the respect she demanded. Militsa loved to talk to Alexandra about the world of the occult and mysticism. She spoke convincingly of true men of God, of prophets and seers from the humble folk, and convinced the empress such men were real and walked among them, men free of the vanity and corruption of court and fashionable society. Militsa insisted not only on the reality of the Antichrist, but that his forces were present in contemporary society. Alexandra listened to this, and she believed. According to Anna Vyrubova, the empress's closest friend, Alexandra considered Militsa practically a "prophetess" and hung on her every word. Militsa even managed to convince Alexandra that the Queen of Italy, the Black Crows' sister Elena, had been possessed by an evil spirit.[8] Upon their return from France, the sisters told the royal couple about the remarkable man they had met while abroad and of their wish to present him to their majesties.

Nicholas recorded their first meeting in his diary on 26 March 1901: "I met with one remarkable Frenchman Mr Philippe! We talked for a long time." Philippe stayed in Russia for about three months and then returned for a second visit in July. Nicholas and Alexandra went to see him on the ninth, the very day of his arrival, and spent the evening with Philippe and the Black Princesses, Pyotr, and Nikolasha at Znamenka. They listened to their exotic visitor for hours, utterly enraptured by his words. Nicholas and Alexandra went to see him again the following night. "What miraculous hours!" the emperor noted in his diary after his second evening with Philippe. On the eleventh, Philippe lunched with the royal family. He spent a long time conversing alone with Alexandra and then was presented to the couple's four girls, including the infant Anastasia born the previous month. "We showed him our daughters," an ecstatic Nicholas wrote, "and prayed together with him in the bedroom!" By now they were already calling him "Our Friend." Nicholas and Alexandra saw Philippe every day until his departure for home on 21 July.

Nicholas was particularly drawn to Philippe. He went to visit him at Znamenka on the twelfth and the two sat alone for over three hours. "The ways of the Lord are inscrutable!" he noted in his diary after returning to the palace. The Frenchman was forever on their minds. On the fifteenth they left a theater performance at the intermission to see him and ended up listening to Philippe's words until 2:30 in the morning. Philippe would speak for hours of the wonders of God, at times reaching the height of religious ecstasy before his rapt audience. They rushed through their official commitments so as to have as much time with him as possible. These visits were the highlight of their day. The tsar even invited Philippe to join him at public ceremonies, as on the fourteenth when Nicholas reviewed the troops at nearby Krasnoe Selo and again at a ceremonial march there on the seventeenth. On the evening of the eighteenth, they had an "important conversation," in Nicholas's words, at Znamenka and prayed with him two nights later. Nicholas and Alexandra saw Philippe off late on the afternoon of the twenty-first. "We all feel as if we've been orphaned!" a despondent Nicholas remarked that evening in his diary. On his next visit to Znamenka eight days later Nicholas found it "strange" not to see "Our Friend" there.[9]

Even though Philippe was gone, his influence remained. Alexandra wrote to Nicholas on 27 August after the tsar had sailed off on the imperial yacht *Standart* to meet Kaiser Wilhelm of Germany at Danzig for discussions on the Far East (Wilhelm was seeking Russian support) and to observe German naval maneuvers: "My thoughts and prayers will be with you the whole time. And I know this is also true for Mr P[hilippe], and this alone comforts me, for else the separation would be too horrible. [. . .] Don't forget, Saturday evening around 10:30—all our thoughts shall take flight for Lyon. How rich our lives have become since we met him, and it seems that everything has become much easier to bear."[10]

From Danzig, Nicholas left for France, traveling with the French President Émile Loubet by train to Compiègne, northeast of Paris, where he was joined by Alexandra. There, on 6 September, Philippe paid them a surprise visit. Nicholas and Alexandra saw him again the next day, when they were introduced to his son-in-law Dr. Emmanuel Henri Lalande, the author of occult books under the pen name "Marc Haven." During his stay Nicholas brought up Philippe in a conversation with French Minister of Foreign Affairs Théophile Delcassé and urged the minister to grant his friend a French medical diploma. Delcassé, as well as Loubet, was shocked by the tsar's request, as well as by the adamancy with which it was delivered. To them Philippe was nothing but a charlatan. Nicholas's request was ignored.[11]

Important conversations. Prayer sessions. Requests of the president of France. It was clear from the beginning how great an effect Monsieur Philippe had had on Nicholas and Alexandra. This was no amusing diversion from the burdens of rule. Quite the opposite. In their new friend, the emperor and empress had found someone who could help shoulder the burden. Philippe had made himself into one of the tsar's chief confidants practically overnight, and he was apparently using this authority to offer advice on how to rule. Notes, purportedly written down by Militsa after a séance at Znamenka, captured some of the words he spoke to Nicholas: "War is coming to England," he predicted, and "Witte is sowing trouble." Count Sergei Witte, minister of finance and later prime minister who implemented policies to industrialize and modernize Russia's economy and political structure, seems to have incurred particular criticism from Philippe. He is said to have described Witte once to the Black Princesses as a deadly "spider" and said that an unclean spirit had taken possession of his soul. Philippe, to the contrary, had been trying to convince Nicholas to resist any political reforms that would weaken the tsar's autocratic power and told their majesties that a constitution would mean the ruin of both Russia and Nicholas himself, words that neither Nicholas nor Alexandra would ever forget. Philippe tried to get Nicholas to see that his future was not as some tame constitutional monarch, but as something grander. He was to become the "radiant Tsar of the East" and the defender of Europe's interests in the Orient. As for the empress, he informed her that she had an infallible ability to read people and could intuitively distinguish friend from foe.

And Philippe's influence did not end there, but extended all the way to Alexandra's womb. One of the talents that recommended Philippe to their majesties was his purported ability to determine the sex of a fetus. How exactly he managed this is not clear. Some claimed he used a series of "hypnotic passes" over the womb, others a mixture of astronomy, hermetic medicine, and psychurgy.[12] After the crushing disappointment with the birth of Anastasia that spring—four children, all girls—Alexandra, Nicholas, and indeed the entire empire were desperate to see a male heir to the throne. Philippe offered them the best hope yet and Nicholas and Alexandra gladly put their faith in his hands.

Philippe returned to Russia in November 1901, taking up residence in a small house near the Alexander Palace at Tsarskoe Selo, the residence of the Romanovs outside St. Petersburg. Nicholas spent the evening of the seventh with Philippe and Nikolasha, Pyotr, and their wives, all recently returned from the Crimea where they had hosted their French friend. They gathered again on the ninth at Znamenka in the company of Philippe, his daughter Victoria, and son-in-law Lalande. Nicholas had good news for his guest: earlier that same day the tsar had secured for Philippe a diploma as doctor from the Military-Medical Academy. To complete the distinction, Nikolasha ordered for him the uniform of a military medical doctor. Philippe stayed for two months, and it was apparently at this time that he convinced Alexandra that she was pregnant and that this time it was a boy. Alexandra was said to have been so overjoyed she kissed his hand. Before he left, Philippe instructed Alexandra to keep this news a secret and not to let her doctors know or examine her. Once he had gone, Nicholas, Alexandra, and the Black Princesses and their spouses could talk of nothing but the miracle-working Philippe.

When they next met in March 1902, Alexandra was indeed pregnant. Her abdomen was swelling and she had stopped wearing her corset. Their friend's prophecy was coming true. Nicholas and Alexandra spent three evenings with Philippe at the end of the month. They stayed up until 1 a.m. on the twenty-ninth listening enraptured by his "teachings," to quote Nicholas. "I could listen and listen to him forever without end," he sighed. They invited Philippe to spend the final moments of his stay in Russia with them in the garden of the Winter Palace. They parted with him on the thirtieth "with sadness," but the warmth of his visit lingered after his departure.[13]

By the spring of 1902 members of the Romanov family and the imperial court had taken notice of the mysterious stranger and had begun to talk. State Secretary Alexander Polovtsov noted in his diary on 8 May that he had heard from a most reliable source that their majesties had fallen completely under the influence of an occultist from Lyon. The Black Princesses had invited him to Russia, where he conducted séances for Nicholas and Alexandra at which he would summon various spirits, most often that of Alexander III so that he could instruct his son how to govern. Witte had heard that Philippe was trying to convince Nicholas that he needed no one to advise him on how to rule other than high church figures whom he, Philippe, would present to the emperor. There was talk of Philippe having established a secretive occult lodge at court and how he had been sent to Russia on a mission by a cabal of Jews and Freemasons to gain control over the tsar.[14]

Among those who believed such rumors was the Dowager Empress. So concerned was she about Philippe's influence over her son that she instructed General Pyotr Gesse, the palace commandant, to look into the man's story, convinced as she was that he was a "Satanist" and an agent of international Freemasonry plotting to bring down the monarchy. Gesse passed the matter on to Pyotr Rachkovsky, head of the tsarist secret police abroad stationed in Paris. It did not take long for Rachkovsky to report back that Philippe was a "dark and suspicious character," a dabbler in black magic, and "a Jew" with ties to the Lodge Grande Alliance Israélite. He included an article from *Le Temps* that described Philippe as a charlatan and a would-be magnetizer as well as information received from the French police. It was rumored that when Gesse presented the report to Nicholas, he took one look at it, tore it up, threw it on the floor, and stomped his feet all over it. Nicholas was said to have then ordered Minister of the Interior Vyacheslav von Plehve to put an immediate end to Rachkovsky's investigation and Alexandra asked Militsa to convey to Philippe their most sincere apologies for any unpleasantness Rachkovsky may have caused him and his family.[15] Plehve fired Rachkovsky in October, largely to please the emperor. The Philippe affair must have played some role in his downfall, though it was but one factor and likely not the main one. That did not prevent talk that Philippe had occasioned Rachkovsky's end. Grand Duke Sergei Mikhailovich, Sandro's brother, began to gossip that Nicholas had ordered Rachkovsky fired within twenty-four hours after reading his report. It was said that Philippe had sent a message to the emperor via Militsa that "the heavens" demanded Rachkovsky's firing.

In July, Alexandra's sister Ella visited Peterhof and tried to talk to her about Philippe's poor reputation. Alexandra wrote to Nicholas on 23 July: "She has heard many very unfavorable things about Him and that He is not to be trusted. I did not ask what one said—I explained that all came from jealousy and inquisitiveness. She said such secrecy had been spun around it. I said no, that we did everything openly and that in our positions there never can be anything hidden, as we live under the eyes of the whole world."[16] Alexandra would have none of Ella's meddling. Just the day before, in a shocking letter that shows just how important Philippe had become to them, she wrote to Nicholas, then on his way to Reval (now Tallinn) on the Gulf of Finland for talks with Kaiser Wilhelm: "It's dreadful letting you go all by yourself, knowing what troubles await you. But our dear Friend will be next to you, and he will help you answer Wilhelm's questions." Russian foreign policy was being placed in the hands of a French magician.

Philippe returned to Russia in early August, and Nicholas and Alexandra were ecstatic to see him. "A happy day," Nicholas wrote in his diary on 12 August 1902, "around 5 o'clock 'our friend' arrived at Znamenka. [. . .] We dined and spent the entire evening at Znamenka in the company of 'our friend.' What a joy it is to see him!" Yet it was during his stay that a crisis descended on the family. By the summer it had become clear that something was wrong with the empress. She had not gotten any bigger in months and there were no signs that the fetus was growing. Nevertheless, the palace moved ahead with plans for another, much-awaited child and imperial manifestoes announcing the birth were prepared. After considerable hesitation, Alexandra finally allowed herself to be examined by Dr. Dmitry Ott, Russia's leading gynecologist, who found that the empress was in fact not pregnant at all. It was a terrible blow. To save face, the palace put out a statement citing a miscarriage.[17]

On 18 August, an embarrassed Alexandra had to tell the Dowager Empress and the other family members the truth. Then she and Nicholas went to see Philippe at Znamenka and he did his best to console Alexandra and Nicholas, insisting they forget all this sorrow. Nicholas found his words "wonderful." But the rest of the family was not so willing to forget the matter. On the twentieth, Nicholas's mother and his sister Xenia came to the palace to get answers about what exactly had been going on with this strange Frenchman behind everyone's backs. The pair insisted there was nothing wrong in their relations with Philippe and that they had never tried to hide a thing, but they refused to say much more than that. Xenia was frustrated. She wrote in a letter that day to Princess Alexandra Obolenskaya, long-time maid-of-honor to the Dowager Empress: "Nevertheless the mystery remains—we still haven't found out exactly what he is! They said he is a very modest man and that it is pleasant to talk to him as he has such understanding and says 'things which do one good'! All the same it's good at least that *la glace est rompue!* [the ice is broken!]" An angry Nicholas wrote in his diary on the twenty-first: "People talk such rubbish about him that it's sickening just to listen, and I don't understand how they can believe the nonsense that they themselves are spouting." And much of what was being spouted was indeed nonsense. Grand Duke Konstantin Konstantinovich (aka K. R.), Nicholas's uncle, believed the talk, for example, that Philippe was attending meetings of the Council of State.[18] He also gave credit to the gossip that Nicholas was sending instructions to his ministers based on Philippe's advice, a story that, in light of Nicholas and Alexandra's own words, may well have been true. State Secretary Polovtsov found the entire business of the bogus pregnancy, which he was convinced had been the product of hypnotism by the "adventurer" Philippe, shameful. "All this would be amusing if it weren't so terribly sad," he remarked in his diary.[19]

Nicholas did not let the concerns of his family bother him. On the twenty-ninth he arrived in Kursk to witness military exercises. "I don't know but I feel so quiet before arriving today there," he wrote Alexandra, "that is the fulfillment of 'our Friend's' promise."[20] What that promise was is not known, but the tsar's words make plain his complete faith in Philippe's ability to predict the future. The day he arrived in Kursk, Ella wrote to the Dowager Empress about her talk with Alexandra and her worries about the tsar meeting someone like Philippe. She understood his desire to meet interesting people "without any position," but felt he had to be careful to do this only with many others around, for otherwise people were certain to talk. God forbid any of these meetings should take on even the slightest hint of being secret, she went on, for if so this could well have "fatal consequences." Ella remained suspicious about Philippe and the nature of his relations with her sister and brother-in-law and she criticized the Black Princesses, whom she called the "cockroaches," for having brought him to Russia. It was being said the sisters were using spiritualism to control the emperor and empress. "*C'est une crime*" were the words Nicholas's mother used to describe the situation at court.[21]

On the final day of August Xenia wrote again to Princess Obolenskaya:

I am no longer in any doubt that what happened to A. F. [Alix] was suggestion, although they themselves are unaware of it. However, she did admit to her sister that she prayed with Ph.[ilippe] on one occasion. It's all so strange and frightening, God knows how it will all end! I'm afraid that their friendship and association with these people will continue—everything will remain as before and we will look like fools. However we are not going to remain silent any longer, although we have to go about it in the right way, which is not easy—they have completely fallen under his influence. There are many things I could tell, only I don't want to write about it.[22]

By the autumn word of Philippe had spread beyond the court and aristocratic society and become public knowledge. The Russian journal *Liberation*, published in Paris and Stuttgart, ran a story in October on how Philippe had become so powerful that the tsar did not dare make a single decision, whether in regard to his personal life or matters of state, without his permission. The country was being governed by a man who claimed to be able to call forth the souls of the dead and to make the empress pregnant by way of "psychological treatments."[23] Although banned in Russia, copies of the journal were smuggled over the border and passed from hand to hand.

On 1 November, the elder Prince Vladimir Meshchersky, an arch-conservative defender of the monarchy and a personal friend of Alexander III, went to talk to Nicholas and Alexandra of the danger a man like Philippe presented to the monarchy. Focusing his attention on Alexandra, he warned her of the fantastical world of gossip that was taking hold due to their French friend and how such dangerous talk was already spreading across the country. Alexandra refused to listen: "I do not give anyone the right to talk about this, no one dares to touch on my private life."

Meshchersky told the empress that she could ignore his words and drive him away, but that she needed to realize the spiritual life of the empress of Russia was not a matter her subjects would, or should, be indifferent to. He then proceeded to tell her of the rumors floating around, including one that in the home of Grand Duke Pyotr and Militsa Philippe was viewed practically as a god, that they never sat in his presence and even bowed before his feet. It was also rumored the three of them had managed to turn Alexandra against Orthodoxy and that the tsar, too, was beginning to waver in his faith. And among the common folk it was being said foreigners had sent a "sorcerer" who had bewitched the empress and taken control of her womb. Yes, he admitted, all of this was pure nonsense, but what if their enemies were able to make use of it, to spread such talk among the educated classes and the *narod*, the vast peasant class, just imagine, the old prince asked Alexandra, the dangers it would present to the prestige, and security, of the autocracy? His warning left Alexandra unmoved.

Nicholas, however, appears to have heeded the warnings. Although it is not clear exactly why and when Nicholas came to this decision, the tsar seems to have realized that he had to send his friend away and cut off all ties with him given the scandal. It is possible a letter from the great holy man of the day, John of Kronstadt, instructing Nicholas to break with Philippe was crucial. They exchanged gifts before Philippe returned to France. Nicholas presented him with an expensive Serpollet steam-powered automobile that he had purchased on a previous trip to Europe. Philippe gave Alexandra some dried flowers that he said had been touched by the hand of Christ himself. He also gave her an icon and a bell, telling her that should anyone approach her who was not a friend, the bell would begin to ring, as if by magic. This, he told Alexandra, would guard them against all enemies. Alexandra had the flowers framed and kept them in her bedroom, and she never forgot about the bell's magic power, using it to safeguard the family throughout the entire reign.[24] Victoria Lalande wrote a plaintive letter to Stana, bemoaning their fate at being sent away for good and railing against what she saw as the injustices done to her father.[25] Alexandra and Nicholas were equally distraught; the empress was in tears as they parted. Philippe, however, left her with a message of hope. You will always be able to find teachers who will help you both in your searches, he said. "Be calm, Your Majesty," he instructed Alexandra, "another friend will come and he will protect you when I am no longer here."[26] The empress took his words as a prophecy. Alexandra appears to have shared Philippe's words and they quickly spread. Grand Duke Konstantin wrote in his diary how it was being said that "Philippe's mission is drawing to a close, that soon he will die and will reappear afterwards to the circle of friends in the guise of another man. What nonsense!"[27]

The general feeling about the Philippe affair was neatly summed up in the middle of November 1902 by Lev Tikhomirov, a former revolutionary turned monarchist and leading conservative ideologue: "That Philippe is the most shameful occurrence for the Imperial Family. He is some sort of foreign charlatan, hypnotist, magnetizer, and magician presenting himself as the possessor of occult powers." Tikhomirov was convinced John of Kronstadt's warning to Nicholas had saved the tsarist family from ruin and he hoped they had learned their lesson and would forget Philippe for good.[28] But they did not forget Philippe. When, in 1907, Nikolasha and Stana were finally able to wed, Nikolasha saw their union as some miracle made possible by the mystical power of Philippe.[29]

If in the reign of Catherine the Great many a young officer at court dreamed of becoming the official favorite of the empress as the way to secure his future and fortune, so in the reign of Nicholas did any number of mystics, stranniki, and startsy hope to occupy the place of seer to the royal couple. After Philippe had gone a series of Russian pretenders appeared at court, including the stranniki Vasia (Tkachenko), and Matryona the Barefooted and the holy fool Mitya "The Nasal Voice" Kozelsky. From childhood Mitya had been deprived of the ability to utter comprehensible speech yet he became known for his prophecies and inspired words that came out of his mouth as strange lowings and bellows that were interpreted for his listeners by a man named Elpidifor. Mitya gained a reputation among the people as a simple man of God, and apparently came to the attention of a highly placed official who brought him to court from the Optina Monastery. Mitya and his inter-preter were apparently presented to the tsar, and Nicholas was taken with the holy fool, but it seems that his status at court was fairly soon eclipsed by the appearance of Rasputin. After his fall from grace Mitya could be seen wandering barefoot through the streets of the capital, even in winter, dressed in a black cassock, his hair reaching down to his shoulders.[30]

5. Alexei

Before leaving Russia for good, Philippe supposedly fell into a trance and experienced a prophecy. Seek the intercession of St. Seraphim of Sarov, he said, and he will give Alexandra a son. But there was one problem: there was no such saint in the Russian Orthodox Church. There had been, however, a great starets by the name of Seraphim in the early decades of the nineteenth century who had lived nearly his entire life in extreme poverty and isolation, first in a hut in the woods and then in a cell in the monastery of Sarov. He had been a true holy man, a humble yet profound spiritual figure, yet he had not passed the test of saintliness: his corpse had failed to remain uncorrupted and had rotted away and thus the church had refused to recognize him as a saint. But Nicholas, to the anger of the Holy Synod, the church's governing body, overrode the decision ("The Emperor can do anything," an angry Alexandra insisted) and ordered that Seraphim be canonized. To some in high society, it seemed Philippe was the true miracle worker. "It would be difficult to know where Philippe ends and Seraphim begins," commented wryly Lady-in-Waiting Yelizaveta Naryshkina.

Nicholas and Alexandra attended the ceremony themselves in July 1903, along with members of their family and a crush of nearly 300,000 pilgrims. It was a profoundly moving religious event, one that helped convince Alexandra of the unbreakable bond that linked the tsar and his people. The canonization of Seraphim was also tinged with political undertones. Continuing a policy begun under his late father, Nicholas sought to bind the dynasty to the Russian masses by harking back to Russia's pre-Petrine past. And Seraphim, who had bemoaned the baleful influence of Western European Enlightenment on Russian spirituality, served that purpose well as part of the tsar's efforts to cultivate the medieval notion of a mystical connection between the tsar and his people. On the evening of 19 July, the royal couple waded into the holy water of the Sarova River, as instructed by Philippe, hopeful that it might bless them, and Russia, with the longed-for sought heir.[1]

Within three months Alexandra was pregnant. On 30 July 1904 at 1:15 in the afternoon, Alexandra gave birth to a son. They named him Alexei. The joy, tinged with relief, was overwhelming. Not only the family, but the entire country celebrated—cannons boomed and church bells rang out across the empire. Back in the nursery, the empress recorded her baby's vital measurements in her notebook: "Weight 4660 gr.; length 58 cm. Measurement of the head 38 cm.; chest 39 cm."[2] But the most important thing about the young boy she could not see or record or measure. Hemophilia.

The disease had been passed on by his mother. Alexandra's grand-mother Queen Victoria had been a hemophilia carrier. One of her sons and two of her daughters, including Alexandra's mother, carried the gene for the disease, and she gave it to Alexandra and her brother Fred-erick. (Alexandra's sister Irene was also a carrier.) Frederick (aka Frittie) first showed signs of the disease in 1872, the year of Alexandra's birth. In May 1873, at the age of three, little Frittie, whom his mother had adored, fell from his mother's window onto a stone terrace. He had not broken any bones and appeared to be all right, but within hours he was dead of internal bleeding. Alexandra's two nephews were also hemo-philiacs. One of them, Prince Henry of Prussia, likely died of it in 1904 at the age of four, not long before the birth of Alexei.

If it came as a cruel shock to his parents that Alexei had been born a "bleeder," it should not have, for the inherited basis of the disease had been established as early as the middle of the nineteenth century. Indeed, a French doctor wrote in 1876 that "all members of bleeder families should be advised against marriage." But it appears that mem-bers of Europe's royal houses were neither given this advice nor did they seek it out, preferring to live in ignorance of the laws of science. As the British geneticist J. B. S. Haldane put it, "The hemophilia of the Tsare-vich was a symptom of the divorce between royalty and reality."[3] Reality intruded quickly into the Romanov household, however. Within the first two months, Nicholas and Alexandra noticed the baby was bleed-ing inexplicably from his navel. Next, he developed bruises and dark swellings under his tender skin. By then it became clear to the parents: Alexei was a hemophiliac. Joy turned to grief.

Grand Duchess Maria Pavlovna (the younger), cousin of Nicholas II and sister of Grand Duke Dmitry Pavlovich, one of Rasputin's mur-derers, wrote in her memoirs:

Even in our house a certain melancholy reigned. My uncle and aunt undoubtedly knew already that the child was born suffering and that from his birth he carried in him the seeds of an incurable illness [. . .] Nobody ever knew what emotions were aroused in them by this horrible certainty, but from that moment, troubled and apprehensive, the Empress's character underwent a change, and her health, physical as well as moral, altered.[4]

If to Nicholas and Alexandra the birth of their son was deeply connected to their friend Philippe, to nearly everyone else it would become connected to his successor. It was said that Rasputin had predicted Alexei's birth and that Alexandra believed his prayers had made it a reality. This, many claimed, was the basis for his influence over the empress. Others told darker tales, insisting that Rasputin did more than pray over the Empress, that he was, in fact, the boy's father.[5] Nothing, of course, could have been further from the truth, for the first meeting between Nicholas and Alexandra and the man who would loom so large in their lives, and that of the country, still lay a year ahead.

The English historian Sir Bernard Pares famously wrote decades ago that "the nursery was the center of all Russia's troubles," asserting that it was the illness of the tsarevich Alexei that brought Rasputin to the palace and his strange ability to comfort the boy that was the foundation of his influence and power.[6] This understanding of the nature of the relationship between Rasputin and the royal couple, and chiefly Alexandra, has long been the accepted view, and while it is true that Alexandra's anguish over her son's health and her belief that Rasputin alone could safeguard him were important, in no way does this begin to explain the much more complex, and profound, need Alexandra felt for Rasputin.

As the story of Monsieur Philippe shows, even before the birth of her son, Alexandra, and Nicholas, too, was in search of a holy man to advise, enlighten, and comfort her. Part of this had to do with her role as a mother, and she was desperate to find someone who claimed the knowledge of how she could produce a son, regardless of their background. But from the beginning, Alexandra had no intention of limiting Philippe's influence to her womb or to her soul, an important fact that has been overlooked. As her letters to Nicholas show, Alexandra looked to Philippe for political guidance and strength, strength not for herself, but for Nicholas, whose weakness and fatalism were only too painfully well known to her. Alexandra loved Nicholas, but she could not help but see how his personal flaws undermined his power, prestige, and effectiveness as emperor, and she was determined to do whatever was necessary to help him, even if this meant finding another man to provide the will he lacked.

And here, in the Philippe interlude, we can see in embryonic form the story of Rasputin yet to come: Alexandra's need for and blind trust in a spiritual advisor, a man of God, who spoke of higher truths and prophecies; her mysticism and intense religiosity; her willingness to insert herself in politics and to use the words of holy men to try to instruct Nicholas on how to rule; the couple's inability to see how their private life was fraught with public implications; the level of mistrust among members of the house of Romanov and how this mistrust engendered ill-feeling and in return gossip that further weakened family relations and would later destroy the bonds among them, and how this gossip quickly spread to educated society and tarnished the image of the monarchy; and finally how attempts to investigate the holy man, and to open the tsar's eyes, only deepened the chasm between the throne and the rest of Russia and would, in the case of Rasputin, eventually help lead to revolution.

6. The Burning Torch

There he is, carrying his pack,
filling the forest trail
with a long, drawn-out song, a soft song
but a sly song, oh, a naughty song. [. . .]

He comes—God help us!—
to our proud capital.
He enchants the empress
of endless Russia.

Nikolai Gumilyov, "The Muzhik"[1]

Sometime between May 1904 and early 1905 Rasputin arrived for the
first time in the historic Tatar city of Kazan on the Volga River, incor-
porated into Russia after a bloody siege under Ivan the Terrible in 1552.[2]
He had apparently been brought to the city by a wealthy merchant
widow by the name of Bashmakova. They had met on a pilgrimage,
possibly at the Abalak Monastery, not long after she had lost her husband. Her grief was enormous, but Rasputin spoke to her and eased her
suffering. She felt drawn to him and became one of his early followers
and began to invite him along, at her expense, on her travels to holy
sites. "A simple soul," Rasputin said of her. "She was rich, very rich, and
she gave it all away [. . .] She inherited more, and gave this away too [. . .]
and should she inherit still more she'll give that away as well, that's the
kind of person she is."[3] In Kazan Bashmakova introduced Rasputin to
wealthy local merchants and prominent clergy. Rasputin made a good
impression. He was a strong, lean, healthy Siberian of thirty-five, proud
and independent. By now Rasputin had taken to calling himself a
starets, and he impressed the people of Kazan with his inner power, his
insight into the human soul, and his knowledge of Scripture. True, he
could be brusque and rude, and was ignorant of the ways of society, but

then he appeared to be a true man of God on a spiritual mission with no time for such petty matters. Word of the Siberian holy man spread quickly and people began coming to him for help. A young couple, grieving over the death of their two small children, sought him out. "My wife's despair grew into insanity," the husband later said, "and the doctors couldn't do a thing. Some advised me to send for Rasputin . . . Imagine this: after speaking with her for half an hour, she became totally serene. Say whatever you like against him, maybe it's even so. But he saved my wife—and that's the truth!"

Among the clergy Rasputin met was Gavriil, father superior of the Seven Lakes Monastery outside Kazan. The two men were alike in many ways. Both were born into the peasantry and had pilgrimaged to the Verkhoturye Monastery and prayed at the relics of St. Simeon of Verkhoturye. They had mutual acquaintances, such as the monk, and later bishop and metropolitan, Melety (Mikhail Zaborovsky), and both men were reputed to possess special healing powers. Gavriil had even attracted the attention of the empress's sister Ella, who often visited him. Rasputin also won over Archimandrite Andrei, born Prince Alexander Ukhtomsky into one of Russia's oldest noble families. Rasputin was a frequent guest at the archimandrite's home, and Andrei even provided Rasputin with recommendations in St. Petersburg. Of Andrei, Rasputin said, "I do not know a single person in whom there is so much love."[4]

Rasputin later recalled that in his meetings with Kazan clergymen, "I mainly spoke with them about love, but they had many surprises from the love I had experienced."[5] Rasputin offers no details about the love he had experienced, but stories later appeared about certain improper acts with women during his Kazan sojourn—questionable meetings alone with various females, taking young ladies to the city's bathhouses and then luring them away from their families after having corrupted them.[6] It is said that Rasputin admitted his sins to Gavriil, about how he stroked and kissed women, although he insisted it was done in a loving and appropriate way. Gavriil believed him, but like so many of Rasputin's early supporters, he, too, would turn against him. Citing the common folk wisdom, he later said that Rasputin was no different than a spider: kill him and God would forgive forty of your sins.

One day, while drinking tea with Gavriil and a group of theology students, Rasputin mentioned his intention to travel to St. Petersburg.

Gavriil disapproved of the idea, thinking to himself: "You'll lose your way in Petersburg, the city will ruin you." All of a sudden, Rasputin leaned in to Gavriil: "And God? What about God?" For Gavriil it was proof Rasputin could read people's minds.[7]

From Kazan Rasputin left for St. Petersburg. "One time I was captivated by an idea and it settled in my heart," Rasputin wrote in his *Life of an Experienced Pilgrim*. His idea was to build a church in Pokrovskoe, for, as Rasputin wrote, echoing the words of the Apostle Paul, he who builds a church will never be conquered by the gates of Hell. Yet Rasputin was poor, how was he ever to get the money—as much as 20,000 rubles—to build the church that he could see fully formed in his heart? Rasputin wrote he had traveled all over the Tobolsk province in search of bene-factors, but the nobles there, though they wasted their money in profligate display, would not give him a single ruble. So he decided to journey to the capital of the tsars.

"And then I come to St. Petersburg and I feel like a blind man on the road, that's how I feel." He went first to the great Alexander Nevsky Lavra (monastery) to pray, carrying nothing but a sack of dirty clothes and a few kopecks, which he spent on candles. As he was leaving, he inquired about a Bishop Sergei just as a policeman happened to be pass-ing by. "What kind of a friend of the bishop can you be," he threatened the poor bedraggled peasant, "you must be a hooligan." A frightened Rasputin ran to the monastery's back gate, where he was struck down by a doorman. Rasputin knelt before the man and told him something about himself and why he sought the bishop. The doorman was moved by Rasputin's words and went to fetch Bishop Sergei (Ivan Stragorodsky), the rector of the St. Petersburg Theological Seminary, who called him in and talked at length with the Siberian starets. Sergei became Rasputin's patron, introducing him to the city's elite and then taking him to the imperial palace and presenting him to the tsar. Nicholas listened to Ras-putin's plan to build a church and gave him the money and Rasputin returned home filled with joy.[8]

It is a moving tale, though far from true. Rasputin did not arrive at the monastery a poor and unknown peasant seeker, but as the con-queror of Kazan bearing a letter of recommendation addressed to Sergei from the influential Bishop Khrisanf, or Chrysanthos (Khristofor

Shchetkovsky), vicar of the Kazan diocese. It was not Rasputin's words, uttered upon his knees to a doorman, that won him entrée to Sergei's apartment, but those of Khrisanf.[9] The time was most likely between the late autumn of 1904 and the spring of 1905.[10]

Ivan Fedchenkov, a seminary student and supporter of the holy fool Mitya, tonsured as the monk Veniamin* in 1907, who later went on to become a metropolitan in the Russian church during the Stalin years, recalled seeing Rasputin in Sergei's apartment at the Lavra: "Rasputin immediately made a very strong impression on me, due both to the exceptional intensity of his personality (he was like a taut bow or spring) and to the sharp insight into others' souls." Without Veniamin saying a word, Rasputin guessed his future plans and the young student was dumbfounded.

> Generally speaking, Rasputin was a truly out of the ordinary person, in terms of his sharp mind and his religious focus. You had to see him, the way he prayed in the cathedral: he stood just like a string under tension, his face turned to the heights, and then, with great speed, he would begin to cross himself and bow.
>
> I think it was precisely in the exceptional energy of his religiosity that lay the main reason for his influence on believers. [. . .] Somehow we have all become "unleavened" or, to use the expression of Our Savior, the salt in us has lost its potency, we are no longer "the salt of the earth and the light of the world" [. . .] We have all cooled down [. . .]
>
> And then suddenly a burning torch appears. What sort of spirit he had, what sort of quality, we did not want to know, nor could we have discovered for we lacked the necessary knowledge. But the magnificence of this new comet, quite naturally, attracted attention.[11]

The practical-minded Bishop Sergei was among the few not impressed by this burning torch from Siberia. It seems he met him only once, and after that never wanted anything more to do with Rasputin.[12] This, however, was not the case for Sergei's seminary colleague Feofan.

Born Vasily Bystrov in 1873 into the family of a poor village priest, Archimandrite Feofan had been a brilliant student at the St. Petersburg Theological Seminary before being made the seminary's inspector in 1905 and then rector four years later. By all accounts Feofan was a true

---

* For clarity, referred to henceforth as Veniamin.

man of God with tremendous spiritual depth. The religious writer and state official Prince Nikolai Zhevakhov called Feofan "a monk of exceptional disposition and enormous authority," a man who exercised great influence not only on the seminarians but within the highest social circles of the capital. Even the writer Zinaida Gippius, someone quite critical of the Russian clergy, called Feofan "a monk of rare humility who lived a serene, righteous life." Gippius never forgot meeting Feofan: "I remember him, he was small, thin, quiet, with a dark, severe little face, and with black hair, so smooth it looked as if it had been glued on."[13] Like other clerics at the time, Feofan sought out religious men from the narod who came unpolished, uneducated, yet full of the living church. Feofan would tell the seminarians that "God's men still exist on earth. To this day our Holy Russia abounds in saints. God sends consolation to his people from time to time in the guise of righteous men, and they are the mainstays of Holy Russia."[14] Feofan surrounded himself with these holy men. He loved talking with them and hearing the way they discussed God and faith; their words took him to another world far from the mundane reality of St. Petersburg. Bishop Sergei invited Feofan to meet Rasputin when he first appeared. Feofan was mesmerized by this man of God from Siberia who went by the name of Brother Grigory. Echoing Veniamin's words, Feofan was amazed by the stranger's psychological perspicacity which bordered on second sight. It was clear from their conversations that the man lacked book learning, but, Feofan recalled after the revolution, he had "a subtle grasp of spiritual experience obtained through personal knowledge."[15] Feofan began meeting regularly with Rasputin, and his wonder at the Siberian holy man grew. Before long he was telling others about Brother Grigory and bringing people to hear his words. Among them were two female relations Feofan invited to the seminary to share the good news of his discovery. As they walked in the seminary's garden, an excited Feofan told them about a man of rare holiness and insight recently arrived from Siberia. "I have never heard anyone pray as he does," he said. After praying with him life itself becomes clearer and so easier to bear, he told the young ladies. Moreover, this stranger had the gift of prophecy: he could read the past and future in every person's face, a gift he had acquired through fasting and prayer.[16]

Feofan began telling anyone who would listen of Rasputin's miraculous powers. In the summer of 1906, while visiting Zhitomir, Feofan stayed with the family of Anna Obukhova. The daughter of a wealthy merchant, Anna was then experiencing a spiritual crisis and was considering becoming a nun. Feofan talked her out of it. "Save yourself in the world," he instructed and then proceeded to tell Anna of a holy man from Siberia—"He is a saint, a true saint"—and recommended they meet, for Feofan was certain Rasputin could help her.[17]

What brought Rasputin to St. Petersburg? It is a question with no clear answer. Rasputin, and some contemporary Russian nationalist historians, would have us believe it was to find the money to build his church back in Pokrovskoe. The historian-playwright Edvard Radzinsky posits a much grander, and infinitely more sinister, aim: "To destroy both Petersburg and that whole world of the tsars [. . .]." Rasputin's daughter Maria offered more mundane reasons—to find a better school for her, having left Maria in the care of a well-to-do family in Kazan, and to please Feofan and other clerics then urging him to come and stay.[18]

The most likely answer lies in some combination of Rasputin's character, his spiritual quest, and the success of his visit to Kazan. Rasputin the wanderer, the seeker, would naturally have been drawn to the idea. He had covered thousands of miles on foot and seen many cities and churches and monasteries. One of the few places that remained was the Alexander Nevsky Lavra. And what Russian would not want to lay their eyes on the imperial capital of the tsars? There was an innate curiosity in Rasputin, but mixed in with it was a clear strain of ambition. He had been to many of Russia's holy places and spoken to many of her holy men, and he had impressed them with his spiritual gifts, gifts that at the time few denied and in which Rasputin took great pride. We will never know whether it was Khrisanf's idea to write the letter to Bishop Sergei or Rasputin's, but it does seem likely that Khrisanf wrote it freely and with conviction (there would have been no reason for him to do so otherwise) and that Rasputin suffered no trepidation or self-doubt about embarking on this important step of his personal journey.

Rasputin's arrival in St. Petersburg, Maria recalled, marked "the starting-point of so many disturbances in his life."

My father was then nearly forty [he was closer to thirty-six]; that is to say his character was already completely formed. Twenty years of pilgrimages and wanderings on foot, his peasant's life, his love of the soil and solitude had developed in him that warm-hearted kindliness, that simplicity of bearing, that bluntness of speech, and at the same time that rather overbearing independence which mark the recluse. There has been talk of his lack of sophistication, his irresponsibility, and it is true where he was concerned with money. But at the same time, he showed in his dealings with men an extraordinary clairvoyance which enabled him forthwith to fathom their most secret impulses. [. . .]

Of rugged bearing, accustomed to speak his mind, never intimidated, because he always plumbed the depths of men's thoughts; such was my father [. . .]

But the capital, sophisticated, worldly, cynical, did not greet a peasant kindly. The mere sight of him turned a great many people off. Dirty, they called him, even though he was not, slovenly, only because he did not style his hair and beard like the smart men of St. Petersburg. His refusal to kowtow to the rich and mighty was described as ill breeding.[19]

In Petersburg, Rasputin lost his way. He told Prince Vladimir Meshchersky, the arch-conservative and openly homosexual confidant of Tsar Alexander III, several years later that, "It's hard to live here. There are no regular hours, no regular days, nothing but holidays that mean the death of the soul [. . .] Fate threw me into the capital. It's so noisy here that men lose their minds . . . It's like a noisy wheel . . . All of this often makes my brain swell."[20]

He was a blind man on the road, as he said himself. The city was loud, it made his head spin, but this attracted Rasputin as much as it repelled, and after tasting its charms Rasputin could never forsake them. No more would he wander as a poor pilgrim, or act as the village teacher of simple morals. The habits that had kept him close to the narod, and independent, free, and ignorant of the temptations of fashionable society and the seductiveness of power, died there, even if he never forgot his life as a wanderer and knew well how to use it to advantage. Gavriil had feared going to Petersburg would lead to Rasputin's ruin, and he was right.

Maria wrote that the move to Petersburg was pivotal in her father's life, for city life corrupted him over time. If, at first, his life differed little from that back in Pokrovskoe, with time her father gave in to temptation and allowed himself "to be caught by some of the seductions of the capital."[21] But the change did not happen right away. Veniamin recalled, of Rasputin's early days in Petersburg: "Pious people, especially women, began to praise this rare man, his circle of acquaintances grew wider. 'He's holy,'—people extolled as his fame grew. And those spiritually hungry individuals within high society sought out this 'light.'"

Prince Zhevakhov noted that while the Petersburg elite was interested in religious questions, they knew little about Orthodoxy and had little contact with the clergy. They were naive, too easily impressed by the starets from Siberia with his strange manners and mysterious pronouncements, and by the way he was not the least bit concerned with wealth and status, by the aristocrats' gilded palaces and lofty titles, addressing everyone as *ty*, the informal *you*.[22] Feofan wanted to show off his discovery and began introducing Rasputin to Petersburg's salons that at the time played a large role in the city's cultural life where the elite from the world of the aristocracy, the church, the arts and culture, the press, and the court and state apparatus would gather, often to engage in spiritual conversations.

The most influential of these belonged to Countess Sofia Ignatieva (née Princess Meshcherskaya) and her husband, Count Alexei Ignatiev, deputy minister of the interior. In their massive, dimly lit apartment at 26 French Embankment met prominent clergy, such as the monk, and later metropolitan, Seraphim (Leonid Chichagov) and Bishop Germogen (Georgy Dolganov), writers and journalists, such as Vasily Skvortsov, editor of the monarchist daily the *Bell*, and figures from high society, such as Lyubov Golovina and Alexandra Taneeva. Many of these people became acolytes and then enemies of the man Feofan introduced them to at Ignatieva's apartment. The countess, drawn to various forms of mysticism, had, so she claimed, prophetic dreams that were discussed there. In one Father Seraphim appeared and said, "There is a great prophet here among us. His purpose is to reveal the will of Providence to the tsar and to lead him on the path of glory."[23] The countess had no doubt who the prophet was: Rasputin.

Rasputin also frequented the salon of the widow Baroness Varvara Iskul von Gildebrand in her sumptuous apartment at 18 Kirochnaya Street. The baroness had wide-ranging interests, from literature and art to politics and church affairs, and guests from a wide range of backgrounds, from grand dukes and duchesses, to state ministers, socialists, priests, and Tolstoyans. Although she did not find Rasputin terribly convincing herself, the baroness found him entertaining and advertised him as a bit of exoticism to her Petersburg friends. She thought it amusing how he would kiss everyone, regardless of their social status, upon greeting and parting, the kind of thing that just was not done in Petersburg circles but, so she believed, was the custom among the common folk in Russia's villages.[24]

Vladimir Bonch-Bruevich, historian, student of Russian religious sects, devoted Bolshevik, and later Lenin's personal secretary, left a detailed account of his first meeting with Rasputin at the baroness's home:

Soon after eight o'clock Rasputin appeared. With a free and light gait he entered Varvara Ivanovna's drawing-room, where, so it seemed, he had never been before, and with his very first words he set upon his hostess as he strode the carpet: "What in the world have you done, my dear woman, covering your walls with so many paintings, it's like a real museum in here, and to think one wall could feed five hungry villages, oh, you, look how you folks live, all while the poor peasants are starving . . .". Varvara Ivanovna began to introduce Rasputin to her guests. He immediately started asking questions: Is Lady A married? Where's her husband? Why did she come alone? Now if we were together, I'd look after you, just as you are [. . .] He carried on his conversations in this manner, very gay, joking, playful and light-hearted. [. . .] My attention was chiefly directed to his eyes. His gaze was always concentrated and direct, and a strange phosphorescent light played the entire time in his eyes. He continually stroked his listeners with his eyes, and at times his speech would suddenly slow down, he would drawl, lose his way as if he were thinking of something else and then fix his gaze on someone, point-blank, stare straight into their eyes for a few minutes, the entire time dragging out his words in a disconnected, confusing manner. Then suddenly he would snap out of it, come to himself, as it were, embarrassed and try to change the subject and start a new conversation. I noticed that it was precisely his persistent staring that had the greatest effect on those gathered, and particularly on the women, who were made most uncomfort-able and anxious by his gaze, yet who then shyly started to watch him out of the corner of their eyes, and sometimes even drew close to him to speak with him a bit more, to hear more of what he had to say. While speaking to someone, he would sometimes suddenly and quite abruptly turn to another, whom he had been looking at 15 or 20 minutes earlier, and, breaking off his conversation, begin

to say in a slow drawl, "No, mother, that's not good, not good at all
. . . That's no way to live, just look at yourself . . . do you really think
responding with an insult will fix matters . . . You need love . . . Yes
. . . Love's what's needed . . . ," and then just as suddenly he would
go back to his previous conversation or start a new one or walk
quickly about the room, occasionally taking a seat for a moment
or bending down, busily rubbing his hands the entire time. All of
this made an impression on those present. People began to whisper
and to say that he had indeed divined the truth in certain matters,
that he had great insight, and an atmosphere of heightened nervous energy began to take hold of the kind that can also be
experienced in monasteries around startsy and seers.[25]

The baroness invited Zinaida Gippius to come meet Rasputin at
her salon in 1912 after his name had become famous—or rather infamous—across Russia. Gippius, along with her husband, the writer
and philosopher Dmitry Merezhkovsky, declined, however. She insisted
that, unlike nearly everyone else in the capital, she had no interest in
joining the throngs curious to get a glimpse of Rasputin, a decision she
saw as a credit to them both.[26]

But they were in the minority. It seemed most people could not get
enough of Rasputin and other strange holy men then making the
rounds of the city's salons. The reason why, according to one journalist,
was quite simple:

> In the gilded drawing-rooms life becomes weary much faster than
> in middle-class apartments and humble little chambers. For money
> you can get whatever life offers. And now we have reached the
> point at which even the most fantastic possibilities fail to satisfy.
> Everything's been tried! In such cases people tend to gravitate to
> that which lies beyond human comprehension, be it a living saint
> or holy fool or epileptic. Just maybe this will offer some new ex-
> perience, will open up some new opportunity, some new reality.
> And it is for this reason that such dark, mysterious figures as Ras-
> putin appear.[27]

Russia, he concluded, was experiencing "strange times."

7. The Mad Monk

At the St. Petersburg Theological Seminary Rasputin met another churchman who was to become one of his greatest allies and one of his greatest enemies. Sergei Trufanov, born in 1880 into a Cossack family along the Don River in southern Russia, lived a life almost as unbelievable as Rasputin's. He entered the seminary in 1901 and became a protégé of Feofan and Bishop Sergei, under whom he was ordained as the monk Iliodor in November 1903. After graduating from the seminary in the summer of 1905, Iliodor was appointed instructor of homiletics at the Yaroslavl Theological Academy and then sent to teach at the Novgorod Seminary in 1906 before being transferred later that year to the Pochaevskaya Lavra in western Ukraine.

The quick succession of posts was not the result of promotions, but a symptom of Iliodor's rebellious nature. The local press in Pochaevsk had this to say about the young monk: "This remarkable man, almost still a boy, with his gentle, pretty, feminine face yet powerful will, immediately attracts crowds of common people wherever he appears. His passionate, inspired words about God, love for the tsar and the fatherland make a deep impression on the masses and light in them the hunger for heroic deeds."[1]

Even his enemies had to admit that Iliodor was an exceptional orator. He could captivate people and convince them to follow him like few others, but it was where he wanted to lead them that was so terrifying. Iliodor had the face of an angel, but the soul of a thug. One biographer has dubbed him a "proto-fascist." In an era known for its anti-Semitism, Iliodor stood out for the extreme violence of his hatred of the Jews. He loudly supported the Union of the Russian People (part of the notorious Black Hundreds) and attacked anyone he saw as its enemy. He began to express his views in a series of articles and booklets depicting Russia as "fettered in Jewish chains."[2]

His 1906 brochure *When Will This Finally End?*, addressed directly to the tsar, offers a picture of Iliodor's Russia. The country, he cried, was being ruined by Jews, journalists, the Duma, and the "criminal humanity" of Russia's legal system. The End of Times is nearly at hand, he warned: "We strongly believe and adamantly preach that the time of the Antichrist shall someday come to Holy Russia." Russia can be saved, it is not too late, Iliodor assured his readers, but the tsar must act and act firmly: violence is the only answer. The death penalty must be reinstated. Anyone who dares to insult the name of God must be "executed in the most ferocious manner." Russia's courts must be returned to their traditional role as "the shortest path to the gallows, the axe, and the bullet." And such punishment ought to be meted out not just to criminals, but also "slanderers, lying newspapermen, and instigators!" Throughout the land, and especially at the imperial court, "everyone in whose veins flows foreign blood" is to be rounded up and banished from Russia. The door to the West that Peter the Great opened two centuries before needs to be slammed shut and for good. To aid the tsar in this epochal struggle, Iliodor placed himself before Nicholas as his most devoted subject, ready to wash from Russia every last vestige of the West. With him, he bragged to the tsar, marched an army not of Black Hundreds, but Black Millions: "We are not the black hundreds, we are millions, we are the black millions, indeed tens of millions."[3]

His former patron Archbishop Antony (Alexei Khrapovitsky) had to admit Iliodor had fallen into the grips of "hysterical insanity." Lenin, however, saw something greater at work, describing Iliodor as the expression of something new in Russia—"dark, peasant democracy of the crudest but deepest kind."[4] The official church was not ready for any peasant democracy (dark or otherwise) and Iliodor became a constant source of trouble. At Yaroslavl, he clashed with the rector, Father Yevsevy (Yevstafy Grozdov), who opposed the Union of the Russian People, which led to his transfer to Novgorod. This would become a pattern throughout Iliodor's life for the next several years as he was moved from place to place, threatened with punishment, and closely monitored until a few years later Iliodor himself renounced his faith in a flash of rage.

The Mad Monk of Russia was the title Iliodor gave to his autobiography. Imbued with the same paranoid megalomania as all his writings, it is a strange mix of fact, error, and shameless lies that proved hugely influential in establishing the myth of Rasputin as the "Holy Devil" of Russia. He wrote it after having fled Russia following a failed attempt on

Rasputin's life. Unable to kill Rasputin, Iliodor set out to destroy him in print.

"My life began in a poor peasant's hut," the aggrieved Iliodor begins, "it blossomed forth among royal palaces, and finally descended to the level of exile and anxious care in a foreign land." Iliodor goes on to imagine his life followed a path similar to Rasputin's—from poverty to power, influence, esteem, and even fame. He, too, like Rasputin, Iliodor remarks, enjoyed the favor of the tsar. Yet this was not enough for Iliodor. Unlike Rasputin, he was not fulfilled by such worldly things. Iliodor wanted something more, he found himself seeking "the light of truth," and it was this search that led him to see the evil truth about Rasputin.[5] He struggled with his conscience, and in the end went to battle against Rasputin in order to save Russia, and for this, Iliodor claimed, Rasputin had him crushed.

Iliodor would outlive Rasputin by over three decades, but he would never escape his shadow.

Part Two

OUR FRIEND

1905–1909

8. To the Throne

On 1 November 1905, while at Peterhof outside the capital, Nicholas made the following entry in his diary:

> Tuesday. A cold windy day. The water has frozen in patches from the shore to the end of our canal. Was occupied all morning.
>
> Dined with Pr. Orlov and Resin. Went for a walk. At 4 o'clock we went to Sergeevka. Had tea with Militsa and Stana. We made the acquaintance of a man of God—Grigory, from Tobolsk province.
>
> Lay down this evening and then worked a good deal and spent time with Alix.[1]

This was the first time Nicholas and Alexandra met Rasputin. They sat and listened to him talk that afternoon for three hours. In a year Rasputin had gone from the bottom of Russian society to the top. It was a journey no one could have foreseen.

We do not know how long Rasputin stayed in Petersburg after his arrival from Kazan. It is possible he went back to Pokrovskoe and then returned later in 1905 or that he remained there the entire time up until this first meeting. We do know that while in Petersburg he lived at the Lavra before moving into Feofan's lodgings in the rector's wing sometime that year.[2] Among the visitors who came to meet Feofan at the seminary were Militsa and Pyotr. The archimandrite and the Black Princess shared a fascination with "life's mystical side," as he put it, and they drew close. Militsa began to invite Feofan to her home and later asked him to be her personal confessor. It was on one of his visits to Militsa that he told her how he had met a man of God named Grigory Rasputin. Militsa was intrigued and invited "Brother Grigory" to her home. Rasputin did not disappoint Militsa, and soon he was a frequent guest. There Rasputin was introduced to Stana and Nikolasha, and they were equally taken with the Siberian starets.[3] The path to the throne now lay open.

While in exile in Sofia after the revolution, Feofan, consumed with guilt over his promotion of Rasputin, denied that he had had anything to do with introducing the Siberian to either the Black Princesses or Nicholas and Alexandra. Indeed, he even claimed that he first met Rasputin at the Black Princesses', which was clearly a lie (he had met him in Sergei's lodgings), but by then almost no one was willing to admit that they had ever befriended or believed in Rasputin and his spiritual gifts.[4]

Vladimir Voeikov, aide-de-camp to the tsar and the last imperial palace commandant (1913–17), told investigators after the fall of the monarchy that it was Nikolasha who first brought Rasputin to the palace, having been talked into it by the Black Princesses. Other sources close to the court confirm that the Black Princesses were responsible for introducing Rasputin to Nicholas and Alexandra with the hope of using him as a tool to strengthen their position with their majesties. It seems the sisters thought the simple peasant would be the perfect instrument in their hands: someone they could use to gather information on life in the imperial household and to help maintain their bond with Nicholas and Alexandra.[5] As part of their plan to control Rasputin, Militsa apparently told him not to meet the tsar and tsaritsa without the sisters present, for, she instructed him, the court was a place of intrigue, envy, and temptations and he would surely be lost without their guidance. But Rasputin did not listen, and the Black Princesses would eventually be profoundly disappointed in Rasputin, for he was much cleverer and more independent than they had assumed, and he had no intention of becoming anyone's tool.

Others have argued that Rasputin's rise was brought about by a group of Orthodox clergymen to counter what they saw as the excessive influence at court of foreign "holy men" like Papus and Monsieur Philippe. Voeikov, for one, was convinced it was for this reason that Feofan introduced Rasputin to the Black Princesses in the hope they would then present him to Nicholas and Alexandra. The tsar of Holy Russia, so church leaders such as Feofan believed, ought to look to true Russian Orthodox Christians, and not French magnetizers, for spiritual guidance.[6] With time the idea took hold and grew, acquiring the traits of a conscious and highly organized plot. In 1914, the *Petersburg Courier* quoted a "Certain Highly Placed Dignitary" on the question of Rasputin's mysterious path to the throne: "Some church clergymen took a simple peasant and turned him into a 'prophet' of mysticism and then used him for their own goals. And so Rasputin is simply the creation of our church 'politics.'"[7] It is worth pointing out that Feofan benefited from Rasputin's rise. It is no coincidence that he was presented to their majesties for the first time less than two weeks after their meeting with Rasputin and that he was asked to be the Romanovs' personal confessor.[8]

There was talk Rasputin had been pushed forward by the Black Hundreds or other nationalist groups and that he had not been the only candidate these forces had been grooming. One of these might have been the mystic Sergei Nilus. Born into a wealthy landowning family, Nilus experienced a religious awakening and left home to wander the countryside as a strannik. He wrote of his religious discoveries in *The Great Within the Small and the Antichrist as an Imminent Political Possibility*, a work that has earned a place in history for its second printing, published in 1905, in which Nilus included the entire text of the infamous anti-Semitic forgery *The Protocols of the Elders of Zion*. The first edition of Nilus's book (without *The Protocols*) was well received in church and conservative circles. One of its admirers was Ella, the empress's sister, who purportedly invited Nilus to Tsarskoe Selo with the intention of introducing him to their majesties as a potential successor to Philippe. Nothing ever came of the matter, however, and it may be the entire story was fabricated. When told about it years later, General Alexander Mosolov, former head of the Imperial Court Chancellery, brushed it away as a pure "fairytale."[9]

To some a tool of the right, to others a tool of the left. This was the argument made by Prince Zhevakhov, one of the chief authors of the most outlandish conspiracy theories involving Rasputin. After the revolution Zhevakhov argued that Rasputin had been the creation of "international Jewry," which used him, unwittingly, for their secret plot to destroy Christian Russia. They were the ones who plucked Rasputin from obscurity and created the myth of his holiness. From the start their plan had been to lead him to the palace, by way of the Black Princesses, with the intention of using him to destroy the monarchy. "Invisible agents of the International worked to fabricate Rasputin's fame, having at their disposal little Jews, bold collaborators, all around Rasputin. They began a subtle and very complicated game and put in motion the revolutionary program they had elaborated long ago."[10]

There was indeed a connection between Rasputin's appearance at court and revolution, though nothing like the fantasy of Zhevakhov's disturbed mind. In 1904–05, Russia fought an unsuccessful and un-popular war against Japan that ended with the humiliating Treaty of Portsmouth. At the same time, Russia was being rocked by workers' strikes in cities across the empire. Then, on 9 January 1905, hundreds of peaceful demonstrators were gunned down by troops outside the Winter Palace. "Bloody Sunday," as it came to be known, helped light the fuse of the Revolution of 1905 that nearly brought down the mon-archy. Millions of workers walked off their jobs, the entire rail system came to a halt, university students went out into the streets to protest, there was unrest in the military and mutiny in the navy (most famously the battleship *Potemkin* on the Black Sea), and all across the countryside peasants rose up, burning the manor houses of the nobles and attacking the representatives of tsarist authority.

The crisis reached a head in the autumn of 1905 when Nicholas finally agreed to concessions. He signed the October Manifesto that, among other things, granted basic civil liberties (freedom of speech, assembly, and religion), allowed the formation of political parties, and invested the recently created State Duma with true legislative and over-sight power. In a very real sense, the October Manifesto turned Russia into a constitutional monarchy. The tsar was still understood to possess "Supreme Autocratic Power," but it was no longer unlimited, and the Fundamental Laws of 1906 created an awkward balance of authority between the crown and the Duma. The manifesto was met by a joyous nation, and the fever of the revolution subsided. Nicholas, however, was devastated. To save his reign he had broken the vow taken upon ascend-ing the throne to uphold autocratic power.[11] He was ashamed and worked for the rest of his life as tsar to try to undo what he had done that autumn and to reassert his undiluted authority.

Throughout October 1905, Nicholas and Alexandra regularly saw the Black Princesses and Nikolasha. They made it through these difficult times together, the most trying days of Nicholas's reign, and it appears that during their conversations Militsa was preparing them to meet a new man of God from Siberia. She must have been telling them of his remarkable spiritual power and how she had come to admire him, of her introduction via Feofan, who also vouched for his holiness. This, it might have seemed to Alexandra, was the friend promised to her by Philippe, the man they needed now more than ever. The prophecy had come to pass.

We do not know what Rasputin and Nicholas talked about at their first meeting. Feofan said later that Rasputin told him that the empress fell under his influence that evening, but it took longer with the emperor. We can get a sense of what they might have discussed from this letter, the first Rasputin sent to Nicholas, dated 5 November, four days after their meeting:

> Great Emperor, Tsar, and Autocrat of all Russia! Greetings to you! May God give you sage advice. When advice comes from God, the soul rejoices, our joy is genuine, but if it is stiff and formal, then the soul becomes despondent and our head is confused. All of Russia worries, she has descended into a terrible argument, she trembles in joy and rings her bells calling for God, and God sends us mercy and scares our enemies with awe-inspiring threats. So they, the mad ones, are now left with a broken vessel and a foolish head, as the saying goes: "The Devil has been busy for a long time but finally ended up flying off from under the back porch"—such is the power of God and His miracles! Don't disdain our simple words. You, as our Master, and we, as your subjects, must do our best, we tremble and pray to God to keep you safe from all evil, to protect from all wounds, now and in the future, so that your life will forever flow like a life-giving spring.[12]

This letter, which has eluded previous biographers,[13] is incredibly important, for it shows that from the very beginning Rasputin did not shy away from addressing matters of state with the tsar. Moreover, he dared to instruct Nicholas on the type of advice he must heed in this troubled time, namely that which comes from God, not that which is "stiff and formal," words that ought to be read as referring to the tsar's ministers. In ruling over his subjects, Rasputin tells Nicholas, he need listen only to God; what is left unsaid is that it is in such a "man of God," as Nicholas first referred to Rasputin in his diary, that His (God's, that is) voice could be heard. The letter also reveals another side of the relation that would develop between Rasputin and the tsar. Rasputin never stopped trying to give Nicholas the confidence he needed to rule, to encourage him to be strong and to have faith in himself and his reign. Indeed, not long after Rasputin's death a story began to circulate that he had owed his place at court to his convincing the tsar not to flee the country at the height of the 1905 violence, assuring Nicholas that all would be well in the end and that he and his family need not fear for their lives.[14] The Okhrana, the tsarist secret police, reported in 1915 that

Rasputin had even advised the tsar on specific policy matters during the Revolution of 1905, telling Nicholas, for instance, that it was "still too early" to grant Russia a constitution.[15] The validity of such a claim is difficult to assess.

The letter is also revealing for what it does not say. There is no mention at all of money for any church. More importantly, there is no mention of Alexei. The conventional interpretation of Rasputin and his relationship with the royal family has long been that it was the sick heir that led them to seek out a miracle healer and that guaranteed Rasputin's place at court. But matters were a good deal more complicated than that. From the first, Nicholas and Alexandra were as drawn to Rasputin for the support and wisdom he gave them about the state of Russia as about the state of the heir. Perhaps even more so. With the country rebelling around them, here came a humble peasant who told Nicholas just what he wanted to hear—of the need to trust in God and his miracles, to be the rightful master of Russia, and to demand submission and obedience in his subjects, for the health of the tsar was inseparable from the health of Russia.

9. Rasputin-Novy

Soon after writing to the tsar, Rasputin left for Pokrovskoe. Traveling with him were several of his new friends from the capital, including Father Roman Medved and his wife, Anna.

A priest at St. Petersburg's Mary Magdalene Apostolic Church, Roman had studied at the seminary, where he became well acquainted with Feofan. Along with Feofan, Roman was close to Father John of Kronstadt. Before the rise of Rasputin, Father John was the most famous religious figure in Russia, the "first modern Russian religious celebrity," to quote his latest biographer. Born Ioann Ilich Sergiev in 1829, Father John (canonized in 1989) became a charismatic priest in the latter decades of the nineteenth century whose sermons attracted enormous crowds and whose hands were reported to have effected all manner of miracle healings. So popular were his services that the church allowed him the unique privilege of practicing mass confession. He was as popular with the poor as with the aristocracy, and his followers literally kissed the ground he walked upon. His image was emblazoned on postcards, placards, and even souvenir scarves, all part of a cult that the priest did much to develop. He was called to the bedside of the dying Alexander III, but his prayers proved useless in saving his life. Upon Father John's death female admirers ransacked his apartment in search of items of clothing that they cherished as holy relics.

During Rasputin's lifetime there was talk linking him to Father John. Some said the elder priest had recognized his successor in Rasputin and even recommended him to Nicholas and Alexandra; others avowed he had denounced Rasputin, saying to his face that his very name was proof of his dissolute ways. Neither story is true, and it appears, based on everything we know, the two men never met. Nevertheless, since the Medveds were close to Father John and saw him regularly, it seems likely that even if they did not introduce the two, then they at least told John about the miraculous Siberian holy man. Father

John must have heard tales about Rasputin, but what he thought of him remains unknown.[1]

Feofan introduced Roman to the Black Princesses and to Rasputin as well. Roman and Anna were immediately taken with Brother Grigory, and he became a frequent guest in their home and then moved in with them at their apartment on Second Rozhdestvenskaya Street sometime in late 1905 or early 1906. His new hosts believed that Rasputin possessed rare healing powers, even across vast distances, and for years Anna would write to Rasputin whenever she or her husband were ill, requesting he pray for their recovery.[2]

Another visitor to Pokrovskoe with the Medveds was Olga Lokhtina. Born in 1867 to a Kazan nobleman, Lokhtina would quickly become Rasputin's most fanatical believer, her life a pathetic spectacle of bizarre behavior that many came to see as the greatest proof of Rasputin's evil influence. She fell under his spell, and if at first Rasputin appeared to Lokhtina as a holy man, with time he became in her eyes a saint, then Christ, and finally God himself. Lokhtina came to believe she was part of a Trinity, with Iliodor as the Son of God and herself as the Virgin Mary. But this was still in the future. In 1905 she was a beautiful and conventional Petersburg wife and mother, married to an engineer by the name of Vladimir Lokhtin. It was that year Olga met Rasputin at the Medveds. She later stated that she was ill at the time with intestinal neurasthenia and Father Roman introduced her to Rasputin certain that he would be able to cure her. Olga was no less impressed with Rasputin than the Medveds, and so she, and her daughter, joined them in November to travel to Pokrovskoe and see how this remarkable man of God lived at home.[3]

"Travelling with Rasputin was a great pleasure," Lokhtina said, "for he gave life to the spirit." She was taken with Pokrovskoe. "I liked the style of his life very much," she told the Commission.

> On meeting her husband, his wife fell down at his feet . . . His wife's humility astounded me. When I am right, I yield to no one. And now here was Rasputin's wife yielding in an argument with her husband, even though it was clear to me that she was in the right and not him. In reply to my . . . astonishment, she said, "A husband and wife have to live with one heart, sometimes you yield, and sometimes he does" . . . We slept where we could, very often in one room, but we slept little, listening to the spiritual conversations of

Father Grigory, who, so to speak, schooled us in nocturnal wake-fulness. In the morning, if I got up early, I would pray with Father Grigory . . . Praying with him tore me from the earth . . . At home we would pass the time chanting psalms and canticles.

She went on:

Yes, he did have the custom of kissing when meeting and even of embracing, but it is only to bad people that bad and dirty thoughts occur . . . It is also quite true that on one of my visits to the village of Pokrovskoe I bathed together with Rasputin and his family, with his wife and two daughters, and in the absence of bad thoughts it did not seem either strange or indecent to any of us. I was con-vinced that Rasputin really was an "elder," both by his healing of me and by the predictions I had occasion to hear that came true.[4]

In a letter to Bishop Antony (Karzhavin) of Tobolsk from 1 June 1907, Olga wrote that Rasputin had "taught me to love in the name of Christ," how to fast, to go to church, and to pray more often before the holy relics. She claimed that Rasputin had miraculously healed her sister's fiancé who suffered from a severe nervous disorder. The doctors could not help him, and he had lost all hope. He was not a believer, but Rasputin instructed him to kiss the simple gold cross on his bare chest and suddenly, before Olga's eyes, he was healed and accepted Christ as his savior.[5] After moving on from the Medveds, Rasputin would stay at the Lokhtins' apartment at 13 Grechesky Prospect from 1907 to November 1908.

On 1 April 1906, Rasputin sent Nicholas an Easter greeting from Pokrovskoe: "Christ has risen! This is where our joy is—that He has risen and is rejoicing with us."[6] That summer he bought an expensive new house (1,700 rubles) for himself and his family on the village's main street.[7] The money had come from some of his Petersburg supporters, quite possibly Olga Lokhtina one of them. On 12 July, Rasputin left Pokrovskoe for Petersburg and six days later he saw Nicholas and Alex-andra for the second time. "We spent the evening at Sergievka and saw Grigory!" an excited Nicholas recorded in his diary.[8]

Among the visitors to the Medveds' home around this time was the writer and philosopher Vasily Rozanov and his family. Rozanov found Roman rather uninteresting (he reminded Rozanov of a frog), but

Rozanov's second wife, Varvara Butyagina, and some of his older children, particularly his stepdaughter Alexandra Butyagina, were attracted to the strong religious atmosphere they encountered among the Medveds, and they began to visit several times a week.

Alexandra, then twenty-three and unmarried, ended up leaving home and moving in with an unusual sisterhood of women somehow connected with the Medved household. Her family now saw Alexandra only on their visits, and they began to notice a strange transformation. She acted not herself, as if she were dead inside or had been turned into a "somnambula." This went on for an entire winter, and no one could explain what had happened to their beloved Alexandra.

Rozanov learned that the circle around the Medveds also included Archimandrite Feofan and a Siberian pilgrim he had never heard of. The fact of the former's presence made him feel better, what with Feofan's irreproachable reputation. At one of their visits to the Medveds, they had seen a remarkable woman leaving the house—she was an elegant lady in an expensive cloak. Rozanov decided to track her down and find out just what was going on in the Medved home. Why, he wondered, were they cultivating an air of secrecy about themselves, holding mysterious gatherings behind locked doors? The lady, it turned out, was Olga Lokhtina. Rozanov met her at her home, and she told him the story of how she had suffered from a terrible illness that no doctors had been able to cure and that had kept her bedridden for years. And then, at the Medveds, she had found the cure through religion. The suffering had been so horrible that she had nearly lost her mind, but prayer and faith had saved her life.

Rozanov did not know what to say. If her story were true, there was no denying the effect the religion being practiced at the Medveds had had on her. Before him stood a beautiful woman. "Her every movement was lovely and elegant. She charmed with her personality, and this charm flowed from her sincerity, her warmth, and the clarity of her mind."

It was not long after that when Rozanov found himself again at the Medveds for tea. There at the table was a new face, "not that of a petty bourgeois, not that of a peasant," he noted. While Rozanov drank and chatted with the Medveds, the stranger finished his tea without saying a word, laid the cup on its side on the saucer, thanked them, and left. Rozanov found him "the drabbest sort of fellow I had ever met." It was only after he had gone that Rozanov learned this was the Siberian wanderer that everyone in the Medved home was so drawn to.

Rozanov began to hear stories about the man, about his incredible spiritual power and the effect he had on people. Soon it seemed everyone was talking about the "miracles" he was performing in Petersburg. But Rozanov began hearing other things as well, namely that the man had a habit of kissing and hugging women and girls. He once asked Father Medved about this, and got an angry response. "His kisses," Roman insisted, "were the most chaste and pure." Roman's faith in Rasputin struck Rozanov as something bordering on an illness: "The priest was adamant about the holy pilgrim's reputation. The slightest doubt about his 'absolute honor' sent him into a rage and he would lose control of himself and begin to curse."[9]

If Rozanov's initial encounters with Rasputin and his followers at the Medveds were contradictory and confusing (although he would later suggest that from the start he was amazed by Rasputin), he was not worried enough to try to force his stepdaughter to return home, even though there was talk that she had been pursued (or worse) by Rasputin. Maybe, Rozanov thought, some sort of sect had formed around the Siberian pilgrim, yet he was not about to take any action against them. The stories about Alexandra, however, would not go away and began to circulate among members of the broader Petersburg religious community.[10] About a year later, in November 1907, Rozanov received a letter from Nikolai Drozdov, archpriest at St. Petersburg's Church of St. Panteleimon the Healer.

> I would like to throw as much publicity as possible on the prophet-impostor from Siberia based on the sad event with your run-away. I am sending you the draft of my text with a request that you add any details that I might have missed and remove anything that might harm this matter. Maybe I shouldn't call the pilgrim by name, which I already did, so that he doesn't make any noise about stones being thrown at him. For we know little about him. From Medved and Ternavtsev* we've heard only one thing—that he is a "saint." We know almost nothing about his words and his deeds; he can hide behind Medved's back in this case with your daughter.

---

* Valentin Ternavtsev was a religious philosopher, official of the Holy Synod, and co-founder of the Religious-Philosophical Society in St. Petersburg along with Gippius, Merezhkovsky, and Rozanov.

We must be cautious. Return the draft to me after you've made any corrections. I'll publish it in the *Bell* or in the secular press.

Drozdov's draft article was titled "The Siberian Prophet."

There is a man from Siberia in the capital who has earned himself the lofty title of a "holy man" among his followers. What he did to "earn" such glory and honor we cannot explain, frankly speaking. Let's hope that those who performed the "canonization" of this saintly man, who was not canonized by the official church, will perform their sacred duty to point out the "holy" aspects of the Siberian newcomer's life and teachings. Our task is different—we would like to make public the doubts and unpleasant surprises that this man raises with some of his actions [. . .]

The Siberian "saint" has a strange habit of hugging and kissing women he talks to even if he is seeing them for the first time. He accompanies his speech with gestures and body movements that have deservedly been called "grimacing" and "apery" by one lady who rejected his moves to kiss her. Sometimes the "saint" enters such an ecstatic state that he acts like he is possessed or raving mad. That is how some skeptics explained some of the photographs of this man.

What sort of behavior is this—this hugging and kissing? Why is it necessary? The admirers of the "saint" would, naturally, explain this "manner" benevolently as an excessive feeling of love for his female companions and call this kissing "holy kissing," which is normal among great "startsy" such as Seraphim of Sarov, Ambrose of Optina. [. . .]

Naturally, we do not dare say that the Siberian "prophet" must be some kind of a mystic sectarian, but there is no doubt that in his "poses and movements," in his kisses and handshakes, there is something quite different from our holy startsy—Seraphim and Ambrose. "The prophet" is not that old. This is the first thing, and the second thing is that he is a layman and a married man: it's unbecoming for him to mimic the kisses of hermits who had rejected the world with all its passions and lust. The kisses of startsy were given, I believe, with great consideration and didn't arouse the feeling expressed by one maiden about the kisses of the Siberian pilgrim: "These kisses and squeezes are disgusting." The kisses of the startsy filled the soul and the body with health, peace, and holy joy. While the kisses of the Siberian pilgrim, supposedly "mimicking the startsy" and with the help of loyal accomplices, resulted in one young woman with a natural inclination to hysteria to leave her parental home, and not only without regret or sadness but with joy about the benefits of her new life and with curses toward her parents' home where she had everything she needed, from her daily bread to reasonable freedom in her life and faith. That evil demon settled in her soul after she met and talked with the Siberian prophet and his admirers: the warm parental house became unpleasant to the young woman after, in the bizarre words of the prophet and his followers, "a new soul began to grow" inside her. She "ran away" from her parents' home, literally as if that home had turned into a Greek Sodom for her. In reality, I want to stress this fact, her family taught her nothing remotely Sodom like. She wanted to have freedom like the famous son from the Biblical story. God prevent that this freedom leads to the "the death of her soul" or to the destruction of all hope.

Drozdov went on in his article to assert that Rasputin belonged to a bizarre religious sect that engaged in wild, orgiastic rites at odds with true religion. He questioned whether Alexandra was growing a new soul or if, in fact, her old one was being purposely destroyed.[11]

Rozanov's reaction to Drozdov's letter and text is unknown. There is no evidence he ever bothered to reply to Drozdov or that his text was ever published. As for Alexandra, she eventually left the Medveds and Rasputin. Rozanov, it seems, had been right not to worry.

Rasputin was back in the capital in the autumn. He asked Roman to pass along a letter he had written to the tsar:

Father-Tsar!
    Having come to this city from Siberia, I would like to present you with an icon of St. Simeon of Verkhoturye the Miracle-Worker, who is worshipped in our region, in the hope that this saint will keep You safe all the days of Your life and support You in Your service for the good and joy of Your loyal sons.[12]

On 12 October, Nicholas summoned Prince Mikhail Putyatin, captain of the Preobrazhensky Life Guards and later head of the Tsarskoe Selo Palace Administration, and showed him the letter. He instructed Putyatin to go to the rail station the next day, meet Rasputin, and bring him to the palace at Peterhof. Rasputin arrived early that evening and was presented to the emperor and empress. He gave them the icon and also brought with him a small icon for each of the children. Rasputin gently caressed little Alexei. The visit with the family lasted a little over an hour; they treated Rasputin to tea before he left. The Court Journal, which recorded every visitor—but rarely captured Rasputin's visits—referred to him as "Rasbudin, a peasant from the Tobolsk province."[13]

A palace footman by the name of Alexander Damer later recalled that at every visit Rasputin would take off his heavy peasant coat on the way into the palace and stop briefly before a mirror in the entry way to look himself over, smoothing his hair and beard, before hurrying up the stairs that opened onto the corridor leading to the inner apartments. He would typically meet Nicholas and Alexandra in the small, comfortable drawing-room next to the tsar's personal office and would leave in the same hurried, business-like manner with which he arrived.[14]

After Rasputin had left Peterhof on the evening of the thirteenth, Nicholas asked Putyatin what he thought of him. Putyatin told the tsar he did not think the starets was sincere and that he likely suffered from "an inflamed brain." It was evident that the tsar did not care for Putyatin's answer, for he was silent and stroked his mustache and beard with the back of his hand, as he often did in such situations. He looked off to the side, and said he was satisfied that Rasputin had brought him the icon. They never discussed Rasputin again. If Putyatin had been sincere with the tsar, he did not let his personal feelings keep him away from Rasputin, for it was around this time he posed with him in a photographic studio. Maybe Putyatin changed his mind about Rasputin or maybe he felt it wise, given the attitude of the tsar, to be seen in his company.[15]

On the sixteenth, three days after meeting with Rasputin, Nicholas wrote to Pyotr Stolypin, Russia's minister of the interior and president of the Council of Ministers (in effect, Russia's prime minister):

Pyotr Arkadevich!
   A few days ago I received a peasant from the Tobolsk district, Grigory Rasputin, who brought me an icon of St Simeon of Verkhoturye. He made a remarkably strong impression both on her Majesty and me, so that instead of five minutes our conversation lasted more than an hour!

He will soon be returning home. He has a strong desire to see you and to bless your injured daughter with an icon. I very much hope that you will find a minute to receive him this week.[16]

Terrorists had blown up Stolypin's summer house on St. Petersburg's Aptekarsky Island two months earlier. The plan had been to assassinate the prime minister, but he survived unscathed. Fifty-four people, however, were killed or wounded; his daughter Natalya had both her legs broken. Nicholas had Natalya sent to live in the Winter Palace to recuperate, which is where Rasputin visited her that month. Neither she, nor her father, a stern character with no use for faith healers, was impressed. She is reported to have asked for a sprinkling of eau-de-Cologne after Rasputin left her bedside.

On his return to Pokrovskoe Rasputin took a detour to Zhitomir in northwestern Ukraine to see Anna Obukhova on the recommendation of Feofan, who had praised Rasputin to her on his visit that summer. She met him at the train station, and he kissed her three times, something she found quite odd. Rasputin took a great interest in her home and asked her about everything, even why she slept on such a hard bed. He then asked her about Feofan, whether she told him everything, to which she said yes. As they walked about the rooms, he said, "I know how to love! I know how to make beautiful love." Anna pretended she did not understand him. He tried to convince her to become his "spiritual daughter," but she declined, which aroused Rasputin's anger, but then, curiously, this passed just as suddenly as it had arrived. He began to speak of the grand dukes and duchesses, calling them by their informal names, which made Anna uncomfortable. He stayed for a few days and never stopped courting Anna. The housemaids were glad once he had gone. They told their mistress he frightened them.[17]

From Pokrovskoe Rasputin wrote Nicholas on 6 December to congratulate him on his saint's day: "Angels praise you and Cherubs at the Throne sing praise to God and we are rejoicing for the sound that is Yours [. . .] and the Tsar rules forever, to the enemy's fear and our glory, and our glory is Your deeds [. . .]".[18] Nine days later Rasputin wrote the Tsar again, this time with a special request.

15 December 1906
Living in Pokrovskoe, I bear the surname of Rasputin while many other residents of that village have the same surname, which may cause some complications. Laying myself at the feet of Your

Emperial Majesty I beg you to give me and my descendants the
right to be called by the surname "Rasputin-Novy."
   Your Majesty's loyal subject Grigory.[19]

The reason for this request is not clear. One of the most widely
repeated stories is that when entering the palace not long before this,
little Alexei, upon seeing Rasputin, yelled out, "*Novy, Novy, Novy!*"—"The
New One, New One, New One!" Some even alleged these had been the
boy's first words, and so grateful and overwhelmed were Nicholas and
Alexandra, that they decided to give the name of "New" to Rasputin. But
as this letter makes clear, Rasputin sought the name change, not the
royal family. It also seems unlikely that Alexei, at two and a half years
old, would have only then started to speak.[20] Perhaps the "New" harked
back to what Philippe had told Nicholas and Alexandra, that after he
was gone a new friend would come to them. Perhaps it was not something new about Rasputin that the name was meant to reflect, but his
status as the *new* friend prophesied years earlier. Whatever the reason,
it seems certain that the request had nothing to do with a wish to erase
his surname, as if he were uncomfortable with the negative associations
that people might infer from it, for Rasputin never stopped going by his
family name and used "Novy" only in conjunction with "Rasputin" and
then only infrequently.

Nicholas passed Rasputin's letter on to his equerry and state secretary Baron Budberg on the twenty-first. Budberg first checked to
make certain it was an appropriate request since double-barrel surnames were traditionally only permitted for nobles, but in this
instance, given the tsar's endorsement, that restriction was waived.
The matter worked its way through the various offices before being
officially granted on 11 January 1907.[21] A grateful Rasputin thanked
Nicholas upon hearing the news: "I'm sending Angels to protect you
all."[22] At the end of March the villagers of Pokrovskoe were called out
of their homes and read an official edict stating that, by order of the
tsar, their fellow villager Grigory Rasputin had been granted a new
name and would henceforth be known as "Rasputin-Novy."[23] It is difficult to imagine what must have been going through their minds
upon hearing this strange news.

Nicholas and Alexandra preferred to call him "Grigory" or "our
Friend," and never did use his surname, either his original or new one.
Yet the name change did seem fitting then, for Rasputin did become

something of a new man around this time, or at least he was embarking on a new phase of his life. He was not the man he had been before meeting and befriending the emperor and empresses. The news did not go unnoticed by the press. The popular Moscow daily *Russian Word* reported the change and asked: "Will Rasputin begin a new life with this change of his surname?"[24]

10. Sects and Whips

In his letter to Rozanov, Father Drozdov suggested that Rasputin was a member of a dangerous sect, infamous for its heretical teachings and sexual perversion. This, more than his own individual personality, explained the Siberian's strange and dangerous ways.

In the middle of the seventeenth century, the Russian Orthodox Church experienced a period of intense crisis that led to the rupture of the church itself. Refusing to accept a series of changes to the traditional liturgical rites and other reforms being advocated by Patriarch Nikon, a considerable minority of Russians broke off from the official church during the great schism—*raskol*, in Russian—and became known as the Old Believers. While it is true that sectarianism in Russia pre-dates the schism, nevertheless, the raskol marked the end of Russian Orthodoxy as a unified community and was enormously important in giving rise to a number of Orthodox religious sects.

From the beginning, the state and the official church viewed Old Believers with suspicion. They were associated with sedition and vice: after refusing to accept Nikon's reforms, Archpriest Avvakum was burned at the stake in 1682. That same decade the state issued an edict that forbade even the existence of religious heterodoxy in Russia. A bounty was put on the heads of sectarians. Those caught were tortured on the rack. If they confessed they were exiled or sent to prison; if not, they were burned. In response dissenters began to preach active resistance and suicide, often by self-immolation. By the end of the century, as many as 20,000 dissenters had taken their own lives. Self-immolation was practiced even into the nineteenth century, and acts of collective suicide were recorded into the twentieth. Russia's sects never managed to emerge from the original shadow of suspicion and remained, in the eyes of the state and the Europeanized elite, a dangerous element.[1]

Sectarians came in a variety of (often bizarre) forms. There were the *beguny* (Runners), for example, who, among other things, renounced all ties to the state and to one's family, as well as to money, printed books, and even their own names. There were the *molokane* (Milk-Drinkers), *dukhobory* (Spirit-Wrestlers), *pryguny* (Jumpers), and the *skoptsy* (Self-Castrators), who sought God through voluntary castration and the cutting off of women's breasts. The skoptsy, like a number of other sects, were themselves the offspring of a larger and more feared sect, the *khlysty*, the whips.

According to legend, in 1631 an army deserter by the name of Danila Filippovich threw the holy books into the Volga River and created his own cult, proclaiming: "I am that God foretold by the prophets and have come down to earth to save the human race, seek no other God." Filippovich instructed his followers to keep all of their rites and commandments in secret, even from their own families. He preached a way of life utterly free of the accepted religious and social norms—not recognizing the rites of marriage, baptism, and confession. Filippovich and his followers believed that Christ was not just alive, but that he was reincarnated in living people among them and that through their rituals he could be made to descend upon them. The sect's leaders in the future were often called "Christ." Their numbers grew. In the second half of the nineteenth century, they were the third largest Christian group in Russia after the official Orthodox and Old Believers. Like the Shakers and the Quakers, names given to these religious groups by their critics, the members of this sect came to be known as khlysty (Whips), a play on *Khryity* (Christs). The movement was also generally known as "New Israel." It was said their strange rites included orgies and self-mutilation. The khlysty would sing and whirl about in circles and then cut off the breast of a naked virgin and collectively eat it, before falling to the ground and engaging in group sex. The mutilated virgin became their "Mother of God," her partner, their "Christ." There were also tales of underground temples and secret gestures.

The khlysty saw themselves as Christians, and despite the talk of their wicked practices were generally seen as such by outsiders. They took all the basic elements of Christianity and remade them, adding new ones. Their church they called a "ship," carrying them through the dangerous sea of Orthodox Russia to salvation on a distant shore; their priest was a "prophet." At the center of their mystical rites (*radenie*, in Russian), practiced in secret in sealed rooms or in cellars, was an intense, whirling dance. Vladimir Bonch-Bruevich once witnessed this "sacred dancing" at a khlyst ceremony and found it "quite elegant, inspired, beautiful, and full of inner fire and striving." The rapid spinning produced in the celebrants altered mental states and caused hallucinations. The speed with which one turned reflected one's level of grace, the faster, the closer to perfection. While some spun, others sang. The spinners would tilt their heads back, their eyes turned upward, and practice a special, intense breathing. As they spun, the spirit would come over them and produce a sort of religious ecstasy. Some were moved to jump, shake, sway, or even run. At times the ecstasy could lead to fits, convulsions, and paroxysms. This mass whirling created a joyful sense of community. In preparation the khlysty (who shunned alcohol and tobacco) fasted as a way to help induce the most intense experience. A crucial element of the khlyst experience was the vat (*chan*), which functioned as a representation of the collective body that was to be achieved during their rites. Two circles were formed around the vat: men in one, close to the vat, women in another, further out. They moved in opposite directions—the men in the direction of the sun, the women, away from the sun.

After the whirling had exhausted itself, the prophets—men and women—would speak. With the rest of the congregation gathered around, either on their knees or bowing to the ground, the prophet would give concrete advice (on farming or the like) or unwind long, vague orations, or prophesy. Some prophets were said to be able to tell who among them had sinned. The prophets spoke in a strange metrical or rhythmic manner, sometimes in rhymes. It was a kind of poetry taken as a sign of their spiritual purity. They would let their minds run free, speaking whatever came into their heads; at times the meaning of what they said was so opaque as to require "interpreters" for the rest of the group. They used unintelligible words or even made animal noises and tweeted like birds.

It was said the khlysts' rites concluded with an orgy accompanied by flagellation (thus, "the whips") and acts of cannibalism. None of this, however, was ever credibly verified, and tales of wanton copulation and group sex are more likely myth than reality. Nonetheless, reports of perversion and sadism among the khlysty were made. In 1825, a denunciation reached Tsar Alexander I that in one khlyst community the prophets, while overcome during their preaching, beat some of the others, dragged them by their hair about the floor, and even trampled on them. But, surprisingly, the victims bore no ill will to their abusers, saying that the Holy Spirit punishes some one day and others the next. In 1911 near Saratov, a khlyst supposedly killed a woman while they were engaged in "reciprocal tortures."

The stories of some of the sectarians are quite fantastical. In 1853, the khlyst prophet Vasily Radaev was arrested and convicted of "khlystovism and depravity." He had been preaching strange ideas of death and rebirth in the villages of the Arzamasky district and fornicating with some of his female followers. He claimed, however, that it was not he who had engaged in sexual acts, but God through him: "It was not my will, but that of the Holy Spirit working inside me." One seventeen-year-old girl he had seduced with the promise she would receive "fiery wings" for her submission. At one of the group's ceremonies, he made a girl undress and then beat her genitals with switches. Despite such things, Radaev was highly regarded in his village as "a righteous man." As he was having sex with his followers, Radaev would say, "Christ took the flesh of Adam [. . .] and I have taken the flesh as well and engage in carnal acts so as to extirpate sin." Doctors examined Radaev at his trial and determined him to be sane. He was flogged and exiled to Siberia, his dutiful wife following after him.

Ilya Kovylin, a Moscow merchant born in 1731 and one of the founders of the Old Believer sect of the Fedoseevtsy, taught his followers that "without sin there is no repentance, without repentance no salvation. There will be many sinners in heaven." It was Kovylin who coined the famous (or infamous) phrase "If you don't sin, you don't repent, if you don't repent, you can't be saved." This Kovylin is immensely important, for his words have mistakenly been attributed to Rasputin, as if he spoke them first, having himself created some new perversion, when in fact they have a much older tradition and represent an idea shared by various sectarian groups.

By 1900, there were perhaps as many as 100,000 khlysty, not to mention other sects with similar practices. Of course, the numbers remain largely a guess since the khlysty, like other sects, were secretive about their membership as well as rites. Yet, not unlike the Freemasons and other such groups, the fact that they shrouded their rites in secrecy aroused a great deal of suspicion and rumor. The state spied on them and monitored their activities out of fear the secrecy was meant as a cover for sedition. One of the biggest challenges the state faced, however, was trying to determine who was a khlyst. Such was the difficulty, that, under the right circumstances, almost anyone could fall under a cloud of suspicion. It was difficult to know how to recognize a khlyst. To that end, the III All-Russian Congress of Missionaries in 1897 came up with a list of ten characteristics:

1. Rumored membership, confirmed if circumstances allow; [. . .]
3. Loose sexual relations, often accompanied by broken family
ties and open adulterous affairs; 4. Avoidance of meat, and particularly pork; 5. Teetotalism; 6. Physical appearance—exhausted, a
yellowish-wan complexion, accompanied by a dim and almost
immobile expression of the eyes. The men's hair is smooth and
heavily greased with oil, the women's heads, covered with a kerchief. They speak in an ingratiating manner, their speech filled with
expressions of false modesty; they sigh constantly, exhibit jerky
movements, nervous bodily tics, and a strange gait, not unlike a
soldier. [. . .] 9. khlysty almost always use pet names for each other;
10. They all have a sweet tooth.[2]

Despite what many thought, the khlysty harbored no seditious
intentions. Regardless, by 1900 the word *khlyst* had become a term of
accusation used against one's enemies irrespective of its validity, a
catchall for denunciation, just as "fascist" became under the Communists, or "Communist" in 1950s America. It could mean a heretic, or the
insane, or the subversive, or the depraved.[3]

Yet at times the assumed power of Russian sects had been embraced
as a force for good. The skopets (self-castrator) Kondraty Selivanov, who
proclaimed himself to be both Jesus Christ and Tsar Peter III, was an
extremely popular figure in the early years of the nineteenth century.
The elite of St. Petersburg thronged to his apartment to listen to Selivanov's prophecies and predictions, and according to legend Alexander I
came to consult with him in 1805 before heading off to fight Napoleon
at the Battle of Austerlitz. The tsar ignored Selivanov's advice not to
engage Napoleon, and the Russian, and Austrian, army was routed by
the French. For nearly two decades Selivanov was a powerful voice in
high society and government circles. He was revered by his followers;
they saved his table scraps as holy relics, just like Rasputin's acolytes did
a century later.[4] When, in 1819, the governor-general of Petersburg
learned that two of his nephews had been attending skoptsy gatherings
and that junior officers of the imperial guards were going so far as to
castrate themselves, the government moved against Selivanov and he
was banished to a monastery the following year for the rest of his life.

For some in the upper classes the intensity and enthusiasm of sects
offered the hope of compensation for the perceived spiritual impover-
ishment of modern life. Like all liminal groups, sectarians were
outsiders and so suspect and dangerous, yet also alluring and alive, in

direct contact with the life-force. In May 1905, the Symbolist poet and editor of the radical newspaper *New Times* Nikolai Minsky gathered at his apartment a group of writers and intellectuals—Vyacheslav Ivanov, Vasily Rozanov, Fyodor Sologub, Nikolai Berdyaev, Alexei Remizov and their wives—for an evening of experimentation. They joined together in a circle, turned off the lights, and then began to whirl about like the khlysty. Next, Ivanov led into the room a young musician, a blond Jew, whom they symbolically crucified before cutting open his wrists, draining the blood into a wine glass for each of them to drink. After this, they kissed. Everyone left pleased (although maybe not the musician), promising to gather again for another khlyst ceremony, when they would once again give themselves over to the mysteries of Dionysus.[5]

Indeed, the Russian Symbolists as a whole interpreted the orgiastic rites of sects like the khlysty as remnants of ancient Dionysian cults on the verge of being engulfed in the rising sea of modernity.[6] Just as the practices of some sects were dying out, their leaders were leaving the countryside for the cities and making contact with the world of Europeanized Russia. It was a moment of exciting cultural discovery. Here is how the writer Mikhail Prishvin remembered this encounter. "They arrive like envoys from another world, one that is unknown yet familiar at the same time, attractive and inaccessible, like our dreams and childhood. They come from a world into which people of written culture —authors and readers—always try to enter but rarely succeed."[7] The intelligentsia projected its own preoccupations onto the sects, seeing in them virtuous, non-violent, communal forms of life that they believed offered a model for a more just social order.

Those intellectuals better informed about Russian sects were less prone to such romantic (and naive) visions. Alexander Prugavin, an expert in the Old Believers and Russian sectarianism, saw society's embrace of sects, and particularly the khlysty, as a grave threat. "Turbid waves of unhealthy, superstitious mysticism, raised on a foundation of hysteria, are spreading ever further, rising ever higher, taking into their grasp [. . .] the highest levels of the intelligentsia, the state, and even the church." At the heart of what Prugavin called "neo-khlystovshchina" was the idea of the struggle against lecherous passions by way of trials of the flesh when men and women attempted to free themselves from their base desires and overcome their lustful instincts by confronting temptation head-on. Prugavin told of women in the capital spending a night in bed with some "prophet" and trying to remain calm and unemotional, even when subjected to all manner of caresses. It was church figures such as Feofan, Prugavin believed, who were chiefly responsible for this development, having sought out and then promoted such figures from the lower orders that they themselves had mistaken for popular saints.[8]

Prugavin's words speak to the perception, held by many at the time, that fin-de-siècle Russia was suffering from a diseased form of religious life. All this concern with peasant holy men, with seers and faith healers, with prophecies and miracles, was a symptom of the bankruptcy of Russian spiritual life, particularly among the upper classes.[9] Moscow University historian Mikhail Bogoslovsky disagreed. He considered the attraction to charismatic figures like Rasputin in literate society to be nothing new, and in this he was correct, as the case of Selivanov shows. For Bogoslovsky, this was a natural, recurring part of Russian life. The reason for the popularity of such religious leaders from the lower depths should not be looked for in the degraded nature of the elite's religious sensibility, he argued, but in the shortcomings of the official church, namely the "stale and dry formalism" of the Russian higher clergy, men he described in his diary as "in reality nothing more than state functionaries, busy signing papers and utterly devoid of any burning religious impulse."[10]

But Bogoslovsky was in the minority. More Russians were coming to share the views expressed by Ippolit Gofshtetter in his article "The Secret of the khlystovshchina" published in the New Times. A grave threat was facing Russia, he warned. The Revolution of 1905 had failed to fulfill Russians' hopes for change, and in their despair and emptiness they had turned to the mysticism of the narod for salvation. These prophets were not what they appeared, however, and Russia was blindly entrusting itself to the "fanatical cruelty of the dark masses." The mystical rites of the khlysty, he cautioned, threatened Russia with "complete and utter destruction."[11]

11. Demons of the Silver Age

The turn of the century was a period of intense spiritual searching in Russia. Intellectuals turned away from the materialist positivism of the nineteenth century and back to the church and other forms of spiritualism in what can be called a true religious renaissance. Many sought to revitalize what was widely perceived as a hidebound, bureaucratic, and spiritually dead official Russian Orthodox Church, to infuse it with a renewed sense of mystery, fervency, and life, while others rejected the church altogether for new forms of spiritual experience that held out the promise of even more powerful encounters with the sacred. Emblematic of the age was the Religious-Philosophical Society, founded by the writers Dmitry Merezhkovsky, Zinaida Gippius, and Dmitry Filosofov in 1901 in St. Petersburg. They became known as the *Bogoiskateli*—God-seekers. Merezhkovsky fashioned himself into a prophet and wanted to create a new religion based on the idea that the Second Coming of Christ was imminent and with it a new Third Testament.[1]

During what became known as Russia's Silver Age, from roughly 1890 to 1914, a period that overlaps almost exactly with the rise and fall of Rasputin, the country's educated classes exhibited a fascination for mysticism and the occult and all manner of the supernatural, from table turning, hypnotism, and chiromancy, to Rosicrucianism, fortune-telling, and telepathy. It was the age of Theosophy, the creation of the Russian-born Helena Blavatsky, a supposed secret doctrine, part Gnostic gospel, part Buddhism, that claimed to synthesize the ancient wisdom once common to all the world's civilizations and that held out the promise of a universal brotherhood. Theosophy's mystic charms attracted many of Russia's leading creative figures—philosophers Vladimir Solovyov and Nikolai Berdyaev, poets and writers Konstantin Balmont and Andrei Bely, the composer Alexander Scriabin, and the artist Vasily Kandinsky. It was the age of Spiritualism, founded in Hydesville, New York in 1848 by the sisters Kate and Margaret Fox, that offered the possibility to communicate with the dead through the help of special "mediums." Spiritualism swept across America, England (Queen Victoria and Sir Arthur Conan Doyle were believers), Germany, and Russia, as people flocked to séances to try to make contact with their lost loved ones, their spirits manifesting themselves by rapping, spectral voices, automatic writing, and even ectoplasmic materialization. So popular did these séances become that the Imperial University in St. Petersburg established the "Scientific Commission for the Study of Mediumistic Phenomena," led by the chemist Dmitry Mendeleev, father of the periodic table.

Hypnotism was more popular in early twentieth-century Russia than in Western Europe and was a particularly common practice among Petersburg psychiatrists. The poet Osip Mandelstam was a visitor to the home of the Petersburg physician Dr. Boris Sinani, famous for his ability to cure his patients merely "by suggestion," as Mandelstam put it. The best known psychiatrist-hypnotist at the time was Vladimir Bekhterev, who used hypnosis as part of his science of "psychoneurology."[2]

The fascination for the occult became widespread, extending well beyond Russia's artists and intellectuals and reaching deep into the middle classes, becoming a truly popular cultural pastime. By 1914, Petersburg counted thirty-five officially registered occult circles and hundreds more informal ones; the craze was not limited to the capital, but by then had seduced Moscow and most provincial cities and towns. If for some the occult was deeply serious, for others it was simply a form of entertainment. Russia hosted a variety of mediums, clairvoyants, and savants for every taste: there was the "Mysterious Dog Jack" able to guess one's age, the year of one's wedding, and even the amount of money in one's pocket; there was the Indian somnambulist Princess Madame Naindra; and there was the Polish medium Yan Guzik, who could summon not only the spirits of Alexander the Great, Napoleon, and Pushkin, but even those of dead animals, some of which were so ferocious that spectators were known to seek medical attention after his séances.[3]

Even Russia's peasants and workers, the vast majority of the population, embraced new spiritual movements and religious practices. Holy pilgrimage attracted ever larger numbers, including the likes of Rasputin, and the belief in spirits, possession, miracles, and magic flourished. Groups of peasants came together to establish their own Christian communities, at times without the blessings of the church or even without the participation of any clergy. In the cities workers, too, took an interest in their spiritual well-being, flocking to mystics and popular preachers promising salvation.[4]

Perhaps the most remarkable of these figures was Alexei Shchetinin. Born near Voronezh in 1854, he moved as a child to Stavropol. After a short stint in prison in 1879, his wife left him and he took to preaching and embarked on a new life as a sectarian khlyst prophet, calling himself "the free son of the ether," a phrase he lifted from Mikhail Lermontov's poem "The Demon" (1829–39). From the start, Shchetinin was a volatile, nasty figure. Out of one corner of his mouth he would denounce competing sects to Orthodox missionaries, and then out of the other denounce the Orthodox to his followers. It was said he tried to keep the missionaries from meddling with his sect by sending young females to seduce them.[5]

He arrived in Petersburg in 1906 and soon attracted a group of followers drawn largely from the city's factory workers transfixed by his sermons. A curious Mikhail Prishvin once visited Shchetinin in a cramped, stuffy apartment on the edge of the city. He found Shchetinin drunk and muttering something vulgar, surrounded by his disciples. One of them, a man by the name of Pavel Legkobytov, spoke up.

> I am that man's slave, I know that there is perhaps no nastier a man on the earth, but I gave myself up to be his slave and now I know the true God, and not just the sound of his name. [. . .] He accepted me, he killed me, I have been killed by him and am now reborn for a new life. And so must you intellectuals die in the same way and rise from the dead with us. Look at all of us, see how we come to know each other through slavery, the vat has boiled us down to our very essence.

Prishvin was shocked at what he was witnessing. This "Christ-Tsar" was a drunken rogue, yet his acolytes believed in him and were happy to give him whatever they had, be it their meager wages or their wives. Shchetinin's favorite motto was "You are greater than I," words he taught his disciples to repeat to help break their will and to convince them to "throw themselves into the vat." He was a sadist who took pleasure in seeing his followers suffer. "I had to undress him myself and then lie down next to him," one female disciple recounted. "He forced me to kiss his body, to suck his member, while citing holy scripture—'unto the pure all things are pure.'"[6]

Some intellectuals, such as Merezhkovsky, found Shchetinin

fascinating. Shchetinin tried to convince Merezhkovsky to join their ranks, saying, "Our life is a boiling vat, we boil ourselves in this vat, we have nothing that belongs just to ourselves [. . .] Throw yourself in with us, die with us, and we shall resurrect you. You will rise again as a leader of the people." Merezhkovsky invited Shchetinin to a meeting of the Religious-Philosophical Society. Zinaida Gippius took him as a second, "democratic edition" of Rasputin, noting that they even dressed the same, although since Shchetinin had failed to make contacts among the church hierarchs so he had moved down, not up, the social ladder, finding his place among Petersburg's workers. "A lively person," she wrote, "evidently of strong will, imperious and possessed by a frenzied passion for talking." In his message of self-abnegation and the symbolic suicide of the individual on the path to a higher plane of life via the community, Gippius believed she discerned Marxist ideals at the heart of Shchetinin's philosophy.[7] Later, after the revolution, Gippius was given the police file on Shchetinin. It included a large photograph of him, dressed as a woman and surrounded by his female acolytes. What she read curdled her blood. No, she realized, Shchetinin and Rasputin were not so alike after all. "The disgracefulness and debauchery of the latter pales in comparison with what Shchetinin did out of his unquenchable and irrepressible lust and depravity that bordered on sadism."[8]

To test the strength of his hold over his followers, Shchetinin required parents to hand their children over to orphanages of his choosing so they would not only lose their children, but not be able to ever track them down and find them again. This was apparently one step too far, and his followers rose up and overthrew him in 1909 for Pavel Legkobytov, the man Prishvin had met earlier. As their new leader one of the first things Legkobytov did was have all the females undergo a collective wedding with the men of the sect.[9]

Shchetinin was arrested and imprisoned in 1912. Alexander Prugavin, the specialist in Russian sects, suggested to his niece Vera Zhukovskaya, who was herself particularly interested in such characters, that she go visit him in prison. Zhukovskaya was thrilled by the idea: "This is one of the last prophets, one might even say the last living gods. His ability to impose his will not only over the souls but the bodies as well of his female acolytes is quite simply worthy of wonder, especially since this man is so debauched. He has been tried in court more than once, even for rape. And now here he is in prison, and not for spreading his dangerous heresy, but for seducing a minor."[10]

Zhukovskaya was shocked by what she encountered behind the bars of his cell. "He stared at me hungrily with two brightly shining, unblinking eyes, unmistakably those of a khlyst." Shchetinin vibrated with a tense energy, like a wolf in a cage, she thought, bouncing from one foot to another. He began to speak loudly, gesticulating and jumping about. He was explaining the secret of life, but his words were a chaos of unconnected thoughts—"a fountain of words"—making it nearly impossible to follow his meaning. His power was at once repulsive yet irresistible: "A sweet, agonizing bliss rose ever higher and higher toward my throat. I thought to myself—you're going to choke and that will be the end. You'll never feel another thing." Zhukovskaya left the prison profoundly moved by her encounter with this captive animal mysteriously endowed with the opposing forces of God and Satan.

Shchetinin had earlier wanted to marry Darya Smirnova, the so-called "Okhtinskaya Virgin," head of a khlyst sect located on the Okhta River, a tributary of the Neva on the eastern side of Petersburg. She was physically beautiful, sporting a green dress, her face powdered and rouged, and with what Prishvin called "cold eyes." Intellectuals like Prishvin, Vyacheslav Ivanov, and the poet Alexander Blok were fascinated by her. They would visit Smirnova and invited her to come speak to the Religious-Philosophical Society. She offered to instruct them in the secret ways to control others and told them, "He who takes me for a woman shall find a woman. He who takes me for a god shall find a god." She spoke to them of the visible and the invisible worlds, of the astral sphere.

In March 1914, Smirnova was tried in a Petersburg court on a number of charges, including religious perversion and the deaths of two women whom she had instructed to fast for forty days. Prishvin appeared in court and spoke in her defense, saying he considered Smirnova a "peasant Eve." Others at the trial disagreed. Vladimir Bonch-Bruevich was called in as an expert witness and testified that during her rituals Smirnova forced her followers to drink not just her dirty bathwater but even her urine. There was talk of sexual perversion. The court found for the prosecution. Smirnova was stripped of her property and exiled to Siberia.

And then there was the strange case of Valentin Sventsitsky, a Russian Orthodox priest, writer, and co-founder of both the "Christian Brotherhood of Struggle" and the Moscow Religious-Philosophical Society, who argued that the path to Christ lay in suffering, sexual sin, and even torture. In 1910, he wrote about those Christians who sought spiritual renewal only by peaceful means:

> Awaken in them cruel lust and the bloody fires of sensual desire. May they at least once after their learned gatherings fall into a wild orgy such that they lose all human form. [. . .] May the Lord send lovers to their wives. And not just one, but many. And not pure, decent lovers, but the most perverted and brutal ones. And may these wives learn to deceive their husbands [. . .] may they learn how to give their bodies over to desecration and pleasure. Poison their "chaste" souls with pleasure, awaken in them the basest instincts. Give all of this to them so that they may be saved.

In 1908, Sventsitsky published *The Antichrist*, a scandalous novel with a Nietzschean hero who freely mixes good and bad—and a healthy dose of sadism—as he seeks to create his own moral universe. Sventsitsky's friend Mark Vishnyak described his faith as the "vulgar wisdom of the common folk: if you don't sin, you don't repent, if you don't repent, you can't be saved."

Women, Vishnyak and others noted, went crazy for Sventsitsky. There were all sorts of outsize rumors about his sex life, and no one could be certain where the truth about his exploits gave way to myth-making. He did, however, seduce three young and attractive women and have a daughter with each of them. None of the women resented each other or thought less of Sventsitsky for his infidelities. The members of the Religious-Philosophical Society, however, felt otherwise, and he was kicked out of the group. Around 1909, he helped start a new movement—Golgotha Christianity—predicated on the belief that for humanity to be saved every person must be equal to Christ and experience his own Golgotha. Their ideas were publicized in the society's weekly *The New Land*, whose contributors included Blok, the Symbolist poet Valery Bryusov, and the future Nobel laureate Ivan Bunin. In its pages the priest Iona Brikhnichyov wrote of Sventsitsky: "To you the mysteries have been entrusted . . ./ To you the word of the Testament has been entrusted . . ./ You are not here by chance./ You are the light of a distant Light./ Go, spread the light./ The hour has struck to act./ Expect no mercy./ There shall be no mercy shown to the prophets."[11]

*

The restless spiritual seeking of the fin de siècle was a pan-European phenomenon. Much of this can be explained by the declining influence of the church, and institutionalized religion in general, throughout the West, but there were other specific domestic factors that lent a greater urgency to this spiritual searching in Russia. Beginning with the end of serfdom in 1861 and stretching into the early years of the twentieth century, Russia, arguably more so than any of the countries of Europe, was experiencing rapid and profoundly unsettling change as a traditional, agricultural society tried to modernize practically overnight. Along with this enormous transformation, the shattering defeat in the Russo-Japanese War followed by the Revolution of 1905 that shook the old order to its foundations left Russians with an inescapable sense of alienation, foreboding, and imminent crisis. The old institutions, and the old beliefs that went with them, no longer seemed adequate to address the troubling questions of a new and, to many, uncertain and frightening world.[12]

The popularity of occultism encouraged the belief that diabolic forces were at work. This belief in turn fueled conspiracy theories, the search for secret plots, and the preoccupation with enemies operating under the cover of disguise. On the political right, it found expression in the idea that Russia's woes were the work of international Jew-Masonry. Although the First World War exacerbated these patterns of belief, eventually whipping them into a national psychosis, the belief in "Dark Forces" appeared several years before the conflict began. Around 1906, for example, Vyacheslav Ivanov and the Theosophist Anna Mintslova wrote the novelist Andrei Bely that *"enemies really do exist who are poisoning Russia with negative emanations; these enemies are Eastern occultists acting on the subconscious of the Russian people, unleashing wild passions beneath the crescent of the waning moon."* They were under attack by "occult arrows shot from the world of darkness that was consciously demoralizing Russia."[13]

The obsession with "Dark Forces" accompanied an obsession with the Devil himself. Satan seemed to be everywhere in the years prior to World War I, from Anton Rubinstein's opera *Demon* (1871–72) to the paintings of Mikhail Vrubel—"Demon Seated" (1890), "Demon Prostrate," and "The Demon Cast Down" (both 1902). Vladimir Solovyov, racked by the collapse of his belief in the traditional church, was beset by visions of demons and came to believe he had even encountered Satan in the flesh. His last literary work was titled *A Short Tale of the*

Antichrist (1899).[14] The noted writer Leonid Andreev dealt with the Devil in his 1909 tragedy *Anathema*, and the composer Alexander Scriabin came to fear his own Sixth Piano Sonata, convinced that it had been corrupted by demonic forces and so he refused to play it in public. Scriabin considered himself to be God (if one is to believe some of his later poetry) and even tried to walk on the waters of Lake Geneva (unsuccessfully), and after attempting to exorcize the demons by way of his Seventh Sonata, he went on to compose a Ninth Sonata in 1913 known as "The Black Mass" with references to devil worship, sadism, and even necrophilia.[15]

Writers such as Alexander Dobrolyubov, Bryusov, and Bely were also obsessed with black magic and the demonic. The third volume of the religious philosopher Mitrofan Lodyzhensky's *Mystical Trilogy*, titled *Dark Forces* (1914), examined all aspects of these influences, including those of the Devil and the Antichrist, on the human soul. Alexander Blok was another writer obsessed with the Devil, and not just in literary terms; he believed a real, undeniable demonic force had been unleashed in Russia. While working for the Commission in 1917, Blok wrote that to understand the final days of the Romanov dynasty required a "demonic" point of view.[16]

Belief in the supernatural, in dark forces secretly directing the course of Russia toward the Apocalypse, in the undeniable presence of the Devil himself—all came together in shaping the popular perception of Rasputin. It cannot be stressed enough that the image of Rasputin that developed in the years before the Great War, an image which remains to this day, was created less by Rasputin the man—by the true nature of his character and the actual record of his actions—than by Russia's diseased zeitgeist of the early 1900s. Cosmic forces were battling for the future of Russia, and the fact that a simple peasant had managed not just to make his way to the tsar's palace, but to so thoroughly win his trust could only mean one of two things: either he was an angel sent from God or he was a servant of the Devil. Iliodor was not being metaphorical when he called the Russian edition of his book *The Holy Devil*.[17] As the years passed, and the crises facing Russia grew, it became ever more obvious to nearly everyone that the peasant from Pokrovskoe could only be the latter. Blok's mother was convinced Rasputin was either the Devil or the Antichrist and the root of all of Russia's troubles. Even Russian Foreign Minister Sergei Sazonov called Rasputin the Antichrist.[18]

During his own lifetime, Rasputin stopped being a man and became the haunting personification of a terrifying era. The *New Sunday Evening Newspaper* captured the phenomenon:

Rasputin is a symbol. He is not a real person. He is the characteristic product of our strange times, when we must endure exhaustion without end, when you feel around you a poisonous miasma, rising up out of the swamp, when the twilight descends all around, and in the half-light strange figures come crawling out from their cramped lairs—ghouls, bats, the undead, and every kind of evil spirit.[19]

12. Anna Vyrubova

It was in the spring of 1907 that Rasputin met the woman who would become one of his most devoted acolytes and greatest defenders. Anna Vyrubova was born in 1884 into a high-placed family. Her mother was Countess Nadezhda Tolstaya, her father, Alexander Taneev, a well-known composer and head of His Majesty's Personal Chancellery, a post held by Anna's forebears since the time of Alexander I.

Rasputin excepted, Vyrubova is perhaps the most controversial and polarizing figure from the court of the last Romanovs. No other person has been drawn in such contradictory fashion or elicited such opposing opinions. Take the assessments of the members of the Commission from 1917. After her arrest following the fall of the dynasty, Vyrubova was imprisoned in the Trubetskoy bastion at the Peter and Paul Fortress. Among her interrogators was Vladimir Rudnev. From the first time he saw her Rudnev was struck by the rare expression of her eyes—"full of unearthly mildness." After checking her statements against other sources and witnesses, Rudnev concluded everything she had told him had been true. Her words, he said, "breathed truth and sincerity." She showed little concern for herself, even though she was subjected to all manner of humiliating and violent behavior at the hands of her guards. She was not bright, but straightforward, honest, and utterly lacking the least hint of cunning. The notion that Vyrubova exercised any sort of influence over Nicholas or Alexandra or Rasputin was, in Rudnev's estimation, laughable.[1]

Alexander Blok, Rudnev's colleague at the Commission, disagreed. "There's not one word of truth in Vyrubova's testimony," he insisted. Blok found the mere existence of a woman like Vyrubova "ghastly"; to him she was nothing but "loathsome."[2] Commissioner Boris Smitten had a similar opinion: "More than just limited, she was obstinate and cocksure [...] superficial and poorly educated."[3] Gippius, who met Vyrubova but could not really claim to know her well, felt she had seen enough to call her call "dim, obstinate, and cunning. The typical Russian

female psychopath one found gathered around 'the starets.'"[4] Grand
Duchess Olga, the tsar's sister, described her as "utterly irresponsible,
childish to silliness, and much addicted to hysterical outbursts."[5]

Equally divergent are the views on her role in the lives of the imperial family. If to Rudnev it was inconceivable that Vyrubova exercised any influence (he shared the opinion of Alexander Protopopov, the last imperial minister of the interior, that she was merely a "phonograph" for Rasputin's ideas), others have sought to depict her as the evil genius behind the throne.[6] Playwright-historian Edvard Radzinsky dubbed Vyrubova the "invisible ruler" of the Russian court and claimed (with no evidence) that she not only hired and fired ministers as she saw fit, but even dominated the empress herself, all the while pretending to be nothing more than a good-natured simpleton. At the heart of Vyrubova's relationship with the empress, he claimed to have uncovered a dirty little secret: Anna was desperately in love with Alexandra.[7] The idea of a lesbian relationship between Vyrubova and Alexandra is not new. It was talked about in the aristocratic salons of the capital in the years soon after Rasputin's appearance and grew to the most absurd lengths. One story that went around Petersburg was that the two women engaged in orgies together with Rasputin, and that it was through these ménages-à-trois that they developed such a close bond.[8] Vyrubova did love the empress, but there is nothing to suggest anything sexual in their relationship. Nor did she ever exert any influence over Alexandra; the empress was beyond doubt the stronger of the two. Vyrubova lived to please the empress, not direct her.

It was in 1905, the same year Alexandra met Rasputin, that the two women drew close when Vyrubova sailed that summer on the *Polar Star* with the royal family in the skerries off the coast of Finland. Vyrubova was drawn to Alexandra. They were both shy, loved music (Alexandra and Vyrubova would spend many hours together singing duets), and shared a deep religious sensibility. Vyrubova's faith grew out of her own personal experience. At the age of sixteen she fell dangerously ill with typhus and was close to death. The doctors told her parents her situation was hopeless. One night Father John of Kronstadt appeared in her dreams and told her she would live. The next morning she asked her parents to call the priest. He came, prayed over her, sprinkled her with holy water, and the following day she made a miraculous recovery. The incident proved to Vyrubova the immense power of faith and that there were men living among them with extraordinary spiritual gifts.[9]

Vyrubova was a maid-of-honor at court and, for a time, one of Alexandra's ladies-in-waiting, but the nature of her importance to the empress was never reflected by any official position. She was quite simply Alexandra's closest friend, her confidante, the one woman she trusted more than any other, even if she found Vyrubova's devotion at times overwhelming. "The Cow," Alexandra called her on occasion, a cruel way to speak of someone who lived to please the empress and her family.[10] Vyrubova was indeed heavy (though not bovine), yet one's opinion of her looks generally depended on one's opinion of her character. Gippius thought her soft exterior hid an iron core of obstinacy and deceit. As for her eyes, these were "wide, open, light [. . .] and blind."[11] Prince Felix Yusupov, a dance partner of Vyrubova's in their youth, found her "extremely crafty," as well as "stout with a puffy, shiny face and no charm whatever."[12] But to Maria Rasputina, Vyrubova had "luxuriant brown hair and gentle intelligent eyes" and, if not a conventional beauty, still "she had a charm, gentleness, a clear voice and attractive manners which won all hearts."[13]

Vyrubova was twenty-two when she met Rasputin in the spring of 1907. The introduction was arranged by Militsa, possibly at the request of Alexandra. Militsa told her she had met "an apostle" through Bishop Feofan and offered to arrange a meeting at her Petersburg mansion on the English Embankment. Vyrubova arrived and the two sat and talked about religious topics over tea for an hour or two. Then, Rasputin came.

> I remember I was very nervous when Rasputin's arrival was announced. "Don't be surprised,"—she said,—"I sometimes exchange a triple kiss with him." Grigory Yefimovich entered— slim, with a pale, exhausted face, wearing a short black caftan; his gaze was extraordinarily piercing, it reminded me of the gaze of Father John of Kronstadt. "Ask him to pray about something specific,"—said Militsa in French. I asked him to pray that I would be able to spend my whole life in the service of Their Majesties. "So it shall be,"—he said, and I left.[14]

It appears the driving force behind the meeting had been Alexandra, not Militsa. Around this time the empress was starting to have concerns that the Black Crows and their husbands were intent on using Rasputin to exercise influence over the palace. By cultivating a relationship between Vyrubova and Rasputin, Alexandra hoped to weaken the Black Crows' hand and to establish a new channel to Rasputin over which she would have better control.[15]

The meeting took place a month before Vyrubova was to marry on 30 April 1907. Her fiancé, Alexander Vyrubov, was a decorated naval officer of the Russo-Japanese War and the cousin of Vladimir Voeikov. The marriage proved short, unhappy, and the source of considerable gossip. Vyrubova later wrote that Rasputin had predicted her marriage would not be happy, but his letters to her from this period belie this claim. "A true Easter," he calls her wedding, and her new husband, "a cross of gold."[16] But after the wedding, when the difficulties in their marriage were becoming too large to ignore, Rasputin wrote counseling patience, insisting that all would be well in the end: "You've truly difficult moments, and our dear Papa and Mama also have them [. . .] Still it's a sweet paradise and God provides, I am a witness that all will end well. Yes, God has wed you in lawful marriage and there you'll find a cedar of Lebanon that brings fruit when it's due; and you like an exemplary cedar will bring joy when the time comes."[17]

It is possible that Vyrubov was suffering from impotence (temporary, that is, for he later had two daughters with another woman), as seems to be suggested by another letter from Rasputin: "God has sealed you in marriage with your wonderful and intelligent bridegroom. [. . .] Don't push or use pressure, and gradually he'll come himself to the sweet table, he's busy now and when he finishes then he'll come and eat of those lessons you provide him."[18]

But Rasputin was wrong. The marriage collapsed the following year. Vyrubova later said her husband suffered from "sexual impotence and an inclination for sadism." Once he tried to make love to her but could not, so he threw Anna on the ground and began to beat her.[19] Gossips said the marriage had been destroyed by Vyrubova's sexual passion for the empress; others that it was her sleeping with Rasputin.[20] Iliodor claimed to have watched as Rasputin grabbed her breasts, stroking them shamelessly in front of others.[21] None of this seems remotely plausible. Rasputin offered Anna comfort, writing on 1 July 1908 that just as the Lord had sent the Holy Spirit to the Apostles, so would she, the "sufferer," whose husband had "slandered" her, find peace by pouring out her "sorrow before the throne of the Almighty."[22] The pain of her failed marriage intensified her already great religious passion and brought her ever closer to Alexandra and Rasputin.

Anna introduced her sister, Alexandra (known as Sana), to Rasputin and she too, along with her husband, Alexander Pistolkors (as of 1908), joined the growing ranks of his followers. The Russian archives preserve her pleading telegrams to Rasputin—

> 24 July 1910. From Petersburg to Rasputin in Pokrovskoe. Am ill. I beg for your help. I want to live. Sana.
>
> 1 November 1910. From Petersburg to Rasputin in Pokrovskoe. I'm in pain. Bedridden. Am terribly afraid. Please pray for me. Sana.[23]

Alexander Pistolkors' aunt Lyubov Golovina (née Karpovich) and her daughter Maria (known as Munya) were also introduced around this time to Rasputin and became devoted disciples as well. Alexander's mother, however, Princess Olga Paley, and her second husband, Grand Duke Paul Alexandrovich, Alexander's stepfather, could not abide Rasputin, nor could Paul's son, Grand Duke Dmitry Pavlovich, one of Rasputin's murderers. To complicate matters still, Alexander's sister, Marianna Pistolkors (m. Derfelden), was extremely close with her stepbrother Dmitry and shared his views about Rasputin.[24] Some later claimed she was even present at his murder. Rasputin divided families as well as the entire country.

In time Vyrubova came to see Rasputin as a saint, and her faith in him was as strong as her faith in God. According to the memoirs of the singer Alexandra Belling, before putting food to their lips Vyrubova and her guests would first have it blessed by Rasputin. Whenever someone expressed an opinion, no one said a word before first hearing what Rasputin thought of it. And when anyone dared discuss with her the negative stories being told about him or brought her critical articles to read, Vyrubova was ready with an answer: "Just as all righteous men are recognized only after their deaths, so too will the holy deeds of the starets come to light after his death, and then the people will understand who they have lost and who they failed to cherish during our dear father's life. His relics will undoubtedly be revealed to create miracles that we have yet to see."[25]

As for Rasputin, he could at times be harsh with Vyrubova, even rage at her, but his affection for her was real and lasting. "I kiss you," he would write, "and love you with all my soul."[26]

13. The Eyes

In July 1907, Nicholas left Russia to observe joint naval exercises with Germany. From Peterhof, a worried Alexandra wrote to him on the seventeenth: "I do hope that all goes smoothly, without any obstacles and unpleasant conversations—Gr[igory] watches over your journey, and all will be well."[1] Later that summer, while the family was sailing in the Finnish skerries, Alexandra approached Nikolai Sablin, a high-ranking naval officer and aide-de-camp of the tsar, and asked him in private whether he had ever heard the name Rasputin and if so, what his opinion of him was. He replied that he had heard about a simple man who had been visiting the royal family but knew nothing more. "This is a very pious, far-sighted, real Russian peasant," she told him. "He knows church worship by heart. Of course, this is not a person from our circle but you may find him interesting to meet."[2] She added that there were people whose prayers, thanks to their ascetic way of living, had special powers, and Rasputin was such a man.[3] She gave Sablin his address and told him to go meet him.

He found Rasputin living with the Lokhtins at 13 Grechesky Prospect. By his reception Sablin could tell that Rasputin had been expecting him. He was friendly and greeted Sablin warmly. Rasputin was slender, almost frail, narrowly built and below average height. He was wearing a long Russian shirt and simple, homespun coat, his trousers tucked into a pair of high boots. His hair was brown and his beard, Sablin noticed, was untidy and unevenly cut and made an unpleasant impression. He spoke to him about religion and God and praised the tsar and his family. Sablin said little. Then, out of the blue, Rasputin asked Sablin whether he drank. The question threw him off and Sablin got ready to go. As he was leaving, Rasputin asked Sablin for five rubles. "Give me, my dear, a fiver, please, I have somehow completely run out of money." Sablin was surprised but gave him the money. Sablin's impression of Rasputin was rather unpleasant.

Since it was Alexandra's wish, Sablin met Rasputin several times.

Sablin later said that the empress wanted him to get to know Rasputin better and obtain a blessing from him. Finally, however, Sablin had had enough and he told Alexandra that having gotten to know Rasputin he did not have a very good impression of him, to which the empress replied: "You cannot understand him because you are far from people like that, but even if your impression was correct, it is still God's will that he is like that."[4]

There was, however, one thing about Rasputin that had impressed Sablin. His eyes. "There was 'something' in them," he had to admit. In this Sablin was not alone. If there was ever one thing everyone could agree on about Rasputin it was that there was *something* about those eyes.

"His eyes pierced you like needles," remarked Lydia Bazilevskaya, a wealthy, beautiful twenty-eight-year-old divorcée upon meeting Rasputin.[5] Prugavin described them as "the green, rapacious fires of a voluptuary."[6] His niece Vera Zhukovskaya recalled: "The starets has especially amazing eyes—gray that can in an instant burn red. His eyes are irresistible: they are filled with their own inner magnetism. When in the presence of women, they catch fire with an unusual passion."[7] Voeikov called them "the eyes of a rogue, always roving and never looking you straight in the face."[8] A reporter for the *Petersburg Newspaper* remarked that "there was something disturbing and alarming in the metallic expression of those cold gray eyes that pierced straight through you."[9] (As to their color, Rasputin's eyes were greenish-gray, of this there is no doubt.)

One female friend wrote in the autumn of 1915:

> Well, there are those eyes of his. Every time I see him I am amazed how expressive they are and what depth they possess. It is impossible to withstand his gaze for long. There is something heavy in it, as if you are experiencing some sort of material force emanating from his gaze, yet his eyes are often shining with goodness, though always with a hint of craftiness, and there is a great deal of tenderness in them. Nevertheless, how fierce they can be at times and how horrifying they are when he's angry.[10]

Maria, too, had to admit that her father's "magnetic eyes" possessed a "disturbing fixity" that made people ill at ease.[11] One woman found Rasputin's gaze so terrifying she ran to church for confession to purify herself after he did nothing more than lay his eyes on her.[12] A certain

Polish countess went to pieces upon being confronted by Rasputin's eyes: "I can't, I can't handle those eyes. They see everything. I can't take it!" she screamed.[13]

Many Russians saw in Rasputin's eyes the source of his power. Expressing a widely held view, his good friend Nikolai Solovyov told the press that "The charm of this man lies in his eyes. There is something in them that draws you in and forces you to submit to his will. There is something psychologically inexplicable in all this."[14] A female admirer commented how the power of Rasputin's gaze was so intense it could make a woman shake and fall into hysterics.[15] Meriel Buchanan, daughter of the British ambassador, caught sight of Rasputin riding through the streets of the capital. "Pale gray, deep-set but amazingly brilliant eyes were looking at me," she recalled, "and while that gaze held me I stood motionless, [. . .] held by a sensation of helplessness so intense."[16]

As to Rasputin's overall physical appearance, opinions differed. Lily Dehn, a good friend of the empress, met Rasputin around 1911 and was struck by how horrible he looked. Other than his eyes, and here, too, she had to admit these "held her in his power," he looked just like a typical Russian peasant of about average height (though he seemed taller than he was), his face thin and pale, his hair long, his unkempt beard a darkish auburn.[17] In early 1912, Rasputin sat for the artist Alexander Raevsky. It was the first time Raevsky had seen him in person, and he was struck by the impression Rasputin made. "What was my surprise when I saw a tall, well-proportioned, strongly-built man without a single gray hair who moved with such remarkable lightness and flexibility. He flew up to the sixth floor in one breath without any sign of being short-winded." Raevsky noticed the nervous energy that coursed through Rasputin. He had "nervous fingers" that were forever stroking his beard.[18] Stepan Beletsky, director of the department of police from 1912 to 1915 and a man who came to know Rasputin very well, also remarked on the unmistakable and pronounced "nervousness of his entire lively, sinuous figure."[19]

Many found his voice appealing. Konstantin Globachev, head of the Petrograd Okhrana during the war, noted his voice was "soft, pleasant, his manner of speech that of the simple peasant, yet intelligent."[20] It was said he spoke in a steady, unhurried way and that he had a fine singing voice as well.[21]

The common stereotype of Rasputin was that he was a "dirty peasant," but this was merely a reflection of the prejudice of the upper classes. Rasputin, according to those who knew him best, kept his body clean and bathed. Indeed, we know for a fact that he frequented the baths both in Pokrovskoe and Petersburg regularly. Even the Russian press—no friend of Rasputin and ready to print the most outlandish lies—commented that his hands, large and powerful with unusually long fingers, "were clean."[22] Rasputin's good friend Alexei Filippov said he was "exceptionally clean: he often changed his linen, went to the baths, and never smelled bad. [. . .] His body was exceptionally firm, not flabby, and ruddy and well-proportioned, without the paunch and flaccid muscles usual at that age." As for his private parts, Filippov noticed nothing exceptional about them, except that they were "without the darkening of the pigment of the sexual organs, which at a certain age have a dark or brown hue."[23] Filippov is silent as to how, exactly, he knew this most intimate detail about his friend.

14. ". . . prayers that purify and protect us."

In September 1907 Rasputin returned to Pokrovskoe. He arrived home as the big man in the village. Some called him *gospodin*, lord, as if he were a nobleman. He was bearing money from Militsa, which he gave to the church, and also helped the villagers with gifts (including cash), built houses for the poor, and paid for funerals. He lived in his new large wooden house of dark gray on the main street that had once belonged to a river pilot. It had two stories and was enclosed by a large fence; the extensive yard included a bath, small barn, and other outbuildings. There were flower boxes on the house, including a large one on the street, and the windows were decorated with elaborate painted frames; the roof was tin. His father, now a widower, Anna having died in 1904, had chosen not to move in with his son, but stayed on in his smaller house located between the Tura and the back of Grigory's place.[1]

The family lived on the ground floor, which had a kitchen and three separate rooms, one filled with icons, including a large and reportedly miracle-working Kazan Mother of God. A wooden staircase covered in multi-colored mats led to the second floor, chiefly reserved for guests. Here there was a small reception room with benches and a larger main hall, its floor covered in the same mats, complete with a writing desk, well-upholstered chairs, a heavy oak buffet, piano, and a large ebony clock. The walls were decorated with paper and crowded with photographs of Rasputin posing with seminarians and clergy from the theological academy, various priests, and members of the capital's aristocratic elite. There was a portrait of the emperor and empress and a number of icons. Next to the window stood a ficus. The Rasputins lived well. Not everyone could accept this, however. Feofan would say to the Commission in 1917 that the Rasputins' home reflected a "semi-indigent peasant's notion of how rich people lived in the cities."[2]

Traveling with Rasputin were Olga Lokhtina and three other women. Akilina Laptinskaya would become one of Rasputin's closest followers, and more, for the rest of his life. Born into a peasant family in the village of Bakhovo in the Mogilyov province in 1879, Laptinskaya was a nurse in Petersburg, having previously served in military hospitals during the Russo-Japanese War. She had first heard of Rasputin quite some time earlier from conversations at the St. Troitsky Commune of Nurses and turned to Lokhtina to arrange a meeting that took place in September 1907. He immediately struck her as a truly unusual man. "Grigory Yefimovich's simple way with people impressed me most of all. He is so full of goodness and pure love for others unlike anything I have encountered in anyone else. His knowledge of life is remarkable, there is not a question to which he cannot give an answer without the least hesitation." When she learned this group of women was going to Pokrovskoe to see how Rasputin lived and to learn from him, she asked to join them. She was not disappointed. Laptinskaya stayed with Rasputin for the rest of his life, becoming a sort of personal secretary and helping to run his household in the capital.[3]

Zinaida Manshtedt, from the city of Smolensk, was the wife of a high-ranking state official described by one acquaintance as "good, pretty, and nice." She became infatuated with Rasputin not long after his appearance in the capital, although not to the point of Lokhtina, and would often come to Petersburg to visit him. After returning home from Pokrovskoe, Zina, as she was called, wrote a letter that reveals much about both the psychology of his female followers and the nature of their relationship with Rasputin:

> Hello, dear Father Grigory!
>
> Thank you, thank you, I thank you without end for your great love that has resurrected the life of my spirit, for your tenderness and care. I returned home healthy and happy and am living here quietly and peacefully. Your last words, that I was wrong to leave, made a strong impression on me. You said it—so it must be true; they echoed in my ears the entire journey and forced me to examine every movement of my soul. Of course, there's much that's worthless in my soul, and I always need your help and your prayers that purify and protect us. I returned home a different person inside. Lord, help me to remain so. Now I'm alive, anger had tormented me and shut me off from everything. I fervently kiss your hands and pray forgiveness for all my filth.
>
> Your negligent Zina[4]

And then there was Khionya Berladskaya, aged twenty-nine and a widow, her husband having committed suicide two years earlier. Khionya suffered terribly after this tragedy, blaming herself for his death. A general's wife took pity on her in the autumn of 1906 and brought her to meet Rasputin. He looked at her intently and said: "What are you thinking? Don't you know that our Lord had twelve disciples and one of them, Judas, hanged himself? And this happened to our Lord, so what about you?" His words changed her life.

> These words were the answer to the thought that had been weighing down my soul, namely that I was guilty for my husband's death. So if something like this could have happened to our Lord, then I, a weak person, could not expect to bring my husband back to life. This immediately became clear to me, and my soul became so utterly calm, something that neither hypnotism nor any medicine had been able to do. Up until then I had not fasted for a year and I could not even enter a church, the sound of the hymns upset me so and I believed I was experiencing heart attacks. For two years I ate almost nothing and reached a point of almost complete spiritual and physical exhaustion. Becoming acquainted with Grigory Yefimovich I felt that he could solve all my life's problems with the right words from the Gospels. For this I feel the most profound love and gratitude for Grigory Yefimovich.

Berladskaya first visited Pokrovskoe in April 1907, staying with Rasputin and his family for four months "to learn how to live," as she put it. This had been a rewarding experience, and so she returned in November. Unlike the other three women, however, Berladskaya would change her opinion of Rasputin and her words would be used to turn others against him as well.[5]

By mid-November, Rasputin was back in Petersburg. One night Nicholas invited his sister Grand Duchess Olga Alexandrovna to dinner at the Alexander Palace at Tsarskoe Selo. After they had finished eating Nicholas asked Olga to come meet a Russian peasant. They went upstairs and found the four Romanov daughters and Alexei in their white pajamas, their governesses preparing them for bed. In the middle of the room stood Rasputin:

> When I saw him I felt that gentleness and warmth radiated from him. All the children seemed to like him. They were completely at

their ease with him. I still remember their laughter as little Alexei, deciding he was a rabbit, jumped up and down the room. And then, quite suddenly, Rasputin caught the child's hand and led him to his bedroom, and we three followed. There was something like a hush as though we had found ourselves in church. In Alexei's bedroom no lamps were lit; the only light came from the candles burning in front of some beautiful icons. The child stood very still by the side of that giant, whose head was bowed. I knew he was praying. It was all most impressive. I also knew that my little nephew had joined him in prayer. I really cannot describe it—but I was then conscious of the man's utter sincerity.

After the children had been put to bed, the three adults went downstairs to the mauve boudoir to talk.

I realized that both Nicky and Alicky were hoping that I would come to like Rasputin. I was certainly impressed by the scene in the nursery and I allowed the man his sincerity. But, unfortunately, I could never bring myself to like him.

    I never felt I was hypnotized by Rasputin. I did not think that his personality had anything irresistible in it. If anything, I found him rather primitive. [. . .] That very first evening I noticed that he leapt from one subject to another, and he did use so many biblical quotations. They did not impress me in the least. . . . I knew enough about the peasants to realize that a great many among them knew whole chapters of the Bible by heart.

Olga was more than just unimpressed. She found Rasputin overly familiar:

It was his curiosity—unbridled and embarrassing. In Alicky's boudoir, having talked to her and Nicky for a few minutes, Rasputin waited for the servants to get the table for the evening tea and then began plying me with the most impertinent questions. Was I happy? Did I love my husband? Why didn't I have any children? He had no right to ask such questions, nor did I answer them. I am afraid Nicky and Alicky looked rather uncomfortable. I do remember I was relieved at leaving the palace that evening and saying, "Thank God he hasn't followed me to the station."

Olga saw him once more after that at Vyrubova's home near the palace at Tsarskoe Selo. At one point when they were left alone, he came over and sat next to her, putting his arm around Olga and stroking her shoulder. She got up and moved off to join the others without saying a word. Although he pressed Vyrubova to see Olga again, she would have nothing more to do with him.

It was around the time Olga met Rasputin that Alexei, aged three, fell in the gardens at Tsarskoe Selo and hurt his leg. Internal bleeding began, then horrific pains. "The poor child lay in such pain," Olga recalled, "dark patches under his eyes and his little body all distorted, and the leg terribly swollen. The doctors were useless." They looked more worried than the rest, whispering among themselves. The hours passed and finally the doctors had to admit there was nothing they could do. Late that evening Alexandra sent a message to Rasputin in the capital, asking him to come immediately. Rasputin came and prayed over the little boy. The next day Olga returned to the palace and could not believe her eyes: "The little boy was not just alive—but well. He was sitting up in bed, the fever gone, the eyes clear and bright, not a sign of any swelling in his leg. The horror of the evening before became an incredibly distant nightmare. Later I learned from Alicky that Rasputin had not even touched the child but merely stood at the foot of the bed and prayed."[6] Olga insisted the boy's recovery could not have been a coincidence. Exactly how Rasputin had helped Alexei recover she could not say, but she never again had any doubt of Rasputin's power to heal.

Talk of Rasputin's late-night visit to Alexei's sickbed soon spread throughout the palace. Some said Rasputin had touched the boy and told him all would be well, although, he added, only God knew the hour of our death. Others insisted that after leaving the boy he had told the empress not to worry, that Alexei would suffer from his illness until the age of twenty but then it would pass and leave not a trace.[7]

What seems beyond doubt is that by the final months of 1907, Rasputin was feeling increasingly confident about his place with the imperial family, so much so that on 15 November he showed up at the palace to visit them without an invitation. Although quite naturally surprised by his unexpected appearance, Nicholas and Alexandra were delighted to see him.[8] He also saw at the palace that day Maria Vishnyakova, nursemaid to Alexei as of 1905. Vishnyakova had earlier been the nanny to the children of Stana, and she recommended her to the empress, who hired her in 1897 as nursemaid to her newborn Tatyana.

Vishnyakova was in her early thirties, gentle, tender, and quite pretty. Upon returning home that evening, an excited Rasputin wrote to Vishnyakova:

> Rejoicing in the Lord, you priceless one in Christ, for you live in glory and nourish the glory of our great Autocrat Alexei Nikolaevich. Ah! What a powerful word and priceless figure, my god-loving little sister in Christ, is that not a profound greeting for such a youth. My sweet one, educate him, this will be your ideal—my golden one, show him small examples of God's edification, in all his children's games seek edification. Allow him to romp a bit more; let him romp about as he wishes. For he sees you as a young woman bedecked by God's glory, and your example is profound, it will remain firmly in his soul [. . .] And for all this you shall be the mother of the land. Listen, god-loving sister in Christ. Dear mama, what does this mean? What supreme sign does your priceless summoning here hold? What a gift the Lord has bestowed on you that you may enjoy the esteem of such exalted parents. [. . .] If we love all, and do not let ourselves become proud, we shall dwell in glory here and in joy in heaven. Of course, the enemy crawls about, he knows we are sublime and are here among the mighty; that is his perfidious nature. But I've yet to find any pride in you, and have found in your soul the warmest greeting for me. From the very first you saw me, you understood me. I wish very, very much to see you again. Ask Papa and Mama for their permission to come to me for I saw you only briefly and could not see you anymore, it was awkward to stay longer.[9]

It is an intriguing letter for a number of reasons. Why, for example, would Rasputin have encouraged her to let Alexei romp given what was already known of his illness and what had just happened to the boy a short time before? Is it really possible Rasputin did not understand the danger this presented? Rasputin is clearly trying to make an ally at court out of Vishnyakova, playing both to the holy mission that she has been entrusted with and to their shared status as close friends of the imperial family. The reference to the enemy is also intended to draw her to him by suggesting there are people at court who are jealous of their intimacy with the family and may well be plotting against them. And what is to be made of Rasputin's comment that Vishnyakova understood him from the first time they met? One thing that is clear is Rasputin's desire to see more of Vishnyakova. If this had been only to discuss the well-being of the tsarevich, there would have been no reason for any embarrassment on Rasputin's part. But Rasputin appears to be implying something different here, something concerning just the two of them, something much more personal. We do not know whether Vishnyakova ever asked for permission to see Rasputin, nor do we know whether she ever acknowledged his letter. Three years later, however, Vishnyakova would go to the empress with serious accusations against Rasputin that would result in an enormous scandal.

Toward the end of the year Rasputin left Petersburg for Kazan. There he met fourteen-year-old Olga Ilyin at her family home. Olga was shocked to see a peasant enter through their front door, something she had never witnessed in her life. People from the lower classes only ever entered through the back. He was bearing a letter from Olga's aunt in Petersburg, who had come to know Rasputin and was taken with him but wished to introduce Rasputin to Olga's father and get his opinion of the man.

Rasputin stayed for dinner. He made Olga uncomfortable. Rasputin looked at her strangely and his manners were atrocious. After soup had been served he pulled out his comb and began to groom himself at the table, much to everyone's displeasure. Over dinner they asked Rasputin about his life and travels. When asked how he, a religious man of God devoted to solitude and prayer, took to Petersburg, he replied: "I asked God about that when I first came to St. Petersburg. 'Why did you send me here?' I asked him. 'Why are you testing me this way?' And he said to me, 'Wherever I send you, that is your place to be. People might hate you, because they'll envy you, but you must endure because you are needed.'"

The Ilyins and their guests were at turns fascinated and repelled by the stranger, at once ready to believe he was who he claimed to be, and Olga's aunt believed him to be, or a charlatan. He told them God gave him the power to read other people's minds. As proof, he turned to Olga's art teacher and called him a sinner, for he was forever starting something but never seeing it through to the end, and this God did not like. His words stunned them: this was all true, they had to admit. With that the others asked him to read their minds, which he did and did well enough to convince everyone that his power was genuine.

Olga saw Rasputin several more times between 1907 and 1910 at her aunt's in Petersburg. Her aunt maintained her faith in Rasputin as a true man of God, and allowed him to visit her home. Olga, however, never trusted him, though she kept this to herself. She was certain he was duping her, showing her aunt only one side of himself. At one of these visits for tea, after her aunt had left the room, Rasputin got up and came to sit next to Olga. She froze with indignation when he asked her to open up and tell him about herself. When she refused he asked her why she was frightened of him.

"I'm not scared of you at all."

"Yes, yes you *are* scared," he replied, "whereas I should be loved. Because I have been sent to you all by the Lord God. That is why everybody should love me more than they love anyone else in the world. The Tsar and Tsaritsa both love me, so you should love me more than you love anyone else."

He moved his hand across the sofa toward her, gazing at her intently, and with that Olga bolted and escaped to her room. She never saw Rasputin again.[10]

15. The Investigation: Part I

The remarkable changes in Rasputin's life did not go unnoticed by the authorities back in Siberia. Questions were being asked about the unusual things taking place at the Rasputin home in Pokrovskoe.

On 23 July 1906, two days before Rasputin was to meet Nicholas and Alexandra for only the second time, the Tyumen district superintendent of police, a man by the name of Vishnevsky, sent a report to the district chief of police regarding the local peasant Grigory Yefimovich Rasputin and the various guests from the capital he had been hosting of late, such as Father Medved, described in the report as the preceptor to the children of Grand Duke Nikolai Nikolaevich, and one Olga Lokhtina, both of whom had been heard to say that the peasant Rasputin "works miracles" in St. Petersburg. Rasputin, Vishnevsky reported, often received money by post from Petersburg, sometimes as much as one hundred rubles or more, as well as gifts that he claimed came from lofty personages, including their imperial majesties. During their visits his guests appeared to spend most of their time in Rasputin's home reading the Gospel and singing hymns.

The report is the first known document by the state authorities concerning the personality and affairs of Rasputin. It is not clear who ordered Vishnevsky to take up the matter of an obscure Pokrovskoe peasant or whether the order came from local officials in Tyumen or Tobolsk or from someone in the capital, although the former seems more likely. Regardless, the district chief of police forwarded Vishnevsky's report to Nikolai Gondatti, the governor of the Tobolsk province. Gondatti did not consider it worthy of his attention or a matter for the civil authorities and he, in turn, forwarded it on 4 August 1906 to Antony (Alexander Karzhavin), bishop of Tobolsk, "for his information." That Gondatti did not bother to follow up on the matter adds further credence to the fact that the investigation had been initiated at the local level, for had it come down from St. Petersburg, Gondatti would certainly have given it his own attention.

Antony did not give the report much importance either, and the business of the peasant Rasputin seemed to end there. It was only a year later, on 1 September 1907, that Antony did take action, writing a letter to the Tobolsk Ecclesiastical Consistory outlining in detail the suspicious behavior of Rasputin, on whom, he noted, he had been collecting information for some time. Antony wrote that Rasputin had learned the teachings of the khlysts "at the manufactories in the Perm province" where he met and came to know "the leaders of this heresy." Later, in Petersburg, Rasputin had begun to attract a group of female followers and they came to live with him for long stretches in Pokrovskoe. Antony was in the possession of letters from these women in which they wrote of Rasputin's special teachings, of his miracle healing, and of his being "a mass of love."

For the past five years as many as eight young women at a time had been living in Rasputin's home. They dressed in black with white head kerchiefs and accompanied him everywhere, calling him "Father Grigory"; he caressed, stroked, and even kissed these women. They held religious gatherings on the upper floor of his home, singing obscure religious songs, during which Rasputin donned a black cassock and a large gold pectoral cross. The peasants of his village talked of his teaching "khlystovism" and how one of the young women, a healthy creature, had fallen ill and died under mysterious circumstances. They told Antony about photographs taken in Yekaterinburg depicting Rasputin "in a full-length black cassock with two nuns on either side of him holding over his head a large paper banner with the words 'Seek the Heavenly Jerusalem.'" Moreover, Father Yakov Barbarin, barred from conducting services and banished to the Valaam Monastery in Karelia by the Holy Synod under the suspicion of spreading the teachings of the khlysty, had been a frequent guest of Rasputin's and had taken part in these nightly rituals.

Based on this information, Antony instructed the consistory to order Father Nikodim Glukhovtsev to begin a preliminary investigation into Rasputin and, should these charges be substantiated, to open a formal investigation that would include the nature of these nightly gatherings. To this Antony added his own personal observations. Rasputin, he wrote, had been to Tobolsk several times and had insisted on meeting the bishop to tell him about his plans to expand the village church and to construct some sort of "women's commune," all of this using his own money. "I was struck by his extremely emaciated face, with its sunken and sickly burning (inflamed) eyes, by his sham endearing manner of speech, full of diminutives and pet names so common to sectarians."[1] Antony also noted how poorly Rasputin read Russian, to say nothing of his inability to write and dismal knowledge of Old Church Slavonic.

Although Antony's meeting with Rasputin had left a bad impression on him, it had not been enough to cause him to launch the investigation into his possible ties to the khlysty. More disturbing to Antony than this meeting were three letters sent to him that summer containing considerable strange detail on Rasputin's recent activities. The first was from a Tobolsk woman by the name of Maria Korovina that August. A local priest by the name of Father Alexander Yurevsky had brought Rasputin to her home twice that month. Her story was troubling. From the very first she found him "a quite strange looking man, both by his clothing and the expression of his face, especially his eyes."

During their conversation he never sat still and was forever making odd gestures with his hands or touching Father Yurevsky. Rasputin came back alone to see her the next day. He told her he was leaving soon and how disappointed he had been with his visit to Tobolsk since so many people there were calling him a sectarian. "What sort of sectarian am I," he asked Korovina, "I just have a lot of love, I love everyone, I love you too and everyone else, so tell me, why does that make me a sectarian?" She replied that while she hardly knew him, she found it odd how he was always touching and stroking people, like Father Yurevsky, and how he had tried to do the same with her. Rasputin replied, "If I reach out and touch your hands, then this is again just because I have so much love [. . .] There's nothing I can do about it. Without touching hands, I have no inspiration."

Rasputin then cited what he said were the words of St. Symeon the New Theologian (949–1022), a Byzantine monk and Orthodox saint, that "an impassive man can be amidst a crowd of naked people and touch them with his naked body and suffer no harm," to which Maria replied: "Yes, I know that, but this refers to someone who accidentally ends up in such a situation, but it does not recommend seeking this out, for what kind of person looks freely for this sort of temptation?" (Symeon had also stressed the necessity for submission to a spiritual father on the path to God, something Rasputin avoided his entire life, for which he would often be criticized and which some clergy claimed was the reason for his spiritual failings.) Despite the obvious tension between them, they kissed upon parting. "In my opinion, G. Y. is not an entirely normal person," she concluded.

Father Yurevsky also wrote a description that month of his meeting Rasputin and their visit to Maria Korovina's. Rasputin had sought him out at his Tobolsk church and from the start had tried to impress Yurevsky with his personal connections to high clergymen such as Bishop Khrisanf and Archimandrite Andrei (Ukhtomsky) of Kazan. He made sure to mention how he visited Grand Duchess Militsa with Bishop Antony (Khrapovitsky). Yurevsky noted that while Rasputin was, of course, boasting, he believed there was more to his words. Yurevsky sensed that Rasputin knew certain persons were gathering information on his possibly being a sectarian, and this name-dropping was intended to convince Yurevsky that Rasputin was accepted as a devout Orthodox Christian by the highest men in the church. He told Yurevsky he had come to Tobolsk to meet an architect about his plan to build a new church in Pokrovskoe. He mentioned to Yurevsky he still needed about 20,000 rubles to fund the work. When Yurevsky expressed doubt about his ability to raise so much money, Rasputin replied vaguely:

"*She'll* give!"

"Who?"

"The Empress."

Yurevsky was shocked and confused by what he had heard and not sure what to think.

At Korovina's, Rasputin boasted of having been to the palace. "Even the Emperor knows me. He is the kindest man and such a great sufferer! He gave me a new surname. I had not requested it. I don't know why he did it. He said to me: you will be called 'New.' Here look," and with this Rasputin pulled out his internal passport for them. They saw he was right. What they could not have known was that Rasputin was lying: he, not the tsar, had requested the new name. Yurevsky asked why Rasputin sought out such mighty people, for, in his words, such acquaintances "seed only pride and self-importance in people." He wondered why Rasputin did not remain at home and tend to the souls of those around him. "They invite me," Rasputin replied, "and they too are people, and their souls seek nourishment, and I love everyone. There's a great deal of love in me. And they love me too."

Maria asked whether the villagers of Pokrovskoe were "spiritually sated." She pressed Rasputin: "Why then don't you nourish the souls of your neighbors, why do you travel to the capital and other cities? For at present people all over the country are searching, and there are false prophets everywhere." Rasputin tried to evade the question, clearly uncomfortable, and he mumbled that in his village the people were not searching.

Rasputin soon left, but only after asking for Yurevsky's blessing: "What sort of person is Rasputin?" Yurevsky wondered. "A sectarian? Or does he see himself as something else?" This one meeting was not enough to say just who he was.

> Regardless, Rasputin left me with the impression of a strange person. His costume was rather original; his speech, incoherent; he is not always able to express his thoughts properly with words, and so he is constantly availing himself of strange movements with the fingers of both hands; all of his movements, even his bowing, are fast, sharp, awkward; his sunken eyes stare at you intently, sometimes impudently. That alone is enough cause to consider him a not entirely normal person. His attraction to various "personages," the constant boasting of his acquaintance with these personages, his desire to stand out among his fellow villagers even if only by a new name—all of this forces one to think that Rasputin, if not a sectarian, is a person who has fallen into "demonic *prelest*."[2]

Prelest, usually translated as "charm" or "fascination," meant here in the religious context "delusion." Prelest was the word the official Orthodox church used to describe those individuals with an exaggerated and unwarranted sense of their own spiritual gifts. Sometimes it was equated with a type of psychosis; its sufferers were seen as unbalanced and disturbed.[3] It was an accusation that Rasputin would never escape.

In late July Antony had also received a letter concerning Rasputin from Yelizaveta Kazakova. Yurevsky knew Kazakova, and he happened to ask Rasputin about her. The mention of her name upset Rasputin; he wondered why Yurevsky was interested to know. "She calls you quite simply delusional," he replied. Rasputin was furious: "Malice fired in Rasputin's eyes, and he lost his emotional balance. With a worried voice, an angry grin on his face, he said: 'She considers me delusional? How's that?'"[4]

Kazakova had first met Rasputin in the autumn of 1903 when he sought her out at her sister's funeral. She did not know what to make of him or why he had approached her. He told her that he was looking for young maidens and women to come with him to the bathhouses where they would receive what he called "full repentance" and learn how "to temper their passions." There was nothing immoral or improper in all this, he assured Kazakova, for he considered everyone to be part of his own family.

Rasputin left and Kazakova looked into this stranger. She discovered that he had been going about preaching in villages to maidens that there were many false pilgrims in the land pretending to be monks as a ruse to seduce them. Rasputin would tell these women that the only way to protect themselves against such snakes, and against temptation in general, was to submit to his kisses until such time that they were no longer repugnant to them. Then, and only then, would they have mastered their passions. When Kazakova next saw Rasputin she told him what she had heard. At first he denied the story, saying this was the "Devil's teaching," but then he came around and admitted it to be the truth. There was nothing to be ashamed of, he told Kazakova, for he took all of the sin from these women and placed it upon himself.

Kazakova believed him and was impressed enough by his words that in May 1904 she traveled with her daughters Maria and Yekaterina to Pokrovskoe to see how Rasputin lived. She found there a large number of important society ladies who surrounded him, attended to his needs, and treated him as a great holy man. They even cut his fingernails and sewed them in their clothing as if they were holy relics. On their walks about the village Rasputin hugged and kissed the ladies openly, saying as he had before there was no shame in this for "we are all of us family."[5]

Kazakova and her daughter Maria visited at least once more, in June 1907. After a week with Rasputin, however, she had a change of heart and saw him in a new and unflattering light. That month she wrote three letters against Rasputin to a local Pokrovskoe priest, Father Fyodor Chemagin, insisting he was not what he claimed to be. When this got no reaction, she sent her letter to Bishop Antony the following month. She said that her initial attraction to Rasputin had been "compassionate love for a lost soul." But Rasputin, she remarked, was far from holy, and she had been badly deceived in him. Her letters were meant as a warning, especially for Khionya Berladskaya, who she feared had yet to see Rasputin in the true light. She desperately wanted her experience, and the "pain" it had caused her, to help open the eyes of those women still believing Rasputin was the holy man he claimed to be. In her eyes, Rasputin had been embraced by "poor suffering upper-class sisters, drowning in the debauchery of the capital, who had flung themselves like flies to honey." A new generation of elites were bowing down before the peasantry, and these ladies had chosen Rasputin as their idol. As Rasputin himself had confessed to her, he was "holy but not tested," and so, to Kazakova, he posed a real danger.[6]

Not everyone saw something wicked in all this. A political prisoner in Tobolsk by the name of Zaitsev knew Kazakova and he told a reporter around this time that he and Rasputin were members of the same sect whose goal was simply moral improvement, and that the relations between the sect's brothers and sisters were "entirely filial."[7]

Zaitsev's opinion, it seems, was not widely shared. Indeed, that summer the nasty talk about Rasputin in and around Pokrovskoe appears to have increased. On 16 June, an anonymous letter was mailed to Rasputin's wife from Tyumen expressing sympathy for her situation and telling her not to worry, for "they" (presumably Rasputin's family) would be comforted by "the entire village." At least one of Rasputin's followers came to his defense. On 1 June, Olga Lokhtina wrote a letter to Bishop Antony saying she had heard about the rumors and defending Rasputin as a true man of God and miracle healer. She wrote she had known Rasputin for two years and had visited his home four times "to live their life, to listen to his teachings." She had seen nothing to change her opinion of him. "Gr. Yef. teaches us love, simplicity, and to have a clean conscience and to love completely, and then a person lives not for himself and is capable of giving up his soul for his friends."[8]

These details are crucial for reconstructing the origins of the investigation into Rasputin's links to the khlysty that ran from September 1907 until May 1908 when it was stopped and lay dormant for four and half years before being revived in September 1912. The investigation's findings, running to 108 folio pages and marked "secret," are gathered in the "File of the Tobolsk Consistory on the Charge against Grigory Yefimovich 'Rasputin-Novy,' a Peasant of the Village of Pokrovskoe in the Tyumen District, of Spreading False Khlyst-like Doctrines and of Forming a Society of Followers of His False Doctrine." The file has had a complicated past, somehow finding its way outside Russia after the revolution and then coming up for sale at Sotheby's auction house in

London in 1994. It eventually returned to Russia and was given to the State Archive of the Russian Federation in Moscow in early 2002, where it has been kept ever since, listed as Collection 1467, Inventory 1, File 479a. Few of Rasputin's biographers have had a chance to examine this invaluable document.[9]

Among the things the file reveals is that the reasons for the investigation are undoubtedly to be found in local events in Siberia and not, as has often been argued, back in St. Petersburg. A popular misconception is that the instigator of the investigation was none other than Grand Duchess Militsa as retribution for his having grown too independent of her. Angered by his impudence, so the story goes, she sought to destroy him.[10] But the file shows definitively that neither Militsa nor anyone else in the capital had anything to do with the initial investigation. In fact, Rasputin continued to enjoy warm relations with the Black Princesses well after 1907. According to information gathered on Rasputin in Pokrovskoe in 1909, Militsa had even visited him there "incognito" in 1907 and was one of the people then still sending him "large sums of money."[11] No, it seems incontrovertible that the investigation was born out of suspicions and feelings of envy centered in Rasputin's homeland of western Siberia.[12]

Rasputin himself said as much in his *Life of an Experienced Wanderer*, written that very year. It was when he returned home with money from Nicholas to build a church, he wrote, that the envious priests began spreading nasty lies about him, claiming that he was a heretic and a member of "the lowliest and dirtiest sects." Rasputin insisted that even Bishop Antony of Tobolsk had joined the priests against him.[13] At a village gathering on 9 May 1907, Rasputin offered 5,000 rubles given to him by the tsar; all he asked of his fellow villagers was that they contribute some money as well. The offer went nowhere when the church elders insisted there was nothing wrong with the church as it was and refused to raise any funds. The villagers were not happy either, insisting what was really needed was a new school. In the end, the new church was never built, and Rasputin used the money to buy reliquiae for the existing village church—large crosses (one of gold, the other silver) and silver lamps for the iconostasis. (The story of the disagreement in the village over Rasputin's proposal appeared in a local newspaper that May, the first time his name was mentioned in the press.)[14] But it appears Rasputin did not give up hope. In a letter to Nicholas and Alexandra from December 1908 Rasputin still spoke of building a church with the money they had provided. It is not yet done, he told them, but will be "soon," and it will be a great consolation to everyone.[15] In the end, Rasputin's church would remain only a dream.

The villagers, or at least many of them, had grown suspicious of Rasputin. What were they to think of a peasant who did not spend his days in the fields or labor at a craft, as they did, and then, on top of this, was able to afford a fine home? Where was he getting this money, from whom, and why? And what had become of Rasputin the humble pilgrim who had traveled by foot on little food, who now only traveled by steamer and rail car and boasted of his mighty friends back in Petersburg? It was all too much. It was not right. Some turned against Rasputin.

In response to Antony's letter of 1 September, Father Nikodim Glu-khovtsev arrived in Pokrovskoe five days later to take depositions from the locals concerning Rasputin.

He went first to speak to Father Pyotr Ostroumov. The priest spoke highly of Rasputin, his family, and way of life. He had known Rasputin since coming to the village in 1897 and had always seen him lead an upstanding Christian life, following all the rites and rituals and holidays. The same was true of his family—his wife, three small children, and his father, and the women who lived with them. He said one might call them "exemplary," strictly adhering to the fasts and regularly attending church. Rasputin worked as a farmer of average holdings; he had done all the work himself but after leaving home more frequently in the past two years the family had started to take on more of the labor. As for his trips to the capital, Ostroumov did say that Rasputin had shown him photographs of himself with Feofan and Sergei of the St. Petersburg Theological Seminary, along with other high church officials.

Nonetheless, he had been hearing talk among the villagers that Rasputin was "a dishonorable man" and someone who had "changed his Orthodox faith." He mentioned they were suspicious of his travels, his sudden wealth, and the women who lived in his home and the way he behaved with them. Some even talked about the tragic fate of a peasant girl from the village of Dubrovskaya. It was said he took her on one of his pilgrimages and forced her to walk barefoot through the snow for miles; she fell ill with consumption and died.[16] Ostroumov, it needs to be remembered, had been an early opponent of Rasputin when his reputation as a holy pilgrim first began to grow.

The sexton Pyotr Bykov also had good things to say to Glukhovtsev, noting that in the six years he had lived in Pokrovskoe Rasputin had been a regular and devout churchgoer with a very fine singing voice. After every service, he would kiss the icons. He did, however, have a rather odd way of praying: "waving his arms about wildly while making grimaces."

Glukhovtsev next interviewed Yevdokia Karneeva, a twenty-eight-year-old who helped out at the Pokrovskoe church. She had a different story to tell. Six years ago she had spent a night at the Rasputin home while traveling through the village on a pilgrimage. Rasputin had tried to kiss her, she said, and when she told him to stop, that it was wrong, he replied that it was not sinful for among them "spiritual kissing" was a common practice. Later, when he was showing her his chapel in the stables, Rasputin jumped toward Yevdokia and kissed her on the cheek. He told her that once while having sex with his wife the Holy Trinity had appeared before him "in the light."[17]

The information Glukhovtsev left with that day was conflicting and not conclusive. So, two months later he returned and spoke with someone who knew Rasputin better. Father Fyodor Chemagin had met Rasputin in 1905 and been to his home many times to attend gatherings dedicated to spiritual readings, prayer, and song. At their first meeting Rasputin told him about his journeys and the important figures in the church he had met, such as Feofan, or "Feofanushka," as Rasputin called him, and showed Chemagin a photograph of himself with Gavriil of the Seven Lakes Monastery. He told Chemagin that he had gone to Petersburg in 1905 for the purpose of making acquaintance with the imperial court and returned from there with Olga Lokhtina and the wife of Father Medved. Around this time, Chemagin happened to stop by one evening when Rasputin was returning home all wet from the baths. A few minutes later, the women living with the Rasputins also arrived, also wet and well-steamed. It was then Rasputin confessed to Chemagin that "he had a weakness for caressing and kissing young 'ladies' and also admitted that he had been with them in the baths." Among the women visiting Rasputin Chemagin named Khionya Berladskaya and Zinaida Manshtedt. Rasputin was fond of caressing them, holding their hands, and calling them by their pet names "Khonya" and "Zinochka." Nevertheless, he had to conclude that Rasputin and his entire house were exemplary Christians—regularly attending services, praying devoutly, and giving often to the church.[18] This last bit of testimony is corroborated by what a Pokrovskoe peasant told Sergei Markov passing through the village in early 1918. "A man of God," he said of the now dead Rasputin, "a kind-hearted person," someone always ready to help his fellow villagers, nearly every one of whom had received gifts of money from him at some point in their lives.[19]

On 1 January 1908, Glukhovtsev wrote a preliminary summary in which he expressed doubts about Rasputin, particularly his behavior with women. There was reason to suspect that he took advantage of some women given his reputation as a holy man of God and miracle worker. The gatherings in his house recalled those held by sectarians, and his personal appearance was also odd and suggestive of someone close to the khlysty. Finally, his recent and rapid accumulation of wealth and the growing number of his followers, from as far away as St. Petersburg, spoke to his considerable success as a self-appointed holy man. In light of this, Glukhovtsev decided to dig deeper, by inspecting Rasputin's home and interviewing him and the members of his household, including his out-of-town guests, all of whom were required to remain in Pokrovskoe until he had completed this phase of the investigation.[20]

The following day, Glukhovtsev, along with Father Pyotr Ostroumov, the village constable, the village elder, and three peasant witnesses arrived at the Rasputin home. Glukhovtsev placed the written summary before Rasputin for him to read, which he did and then signed, "GRIGORY." He was informed they were here to inspect his home and take testimony from everyone inside. It was a terrible moment for Rasputin. Berladskaya recalled: "Grigory was horribly frightened, his face was terrible [. . .] He feared they would send him to prison."[21] The men began by examining the walls covered with icons, religious pictures, and photographs of Rasputin with important church and worldly personages; they went through his shelves and cupboards. They found nothing in the least suspicious. Then, for the next two days, they questioned everyone, starting with Rasputin.

He told them he was forty-two (in fact, he would turn thirty-nine in a week), married, and a practicing Orthodox believer. He had begun to undertake pilgrimages fifteen years ago, first just in Siberia and then in recent years only to monasteries in Petersburg and Kiev. He also took

in pilgrims passing through Pokrovskoe. Two young women from the
peasant community of Kumarskaya lived with them, Yekaterina and
Yevdokia Pecherkina, helping about the house in exchange for food and
clothing. Yevdokia was an aunt of Rasputin's friend Dmitry Pecherkin;
Yekaterina, his sister. Rasputin chose not to keep any male helpers, for
he was often away and his kin feared having other men about. He was
frequently visited by his "brothers in Christ," Ilya Arapov, Nikolai Rasputin, and Nikolai Raspopov, and together they would sing religious
songs and hymns and read the Bible and interpret it, as best they could.
Most of the time now, Rasputin told them, he was away at various monasteries to visit acquaintances with whom he would talk about all sorts
of spiritual matters. The trips were almost always at their insistence and
people were always inviting him to come see them. Yes, he admitted, he
often had visitors, friends typically, like the ladies staying with him now
who had come to see him and his family and "to learn from me about
God's love." Women he knew well he kissed on the cheek upon greeting and parting, "out of true love;" those he did not, he never kissed. He
said he had no recollection of claiming to have seen the Holy Spirit, but
he admitted that "I am a sinner, I make mistakes, but when a righteous
person stops me, I do change my ways." Finally, Rasputin told Glukhovtsev that he had stopped eating meat fifteen years ago, and five years
after that had given up smoking and drinking, since, he admitted, "I was
a nasty fellow when drunk."[22]

Rasputin's father could not tell them why his son was usually gone
other than it had something to do with "praying to God," and his wife
Praskovya added that her husband's travels were increasingly the result
of having been summoned by "lofty personages" and not just of his own
choosing. She, too, had traveled across Russia—once in 1906 to receive
medical treatment, and a second time in November 1907 to see her
husband in Petersburg, where they were the guests of Olga Lokhtina.
As for the Pecherkins, they were treated like their own daughters, with
love and affection. The only gatherings they held were with their three
male "relatives," who came to sing and read the Bible and engage in
"spiritually-uplifting conversations."

Rasputin's visitors—Olga Lokhtina, Khionya Berladskaya, the Sokolova sisters (Yekaterina and Yelena), and Akilina Laptinskaya—were also
questioned. Lokhtina stood by her letter of 1 June 1907. The Sokolova
sisters, both in their twenties, had met Rasputin the previous year upon
the recommendation of Feofan. From the first they were taken by "his

answers, his simplicity, and his complete love for all people." They, too, had come to learn how to live like Rasputin. As for Berladskaya, yes, she said, Rasputin kissed them, but added "I do not find it odd, for it is natural with him and has been adopted from our holy fathers." Indeed, in a light-hearted way they would at times call Rasputin "our father." Laptinskaya concurred with everything the other women had told the men, and then added that as to his habit of kissing the women he knew, she found nothing at all strange in this, for it was done in a spirit of pure brotherly and Christian love. And, she commented, did not educated people in the cities do the same, kissing and embracing when they met and parted with friends and family?

All of this seemed convincing, but there was still the earlier testimony of Yevdokia Karneeva, and so on 4 January Glukhovtsev met with her once more to hear her story a second time. She told him it had been six years ago that she had stayed a day with the Rasputins while on a pilgrimage to Kiev. It was the busy season, and Rasputin was mostly out in the fields, but he would often run home to check on things, each time trying to get her to kiss him. She resisted, insisting it was not right, but he told her that "among us spiritual pilgrims seeking to save ourselves there is a type of spiritual kissing, like the way the Apostle Paul kissed St. Thekla." Karneeva repeated how while climbing up out of the chapel beneath the stables, he had grabbed her and kissed her cheek. It was then Rasputin told her of the appearance of the Holy Spirit. Later that day, Glukhovtsev brought Karneeva and Rasputin together for what the Russians called an *ochnaia stavka*, a sort of face-to-face confrontation, to try to get to the bottom of her claims. Seated directly across from Rasputin, Karneeva repeated everything she had told Glukhovtsev. To each of her statements Rasputin said little more than "That was all long ago, I don't recall a thing," or "I don't remember a thing from that far back," or simply "I don't remember that."

Next Glukhovtsev spoke once more to Ostroumov and Chemagin. Ostroumov stood by his earlier testimony and had nothing more to say; Chemagin, however, added that in private conversations Rasputin had admitted to him that he had made "various mistakes"—namely, that he kissed different women and that at times in church he stood about "absent-mindedly." All of this testimony was then put before Rasputin who rejected the claims that he was a khlyst or had spent time in the baths with various women as mere "slander."[23]

Glukhovtsev completed his report on 10 January 1908 and sent it to

the Tobolsk Consistory. From there the report and the various testimonies were forwarded to Dmitry Berezkin, an inspector at the Tobolsk
Theological Academy, for review before being submitted to Bishop
Antony. In his opinion of 28 March, Berezkin concluded that there were
still too many unanswered questions to warrant moving on to a full
formal investigation of Rasputin. While it was beyond any doubt that
Rasputin and his followers formed a special "society" with their own
religious-moral structure that was "distinct from Orthodoxy," one
could not say for certain they were khlysty. Yes, Rasputin's appearance
and mannerisms fit the model of the typical khlyst, but the investigation, in his opinion, had failed to dig deep enough and come up with the
necessary proof to say definitely just what they were dealing with. What
precisely were the hymns and canticles being sung? What sorts of religious texts were they reading? What interpretations did Rasputin give
them? And might there not be a hidden khlyst ritual space in one of the
outbuildings on Rasputin's property? In his opinion, a new preliminary
investigation was warranted, but this time by someone who was a
specialist in sects, which, he noted, Glukhovtsev was not.

The consistory reviewed Berezkin's opinion and agreed with him.
In a finding from that May, the consistory endorsed the idea of a new
investigation and asked Berezkin to lead it. A certain Smirnov, chief
author of the finding, noted that the attention of so many women had
caused a harmful change in Rasputin: "Such deference, respect, and
even veneration had to first give birth to and then strengthen in him the
conceit of Satanic pride and lead him to fall into 'demonic delusion.' It
is not surprising that, especially since 1905, Grigory Novy adopted the
role of some exceptional mentor, spiritual leader, advisor, and com-
forter." On the other hand, it had to be admitted that he lived the life of
a true and good Orthodox Christian, attending services, praying, fasting, and donating to the church. None of this added up. Much about
Rasputin did not make sense. It was not at all clear who he really was.[24]
The May finding came to the conclusion that the investigation had been
too formal and had focused too much on external, physical evidence.
Another investigation, one that probed deeper and more thoroughly,
was necessary.[25]

But for some unknown reason the consistory's May finding was
ignored and nothing further was done about Rasputin. The investigation into Rasputin's links to the khlysty stopped and would lie dormant
until the autumn of 1912. The secret investigative file on the case is

mute as to what killed the matter in 1908, and no other sources that might provide the answer have ever been found.[26] It has been suggested that Lokhtina raced back to Petersburg that spring and got word to the throne, and this put an end to the investigation. This is possible, but only one theory. Another suggests Feofan, possibly joined by other high clergy in the capital, convinced the tsar to halt it. The later Duma President, and implacable foe of Rasputin, Mikhail Rodzianko, claimed that the tsar put a halt to the affair by offering Bishop Antony a choice: either stop the investigation, for which he would be promoted to the see of Tver, or be forced to withdraw to a monastery. Although Antony was promoted to Tver in late January 1910 upon the retirement there of Archbishop Alexei (Alexei Opotsky), there is no documentary proof to substantiate Rodzianko's claim, a claim, it ought to be noted, made only after the fact and so likely a retrospective attempt to assert causality.[27] What does seem beyond doubt is that while the investigation had begun in Siberia, it had been stopped in St. Petersburg. The documents prove the authorities in Siberia were preparing to continue to dig into the life of Rasputin, and only more powerful forces back in the capital, or the palace, could have ordered them to cease.

Although it had been put on hold, news of the investigation leaked out. The newspaper *Siberian Virgin Soil*, for example, published a short article in January 1910 describing how Rasputin's home had been searched due to suspicions he belonged to the khlysty, although the story did state that nothing compromising had been found. And Father Pyotr Ostroumov discussed the investigation with Alexander Senin, a political exile in Siberia, and he wrote it up for the pages of *Southern Dawn* in June 1910.[28] Stories like these fed people's curiosity.

"Rasputin, formerly a peasant farmer," *Siberian Virgin Soil* commented, "is now a mysterious character, even for the villagers of Pokrovskoe, among whom he grew up. [...] The secret of how the 'simpleton' Grishka was transformed into 'father' Grigory remains a mystery and gives rise to the wildest rumors concerning the life of the 'holy man.'"

16. The First Test

The investigation inflicted no apparent harm on Rasputin, and he continued his rise in Petersburg and at court. From what little is known it seems that during the early years in Petersburg Rasputin behaved modestly. Of these days Colonel Dmitry Loman, an admirer of Rasputin serving in the office of the palace commandant, recalled:

> At that time Rasputin behaved beyond reproach and did not permit himself to get drunk or to act out. Rasputin made a very good impression on me. Like a doctor making a diagnosis of a physical illness, Rasputin was received by spiritually ill people and he immediately divined what they were searching for and what was disturbing them. His simple manner with people and his tenderness toward others calmed them.[1]

Nonetheless, given the investigation of the previous year, Alexandra decided to settle matters for herself and sent Feofan along with Rasputin to Pokrovskoe in the late winter of 1908 to observe his life there and report back to her. Before Rasputin left, Alexandra presented him with a shirt she had sewn herself. He wrote to thank her: "A shirt—a raiment—the joy of eternal life, your sewing is a golden coin. I cannot express my gratitude for this favor."

The trip seems to have gone well, although the shirt caused Rasputin nothing but trouble. He showed it around to his fellow villagers, but few believed that the empress had sewn it for him and those who did believe grew envious, as Rasputin noted in a letter of 8 March:

> Hello Mama and Papa, my sweet and dearest ones! [. . .] They could not tolerate the shirt, because this is too huge a phrase for them and an unexpected object, the likes of which has never been since the beginning of time until now, because, in actual fact, despite all expectations, this shirt has such importance, like a large, extraordinary weight. Here it makes your labors grow, there it's a piece of gold; and with the future Second Coming, the most precious

piece of gold and cover for all my sins. All of them understood this, and since they've never done the like to a close friend, they became furious.[2]

While passing through Nizhny Novgorod on their return, Feofan supposedly decided to break their trip and travel south to visit the Diveevo Convent near Sarov. Rasputin chose not to accompany him and went straight on to Petersburg. Later, it was said that Rasputin did not make the journey since the local bishop had once warned Rasputin never to return. And when Feofan met the mother superior she hurled a fork on the floor, spitting: "That's how you need to throw out your Rasputin." These stories, often repeated in biographies of Rasputin, are most likely apocryphal since after returning home Feofan gave Alexandra a favorable report of what he had seen and heard on his travels.[3]

On 12 March, Rasputin and Feofan saw Nicholas and Alexandra at Anna Vyrubova's modest home located at 2 Church Street near the Alexander Palace in Tsarskoe Selo. "It was so nice!" Nicholas remarked of their gathering in his diary.[4] The exclamation point is telling. Nicholas almost never used them in his diary, and so it offers a solid clue to the depth of feeling he had developed for Rasputin. Rasputin must have been pleased by his reception as well, for just days earlier he had written to Nicholas and Alexandra to express his regret for some poorly spoken words and to seek their forgiveness—"I wasn't understood in the way I deserved, don't judge me by my sins but by God's mercy—talk to each other and find consolation in this." He sent along with his letter an icon he had had painted for them depicting Christ blessing Nicholas, Alexandra, and Alexei along with the words, "Christ himself saves and spares them." It had been occasioned by an accident the previous September when the *Standart*, the imperial yacht, ran aground and the family had to abandon ship. Rasputin wrote that this icon was to be a reminder that God watches over them. "Your faith will never run out. And this will be a reminder to you that He is always with you, saving, protecting and preserving." He instructed the tsar to later give the icon to Alexei to keep "as a memento." Rasputin ended, "Jesus Christ, the Son of God, have mercy on me, a sinner, save me."[5]

Nicholas and Alexandra saw Rasputin again on 10 and 23 May, both times at Vyrubova's when they sat in the evening and spoke with him for a long time.[6]

*

It was around this time that Prince Nikolai Zhevakhov, a mystic obsessed with visions of the apocalypse and frequent pilgrim to Russia's monasteries, first met Rasputin one evening at the home of Alexander Pistolkors, Anna Vyrubova's brother-in-law.

> What struck me as strange was not Rasputin, who behaved so well I felt sorry for him, but the way those gathered there behaved toward him. Some detected in every meaningless word he uttered a prophecy or hidden meaning, others, seized by reverential trembling, timidly approached him, bowing at his hand ... Like a hunted rabbit Rasputin looked around from side to side, apparently embarrassed, yet at the same time concerned he might destroy the charm of his character, which he was not sure exactly what it was based on, with an incautious word, gesture, or movement. Were there people there that evening just pretending, I don't know ... Maybe there were ... But the majority truly and sincerely believed in the holiness of Rasputin, and this majority comprised a select representation of the very highest layer of the capital's society, people of the purest and loftiest religious sentiment, guilty of only one thing: not one of them had the slightest understanding of the true nature of a "starets" and his world.

Pistolkors invited the prince to join them next at the home of Baron Nikolai Rausch von Trauenberg, an official in the ministry of finance, on Vasilevsky Island where Rasputin was to speak. At the time, Rasputin's sermons, if one could call them that, caused a sensation. He did not speak for long, but limited himself to apothegms and a few abrupt, disjointed words, always vague and mysterious. The drawing room was full of aristocrats and what Zhevakhov also called "some suspicious types," all of whom were staring at Rasputin, trying to get his attention. One of them was talking loudly to no one in particular about how he had been healed by Rasputin. When Rasputin heard this, he interrupted him in a sharp tone. Off to one corner stood a strange woman with wide eyes aimed at Rasputin, clearly in the grips of ecstasy and struggling to control herself. Pistolkors whispered in the prince's ear that that was Olga Lokhtina who had left her husband and family to be with Rasputin. Zhevakhov could not believe his eyes. He was convinced he had landed in a madhouse.

Rasputin was seated at a table loudly cracking nuts with his hands. Upon seeing Pistolkors and Zhevakhov, he gruffly pushed the young ladies out of the way and told them to come sit with him. He asked them why they had come—to stare at him or learn how to save themselves in the world. "He's a saint, a saint!" Lokhtina cried out. "Hold your tongue, fool," Rasputin snapped. Rasputin proceeded to tell them that only a few could leave the world behind and join a monastery. Most were obliged to remain in the world. But how could they save themselves, surrounded by so much temptation? It was not enough to live a God-pleasing life, as one was instructed in church, for what, precisely, was that? What did this mean in concrete terms? Just how was one to find God? As he spoke, everyone in the room fell silent and leaned in to listen to his words.

After church, having prayed to God, he told them, go out on some Sunday beyond the city limits, out into a clean field. Walk and walk until you can no longer see the ugly soot of the city's smokestacks and before you lies the beckoning blue horizon. Stop and think of yourself. You will realize just how small and insignificant you are, how helpless, and the capital will appear before you as an anthill, its inhabitants a buzz of scurrying insects. What then, Rasputin asked, what will become of your pride and vanity and your power and position? You'll look up to God in the heavens and see for the first time He is everything your soul needs. You will feel this inside, and you will experience tenderness. This is the first step to God.

Carry this feeling back with you into the city and guard it with your life, he continued. Everything you do and say, let it come through God that you have allowed inside you and so shall your actions and words be transformed from those of this world, to that of the next, and so shall you be saved, for your life will no longer be devoted to the glorification of your passions, but to the service of God. Remember, he told them, Christ had taught that the kingdom of God is within you. Find God, and live within Him and with Him.

With that Rasputin stopped. Zhevakhov was moved. Rasputin had said nothing new, nothing that had not been said many times before, but it was the way he had said it, the simplicity, the concrete terms in which he expressed it, without any dead theology and citation, that was so rare and powerful. It was his gift for drawing on his own lived experience when popularizing the truths of the Bible that Zhevakhov considered his secret and the reason for his influence. He could easily now understand how women like Lokhtina, prone to "religious ecstasy," would consider him holy.[7] Zhevakhov himself would become a devoted follower of Rasputin, for which he would be rewarded in September 1916 when was appointed Deputy Chief Procurator of the Holy Synod, having served up until then only as a minor official.

Another man drawn to Rasputin then was Archbishop Germogen. "That man is a slave to God," he told Zhevakhov, "you have sinned if you even think about condemning him." Germogen, born Georgy Dolganov in 1858, had only just met Rasputin as well. He would become one of his most devoted supporters and later one of his greatest foes. Like Feofan and Iliodor, his protégé, Germogen was a graduate of the Petersburg Theological Seminary, and like Iliodor, he was an extremist in his religious beliefs. Before being tonsured as a monk in December 1890, he castrated himself with his own hands in an attempt to achieve moral perfection through mortification of the flesh. This gave rise to talk that Germogen was in fact a member of the skoptsy, the sect of self-castrators.[8] In the early 1890s he served as Inspector of the Tiflis Seminary in Georgia. Among the young seminarians was Josef Vissarionovich Djugashvili, later and better known as Stalin. Germogen caught little Josef with a copy of Victor Hugo's novel *Ninety-Three*, forbidden by the monks for its favorable depiction of French revolutionaries, and had him locked in the punishment cell. In March 1903, he took up the see of Saratov and Tsaritsyn, a post he would hold until his fateful clash with Rasputin in early 1912. An anti-Semite and nationalist, Germogen was a loud supporter of the extreme-right Black Hundreds and he preached xenophobia and blind commitment to the Russian autocracy. In the early years of the century he was one of the most influential and powerful figures in the Russian Orthodox Church.[9]

To moderate members of the higher clergy, Germogen was a deeply flawed figure. Although a great ascetic, he was unbalanced and prone to violent rages. Many felt his embrace of right-wing politics destroyed his Christian faith; he hated the intelligentsia and thought every revolutionary ought to be hanged. Archbishop Antony (Pavel Khrapovitsky) once wrote a friend: "Germogen is a self-deceiving fool, extremely limited and not quite normal: he castrated himself while a student at Novorossiisky University and in so doing deprived himself of a normal temper."[10]

Germogen met Rasputin in 1908 through Feofan, a man whose judgment he greatly respected, and for a while he was not disappointed. Rasputin, Germogen said, truly had "the spark of God" in him, along with many other talents, and on several occasions had found the answers to Germogen's spiritual suffering. "He conquered me," Germogen said, just as he "had conquered others." But then Rasputin changed and Germogen claimed he saw him for who he truly was. "I, too, had been wrong, but, thank God, in time I came to understand him."[11]

If some like Prince Zhevakhov and Archbishop Germogen added their names to the list of Rasputin's acolytes in 1908, there was growing talk in Petersburg circles of troubling aspects of the Siberian's story. Indeed, some of this talk made its way to Zhevakhov himself.

Princess Yelizaveta Naryshkina ("Zizi") was the most senior lady-in-waiting at the Russian court. Born in 1840, she had served in the retinue of Empress Maria Fyodorovna and then, in 1909, Alexandra made her "mistress of the robes," the most important rank in the empress's entourage of 240 ladies, responsible for overseeing the empress's official court life. Naryshkina, one contemporary noted, had "shrewd eyes" that saw "everything."[12] And she did not like what she was seeing. She told Zhevakhov that Rasputin was making frequent visits to the palace to see Alexandra, but he was always let in through a back door so his name would not appear on the official court diary of visitors. Zhevakhov was stunned that she would say such a thing to him, a man she was meeting for the first time. He strongly cautioned her about the danger of such talk: "Believe me, Yelizaveta Alexeevna, that such talk about Rasputin is more dangerous than Rasputin himself. That is the private sphere of Their Majesties, and we have no right to touch upon it. If people talked less about Rasputin, then there would be less food for all those legends that are spread about specifically in order to discredit the prestige of the dynasty."[13]

Dr. Yevgeny Botkin, the court physician, shared Zhevakhov's concern. He simply would not stand for any gossip about their majesties in his home and was deeply disturbed to hear it in anyone else's. Dismayed at such talk, he told his family: "I don't understand how people who consider themselves monarchists and talk about their worship of His Majesty could so easily believe all the gossip that's being spread and help to spread it further themselves, casting aspersions on the empress, and then not realize that by offending Her they are in this way offending Her August Spouse, whom they claim to worship."[14]

One such monarchist couple were General Yevgeny Bogdanovich and his wife, Alexandra. Yevgeny was a member of the Council of Ministers, a warden of St. Isaac's Cathedral, and the publisher of a series of monarchist-orthodox publications. Such was his reputation in the church that Father John of Kronstadt called him "the sower of the good word." Vladimir Dzhunkovsky, former adjutant to Grand Duke Sergei Alexandrovich and the governor of Moscow from 1908 to 1913, described Alexandra as a "a holy woman, capable of warming the hearts of both the high-born and the most common men with her Russian charm." Yevgeny and Alexandra were ardent nationalists and prominent supporters of the far-right Union of the Russian People.

For three decades they hosted one of the capital's most influential salons that, from 1908, met in their home at 9 St. Isaac's Square. The Bogdanoviches held open breakfasts where the latest gossip was freely exchanged; every possible subject was open to discussion. A more select circle was invited to stay for dinner. Among the salon's habitués were Count (later Baron) Vladimir Fredericks, minister of the imperial court from 1897; Prince Vladimir Meshchersky; Lev Tikhomirov; Vladimir Purishkevich, one of the founders of the Union of the Russian People and conspirator in the murder of Rasputin; Mikhail Menshikov, a conservative publicist; and Boris Stürmer, future prime minister. The Bogdanovich home, which Yevgeny described in a letter to the tsar in 1910 as "the gathering place for all that is patriotic in our Fatherland," would become one of the main incubators for the gossip—and slander—about Rasputin. The Bogdanoviches had access to the most intimate details of court life from a number of sources, including Alexandra Bogdanovich's sister Yulia, a maid-of-honor; Vladimir Dedyulin, the palace commandant from 1906 to 1913; and Nikolai Radtsig, the tsar's valet for over thirty years, from 1877 until his death in 1913. "My old loyal friend," Nicholas liked to call him.[15] Little did he know.

On 8 November 1908, Radtsig brought some particularly disturbing news to the salon. He had recently become friendly with Vyrubova's maid, Feodosia Voino, and once, after describing her mistress as a good and serious woman, the maid laughed and said she had seen photographs that would make him change his mind. Voino said that Vyrubova had begun to keep the company of a strange peasant and then produced a photograph of the two together. Radtsig could not believe it. The man had the most beastly eyes, he told those gathered, and the most hideous appearance. Vyrubova was careful not to keep the photograph out in the open, but tucked inside her Bible. Vyrubova, so it was said, had even sewn the man a silk shirt. The worst part of Radtsig's story was that the empress was there at Vyrubova's during his visits, although, Radtsig (mistakenly) assured them, he had yet to be granted entry to the palace.[16] The talk did not end there. Before the year was out Madame Bogdanovich was hearing tales passed on by this same maid that Vyrubova and the empress had become lovers.[17] Incredible as it seems, the Bogdanoviches and their guests entertained the possibility that such stories were true.

Radtsig would continue to dispense salacious gossip to the Bogdanovich salon for years. In December 1910, he told them how everyone at the palace disdained Vyrubova, but that she was constantly with the empress and so no one dared go against her. Every morning at 11:30, the emperor went to his study and the empress and Vyrubova retired to her bedroom. "What a pathetic and shameful picture!" Alexandra Bogdanovich wrote in her diary, clearly assuming some sort of sexual affair between the two women. As for talk about the empress's health, Radtsig said that she was not terribly ill at all and it was more of an act on her part. The only illness the empress suffered from was of a "psychiatric" nature. She lay about as if nearly dead, he told them, and then suddenly jumped up from her bed as if there was nothing the matter, and then just as quickly collapsed as if stricken.[18]

Dedyulin was also having conversations about the stranger visiting Vyrubova with General Alexander Gerasimov, head of the Petersburg Okhrana. Dedyulin found the entire business curious. He had tried to discover more about the man, but had come up with nothing. Dedyulin began to fear the supposed holy man might well be a terrorist plotting an attempt on the life of the emperor. Dedyulin contacted Gerasimov, who had also never heard the name Rasputin, and asked him to make inquiries and find out just who he really was. Their fear was not without justification. A peasant by the name of Anna Rasputina was a known Socialist Revolutionary terrorist, responsible for trying to assassinate Grand Duke Nikolai Nikolaevich and Minister of Justice Ivan Shcheglovitov. She and several others were caught before they could act, and Anna was hanged along with sixteen other terrorists on 17 February 1908.[19] The surname, the social background, the timing of Rasputin's introduction to the sovereign (as best they knew)—all of it seemed suspicious and potentially dangerous.

Gerasimov requested information from Siberia and later claimed in his memoirs he received a report detailing Rasputin's dissolute life there—stealing, drinking, and seducing girls. He learned that Rasputin had been imprisoned more than once for his offenses and had then been ultimately forced to flee his home village. (This was, of course, not true, and Gerasimov is clearly making things up in his memoirs.)[20] At the same time, Gerasimov had his agents quietly follow Rasputin in Petersburg. Here, too, so he writes in his memoirs, a similar picture emerged of Rasputin as a crude and debauched fiend. Rasputin, Gerasimov concluded, should not be allowed "within cannon fire" of the imperial court.

Gerasimov took his findings to Pyotr Stolypin, the prime minister. According to Gerasimov, he managed to convince Stolypin to bring up the matter of Rasputin with the tsar, which he did at his next meeting. Nicholas, however, told the prime minister that Rasputin was of no concern to Stolypin. "But why, exactly, does it interest you?" he purportedly asked his minister. "For this is my personal business and has absolutely nothing to do with politics. Are we, my wife and I, not permitted to have our own personal acquaintances? Is it really the case that we can not meet with everyone who interests us?"

Stolypin was touched by the tsar's naivety. He tried to explain to Nicholas that the sovereign of Russia could not simply do whatever he wished, even in his private life, for he was the personification of Russia herself, all of his subjects had their eyes directed at him and so he must never come in contact with anything that could sully his image and damage the moral authority of the throne. Nicholas was clearly moved by his words and promised never to see Rasputin again. Stolypin left convinced he had opened the tsar's eyes to the danger inherent in Rasputin and certain the tsar would act accordingly. Gerasimov, however, was not so sure, and he had his agents increase their surveillance. Sure enough, not only did Rasputin not stay away from Vyrubova's but he continued to see the empress there.

Meanwhile, Nicholas asked Dedyulin and his aide-de-camp Colonel Alexander Drenteln to meet with Rasputin and form an opinion of him. Both came back with critical words. "That is a clever but cunning and deceitful peasant," Dedyulin told the tsar, "in possession of some power of hypnotism as well, which he makes use of."

Gerasimov next approached Stolypin with the idea of banishing Rasputin from the capital, a move Stolypin had the legal right to take as minister of the interior. (Stolypin held the two most powerful ministerial posts at the time.) After some hesitation, Stolypin agreed. Rasputin, however, seems to have learned of their plan and began to move about erratically, sleeping in the homes of his well-connected followers and staying one step ahead of Gerasimov's agents. Once while returning from Tsarskoe Selo he managed to slip past the police in the rail station and jump into the waiting automobile of Grand Duke Pyotr Nikolaevich and drive away. The agents staked out the grand duke's palace for the next three weeks waiting for Rasputin to exit, only to learn from the governor of Tobolsk that Rasputin had recently arrived in Pokrovskoe. Somehow he had given them the slip.[21]

The actions of Stolypin and Gerasimov had been the first serious test of Rasputin's place at court. And his first serious victory.

The meetings with Rasputin continued. Nicholas recorded in his diary for 4 August 1908 that he returned to Peterhof at 6:30 p.m. to find Alexandra and Rasputin alone together in conversation.[22] It is a startling revelation. Rasputin and Alexandra meeting alone, in the palace, without the tsar, and he utterly ignorant of the fact. What could Alexandra have been thinking? How could she not see that such a thing would be talked about, and distorted, by the suspicious minds at court and from there make its way out into society? As for Nicholas, far from angry or upset or even disappointed in his wife, he appears to have viewed this as a happy coincidence, his coming home early enough to be able to join the two of them.

They next saw Rasputin on 6 November, this time together at Vyrubova's, where they talked for a long time. When he was away, Rasputin would write comforting words to them both:

"I am calm, you are learning wisdom from me, but later there will be various adversities, only then will you be ready, you will see this and will understand."[23]

"What you love, there one finds sorrow and God takes it away because you are strong and brave in spiritual joy."[24]

That Christmas, Nicholas and Alexandra joined Rasputin at Vyrubova's to light the tree, staying until midnight. "It was very pleasant," Nicholas wrote.[25] Nicholas's sister Olga was at Vyrubova's that year as well. To her, the evening proved less than pleasant.

Rasputin was there and he seemed very pleased to meet me again, and when the hostess with Nicky and Alicky left the drawing room for a few moments, Rasputin got up, put his arm around my shoulders, and began stroking my arm. I moved away at once, saying nothing. I just got up and joined the others. I'd had more than enough of the man. I disliked him more than ever. Believe it or not, on my return to St. Petersburg I did a strange thing— I sought my husband out in the study, and told him all that had happened at Anna Vyrubova's cottage. He heard me out and with a grave face he suggested that I should avoid meeting Rasputin in the future. For the first and only time I knew my husband was right.[26]

17. "better ten Rasputins . . ."

Anna Sederkholm was the twenty-eight-year-old wife of an officer in the imperial guards serving at Tsarskoe Selo when she met Rasputin at Olga Lokhtina's apartment in January 1906. She mentioned to Rasputin that her husband had been having troubles in his service and complained of their difficult situation. "What, do you expect to be happy about everything in your life?" Rasputin asked her gruffly. "In what way are you better than others? You are close to God." Lokhtina began bringing Rasputin to visit Sederkholm along with some of his other acolytes such as Sana Pistolkors and Zina Manshtedt. During their visits Rasputin would read the Bible to them and talk of religion.

Sederkholm got the feeling that Rasputin was cultivating her to become a member of his circle. She was intrigued but skeptical. Soon the group grew to include Vyrubova and the nursemaids to the Romanov children: Anna Utkina, Alexandra Tegleva (aka Shura), and Maria Vishnyakova. Utkina and Tegleva appeared to be uncomfortable and were at a loss for what to do or say around him. But Vishnyakova, according to Sederkholm, was different: it was obvious she believed in him as if he were a saint and had no doubts about his power to safeguard the health of Alexei.[1] Sederkholm found a good deal of what she saw rather odd. Lokhtina would kiss Rasputin's feet. Once she was so aroused she claimed to see an aura around him. "He's been transformed," Lokhtina cried, "he's been transformed. He is Christ." Sederkholm telephoned Vyrubova to tell her she must come at once and see what was happening. Vyrubova was evasive and said she was busy at the moment; Sederkholm got the feeling she did not want to have anything to do with the situation.

In May 1909, the empress decided to send a group of women to Pokrovskoe to observe how Rasputin lived and convince themselves of his holiness.[2] The party consisted of Vyrubova, her maid, the elderly Madame Orlova, Anna Utkina, and a woman named Yelena, the daughter of a priest, who had met Rasputin at the palace. It appears Maria

Vishnyakova was also a member of the party. Vyrubova visited Sederkholm to tell her the empress wished her to go as well. Alexandra even
offered to pay her expenses. Anna, somewhat reluctantly, agreed to join
them. Vyrubova informed Anna that the empress was very pleased she
had decided to make the trip and of the imperial favors that awaited her
upon their return.

They took the train to Perm where they met Rasputin, and he joined
them in their railway carriage. He talked a great deal of the Weeping
Kazan Mother of God icon he had at home. At Yekaterinburg they
changed trains and split into two compartments: Rasputin, Yelena, and
Sederkholm in one, Vyrubova, Orlova, and Utkina in the other. (In
which compartment Vishnyakova rode is not known.) Yelena, who
Sederkholm could tell was in the throes of "religious ecstasy," was overjoyed to be with Rasputin; Anna was not. Rasputin and Yelena climbed
into the upper berth and began to "carry on outrageously," and Sederkholm protested and told Yelena to climb down, but she refused, saying
she was happy where she was. Sederkholm fell asleep to the sounds of
their rustling over her head. Later that night Sederkholm woke with a
fright. She could feel a man's coarse beard on the pillow next to her. She
jumped out of bed and began shouting at Rasputin, demanding he tell
her in what holy books had he read that such a thing was appropriate.
Rasputin said nothing and retreated to his berth, leaving Sederkholm
alone for the rest of the trip. The next morning she told Utkina and
Vyrubova what had happened, but neither took it seriously. Vyrubova
told her, "He came to you to commune with the spirit. It is a divine act."

At Tyumen they chose to travel the rest of the way by wagon with
Rasputin at the reins. It was a bumpy, dusty ride, and the old Orlova
moaned the entire way. Rasputin grew angry. "Why did I bother to take
her with me!" They arrived at Pokrovskoe at two o'clock in the morning.
The women were led upstairs and put to sleep on simple mattresses
spread out on the floor under the glow of icon lamps.

In the morning Rasputin told Sederkholm to go bathe in the river.
As she was washing, a woman appeared with her buckets. "My dear,
where are you from?" she asked. Sederkholm told her she had come
with some other ladies to visit the Rasputins. The woman gave her an
unhappy look, grabbed her buckets, and walked off. Sederkholm could
tell not everyone in the village was in love with their host.

Later that day Rasputin went to the baths with Praskovya and
Yelena. His wife washed him there, while Yelena sat outside on a bench.

Just then Vyrubova ran to the others back in the house telling them to come quickly for Rasputin had experienced a vision and was about to preach. Utkina started to cry, saying she did not want to go. Vyrubova tried to persuade her, but eventually gave up, and none of them went to hear him. After the group returned from the baths, they all drank tea upstairs before going to visit the village church along with two of Rasputin's "brothers in Christ." Outside Rasputin gave each woman a kerchief and Vyrubova took their photograph as a memento. The day's main meal consisted of white buns with raisins and jam, pine nuts, and fish pies. Rasputin instructed Sederkholm to sit at the far end of the table; she got the sense that he was not pleased with her wary attitude. She was struck by his table manners. He tore the food to bits with his hands and licked the spoon before using it to serve the others.

Many shared Sederkholm's reaction to Rasputin's manners. He never mastered the niceties of the napkin and utensils, and ate as a peasant, always with his hands, greasy with food, that he would then lick clean or wipe on the table cloth, slurping and smacking his lips, his beard flecked with bits of his meal. A reporter claimed he once saw Rasputin handed an apple and a knife. Rasputin took the knife, and cut off the top, then laid the knife down and tore the apple into bits with his hands for the others. Some observers saw in this a conscious strategy. Archpriest Ioann Vostorgov said he tried to teach Rasputin how to behave at table, but Rasputin knew that part of his attractiveness was his very crudeness. Turning him into a gentleman would only strip him of this color. Vostorgov insisted Rasputin was too clever not to understand that his power lay in being "the first man in the village, not the second in the city."[3]

Their day in Pokrovskoe ended with the singing of canticles—Sederkholm noted how Rasputin waved his arms about as if he were conducting—and then prayers before the miracle-working Weeping Kazan Mother of God icon. Rasputin began the prayers, which they would repeat after him. He prayed fervently, bowing and crossing himself slowly at first and then ever faster. Sederkholm did not notice anything that suggested Rasputin was a member of the khlysty. The following day they took a boat ride on the Tura River (Vyrubova was deathly afraid of capsizing and drowning) and caught some fish.

Olga Lokhtina was already in Pokrovskoe when the women arrived. She sent a telegram back to Petersburg describing how they celebrated Trinity Sunday, a major holy day in Russia when the peasants would decorate their homes and churches with fresh flowers, grasses, and twigs: "I feel marvelous today and could write and talk for nine hours. Father Grigory gave me, Zina, Meri [Vishnyakova], and Lena shoots from his ficus and sprigs at noon on 19 May that we handed out at the church here in Pokrovskoe." She included in her telegram a list of relics she had saved during her stay:

1/ Leaves from some birch switches. 1909 May 7
2/ A flower from the bird cherry tree in the garden of G. Y.'s home in Pokrovskoe. He gave them to us himself
3/ Little sunflower husks. G. Y. cracked them and put them on the table in front of me—2 halves
4/ Hairs from the beard of G. Y.[4]

Sederkholm was not about to save any of Rasputin's hairs, and she worried her distrustful attitude was ruining the trip for the others. She wondered if this was the reason for Vyrubova's strange behavior. "Vyrubova was very nervous in Pokrovskoe, she was afraid of something and was not herself. Rasputin was in a bad temper. Apparently because of me. More than once Rasputin's wife said to her husband, 'Ah, Grigory, you're wasting your time with her!'" referring to Sederkholm. As for Praskovya, Sederkholm found her "very kind." She had greeted them all warmly and like a true mistress of the house. They stayed three days and then left for home. Along the way, Rasputin tried to kiss Sederkholm; she hit him, and he never did it again. Sederkholm was by now convinced that Rasputin was no holy man. Still, she had to admit he had the gift of clairvoyance. Once she witnessed how Rasputin had been presented with a photograph of several persons unknown to him. Rasputin stared at the faces, and then pointed to a certain "Mr. X.", saying, "This one doesn't believe in God." He was right, for the man he pointed to was an atheist. There was no logical explanation for it, she said.

When she returned Sederkholm wrote a letter thanking the empress for her largesse and also to say that Rasputin was not worthy of her trust. She did not go into any details, saying it was too difficult for her, but added in her letter that Madame Orlova would confirm what she said. Orlova, however, got cold feet and refused, telling the empress that Sederkholm's poor experience was due to her being so "nervous." Sederkholm then asked Utkina to talk to Alexandra, but she was too frightened and claimed ignorance. Vyrubova, however, did tell Alexandra about Sederkholm's reaction to Rasputin, but she explained this away as a result of her ignorance of "the innocence and naivety of the folk, of their saintly naivety." Vyrubova did not give up trying to open Sederkholm's eyes to Rasputin's holiness, but she failed. Sederkholm would have nothing more to do with him.

Vyrubova made another trip to Pokrovskoe a few years later, this time with Munya and Lyubov Golovina and Baroness Iskul von Gilde-brand. Munya was taken by the honest simplicity of their lives. They visited his friends and relatives, went fishing on the Tura, and drank *brazhka*, home-brewed peasant beer that made the women's heads spin. Munya found Praskovya a "serious and pleasant woman" and most wel-coming. When Lyubov told her how Rasputin had talked Munya out of joining a convent, Praskovya replied:

> See, that's why Grigory had to leave us, to take care of all of you! And little Alyosha, he's so sick, if he [Rasputin] were not next to Him, what would happen? But Auntie Lyuba [Lyubov], is it true there are wicked people who are in charge there and are preparing to shout against our dear Emperor and such things and are always abusing Grigory as much as they can? Tell them to stop, tell them it's against God's will!

Munya left full of warm impressions of life in Pokrovskoe. She felt she better understood what Rasputin meant when he would say, "Simplicity is from God, one must be simple, as a small child, to enter the Heavenly Kingdom." The words were from the Bible, but they only came alive for her then and there.[5]

Rasputin stayed in St. Petersburg for roughly a month before returning to Siberia with Feofan. The two men had together visited Nicholas and Alexandra at Tsarskoe Selo earlier that year, on 4 February 1909. It was a happy occasion: that day Feofan had been named rector of the St. Petersburg Theological Seminary.[6] Later that month Feofan was appointed bishop of Simferopol. Some saw in Feofan's rise the work of his protégé Rasputin. It was noted that the royal family had asked Feofan to be their personal confessor on 13 November 1905, just days after Rasputin's first meeting with Nicholas and Alexandra.[7] Rasputin and Feofan were next at the palace on 23 June, along with the starets Makary from Verkhoturye. Veniamin later claimed Rasputin had purposely brought Makary to Petersburg to show Nicholas and Alexandra what good, pious friends he had and thus counter the whisper campaign against him.[8] There is no evidence to prove or disprove such a claim. Soon after their meeting at the palace the three men left St. Petersburg for Verkhoturye. There they had their photograph taken, and Rasputin and Feofan then traveled on to Pokrovskoe.[9]

On their return to St. Petersburg Feofan broke off from Rasputin to visit the monastery in Sarov on his own, as he had possibly done the previous year. He went to pray alone in the cell of St. Serafim. He was gone for so long that the monks began to worry something had happened to him. Indeed, Feofan had prayed so hard that he passed out, and when he finally came to he was unable to explain to the brothers what had happened to him. Eight years later Feofan told the Commission that he had gone to the cell to pray to God and St. Serafim for help in understanding Rasputin and there the truth was revealed to him: "Rasputin [. . .] was on the false path."[10]

Back in Petersburg, Feofan summoned Rasputin to a meeting. Joining them was Veniamin. They began questioning him on his suspicious ways with women (the trips to the baths, stroking their hands, kissing), actions they had noticed themselves and heard talk of and could now no longer ignore. (It ought to be noted that such was Feofan's "asceticism" he refused even to shake a woman's hand or share a train compartment with her.) Rasputin admitted that it was true, he did go to the baths with women, to which they told him this was unacceptable from the point of view of the holy fathers, and Rasputin promised to stop. They left it at that. Feofan later said they did not judge him too harshly because he was a simple peasant and they had read about men in the Olonetsk and Novgorod provinces with similar practices, and this was not a sign of moral degeneracy, but of the patriarchal nature of peasant life. "Moreover, it was clear from the Lives of the ancient Byzantine holy fools Saint Simeon and Saint Ioann," Feofan told the Commission, "that both had gone to bathhouses with women on purpose, and had been abused and reviled for it, although they were nonetheless great saints." Rasputin told Feofan that he went to test himself by looking at the bodies of women, to see whether he had extinguished his passion. Feofan warned him this was dangerous, "for it is only the great saints who are able to do it, and he, by acting in that way, was engaging in self-deception and was on a dangerous path."[11]

After their return that summer, Feofan and Veniamin called Rasputin to them for a second time. Reports of Rasputin's improper behavior continued to reach them and they now accused him of "spiritual delusion." One of the things that had come to Feofan's attention was that Rasputin was reportedly instructing his female followers not to confess to their priests the sin of adultery, saying they would not understand and it would just upset them. "Feofan is a simpleton," Rasputin was claimed to have told them, "and he won't understand these mysteries; he'll condemn them and so condemn the Holy Spirit and commit a mortal sin."[12] They told him that this was his last chance to change his ways, otherwise they would cut off all relations with him, publicly denounce him, and present everything they knew to the tsar. The press later reported (most likely with great exaggeration) Feofan saying to Rasputin: "Don't come near me, Satan, you are not blessed, but a deceiver."[13] A stunned Rasputin, so Feofan later stated, broke down and began to cry. He admitted to making mistakes and promised to change his ways, to renounce the world, and to submit to Feofan's authority. Satisfied with Rasputin's response, Feofan and Veniamin asked Rasputin to pray with them.

But word soon got back to Feofan that Rasputin had neither renounced the world nor changed his ways. He was also told that Rasputin was taking actions to protect himself against Feofan, and so he decided to speak directly to the tsar himself. But when he arrived at the palace he was received not by Nicholas, but Alexandra, along with Vyrubova. Feofan spoke for about an hour, trying to prove to the empress that Rasputin was in the grip of spiritual delusion. Alexandra would have none of it, insisting that this was all lies and slander. Feofan was convinced Rasputin had warned her, and so she had been prepared for him. Feofan saw Rasputin just once more, and only to call him a deceiver to his face. Rasputin wrote to beg forgiveness and seek a reconciliation, but he was ignored.

It was apparently that summer that Feofan shared his concerns with Antony (Vadkovsky), metropolitan of St. Petersburg, one of the most important figures in the church. In August, Antony, convinced of what Feofan had shared with him, came to see Rasputin as an expression of society's unhealthy preoccupation with mysticism. These concerns were shared by the new head of the Synod (as of 5 February 1909), Sergei Lukyanov. Nicholas and Alexandra were supposedly not pleased with Lukyanov's appointment since he, together with Stolypin, had wanted to bring Rasputin's actions to light for some time. With the help of Antony, Lukyanov gathered compromising materials on Rasputin to give to Stolypin, who tried to use them to open the eyes of the emperor a second time, but failed. Antony also, with the tacit approval of Lukyanov, reprinted in the capital's religious press a few anti-Rasputin articles from the major newspapers.[14]

Rasputin saw little of Nicholas, Alexandra, and the children that summer of 1909, and their separation continued when the family departed Tsarskoe Selo early in the autumn for Livadia in the Crimea. In the first week of October Nicholas left for an extended trip without them. A worried Alexandra wrote to him: "Sweet Treasure mine, my Huzy, dearly beloved One, God bless and keep you. Gr[igory's] prayers watch over you on your journey, into His keeping I give you over."[15]

Rasputin spent several weeks that autumn in the Petersburg apartment of Vladimir Korolenko, writer, editor of the liberal *Russian Wealth*, former revolutionary, and champion for human rights, and his wife, the radical populist Yevdokia Ivanovskaya, located at 7 Kabinetskaya Street.[16] Whether Korolenko and his wife were there at the time is not known (they lived chiefly in Poltava after 1900), but it would not have mattered to Rasputin, who gave little attention to party affiliation and could befriend people from across the political spectrum. In November, Rasputin departed for Saratov, where he met Germogen and then the two traveled to Tsaritsyn to visit Iliodor. Iliodor's extremist talk had kept him in trouble ever since leaving the Petersburg Theological Seminary. In 1907, the Synod transferred him from the Pochaevskaya Lavra to Zhitomir and placed him under the personal supervision of Father Antony (Khrapovitsky). He was here for less than a year before being moved again, this time to Tsaritsyn, where he was appointed a missionary-preacher at the Monastery of the Holy Spirit under the supervision of Germogen, then the bishop of Saratov. Tsaritsyn may have been chosen given its minuscule Jewish population, but this made no difference to Iliodor and now he directed his attacks on local journalists, clergy, businessmen, and officials.[17] "I was transformed into a monster of audacity," he later wrote of this period.[18]

Iliodor first became nationally known in August 1908 following a violent clash with police at his monastery. After this the governor in Saratov sought Stolypin's help to remove Iliodor from Tsaritsyn, but Germogen and others came to his defense, and Iliodor remained. Then, at the end of November 1908, the Synod ordered Iliodor transferred to the diocese of Minsk after a number of speeches attacking Stolypin. Iliodor appealed and the decision dragged on into the spring of 1909. Germogen protected Iliodor as best he could and then encouraged him to go to Petersburg and seek the help of Rasputin after no one else was willing to come to his defense. Rasputin arranged a private audience for Iliodor with the empress. They met at Vyrubova's house on 3 April, at which Alexandra made Iliodor promise not to attack the tsar's ministers any more, to which he agreed, and to listen to and obey Rasputin: "You listen to Father Gregory [. . .] He will lead you to the light. He is the greatest living ascetic. He keeps meditating all the time over the welfare of Russia. A saint he is, a great prophet."[19] Such, according to the less than reliable Iliodor, were her words. Rasputin had won. Nicholas over-rode the decision of the Synod and Iliodor was permitted to stay. "He was like an angel," Iliodor wrote later of Rasputin after his intervention, "the right hand of my Saviour."[20] The mad monk returned to Tsaritsyn more emboldened than ever.

Germogen and Rasputin arrived in Tsaritsyn in early November and stayed until the end of the month. In 1912, Iliodor would write that it was one night during this visit that Rasputin snuck into the bedroom of a twenty-nine-year-old nun in the home of a merchant by the name of Lebedeva and tormented her for four hours.[21] He stated he only learned of this much later or else he would have broken with Rasputin right then. It is impossible to verify Iliodor's account.

At the end of November, Rasputin and Iliodor left Tsaritsyn for Pokrovskoe and Germogen returned alone to Saratov. As they journeyed to Siberia Rasputin told Iliodor the truth of his relations with Nicholas and Alexandra. "The tsar considers me to be Christ. The tsar and tsaritsa bow at my feet, they sink to their knees before me and kiss my hands. [. . .] I have carried the tsaritsa in my arms. I have held her, cuddled her, kissed her."[22] Iliodor's words are pure fantasy, as was the description he gave in his book of his stay in Pokrovskoe, in which he claimed Rasputin sent the Pecherkin women to his room at night to have sex with him and tried to convince him to join the khlysty. He smeared Rasputin's son Dmitry, calling him lazy, debauched, and vile. Rasputin, according to Iliodor, regaled him with the stories of his many orgies, about how he had sex with Vyrubova and others in the baths and how once in the cell of Makary at Verkhoturye several women wrapped their naked legs around his face and other body parts. Iliodor stated that "his genital member did not function," yet somehow Rasputin still managed to have sex with large numbers of women.[23]

More believable is Iliodor's description of how Rasputin showed Iliodor the shirts the empress had sewn for him and letters he had received from her and the children, as well as from several grand dukes and duchesses. Iliodor begged Rasputin to give him the letters, and he did, except for one letter from Alexei. These letters would soon be the cause of a major scandal. The last night there Iliodor met Father Pyotr Ostroumov, supposedly against Rasputin's wishes. According to Iliodor, Ostroumov called Rasputin a villain, libertine, and a drunkard. The next day, on 15 December, Iliodor and Rasputin left Pokrovskoe. Iliodor would never return to Rasputin's home. Unbeknownst to Rasputin and Iliodor, the police had been monitoring their stay in Pokrovskoe. They recorded their departure for Russia and also tried to gain information about the purpose of Iliodor's visit. According to files in the Tyumen archives, Iliodor had come to Pokrovskoe promising to donate the 20,000 rubles needed for Rasputin's long-dreamed-of new church.[24] No money, however, was ever received.

The two men returned to spend Christmas at Tsaritsyn. When Rasputin departed for Petersburg on 30 December, Iliodor helped organize a lavish send-off with some fifteen hundred followers for the man Iliodor called a "fervent servant, brother Grigory." Iliodor told the gathering at the station how sorry he was to see Grigory depart, and how those who did not go to listen to him talk about "God's Word" were "atheists, villains, our enemies and the enemies of the Orthodox Christian faith." The crowd sent him off with the song "Many Years."[25] That evening Rasputin arrived in Petersburg. Iliodor would later write that it was then, in the final months of 1909, that he began to have his first doubts about Rasputin.

If Iliodor is to be believed, this public embrace of Rasputin hid his growing private doubts. In The Holy Devil, Iliodor wrote that he prayed to God in late 1909 to reveal to him whether Rasputin was an angel or the Devil. "The Devil incarnate" was His answer.[26]

According to Pavel Kurlov, deputy minister of the interior from 1909 to 1911 (and lieutenant general from 1910), in late 1909–early 1910 Stolypin received an order (Kurlov does not say from whom) to end the police surveillance of Rasputin, a directive that Stolypin passed on to Kurlov to carry out. A few days later, Stolypin asked Kurlov to join him in his office that afternoon, for he had arranged a meeting with

Rasputin and wanted Kurlov's opinion of the man. Pretending to be examining some papers in the corner of his boss's office, Kurlov listened carefully to Rasputin for over an hour as he tried to convince Stolypin that he was falsely held in suspicion even though he was a humble, harmless soul. Stolypin said hardly a word, other than to tell Rasputin upon parting that if this were all true and his behavior were correct he had no reason to worry about being bothered by the police. After Rasputin had gone, Stolypin asked Kurlov for his opinion. Kurlov told him that Rasputin belonged to a certain type of cunning, calculating Russian peasant, but that he did not appear to him to be a charlatan. "Nonetheless," Stolypin replied, "we'll have to find a way to deal with him." (The accuracy and disinterestedness of Kurlov's assessment have been questioned. General Gerasimov of the Petersburg Okhrana, who had earlier set up police surveillance of Rasputin upon the order of General Dedyulin, was convinced Kurlov owed his appointment in 1909 to powerful friends of Rasputin and it was his influence in late 1909 that allowed Rasputin to avoid being exiled from the capital.)[27]

Stolypin never left any memoirs on Rasputin, and so we have only what others claim he said. Here is what Mikhail Rodzianko said Stolypin told him:

> He ran his pale eyes over me, mumbled mysterious and inarticulate words from the Scriptures, made strange movements with his hands, and I began to feel an indescribable loathing for this vermin sitting opposite me. Still, I did realize that the man possessed great hypnotic power, which was beginning to produce a fairly strong impression on me, though certainly one of repulsion.[28]

Maria Bok, Stolypin's daughter, recalled bringing up the subject of Rasputin with her father on a few occasions. In the summer of 1911 shortly before his assassination, she asked him once more:

> Hearing Rasputin's name my father made a wry face and said with deep sadness in his voice: "Nothing can be done about it. Every time I had an opportunity to warn the tsar, I did. And here is what he told me recently: 'I agree with you, Pyotr Arkadievich, but better ten Rasputins than one of the empress's hysterical fits.' That's what the reason was. The empress is ill, seriously ill, she believes that Rasputin is the only person in the whole world who can help the heir and it is beyond human capacity to dissuade her about it."[29]

It was also reported that Nicholas said to Stolypin: "I have no doubt, Pyotr Arkadievich, that you are sincerely dedicated to me. Maybe everything you are saying is true. But I am asking you never to talk about Rasputin to me. I cannot do anything about it anyway."[30] Nicholas's quip about hysterics did not remain between the tsar and his prime minister but quickly spread throughout society. The tsar of Russia, so it seemed, was letting his fear of his wife determine how he ruled the empire.

Vasily Shulgin could barely believe what was happening before their eyes. "There's this terrifying knot . . . The Emperor insults the country by allowing into the palace, access to which is so difficult even for the best people, an exposed libertine, while the country insults the Emperor with its awful suspicions . . . And so the bonds, slowly built up over centuries, that hold Russia together are coming undone . . . And why? All because of one man's weakness toward his wife . . ."[31]

Part Three

SCANDALS

1910–1911

18. Trouble in the Nursery

Rasputin saw Nicholas and Alexandra often in the first two months of 1910—seven times in January, four times in February. Typically Rasputin would come visit them in the evening, and not necessarily to see them both. On 6 January, for example, Nicholas wrote in his diary: "At 9:30 we went into town. After this Grigory came to see Alix, we sat with him for a long time and talked." These long evening conversations were common then. On 14 February, Rasputin came to the palace to say goodbye before returning to Siberia.[1]

During his visit home, the local police were busy digging into Rasputin's past. On 7 March 1910 Captain A. M. Polyakov reported to the head of the Tobolsk Provincial Gendarmes Administration that Rasputin was forty-five years old, a peasant from Pokrovskoe in the district of Tyumen, and lived much like the other peasants there engaged in farming. He frequently traveled to Russia, where he had high-placed friends, including Grand Duchess Militsa Nicolaevna. He "commands respect, is materially well off, and is shown great esteem. From every corner of Russia he receives large amounts money from various people, including high-placed individuals; among the common folk he is considered 'righteous' and 'wise'; he sometimes travels to Russia, visits Moscow and Petersburg, talks with high clergymen there, and in the spring of 1907 Her Imperial Highness Gr. D. Militsa Nikolaevna deigned to visit him in Pokrovskoe incognito." Polyakov did not fail to mention that Rasputin was leading a "sober" life.[2]

Rasputin was back at Tsarskoe Selo the day Polyakov wrote his report.[3] His return occasioned tension among the family and their closest servants. It seems some of the Romanov daughters had been keeping secrets, secrets about "our Friend." The day Rasputin arrived Alexandra wrote to her daughter Maria to inform her of Rasputin's arrival and to instruct her on the need to be a nice little girl and not to keep any secrets, for she did not like secrets.[4] The following day, Tatyana wrote a letter to her mother begging her forgiveness (she does not say for what) and promising never to do it again. "I am so afraid that S. I. can speak to Maria about our friend some thing bad," she fretted. "I hope our nurse will be nice to our Friend now."

"S. I." refers to Sofia Ivanovna Tyutcheva. By the spring of 1910 Tyutcheva had become convinced of Rasputin's immorality and the danger he represented to her charges. She was deeply concerned that Rasputin was permitted in the nursery and she was not shy about saying so. Nicholas's sister Xenia wrote in her diary on 15 March 1910:

> I sat for a long time with S.D.* She is still under the shock of a conversation with S. I. Tyutcheva in Tsarskoe yesterday, and everything that is going on there: the attitude of Alix and the children to that sinister Grigory (whom they consider to be almost a saint, when in fact he's only a *khlyst*!).
>
> He's always there, goes into the nursery, visits Olga and Tatyana while they're getting ready for bed, sits there talking to them and *caressing* them. They are careful to hide him from Sofia Ivanovna, and the children don't dare talk to her about him. It's quite unbelievable and beyond understanding.
>
> They are all under his influence and pray to him. I was simply crushed by this conversation.
>
> Olga and I had dinner at the Anichkov. As I only had one thing on my mind, it was all I could talk about. But who can help? It's very difficult and "ticklish" for the family. There are the most terrible rumors about him![5]

News of the troubles at court was being talked about back in the city. Salon hostess Alexandra Bogdanovich noted in her diary on 20 March 1910 that she had heard the palace servants were aghast at the behavior of Rasputin and the empress's support of him. It was said this "rotten man" was permitted access to the palace at all times and even visited the empress in her bedroom and the tsar had no qualms about such things. Bogdanovich had heard that on a trip to Pokrovskoe Rasputin had "insulted" several of Vyrubova's maids and that one was now pregnant with Rasputin's child. The talk at court had it that Rasputin was openly telling everyone that Vyrubova had agreed to take the baby after it was born and raise it as her own child. More than an immoral person, Rasputin was even meeting at length with the tsar and giving him political advice, Bogdanovich noted. Others, too, were starting to

---

* Alexandra's Lady-in-Waiting Sofia Dmitrievna Samarina.

recognize his authority. It was said that Count Sergei Witte was seeking to curry favor with Rasputin in the hopes of returning to a position of power. "And this is all taking place in the twentieth century! It's simply horrible!"[6]

Matters in the nursery only got worse. Along with Tyutcheva, Maria Vishnyakova, the lovely nursemaid to little Alexei who had been charmed by Rasputin, was at the center of the trouble. Little reliable information exists of their relationship, although all sources suggest Vishnyakova had been an ally, and likely a good deal more, of Rasputin. Indeed, the Okhrana believed at the time that Vishnyakova had been the one responsible for introducing him to court.[7] But by March 1910 something had happened to poison their relations. Just what this was, and precisely when and where it happened, remains murky. Iliodor claimed that Rasputin raped Maria in the summer of 1907 or 1908—either in Verkhoturye or Pokrovskoe.[8] Tyutcheva told the Commission in 1917 that it was during a visit to Pokrovskoe in 1910 that Rasputin crept into Maria's room one night and took advantage of her.[9] (Tyutcheva misspoke: this would have to have been in 1909, not 1910.) Several years after Tyutcheva's testimony, the former empress's personal maid Madeleine (Magdalina) Zanotti also claimed that Maria herself had told her how Rasputin seduced her, although she noted this had happened not in Pokrovskoe, but in the Alexander Palace itself. Maria, according to Zanotti, called Rasputin a "dog."[10] Maria told the Commission a similar story. She stated that it was indeed while on the trip to Pokrovskoe that one night Rasputin crept into her room and started to kiss her and then, with Maria in hysterics, took her virginity. On the ride back, she said, Rasputin ignored her, sharing his berth on the train with Zinaida Manshtedt.[11]

If Rasputin did assault Maria on the trip to Pokrovskoe in 1909, the question is why she did not say anything or make any sort of complaint about Rasputin for practically an entire year.[12] Perhaps she was too frightened, or felt it had been her fault, or did not think anyone would believe her. Perhaps it was only by the early months of 1910, when her fellow governess Tyutcheva was upset enough about Rasputin that she felt she had to speak up, that Maria felt she could finally unburden herself. Tyutcheva told another story altogether to the Commission.

> Once on entering the children's wing, I came upon a terrible commotion. Vishnyakova told me with tears in her eyes that she . . . and

the other devotees had participated in rites of "rejoicing." That
what she had accepted as a command of the Holy Spirit had turned
out to be simple debauchery . . . I understood from her account
that Feofan, who was her confessor . . . had in his humility sent
them to Rasputin, whom he considered to be one of God's elders.
Rasputin forced them to do whatever he needed, passing himself
off as someone acting at the command of the Holy Spirit . . . At the
same time he warned them not to tell Feofan, covering it up in
sophistry: Feofan was a simpleton and would not understand such
secrets and would condemn them, thereby passing judgment on
the Holy Spirit and committing a mortal sin.[13]

Whatever the reason, Maria did complain to Alexandra about Rasputin at this time. Did she tell the empress she had been raped, or did
she bring Alexandra a critical article on Rasputin from the *Petersburg
Leaflet* as society gossip insisted at the time?[14] Of this, we cannot be
certain. Whatever Vishnyakova said, the empress refused to believe
her. According to Tyutcheva, Alexandra told Maria she put no stock in
such gossip, that such talk was just the work of "dark forces" intent on
destroying Rasputin, and she forbade Maria from ever again bringing
up the matter.[15] Nicholas's sister Olga many years later insisted Maria's
story of being raped was not true. Yes, there had been a scandal involving Maria, Olga admitted, but this had had nothing to do with Rasputin
but a Cossack of the imperial guard instead, in whose bed Maria had
been discovered.[16]

Zanotti asserted, as if to prove the scope of Rasputin's power, that
Maria was fired for mentioning the matter to the empress, although this
is clearly incorrect, for Maria remained Alexei's nanny for another three
years and was then let go not for anything having to do with Rasputin,
but chiefly because Alexei had outgrown his need for her services.[17]
Valentina Chebotaryova, who worked in the Palace Hospital at Tsarskoe
Selo during World War I and knew Maria Vishnyakova, wrote in her
diary not long after the February Revolution that ever since the "awful
drama" at Rasputin's in Pokrovskoe Vishnyakova had never been quite
normal again. It is not clear whether Chebotaryova knew this first
hand or was simply parroting common gossip. As of 1917 Maria
was tormented about leaving her life behind and joining a convent.
Chebotaryova asked whether she still loved Alexei, to which she replied:
"More than ever!"[18]

*

Whatever the truth of what transpired between Rasputin and Vishnyakova in the spring of 1910, there is no doubt that his visits had become
the source of great tension and discussion. From Rasputin's own letters
to the children we know that he did visit them in the nursery and that
they engaged in play and even some roughhousing. He wrote in February 1909: "My dear golden kiddies, I live with you. My sweet little
Alexeiushka and kiddies, I live with you and often recall the nursery
where we lay about. I live with you. I will come to you soon." He would
write them brief notes on the importance of faith and love and the need
to trust God's mysterious ways: "What matters is not power, but belief
and love. [. . .] The paths of God are inscrutable; it seems things are bad,
but then they turn out to be holy."[19] He wrote to them often of the
beauty of nature, as in this letter to Maria: "My dear pearl M! Tell me
how you talked to the sea and to nature. I miss your simple soul. Will
see you soon. Kissing you from the bottom of my heart."

He would try to comfort the children, and Nicholas, when their
mother was ill:

"My sweet children, [. . .] little angels protect you, and God is with
your Mama in her bed. She is merry but we are in pain because we look
not with God's eyes but with ours. Mama is lying with angels and rejoicing but we are in sorrow. Papa, don't be downhearted! Mama is fine,
and she is an adult, just be patient for a while and she will get well." (As
for Alexandra, she once wrote Olga in early 1909 that God sends us
illnesses "for the good," and we must be certain of this and trust that we
shall get well when God deems the time has come and so we must all be
patient. Still, she added that she will be "very happy" as soon as she can
see "our Friend" again.)[20]

As in his letters to their parents, so too in those to the children Rasputin divided the world into true Christians and their enemies, into "us
versus them" ("All the world curses, yet we cover ourselves under the
hand of Christ—under love."), while always preaching tolerance for all
religious beliefs ("Every faith comes from the Lord, one must never criticize another faith."). He sent letters praising "Olya," his pet name for
Alexei, as in this one from the spring of 1909:

Olya will triumph with them because Olya will follow very closely
their example because he is not an ordinary earthly being; there
has never been such a tsar and there will never be another one.

The look in his eyes is similar to Peter the Great's, though Peter

was very wise but his deeds were very bad—if not to say lowly [. . .]
But your Olya does not allow any wrong-doings to even come
close to him unless someone sets him a bad example. [. . .] I keep
Alexei in my soul, may God let him grow as a cedar of Lebanon,
and may he bear fruit so that all Russia would rejoice for this
fruit.[21]

Rasputin encouraged Alexei to find strength in the life of Christ: "My dear
little one! Look at our dear God, see his wounds. Once he suffered
patiently, and then he became strong and all-powerful. And so you too,
my dear one, and so you too will be cheery and we'll live together."[22] At
times he wrote to the girls individually, as in this letter to Olga from 1909:

> The quietness of God—We love God, and this love is gentle. Olga,
> pray so that light shines above your house and brings you joy.
>   The beggars are kind and their joy is immeasurable. We are all
> beggars but one who does not consider himself a beggar is a tor-
> turer and has brought himself hell on earth, has not yet died but
> has brought hell on earth.

And this to Maria around the same time: "Ma, my dear, don't fear the
enemies, for God and I are with you. This is why they rage and the hea-
thens keep away, and you will always be a Maiden, and so you'll know
peace. No sound, only God. Who is with God is not frightened of me,
who does not remember God, but is afraid of people, for them God is
not a fortress."[23]
Several of his letters to Tatyana have survived as well:

> Tanya, Tanya's where, where, in Pokrovskoe I'm at home and I see
> you, my little friend, you did not yell to me loud enough, I did not
> hear and did not receive your telegrams, but my friend, friend, I
> miss you. Our little God is in heaven, and you are in the Crimea,
> you are far away. Dear God is with us and in us, and we don't see,
> but it will happen soon and our dear little God will come to us [. . .]
>   Dear little friend, now as before I am with you, even this
> moment I am with you in my thoughts, your life of love overflows,
> it feeds hope in the supreme creator, the Lord be with you.
>   Your day was chosen out of love and the angels rejoice, may
> love serve as your fortress.[24]

Alexandra had complete faith in Rasputin and the beneficial influence he had on the children. She wrote once to Olga, her eldest child:

"Remember above all to always be a good example to the little ones, only then will our Friend be contented with you."[25] Sometimes Nicholas and Alexandra would go together with Rasputin to see the children in the nursery. On at least one occasion, Rasputin met alone with Olga for a long time, something that brought Alexandra nothing but joy. And the children apparently were joyous as well. On 25 July 1909, while their father was away, Olga wrote to him of their great excitement that "Grigory" was coming to see them that evening. "We are all wonderfully happy to see him yet again."[26]

The last head of the Petrograd Okhrana, Major General Konstantin Globachev, responsible for surveillance over Rasputin, noted that his relations with the royal family were always "most proper," but this was immaterial; appearance was everything.[27] And with time, the stories grew ever uglier and more unbelievable. In 1912, the Socialist Revolutionary newspaper *For the People!* wrote that Rasputin tried to have his way with Olga, but was threatened by a number of guards officers when they found out.[28] During the war rumors about Rasputin having raped the girls were widespread. Even men who should have known better believed them. One Russian general recorded in his diary the rumor (which he did not think impossible) that the Grand Duchess Tatyana was pregnant with Rasputin's child.[29]

Even if she knew such talk to be nonsense, Tyutcheva was, nonetheless, not at all pleased that Rasputin was permitted into the nursery; it did not seem appropriate that this controversial peasant should be given access to the private rooms of the tsar's daughters, now on the verge of womanhood, whose reputations (and bodies) must be guarded with the utmost care. And in this she was right. After hearing Vishnyakova's story about what had happened in Pokrovskoe, Tyutcheva felt she now had no choice but to act, and so went to Alexandra. Although the empress would hear none of Tyutcheva's words, it seems the emperor wanted to know more of the matter himself. He had Tyutcheva come to him the very next day. She told the Commission about their meeting.

"Sofia Ivanovna, you will already have guessed why I have sent for you," Nicholas said as she entered his study.

"What is going on in the nursery?" I then told him everything that had happened. "So you also do not believe in the sanctity of Grigory?" asked the Emperor. I answered negatively and the Emperor said, "And what if I told you that all these difficult years I have survived only because of his prayers?"

"You have survived them because of the prayers of the whole of Russia, Your Majesty," I replied. The Emperor started to say he was convinced it was all a lie, that he did not believe these stories about R, that the pure always attracts everything dirty."[30]

Sofia replied:

"You, your majesty, are too pure of heart and do not see what filth surrounds you."

"Am I then the enemy of my own children?" he asked.

He asked me never to mention Rasputin's name in conversation. In order for that to take place, I asked the sovereign to arrange things so that Rasputin would never appear in the children's wing. Before that the tsarina had told me that after six I was free, as if hinting that she did not wish me to visit the children after that hour. After my conversation with the sovereign, I went to the nursery whenever I wished. But the distance between the family and me continued to grow.[31]

Sofia continued to talk about Rasputin to her friends and word continued to spread. Vyrubova recalled visiting her Moscow relatives and being asked whether it was true that Rasputin was at the palace nearly every day and was even permitted to bathe the children. Stunned, she asked them where they had heard such nonsense, and they told her from Tyutcheva herself. Tyutcheva was from an old Moscow noble family and had come to the court upon the recommendation of Alexandra's sister Ella, a foe of Rasputin. These connections would help make Moscow a major center for opposition to Rasputin and, with time, Nicholas and Alexandra as well. (Indeed: in March 1910, Ella, clearly implying Rasputin, wrote to Nicholas telling him "that not all who seem holy are.")[32] Vyrubova insisted that after her conversations with Nicholas and Alexandra, Tyutcheva continued to spread intrigue and sow mistrust at court and among the royal family. She created scandals and stirred up the other nannies, she tried to turn members of the imperial household staff against Alexandra, as she did with Princess Obolenskaya, a long-devoted maid-of-honor to the empress. The grand duchesses supposedly complained to their mother of Tyutcheva's machinations, which went so far as to try to turn them against their own mother.

The rumors surrounding the scandal swirled. Tyutcheva presented herself as a victim of Rasputin, and many believed her. Tyutcheva was blind to the fact that her talk, which was driven by true love and devotion to the girls, was in fact giving rise to the corrosive rumors that she believed she had been trying to stop by speaking to Alexandra and Nicholas. Paradoxically, by trying to open people's eyes to the danger Rasputin presented, she was fanning the flames. Vyrubova wrote that all the ridiculous gossip about Rasputin and the children originated with Tyutcheva and no one was more responsible for spreading the "monstrous gossip" about the royal family than she.[33] The emperor's valet Radtsig told those gathered at the Bogdanoviches' salon in June 1910 that everyone at court now hated the empress and that she continued to be angry with everyone who dared to say anything bad about Rasputin. Both Tyutcheva and Vishnyakova, he informed them, had been sent away for two months for daring to speak up against Rasputin. It was being said Vyrubova was to take the place of Tyutcheva. "The poor children!" Alexandra Bogdanovich scribbled in her diary.[34]

To the empress's friend Lily Dehn, the scandal was due solely to Tyutcheva's own meddling and envy.[35] She was, however, largely alone in this opinion. To most, Tyutcheva was a hero. Strained though the relations were now between Tyutcheva and the empress, she maintained her post as the girls' governess for another two years.

During her conversation with the tsar about Rasputin that spring, Tyutcheva saw a letter on Nicholas's desk from Feofan. This was apparently the second time he had written the tsar to denounce Rasputin. In his letter Feofan repeated his claim from the previous year that Rasputin was in the grips of "spiritual delusion" and now also stated that he was "a criminal in both the religious and moral sense of the word." Rasputin, Feofan warned, was "a wolf in sheep's clothing." Feofan had originally asked Tyutcheva to deliver the letter to Nicholas, but she had refused, given the trouble she was in already. Someone else had done it for him. Nicholas told Tyutcheva he was shocked by Feofan's words, for he had always spoken so fondly of Rasputin in the past.[36]

Feofan had received new information that not only confirmed his suspicions of the previous year, but presented a much darker image of

Rasputin than he had imagined. Such had been Feofan's shock upon learning these new details, and then realizing that neither the emperor nor empress would deign to acknowledge them, that he fell ill and suffered a paralysis of the face.[37] The new information that Feofan had received was a written confession by Khionya Berladskaya, once one of Rasputin's most devoted acolytes. She now called Rasputin a khlyst and a sex maniac, a prisoner of his own "devilish delusion." Berladskaya detailed Rasputin's violent nature, noting how he liked to beat Praskovya and the other women around him and kept them all virtual hostages at his home in Pokrovskoe. She claimed that several years earlier Rasputin had raped her on the train from Petersburg to Pokrovskoe. The veracity of Berladskaya's account is highly questionable; her words seem embellished for obvious effect. Vladimir Bonch-Bruevich characterized her confession as a bunch of lies and extreme exaggerations.[38] Veniamin had made a copy of Berladskaya's confession for Feofan to keep, and the original was delivered to the Metropolitan of St. Petersburg, Antony (Vadkovsky), and through him presented to the tsar. According to Iliodor, Nicholas summoned Rasputin and held out the notebook with Berladskaya's confession, asking him whether he ought to read it. Rasputin replied by asking the tsar whether he enjoyed reading in the lives of the saints about how they had been mocked by slanderers. No, the emperor said, and with that threw the notebook into the fireplace.[39] As with everything Iliodor wrote, one must approach this scene with considerable skepticism.

It appears that another damaging testimony against Rasputin had been given by a Yelena Timofeeva, a graduate of a St. Petersburg religious school for girls and the sister-in-law of Vasily Spiridonov, a local clergyman. She became one of Rasputin's early followers, and he was exceedingly fond of Yelena, calling her "my little dove," before she suddenly disappeared. It was said that she had confessed to Feofan to being abused by Rasputin and Lokhtina and that he convinced her to leave Rasputin and join a convent. Vyrubova later recalled Yelena and noted that she had indeed been a fanatical believer in Rasputin, but turned away from him not because he had assaulted her, but after he embarrassed her in front of others about a young student Yelena had developed a crush on. Where the truth lies in all this is impossible to say.[40]

Feofan and Veniamin next tried to enlist Iliodor in their campaign and shared with him the confession of Berladskaya and Vishnyakova's story. Rasputin, they wrote Iliodor, had revealed himself to be "the veritable Devil." Rasputin apparently learned of their efforts to court Iliodor, and so he wrote to his friend: "My dear Iliodorushka! Don't believe the slanderers. They are libeling me. And do you know why? Out of envy! I am nearer to the imperial family than they are; the czar and czarina love me very much and care nothing for them. That's why they have risen against me, that's why they are planning to overthrow me. Don't you believe them. This sin will be their undoing."[41] Iliodor stuck by Rasputin for reasons that are not clear. Iliodor later wrote it was his fear of what Rasputin might do to him that kept him from joining Feofan, although it is just as likely he was still not convinced of the accusations being leveled against his friend.[42] Iliodor would defend Rasputin loudly throughout 1910 when he became the target of a massive campaign in the press. He never showed the slightest wavering in his belief in Rasputin's holiness.

In May, the newspaper *Speech* reported that after Feofan and Veniamin attacked Rasputin, Iliodor came to Petersburg "incognito" to defend Rasputin and had been able to revive his reputation at a time when Rasputin was no longer being received in the city's salons. A seething Rasputin, the newspaper wrote, had threatened Feofan: "I'll show you, you meek ascetic, I'll show you. I'll teach you the necessary respect in dealing with the starets. I'll return to Petersburg and then nothing will save you from me."[43] The quote is obviously fabricated, and Iliodor most likely never traveled to the capital to restore Rasputin's status. Regardless, this period marked the height of Iliodor's bizarre career. He had completed a new monastery at Tsaritsyn that could accommodate 7,000 pilgrims. Its shop sold religious trinkets and souvenirs, including an image called "Holy Russia" that featured a Christ-like figure with an unmistakable resemblance to Iliodor. He considered himself a candidate for sainthood, and many in Tsaritsyn agreed with him. Upwards of 10,000 worshipers would come to hear his angry, hate-filled sermons. At times he even dared to exhort his flock to rebellion. He was outrageous. Iliodor hung a large portrait of Lev Tolstoy and encouraged his parishioners to spit on "the great atheist and degenerate" as they walked past.[44] Iliodor believed he was now untouchable. The future was his.

Having failed with Iliodor, Feofan next turned to Germogen. He obviously knew that Germogen was a supporter of Rasputin, but Feofan wrote that he hoped the new information he was sharing with him would open Germogen's eyes, just as he, too, had changed his

opinion of Rasputin. Upon learning of Feofan's effort, Rasputin reportedly traveled to Saratov to see Germogen himself and to try to convince
him that the charges being leveled against him were baseless. Germogen
would later claim that it was after meeting with Rasputin and confronting him about the information provided by Feofan that his estimation
changed. He said that he now saw Rasputin for who he really was,
stopped receiving him, and tried, unsuccessfully, to enlighten Iliodor as
well.[45] Echoes of the falling-out were reported in the press in early June,
quoting Germogen as saying, "For truth, he is the son of the Devil."[46]
But the reporting was premature, and despite his own characterization
of events, Germogen would not fully break with Rasputin until the end
of 1911.

Speaking out against Rasputin took courage on the part of Feofan, but
he was willing to risk his warm relations with the emperor and empress
for what he believed to be the truth. Feofan did not suffer for his honesty. True, he was replaced as Alexei's confessor that year by Father
Alexander Vasilev, but he was kept on as the confessor to their majesties until 1914. In November, Feofan was made bishop of Tauride and
Simferopol and although this appointment has at times been presented
as punishment, this was not the case. Feofan and Alexandra, in fact,
remained close after November, and Feofan himself did not take the
new assignment as a sign of disfavor. Indeed, it seems to have been just
the opposite. The new post in the Crimea was an indication of their
majesties' concern for Feofan, for the Petersburg climate was extremely
hard on him and it was decided he would fare better in the mild south.
On their later visits to the Crimea, the tsar's children gathered special
berries from the woods for Feofan's health, and he was given access to
the tsar's automobile for trips up into the mountains.

Feofan tried not to put too much blame on Rasputin for the direction his life had taken. There were, in his opinion, other, more critical
forces at work.

He was not a hypocrite, not a scoundrel. He was a true man of
God, having come from the simple people. But under the influence of high society, which could not understand this simple man,
a terrible spiritual catastrophe took place and he fell. And the
milieu that had brought this about looked upon it with the most

frivolous attitude. For high society this was nothing but a "laugh." Such a fall, in the spiritual sense, can nevertheless lead to very serious consequences [. . .][47]

Rasputin, in other words, had been the victim. This was to become a fairly common notion, namely that Rasputin, the simple Russian peasant, had been destroyed by his contact with the corrupt Europeanized elite of the capital. It is a notion not without merit.

19. The Press Discovers Rasputin

Despite the scandals in the nursery, the salon gossip, and Feofan's campaign, it was still possible to find people in Russia at the beginning of 1910 who did not know who Rasputin was. Indeed, you could even find such people within the Romanov family. The tsar's uncle Grand Duke Konstantin Konstantinovich (K. R.) noted in his diary for 19 January 1910 that he had been told two days before by the bishop of Kronstadt, Vladimir (Putyata) "about the rumors concerning some God's fool, Grigory, a simple peasant introduced to the Empress A. F. by Militsa and who is said to have great influence over the Tsaritsa's household. I was somewhat unpleasantly surprised that the bishop touched on a subject completely foreign to us, one in which it is quite difficult to distinguish where the truth ends and the rumors begin."[1]

This was all about to change. On 2 March 1910 the *Moscow Gazette* published a lengthy article under the title "The Spiritual Touring-Actor Grigory Rasputin." Before the month was out, practically the entire country knew the name of Rasputin.

"There has been frequent mentioning in society of late of one 'starets' Grigory with the surname 'Rasputin-Novykh,'" the story began. "Grigory only recently petitioned for this surname to replace his previous one—Rasputin. We can only regret the change since his original surname much more accurately corresponded with the lifestyle of this 'starets.'"[2]

Mikhail Novoselov, the article's author, presented three documents about Rasputin, his teachings, and his character that had been written by three unnamed persons—a Tsaritsyn journalist, a student, and a fellow starets—all, he claimed, well acquainted with the Siberian holy man. The documents painted a damning picture of Rasputin as a cunning charlatan, avaricious social climber, and lecherous womanizer who resorted to hypnotism, along with lascivious stroking, to cultivate an image among his almost exclusively female followers as a true man of God, supposedly bringing these women into a "heavenly condition," while being, in fact, a pseudo-prophet whose notions had nothing in common with true Christian faith but were characteristic of a man in the throes of "spiritual delusion." Rasputin was said to be lazy and a bad family man, having abandoned his home and failed to provide for his family; his children were "naughty little miscreants." His lechery was responsible for destroying a good many families and women's lives. Novoselov concluded by writing that an archpriest (Feofan, perhaps?) had recently told him that Rasputin was "a khlyst and a sex maniac." Though the facts, according to Novoselov, were beyond doubt, he feared neither the church nor the state authorities, given their usual "cowardice," would do anything about Rasputin, so he was addressing his words to "the moral consciousness and healthy minds of the average priest and his parishioners."

It was a damning picture indeed, even if almost none of it was true. Not that this seemed to matter to its author. Born into the Russian clergy on both his mother's and father's sides, Novoselov had been a religious seeker from his early years. After completing St. Petersburg University he fell under the influence of Leo Tolstoy. The two men exchanged letters, and Novoselov was later arrested for distributing some of the great writer's illegal works and exiled from the capital. At the age of thirty he broke with Tolstoyanism and flirted with the ideas of the religious philosopher Vladimir Solovyov and the Religious-Philosophical Society. He knew not only John of Kronstadt, but the "God-Seekers" as well, men like Berdyaev, Rozanov, and Sergei Bulgakov. He was also part of the Moscow circle around Ella, the empress's sister. Berdyaev wrote that Novoselov's apartment had the feel of a monk's cell; he surrounded himself with startsy, ascetics, and other devout religious types. Novoselov had no patience for the church hierarchs, recognizing only the spiritual authority of such humble holy men.[3]

Novoselov had had his doubts about Rasputin from as early as 1907, which he had apparently been sharing with others well before 1910. He began gathering material and writing a denunciatory text about Rasputin, but this had been seized by the police before he could publish it.[4] His hatred of Rasputin knew almost no limits. General Bogdanovich said that Novoselov actually believed Rasputin to be the incarnation of the Devil.[5] This antipathy was due in large part to Novoselov's sympathy for the religious world Rasputin sprang from and which he claimed to represent: for a man like Novoselov, Rasputin's identity as a starets amounted to a form of spiritual treason, it was a travesty of the most despicable sort and an insult to all true popular holy men.

Lev Tikhomirov, the *Moscow Gazette*'s editor, was also a key figure behind the article. He would later claim that he had been the first to unmask Rasputin with this publication.[6] If Novoselov hated Rasputin for being a false expression of popular religion, Tikhomirov hated him for what he saw as Rasputin's perversion of his idea of "popular autocracy." Tikhomirov had started out as a radical populist before becoming a monarchist, and so while the notion of a peasant making his way to the palace and forming a bridge between the peasantry and the tsar was the very thing Tikhomirov had hoped for, it was the particular peasant who had managed this that so infuriated him. In Tikhomirov's eyes it amounted to a grand betrayal.[7] Tikhomirov saw Novoselov on 25 March and told him that from what he knew the article had had no effect with their majesties. He was not sure whether Nicholas had even seen it, though he knew if he had it would have made him furious.[8]

For the rest of the public, the article amounted to a bomb going off. Excerpts were reprinted in other Russian newspapers, including some in St. Petersburg, that added fuel to the fire.[9] Iliodor sprang to Rasputin's defense in the press, insisting Rasputin was indeed a true starets who had so completely subjugated his carnal instincts that he no longer even slept with his own wife.[10] According to the newspaper *Russia's Morning* on 23 March, Iliodor had also delivered a sermon threatening to strap Novoselov and the paper's editors to "the pole of Russian shame" and beat them till they bled. Iliodor saw the article as an act of treason against the *Moscow Gazette*'s late editor, Vladimir Gringmut, a former leader of the Black Hundreds. Iliodor was certain Novoselov's primary target had been the Black Hundreds and not Rasputin, a convenient proxy.[11] (Rasputin never was a member of the Black Hundreds, although his name would at times be brought up in connection with the reactionary group given his close ties to Iliodor and Germogen.) When Tikhomirov read the story he was dumbfounded: he glimpsed in it, quite presciently, in the blind hatred provoked by the scandal, the death knell of the Romanov regime. He wrote in his diary:

> There's your "Old Russia of the Black Hundreds!" What is this absurd dark force not capable of? [. . .]
> I don't know how the church will manage, but the monarchy,

it seems, is finished, unless by way of some miracle a strong, wise savior with a powerful hand and a powerful mind should appear.[12]

So overwhelming had the response been to his article that Novoselov published a follow-up on 30 March—"One More Thing About Grigory Rasputin." He noted that he had been receiving a great many letters from others who knew Rasputin that corroborated what he had written in his first article. This second article insisted it was not in any way motivated by some party attack on the Black Hundreds, but directed solely against Rasputin. It also stressed that even Feofan, once one of Rasputin's greatest patrons, had seen the light about Rasputin and was now speaking out against him and had severed all ties to the bogus starets. After reading Novoselov's article, Feofan wrote him to say that Rasputin was beyond saving: "He falls ever further into delusion and under the spell of a demonic power, he has passed over to the dark side for good and insists, through his utterances of falsehoods, on dwelling in the land of lies."[13]

The *Moscow Gazette* did not stop there. It returned to the matter on 30 April, singling out for ridicule words from a speech of Iliodor's recently printed in some of the Tsaritsyn newspapers in which he stated that yes, it was true Rasputin "loves women very much, caresses and kisses them, but not in the manner of sinful people, but with some sort of special holiness." This, the paper insisted, only served to prove he was a khlyst, and as such belonged to a sect deemed by law to be harmful and impermissible. Tikhomirov and the newspaper demanded answers: Why isn't the Synod investigating Rasputin? Why isn't the Chief Procurator concerned? If what has been published were true, and Rasputin were indeed a khlyst, then how can the Synod allow its priests such as Iliodor to publicly defend him? "The personality of Grigory Rasputin must be brought to light and this seduction must be stopped," cried the *Moscow Gazette*.[14]

Tikhomirov had tried to use the press to open the eyes of the tsar to the truth (as he saw it) about Rasputin and the danger he represented to the throne. He failed. Once news of the scandal reached him, Nicholas was deeply disappointed by Tikhomirov's actions, and the tsar now refused to see him. Tikhomirov was hurt and saddened by the news, but felt no regret: "Fine then, so be it. I simply must expose spiritual depravity." Stolypin later told Tikhomirov that his act had been heroic, but in losing the favor of the tsar it had cost him dearly. The disappointment was mutual, though greater for Tikhomirov: he lost all faith in his sovereign, and in this disenchantment one sees how Rasputin helped to turn the emperor's loyal supporters into foes. Tikhomirov spoke of his profound disillusionment and pessimism for Russia's future in his diary:

> With such an emperor nothing but revolutionary "sedition" is possible. [. . .] A "Russian *intelligent*" has come to the throne, not, of course, some revolutionary type, rather a "liberal," weak-willed, friable type, one with a "beautiful soul," who has absolutely no understanding of the true laws of life [. . .] There is no tsar, and no one wants one . . . And the church . . . it too is crumbling. Faith is disappearing . . . Oh, Russian people![15]

The attack launched by the monarchist *Moscow Gazette* was soon followed by similar attacks in the liberal press, chiefly in *Speech*, the newspaper of the Constitutional Democrat (Kadet) party. Between 20 May and 26 June, *Speech* ran ten articles titled "Rasputin-Novykh" claiming to be the first in-depth look at the life of the "criminal starets." The series detailed in lurid fashion the strange harem of twelve beautiful young women selected from across Siberia that Rasputin kept prisoner at his Pokrovskoe home. They lived in great luxury, yet trembled under his violent will. No one, not even his wife, dared say a word in protest. His power was limitless. "He can do everything," one of the women was reported as saying. She, like some of the others, wanted to escape, but knew this was impossible. Rasputin had also recruited two male followers, startsy like himself, and had given them permission to keep two "sisters," along with their legal wives, for their own pleasure. The articles admitted that Rasputin did possess special gifts, notably his ability to tell people's fortunes, but stressed his perverse moral vision. "I have in me an element of Jesus Christ, and only through me can one be saved. And so it is necessary to merge with me in both body and soul. Everything that flows from me is the source of light washing away all sins," *Speech* quoted Rasputin as saying.[16] The author was identified only as "S. V." It is possible that the man hiding behind these initials was Father Vladimir Vostokov, a liberal priest who was to become one of Rasputin's most implacable foes and then, following the Bolshevik coup, a noxious proponent of the "Jewish-Masonic" plot to destroy Russia.[17] The series in *Speech* proved wildly popular and was soon reprinted by a number of publications in cities across Russia.[18]

The Yekaterinoslav newspaper *Southern Dawn* ran a lengthy article in several installments on the life of Rasputin between 30 May and 4 June. The author, Alexander Senin, claimed to have lived for a time in Pokrovskoe and met Rasputin in early 1907. Senin's piece was full of lies and outlandish tales and repeated much of what had appeared in the other articles that spring. He included a story about two healthy young girls who went to live with Rasputin, grew sick and weak and then died in mysterious circumstances, and about another girl who became pregnant while living with the Rasputins and strangely disappeared without a trace.[19]

Speech reported in May that Rasputin had looked to Iliodor and Germogen to come to his defense. Germogen had supposedly already arrived in the capital to rehabilitate Rasputin; and having made such strong speeches on Rasputin's behalf in April, Iliodor was expected soon as well. Their intentions, however, were said to be partially self-serving. The story noted how for the past two or three years, Germogen and Iliodor had felt themselves to be especially powerful, and this was due in large part to their connections to Rasputin. Back in Tsaritsyn that spring, Iliodor continued his public defense of Rasputin, *Speech* wrote, going so far as to liken him to an Old Testament prophet and calling him a saint.[20]

The monarchist writer, publisher, and Orthodox missionary Vasily Skvortsov offered his interpretation of Rasputin on the pages of *Tsaritsyn Thought* in July. He considered Rasputin a man with a highly refined psychological "flair," an example of those startsy, all quite gifted, from the "depths of the world of the khlysty." In this regard, he saw Rasputin's prototype in a starets by the name of Stefan. First appearing about twenty-five years earlier, he, too, had attracted the attention of the authorities, was investigated and then exiled to Suzdal, where he took orders and still lived as a monk in the local monastery. Stefan had been a miracle worker, with the aid of hypnosis. He would hypnotize women seeking his spiritual help, and then, under hypnosis and with the use of strange passes of his hands, convince them that their soul had been invaded by a "demon" and their only hope was to permit him to exorcize it. This he did by conversing with the demon as he stroked the woman's chest and shoulders, slowly making his way down the body. Only after he had had sex with the woman could he claim to have driven out the evil presence. Skvortsov wondered whether Rasputin, like Stefan, had been employing the same method with his victims. In a follow-up article, the newspaper elaborated that this very Stefan had raped two hundred young women after luring them to his monastery with his "Rasputinist theories on the sanctity of the flesh." Stefan and Rasputin, *Tsaritsyn Thought* concluded, were two of a kind.[21]

By now the foreign embassies had taken notice. In a report dated 7 April/25 March 1910, the Austrian ambassador, Leopold Graf Berchthold, wrote to Vienna with news of the growing scandal: "As before the frequent presence of a suspected priest from a sect outlawed by the police in the intimate sphere of the Empress has been causing great concern for ladies at court and every attempt to alert the Sovereign Lady to the harmful effects of such interaction has been completely fruitless."[22] If the ambassador thought Rasputin untouchable, the press was reporting that he was finished. *Tsaritsyn Thought* ran a story under the title "The End of Rasputin" on 13 June. "The debates in Tsaritsyn have ended," it began. "Everyone has been forced to recognize that Rasputin is a rogue, a reprobate, a vile hunter after money and women."[23]

Nicholas was furious as the newspaper campaign grew throughout the spring. He sent Stolypin a note stating in the strongest language that he had had enough of the articles, that no one had the right to comment on his private affairs, and that he was to stop such articles at once. The tsar also let his prime minister know that he should have put an end to the business already.[24] But things were not that simple. The political reforms following the Revolution of 1905 largely guaranteed freedom of the press, although publishers continued to be harassed and fined and at times even shut down for exceeding the boundaries of what was deemed tolerable. Indeed, under Stolypin in 1907–09 hundreds of newspapers had been suspended and over three hundred editors had been sentenced to prison. Editors of some of the leading papers—Alexei Suvorin of *New Times* and Iosef Gessen of *Speech*, for example—were already under Okhrana surveillance in 1910. But the chief of the police department's press division pointed out to Stolypin that even if some of the Rasputin articles contained elements that might be considered criminal, it was only once the newspapers had been printed that this would become known to the police and by then it was too late to prevent copies from getting out to the public.[25]

Nevertheless, Stolypin had to do something. He met with Alexei Belgard, head of the State Administration for Matters of the Press, and asked for his advice. Belgard agreed that it was not legal to simply shut the newspapers down, so they decided to make a list of the most important papers and speak to each of the editors individually, asking them to refrain from touching on the matter of Rasputin in the future. Some, like Prince Meshchersky of the *Citizen*, reluctantly agreed; others, like Iosef Gessen of *Speech*, on the other hand, said he would be happy to stop writing about Rasputin, as soon as he disappeared and there was no more reason for the press to concern itself with him.[26] At the same time Stolypin instructed Alexander Makarov, the deputy minister of the interior, to write to the Moscow City Governor Alexander Adrianov to inform him of "the complete undesirability of the appearance in the organs of the periodical press of any articles or reports on the peasant of the Tobolsk province, Tyumen district, village of Pokrovskoe by the name of Grigory Yefimovich Rasputin-Novykh." Should this happen, however, Adrianov was ordered to immediately get in contact with the responsible editors and publishers and inform them of this wish, but "Do so in the most polite and correct while at the same time convincing and insistent manner, without, however, resorting to threats of administrative punishment, influencing said editors and publishers by way of your powers of persuasion and authority."[27] On 15 December, Adrianov called in Tikhomirov and apprised him of the government's wish. "This is simply terrible," Tikhomirov replied.[28]

The police began to search the press for the slightest mention of Rasputin. Every article no matter how small or insignificant would be clipped and saved in special folders in the police archives. And it did not end there. The police started monitoring the foreign press as well. These publications, chiefly in Europe and Britain, were scanned for references to Rasputin, the articles then cut, translated into Russian, and filed. An interview the revolutionary exile Vladimir Burtsev gave the French paper *L'Humanité* in April 1912, for example, ended up in the Okhrana files on Rasputin, along with a scandalous article by Princess Catherine Radziwill from the Swedish *Dagens Nyheter*. When, in 1912, Russian agents in Germany overheard talk of a sensationalized novel about Rasputin soon to be published there, an order went out from the secret police to agents in Berlin, Paris, and St. Petersburg to uncover every detail about the book. On 9 November 1913, an overview of the foreign press prepared for the minister of the interior included an article from the *Rheinisch-Westfälische Zeitung* chronicling Rasputin's growing influence over the Russian emperor and empress.[29]

By that autumn the press campaign against Rasputin had died down, although the reasons why are not clear. It may be that the measures of the ministry of the interior had had the desired effect or it may have had something to do with the fact that the royal family had left Russia to take the waters in Germany.[30] Whatever the reason, the lull marked not the end of hostilities, only a brief ceasefire. The first shots in the war over Rasputin had been fired, and nothing would stop his enemies now.

20. In Search of Rasputin

Just like Tyutcheva and Feofan, the press had failed to force Nicholas and Alexandra to break from Rasputin. Nonetheless, the press could not help reporting with unwarranted glee in May 1910 that Rasputin had been arrested and exiled to Pokrovskoe without the right of return.[1] Rasputin was, indeed, absent from court from the spring of 1910 until February 1911, which may well have been by some sort of mutual understanding between him and their majesties to stay away until the scandals had died down. In May, Rasputin left Petersburg for a meeting with Germogen and Iliodor in Saratov and from there returned to Pokrovskoe for the summer. He was missed at court, where Alexandra was ill. On 8 August, Nikolai Sablin wired Rasputin from Petersburg: "Pray. Lift Mama's spirit. She's not well. With you in my thoughts. We often recall you, very sad without you. I kiss you. Are you coming?"[2]

Rasputin did come to the capital, though it is not known whether he visited the palace. The police tracked him down in the third week of August to an apartment on 8 Kuznechny Lane that belonged to Georgy Sazonov and his wife, Maria.[3] Sazonov was a mediocre writer and publisher described by Count Witte as an "abnormal" man. He started out on the extreme political left in the later years of the nineteenth century before migrating to the right following the 1905 Revolution, drawn first to the Black Hundreds and figures like the politician Vladimir Purishkevich and then increasingly to various right-wing religious types like Iliodor and Germogen then on the rise and to whom Sazonov hoped to hitch his fortunes.[4] The Sazonovs were friendly with the Lokhtins, and it was Olga who told Georgy that Rasputin would like to meet him.[5] Rasputin came to the Sazonovs and it was clear he felt himself welcome there. Sazonov knew he was taking a risk given all the talk about Rasputin then in the air but he did not let this stop him, and he did not regret his decision.

I found myself looking into the characteristic face of a hermit from a Byzantine painting, gaunt, stern with deeply-seated, penetrating eyes. What struck one most was his exceptional nervousness, the jumpiness of his movements. The stamp of his soul was that of a mystic. Devout faith yet the absence of the signs of religiosity. The sincerity of his tone. His speech was abrupt, disjointed, and seemed to jump about. No narcissism, no masks. None of this matched the description the press had given of him. The stamp of his soul, his entire nature, his human form, it was entirely different.[6]

Sazonov invited Rasputin to stay with them. The household was impressed by his devotion. A servant came one day to tell Georgy about how their new guest did not sleep nights but stayed up praying. On visits to the family dacha, Rasputin would go out at night into the woods and pray intensely for hours at a time. Feofan had noted the same thing about him, commenting that the depth of his praying was something he had only rarely seen among the most holy of monks. It was not long before rumors started that Rasputin was having an affair with Maria Sazonova. This cannot be verified, but what is known for certain is that Rasputin and the Sazonovs remained on friendly terms up until Rasputin's death and Sazonov never doubted Rasputin's morals.[7] Witte characterized Sazonov's relationship to Rasputin as "something analogous to the curator of a museum showing off his exotic creatures." If Witte is to be believed, Sazonov used his connections to his new houseguest to further his own career well beyond where his modest talents could have taken him.[8]

One of the men he introduced Rasputin to then was the publicist Mikhail Menshikov. A member of the Bogdanovich salon, Menshikov had heard all the gossip about Rasputin and was curious to finally meet him. They dined together and talked for a long time. Menshikov was struck at how young Rasputin was, not at all like a starets was supposed to be, and how this nearly still wild Siberian peasant could have managed to have risen up so high. As they talked, Menshikov became increasingly amazed by Rasputin. He dubbed him a "natural philosopher from the very bottom of the peasant masses," barely literate but someone with a great knowledge of Scripture and a gifted mind. Some of Rasputin's expressions Menshikov found undeniably original and even profound, strangely similar to the kind of thing said by ancient oracles, a modern-day Pythia, the prophetess at Delphi. There was something a bit cunning in him, Menshikov thought, but not in a bad way, and he came away believing Rasputin was just the sort of man capable of waking up the great majority of Russian Orthodox believers from their "lethargic sleep." The only thing he did not like about the man were his boots—tall, stiff, shiny, and black, what Russians called "bottles"—that were too fancy, too elegant on a supposed starets from the people.[9] No, the Rasputin Menshikov had met in no way corresponded with what he had heard about at the Bogdanoviches' home. He later said as much during a salon gathering, insisting Rasputin was in fact a sincere, true Christian. His words were met with skeptical silence.[10]

Sometime later Rasputin asked Sazonov whether he might not bring his daughter Maria to live with them as well, to which he agreed, in part because he had a daughter just around the same age, and the girls became fast friends. Her father had earlier taken Maria to Kazan to go to the Mariinsky School, but she was lonely there so he brought her to Petersburg, where she was enrolled in the Steblin-Kamensky School on Liteiny Prospect. Later, her sister Varvara joined her there and both of them became boarders, coming home to see their father and the rest of the family on holidays. The sisters had originally gone to the local village school in Pokrovskoe, but, according to Maria, the empress had decided they should get a better education and it was at her urging that Rasputin put them in a fine school in the capital. Dmitry was sent to Saratov to study under Germogen, but he never took to book learning and missed life at home and so returned to Pokrovskoe. Praskovya did visit the capital several times with her husband, although she preferred Pokrovskoe. So, too, did Rasputin's father. Yefim visited Petersburg only once. He found the noise and commotion overwhelming. Maria wrote that before daring to cross the street, he made the sign of the cross and then cautiously headed out into the swarm of automobiles.[11]

The police reported on 24 August that Rasputin had left Petersburg for Moscow. The Moscow Okhrana was notified, but as late as 24 October they were still unable to locate him. The Okhrana sent agents to check at Tsarskoe Selo; here, too, they found no trace.[12] Rasputin's whereabouts throughout the final months of 1910 became a matter of considerable speculation. *Russia's Morning* reported on 14 September that Rasputin had earlier been banished from the capital and other

major cities in central Russia and that for over two months he had been
lobbying to be permitted to return and had, indeed, finally arrived back
in St. Petersburg.[13] The next day *The Rudder* wrote to correct that story,
insisting Rasputin was actually renting a dacha near Vyritsa, about an
hour's train ride south of the city. "The goal of his arrival," the newspaper pronounced with false authority, "is to rehabilitate himself."[14]
That same day another paper reported that Rasputin's attempts to
secure a meeting with the Synod, a step in his rehabilitation, had failed;
he had been forbidden once more from living in the capital and had
decided to settle outside the city of Tver.[15]

Meanwhile, the police kept looking. As minister of the interior,
under whose authority were the various police agencies, including the
department of the police, the Okhrana, and the corps of gendarmes,
Stolypin ordered his agents to find Rasputin.[16] On 24 October, Stolypin
received a secret report from the St. Petersburg Okhrana stating that
Rasputin was not in the capital or its environs. Okhrana agents had
been to question Sazonov on his whereabouts. Sazonov told them Rasputin had stayed with him in August and then left for Moscow, but that
he was now back "in his homeland." Sazonov said he was expecting
Rasputin's wife from Siberia any day. The Okhrana had also heard
reports that Rasputin had been to Tsarskoe Selo on his last visit, but an
agent sent there to inquire on the validity of the rumor found it to be
baseless. Finally, telegrams had been sent to Moscow and Tobolsk for
any further information on Rasputin's whereabouts. Stolypin instructed
that should Rasputin return to the capital he was to be placed under
"very careful surveillance."

Two days later another confidential report was prepared and then
soon after recorded in the "Secret Journal" of the police department's
Special Section (*Osobyi otdel*):

> Herewith the details I have gathered by secret method into the
> investigation of the case of Grigory Yefimovich Rasputin-Novy,
> peasant of the Tobolsk province, Tyumen district, volost and vil-
> lage of Pokrovskoe:
>
> Physical description: 38–40 years old, height—tall, hair—
> light-brown, eyes with deep sockets. It is not known where he is
> now or is living, but this could be discovered: by interviews with
> various people, secret observation, etc. Information is now to hand
> that Rasputin is currently living with his female friend Olga Vladi-
> mirovna Lokhtina, the wife of an engineer, who lives somewhere

on the S[mall] Okhta [River], although, most likely, without being legally registered. 5 days ago he, Rasputin, was seen riding in a cab to the ferry near the church of St. Mary Magdalene on the S. Okhta. He was likely riding from Lokhtina's to his follower and patroness, the former maid-of-honor Anna Alexandrovna Vyrubova, who lives in Tsarskoe Selo at No. 2 Church Street. The fact that she, Lokhtina, lives on the S. Lakhta [*sic*] was said by her acquaintance and follower of Rasputin—a certain Yekaterina, a teacher or instructor at the profess.[ional] sewing school on Liteiny Pr. in house No. 58. And Lokhtina's husband—engineer and State Councilor Vladimir Mikhailovich Lokhtin, who lives at the corner of 5th Street and Grechesky Prosp., could also provide valuable information on this case since he is not living with his wife at the moment. Lokhtina herself has become a fanatic and considers Rasputin almost Our Savior Jesus Christ, although everyone actually considers Rasputin a criminal and khlyst; he abused the sister of the wife of Father Vasily Grigorevich Spiridonov,* who lives at Sivkovskaya Street, No. 32 near St. Sergei of Radonezh Church, and other women.

Many people know Rasputin and have been most hospitable to him until recently, for instance, homeowners—D. N. Novikov, Pavel Polikarpovich Smirnov, the merchants Petrov, the former publisher of the newspaper *Russia* Georgy Petrovich Sazonov and others. This Rasputin was even frequently received at the Imperial Court through Maria Ivanovna Vishnyakova, the governess of His Imperial Highness and Heir, Grand Duke Alexei Nikolaevich.

Upon reading the report, Stolypin ordered a secret investigation into the case of Rasputin.[17]

At the same time efforts were also being made by the police in Siberia to find Rasputin. Major General Velk in Tobolsk cabled Captain Chufarovsky in Tyumen on 25 October to have him find the "peasant Grigorii Yefimovich Novy." Three days later Tyumen police reported that other than one trip that summer to Petersburg, Rasputin had been in Pokrovskoe since spring.[18] (So much for the report of his being sighted earlier in the month riding through the streets of St. Petersburg. The tsarist police were frequently as ignorant of Rasputin

---

* Rasputin's former acolyte Yelena Timofeeva.

and his whereabouts as the press.) On 28 October, a telegram arrived from Tobolsk confirming Rasputin was in Pokrovskoe.[19]

Two days later, on 30 October 1910, the Petersburg branch of the Okhrana, headed by Mikhail von Koten, issued a "Top Secret" order to gather more information on Rasputin and his whereabouts and to establish where he had been throughout the summer and early autumn. Replies soon came in. The first was from Alexei Prelin, a junior officer in the Tyumen City Gendarmes Administration, sent from Pokrovskoe on 13 November to the head of Tobolsk Provincial Gendarmes. Prelin reported that in early August Rasputin had left with his daughter Maria to take her to study in Kazan. Then he visited Petersburg and returned to Pokrovskoe, where he had most recently been seen "making merry" and marking the holidays together with three nuns.[20]

Prelin's description of Rasputin's mood is curiously at odds with that reflected in "My Life in Fear with Jesus," a short piece that Rasputin wrote on 4 December 1910 while in Petersburg.

> I have trust in you, God, and I am not ashamed of it. I will praise You, my enemies don't leave me in peace. They are trying to catch me day and night, wherever I go, my words would be distorted and presented in their own way, people have become like beasts and God's grace is far away. I will say in my soul: Jesus, be my Creator and Protector, and the enemies will follow me and will have raids to catch me and will shoot arrows into my soul and will penetrate me with their sly gazes and will want to take the truth away; but they cannot, they won't be able to take it [. . .] While evil tongues spread slander, many have died from sorrow: but this is a martyr's crown.
>
> Jesus also suffered and had hard moments with his cross. And His cross remained on those that loved Him and it still is with those who suffer for Christ. There are enemies who still chase and catch Christians. God, thousands have ganged up against me [. . .] how long will the wicked triumph, show us God's fledglings. [. . .] How have all my enemies come together putting spies everywhere. The spies are happy about the victory of their courage, let's take the simpleton and put ashes on his head instead of balm. [. . .]
>
> Nowadays one is not tortured with spears but with words — they hurt more than arrows. And all the words are arrows that hit stronger than a sword.
>
> Jesus! Save those close to you![21]

It had indeed been a trying year for Rasputin, perhaps the most difficult of his life. He was feeling attacked from all corners. His name, covered in infamy, was by now known across the empire, and his enemies felt not the least compunction in writing the most outlandish lies about him in the country's newspapers. The police had taken notice as well, and but for a few brief spells, he would be watched, followed, tracked, and monitored by agents of the state for the rest of his life. Having lost his anonymity, Rasputin would never again know peace.

Rasputin shared his words with the empress and she wrote them down to save. Alexandra commiserated with him and believed in the truth of what he had written. By the end of the year, Rasputin had regained whatever trust he might have lost with their majesties. The writer Ippolit Gofshtetter met Lev Tikhomirov in Moscow to tell him that Rasputin once more enjoyed the "tender love" of the emperor and empress and had amassed "enormous influence." Distraught, Tikhomirov wrote in his diary on 13 December: "They can't be saved. 'Mene, tekel, peres.'* Oh, what a reign with all these Grishka Rasputins!"[22]

---

* From Daniel, 5:26–28. A reference to the three words that mysteriously appeared on the wall during a feast of the Babylonian king Belshazzar that foretold the fall of his empire in the sixth century BC. It was Daniel who managed to decipher the words and their meaning.

21. Prince Yusupov

The Yusupovs were one of Russia's wealthiest and oldest aristocratic families, claiming a lineage that went back to a nephew of the Prophet Mohammad and the rulers of ancient Egypt. The family joined the court of Ivan the Terrible in the sixteenth century, having first come to Russia centuries earlier as warlords for the conquering Mongols from the east. The family converted to Orthodoxy and were granted the title of prince and vast lands by the subsequent tsars. Prince Felix Yusupov's mother, Princess Zinaida Yusupova, was beautiful if vain and controlling. According to the Spanish Infanta Eulalia, the daughter of Queen Isabella II of Spain, Zinaida possessed "the majestic splendor of a Byzantine Empress. [. . .] She lived in extraordinary luxury, in a setting of unsurpassed splendour [. . .] The magnificence and luxury of Russia, blended with the refinement and distinction of France, reached its culmination point in the Yusupov palace."[1] The furniture in her petite salon in the family's Petersburg palace on the Moika had belonged to Marie Antoinette.

In 1882, the princess, aged twenty-one, married Count Felix Sumarokov-Elston, whose father, Count Felix Nikolaevich Elston, was believed to be the illegitimate son of King Frederick Wilhelm IV of Prussia and a lady-in-waiting at court. Felix père took the surname Elston from his English nanny to which he added Sumarokov upon his marriage to Countess Yelena Sumarokova. The Sumarokovs were a distinguished Russian family, but nothing to compare with the Yusupovs, and so the tsar granted Zinaida, an only child and the last of the princes Yusupov, and her new husband the right to bear the joint title Princes Yusupov and Counts Sumarokov-Elston.[2] Felix was a cold, rigid man, but he was not without a sense of romantic extravagance: he once bought his wife a mountain for her birthday.[3] For many years he served as an adjutant to Grand Duke Sergei Alexandrovich and then later, after the grand duke's assassination, as governor-general of Moscow, an office the count was fired from after his failure to prevent horrific anti-German riots in 1915.

The couple had two sons: Nikolai, born in 1883, and Felix, in 1887. Nikolai had been the jewel of his parents' eye. He graduated from the law faculty of St. Petersburg University, was a gifted writer (publishing under the pen name "Rokov"), an amateur actor and founder of a comedy troupe. He had plans to join one of the elite guards regiments when he was killed in a duel in June 1908 at the age of twenty-five by Count Arvid Manteifel, after falling in love with the count's wife, Countess Marina Heiden.[4] Zinaida was devastated and never fully recovered. She turned to holy men for spiritual guidance, eventually placing her faith in John of Kronstadt, who she, and Felix, believed was capable of miracle cures via prayer. Both mother and son were convinced his prayers had once saved her life when the doctors had announced she was beyond all hope.

Young Felix was nothing like his golden brother. As a child, Felix wrote in his memoirs, he was sickly, spoiled, ill-behaved, and a bad pupil. And as he grew, these traits only worsened. "I was wayward," he recalled, "and extremely lazy." Not surprisingly, this caused his parents considerable anguish. The Felix Yusupov that is described in his memoirs borders on a caricature of the vain and spoiled aristocrat for whom everything is permitted, nothing is to be taken too seriously, and the entire world and all the things (and people) in it have been created for his own use and enjoyment. Nothing held his attention for long, and Felix's life amounted to a search for intense experiences and thrill-seeking that began with cross-dressing and eventually ended in murder.

Among his pastimes as a youth was to dress up as a sultan and adorn himself with his mother's jewels and force the family's Arab, Tatar, and African servants to play the part of slaves to his omnipotent Oriental satrap in the decadent Moorish room at the Moika palace. The role playing, what he liked to call "tableaux vivants," once went so far Felix almost stabbed to death a servant acting the part of a disobedient slave. Only the unexpected appearance of his father ended the charade, to the great relief, no doubt, of the family servants.[5]

Not lacking imagination, Felix enjoyed fleeing into the identities of others, often men stronger and more powerful than himself. At the family country estate of Arkhangelskoe outside Moscow he pretended to be his ancestor Prince Nicholas Yusupov, a fabulously wealthy patron of the arts who a century earlier reigned over his estate like an absolute monarch. Prince Nicholas had kept a theater troupe composed of his own serfs, and Felix liked to sit in the empty theater and imagine the serfs had come back to life and were now singing and dancing for him. At times, he dreamed he was the star singer of the theater, and was "so carried away by my imagination that the ghosts of past audiences seemed to come to life and applaud me." When the dream came crashing down, Felix would be crushed. His first sexual encounter (if we can believe his memoirs) was a ménage à trois with an Argentinean man and his concubine at a hotel in Contrexéville at the age of twelve. So overwhelming was the experience that "in my youthful ignorance, I failed to discriminate between the sexes."

As adolescents he and his cousin Vladimir Lazarev enjoyed putting on Princess Yusupova's jewels, velvet pelisses and wigs, and strolling Nevsky Prospect in the hope of catching the eye of the men there trying to make a date with one of the many prostitutes. One time, when they began attracting more attention than they could handle, the boys fled to a grand restaurant, where they were invited to dine in a private room with a group of young officers. Although he was punished for this, once he had a taste Felix could not stop. His brother's lover began dressing him up and out he would go. "I began to lead a double life: by day I was a schoolboy and by night an elegant woman." Even while visiting Paris, young Felix preferred visiting the Opera and the *café-concerts* in drag. Back in Petersburg, he so impressed the manager of The Aquarium Cafe that he was given a two-week engagement as a singer, the manager having no idea that he had not only hired a man, but one from one of Russia's most illustrious families. His career as a cabaret singer was cut short after his identity was discovered, though the fondness for cross-dressing persisted.

His brother kept a watchful eye on him, fearful how far Felix might take matters, but he could not always keep him out of trouble, like the time Felix accepted an invitation from four guards officers, led by a notorious Don Juan who was courting Felix "assiduously," to dine at The Bear. They took to a private room, but just how far the merry-making went, Felix carefully leaves out in his memoir. Felix's double life eventually became known to his parents, and his outraged father upbraided him as a disgrace to the family, a "guttersnipe and a scoundrel," deserving of exile to a Siberian convict settlement. He tried to cure his son with icy showers every morning. His life in drag came to an end, and in an attempt to please his parents, he tried to take an interest in women, though, as he wrote, this only made his life "even more complicated" since "being accustomed to adulation, I quickly tired of doing the courting and cared for no one but myself. [...] I liked to be a star surrounded by admirers."

Both Yusupov brothers were drawn to spiritualism and attended séances. Each promised that were he to die first, he would come back and appear before his brother. (Felix later claimed that his brother did in fact come to him one night in spirit form.) Felix apparently took this interest further than his brother, immersing himself in the occult and theosophy and yoga. Madame Freya, a clairvoyant in Paris, told him: "In a few years you will take part in a political assassination and will go through a terrible ordeal which will end in a complete victory for you." Convinced he was illuminated by a divine truth, he set out to develop what he believed were his own latent superhuman powers through a series of breathing exercises, eventually convincing himself that he had developed considerable hypnotic power that gave him control not only over his own perception of pain, but such force of will that he could control other persons as well. In his memoirs Yusupov claims that during his years in England as a student at Oxford he was inexplicably endowed with a strange ocular phenomenon of premonition: once while dining with a friend of his parents a strange cloud appeared before him. He took this as a bad omen, and indeed, within days the man was dead. If there was one power greater than himself, then it was opium, which he first tasted in Paris before the war, and could not stay away from despite his best efforts.[6]

Anna Vyrubova had known Felix for years and considered herself to be an old and trusted friend. She wrote him heartfelt letters upon the death of his brother, and offered not just her sympathies but advice as well:

> The time has come for you, dear Felix, and may God give you the strength to organize your life now as God requires. So much has been given to you, and more will be asked of you than of anyone else. Until now you have been nothing but a child who has thought only about how best to have fun and pass the time, isn't that right? Now that the Lord has called dear Nikolai to him it is on you alone that all the responsibilities to your parents lie, and also for all those things that God has given us.[7]

Although truly saddened by his brother's death, the younger Yusupov could not help but realize that this meant he was now the sole heir to the family fortune: "I realized that all this would some day be mine [. . .] The idea that I would one day be one of the richest men in Russia went to my head like wine. [. . .] Wealth, splendor, power: I could not imagine life without them," he confessed. Felix sought spiritual guidance from Ella, Empress Alexandra's sister, after his brother's death. She urged him to place his faith in God, to believe and trust in his infinite love and wisdom. Although he found some relief in her words, he feared God would never forgive him his sexual transgressions. He confided this to her, but Ella encouraged him to have no fear, for "Anyone who is capable of doing much evil is also capable of doing much good, if he sets about it the right way. No matter how serious the offense, it is redeemed by sincere repentance. Remember, the only thing that defiles the soul is spiritual sin; it can remain pure in spite of carnal weakness."[8] Her words could well have been spoken by Rasputin himself.

The Yusupovs were frequent guests at the Ilinskoe estate of Grand Duke Sergei Alexandrovich and his wife, Ella. It was here Felix met Grand Duke Dmitry Pavlovich and his sister Maria Pavlovna, who lived there with their aunt and uncle—their father, Grand Duke Paul Alexandrovich, having been forced to leave Russia due to his morganatic marriage to divorcée Olga Pistolkors (later Princess Paley) in 1902. Dmitry and Maria's father, the youngest son of Tsar Alexander II, had first been married to Princess Alexandra of Greece—a daughter of King George I and Queen Olga Konstantinovna, a Russian grand duchess— who died in 1891 while giving birth to Dmitry at the age of twenty-one. Maria remembered her "Aunt Ella" as haughty, cold, and vain, if beautiful: "[. . .] one of the most beautiful women I have ever seen in my life. She was tall and slight, of blonde coloring, with features of extraordinary fineness and purity." Her "gray-blue" eyes had a "cold, hard look" that "chilled me to the heart." One had the sense she kept herself hidden behind a mask. All of this changed when Sergei was blown up by a terrorist's bomb in the heart of Moscow in February 1905. Ella, who heard the blast and went out to collect the bloody scraps of his shattered body from the snow, turned away from worldly things, devoted herself to religion, and founded the Convent of Martha and Mary dedicated to aiding Moscow's poor. She also drew close to her niece and nephew; Maria wrote that henceforth Aunt Ella and Dmitry were "bound together by a bond of real affection until the day when events separated them forever." According to Felix, Dmitry simply adored Ella.

Dmitry grew to be tall and handsome. Before the outbreak of World War I, he served in the Imperial Horse Guards and lived with the royal family in the Alexander Palace. Maria described her brother in these years as "a dashing young officer," full of confidence, brio, and charm. He was treated like a son by Nicholas and Alexandra, both of whom were captivated by his playful personality.[9] Dmitry's letters to his "dear Uncle," sprinkled with sexual innuendo and scatological humor, reveal the great warmth and ease the young man felt toward the tsar.[10] It was rumored in 1912 that Dmitry was betrothed to their eldest daughter, Grand Duchess Olga. Alexandra, however, was apparently against the match, for there were elements of his life she did not approve of. It has been suggested that Dmitry was bisexual and was then in love with Felix, which was the main reason for the empress's disapproval.[11] This may be, but it cannot be said for certain. What is beyond doubt is that Alexandra never stopped worrying about what she called Dmitry's "evening escapades." She was convinced Dmitry was far too impressionable and too easily susceptible to the whims of whomever he was most drawn to at the moment. As late as February 1916 she was writing to Nicholas to send Dmitry back to his regiment as she was hearing "shocking" stories about him in town. "Town & women are poison for him."[12]

The empress's characterization of Dmitry is corroborated by what Felix later had to say:

> Dmitri was extremely attractive: tall, elegant, well-bred, with deep thoughtful eyes, he recalled the portraits of his ancestors. He was all impulses and contradictions; he was both romantic and mystical, and his mind was far from shallow. At the same time, he was very gay and always ready for the wildest escapades. His charm won the hearts of all, but the weakness of his character made him dangerously easy to influence. As I was a few years his senior, I had a certain prestige in his eyes. He was to a certain extent familiar with my "scandalous" life and considered me interesting and a trifle mysterious. He trusted me and valued my opinion, and he not only confided his innermost thoughts to me but used to tell me about everything that was happening around him.

Of the thirty-seven pages devoted to his forebears in Felix's memoirs, only two discuss his father's side of the family. Felix had almost no relation with his father, and a suffocatingly close one with his mother. She was the one true love of Felix's life, and, after the death of Nikolai, Felix was hers. Like Empress Alexandra, Zinaida suffered from nervous fits that, though they had no physical basis, were profoundly debilitating. The only one who could soothe her in such moments was her beloved boy.[13] "Alas, she was a tragic mother—she spoiled her children far too much," Grand Duchess Olga Alexandrovna remarked.[14] At the age of twenty-nine, Felix was still writing his mother to stomp his feet and insist he was a man: "Really, I'm no longer a little baby who must be afraid that he might be punished. Don't forget that I'm almost 30, that I'm married, and that we are entitled to our own private lives."[15]

Zinaida had wanted to control everything. She decided when he was to get married and to whom. Felix went along with as much enthusiasm as he could muster. Irina Alexandrovna was the daughter of Grand Duke Alexander Mikhailovich (Sandro) and Grand Duchess Xenia Alexandrovna, thus making her a granddaughter of Alexander III and a niece of Nicholas II. She was eight years Felix's junior, and she was beautiful. The only competition for her hand was Felix's friend Dmitry, but in the end she chose Felix. They were married on 9 February 1914 at the Anichkov Palace. The tsar led her down the aisle. They honeymooned in France, Egypt, and the Holy Land. Felix found Jerusalem unpleasant. He was repelled by the disease and the "horrible stench" of the poor; their audience with the patriarch he found "tiresome."[16]

The Yusupov household was staunchly anti-Rasputin. Felix's father could not bear even to hear the name spoken in his presence, and his mother let the empress know of her hatred for the man, which poisoned their relations for good.[17] Felix's attitude toward Rasputin was profoundly shaped by his parents, and by Ella, too, and so it is something of a surprise that he seems to have sought out an introduction to Rasputin. The woman who brought the two men together was a dear friend by the name of Munya Golovina.

Golovina had known Felix and his brother for years, and she had harbored a secret love for the older Yusupov at the time of his death. In her memoirs, Golovina writes how the three of them, always ready for new experiences, went one dark day late in 1907 to visit a mysterious new magician-occultist by the name of Chinsky. Disguised to hide their identities, they visited Chinsky's small studio and had him tell their fortunes. He told them they stood on the precipice of a large catas-trophe, but they could avoid it if they would return and permit him (for a fee) to instruct them in the ways of the occult. Nikolai was thrilled by Chinsky and they continued their visits, telling Chinsky of their lives, passions, desires, and fears, and permitting him to offer guidance and instruction.

Munya was terribly grieved by Nikolai's death. She asked her mother, Lyubov Golovina, to take her to Italy so she could try to put it behind her. Upon her return to Moscow, Felix picked her up in his auto-mobile and drove to Arkhangelskoe, where Munya prayed over Nikolai's grave. She continued her engagement with spiritualism and the occult, seeking answers to her suffering. She later wrote that she had made great strides in her mental powers: by asking herself questions and then concentrating all the energy of her mind on the answers, she was able to practice the art of "automatic writing," words mysteriously appearing on the page with no one holding the pen. Still, she was not fulfilled, her life nothing but pain and confusion. She considered entering Ella's convent.

It was then she heard from her cousin Alexandra (Sana) Taneeva, the sister of Anna Vyrubova, about a mysterious holy pilgrim who had come to Petersburg and won the trust of the emperor and empress. She went to Sana's one day to meet him. From the moment she saw him Munya was moved by his person. He seemed to her "full of mystery and drawn to the supernatural." It was crowded, and so Munya was not able to tell him of her plight, but he put his hand on her head and told her she would be one of the chosen and that he would see her again. Munya was distraught. She needed his advice on whether or not to join the convent, and so she prayed God to lead her to him. Her prayers were answered. She next saw him with a group of followers in the Kazan Cathedral. She went up and spoke to Rasputin, and together they left the cathedral for the Golovins' home so he could meet her mother and discuss her problems. "For me this was a door into a new world," Munya confessed, "I found my spiritual guide in the person of a Siberian peas-ant who already in our first conversation amazed me with his insight. The authoritative look of his gray eyes equaled, in their power, that of his inner will that utterly exposed people before him. It was for me a great day."

Rasputin made Munya promise to stop attending spiritualist séances and practicing automatic writing under the influence of spirits.

He told her these things they called spirits were in fact demons, tricking us into thinking we were in contact with the souls of our departed loved ones. Only those rare persons with pure souls free of the sins of the world could make contact with these true spirits, Rasputin told Munya and her mother, and for others to even try was to engage in sin. As for joining Ella's convent, here again Rasputin instructed her to stop and follow his advice: "The vows we make to the Lord are not always to be found in convents [. . .] they are in fulfilling our daily duties, in the joy of life, such as loving to praise God and in experiencing the happiness of feeling His presence, the secret buried essence of which is to always keep your heart open to every good deed, and to have an affectionate word for everyone." From that day Munya and Lyubov remained devoted to Rasputin for the rest of their lives.

In a later draft of her memoirs written many years after this description, Munya added a few more words that she claimed Rasputin had spoken that day: "She will bring me greater evil than all the others, for she will be the cause of an inevitable event."[18] This event was, of course, his own murder. It seems unlikely that Rasputin uttered such words that day. What Munya was expressing here was not Rasputin's prophecy, but her own guilty conscience for having introduced Yusupov to Rasputin.

Having been cured of her existential anguish by Rasputin, Munya desperately wanted to introduce him to Felix to help him cope with the loss of his brother. As for Felix, he told investigators after Rasputin's murder that "Rasputin interested me as a personality, famous to all at the time and having enormous hypnotic powers." He mentioned nothing about the trauma of his brother's death (involvement in which some suspected him), but only certain undisclosed "ailments," and so with Munya's insistence, he agreed to meet.[19] When and where this happened is not clear. Felix stated more than once that he met Rasputin at the Petersburg home of the Golovins, but his testimony about when this was varies, from Christmas 1909 to as late as 1911, a date also mentioned by Munya in her testimony to the police following Rasputin's murder.[20]

Felix wrote in his memoirs that he was immediately irritated by Rasputin's "self-assurance." This seems quite plausible. The aristocratic Felix would have expected nothing less than subservience from a peasant, something, however, foreign to Rasputin's character. In his first lines on Rasputin, Yusupov lies, claiming he spotted on his head a "great scar," which he writes was the result of a wound "received during one of his highway robberies in Siberia." Rasputin's face, so Yusupov said, was "low, common," his features "coarse," his eyes "shifty," his overall impression that of a "lascivious, malicious satyr." To read Yusupov on Rasputin is to be presented with a man more animal than human.[21]

Munya told police after Rasputin's murder that following this initial meeting the two men met about twice a year at her home for the next several years. Yusupov visited Rasputin only on a few occasions, and then always together with Munya.[22] They would take the back stairs to avoid the Okhrana agents, as Rasputin recommended, and Yusupov would dress in such a way so as not to attract attention. Maria Rasputina confirmed the secrecy that Yusupov adopted when visiting her father. She found him "lithe and elegant, and with rather affected manners," but never imagined he was capable of murder.[23]

Given the unreliability of Yusupov's memoirs (more on this later), the letters Munya wrote to Yusupov about Rasputin provide the best evidence on the men's relations. It is clear that Munya not only helped make the introduction, but, as Rasputin's disciple, was intent on opening Felix's eyes to what she believed to be the truth about him and not the gossip he had heard so much of at home and in society. On 20 August 1910 she wrote:*

> Dear Felix Felixovich
>
> I am writing you to ask that you don't show <u>anyone</u> that piece of paper I handed you at Ala's [Alexandra Pistolkors]. Your new acquaintance visited us today and requested this, and I, too, think that the fewer conversations about him the better. I do so want to know your opinion of him; I think you were not able to take away an especially good impression, for this you need a special mood and then you get used to a different way of relating to his words, which always imply something spiritual and do not relate to our ordinary, everyday life.
>
> If you have understood this then I'm terribly happy, happy too that you saw him, and I believe that it was good for you and for your life, just don't abuse him, and if he is not pleasing to you—try to forget it.

In early September 1910, as Yusupov was preparing to return to Oxford, where he had been studying since the previous year, Munya wrote to him from her family's home in the countryside:

---

* The letter provides the best evidence as to when Yusupov and Rasputin likely met.

Upon arriving home I found your letter that was forwarded to me from Petersburg. Having read what you wrote about our friend, I recalled that he had written a few words on the back of your photograph that was among a series of others I showed him and he wrote on the back of several of them. He wrote you something very nice, and I do not even have the right to hold on to something for so long that belongs to you. [. . .] I was not in the right temper for prayer without our friend here—in his presence I pray so joyfully, so easily, and I was sad that he was not here and that we did not meet him and pray together at least once, I had no one to share my impressions with even though the people taking part in this religious experience were spiritually together.[24]

The photograph and Rasputin's inscription are reproduced in Yusupov's memoirs. Felix, standing alone on an empty city street, dressed nattily in a dark suit and tie, sporting a straw hat and walking stick, a small black case in his left hand, looks every inch the wealthy, polished, and confident young aristocrat about town. On the back, in his usual scrawl, Rasputin has written: "Bless you my child live not in delusion but in the joy of pleasure and light Grigory."[25] Typical of Rasputin's utterings, the precise meaning is vague, but his use of the word *zabluzh-denie*—delusion or error—might refer to Yusupov's sexual habits that Rasputin would have deemed sinful.

From Munya's letters it is clear Felix was struggling over just what to think of Rasputin. From his family he had only heard the worst rumors, but here was his old friend insisting these were all lies, that he was not the man people thought. Munya loved them both, and she was adamant that she make them love each other. Felix was being torn in two directions. Rasputin sensed Yusupov was wary, if not worse, and Munya did her best to try to encourage a friendship between them: "Our Friend has departed," she wrote while away in the Crimea, "he knows, but he too is not pleased that you did not tell me. I asked him to pray for you, so that all will be well for you, and he instructed me to tell you that 'he ran from society, and then crept right back in,' but I try to convince him and others that you are a very, very kind and good person, so do prove this and come soon—Yalta is not far from us. May God protect you. Maria."[26]

Sometime around the middle of June 1911, Munya, while visiting Boulogne sur Seine, wrote a long, angry letter to Felix in England about how he had been saying mean things about her and Rasputin to others:

How could you say so many unjust and cruel things! I read your letter several times in order to understand under what sort of influence you wrote it. Some day, another time, I do hope we will talk all this over in detail, and for now I will only say that you have accused me for no good reason—I have done nothing wrong. If you think that I am ruining myself as a result of my acquaintance with G. Yef. and my respect for him as a man of prayer and fellow believer—then so much the worse for you; I cannot change my opinion of a man whom I know just because of some second-hand gossip, for if I were to believe in all the things people say then I'd be forced to be disappointed with you! But I only want to always believe my inner feeling and that feeling tells me that G. Yef. pleases God. As for my making myself into his slave, that is not true. Everything I do I do it consciously and voluntarily. One needs a leader to grow spiritually, but this does not mean to enslave oneself, but only to recognize his spiritual experience as greater than yours, maintaining for yourself the freedom to perfect yourself on your own and to analyze your own feelings. He wrote me recently and asked me to tell you not to forget him when you are not well, and together with him to think about Our Creator and then all will be well! Don't sin against him any more, I don't like hearing from you those words I hear others speak. [. . .] I am glad you wrote me everything that you have been thinking, but it hurt me that you think that way. Those are not your ideas, at least not those that you had when you visited me last. You yourself wanted to see him, you wrote that, and even said that you were going to convince your mother to meet him, and were disturbed by the lies that pursued him and now such a sudden change! From all this I might think you don't even know him!

What great significance you give to society! Do you really still not know that today it despises you, tomorrow extols you, and is always happy to judge anyone no matter how lofty their position! What disappoints me most of all, of course, is the attitude of your mother to everything that has happened, it's so painful, nonetheless, I ask myself whether your mother is angry only because you met G. Yef. or is it your friendship with me (what a good friendship!) that she finds so unpleasant? I'd like to get to the bottom of all this, to know what I'm being accused of, why you were not allowed to see or speak with me? Can it really be you never do the

least thing that might upset your mother were she to find out? [. . .]
I simply can't believe that you so easily gave up your own view as
an adult and did not defend me, and then so mercilessly judged me
your very self [. . .] It's natural for you to love your mother more
than anyone on earth, especially such a mother as yours, but are
you expected to do something nasty, evil, against your own nature
out of this love for her? I myself love and respect your mother too
much to allow the thought that she would consciously insult
someone, particularly me, toward whom she was always so kind,
even after she learned of my acquaintance with G. Yef. [. . .] I
worship my mother, but if it seems to me that she is mistaken, I will
use all the power of my love to convince her to change.[27]

Munya never gave up trying to convince Felix of Rasputin's goodness and to reconcile the two men closest to her heart. Sometime after
the above letter she wrote again to Felix:

Why is it that when whole masses practice spiritualism, and our
entire youth makes use of every method to over excite their nerves,
ruin their health and soul, no one's concerned, and the only danger
people are able to see is one poorly educated man reminding them
about God, about the spiritual life of prayer, about reading more
religious books, about going to church and keeping the fasts all
while not hating anyone, and gathering to talk more often about
God and the life to come. For me all the rest is so ridiculous that
I don't even understand it, and I'll forever grieve should people's
empty gossip have any influence on you and should you believe
it [. . .]

    God bless you, I am sending you a little book in which I wanted
to copy down for you the thoughts of your "new acquaintance" and
one letter, sent to you, that I have rewritten; I've not managed to
rewrite all the rest. Read it all and write to me your opinion—
beneath the naive form are profound thoughts and much truth.[28]

On 3 October 1913, Munya wrote Yusupov from her room in Yalta's
Hotel Russia:

My Dear Felix Felixovich,
    I would not have written to you for anything in the world if it
weren't for our friend who wants me to send you his letter, and I
simply cannot ignore or disobey him, all the more so since you,

perhaps, might want to see him and take advantage of his short stay in Yalta? He is leaving soon [. . .]²⁹

Munya's opening words suggest the anger and hurt she was feeling toward Felix after years of failing to get him to see Rasputin as she did. As for Rasputin, it seems he had not given up on trying to win Felix over. What was it about the prince that continued to interest him? Rasputin, after all, had the trust of not just many other well-born and rich Russians, he had the love of the royal family, so what would Yusupov's friendship have meant to him? To this question there are no clear answers, but Rasputin's good disposition toward Yusupov does help explain why he would later embrace the man who would kill him after he had appeared to have changed his opinion of Rasputin and come back into his life. Munya never did manage to turn the two men into honest friends. Felix met Rasputin a few more times after 1913, but then broke off all contact with him in January 1915.³⁰ He would not meet Rasputin again until he had decided he was going to kill him.

22. Holy Land

In early January 1911 the royal family returned to the capital from their palace of Livadia in the Crimea. Nicholas was not back long before he was once more beset by scandals that could not be ignored.

Iliodor had continued his outlandish public attacks on tsarist officials and the church hierarchs and by January the Synod had had enough. It was high time to bring the renegade priest to heel. On the twentieth the Synod decided to punish Iliodor by moving him from Tsaritsyn to the remote Holy Spirit Monastery in Novosil in the Tula province.[1] Upon hearing the news, a terrified Iliodor twice cabled Rasputin in Pokrovskoe to beg for help: "The Synod moved me to Tula today. Papa [the tsar] has not yet confirmed it. Ask him my dear Friend not to move me." That same day, Olga Lokhtina also wrote Rasputin to help Iliodor. She told him that even though the tsar was angry at Iliodor, the renegade monk would refuse to leave no matter what—even if every brick of his monastery were to be covered with his own blood, he would not budge. Iliodor was ready to see that the monastery became his grave.[2] Rasputin apparently did send a telegram urging the tsar to reconsider the Synod's decision, although the telegram has never been found. Vyrubova, too, asked Nicholas not to act before hearing more from Rasputin. But in the end, no one could sway Nicholas, and, for once, he supported the Synod and endorsed its decision to transfer Iliodor on 22 January. Just as he had defied the Synod, Iliodor now refused to acknowledge the authority of the tsar himself. "Heroes don't surrender," he said. "They die. I shall not go to Tula alive!"[3] By the end of the month, the story was appearing in the press. The *Russian Word* wrote on 29 January that Iliodor was trying to enlist Rasputin to overturn the decision.[4] A week later the same newspaper stated that Rasputin had left Siberia to visit Iliodor in Tsaritsyn.[5] At the end of the month, the newspapers were reporting that Iliodor and as many as 10,000 of his followers had locked themselves up in the monastery and declared a hunger strike.

Unsure just what was transpiring in Tsaritsyn, and caught between the opposing advice of the Synod and Rasputin (as presented by way of Alexandra and Vyrubova), Nicholas decided to send his own man to investigate. He chose for the job his trusted aide-de-camp Alexander Mandryka, a captain in the Fourth Life-Guards Imperial Family's Rifle Regiment and a man of the highest integrity.[6] According to Vladimir Gurko, deputy minister of the interior under Stolypin, however, the choice of Mandryka was not as straightforward as Nicholas believed. Gurko later claimed that Rasputin had suggested Mandryka to the empress, knowing she would pass this on to Nicholas and the tsar would think that it had been his idea. Rasputin had wanted Mandryka chosen since the officer's cousin Maria, the abbess of the Pokrovsky Convent in Balashov in the Saratov province, was devoted to Germogen and especially Rasputin and so, according to Gurko, would be able to influence Mandryka's report.[7]

Mandryka left for Tsaritsyn at the beginning of February. He met with Iliodor accompanied by Nikolai Kharlamov, deputy director of the department of police sent there earlier on the order of Stolypin to try to resolve the crisis, and deputy governor of the Saratov province, Pyotr Boyarsky. According to Iliodor, Mandryka told him he had come to pass along the tsar's order that he was to leave immediately for Novosil, to which Iliodor replied that he did not believe this to be the tsar's wish, but that of "that aggressor Stolypin." Iliodor then proceeded to inform Mandryka he would not recognize any order for him to leave Tsaritsyn no matter who it came from.[8] Kharlamov found Iliodor bright and gifted, especially when it came to working up the crowd, but unbalanced and excitable. From his interviews with others in the city Kharlamov learned that the success of the past few years had gone to Iliodor's head, and he now believed he could do anything. Kharlamov noticed how Iliodor bragged about his intimacy with the royal family, making up stories to impress people, like one about the empress and one of her daughters visiting him disguised as poor pilgrims the previous summer. Iliodor's increasing belligerence toward tsarist ministers, "Jew-newspapermen," and the rich was, Kharlamov learned, a response to the changing political situation since 1905. With the failure of the revolution, and suppression of the revolutionary movement, Iliodor had consciously decided he needed new enemies to help build a mass following. It was all done with the utmost calculation.

Mandryka returned to report on his trip to the tsar. For almost two hours he told Nicholas and Alexandra about the situation in Tsaritsyn with Iliodor. He did not fail to mention that supporters of the wayward priest had tried to influence his report, including Vyrubova and Mandryka's cousin the abbess, who had apparently tried more than once to incline Mandryka to go easy on Iliodor, even coming to the capital after Mandryka's return to speak to him. Mandryka did not, of course, ignore the role of Rasputin in these efforts to sway him and then dared to go even further, saying to the emperor: "Forgive me, Your Majesty, for my harsh words, but he is a big scoundrel." To this the tsar gave no reply. Mandryka was supposedly so worried about how his words would be met he broke down in tears. Neither Nicholas nor Alexandra was upset, however, and the tsar thanked him for his honesty.[9]

The story of Mandryka's audience with the royal couple grew over time and became part of the Rasputin legend. Mikhail Rodzianko, for example, embellished the story by claiming that Mandryka brought up having uncovered Rasputin's khlyst activities in Tsaritsyn, something Mandryka did not do, nor is there any evidence he ever said anything of the sort during his report.[10] Gurko has Mandryka not just in tears, but on the verge of a nervous collapse, such was the passionate hatred with which he told Nicholas and Alexandra about Rasputin and the wild orgies he had been engaging in with young nuns around the time of Mandryka's mission to Tsaritsyn. Gurko also claimed that the abbess won an audience with the empress thanks to Rasputin and Vyrubova and she did her best to undermine her cousin's report.[11]

In the end, it was Germogen who managed to talk Iliodor into leaving for Tula, where he arrived on 12 February.[12]

Amidst all this drama, Stolypin, according to Rodzianko, decided it was time to bring up the matter of Rasputin with Nicholas once more in the hopes of finally convincing the emperor to be rid of him. He compiled a file on Rasputin and presented it to Nicholas. The tsar quietly listened to his prime minister and then told him to meet with Rasputin and see for himself what kind of man he was. Stolypin set up a meeting with Rasputin and informed him he had documents in his possession that would reveal Rasputin's connections to the khlysts. Then he gave him a way to save himself: Rasputin could immediately leave Petersburg for home and never return. The threat, however, failed, and Rasputin refused to go. Stolypin was the most powerful man in the empire after the tsar, but he was not powerful enough to get rid of this peasant, and Rasputin knew this, for as long as he had the love and respect of the tsar and tsaritsa, no one could touch him, or so he believed at the time. As for Stolypin, he had been warned by others in the government not to confront Rasputin, and they had been right. The only thing Stolypin gained from his threatening Rasputin was the enmity of the empress.[13]

If Stolypin's confrontation with Rasputin, which has been told and retold in every biography, did indeed happen, it could only have been in the first days of February when Rasputin returned to the capital. He had most likely not seen Nicholas and Alexandra since the spring of 1910 and the press scandals of that season, and he first visited them again after dinner on the night of the twelfth—the same day Iliodor arrived in Tula with Germogen. They talked for a long time.[14] The royal couple appear to have been truly glad to see him after such a long absence. Rasputin presented Alexandra with a blank notebook in which she could record his words. He inscribed it to her on the front page: "Here is my peace, the source of glory, light in the light. A gift to my sincere mama. Grigory." On the next page Alexandra began with these words of her friend: "My minute is hard, my days of grief! There's no greater grief than when your own do not recognize you."[15] The following day, Rasputin departed. A despondent Alexandra wrote to her daughter Maria to say that she, too, was "very sad that our dear Friend is going away—but while he's gone we must try to live as he would wish. Then we shall feel that he is with us in our prayers and thoughts."[16]

Rasputin was about to embark on the longest journey of his life, a pilgrimage to the Holy Land. The reasons why he chose to go, and why then, are murky. It has been posited that Rasputin's enemies had set him up at the apartment of a Finnish ballet dancer by the name of Lisa Tansin, getting him drunk and taking pictures of him naked with some prostitutes. When the tsar found out, he suggested Rasputin leave until the scandal died down.[17] Gurko claimed Rasputin was ordered out of the capital in connection with Mandryka's report.[18] In her memoirs Munya Golovina writes that the decision to leave came just after Yelena Timofeeva, Rasputin's much beloved young follower, had disappeared without word upon the urging of Feofan. Rasputin, according to Golovina, was devastated by this. Just then, he was summoned to the palace to see their majesties. They treated him with all the love of the past, but then informed Rasputin that they had approved the wishes of the ministers that for his, and their benefit, he should undertake a pilgrimage to the Holy Land, and to depart immediately. Rasputin did not argue. It seems beyond doubt that the troubles of the past year were the key reason for the trip. Nicholas and Alexandra may have agreed with the advice of their ministers to send Rasputin away for a time, or at least they did not care to fight it. His absence might well quiet the various scandals, and visiting the lands where Christ had lived and died might also help burnish their friend's image as a man of God. Rasputin saw several of his followers before leaving Petersburg. "The ministers are sending me to Mt. Athos and Jerusalem," he told them. "They think a little trip will do me good."[19]

It was not rare for Russians to travel to the Holy Land in those days. About 2,000 Russians made the pilgrimage every year with the help of the Imperial Orthodox Palestine Society. The society had accommodation for 7,000 pilgrims in Jerusalem and for 1,000 in Nazareth. When Rasputin was there in 1911, there were over 9,000 Russian pilgrims in Jerusalem; more than 4,000 stayed for Easter.[20] Rasputin would be away for over three months. The journey, most probably paid for by the tsar and carried out in relative comfort (he traveled overland by train, not on foot like the mass of Russian pilgrims), made a deep impression on him. He wrote often to Nicholas and Alexandra and to Anna Vyrubova along the way, and later his writings from the trip were published as a small booklet, edited and paid for by Alexandra, titled *My Thoughts and Reflections*. The booklet was never sold, but given out by Rasputin as a gift to his admirers.[21]

Rasputin left Petersburg on 13 February for Kiev, the cradle of Russian Orthodoxy, arriving on the eighteenth, where he toured the spectacular Kievo-Pecherskaya Lavra, and from there headed to the ancient Pochaev Monastery in western Ukraine to pray before its icon of the Virgin Mother, and then southward to Odessa on the Black Sea coast. Here he joined some six hundred other Russian pilgrims and embarked on a steamer for Constantinople.[22] It was Rasputin's first time at sea. He found the experience amazing.

What can I say about my silence? As soon as I started from Odessa on the journey along the Black Sea—there was silence at sea and the soul was rejoicing and sleeping in that silence, I can see small sparkles glistening as gold and there is nothing else to look for. [. . .]

The sea consoles you without any effort. When you wake up in the morning, the waves are talking and splashing and making you happy. And the sun shines in the sea, and slowly rises, and the human soul forgets everything at that moment and looks at the glimmering sun and the soul starts rejoicing and the person feels like he is reading the book of life—an indescribable picture! The sea wakes you from the sleep of vanities, many thoughts come to your mind on their own, without an effort. [. . .]

How amazing the silence is . . . Not a single sound comes from a bird, and a person starts walking to and fro on the deck deep in his thoughts; he remembers his childhood and all the vanity and compares the silence he is having with the world full of vanity and he quietly talks to himself and wishes to unload his heart (and relieve his boredom) from the feelings accumulated through interaction with his enemies [. . .]

One sees the shores and the shining trees—who wouldn't rejoice? [. . .] we look at God's nature and praise God and his Creation and the beauty of nature, which cannot be described by any human mind or philosophy.

It may have been beautiful, but the voyage made him seasick.

They disembarked in Constantinople to view Hagia Sophia. Rasputin was moved: "What can I say with my little human mind about the wonderful magnificent Sophia Cathedral, the only one unique in the whole world. The Sophia Cathedral is like a cloud on a mountain—the best one in the world." Although it pained him to see the cathedral in the hands of the "infidel Turks," he put the blame for this on the Christians themselves, for it was their sinful pride, he wrote, that caused God to take it away from them and give it to people of another faith who had mocked and desecrated his image. Surely, he believed, the cathedral must once more be in the hands of the Orthodox, but for that patience was required, and repentance for their sins.

From there they sailed out into the Aegean Sea and down the Turkish coast, past Mitylene, Smyrna and Ephesus, the islands of Chios and Patmos, moving through the lands once traveled by St. Paul in the first century. He felt himself swept back to the early church, amazed by the faith, power, and suffering of the first Christians: "My God, how much faith the apostles kindled here, on these shores! They turned unlimited amounts of people into Christ lovers and that is why there are martyrs everywhere, on both sides of the Mediterranean Sea."

But after the Apostolic Age it had been all downhill. "The Greeks became very proud of their philosophy. God got angry and gave all the products of the apostles' labor to the Turks." The Greek bishops, it was true, were educated and followed decorum, but, according to Rasputin, they lacked the spiritual essence of faith. Here, the bishops were focused on outward signs—they wanted fine crosses, not poor robes—and Rasputin had to admit Russia was not immune either. The church back home, he wrote, was "lacking in spirit," it was too concerned with "formal decorum," which was the reason the churches were so often empty. So many bishops were lazy, as well as afraid of those simple monks in whom the true "sacred flame" burned.

Sailing southward they passed Rhodes ("Rhodes has everything one can imagine"), Beirut, and then landed at the ancient port of Jaffa. From there, they traveled overland to Jerusalem. The emotion at the moment of arrival was more than Rasputin could bear, and he broke down in tears:

> I ended my journey by arriving at the holy city of Jerusalem via the main road.
>
> [. . .] I can't describe the joy I experienced—ink cannot describe it, and every pilgrim will shed tears at such a moment.
>
> [. . .] God suffered here. Oh, you can picture God's Mother at the Cross. Your imagination is vivid here, especially how he had to suffer for all of us in Attica. [. . .]
>
> How can I describe the minute when I approached the Holy Sepulcher!
>
> Thus I felt that the Sepulcher is the tomb of love and this was such a strong feeling that I was ready to hug everyone and felt such love toward people that everyone seemed to be a holy man because love does not allow you to see people's weaknesses. Near the sepulcher you see with your heart lovingly all the people and they feel this even when they get home. [. . .]
>
> Oh, what a big impression Golgotha makes! [. . .] Once you cast a glance at the place where the Mother of God stood, your tears start falling on their own and you see it all in your mind's eye.
>
> God, what a deed took place; the body was taken down and stretched on the ground. What sorrow it can bring and what tears where the body lay! God, God, what is it for? God, we will not sin again, save us with your suffering![23]

Such was the power of the Holy Land, he felt as if the royal family were there with him:

> My dear little ones, I have reached the city of the Sacred Word [. . .] God, the Holy Sepulcher is such joy and you were standing next to me: Annushka, you were there, and Mama and Papa, and you were all mine, we could not have been closer to each other or I could even touch you with my finger because love is above all; Mama, understand, Annushka, there is no shame here, no, kissing you, all mine, everyone. Grigory.[24]

He visited Gethsemane ("one is afraid to step on the ground, every bulrush is sacred"), the River Jordan, Jericho, and Bethlehem. Rasputin's thoughts were directed not solely to Christ. "The Jewesses here are especially pretty," he wrote to friends back in Petersburg.[25] On 10 April the Orthodox Christians celebrated Easter in the Holy Land. It was, like everything for Rasputin, a profoundly moving experience, though not without its disappointments. He was shocked to find not everyone as awed by the significance of these holy places as he was. He was put off by the endless hawkers of religious trinkets and being harassed by women chasing after him and the other pilgrims with their kitschy gewgaws. Nuns were selling wine in the most holy of places, and since it was cheap everyone seemed to be drinking it. All this just confirmed Rasputin's belief that the Devil was everywhere. Temptation was inescapable. Rasputin's description of the immorality he saw about him was no exaggeration: there was plenty of wild drinking, concubinage, fighting, and general mayhem to greet pilgrims to the Holy Land in those days.[26]

And just as he had been disappointed by the spiritual emptiness of the Greek churches, so too was he disappointed by what he saw of a Catholic Easter mass. "What can be said about their Easter? In our celebration everyone, even non-Orthodox, is happy, their faces are lit [. . .] while they have not joy in their main cathedral, there is no commotion there, and one can see that they have no Easter in their hearts [. . .] We are so happy being Orthodox! No faith compares to ours!"

Rasputin drew important lessons for Russia from his pilgrimage. He found in pilgrimage a way of fostering faith among the people of Russia and so of building reverence for the throne, especially among the poor, and he urged the government to support and encourage Russians to travel to the Holy Land. Upon returning to their native villages, these pilgrims, full of renewed spiritual force and, he believed, renewed faith in the motherland and its *Tsar-Batyushka*, would act as ambassadors for Orthodoxy and the monarchy. To that end, Rasputin felt the difficult conditions of the Orthodox pilgrims ought to be improved. The price of the journey should be lowered, missions should stop charging the pilgrims for hot water, for room and board, and they should not be conveyed by the hundreds "as cattle in the lower hold."[27] Wealthy pilgrims traveled in great comfort, the poor suffered. This, Rasputin believed, was not right.

On the evening of 4 June Rasputin returned to visit Nicholas and Alexandra at the Alexander Palace. They were overjoyed to see him again after so many months.[28] He brought with him gifts; for Alexei, a ball, comb, top, and a small box of paints. The boy was thrilled.[29] They were not the only ones glad to have him back. Sofia Buksgevden noted that after his return, the number of Rasputin's followers grew noticeably, for they were all eager to hear about his adventures.[30] For some, the fact of Rasputin's pilgrimage proved the truth about his profound faith and added to the intensity of the spiritual aura around him. If the tsar's ministers had insisted on the pilgrimage as a means to curtail Rasputin's influence, they had failed.

23. Rasputin in His Own Words

Contrary to popular perception, Rasputin was not illiterate. Although he never attended school, he did learn to read and write, and during his many years as a pilgrim absorbed a great deal of holy scripture. He wrote poorly, it is true, with little understanding of grammar. Sentences ran on, verbs failed to agree, proper declension was ignored, punctuation did not exist. His spelling was appalling. Perhaps this explains much of the reason why previous biographers have largely ignored his writings, dismissing them as the incoherent scribblings of a semi-literate peasant.

The press at the time made this very point. A commentator in the *Stock Exchange Gazette* noted that Rasputin's writings exhibited "no special excitement, no special depth, no originality." The newspaper asked how it was possible Rasputin's anonymous editors could not have noticed "that 'the emperor was naked,' yet still they invite us to admire the phantom 'clothes of the king.'?"[1] In 1911, *Evening Time* wrote that Rasputin had developed his teachings while a pilgrim, thinking he had come up with some new philosophy when in fact he was just repeating the ideas of the second-century heretic Marcion, who asserted that to raise one's spirit one must first destroy one's flesh by whatever means possible.[2] It is true Rasputin was no original or important thinker and he added nothing to Orthodox theology, yet he had strong opinions about faith and society and the Russia of his day, and his writings offer perhaps the best window into Rasputin's mind. Rasputin was never a preacher, and he only rarely spoke before large public gatherings, but he was not indifferent to what he had to say, and, with the help of followers such as the empress, he saw that a few booklets of his words were printed during his lifetime.[3] Olga Lokhtina told the Commission that Rasputin liked to write down his thoughts in a little notebook, which she would transcribe, correcting the grammar but making no other changes, and these were published as *Pious Meditations* in 1911.[4]

In 1915, with the backing of the empress, Rasputin's *Thoughts and Reflections* chronicling his trip to the Holy Land was printed.

Alexandra collected Rasputin's sayings in the notebook he had given her in February 1911. This notebook meant a great deal to the empress. She wrote Nicholas on 5 May 1915: "These days are so long and lonely [. . .] When my head aches, I write down the aphorisms of our Friend, and the time goes by faster." After the revolution, she took the notebook with her into exile as a source of comfort.[5] It is not easy reading, and his words are often nearly impossible to render accurately into English. Much of his speech, as recorded not only here but in other sources, is at times impossible to follow—it is often vague, confused, elliptical, incomplete, impenetrable. (For the sake of clarity, Rasputin's language has been ironed out in the quoted passages below.) Nonetheless, certain themes emerge. Rasputin repeatedly stressed the power of prayer and faith, the wonders of almsgiving, the saintly quality of work, and the importance of mercy. Rasputin rarely spoke of sin, but was obsessed with the Devil, what he referred to as *bes*, literally "demon," a real, powerfully present force in the world around them that must be resisted at every moment.[6]

Love is at the heart of Rasputin's message.

Love paradise, it comes from love, we go where our spirit goes, love clouds, we live there.

Love is great suffering, it doesn't let you eat, it doesn't let you sleep.

It is mixed with sin. Still it is better to love. A person makes mistakes in love and suffers from them, and his suffering purges his mistakes.

God, [. . .] teach me how to love and then all the wounds from love would not hurt me and the suffering would be pleasant. I know that there is suffering and struggle in love (I have suffered myself) but I am born from love and from the loved ones [. . .]. Don't take love from me—let the suffering of the closest ones teach me love and I suffer and love, though I err, but according to the Apostle's words: "Love forgives many sins."

Love is everything, love will protect you from a bullet.

From love flowed help for one's fellow man, and particularly alms. Rasputin had much to say about almsgiving, and it was a central theme of his message. In 1910, these sayings were collected in *The Marvelous*

Deeds of Alms written down by Grand Duchess Tatyana Nikolaevna in her notebook.

> He who gives, that man has many times experienced for himself that the giving hand does not grow poor, but receives very much.
> But the Devil through temptation does not leave us alone and sends all manner of phantoms, saying "you go through the world alone, don't give," or he conjures up a drunk or unworthy lazy types and says even louder "you'll go broke yourself."
> The Heavenly Kingdom is not given for nothing, different types of crosses are needed, and almsgiving is greater than any other deed.

The Devil tried to stop one from giving to the needy, just as he was forever trying to trick one into abandoning God and following the wrong path. "It is so painful to suffer! The Devil is very experienced, he has lived for centuries and he always takes away from man what he truly loves. Many people cannot overcome this, kill themselves, these people haven't made friends with God. Friendship with God—harsh persecution and loss of what you love "

It was due to the Devil that Rasputin believed he faced so many enemies, a theme he returned to again and again.

> Sorrows are God's palace! [. . .] I am living through terrible slander. It's incredible what people write about me. God! Give me patience and shut the mouths of my enemies! Or give me heavenly help, that is prepare for me the eternal joy of Your delight.
> Oh, the miserable Devil has raised all Russia against me, as if against a criminal! The Devil and everyone are preparing eternal bliss! That's how the Devil will always lose. God! Save your own!
> The truth is always with the martyrs and the godly men, they will endure the harassment—and be crowned in the end.[7]

Rasputin frequently admitted that he too was not entirely free of the Devil's clutches. More than once did he say, "I am also tempted by the enemy." The enemy was envious of those who seek God, as Rasputin saw matters, and so however one might try to reach God, the enemy will send pain and suffering: he who bows low will be sent back pain, he who fasts will be visited by indescribable thirst, he who tries to avoid bodily desires will be sent members of the opposite sex with tempting thoughts. In his *Life of an Experienced Pilgrim* Rasputin offered advice on how to resist such things based on his own experience:

> One should try everything: pray a little but hit yourself only when nobody is around, do it strongly, correctly and use physical force, so that even the floor can shake, but try to do this when nobody is around, then it will be fine and everything [temptations] will go away, and you will gain experience and accept all this with joy because the enemy has taught you but failed to tempt you—he has made you love God even more.[8]

Rasputin's preoccupations with suffering, the work of the Devil, persecution at the hands of one's enemies all resonated with Alexandra. She viewed the world much as he did, and one can see how Rasputin's words would have been welcomed by her and how they helped to create a bond between them. Alexandra saw herself as surrounded by enemies intent on harming her, her family, and Rasputin too. She saw the world in stark black-and-white terms of sin and virtue. As the years passed Alexandra became more judgmental of anyone she felt belonged in the former category. Her long-serving maid Madeleine Zanotti, who knew the empress from her early years as a young lady in Darmstadt, noticed how the empress found it ever more difficult to tolerate anyone's ideas but her own. Persons who did not share her opinion were to be removed from her environment.[9] Outside her immediate family, Rasputin was the only man who managed not to fall short of the empress's impossibly high standards.

If the shared feeling of persecution that helped unite Rasputin and the empress was beyond doubt, what is less clear is the extent to which Rasputin cultivated this aura of martyrdom for this very purpose. The feelings he expressed were certainly genuine, and not without warrant, but to what degree, if any, did he amplify them to help maintain his place in the hearts of both Alexandra and Nicholas? This is difficult to say. On a few occasions Rasputin directed his words at Alexandra and in these instances it is clear he was both offering comfort at times of adversity and playing to her vanity:

> So nowadays we hear and see troubles on earth, which are frightening and hard, and God's greatness came on our Empress because we hear about her mercifulness [. . .] it is our lawlessness and sins that caused them and God left and everybody came out pitiful and ashamed. She was affected, our Mother Empress, deep in her heart

and soul. [...] having experienced all the tribulations, she fell ill and shook her inner energy. She keeps hoping and anticipating with her faith and expectation and grace. She doesn't turn to earthly doctors but Her labor will grow and her soul will resurrect.

And:

She feels God like us, simple people, but when she talks, she merges with God's grace. Nobody has known glory as our Mother Empress has. And often the enemy tries to put other weaknesses on her. But she is a fighter, she has learned from experience, and she fights cleverly, in a holy and skilful manner. She is an example to various acquaintances and tells them to understand by her experience and by her artfulness. Thus she gives an example now to children, teaches them not to be hurt but points to the bliss gained through patience. God creates wondrous things all over our Mother Russia. There were times when people suffered, but thanks to their holy prayers those days are past, the Lord will put an end and we will suffer no more and God will not let us pass into the hands of the infidels forever and ever. As there were anointed ones in the past so shall there be today. Amen.

One can imagine how such words pleased Alexandra.

If Alexandra had difficulty accepting others' imperfect selves, Rasputin was more forgiving, and despite his talk of persecution, Rasputin's writings are devoid of any desire for retribution. Vengeance was a foreign concept to Rasputin. All would be settled in the end by God himself. This was a form of grace lacking in the empress.

Except on a few occasions, Rasputin showed compassion for others, a sentiment that sprang from his recognition of man's imperfection. Sinful creatures, we cannot all be true Christians and experience the beauty of God's love and wisdom. "Gold is known to everyone but diamonds are not that clear to all though they are valuable. Similarly, spiritual life is not accessible to everyone." Those most likely to find God were the humble and the poor. The common man carried God inside him much more easily than the rich and the mighty, and Rasputin used this understanding of spirituality as a weapon against Russia's aristocrats, intellectuals, merchants, and priests. Rasputin spoke much of the supremacy of love, but when speaking of particular social groups his words were often devoid of such feeling.

What happiness it is to raise the souls of aristocrats. [...] Why?
Because, first of all, they are not allowed to talk to simple people.
What is a simple person? He cannot say foreign phrases but speaks
simply and lives in harmony with nature and it feeds him and his
spirit is raised in wisdom. [...] That is why they say: the more
important, the stupider. Why stupider? Because wisdom is in
simplicity.

   Pride and haughtiness lead to losing your mind. "Oh, I'd like
not to be proud but my grandfather spent time with ministers, I
was born into such a clan, they lived abroad." Oh you unfortunate
aristocrat! Since they lived that way so must you! And so you have
run your country estate into the ground, you lose your minds.
[...] Ah, Satan knows how to catch aristocrats. There are some,
though they are rare—you need to search for them with a light in
the daytime, as they say—who present themselves simply; they
don't forbid their children from going to the kitchen to learn
simplicity from the cook. These people have an upbringing and
knowledge of simplicity, their mind is sacred. A sacred mind feels
everything and these people are the commanders of the world.[10]

And:

Oh, you, aristocrats! I got drunk in a small tavern for 3 kopecks,
and you did it abroad, in Berlin, have you forgotten this? [...] The
damn aristocrats haven't seen the light yet. [...] God sees the
truth—let the bones of your grandchildren lie in peace, but know
the truth and don't touch the Christian man and Orthodox people!

   In an interview with the *Petersburg Courier* in June 1914, Rasputin is
reported as saying "every aristocracy feeds off the common man."[11]
According to Vladimir Bonch-Bruevich, Rasputin liked to say, "One
must live for the common people, one must think about them."
Bonch-Bruevich had no doubt he meant it.[12]

In the spring of 1915, Rasputin began visiting the Petrograd studio of
the Danish artist Theodora Krarup. She was close to the Dowager
Empress, a fellow Dane, and had painted several portraits of members
of the royal family, and now Rasputin came to her offering three
hundred rubles for his own portrait (a good deal less than she usually
charged for a commission.) They quickly developed a warm bond and

Rasputin became a regular visitor to Krarup's studio. In the end, she would paint his portrait twelve times. One of these, she gave to the tsarevich Alexei.[13]

The shabby poverty of her place moved Rasputin, symbolizing for him Krarup's humility and highlighting her honest labor. He contrasted Krarup with what he perceived as the self-aggrandizing ways of Russia's generals during war:

> Our strength is only in our talent. Why is there no warrior and no victor nowadays. Because that beauty is missing, the beauty in their hearts is not for victories but for slipping someone the knife so he doesn't get a promotion or a medal [. . .] Really, take a look at the artists, women and men, they are so poor, no crosses, no medals, just their materials—their material is paint, and their talent is in their spirit. Jesus! Why didn't you put victory into the generals' heads and not knives. They are so far from being brothers of the artists—male and female! Look at a true artist: you come to his studio and see his paintings around you, he only has a bed, a mattress, like in trenches, he doesn't get crosses and does nothing to earn fame, while the generals are the ones who are supposedly saving us . . . but I am not sure [. . .]

Krarup was taken with Rasputin from the start. He typically came to see her together with Munya Golovina. As he posed for the artist he would talk about life in Russia, and the one theme he returned to over and over was his anger over the nobility's exploitation of the peasants. In Krarup's opinion, Rasputin was a Christian socialist.

The humble beauty and comfort Rasputin experienced in Krarup's studio he also felt at home in Pokrovskoe. In a piece he called "A Walk through My Village" dated 27 October 1911, he recounted what he saw through the windows of his fellow villagers one evening. He went out thinking about "peasant labor" and was warmed to come across sights of young boys studying Scripture, a man repairing a sledge, women weaving mats. Here, in these simple huts, he saw joy and God's light. Even the women, who laughed and sang secular songs as they worked, were pleasing to God, for He approved of their labor. "What peasants do in the evenings is full of holy work and righteousness." And then he passed the house of the priests. Here he saw three clergymen chatting and playing cards for money. "Their faces were lit with hazard" and their house by a "non-transparent light." Yet Rasputin was not too damning.

"Let us not judge too much," he instructed, "but we will not follow their example, we will wait until they act properly and learn from them when they are in prayer, not with cards."

Rasputin frequently spoke harsh words about Russia's priests:

> Many of us talk about love but have only heard what it is, but we are often far from love. It mainly comes to experienced people but it will not come to the person who lives in comfort and in serenity, even if he is a priest. Because there are two kinds of priests—some are hired by their parishes, and others have developed to be a priest by their lives, he is a genuine priest and he tried hard to serve God; but the one who is hired often informs on him and criticizes him. Those who are chosen by God know the ultimate love, one can go and listen to them and they will not preach from a book but from experience, because love is not received easily.

It is obvious Rasputin is speaking about himself here and placing himself above official clergymen, and particularly those who spoke out against him. Rasputin has given way to pride in this instance, a sin that he was quick to point out in others, the aristocrats, generals, priests, and intellectuals, who also came in for criticism. "Being educated does nothing for righteousness at all! I am not criticizing men of letters, one should study, but an educated man does not have access to God. He has learned only letters but cannot call God. The letter has confused his mind and bound his feet and he cannot follow the steps of God."[14] Once he counseled: "Don't philosophize—you'll just get tired."

In the spring of 1913, Rasputin visited the Petersburg Foundling House for abandoned and illegitimate children. The sight of the tiny, unwanted babies moved him to tears. He was sad so few people knew about the place or ever bothered to visit "this house where humankind is rising." He expressed the view that these children were ignored and unloved since they were the result of "the frenzy of uncontrollable flesh, they come from sin, from everything that we call sin and that everyone fears." Rasputin did not deny the sin that lay behind their birth, but he stressed that no one was free of sin and that God was forever merciful.

"Their faces show no more traces of sin," he said, "the flesh has freed itself from frenzy." They were all "defenseless little creatures." He praised the wet-nurses and the doctor there: "The people are simpler, calmer than the higher classes. And you trust the wet-nurses more than those who command them. Power spoils a person's soul, burdens it, one does not need power here but love. Those who understand this will be blessed throughout their life."

Rasputin defended these weakest members of society against the prejudices of the day. No, these children were not to be despised and discarded, he insisted, for they were in fact of special value:

> The great harvest of love cannot be collected in distant granaries. This leads to the loss of many young crops, souls that could have survived and become a decoration for posterity die. Just think: the healthiest children come from secret love because it is strong. The open one is ordinary. When it is open, your feelings are reluctant, you give birth weakly. [. . .] The greatness and glory of the state are built by the strength of a spirit, love for children and childhood. Build faster and more such angel refuges. There is no sin in them, they are not for sin. Sin is in blaming the unusual, when someone's soul and body are rejected because they are unusual. But we are afraid of this. Why should we be afraid when we must rejoice and lift up praise to the Creator and the Maker of everything?[15]

Rasputin was something of a Russian Rousseau with his praise of nature and the common man, his awe at the innocent purity of childhood, his distrust of the educated classes and the aristocracy, and his call for simplicity and the return to some original purity.[16] It should be noted that such ideas did not make Rasputin unique. John of Kronstadt, for example, expressed similar views, denouncing the soullessness of Russia's educated classes and their corrupting influence on the lower orders and their morals.[17] That Rasputin's views were shared by others does not invalidate them, but shows instead how he was preoccupied by concerns then gripping much of Russian society. It can be tempting to discount Rasputin's words as cynical hypocrisy, empty phrases he put no faith in and used simply as a part of his cunning strategy to gain influence and notoriety. But this would be a mistake. Like everyone, his words and deeds did not always agree, but more often than not they did.

24. Iliodor's Triumph

On 15 February, just days after arriving in Novosil, Iliodor sent a pleading telegram to Rasputin in care of Sazonov in Petersburg: "My dear friend, come to me as fast as you can; it's very difficult."[1] But the telegram arrived too late. Rasputin had already left for the Holy Land. And so Iliodor turned to others. With the help of Lokhtina and Iliodor's brother Apollon, a former student at the Moscow Theological Seminary, he planned his escape. Iliodor removed his cross, donned a pair of dark glasses and a large fur hat and fled Novosil for Moscow where the three of them caught an express train and headed south to Tsaritsyn.[2] How Iliodor managed to get all the way back to Tsaritsyn undetected is something of a mystery. In his memoirs, Governor of Saratov province Pyotr Stremoukhov wrote that it was Kurlov, then deputy minister of the interior under Stolypin, who was responsible. Kurlov secretly ordered his agents (as second in command at the ministry he was in charge of the police agencies) to let Iliodor return to Tsaritsyn as part of his plan to undermine his boss Stolypin and strengthen his own position. Kurlov, Stremoukhov claimed, saw potential patrons at court in the figures of Iliodor and Rasputin.[3]

Upon reaching Tsaritsyn on 12 March, Iliodor barricaded himself in his monastery, now surrounded by tens of thousands of supporters. That same day he sent a telegram to Rasputin: "Having gotten past the patrols and hundreds of agents, protected by the Virgin Mother, I have arrived safely at my cathedral. The people are joyously running to me now in masses. In the city the police, gendarmes, and guards are covered in shame; finish this business." He sent a second, desperate telegram later that day: "Avert a great calamity."[4]

Meanwhile, Iliodor seemed intent on provoking the great calamity he wanted Rasputin to avoid and continued his incendiary sermons. The emperor is in the hands of the "Yid-Mason" ministers, he screamed, the most dangerous of whom was Stolypin. Iliodor called for all of them to be flogged with rods, Stolypin being given special beatings to expel his "Masonic spirit." Stremoukhov was ordered not to allow any more followers to join the crowds and not to attempt to touch Iliodor until further notice. Stolypin asked the procurator of the Synod to engage Germogen to help defuse the situation. The effort failed. Kurlov then ordered Stremoukhov to send the police to storm the monastery at night and seize Iliodor. Knowing this would end in a bloodbath, Stremoukhov refused to obey. It is possible a bloodbath is just what Kurlov had wanted, hoping to lay the blame for it at the feet of Stolypin. Iliodor whipped up his followers, telling them they alone could save him and so guarantee for themselves a place in Heaven. Iliodor had turned his monastery into a fortress. His followers, many of whom were now armed with rifles and clubs, ringed the entire building, prepared to repulse any attempt by the police to arrest Iliodor.

According to Kurlov, the police were intercepting telegrams to Rasputin from Iliodor and Germogen, who had joined his protégé, begging him to intercede with the tsar. But Rasputin was now too far away to help; their telegrams appear never to have reached him during his pilgrimage. (The fact that Iliodor was unaware Rasputin had left for the Holy Land lends credence to the idea that his decision to leave was taken at the last moment.) Iliodor wrote, however, that Rasputin did respond to his calls for help and was cabling the tsar in defense of the rebellious priest and also wrote to assure Iliodor that he would save him.[5] On 27 March, the *Russian Word* printed what it said was a telegram from Rasputin in Jerusalem to Iliodor: "God is your only hope. Pray to the Suffering Mother of God. Blessings to all from Father Grigory. They're [Nicholas and Alexandra] angry in Petersburg for disturbing the peace. They wanted to give you the requested money. They're talking—why didn't he ask it to be sent?"[6] Gurko later alleged that Rasputin wired Alexandra, telling her that if Iliodor was not forgiven and permitted to stay in Tsaritsyn, the tsarevich would face "a great danger." It was Rasputin and Vyrubova, Gurko wrote, who would save Iliodor, although he provides no evidence for this.[7] Iliodor wrote years later in *The Mad Monk* that Rasputin sent this telegram to Nicholas: "It is my wish that Iliodor remain in Tsaritsyn." Iliodor makes for a most unreliable source, however. He also claimed in his book that he never asked Rasputin to help him during the crisis and had no idea that Rasputin had interceded on his behalf, words that his telegrams in Russia's archives prove to be lies.[8] And he contradicts what he wrote in a long letter in January 1912 where he states that even though Lokhtina and others begged Rasputin to help Iliodor, he did nothing.[9]

On 26 February, Stolypin wrote to the tsar about his thoughts on the scandal and the dangers it represented. For the prime minister, the Iliodor affair offered terrible proof of the church's weakness and disorder. Something clearly had to be done, and this included the removal of Sergei Lukyanov as chief procurator, but he could not stress enough to the tsar that this could under no circumstances happen now, for this would be interpreted by all, and especially by Iliodor, as a sign that the rebellious priest had won, and so embolden him, and other opponents of the state and church, and only further weaken the authority of these institutions. They had to do whatever necessary to avoid the worst possible scenario. "In Russia," Stolypin wrote, "nothing is more dangerous than the appearance of weakness." And not only did this concern the church, but the tsar himself, whose authority Iliodor had been so brazenly defying.[10]

The stand-off dragged on into the spring. Stremoukhov returned to Petersburg in late May to discuss the situation with Stolypin. He simply could not understand how the tsar could permit Iliodor to continue denouncing him and his authority. Many began to believe the rumor, apparently begun by Iliodor himself, that the reason Nicholas was loath to touch Iliodor was that he was in fact his stepbrother, the illegitimate son of the late Alexander III. Stremoukhov wanted to know why Stolypin was not doing anything about it, but the prime minister replied he had done everything he could. He told him that his hands were tied, that to move against Iliodor would be to knock down a hornets' nest, unleashing the fury of the right and left against him, and so greatly damage his power at court. They decided that Stremoukhov would talk to Nicholas, and not just about Iliodor, but his allies Germogen and Rasputin as well. But then, the day before his audience with the tsar, Stremoukhov received an anonymous phone call instructing him to only mention Iliodor and Germogen, not Rasputin. Stremoukhov asked who was calling, but the line went dead. A surprised Stremoukhov could not be certain, but he believed it had been Stolypin on the other end of the line, calling to warn him against discussing Rasputin with the tsar.

Stremoukhov told the tsar that he had come to report on the matter of Iliodor, but before he could say another word, Nicholas told him there was nothing to say, that he had already pardoned him. Stremoukhov could hardly believe his ears.[11] Incredibly, Nicholas had backed down and decided to permit Iliodor to remain in Tsaritsyn. The rebel monk had won in his battle against the tsar, his ministers, and the Synod. Nicholas's decision dealt a harmful blow to the prestige of the Synod and the throne. In a weak attempt to hide what had really happened, the official decree from the Synod issued on 2 April stated that Iliodor was to be allowed to leave Novosil for Tsaritsyn where he was to be placed under the authority of Germogen. The tsar, so it was explained, had heard the wishes of the people and acted accordingly. Of course, everyone knew that Iliodor had been in Tsaritsyn for several weeks already. Several prominent clerics chose to place the blame not on the tsar, where it truly lay, but on Rasputin, although there was no evidence that he had had anything to do with the decision.[12] Iliodor had been saved not by Rasputin's strength, but by Nicholas's weakness. Whatever Rasputin's role, given the closeness of their relationship, Iliodor's victory was quite understandably seen as a victory for Rasputin. Iliodor, however, appeared the ultimate victor. He knew this, and it went to his head.

The concerns of the larger Romanov family grew during this latest scandal. On 26 February, the same day that Stolypin wrote to the tsar, the Dowager Empress went to the Alexander Palace to warn her son and daughter-in-law about the danger Rasputin represented and to ask that they promise to send him away for good. Alexandra fought back and vigorously defended Rasputin, while Nicholas sat in silence. It pained Maria Fyodorovna to watch how her daughter-in-law dominated her son. Nicholas never once mentioned Rasputin in any of his letters to his mother. The subject for him was taboo. His mother wept: "My poor daughter-in-law does not perceive that she is ruining the dynasty and herself. She sincerely believes in the holiness of an adventurer, and we are powerless to ward off the misfortune, which is sure to come." It was possible she was then recalling that upon her arrival in Russia from her homeland of Denmark in 1866, an old woman had foretold that her son would rule over Russia with great wealth and power, only to be cut down by "a moujik's hand."[13]

Over lunch on 20 May, Maria Fyodorovna had a long talk about Rasputin with the tsar's uncle K. R. He wrote in his diary: "She is distressed that they continue to receive in secret some God's fool, Grisha, who orders the Empress A. and the children to keep it secret and not to say that they have seen him. It can hardly be beneficial to accustom the children to such dissimulation. Stolypin reported at some point to the Emperor that this Grisha is a rogue, but was told in reply to leave Grisha alone."[14]

Iliodor's victory meant Lukyanov's defeat. On 2 May, he was dismissed and replaced by Vladimir Sabler. Rumors began to spread that the selection had been made under the influence of Rasputin; some even claimed that before his official appointment Sabler had been "anointed" in the front hall of Rasputin's apartment.[15] This would have been difficult, however, since Rasputin had yet to return to Russia. Soon after Lukyanov's dismissal a triumphant Iliodor visited Petersburg. He was warmly welcomed into the salon of Countess Sofia Ignatieva and embraced by Stolypin's reactionary foes. He later claimed to have been received by Nicholas himself at Tsarskoe Selo.[16] The audience took place only in his overheated imagination.

After his meeting with Nicholas and Alexandra on 4 June, Rasputin hurried to Tsaritsyn to see Iliodor, arriving on the fourteenth. He stayed for two weeks. The press never let them out of sight.[17] On the eighteenth Rasputin gave a sermon before two hundred women about his journey to the Holy Land. On the twenty-fifth, he, Iliodor, and Germogen, accompanied by some forty women, traveled by boat to Dubovka to visit the sisters at the Holy Voznesenksky Convent. The press reported how in the convent's fields Iliodor went out to scythe some oats and then handed the tool to Rasputin. He made one or two awkward passes before banging the scythe against the ground and breaking it. The intended message was clear: Rasputin was no real peasant. The article focused on the warm reception Rasputin received from the sisters; they followed his every step and hung on his every word. Iliodor, they wrote, grew weary at the scene and they made to leave. A large crowd saw them off that night for the return trip, and as many as two hundred women joined them on the steamer back to Tsaritsyn. Rasputin made a few remarks after Iliodor's sermon to his followers on the night of the twenty-eighth. He then met with the women, one on one, in the corner of the church to tell them their future and give them advice on their troubles.[18] In the large yard outside the church Iliodor informed the crowd that tomorrow Rasputin would leave them and there was to be a special prayer service and procession to the wharf. The next morning following the liturgy Iliodor made another speech before a crowd of several thousand. It was more political rally than religious service. There were speeches praising Rasputin for defending Iliodor against the

Jews and "Kike Press." Iliodor called Rasputin "our much-loved friend and brother in Christ."

"When the atheists and yids slandered you," Iliodor cried, "all your friends hid. Only we could not and did not want to hide from the enemies, and we began to scream loudly about you for the world to hear and rose up to defend you. As over me, so over you, in recent days black clouds appeared but we have now defeated them." Rasputin was, in Iliodor's parting words, "a great man with the beautiful soul of an angel" and "a true envoy of God" who had left his family and wandered so as "to teach the people mildness, love, and humility." Rasputin, holding an icon aloft, complimented Iliodor in return, noting that he was amazed that in such a "corrupt city as Tsaritsyn" there is "such purity as Iliodor." Iliodor's followers presented Rasputin with an expensive tea service and then gave him a hero's send-off. The two men rode from the monastery through the entire city in a carriage bedecked with artificial flowers and greenery, accompanied by a crowd of women and girls singing patriotic songs and shouting "Hurray!" Most of them wore on their breast the badge of the local chapter of the Union of the Russian People. Several photographers had arrived to record the scene at the wharf as Rasputin boarded the steamer *Emperor Nicholas II*. A reporter for *The Church* recorded Rasputin's features:

> Rasputin's face—deathly pale and lifeless—is that of a man who doesn't like people to look him in the eyes. When you meet his glance, he immediately looks away to the side, as if he fears an unexpected, awkward question. Sharp features, a long nose and sunken gray eyes, most of the time gazing downward and only occasionally and furtively looking around to take in quick glances to the sides, that is the portrait of Rasputin.

The reporter continued:

> "Grigory Yefimovich!" Iliodor's sharp voice rang out. "Grigory! Do you know who your enemies are?"
>
> "I know!" just as loudly Rasputin answered and nodded his head.
>
> "And here they are with me!" Iliodor screamed again and held his closed fist high over the crowd. "And this is what will become of them." With that he suddenly spread his fingers and threw a wad of small pieces of paper that twisted and turned in the air and fell

to the ground on all sides. Iliodor was engulfed in a wave of approving cries and laughs.

The crowd sang the traditional hymn "Many Years" to Rasputin as he waved his bouquet in parting. Women managed to break through the line of sailors and run up to him, kissing his hands and the hem of his caftan and thrusting loaves of bread and packages into his hands. He bowed and thanked them all. As the steamer finally pulled away, Iliodor screamed one last time, "Grigory! Stand as strong as ever! And fear nothing!"[19]

Days later Iliodor undertook a rowdy pilgrimage—a sort of victory tour in his battle against the church and state—along the Volga River in a converted steamer accompanied by Olga Lokhtina and as many as 1,700 followers. Along the way Iliodor held up a bag that was said to be carrying as much as 3,000 rubles, money the empress had given to Rasputin to subsidize Iliodor's trip.[20] It was an ugly procession. Young toughs went along the shores shouting at onlookers to remove their hats and show their respect for Iliodor; those who failed to do so were roughed up. From the steamer they screamed: "Accursed yids! Anathema!" Iliodor stopped at Nizhny Novgorod and was warmly received by the local governor, Alexei Khvostov. Together they appeared on the balcony of the governor's mansion to receive the adulation of the crowd. Khvostov's and Iliodor's paths would cross again, under more sinister circumstances in early 1916. Iliodor was at the height of his career and everything seemed possible. As one journalist put it that summer, the only thing that existed for Iliodor was "his own ego."[21]

25. Two Murders

From Tsaritsyn Rasputin returned to Siberia for a month. On 4 August 1911, he was back at the Alexander Palace, where he sat with Nicholas and Alexandra for well over an hour after dinner.[1] A few weeks later Nicholas and Alexandra traveled to Kiev for the unveiling of a statue to Alexander II in connection with the fiftieth anniversary of the emancipation of Russia's serfs. Rasputin joined them. Soon after, he published his impressions of the visit in a small brochure titled *Great Days of Celebration in Kiev!* The brochure, printed in 20,000 copies in Petersburg, elicited this response from one newspaper: "It's unlikely that this debauchery [*rasputstvo*] of the word will elicit anything but laughter and indignation."[2]

"The visit of the Tsar helps renew the Motherland," Rasputin wrote. "Soldiers feel strong and filled with light. During these days they are ready to serve for the rest of their lives, they have been caught by a strong positive force and the bravery of warriors. Nothing can bring so much renewal as a visit of the Father-Tsar himself. Nobody can understand how and why—but everyone gets a solemn force from the Father-Tsar!"

Rasputin praised the tsar's visit and encouraged him to do more of the same, to get out and move among his people as something vital to his reign that would inspire his Christian subjects and help defeat his enemies:

> No Christian can even describe what happened in his heart when he saw the Father-Tsar! And those who are evil and godless experience such malice—they want to spread disturbances but have no power because the crowds of people are so full of joy: the evil and the envious cannot do evil things and their numbers drop now like ice thawing under heat, because the joy and the cries of "hurray" are like lightning and thunder. As the thunder strikes, we cross ourselves and when the "hurrays" come—it's our strength.

The evil are weak and they run from the "hurrays" like the Devil runs from prayers; Russia's enemies shudder and run and hide. [. . .]

How can you explain that? Only by the fact that the Orthodox faith is great and a God's Chosen and Anointed Man has appeared within it. There are no words to describe this and nothing can be compared with it. God, we are so happy! [. . .] His trip wakes up everyone who has been sleeping. Probably if he were to travel more often, he would see how he is waited for and loved and how the light of this love illuminates everything. [. . .]

Our Father-Tsar has passed by us with joy and has revitalized us with his visit over and over. God, reveal your mercy to us! Give courage to our Father-Tsar to visit us more and more often and survey the ready garden that belongs to him.[3]

As the references to enemies suggest, the brochure was dedicated not only to praising the tsar, but contained a darker message as well, one connected with a spectacular crime that had gripped the city that summer. In March 1911, thirteen-year-old Andrei Yushchinsky was found murdered in a city cave, his body horribly mutilated. While the police searched, unsuccessfully, for his killer, the local chapter of the Union of the Russian People began to spread the story that Andrei had been murdered in a Jewish ritual killing. The Black Hundreds called for pogroms against the city's Jews and soon the story was being carried by newspapers across Russia and attracting the attention of ministers back in the capital. In July, a month before the Romanovs arrived in Kiev, the police arrested a Jew by the name of Mendel Beilis and charged him with the killing. Beilis was clearly innocent, but he would be held for over two years until finally freed, during which time the "Beilis Affair," as it was known, became a world-wide cause célèbre among critics of the tsarist regime.[4]

Rasputin's name became attached to this gruesome affair, as with nearly everything that happened then in Russia. It was said that the day Andrei was murdered, Rasputin came across his mother on the street in Kiev and gave her five rubles. When the man Rasputin happened to be walking with asked him why he had given her the money, he replied that the poor woman did not know what he did: that she would not find her boy waiting at home as she expected for he had just been murdered.[5] It is a neat tale, even if pure fiction.

Rasputin spoke directly to the Beilis Affair in his brochure. He heaped praise on the Union of the Russian People, calling them "Allies" and "the true servants of the Church and the Great Tsar-Batiushka." The Union was like "the greatest saint." He encouraged the tsar to meet with the Black Hundreds and other nationalist groups, such as the Union of the Archangel Michael, to become their patron, and to encourage the formation of similar groups across the empire:

> These circles are necessary as protection from the Jews; the latter fear them a lot. When they walk through Kiev, the yids whisper and tremble; the army is not feared as much because they have military discipline and cannot do much, but the Union of the Russian People does not have discipline. There should be as many circles as possible and they should not quarrel among themselves, and then the yids won't even dream about asking for equality.[6]

The story of Rasputin and the Jews is a complex one. These words—and it should be assumed that they were his words—are the only public anti-Semitic comments he ever made. Nevertheless, Rasputin clearly was at home among Russia's most anti-Semitic clergymen in those years. He later turned away from this milieu, but he never openly denounced the views of men like Iliodor. Was Rasputin himself ever a member of the Union of the Russian People? Some have claimed he was, but there is no solid proof.[7] At times the press described Rasputin as a tool of the Black Hundreds at court. In May 1914, the press reported that Rasputin was a member of the Moscow branch of the Union of the Russian People and had had meetings with the deputy director of the rightist Russian Monarchist Union while on a visit to the city.[8] An anonymous letter sent to the department of the police in November 1915 asserted that Rasputin was a member of the Union of the Archangel Michael and had pledged himself to their cause of saving Russia from chaos and revolution.[9] There is no evidence to corroborate any of these allegations. If anything, Rasputin's close relations with many Jews in his later years, and his speaking out in their defense, raises considerable doubt about such reports.

The murder of young Andrei was not the only killing in Kiev that season with serious political repercussions. On the night of 1 September, Nicholas, his daughters Olga and Tatyana, and various dignitaries visited the Kiev Opera House for a performance of Nikolai Rimsky-Korsakov's *The Tale of the Tsar Saltan*. During the intermission, Dmitry

Bogrov, an anarchist and secret spy for the Okhrana, approached Stolypin and shot him twice with a revolver. Four days later Stolypin died. Stolypin's assassination has long been the subject of considerable speculation, especially concerning just whom Bogrov was working for that night: revolutionaries and Jews antagonistic to the regime or right-wing elements in the government itself opposed to Stolypin's reforms. The fact that Bogrov managed to enter the heavily guarded theater with a revolver has led some to believe that it was Kurlov himself who was behind the murder.[10]

Rasputin's presence in Kiev did not go unnoticed. Iliodor later implied that Rasputin had somehow been involved in the murder, and Prince Felix Yusupov wrote in his memoirs that Bogrov and Rasputin had been friends, and it was for this reason the tsar later halted the investigation into the killing.[11] It was also said that Stolypin had been murdered for trying to take on Rasputin.[12] There is no evidence at all that Rasputin even knew Bogrov, much less was his friend. The Provisional Government later investigated the matter but could not find the slightest trace linking Rasputin to the killing.[13]

Still, some said that while Rasputin may not have been involved, he did foresee Stolypin's end. Vasily Shulgin, a rightist Duma member, wrote that in the autumn of 1913 he was visited by a postal clerk from Kiev. The man told Shulgin that he had stayed in the same house in Kiev as Rasputin in 1911. One day, while they were standing on the street, the imperial carriage passed by, followed by another carrying Stolypin. Rasputin, the man told Shulgin, "suddenly began to shake, crying, 'Death is following him! Death is riding behind him! Behind Peter!'" Later that night the clerk heard Rasputin groaning, "Oh, there will be a tragedy, a tragedy." He asked Rasputin what the matter was, and he replied, "Oh, calamity, death is coming." The next evening, Stolypin was shot.[14]

The gossip at the Bogdanovich salon had it that after Stolypin died, Alexandra sent for Rasputin to get his advice on who should replace him.[15] The German ambassador, Hellmuth Lucius von Stoedten, wrote to Reichskanzler Theobald von Bethmann Hollweg that the tsar had sent "the monk" Rasputin to meet the man Stolypin had earlier thought would make a good candidate to take his place after he left office. Rasputin went and met him and then told the tsar he found the man "acceptable." The killing of Stolypin, the ambassador averred, had only reinforced in the emperor and empress the necessity "to trust the monk's protection and to listen to him."[16]

Vladimir Kokovtsov, then the minister of finance, became the new prime minister. The son of a poor noble family, Kokovtsov was bright and capable and a man of irreproachable integrity, traits that would help spell his downfall less than three years later.[17] Kokovtsov, and Alexander Makarov, the new minister of the interior, had not been in office long when they were confronted with the problem of the mounting number of stories in the press about Rasputin and his influence at court. The stories, Kokovtsov recalled, were unpleasant for both of them, and they knew that, eventually, they would be forced to deal with the matter. Indeed, Nicholas was angry and ordered Makarov to stop this "persecution" by the press. They tried to convince the editors of the most vocal newspapers, then *Speech* and the *Russian Word*, to stop but they refused, replying that the ministry of the interior was overstepping its authority. The editors said the problem could be solved quite easily: send him back to Tyumen and they would stop writing about him. This, of course, the ministers knew was impossible. Kokovtsov then called in Alexei Suvorin, editor of the popular *New Times*, and his assistant Mazaev and tried to show them how their constant articles about Rasputin only served "to advertise" him and, what was worse, played into the hands of the revolutionaries by weakening the prestige of the monarch. They agreed in principle, however, but the two men claimed to be innocent and insisted (insincerely) that the ones truly at fault were *Speech* and the *Russian Word*.[18] In the end, the press carried on as before.

That autumn Feofan made one last attempt to talk to the emperor and empress about Rasputin. At the beginning of 1911, Feofan had spoken before the Synod and asked that it express its official displeasure to Alexandra about Rasputin's behavior. His fellow hierarchs, however, demurred, telling Feofan that in his role as the royal couple's confessor, he ought to bring up the matter with them himself. He spoke with Alexandra for an hour and a half about Rasputin at Livadia, but his words were wasted. She insisted he was spreading slander and was deeply offended by Feofan's words. Alexandra became angry; at times she would call Feofan "loathsome." Feofan, however, bore Alexandra no ill will, and neither did Rasputin toward his former patron: "He feels malice toward me now," he said in 1914, "but I am not angry with him, for he knows so well how to pray. His prayers would be stronger if he did not have it out for me."[19]

26. Confronting the "Antichrist"

On 3 November, Iliodor sent a warm telegram from Tsaritsyn to Rasputin in Pokrovskoe: "Dear friend, I heartily thank you for your love. Forgive me but I can't come; I long to see you but affairs keep me here. Send me Annushka's address. For God's sake, don't be offended. [. . .] Loving you with all my soul, Hieromonk Iliodor."[1] The two did not manage to meet again until 16 December in Petersburg. What transpired that day makes for one of the most bizarre and mysterious events in Rasputin's life.

Rasputin had apparently just arrived early that day from Yalta and telephoned Iliodor asking whether they might meet. It was agreed that they would gather that evening at the residence of the Yaroslavsky Synod on the Nikolaevsky Embankment of Vasilevsky Island, where Germogen was staying at the time. Iliodor apparently met Rasputin in town and together they went to see Germogen. When they arrived Rasputin noticed something was amiss. Along with Iliodor and Germogen were two others: Ivan Rodionov, a Don Cossack, Black Hundred writer and reporter for the *New Times*, and ally of Iliodor (he had given public lectures and published a book defending Iliodor during the Tsaritsyn crisis), and the holy fool Mitya Kozelsky.[2] According to police files from January 1912, Rasputin and Mitya had been close friends for several years, but then Rasputin had come upon Mitya hugging and kissing one of his "sisters" and accused Mitya of "debauchery," to which Mitya replied he was only "killing the flesh" as Rasputin had taught him. Then, Mitya started a campaign against Rasputin, telling his own followers that he was not "a holy starets" but "a rogue." It was said Rasputin used his connections at court to see to it that Mitya was expelled from the capital.[3]

Both Iliodor and Rodionov left accounts of what (supposedly) happened next. Rasputin was on edge, Iliodor wrote. His eyes shot glances about the room and he appeared confused. They cornered Rasputin, and Iliodor told Mitya to begin. "Ah! You are an ungodly man! You have maltreated many women; many nurses; you live with the czarina. You're a rascal," Mitya, limping and waving a shriveled arm, screamed at Rasputin, who began backing up toward the door. (How Mitya the Nasal Voice communicated this without his interpreter is not explained.) With his good arm, Mitya grabbed Rasputin and dragged him over to an icon and began to scream even louder: "You're an ungodly man. You are the Antichrist." Trembling, Rasputin pointed at Mitya and mumbled: "No, you are an ungodly man. You're an ungodly man." In a different text, Iliodor wrote that Mitya tried to grab Rasputin's penis.[4]

It was Iliodor's turn next. He accused Rasputin of forcing his friendship on him, of threatening him should he try to break free of Rasputin. He had not been strong enough to rid himself of Rasputin, but now, he said, in the company of his friends, he stood before him as his accuser and prosecutor, and enumerated Rasputin's many evil deeds. "Grigory," Iliodor concluded, "I defended you. I shall also destroy you, and all your followers with you." Trembling, pale, biting his finger nails, Rasputin, in Iliodor's account, quaked with fear. Germogen held aloft a cross and asked Rasputin, the "Devil's disciple," whether he was ready to confess that what Iliodor had just spoken was the truth. "Yes," he said in a voice as if "from beyond the grave, 'Yes, the truth, the truth; everything is true.'" With that, Germogen grabbed Rasputin and began beating his head with the cross and shouting, "Devil, in God's name I forbid you to touch women. I forbid you to enter the imperial palace or to have anything to do with the czarina. You are a murderer." Next, before an icon, he ordered Rasputin never to enter the palace again without the permission of Germogen or Iliodor. Rasputin, pale as death, kissed the icon and promised.[5] Here Iliodor breaks off his story.

Rodionov (as presented in the memoirs of Mikhail Rodzianko) gave a somewhat different account. Here, Germogen, not Iliodor, takes the starring role in confronting Rasputin. More importantly, Rodionov depicts Rasputin not as cowering and afraid, but defiant and belligerent, refusing to acknowledge the charges against him and the injunction to stay away from court and even threatening to destroy Germogen for turning against him. He set upon the bishop and began to beat him savagely with his fists, before being pulled off by the others. Rasputin cursed that he would get even with them as he fled.[6] Over time other, more disturbing elements were added, namely that the men had tried to castrate Rasputin but he had somehow managed to escape.[7]

It seems fair to assume that Germogen, like Feofan, had by now come to see Rasputin as unworthy of his holy reputation and his place at court and had become convinced that Rasputin's proximity to the royal family was damaging the authority of the throne. A monarchist, again like Feofan, he believed that it was his duty to confront Rasputin in defense of the dynasty. In both men's actions, it is doubtful personal ambition played any role. The same cannot be said of the others involved. It is possible Mitya, nursing a grudge against Rasputin in the wake of the Monsieur Philippe scandal, had designs on trying to replace Rasputin at court, something Iliodor and others believed to be the case.[8] But if anyone was motivated by selfish reasons it was Iliodor. One theory is Iliodor turned against Rasputin after he had refused to help win money for Iliodor's proposed newspaper, *Thunder and Lightning*, and for future pilgrimages.[9] Iliodor himself gave a number of reasons. He wrote that after his victory earlier that year the tsar had promised to make him an archimandrite, but then Rasputin intervened to convince the tsar to rescind the order. "The saint gave and the saint took away," Iliodor commented years later.[10] He told another tale according to which Rasputin had tried to seduce the wife of a bishop that summer at the Pokrovsky Convent in Balashov, but was caught in the act by Iliodor and Germogen, who had set a trap for Rasputin to test whether the rumors about him were true.[11] Iliodor at another point wrote that he decided to turn on Rasputin when Mitya confirmed for him the rumor that he was sleeping with the empress. "I defended him more than anyone, and so I will destroy him," he swore.[12]

Iliodor is just as unconvincing when he writes that he had seen the truth about Rasputin in early 1910, but did nothing about it out of fear for his life.

None of this is plausible. Based on all the evidence, it seems most likely that Iliodor decided to move against his longtime friend shortly before this fateful encounter. And the idea for the confrontation (*pace* Iliodor in his *Mad Monk*) almost certainly belonged to Germogen, who convinced Iliodor to join him and come to Petersburg for the occasion.[13] The key to Iliodor's motivation lies in the shifting fortunes—or, better, "perceived" fortunes—of Rasputin and Iliodor. Many, Iliodor among them, saw Rasputin as having fallen into disfavor with his royal patrons since the spring of 1910. It is possible Iliodor read Rasputin's decision to undertake his pilgrimage to Jerusalem as yet more evidence of displeasure at court. At the same time, Iliodor saw his own star as on the rise. Not only had he been victorious in his standoff at Tsaritsyn, but he had been embraced by important figures of Petersburg society. In May Iliodor had heard talk that Nicholas was even considering raising him to the rank of metropolitan.[14] Following his summer pilgrimage, Iliodor felt that nothing and no one could stop him. It is interesting to note that in his letter of 3 November Iliodor asked Rasputin for Vyrubova's address. Was he planning on cultivating her as the crucial next step to the palace? Iliodor came to the conclusion that now was his chance to defeat Rasputin and take what he saw was his rightful place alongside Nicholas and Alexandra. The offer from Germogen came at just the right time.

Or so Iliodor thought, for he overplayed his hand. Iliodor would pay dearly for his mistake.

Part Four

A TIME OF MIRACLES

1912–July 1914

27. Germogen's Fall

On 7 January 1912, Germogen learned that four days earlier he had been relieved of his office as bishop of Saratov and removed from membership in the Holy Synod. He was shocked and angry and he knew who was responsible. Instead of keeping the matter within the ranks of his fellow church hierarchs, Germogen went public and gave an interview on the eleventh to the *Stock Exchange Gazette*: "I consider those chiefly responsible to be V. K. Sabler and that most notorious khlyst Grigory Rasputin, the most dangerous religious perverter of faith and the disseminator of the new *khlystovshchina*. [. . .] I repeat, he is the most dangerous and committed khlyst. [. . .] He hides his depravity behind an aura of blasphemous religiosity."[1]

The timing was indeed suspicious. The sacking came just weeks after the confrontation on Vasilevsky Island, and Germogen assumed this was Rasputin's revenge. Germogen was certain that Rasputin had gone immediately to Alexandra and told her what had happened and had her lean on Nicholas to have him punished. But there is not a single piece of evidence that Rasputin ever did such a thing. There is nothing to even suggest he had any contact at all with either the royal couple or Vyrubova between these two events. Germogen was mistaken. The cause of his downfall lay not with Rasputin, but with himself.

In the previous year the Synod proposed a series of changes in church practice, most importantly approving the creation of deaconesses and burial services for non-Orthodox Christians. Germogen was vehemently opposed to the reforms and sent a telegram to the tsar on 15 December 1911 asking him to intervene and stop the changes, which he described as "heretical," and to defend the Russian Orthodox Church against its enemies responsible for these innovations. The Synod was outraged at Germogen's taking an internal church matter to the tsar and voted to remove him. (Trouble with Germogen had been brewing: nearly every meeting of the Synod he attended resulted in clashes with his fellow hierarchs.) Adding fuel to the fire, on 14 January the full text of Germogen's telegram was printed in the pages of the *New Times*. This was now more trouble than Nicholas would allow, and the next day he telegraphed Sabler telling him that he wanted the Synod to have Germogen sent immediately from the city and order brought back to the body. That same day the Synod met. The clerics decided that both Germogen and Iliodor were to return to their homes by the end of the next day. Germogen, however, refused to obey. He demanded an audience with the tsar and then told the press he was not leaving until his demand was honored.[2]

The affair exploded onto the pages of the press. Reports were now appearing that the real reason Germogen had been fired was his opposition to plans by the Synod to have Rasputin made a priest.[3] Rumors gripped the city. Rodzianko claimed that a member of the Synod told him that at a secret meeting Sabler had proposed initiating Rasputin into the priesthood. The Synod was outraged and rejected the idea, even though Sabler insisted it had come from a "high source." At this meeting, Germogen had then reportedly delivered a fiery speech denouncing Rasputin's debauchery. In the end, Rasputin never did become a priest or monk, although people continued to talk. On 16 February, the *Petersburg Newspaper* ran a story purporting to quote Rasputin that it had been Germogen's plan, and not his, to join the priesthood. Rasputin put an end to any such talk by telling Germogen: "I've still not learned all the letters in the alphabet. Me . . . really? . . . I'm no priest."[4] A priest by the name of Ivan Dobrov wrote to Archpriest Ioann Vostorgov in Moscow that the idea belonged to the tsar since he wanted to make Rasputin his personal confessor. Once Germogen learned of this he was shocked and so made the news public, and this was the real reason he had been punished. "It's impossible to even imagine," the dismayed Dobrov sighed.[5] Two years later a story appeared in the press that Rasputin had finally become a priest back in Pokrovskoe in a ceremony conducted by Varnava, bishop of Tobolsk, and would soon divorce his wife and join a monastery.[6] It was a rumor that refused to die.

The reference to Varnava was not coincidental, for the bishop was Rasputin's ally, and Varnava's rise in the church hierarchy was attributed to his influence. Born Vasily Nakropin into a peasant family in Russia's northwestern Olonetsk province, Varnava was lit by an intense belief from his early years. He started out as a lay brother at the nearby Klimenetsky Monastery, rising to the level of hieromonk in 1898 and then becoming the monastery's senior priest the following year and later archimandrite. In 1908, upon the recommendation of Vladimir (Bogoyavlensky), the metropolitan of Moscow, Varnava was made the senior priest of the Troitsky Novo-Golutvin Monastery in the town of Kolomna outside Moscow. Varnava was beloved by his parishioners, particularly for his impassioned sermons and the simple, direct way with which he discussed matters of faith, and became a frequent guest in the homes of Moscow's upper classes. According to one source, Varnava also proved to be an excellent administrator of the monastery.

Varnava's career was rather surprising given his almost total lack of education. He never attended seminary and it is not even clear whether he finished rudimentary schooling. He was barely literate; it was said he began every word with an upper case letter and ended every word with a period. And there were other curious things. Slight and short with a high-pitched voice, Varnava, it was rumored, liked to wear women's clothing, throw wild parties in the monastery, and take boys to his bed. Father Georgy Shavelsky, the last protopresbyter of the Imperial Russian army and navy, characterized Varnava in a letter to Father Vostokov as a cunning and nasty figure of unhealthy ambition. He said Varnava was the confessor to "that Mason Count Witte, and is himself an atheist-Mason." Shavelsky even claimed Varnava had sexually abused and then murdered a beautiful young altar boy at Kolomna, his body discovered lodged under a mill wheel.[7]

Varnava and Rasputin met in one of the capital's salons, and if they did not become friends, the two men of similar backgrounds apparently realized they could be of use to each other: Rasputin could help advance Varnava's career, Varnava could defend Rasputin against attacks from within the ranks of the church. Rasputin introduced him to Nicholas and Alexandra as just the type of man needed to inject new life into the hidebound ranks of the clergy. Alexandra found Varnava unctuous and duplicitous, but Rasputin managed to convince her and Nicholas to have the Synod promote him to the rank of bishop. Nicholas instructed Chief Procurator Sabler to bring the matter up at the Synod and see that it was done. Sabler was shocked. He knew there was no way the Synod would ever endorse a figure like Varnava.

Reluctantly, Sabler brought Varnava's nomination before the Synod without mentioning on whose recommendation. Archbishop Antony (Khrapovitsky), ignorant of what and who lay behind the nomination, asked Sabler to remove it from discussion, and this was done. Sometime later, the tsar asked Sabler why Varnava had yet to be appointed bishop. When Sabler told him, Nicholas grew angry and insisted that God had placed him over the Synod and not the other way around. Soon after, Sabler brought up the matter of Varnava again. A surprised Antony asked Sabler who was behind the recommendation, and now the chief procurator broke his silence and told him it was the wish of the tsar. The eleven members of the Synod could hardly believe their ears. Dmitry, the bishop of Kherson, asked: "And then must we ordain Rasputin?"

Sabler had been prepared for this. He opened his portfolio and pulled out a letter of resignation addressed to the tsar. Should the Synod not endorse Varnava, Sabler told them, he would have to resign as it would no longer be possible for him to serve any further as an intermediary between the emperor and the Synod. Fearing a public scandal, and that Sabler would be replaced by someone worse, the prelates backed down. "We would make a black boar bishop to keep you in your position," Antony said, and in mid-August 1911 the Synod elected Varnava bishop of Kargopol and vicar of the Olonetsk eparchy. Antony and his fellow Synodians were disgusted. "It is now clear that Rasputin installed Varnava in the episcopate," Antony wrote to Flavian, the metropolitan of Kiev. "Rasputin is to blame for the Holy Synod's rascally behavior. He is a khlyst and takes part in their rituals."[8]

The Synod had given Germogen twenty-four hours to leave the capital but he still refused to go before speaking to the tsar. He sent Nicholas another telegram, expressing his devotion and loyalty and repeating his request. He tried to break down the tsar's refusal by offering "to tell him a secret." The tsar was not to be moved. On 17 January, Nicholas wrote to Sabler: "I don't care to know any secrets. Nicholas." Germogen next appealed to Alexandra, citing his poor health and requesting a stay in his banishment, but she too refused to see him, instructing him to obey "the powers established by God."[9] Again Nicholas ordered Sabler to send Germogen somewhere far away from both Petersburg and Moscow. Germogen now realized he had no more cards to play. On the twenty-second, General Dedyulin and Sabler visited the office of minister of the interior Makarov with an order that Germogen be sent from the city that day. Dedyulin passed on the tsar's words that he would not tolerate any further delays and that Makarov was to remove him by force if necessary. Around 11:30 that night, Germogen arrived at the Warsaw station, accompanied by Mitya Kozelsky, Dr. Pyotr Badmaev, and several policemen. He hesitated before boarding the train, as he thought he might escape his fate, but Mitya made sure he got on. "One must obey the Tsar, and submit to His will," he kept repeating to Germogen. And with that Germogen was gone. He journeyed to the St. Uspensky Monastery at Zhirovits in the Minsk province. Here he would stay until 1915, living quietly in two small rooms, serving in the church, and giving sermons to the local parishioners.[10]

The empress's sister Ella was profoundly disturbed by the scandal. A friend of hers in Moscow wrote to Hieromonk German in Sergiev Posad: "Her grief and alarm is beyond description. She is ready to cry and I do not doubt that Her prayers overflow with tears." He noted that Ella had said one might still open the tsar's eyes to Rasputin, but then all it takes is a word from the empress, "in her powerful and confident tone," and then he falls under her spell. As for the empress, it was far too late. "To talk to her is an empty waste of time and nerves—the hypnosis of mystical khlystovism, that is so persistent, is stronger than any logic." And so, Ella said nothing. "The situation is truly tragic."

Ella asked her old friend Archimandrite Gavriil to pray for the tsar as this was "a very difficult time, one might even say threatening, for all of Russia." The Novoselov attacks of 1910 and now this latest scandal were too much, she wrote.

> There's been such violence, such shame already, that all the be-
> lievers in Moscow are filled with outrage and the indignation
> against the TSAR and TSARITSA has seized everyone. Everyone
> pities them as dupes, and all the anger is directed against Rasputin,
> who They so ardently defend and believe in as the way to save their
> souls. (All this is secret.) Pray, that the Lord will open Their eyes
> and minds and give Them the strength to withstand all shame and
> repentance. Oh, if only They were to do this. How dear and longed-
> for they would become for all Russia, that would also repent and
> pray for forgiveness. Bring Them to Their senses, instruct Them,
> Lord.

But Ella had little hope of such an outcome. She feared they would continue to defend "Grishka," and in so doing widen the chasm that had opened up between the tsar and his subjects, "all to the malicious joy of the enemies of Russia and Orthodox faith."[11]

The fate of Germogen provoked public outrage, and for weeks the press fanned the flames. Typical was this story by Novoselov for the *Voice of Moscow*:

> Why are the bishops, who are well informed of the activities of this impudent cheat and seducer, silent? Why are the guards of Israel also silent when in their letters to me they openly call this false-teacher a false-khlyst, sex-maniac, and charlatan? Where is His Holiness, if due to negligence or faint-heartedness he is not guarding the purity of the faith of God's Church and permits a depraved khlyst to carry out his dark deeds in the cover of darkness? Where is his ruling right hand, if he is not willing to lift a finger to expel an impertinent seducer and heretic from the church's garden? Is it possible he is not adequately informed of the activity of Grigory Rasputin? If that is the case, please forgive me for my inappropriate, presumptuous words and I humbly ask to be summoned by the high church administration so that I may present the details that prove the truth of my judgment about this khlyst-seducer.[12]

On 18 February, a long article under the title "At Grigory Rasputin's" appeared in the *New Times*. The author, listed as "I. M-v.," was one Ivan Manasevich-Manuilov. The Jewish Manasevich had been adopted as a boy by a wealthy Russian merchant named Manuilov, who left him an immense fortune that Manasevich managed to go through on gambling and drinking. Later converting to Lutheranism, he moved to the capital and became a protégé (and, it has been suggested, lover) of the elderly and openly homosexual Prince Vladimir Meshchersky, with whose help he launched a remarkable career as a spy, police informant, and journalist in Russia and abroad. Short, soft, and black-haired Manuilov was an infinitely protean, chameleon-like figure, a double-, triple-agent known as "the Mask" and "the Russian Rocambole" after the famous adventurer-schemer created by the nineteenth-century French writer Pierre Alexis Ponson du Terrail. Despite his public reputation as a reporter, Manuilov also secretly worked for the Okhrana and the ministry of the interior focusing on counter-intelligence operations. He had considerable success and was awarded the Order of St. Vladimir

4th Class by the emperor for his services to the state. Unprincipled, unscrupulous, venal, Manuilov was both admired and feared. "Loathsome" was the word Alexander Blok used to describe him.[13] Manuilov would in later years become a confidant of Rasputin, but at first he worked with his enemies. Under Stepan Beletsky, director of the department of the police from 1912 to 1914, Manuilov was tasked with writing negative stories about Rasputin for the press, particularly the *New Times*. He also hounded Rasputin in the streets of Petersburg with a photo camera, causing Rasputin to complain to the police.[14]

"At Grigory Rasputin's" read as if it were Rasputin's reply to the crisis. There were lengthy quotes attributed to him in which he both defended himself and attacked Germogen and Iliodor: "What sort of monster am I . . . With my spirit I'm actually closer to God, and they, my enemies, know that they are lying . . . And as long as someone is in the power of lies, then nothing good can come of this . . . It will devour him. God closed Bishop Germogen's and Iliodor's minds . . . [. . .] Malice overtook their hearts." The article was far from convincing or, much less, flattering, with (most likely manufactured) quotes such as: "I am a sinner . . . Great sin has tormented me more than once and has been stronger than me."[15] Manuilov's article was translated into English and French and appeared in newspapers abroad. Rasputin was greatly angered by the whole business. The idea for the article it turned out belonged to Yevgeny Bogdanovich, and he had then gone to Beletsky to see it carried out.

Bogdanovich wrote to Lev Tikhomirov in February to complain and spread even more gossip: "What's going on! That awful Anyutka [Vyrubova] is responsible for all this. Grishka is their master, or what else might he be? She (the empress) sits with him, behind a locked door. The Emperor comes and knocks, She doesn't let Him in . . . Sitting with Grishka . . . She doesn't let the Tsar come to her even at night. And Grishka puts the children to bed, tucks in the covers. What in the world!" With this, Bogdanovich began to cry. "Just think," he wailed, "this is the Throne, after all, the Russian Tsar, might, purity, holiness . . . And what's happening? Where is the eminence? The might? Dirt. Filth. The foul Grishka reigns." Bogdanovich was so distraught he wrote that month to the tsar, imploring him to get rid of Rasputin, going so far as to say that he ought to disappear from the face of the earth. Nicholas was not angered by the letter, putting it down as the words of an old crank. Yet, after Bogdanovich wrote the tsar once more about the matter in October 1913, Nicholas put him in his place, informing him that he would not tolerate any more letters about Rasputin. He added that he was forty-six years old, and so had no further need for any mentors.[16]

As for Rasputin, it seems he bore no ill will toward Germogen. Beletsky told the Commission that he attended a dinner a few years later where Rasputin and Seraphim (Chichagov), the archbishop of Tver, were present. When the subject of Germogen came up, Rasputin had nothing to say other than, "God alone will judge us both." Serafim was moved by Rasputin's magnanimity. Germogen was less forgiving. Rasputin, he said later that year, was the "enemy of everything good."[17]

28. Iliodor, Apostate

While Germogen was boarding the train for exile, things were unraveling for Iliodor as well. Having lost the protection of Germogen, and the support of Rasputin, Iliodor too was to be sent away from the capital to the Florishchev Monastery in the Vladimir province. He was not to leave the walls of the monastery and never again to show himself in Petersburg or Tsaritsyn. Iliodor, however, had other ideas in mind. In one of his typical grand gestures, he informed the press that he would be leaving not by train but was setting off for Florishchev on foot through the snow and ice. This was a ruse meant to confuse the authorities, and with the help of Rodionov and Mitya Kozelsky, he snuck off in disguise to the apartment of Dr. Badmaev at 16 Liteiny Prospect. Iliodor begged the doctor to hide him and intercede on his behalf at court.

A self-styled doctor of Tibetan medicine, the bright and well-educated Badmaev began his career in the reign of Alexander III. He established a laboratory where he developed various Eastern herbal remedies that became the rage among the capital's fashionable crowd. His medical work was not his chief interest, but more a way of making the acquaintance of the well-connected and through them access to lucrative business dealings. When he learned of Nicholas and Alexandra's interest in holy men and mystics, he saw that by attaching himself to such figures he could secure his own influence at court, and it was this that led him first to Iliodor and then to Rasputin. Badmaev was not foreign to scandal. In 1902, he sued a medical doctor by the name of Krandel over a series of articles he had published in *News of the Day* asserting Badmaev had no qualifications to practice medicine. One of Badmaev's patients went public with his doubts and denounced him as a fraud. The Tibetan quack began losing so many patients he contemplated closing up shop and moving to Paris.[1] In 1911, Badmaev petitioned the authorities to open a "Society for Followers of Tibetan Medicine" together with a series of pharmacies, clinics, and out-patient centers in Petersburg and other towns, but the project was rejected by the medical board. Not to be denied, Badmaev turned to Kurlov and Dedyulin, the palace commandant, for help in appealing the decision, and in the end the board did permit him to open a research society into the study of Tibetan medicine. Despite the board's skepticism, Badmaev continued doing brisk business at a clinic outside St. Petersburg, treating many of the elite with various powders and elixirs.[2] "An intelligent and cunning Asian," Alexander Blok called him, "whose head was filled with political chaos and on whose tongue was always a joke, and who busied himself not only with Tibetan medicine and the Buryat school but also concrete pipes."[3]

Badmaev promised to help Iliodor. He told him to write down everything he knew about Rasputin and he would pass this on to Dedyulin and make certain he gave it to the tsar. This was the only way to save himself, Badmaev told Iliodor, and destroy Rasputin.[4] Having failed to leave the city and gone into hiding, Iliodor was now the subject of an intense manhunt by the Petersburg police. Rasputin had lost all patience with his former friend. "Dear Papa and Mama! Iliodor has been making friends with demons," he wrote. "He's rebelling. Such monks used to be flogged. The Tsars did just this. [. . .] He's a rebel. Grigory." And then again: "If you pardon a dog, Sergei Trufanov [i.e. Iliodor], then he, the dog, will eat everyone."[5]

Having received Dedyulin's specific instructions on what to write, Iliodor sat down on 25 January and composed over a feverish four hours a text he titled "Grisha." Written as a letter to an unnamed "highly placed personage close to the Court," the exposé purports to recount Iliodor's relationship with Rasputin since he first heard his name talked about in the halls of the Petersburg Theological Seminary in 1904. Nothing in the text can be taken for the truth. It is a long list of misinformation, gossip, innuendo, and outright lies. Rasputin is depicted as a sadist, a rapist, a khlyst, and the empress's lover. Iliodor presents outlandish scenes (how, for example, in Makary's cell at Verkhoturye Monastery Maria Vishnyakova wrapped her naked legs around Rasputin's face), fills Rasputin's mouth with impossible words ("The Tsar considers me to be Christ. The Tsar and Tsaritsa bow at my feet [. . .] I carried the Tsaritsa in my arms [. . .]," etc.), and makes absurd claims ("His genital member does not work"—this of the man he asserts is sleeping with the empress, among others). Not content to slander Rasputin, he takes aim at his children—he describes Dmitry as a debauched, corrupt foul-mouth and Maria as a "vile, disgusting girl."

The only bit of truth in Iliodor's letter is this prophetic warning of where matters were leading: "He needs to be removed from the presence of the Tsars and punished as a libertine who dared to consider himself a righteous man and thus crawl his way to the Tsars. If Grishka is not removed and hidden away now, then the Tsarist Throne will topple and Russia will perish."[6]

Iliodor's letter never reached the tsar. For some reason the agreement between Badmaev and Dedyulin broke down, and the letter remained in Badmaev's possession. Frustrated and convinced that Iliodor's unmasking of Rasputin should not be wasted, Badmaev sent a copy of the letter to Mikhail Rodzianko and other members of the Duma. The reaction was overwhelming and placed Rasputin once again at the center of a national scandal.[7] Iliodor himself sent a copy to the Synod in April 1914 and a month after that it began appearing in Russian newspapers. By then, every literate Russian had a chance to read it.[8] Even after sending out copies of the letter to the tsar's foes, Badmaev made one last attempt to make a deal with the palace. On 17 February, he wrote to Nicholas to defend Germogen and Iliodor as "fanatics of the faith," deeply devoted to the tsar, who had felt it their duty to protect the throne by trying to convince Rasputin to stay away. For this, Rasputin had them destroyed. Badmaev told the tsar that he, Badmaev, given his contacts in society, the clergy, the government, and the Duma was the only man to "liquidate this entire affair" before it was too late.[9] Badmaev's letter went unanswered.

Next, Badmaev tried to intercede with Dedyulin, telling him that forcing Iliodor to leave would only make a martyr of him, something that would play into Iliodor's hands. But Dedyulin would not budge, noting that the man was "harmful to any normal, so-called peaceful state structure." With that, Badmaev gave him up.[10] In the end, Iliodor had no choice but to acquiesce and leave for Florishchev. This did not mean, however, he had surrendered to Rasputin.

From Florishchev Iliodor continued to write to Badmaev with more stories of Rasputin's nefarious character and outlandish behavior. Then Iliodor reached for another weapon. He wrote Badmaev that while visiting Pokrovskoe he had received from Rasputin's own hands on the morning of 7 December 1909 several letters of the empress and the grand duchesses.[11] Others have questioned this account. In 1919, Maria said that her father, "out of his honest simplicity," had shown Iliodor the letter from the empress and he had stolen it.[12] Rasputin said the same thing in a letter to Olga Lokhtina in early 1913: "he's a bastard, he steals letters [. . .]."[13] It is likely Rasputin, boasting of his intimacy with the royal family, showed the letters to Iliodor and maybe even lent them to him and Iliodor never bothered to return them. Given Iliodor's duplicitous character, it is even more likely he pocketed them when Rasputin was not looking. The cunning monk knew they might well come in handy later.

There was one letter from Alexandra and one from each of the four grand duchesses, apparently all written in 1909.[14] Those from the girls were rather harmless. They spoke of how they missed Rasputin, of how he visited them in their dreams, of how they try to be the good girls he tells them to be, of how hard it is to see their mother so ill. Grand Duchess Olga asked him for advice on how best to behave toward her crush Nikolai, who was literally driving her crazy.[15] Alexandra's letter to Rasputin, however, was far from harmless:

> My beloved and unforgettable teacher, savior and mentor. How tiring it is for me without you. My soul is calm and I can rest only when you, my teacher, are seated next to me, and I kiss your hands and lay my head on your blessed shoulders. Oh, how easy things are for me then. Then I wish for only one thing—to fall asleep, fall asleep forever on your shoulders, in your embrace. Oh, what happiness it is just to feel your presence near me. Where are you? Whither have you flown? It's so difficult for me, such longing in my heart . . . But you, my beloved mentor, don't say a word to Anya* about my sufferings without you. Anya is good, she is kind, she loves me, but don't tell her of my sorrow. Will you soon be here near me? Come soon. I am waiting for you and am miserable without you. Give me your holy blessing, and I kiss your blessed hands. Loving you for all times. Mama.[16]

Iliodor wrote Badmaev that he no longer had the originals, having handed them over to Rodionov, and he had in turn given them to a certain clergyman, whom Iliodor did not name.[17] Iliodor had, however, made copies that he sent to Badmaev with the following letter:

These letters, it seems to me, don't represent very much on their

---

* Vyrubova.

own, but when you take into account to whom, to what sort of unrepentant libertine they were written, then your skin turns to ice and one fears terribly for the fate of the altar of the Russian people—for the blessed Tsarist family. For nothing is more sacred. [. . .]

I beg you to finish off Grishka as soon as possible. He is getting stronger with every passing day. His army grows. His name is spreading among "the lower orders." I'm not so concerned for my fate, but Theirs! The most grandiose scandal might erupt and everything could end with the most terrible revolution. For God's sake, get rid of Grishka as soon as possible and shut his mouth. Every day counts.[18]

The originals supposedly ended up in the hands of Minister of the Interior Alexander Makarov. How they got there is not clear. Did the unnamed clergyman hand them over, or Rodionov himself, or, as Stepan Beletsky wrote in his memoirs, were they passed along by a Cossack officer and a Mr. Zamyslovsky working in collaboration with a certain "Madame Karabovich" in Vilnius?[19] Or was it someone else altogether, as Kokovtsov wrote in his memoirs, some unnamed man who gave them to Makarov quite readily, saying, "These people [Rasputin, Iliodor, and their allies] will think nothing of strangling me if I don't return the letters to them."[20]

Makarov telephoned Kokovtsov in the early days of February to tell him to come to his house (Makarov was home sick at the time) for he had something vital to show him. There, he presented the prime minister with the original letters. Kokovtsov read them over. He saw that Alexandra's letter matched exactly the copy of it that Duma member Alexander Guchkov had been spreading about Petersburg. The letter released into society the poisonous notion that the empress was having sex with a debauched Russian peasant in the palace, for this is how they were read in salons and drawing rooms across the country. Practically everyone, it seems, was ready to think the worst about the empress. No one came to her defense.

"I sit down to write with a sorrowful, defeated feeling," Alexandra Bogdanovich's diary reads for 18 February:

I've never been forced to live through such a shameful time. Russia is not being ruled by a tsar, but the adventurer Rasputin, who loudly announces that the empress needs him less than he, Nicholas, does.

Is that not horrifying! The tsaritsa's letter to him, Rasputin, is being shown around in which she writes that she can only find peace when she rests on his shoulder. Is that not shameful!

At present all respect for the tsar has been lost. Yet here the tsaritsa announces that the tsar and heir are healthy and alive thanks only to Rasputin's prayers, and that Rasputin dares to openly say that he is needed more by Nicholas (the tsar, that is) than the tsaritsa. That phrase could make one go crazy. What impertinence![21]

Makarov and Kokovtsov began to discuss what to do. At first Makarov proposed simply hiding them to make certain they did not fall into the wrong hands, but Kokovtsov rejected this as potentially opening them up to charges of concocting some sort of nefarious plot. Next, Makarov expressed the idea of presenting them to the emperor; this too the prime minister objected to, noting this would place the emperor in a very difficult situation and he would invariably tell the empress, which would harm Makarov. No, Kokovtsov recommended Makarov request an audience with the empress and hand the letters to her himself and tell her how they came to be in his possession. This Makarov promised to do.

But Makarov did not keep his word. At his next meeting with the tsar, according to Kokovtsov's memoirs, Makarov told him the story of the letters and presented them to him in an envelope. Nicholas, who had been in a fine mood, turned white and nervously removed the letters from the envelope. Looking at the empress's handwriting he commented: "Yes, this is a genuine letter," and angrily tossed the envelope in his desk drawer. The tsar's words put to rest any doubts Makarov and Kokovtsov might have had as to the letters' authenticity. Although the letter Nicholas received may well have been Alexandra's, as Kokovtsov alleges in his memoirs (and as one of the few truly honest men in this history we ought to be hesitant not to take him at his word here), there is no way of knowing for certain whether the letter Nicholas read was the same one Iliodor sent to Badmaev and that then began circulating in subsequent copies throughout the country, for the fact is the original was never seen again. Iliodor's "copy" is all that exists, and in light of his reputation, its veracity is highly contestable. How far did Iliodor's copy match or diverge from the original? Of this, no one will ever know.[22]

The memoirs of Duma President Mikhail Rodzianko further complicate the matter. He wrote that Iliodor had managed to take

Alexandra's letter from Rasputin not in Pokrovskoe but during the confrontation at Germogen's residence on 16 December 1911. The letter, together with those of the grand duchesses, ended up with Rodionov, who then handed them over to Rodzianko in early 1912 when he was gathering evidence against Rasputin. Rodzianko claims that after telling the Dowager Empress he had Alexandra's original letter in his possession, she asked him to destroy it. "Yes, your Majesty, I will destroy it," he told her, but then, so he writes, he went back on his word and kept the letter, never showing it to the tsar. In his memoirs, written in exile in the early 1920s, Rodzianko states Alexandra's original letter was still in his possession. And he makes one more interesting remark about this letter, namely, that "distorted copies of it were being circulated" in society.[23] Where the truth lies in all this is impossible to say: Did Makarov give Kokovtsov a false rendering of his audience with the tsar? Did Kokovtsov get something wrong when recounting these events in his memoirs? Did Rodzianko lie in his memoirs when he claimed to still have in his hands Alexandra's letter? What can be said is that there is no way of knowing whether the letter attributed to Alexandra quoted above was in fact hers or one of the sexed-up bogus copies then being passed from hand to hand in Russian society.

It is also not clear why Makarov ignored the advice of the prime minister. Was he trying to strike a blow against Alexandra by going to her husband? Was he, as has been proposed, trying to open the tsar's eyes to a physical relationship between Alexandra and Rasputin in the hope Nicholas would send both of them away?[24] This seems unlikely, for Alexandra's letter did not prove they were lovers. Rather, as Kokovtsov correctly put it, the empress's words speak to something else entirely: "They showed all her love for her sick son, and all her striving to find in her faith in miracles a means to save his life. They showed the exaltation and religious mysticism of this deeply unhappy woman."[25] Both Kokovtsov and Gurko later wrote that Makarov's act so angered the empress that it led to his dismissal, but this does not appear to have been the case at all. In fact, Makarov held on to his post until the middle of December—a full ten months—and would be let go not over the incident of the letter, but due to matters connected with the investigation into the assassination of Stolypin and, in particular, the role played by Kurlov, whom Makarov believed to be responsible.[26]

*

Life at Florishchev was harsh and humiliating. Iliodor was confined to a small, damp room with iron-barred windows. He slept on bare planks and had no contact with the monks. He stopped attending services and gave up on the practice of his faith. He did, however, have a few visitors, including Lokhtina and some reporters, who managed to sneak their way in.[27] Among them was the journalist Stepan Kondurushkin. Moved by Iliodor's plight, he wrote to Maxim Gorky on 20 March to seek his help. He described Iliodor as "a man sincere and passionate in his belief." Rasputin, Iliodor told Kondurushkin, had so destroyed his faith in Russia's holy institutions—the throne and the church—that he was considering writing a book by the title of "The Holy Devil" to expose his enemy. The book, which he would print abroad, would create, Iliodor assured him, more than an enormous scandal—it would ignite a "political coup." Iliodor knew the risks he was taking in speaking this "terrible truth," but he was prepared. "I am prepared for anything, for everything has been taken from my spirit, my ideal, that I lived for, and all I have left is exile, frayed nerves, and a pained, pained heart." Kondurushkin found the idea rather naive (he wrote it would create nothing but "fruitless noise"), but still he wanted Gorky's opinion. Gorky replied that it was a necessary and timely project, promising to do whatever he could to see it was published abroad. "Do act! For truth, it's very good!" Gorky wrote.

Iliodor would write his book and it would be published, although only years later and under circumstances none of them could have predicted. Regardless, Kondurushkin did not abandon Iliodor. He began to write articles in defense of Iliodor for *Speech* and gave public lectures on his story, describing him as the leader of "a popular protest against faithless democracy." Among those attracted to his work on Iliodor were Sergei Melgunov and Alexander Prugavin, two figures committed to the defense of civil rights in Russia and whose lives would later cross paths with Iliodor as well.[28]

Despite everything he had written in his scandalous letter from January, despite everything he had told Kondurushkin, Iliodor made one last effort to reconcile with Rasputin. On 19 November, he wrote a final letter to his old friend and ally—"I beseech you, dear friend, take note of a man reaching out to you."[29] Rasputin did not reply. That evening, Iliodor sat down to write a letter to the Synod renouncing his office in

the church. Ignoring his inkwell, he took a razor, cut his arm, and wrote
in his own blood.

> For ten months I have appealed to you to do penance.
> I have implored you, begged you, to defend Christ's bride,
> the Russian Church, from the violence and desecrations
> of the libertine Grishka Rasputin. You have not repented;
> you have not even expressed a desire to do so. All I can
> say to you now is, "May your abode be empty!" May
> eternal truth judge you! Now I renounce your faith.
> I renounce your church. I renounce you as prelates. Under
> your mantles you have concealed the "holy devil" Grigory
> Yefimovich Rasputin, knowing that this vessel of lawlessness,
> pretending to consecrate human bodies, has ruined
> many. You have known this, but you have shielded him
> while intriguing to damnation the champions of the purity
> and innocence of Christ's bride, the exposers of the "holy
> devil." While the body of the church trembled like a
> wounded bird, like a dove in a hawk's claws, like an innocent
> maiden before an insolent violator, you solemnly, at
> the Synod, extolled the hunter, the hawk, the violator, and
> called him confessor. [. . .]
> You may perhaps be permitted thus to make sport of others,
> but not of me, not of me. I shall not allow you to mock my
> ideals. And therefore, from now on, I recognize neither
> your God nor you as his prelates.[30]

The following month Iliodor was defrocked. Rasputin wrote to
Nicholas and Alexandra: "Dear Papa and Mama. Iliodor's the Devil. An
apostate. He's damned. He must have gone mad. He needs a doctor, or
else all's lost. The Devil will dance to his tune."[31] When asked about
Iliodor's behavior, the *Petersburg Newspaper* reported Rasputin as saying:
"No matter how great a sinner I have been, and all of us are sinners, no
matter how people or fate have oppressed me, or circumstances were
such, still I have not renounced my faith nor would I ever." It seemed
Rasputin was loath to condemn Iliodor. "Good luck to him, to Iliodor.
God will judge."[32] It is doubtful these were indeed Rasputin's own
words, for in early 1913 he sent Iliodor a number of short nasty letters
threatening to shove a wooden stake up his "ass" and calling him
"satan." He also wrote to Lokhtina insisting she stop visiting him and

see the truth about Iliodor, for he was a "dog" who ought to be "hanged."[33] Although Germogen would not go that far, he too had to admit Iliodor had sided with the atheists and fallen "into the deepest abyss."[34] The press described Iliodor's downfall thus: "At first, friends, moving along hand in hand. Then, fierce, ruthless enemies to the grave. They were enemies since both were moving toward the same goal, and one ended up superfluous."[35]

Iliodor had given up his faith and his priestly name, becoming once again Sergei Trufanov,* and then he left the Florishchev Monastery for his native Cossack village of Bolshoy in the Don region, some hundred miles northeast of Rostov-on-Don. He built a house for himself next to that of his parents and called it New Galilee. He got married and tried to settle down, but he did not forget his enemies. Iliodor seethed with anger. He had been wronged, so he felt, and as the months passed he began to plot his revenge. Seeing himself as a modern-day Yemelian Pugachev, the rebel Cossack who unleashed perhaps the greatest rebellion in Russia during the reign of Catherine the Great, he decided he would start a revolutionary movement to shake the country to its foundations. He purchased 120 bombs and planned to begin by assassinating sixty lieutenant-governors and forty bishops across the country. The attacks would commence on 6 October 1913: the name-day of the tsar. A hundred men disguised as priests would hurl their bombs just as the officials were leaving the churches to mark the occasion. The terror would unleash revolution across Russia. But the police uncovered the plot after Iliodor was sold out by one of his followers. He was arrested and held in his village to await sentencing. It was there, he wrote later, that he was approached by a woman named Khionya Guseva. She came to Iliodor with a vow to help by taking vengeance on the man responsible for his troubles: Grigory Rasputin.[36]

---

* To avoid confusion, Sergei Trufanov will still be referred to here as Iliodor, unless his given name is used in quoted material.

29. *Quousque tandem abutere patientia nostra?*

On 3 January 1912 (the same day Germogen had been removed from the Synod), Mikhail Novoselov, publisher of the series Religious-Philosophical Library, arrived at the printing office of the Snegirev publishing house in Moscow carrying the typescript of a booklet titled *Grigory Rasputin and Mystical Libertinage*. He placed an order for 1,200 copies, to include two portraits, and left. He had been careful to keep the original copy of the manuscript safely hidden in his Moscow apartment. As the title suggests, the book was an attack on Rasputin, comprising a number of previously published newspaper articles with additional commentary, letters from an unnamed Siberian church figure (possibly Bishop Antony [Karzhavin]), and the anonymous "Confession of N." by Khionya Berladskaya. It contained the usual charges: that Rasputin was a khlyst, a sex-maniac, a prisoner of "demonic delusion," that he was a monster who beat his wife and other women whom he held hostage in his Pokrovskoe home. Its veracity left much to be desired; Vladimir Bonch-Bruevich quite fairly characterized it as a bunch of lies and extreme exaggerations.[1]

The Okhrana soon got wind of the booklet (many in Moscow had been talking about it) and ordered the Moscow authorities to find the manuscript and seize all copies before it could be published. In the early hours of 16 January, after a secret order went out to the Moscow police to search the city's printing houses, the typescript was found and confiscated at Snegirev's. The entire print run had not been completed, but all the copies were taken to police headquarters and, purportedly, destroyed; even the printer's set type was broken apart. Georgy Snegirev along with Novoselov were brought in for questioning. The police wanted to know what had become of the original documents and if there were more copies about. Novoselov refused to say, and in the end, the police never did manage to recover his manuscript copy.[2] Word of the confiscation spread quickly. Among those terribly upset by the news was Ella. She had read Novoselov's manuscript and hoped that its message would get out and force Rasputin from court. She then advised Novoselov to make a copy of the materials and take them to Minister of the Interior Makarov and demand an explanation for the seizure, since he did not have the right to suppress freedom of speech if it did not concern the emperor or state order.

January had been a particularly difficult month for the tsar, as concerned Rasputin. He had grown angry over the number of stories on Rasputin in the press and his ministers' inability to put an end to them. Prime Minister Kokovtsov recalled encountering a downcast Makarov in the middle of the month, having just received a pointed note from Nicholas demanding Makarov finally take the necessary measures to subdue the press. Attached to the note was a copy of an even more angrily worded letter on the same matter Nicholas had sent to Stolypin on 10 December 1910. Makarov did not know what to do. Kokovtsov advised him that at his next meeting with the tsar Makarov should tell him that it was pointless either to try to convince editors not to publish on the subject or to confiscate newspapers once they were out, for this only aggravated the situation, turning public opinion against the dynasty and unnecessarily causing conflict with the government. Kokovtsov himself told the tsar that, and should the tsar refuse to listen, then Makarov would be wise to offer his resignation.[3] Makarov had no stomach for confronting the press over Rasputin and tried to place the responsibility completely on the shoulders of Alexei Belgard, head of the State Administration for Matters of the Press. Belgard told Makarov that he and Stolypin had tried to talk to the key newspaper editors in 1910, and that this was their only hope, although he had no intention of doing this on his own without the minister's support.

According to Belgard, after the two men spoke Makarov did decide to act and that very day sent a telegram to the governor-general of Moscow ordering him to take all necessary steps to stop the slightest mention of Rasputin from appearing in the local press.[4] The following month, the Moscow Okhrana investigated the *Voice of Moscow* simply for publishing two portraits of Rasputin. And in May, a Colonel Zavarzin wired from Berlin to the director of the police department in Petersburg that his agents had learned the publishing firm Ladyzhnikov there was planning to publish a "sensationalized novel" on Rasputin that was sure to be immensely popular. The colonel promised to investigate further.[5]

The problem, of course, was since the October Manifesto of 1905 Russia enjoyed freedom of the press and it was no longer possible to simply impose the tsar's will on the increasingly vibrant press. Novoselov knew this, and so he did not give up easily. He took the brief introductory letter to his booklet and gave it to the *Voice of Moscow* (published with the financial backing of Alexander Guchkov) who printed it under the title "The Voice of an Orthodox Layman" on 24 January. Realizing that the press was now being carefully monitored for anything on Rasputin, Novoselov submitted his piece not as an article, but a letter to the editor, a part of the newspaper that was afforded greater leeway than the main sections. The letter opened with a question: *Quousque tandem abutere patientia nostra?*—How Long Will You Abuse Our Patience?—the famous line from Cicero's Catiline Orations from the first century BC. "These indignant words are involuntarily torn from my breast," the letter read, "by a sly conspirator against all things sacred, against the Church, an evil corruptor of people's souls and minds, Grigory Rasputin, who impudently uses the Church itself as a cover." Novoselov expressed his outrage at this "criminal tragicomedy" and at the inaction of the Synod, asking why it had not taken action against this "bold fraud and corruptor," this "servant of lies." If this was due to the Synod's ignorance of Rasputin, then the author of the letter asked they request his presence and he would open their eyes about the true facts behind this "cunning seducer." Excerpts of Novoselov's letter also appeared that same day in *Evening Times*.[6] The next day the ministry of the interior launched an investigation of both newspapers. The Central Office for Press Affairs seized the printed papers and their editors were called in for questioning and threatened with legal action. The offices of the *Voice of Moscow* were thoroughly searched, and the Moscow governor-general suspended the newspaper for a week. The action of the authorities only increased the public's attention to the story. The remaining copies fetched large sums on the black market and the letter was secretly reprinted and widely circulated.[7]

The Duma responded immediately, its members gathering the same day to protest actions they deemed an illegal suppression of free speech. The matter was officially taken up by the Duma on 25 January. The Duma deputies had, quite naturally, long talked about Rasputin, but only in the lobbies, privately among themselves, and never from the rostrum, for this would have been too direct a challenge that could well have threatened the existence of the Duma itself. It was not enough to be indignant about Rasputin, the deputies needed sufficient political grounds to do so. Now the Duma felt it had such a justification. "What kind of strange personage is this Grigory Rasputin that he is beyond the power of the press and is placed on a mysterious and inaccessible pedestal?" deputy Vladimir Lvov, chairman of the Commission on Russian Orthodox Church Affairs, asked. "It is to pull him down from his pedestal that we call for an inquiry. . . . In my opinion, silencing the press, which is our only means of uncovering the truth in this dark matter, is unworthy of a great country, and therefore I hope that you will agree to the necessity for haste and, indeed, for an official inquiry."

Next Guchkov got up to make a fiery speech:

> Russia is going through dark, difficult days. The public conscience is deeply aroused. Some sort of evil spirit from the Middle Ages has risen before us. Something is wrong in our country. Danger threatens our sacred things. And why are the bishops' voices silent, why are the government authorities inactive? . . .
>
> Duty demands that we raise the voice of our conscience so that it will allow public indignation, which is steadily growing, to be heard.[8]

According to gossip in Moscow, when Nicholas heard this he said, "Hanging Guchkov is not enough."[9] Every deputy but one (the Right Octobrist Baron Nikolai Cherkasov) voted in favor of the inquiry.[10]

A man chiefly motivated by limitless personal ambition, Lvov together with several other deputies wrote an appeal and gave it to Duma President Rodzianko for him to present to Makarov. The Duma demanded an inquiry into the ministry's role in the unlawful confiscation of the newspapers. They sought answers from Makarov to two questions: 1. Did the minister know that representatives of his ministry demanded that the editors of papers in Petersburg and Moscow not print any stories on Rasputin and that failure to do so would lead to confiscations and being called to account? 2. And if he did know this, then what steps have been taken to reinstitute the lawful order? To this appeal the Duma appended a copy of Novoselov's letter, which had been read aloud that day before all the deputies, who responded with universal applause.[11] Some members of the Duma surreptitiously slipped their appeal for an inquiry, along with Novoselov's letter, to the editors of the *Petersburg Newspaper*, where they were published on the twenty-sixth for all to see.[12] Rodzianko handed Makarov the Duma's appeal, but in the end, nothing came of the call for an inquiry.[13] A line, however, had been crossed: for the first time the Duma had dared to touch on a matter concerning the personal lives of the ruling family.

The warning that Kokovtsov had given Makarov about producing a major scandal with the government over Rasputin was becoming reality. Rasputin was managing to do something no one else could: unite the fractious opposition to Nicholas. Everyone—liberals, conservatives, left and right, traditional Russian Orthodox and skeptical modern cosmopolitans—came together like never before. And the confrontation was now being played out at the highest level: between the Duma and the tsar. This was the third major clash over Rasputin—first with the Synod, next with Stolypin, and now with the Duma—and this one would be the most destructive of them all. Novoselov was lionized. The Moscow Theological Academy elected him as an honorary member. The editors of the country's newspapers were not cowed, but emboldened to keep publishing on Rasputin, even if it meant paying heavy fines. Not only did they share the indignation of the nation, they could see the money to be made: Rasputin sold newspapers.

But there were some who saw the danger in the public attacks on Rasputin. One of them was Novoselov's friend Lev Tikhomirov, publisher of the *Moscow Gazette*. He had attacked Rasputin on the pages of his paper in 1910, thinking this would destroy him, but once he realized that this would never work he stopped for he saw that in publicly vilifying Rasputin what he was really doing was undermining the sacred aura of the Russian throne.[14] The monarchist Tikhomirov held his tongue upon coming to this realization; Russia's revolutionaries, however, did just the opposite. Rasputin, they realized, was the perfect tool in their struggle to bring down the regime. Sergei Bulgakov, the Orthodox philosopher and economist, wrote that the *intelligent* critics saw this. Thus, when Guchkov asked Ella for information for the Duma's appeal, she refused to cooperate, for she knew the greater danger a public scandal presented, opting instead to work against Rasputin in secret and behind the scenes, and so, she hoped, preserve as much of the prestige of the royal house as possible.[15] Some went even further. The conspiracy-minded Prince Zhevakhov claimed that Rasputin's critics, intent on loudly demonstrating their loyalty to the dynasty and love for the tsar, were actually playing directly into the hands not only of the Duma and the "Jewish press," but those of the "International," that (mythical) secret worldwide network of Jews, banks, and Freemasons bent on the destruction of holy Russia.[16]

By the end of January 1912, Rasputin's name was known in every village of the empire, and everyone had heard the dirty rumors not just of the "sexual comfort" he provided the society ladies of the capital, but also of his "intimate visits" to the imperial court.[17]

Members of the extended Romanov family were growing increasingly worried. The tsar's sister Xenia noted in her diary on 25 January how terrible it was that now everyone was talking about Rasputin. The things they were saying, even about Alexandra, were horrendous. Everywhere she went the subject was the same: Rasputin. "How will it all end?" she wondered.[18]

Matters were growing more tense by the end of the month at court. The papers continued to write about Rasputin and the Duma was now calling that he be sent away from the capital. On the twenty-ninth, Nicholas again spoke to Makarov about muzzling the press: "I simply do not understand—is it really not possible to carry out my will?"[19] He ordered Makarov to discuss with Kokovtsov and Sabler what could be done. Kokovtsov had little hope. The rumors then had it Sabler owed his position to Rasputin, even getting down on his knees before Rasputin to express his gratitude; moreover, his assistant, Pyotr Damansky, was Rasputin's man too, and so unlikely to be of help. But he was wrong. Sabler was unequivocal: Rasputin, he thought, must leave for Pokrovskoe for good in order to protect the prestige of the throne and he was prepared to tell this to the emperor.

Late on the thirtieth, Kokovtsov and Makarov went to speak to Baron Fredericks, that ancient yet irreproachably honest and faithful head of the Russian court, to enlist his help. He told them he completely shared their opinion of Rasputin and the danger he presented and promised to speak to the emperor at the first opportunity. The baron did just as he had promised, and telephoned Kokovtsov on 1 February to inform him of his utter failure; the emperor and empress were irritated and upset by the matter and rejected out of hand the views of Fredericks and the others. The royal couple blamed the mess on the Duma, and especially Guchkov, as well as Makarov for being too weak to bring the press to heel. Nicholas refused to consider sending Rasputin away; if today it was Rasputin, then who might they be forced to banish in the future? For the tsar it was a matter of principle.[20]

As for Rasputin, he had been in St. Petersburg the entire month, still

1. Rasputin's native village of Pokrovskoe on the Tura River as photographed by the great Russian photographer Sergei Prokudin-Gorsky in 1912. (For color version, see endpapers.)

2. Possibly the earliest surviving photograph of Rasputin, most likely taken around the turn of the century. Note that he has already adopted what will become one of his most characteristic poses.

3. Before there was Rasputin there was Mr. Philippe, necromancer, seer, and advisor to Nicholas and Alexandra, whom the royal couple called "our Friend," just as they later did Rasputin.

4. Tsarevich Alexei, Alexandra, Nicholas.

5. The Black Crows, Militsa and Anastasia.

6. Grand Duke Nikolai Nikolaevich.

7. Rasputin at home in Pokrovskoe holding Varvara and flanked by Maria and Dmitry, ca. 1910.

8. The Rasputin home in Pokrovskoe.

9. Rasputin seated between Colonel Dmitry Loman (left) and Prince Mikhail Putyatin (right), most likely from 1906.

10. Rasputin together with two of his closest allies and, later, bitterest foes, Bishop Germogen and the "mad monk" Iliodor, from around 1908. Note Rasputin's vaguely clerical attire.

11. Rasputin in the palace nursery surrounded by Alexandra and the children, ca. 1909. Alexei's nanny, Maria Vishnyakova, sits smiling, lower right; to her right, a glum Tatyana and a happier Maria, her bare feet peeking out from under her white dress. Olga stands on a piece of furniture behind Rasputin.

12. A strangely haunting image of Rasputin, possibly at the palace on the same day as the nursery photograph.

13. Empress Alexandra and Anna Vyrubova.

LEFT 14. After the assassination of her husband by revolutionaries in 1905, Grand Duchess Elisabeth (known as Ella), Alexandra's older sister, took holy orders and became the abbess of a convent in Moscow. Ella's hatred of Rasputin poisoned her relations with her sister.

RIGHT 15. Olga Lokhtina, one of Rasputin's first and most fanatical followers, shown here ca. 1913 after having left her family and Rasputin to be near Iliodor. Lokhtina's strange behavior (she suffered from undiagnosed mental illness) and bizarre dress made her the most notorious, if not the most pathetic, of Rasputin's ladies.

16. The frontispiece to Mikhail Novoselov's *Grigory Rasputin and Mystical Libertinage* that was seized by the Moscow Okhrana from the publisher in January 1912 and destroyed. Only Novoselov's manuscript copy survived. This incredibly rare photograph seems to show Rasputin posing as a monk, but the image is most likely a clever fake.

17. One newspaper's illustrated comment on the early 1912 Duma scandal surrounding Rasputin, shown here shaking hands with Alexander Guchkov under the heading "Heroes of the Day." The drawing of Rasputin is based on Raevsky's much talked-about portrait from the same time.

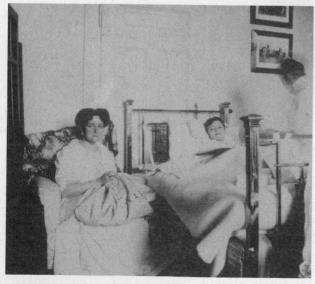

18. A bed-ridden Alexei with an unmistakably distraught Alexandra and nursemaid, possibly taken at Spała in September 1912. "God has seen Your tears and heard Your prayers. Do not be sad," Rasputin wrote to the empress from Pokrovskoe. "The little boy will not die."

19. The "former" Iliodor. The disgraced monk depicted on the cover of the popular magazine *Sparks* in February 1913. Before returning to his homeland in the Don River region, Iliodor had postcards made of himself in his new, worldly attire that he mailed to his many followers. "And still truth will live for all time. Grief to those who fail to submit to it!" he penned in the lower righthand corner, informing the world it had not heard the last of him.

20. Rasputin's doodles. The text reads: "Sunday. 9 March 1914. 1 a.m. English Pr., No. 3, 5th floor. Drawn by Grigory Yefimovich Rasputin."

21. Petersburg gathering, March 1914. Among those pictured are: Alexandra (Sana) and Alexander Pistolkors (far left); next is Leonid Molchanov; and then Prince Nikolai Zhevakhov, his face partially obscured by Anna Vyrubova in white. Lily Dehn is standing in the doorway in white; in front of her is Rasputin's father, Yefim. Munya Golovina sits with folded hands (second woman to the left of Rasputin), while Akilina Laptinskaya is at Rasputin's feet. The three women in the back far right are Madame and Nadezhda Loman, Colonel Dmitry Loman's wife and daughter, and possibly Anna Reshetnikova, with whose mother Rasputin frequently stayed in Moscow.

22. An iconic image of Grigory Rasputin from approximately 1910. The photography studio of C. E. de Hahn, located near the Tsarskoe Selo train station, where the photograph was most likely taken, served the imperial family exclusively. It is possible that Rasputin was captured here by Alexander Yagelsky, "Photographer of His Imperial Majesty" from 1911 on.

23. Rasputin in peasant dress.

24. No Orthodox priest would have thought to strike such a pose before a photographer: Who, exactly, is Rasputin supposedly blessing? The image only further undermined his credibility among official church figures.

СУДЬБА О. В. ЛОХТИНОЙ.
Со снимка, предоставленнаго «Огоньку».

О. В. Лохтина въ гостяхъ у Гр. Распутина.

25. "The Fate of O. V. Lokhtina." Rasputin was widely, though erroneously, believed to be a hypnotist. Here, in a cleverly faked photograph published in the popular magazine *Little Flame*, Rasputin hypnotizes Olga Lokhtina.

26. Rasputin in unconventional attire.

27. Rasputin on the Tura River near Pokrovskoe, taking a break from fishing with one of his Petersburg acolytes. Note the radiant smile.

BOTTOM LEFT
28. Archimandrite Feofan (Bystrov).

BOTTOM RIGHT 29. Archbishop (later Metropolitan) Antony (Khrapovitsky).

30. Bishop Alexei (Molchanov).

31. Archbishop Varnava (Nakropin).

32. Metropolitan Pitirim (Oknov).

33. Vladimir Sabler, chief procurator
of the Holy Synod (1911–15).

34. Alexander Samarin, chief procurator of the Holy Synod (1915).

35. Count Sergei Witte, Russia's first prime minister (1905–6).

36. Pyotr Stolypin, prime minister and minister of the interior (1906–11).

37. Count Vladimir Kokovtsov, prime minister (1911–14) and minister of finance (1906–14).

38. Ivan Goremykin,
prime minister (1906, 1914–16).

39. Vladimir Dzhunkovsky,
governor of Moscow (1908–13) and
deputy minister of the interior (1913–15).

40. Vladimir Sukhomlinov,
minister of war (1909–15).

41. Boris Stürmer,
prime minister (1916).

42. Alexander Protopopov,
minister of the interior (1916–17).

43. Alexander Guchkov.

44. Mikhail Rodzianko,
chairman of the Duma.

45. Pavel Milyukov.

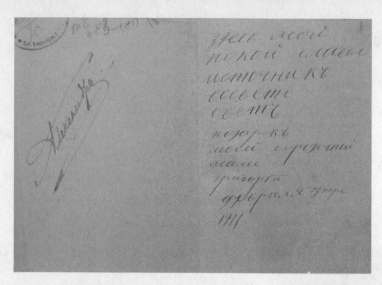

46. "Here is my peace, the source of glory, light in the light. A gift to my sincere mama. Grigory," Rasputin's words on the notebook he presented to Alexandra in February 1911. Her signature is on the verso. When writing to their majesties, Rasputin always made sure to use his best penmanship.

47. One of the few surviving color portraits done of Rasputin during his lifetime. The artist, Yelena Klokacheva, a graduate of the St. Petersburg Academy of Fine Arts, is known today chiefly for this work, done with pencil and crayon in 1914.

48. One of two surviving portraits of Rasputin by the Danish artist Theodora Krarup, done in her Petersburg studio in 1914.

49. Khionya Guseva in custody after attempting to murder Rasputin in Pokrovskoe on 29 June 1914.

50. A headline from the *Petersburg Courier* following Guseva's attack. Rasputin is accompanied by his daughter, Maria, and "his secretary" Apolinaria Nikitishna Lapshinskaya. The Russian and foreign press found the story of Rasputin's near-murder irresistible.

Покушеніе на убійство Григорія Распутина.

(ТЕЛЕГРАММЫ ОТЪ СОБСТВЕННАГО КОРРЕСПОНДЕНТА).

Матрена Гр. Распутина.
Дочь „старца".

Гр. Е. Распутинъ.

Аполинарія Никитишна Лапшинская.
(Секретарша Гр. Распутина).

Прибытіе тобольскаго губернатора

СТРОГУЮ ИЗОЛЯЦІЮ ГУСЕВОЙ, МНѢ УДА-
ЛОСЬ БЕСѢДОВАТЬ СЪ НЕЮ И УЗНАТЬ МО-

Мнѣніе товарища прокурора.

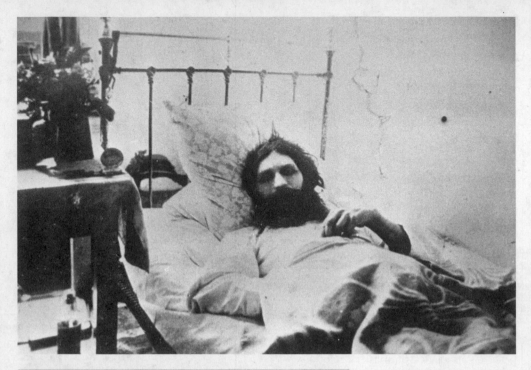

51. Rasputin recovering in his hospital bed in Tyumen.

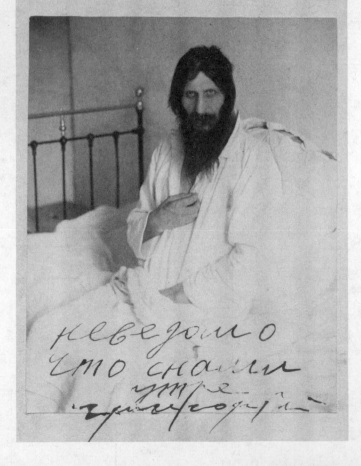

невѣдомо
что снами
утре
григорий

52. Rasputin in the hospital. He signed a number of the same photographs with various expressions. This one reads: "God knows what is to become of us in the morn, Grigory."

at the Sazonovs on Kirochnaya Street, and the police had been tracking his every move. Late that month they followed him to the "family baths" on Shpalernaya Street with Sazonov's wife, which led them to conclude he had taken her for his lover. They followed him in the company of his female followers to various churches, including the Church of the Savior on the Spilt Blood on the Catherine (now Griboedov) Canal, built on the site where Tsar Alexander II had been blown up by revolutionaries in 1881. They attended services there and lingered to pray before the icons. And the police records also indicate that Rasputin was spending time with other women, prostitutes that he had picked up on the street: two on 4 February named Botvinkina and Kozlova, and a certain Petrova on the sixth.[21]

Nicholas and Alexandra, together with the children, saw Rasputin at the Alexander Palace on 11 February. "It was a great comfort to see him and listen to him talk." The scandals swirling around them had apparently left no mark on their relations. Four days later Nicholas's mother came to the palace to talk to her son and daughter-in-law. Xenia recorded the event in her diary:

> Mama talked about her conversation yesterday. She's so pleased that she spoke out. Now they have heard and know what is being said, though Alix defended Rasputin, saying that he's an exceptional man and that Mama should get to know him etc.; Mama's only advice was to send him away now, when the Duma are waiting for an answer, to which Nicky said that he couldn't see how he could do it, while she declared that they couldn't give in.
>
> In general everything she said was besides the point, and there's obviously a lot she doesn't understand—she castigated society (dirty-minded gossips), Tyutcheva for talking too much and lying, and the ministers "all cowards."[22]

On 12 February Kokovtsov was surprised to receive a letter from Rasputin announcing his plan to leave the city for good and requesting a meeting before he departed, so that they might "exchange some ideas." Three days later Rasputin arrived at the prime minister's office. Also present was Kokovtsov's brother-in-law, Valery Mamontov, there on Kokovtsov's request as a witness.

> When Rasputin entered my study I was shocked by the repulsive expression of his eyes, deep-set and close to each other, small, gray in color. Rasputin kept them fixed on me for some time, as if he

intended to hypnotize me or as if he were studying me on seeing me for the first time. Next he threw his head sharply back and studied the ceiling; then he lowered his head and stared at the floor; all this in silence. As I had no idea how long this would continue, I said: "You wanted to tell me something?"

But Rasputin sat mute, turning his gaze back to the ceiling. Mamontov then asked whether it were true he was planning on returning to his village.

"Well, shall I go? Life has been hard for me here; people make up stories about me."

"Indeed, you will do well to go away," I replied. "Whether people tell lies or the purest truth about you, you must recognize that this is no place for you; you do harm to the Tsar by appearing at the palace and especially by telling everybody about your nearness to the Imperial family."

"What do I tell? To whom? It is all lies, calumnies! I do not insist on going to the palace—they summon me," Rasputin almost screamed.

They sat staring at each other, Kokovtsov convinced Rasputin was trying to hypnotize him. In the end, Rasputin acquiesced: "All right, I shall go. But mind, let them take care not to call me back, since I am so bad that I harm the Tsar." Kokovtsov summed up his opinion of Rasputin:

In my estimation he was a typical Siberian tramp, a clever man who had trained himself for the rôle of a simpleton and a madman and who played his part according to a set formula. He did not believe in his tricks himself, but had trained himself to certain mannerisms of conduct in order to deceive those who sincerely believed in all his oddities. Others, of course, merely pretended to admire him, hoping to obtain privileges through him which could not be obtained in any other way.[23]

News of the meeting spread and took on additional color. The Austrian ambassador wrote back to Vienna that such was Rasputin's stench Kokovtsov had to open all the windows of his office the minute the peasant departed.[24] Others were trading in darker speculations. It was being said that Kokovtsov had offered Rasputin 200,000 rubles to leave.[25] Rasputin was revolted by the notion. "Abandon the Emperor and Empress? What sort of scoundrel do they take me for?" he told Munya Golovina, tears running down his cheeks.[26]

On 17 February Kokovtsov informed Nicholas of his meeting with Rasputin. Before Kokovtsov could start, Nicholas interrupted his prime minister to ask whether it was true that either he or Makarov had ordered Rasputin sent away, to which Kokovtsov said no. Then, after listening to the prime minister's details of the meeting and Rasputin's voluntary decision to leave for Pokrovskoe, the tsar asked Kokovtsov of his opinion of him.

> I told him I was left with a very unpleasant impression, and it seemed to me after a conversation that lasted about an hour that I had before me a typical representative of a Siberian tramp, whom I knew from working in transit prisons, prisoner transport, and among the so-called "rootless" people who hide their guilt-stained past and who are prepared to use any means to achieve their goals. I even told him that I wouldn't be comfortable meeting with him in private because of his repulsive appearance, his insincere methods of some sort of hypnotist that he had picked up somewhere, and because of his inexplicable holy foolishness, that would disappear when he slipped into simple and even reasonable conversation on everyday topics, and then just as quickly reappear. In order not to give reason to be accused of bias or exaggeration, I told the Emperor that while I censure Rasputin for his desire to show off his relations with people who do him favors, I censure even more those who seek his protection and try to pursue their selfish interests using his seeming influence.

As Kokovtsov spoke, Nicholas gazed out the window without saying a word, a sign he was displeased. But after the prime minister had finished, Nicholas thanked him for his honesty. Then, if Kokovtsov's memoirs are to be believed, the tsar lied to him, saying that he hardly knew "that man" and had seen him only two or three times, and then only briefly. This was the last time they ever discussed Rasputin, even though Kokovtsov would remain in office for another two years.[27]

The Okhrana reported Rasputin left for Pokrovskoe on 18 February. Before he departed he sent a letter to Nicholas and Alexandra:

> My dearest Mama and Papa! How strong the Devil is getting, may he be condemned. And the Duma serves him; there are many revolutionaries and Jews there. What do they care? Only to get rid of

God's Anointed. Guchkov, their master, a crook, spreads slander and disturbances, and makes inquiries. Papa, it's your Duma, do what you want. What kind of inquiries can there be about Grigory? This is a devil's prank. Command. No inquiry is needed. Grigory.[28]

On the twenty-second, Rasputin arrived home in Pokrovskoe.[29]

Even though he had left the capital, Rasputin's image remained behind to the great fascination of the Petersburg public. In February, the Spring Exhibition of the Academy of Fine Arts opened. The critics panned that year's collection and attendance was low. Something had to be done to save the exhibition, so on the nineteenth a new painting went up. It was a full-scale portrait of Rasputin by the artist Alexander Raevsky. Suddenly, the exhibition was thronged with viewers.

On the twenty-ninth, the *Stock Exchange Gazette* published a lengthy interview with Raevsky about his creation. He had been given the commission by one of Rasputin's female acolytes who wanted the great starets captured on canvas. The portrait was completed in ten sessions at Raevsky's studio, Rasputin arriving each time by automobile. The process, Raevsky remarked, was not easy, for his subject was incapable of sitting still. He was in constant motion, his "nervous energy" was "terrible." Electricity exploded from his very core; sparks flew from his finger tips. Yet, when he touched you, or kissed you, this electricity had a strange pleasing, calming effect. Raevsky was taken by the childlike quality of Rasputin and impressed by his profound humanity. When, at one of their sessions, someone began to attack the Jews, Rasputin suddenly became angry and interrupted the speaker, "That's not true! Before God all people are equal!" The sessions were crowded, for many of Rasputin's lady friends would come along to watch the artist at work. Raevsky told the newspaper that he had long tried to uncover just what it was about Rasputin that made him so unusual.

"I tried to discover wherein lies the secret to Rasputin's amazing fascination," he said. "To be fair to him, he stands apart from all others thanks to a certain inspired intuition. From the moment you meet him he takes control of your soul and he can feel its most secret places and tell you about your sorrows, doubts, and joys."

As for Rasputin, he was exceedingly pleased with the portrait ("Now that's an artist!" he purportedly exclaimed), as were his ladies, one of whom offered Raevsky a great deal of money for it, but he refused to sell. Not all the visitors, however, liked the idea of a life-size Rasputin hanging in the exhibition space. It was said that when the curators learned the Dowager Empress was going to be visiting, they made sure to take it down, but then just as quickly put it back once she had left. They knew what the public wanted.[30]

30. The Blow to the Alcove

Rasputin's departure gave rise to all sorts of speculation. On 18 February, *Evening Times* quoted an anonymous woman, said to know Rasputin well, that the common perception that Rasputin had finally been defeated was utterly incorrect. Far from it, in fact. Although the press campaign and the Duma's inquiry had done much to damage him, he was far from defeated. His departure was nothing but a "subtle maneuver." He would leave and let things quiet down; then, he would be back. Everyone ought to take note: "The fight against him is still far from finished."[1]

A confidential denunciation to the police dated 24 February concurred. If Rasputin's departure signaled the victory of the party of the Dowager Empress, then the fact that Rasputin was seen off at his train by Vyrubova and her sister Sana and that he was presented with a bouquet of white roses sent from the palace could only be interpreted as a sign that Alexandra had not conceded defeat. The "Rasputin epic," it averred, was not over. Indeed, one could not count out Rasputin's own (surely apocryphal) words reported by the *New Times* that he was leaving simply to fetch his daughter and bring her back to be raised along with the daughters of the empress, just as Alexandra had promised. Rasputin was even planning to join Nicholas and Alexandra that spring in Crimea. One thing, however, could not be ruled out: that the Rasputin controversy could lead to the "catastrophic ruin" of the entire state order.[2]

The next to take up the matter of Rasputin with the tsar was Mikhail Rodzianko. Born in 1859, the child of an old Russian noble family, Rodzianko had been given a fine, aristocratic upbringing, served in Her Majesty's Regiment of the Cavalry Guard, and was later appointed chamberlain of the imperial court. With the creation of the Duma, he was elected from the Yekaterinoslav province and was one of the founders of the Union of 17 October, the so-called Octobrists, a group of Duma members seeking to change Russia through gradual reform. Rodzianko's own specific views have been characterized as those of English country Toryism, and he stood as a liberal or moderate opposed to the voices on the political right and far left. In 1911, Guchkov stepped down as president of the Duma and was replaced by Rodzianko, who would hold the position throughout the rest of Imperial Russia. Tall, imposing, and quite heavy (he supposedly introduced himself to little Alexei as "the fattest man in Russia"), Rodzianko tried to use his physicality to lend authority to the Duma, especially in his regular meetings with the tsar. In the end, he failed, unable either to understand his imperial master or to be taken seriously by him.[3]

Following the banishment of Germogen, Rodzianko was visited by an agitated Vladimir Purishkevich from the Duma. In a voice trembling with horror, Purishkevich asked:

> Where are we going? Our last mainstay, the Holy Orthodox Church, is being destroyed. There was a revolution which attempted to undermine the Crown; it failed. [. . .] the powers of darkness are now attacking Russia's last hope—the Church. And the most terrible part of all is that this seems to emanate from the Throne itself. A charlatan, a khlyst, a filthy, illiterate peasant is playing his dirty tricks on our prelates. Into what abyss are we being driven? Oh, my God! I want to sacrifice myself and kill this vermin, Rasputin!

And Purishkevich would, together with Felix Yusupov and three others, kill Rasputin four years later.

In his oft-quoted memoirs, Rodzianko presents himself as the voice of calm and reason, talking a fiery Purishkevich out of any rash action and, in another section, convincing an overly aggressive Guchkov to wait before issuing the Duma inquiry into Rasputin as this would needlessly fan the flames of public opinion. Rodzianko seemed convinced that he, together with the Duma, could persuade Nicholas to do the right thing. To that end, he began gathering a dossier on Rasputin with the help of Guchkov, Badmaev, Felix Yusupov, and Rodionov. Rodzianko even had an agent of Count Sumarokov collecting information from abroad. Rodzianko claims he managed to bring together a large amount of damning material on Rasputin, including scores of letters from the mothers of daughters seduced by him and photographs showing him among his khlyst followers and one in a monk's habit with a cowl and a gold pectoral cross. He also received a letter from the exiled

Germogen, begging him to go and speak the awful truth to the tsar and warn him of the danger.[4] While busy with this task Rodzianko met with the Dowager Empress. She had heard of his plans and tried to talk him out of it, insisting the tsar was so pure he would never believe it and would only become upset. He told her things had gone too far; the dynasty was threatened and he asked her to bless him, which she did.[5] By late February word of the impending audience was spreading in Petersburg society. Admiral Konstantin Nilov, the devoted dipsomaniac courtier who was an almost constant presence around the tsar, was less than optimistic about Rodzianko's chances. He commented at the time that he too had tried to open the tsar's eyes, in vain. In the end, it seems, he simply made peace with the situation, remarking grimly: "There'll be a revolution, they'll hang us all, it doesn't matter a bit from which street lamp."[6]

Rodzianko had asked Prime Minister Kokovtsov and Metropolitan Antony (Vadkovsky) from the Synod to join him in his appeal to the tsar, but they refused. And so he went alone to see Nicholas at 6 p.m. on 26 February. That morning he visited the Kazan Cathedral with his wife to pray for success. The audience lasted for almost two hours. After making his usual reports, Rodzianko deigned to ask permission to speak of Rasputin:

> Your Majesty, the presence of this man of more than tarnished reputation in the most intimate Court circles is an event unparalleled in the history of the Russian Monarchy. [. . .] Rasputin is a tool in the hands of Russia's enemies; he is their instrument for undermining the Church and the Monarchy itself. No revolutionary propaganda could achieve as much as Rasputin's mere presence at Court. Everyone fears his intimacy with the Imperial Family. Public feeling is running very high.

Rodzianko next proceeded to list the prelates who had been unjustly punished for speaking against Rasputin—Germogen, Iliodor, Feofan, Bishop Antony—asserting that anyone who even dared say a word against him was wronged. He stated Rasputin was a khlyst and began to read the letters he had collected as well as extracts from Novoselov's booklet. Rodzianko pointed out that attempts to muzzle the press only made matters worse, for it seemed to confirm in the public's mind the gossip about his relations with the royal family. He told Nicholas about how the investigation into Rasputin's connections to the khlysty had mysteriously been halted. Next, he produced a cutting from a foreign newspaper that dealt with a congress of Freemasons in Brussels at which it was openly discussed how Rasputin was being used as a tool for the secret society's aims in Russia.[7]

This was too much for the tsar. He began nervously lighting one cigarette after another.

Rodzianko stressed his loyalty to the throne and church, and insisted it was his fervid desire to protect them both that led him to speak, and begged him to banish Rasputin. Nicholas said he believed the sincerity of Rodzianko's report, but he could not make such a promise. On the twenty-eighth, Rodzianko learned from his old friend Palace Commandant Dedyulin (who, it warrants noting, many believed had befriended Rasputin to advance his own place at court, a fact Rodzianko either ignored or was strangely unaware of)[8] that Nicholas had ordered he be given all the Synod's secret documents on Rasputin to help with his investigation, but the tsar asked only that Rodzianko keep this matter to himself and not discuss it with anyone else. The next day, Damansky, the Assistant Chief Procurator of the Synod (described in Rodzianko's memoirs as a devoted follower of Rasputin) delivered the documents and Rodzianko immediately instructed his staff to make copies of everything.

The following day, Damansky, along with Father Alexander Vasilev, the tsarevich's confessor, showed up unexpectedly at the Duma demanding the documents back. The order, Damansky said, came from the empress herself, but Rodzianko refused to comply, saying Alexandra was as much a subject of the emperor as he, and it was the emperor's wishes he was following. As for Vasilev, he had also been sent by Alexandra and told to convince Rodzianko that Rasputin truly was a man of God. Upon hearing this Rodzianko exploded, listing all of Rasputin's crimes and practically throwing the men out of his office.[9]

Among the documents Rodzianko had received was the khlyst investigation file from the Tobolsk Ecclesiastical Consistory, where it had lain untouched since the spring of 1908. (Strangely, records in the Russian State Historical Archive report that the file was sent on 18 February and arrived in Petersburg on the twenty-fifth, the day *before* Rodzianko's audience with the tsar. Had Rodzianko acted preemptively without waiting for Nicholas's approval?)[10] Nicholas was convinced that upon reading it, Rodzianko would see that Rasputin was not a khlyst. But Rodzianko was not content just to read the file. He wanted to dig deeper: to request the preliminary materials upon which the final version of the file had been based, to interview witnesses, to summon competent experts. Kokovtsov cautioned him against this, saying it would cause an enormous, and needless, scandal, and destroy the trust the tsar had placed in him. Better he do as instructed, Kokovtsov said: read the file, come to his own conclusion, speak to the emperor, and only then decide whether any further steps were warranted. Rodzianko listened to Kokovtsov, but still felt he needed help in making sense of the material, and so asked his fellow Octobrists in the Duma Nikolai Shubinsky and Guchkov to help him, and the three began to read it and prepare a report for the tsar.

All of this went to Rodzianko's head, according to Kokovtsov:

> Rodzianko was telling everyone right and left about the assignment he had and talked immodestly about being destined to save the emperor and Russia from Rasputin with his report. He fussed over his "assignment," showing me 2–3 pages of his draft report that contained a very unfavorable evaluation of Rasputin, and he waited for the clean version of it to be prepared for his personal audience with the emperor.[11]

In copying the file and sharing it with other members of the Duma, Rodzianko had violated not only the tsar's explicit instructions but his trust as well. His dishonesty would further fan the flames of scandal.

The following year Dedyulin was replaced as palace commandant by Vladimir Voeikov, the son-in-law of Baron Fredericks, minister of the Imperial Courts. Voeikov recalled Rodzianko's less than justified opinion of Rasputin:

> The two of us sat in his office for two-three hours, and I was forced to listen to his lecture on the danger of Rasputin and how he should be dealt with: it turns out I was supposed to drive Rasputin from the palace and prohibit the emperor and empress from meeting with him.
>
>   In reply to my request for advice on how I was to carry this out, he, of course, avoided giving me a straight answer. In general, my conversations with M. V. Rodzianko left me with the impression that Rasputin himself did not concern him so much, but he was using his name to create as much noise and scandal as possible around the tsar and tsaritsa.

As for the secret file from the Tobolsk Ecclesiastical Consistory, Voeikov was convinced it was full of unfounded accusations, but in those days, one simply did not mention such things: "During those wild times it was considered completely inadmissible to announce that all the false rumors about the ruling circles were being spread on purpose and that they had nothing to do with reality."[12] Kokovtsov shared Voeikov's opinion of Rodzianko. He was convinced the Duma President was motivated as much by vainglory as by loyalty and this led him to not only exaggerate but even lie about Rasputin.[13] According to Lily Dehn, this was a problem common to all who tried to warn Nicholas about Rasputin:

> When they told him about the disgraceful things Rasputin was committing "on the side," he did not want to believe them. And why? For one simple reason: the colors used to paint Rasputin were simply too dark. Had those "well-wishers" not tried so hard, then, maybe, the emperor would have listened to their words. He who has given himself the goal of breaking apart two friends commits a big mistake if he depicts the one he is trying to destroy as a completely worthless individual. It is much easier to achieve the desired result if in condemning him or her, you also add a bit of praise.[14]

Fredericks had the following to say to the tsar's aide-de-camp Anatoly Mordvinov when the subject of Rasputin came up:

> You know I love the Emperor like a son and so I did not resist asking His Majesty just what sort of figure this Rasputin was. The Emperor answered calmly and simply: "Yes, it's true, too much and too much erroneous, as usual, is always said about any person from outside the usual milieu whom we deign to occasionally receive. The Empress likes his sincerity as a common man . . . She believes in his loyalty and in the power of his prayers to protect our family and Alexei . . . But this is nothing but our private affair. It's remarkable how people like to involve themselves in things that have nothing to do with them. Whom can he bother?"[15]

The outlandishness of the stories made them all the harder to believe since the royal family never saw this side to Rasputin. Lily Dehn again:

If I were to say that I never saw anything inappropriate about Grigory Rasputin, then people would call me a liar or a stupid woman. Indeed, the latter description would be the kindest sort of thing they would likely say about me. But nonetheless it is the honest truth that we never saw any negative sides in his nature. Perhaps this is because some people have a dual nature. I've heard about people who were perfect angels in the flesh, but the minute they walked out their front door they would throw themselves into such vice that a modern-day French novel would seem like nothing.[16]

After studying the secret file and other documents, Rodzianko compiled a condensed report for the tsar (its overly emotional language first had to be toned down by Yakov Glinka, assistant to the Duma President) on 8 March and wrote to request an audience. He was received soon after by the tsar, who thanked him graciously for his efforts, noting his speed and thoroughness, and promising to send for him as soon as he had read it. Rodzianko returned triumphant to the Duma and waited. And waited, for days in fact, for there was nothing coming from the palace but silence. Nicholas was stonewalling. Rodzianko was outraged. He went to tell Kokovtsov about the matter, insisting this was clearly an insult to the authority of the Duma and threatening to resign. Kokovtsov promised to bring up the matter with the tsar, and as Rodzianko was leaving a messenger from the tsar arrived bearing a large packet. Inside Kokovtsov found Nicholas's reply scrawled on Rodzianko's earlier request for an audience: "I do not wish to receive Rodzianko, especially since I saw him but a few days ago. Let him know this. The conduct of the Duma is deeply revolting, especially the repugnant speech of Guchkov about the Holy Synod. I shall be very glad if my displeasure is made known to these gentlemen; I am tired of always bowing and smiling to them."[17]

Rodzianko never forgot, nor forgave, how he had been treated by the tsar.

Alexandra Bogdanovich recorded the talk in her diary on 12 March:

There were many people today. The topic of conversation continues to be Rasputin, who returned yesterday to Petersburg and that day drove out to Tsarskoe Selo. It's dismal to write about the tastes of the tsaritsa, how she can put up with that khlyst.

[. . .] One can understand the tsar. In the words of Countess

Miloradovich, who heard from the wife of Duma President Rodzianko about her husband's audience with the tsar, when
Rodzianko laid out for the tsar what sort of man Rasputin was, the
tsar completely disassociated himself from Rasputin, saying that
he never sees Rasputin. But how can he permit Grishka in the
palace? For clearly he saw from what Rodzianko had to tell him
what a harmful man he is and what sort of sect he belongs to.
Everyone says one and the same thing, that the tsar has a great deal
of self-control but no will whatsoever—he's is utterly weak-willed.
It's terrible! Tomorrow the tsarist family is leaving for the Crimea
and Rasputin too. All the tsar need do is to tell Dedyulin to get rid
of that creature and that would be the end of it. But here's the problem—he lacks the will. It's horrifying when you take a close look
at the difficult situation of Russia!

And the news seemed to only get worse. A week later Bogdanovich
recorded in her diary that Princess Yelizaveta Obolenskaya (aka Lily O.),
a maid-of-honor to Alexandra and the daughter of adjutant-general
Nikolai Obolensky, was saying that the empress herself was a khlyst.
Obolenskaya had read two articles in the *New Times* titled "Khlystovshchina" and immediately recognized in their description of the sect the
empress herself. Unable to remain silent, she even wrote of her concerns
to the empress, twice, and her letters brought down great displeasure on
Obolenskaya. It was said she would be forced to leave court.[18]

The speech by Guchkov that had so angered Nicholas took place on
9 March at the Duma and came to be known as the "The Blow to the
Alcove." Such was the intensity of Guchkov's criticism that even his
fellow Octobrists were stunned.

Alexander Guchkov was born in 1862 into a wealthy Moscow
merchant family. Educated at Moscow University in history, he was a
brilliant student and went on to study in Berlin and Heidelberg. Undeniably talented, he was not an easy man. Guchkov has been described
as "mercurial, quarrelsome, and high-strung. He was also a braggart,
a bully, and a serial adulterer, whose daughter later ruefully reminisced
that the Guchkov family 'never returned to the same sea-side resort two
summers running, because the second summer all the babies in prams
looked embarrassingly like me.'" Touchy, vainglorious, and insecure
about his honor, Guchkov challenged several men to duels. He imagined

himself to be a terribly important global figure and had to be present at all the world's hot spots: fighting for the Boers in South Africa in 1899, arriving in time in Manchuria in 1900 to take part in the Boxer Rebellion and the nationalist revolt in Macedonia in 1905. He liked to boast of his vast expertise on military matters, and always sought the limelight on such discussions whenever they came up in the Duma.[19] None of this, however, prepared anyone for what Guchkov had to say that day from the rostrum:

> One wants to talk, one wants to shout that the church is in danger and the state is in danger too . . . You all know what terrible drama Russia is going through . . . and in the center of this drama is a mysterious tragicomic figure who seems to have come back from the other world and or is some vestige of the Dark Ages, a strange figure in the light of the twentieth century . . . Perhaps he is a fanatical sectarian spreading his dark deeds, perhaps he is a roguish swindler busy making profit. What paths has this person taken to reach this key position, having seized such influence that even top state and church authorities bow down before him? Just think for a moment—who is running things at the top, who is spinning that axis that brings along with it . . .

At this point the Black Hundred deputy Nikolai Markov (Markov the Second) yelled out from his seat, "That's just women's gossip!" but his words were lost in the general excitement.

Guchkov continued:

> . . . a change of direction and a change of faces, some people's fall and others' rise? If we were facing an isolated phenomenon that had grown up out of the diseased soil of a religious quest or exalted mysticism, we would have stood by in sad silence, with our heads bowed, as if we were at the bed of a severely ill beloved person. Perhaps we would have cried and prayed, but we wouldn't be talking. But Grigory Rasputin is not alone. Isn't there a whole gang, a motley group behind his back that has taken his person and his charms into their own hands? Insatiable highfliers, longing for the power that has slipped out of their hands, shady wheeler-dealers, washed-up journalists . . .

"Sazonov!" the centrist deputy Pavel Krupensky shouted from his seat.

"Entrepreneurs of the starets!" Guchkov went on,

They are the ones who prompt what he has to whisper further along. It is an entire commercial enterprise, deftly and skillfully playing its game. Facing such a scenario, it is our duty to shout the words of warning: the church is in danger and the state is in danger! Because no revolutionary or anti-church propaganda for several years has managed to do what has been done during the past few days!

"That's true!" voices rang out from the floor.

Guchkov did not stop. "Gegechkori* was right from his perspective when he said, 'Rasputin is useful.' I can even add: the more dissolute [rasputnee], the more useful for Gegechkori's friends."

"That's right," shouted one of the rightist deputies.

Guchkov stated that few men were brave enough to speak out (the obvious went unsaid: he was one of them), and then he accused Sabler of doing nothing and surrounding himself with lackeys. "For the years 1911–1912 a Russian chronicler will write: During these years the Orthodox Church under the Chief Procurator of the Holy Synod, the Actual Privy Counselor Vladimir Karlovich Sabler, reached a level of humiliation never known before."

A stunned Sabler called out that Guchkov did not know the facts. But the effort to defend himself was useless and his protestation went ignored. The next day the city's residents read most of Guchkov's speech in the *New Times*.[20]

The speech marked the point at which Guchkov became a personal and not just political enemy of the tsar and tsaritsa—his words had been directed squarely at their "alcove," their most private space. Combined with Rodzianko's actions of the previous weeks, it also marked the final straw in Nicholas's relations with the Duma, damaging them forever beyond repair. Never again would Nicholas receive its president.

Rodzianko later claimed he tried to talk Guchkov out of this radical step. He told him such an act would amount to another diamond necklace affair, a reference to the scandal surrounding Queen Marie Antoinette in the 1780s that caused considerable damage to the prestige of the French throne shortly before the revolution. As for Guchkov, he told the Commission in 1917 he had had no choice. The forces gathered around Rasputin threatened to ruin the country, and the government

---

* The Georgian revolutionary and Social-Democrat (Menshevik), Yevgeny Gegechkori, a deputy to the III Duma.

and its ministers, in his opinion, were either too blind, too lazy, or too afraid to declare war on them, thus he did what was necessary. When he had been told that the tsar wanted him hanged, he replied: my life belongs to the emperor, but my conscience belongs to me and I will continue to fight.[21]

But just who was he fighting, and why? Nikandor Savich, Guchkov's Octobrist colleague in the Duma, wrote that the true motivation behind Guchkov's speech had not been Rasputin but the tsar himself. Guchkov felt Nicholas had not shown him due respect in the past and this was his way of trying to settle the score. Although political on the surface, the speech was at its heart profoundly personal. Guchkov may have warned Rodzianko of his plans, but he did not share them with his fellow Octobrists, and they listened with disbelief to his words. Savich, and others as well, knew the palace would never forget, much less forgive, the speech. "From now on," he wrote in his memoirs, "not only Guchkov, but the entire Duma would have an irreconcilable foe in the Empress, and every last hope of improving relations between the Tsar and the representative government had been lost."[22] Such was the enormous price Russia would pay for Guchkov's bruised honor.

Guchkov's motives were not at all what he claimed, and his characterization of Rasputin and his influence were equally dishonest and mistaken. Rasputin the evil khlyst, Rasputin the man behind the throne, running the government, dispensing favors, determining the fate of ministers, allowing a band of crooks to rob the state coffers—none of this was true, all of this was nothing more than gossip, and Guchkov knew this to be so, but it did not stop him. Guchkov said the actions of Rasputin and Sabler were ammunition in the hands of revolutionaries like Yevgeny Gegechkori—the more *rasputnee*—depraved—the better. Yet this is just what Guchkov had given the state's enemies, and not just to those on the left, but on the right as well. The church was in danger, the state was in danger, these had been Guchkov's words, and with his speech, he had increased danger.

The reaction was enormous. On the eighteenth, the *New Sunday Evening Newspaper* published a caricature of Guchkov and Rasputin shaking hands along with a short satirical verse inspired by Lermontov's famous poem "The Dispute" lampooning the affair.[23] Guchkov had given the regime's enemies much they could use. A top figure among the Social-Democrats commented: "Grishka Rasputin is the best friend and confederate of the Social-Democrats because he is doing more to bring about a second revolution than we are."[24] Shulgin noted, "The emperor offends the country by allowing into the palace, a place that even the very best subjects have trouble gaining access to, a reprobate from the streets."[25] Rasputin's friend Sazonov was possibly the only person who came to his defense. He wrote a short article titled "The Truth about Grigory Novykh /Rasputin/" that was printed in one of the day's many short-lived periodicals. He refuted the charges against Rasputin and called attention to the disinformation and dirty tricks the press had been engaged in, such as a picture published in *Little Flame* depicting Rasputin in a bathhouse holding up a Bible and preaching to his female followers.[26] But no one cared to hear what Sazonov had to say.

The Duma scandal did not escape the attention of the foreign ambassadors, and Rasputin became an important person of interest for the first time. On 29 March, the Austrian ambassador sent a long secret report to the minister of foreign affairs in Vienna detailing Guchkov's speech and its fallout and offering the best intelligence he had on the mysterious Rasputin:

> There is little to be known about the origins of this man. He is a Siberian peasant (some believe a former prisoner) who apparently has a certain suggestive or hypnotic power and—what is the main thing—is a religious fanatic said to belong to the sect of flagellants. He is believed to combine an overall lack of education with a natural talent and an amazing knowledge of the Bible.
>
> A circle of women at the Imperial Court has been formed from which Rasputin recruits his female disciples. The most bizarre rumors are circulating about Rasputin's pursuits with this circle and I am assured that this magnetizer often acts there as an intimate masseur and that the border between religious ecstasy and sexual perversity is not always clearly drawn.[27]

The British ambassador, George Buchanan, also wrote his first report on Rasputin, describing him as one of the contemporary "mediaeval neuropaths," along with Germogen and Iliodor, then popular in Russian society, and as the son "of a good and wealthy Russian family." Back in London an official had crossed out these final words and written: "a mere Siberian peasant."[28]

*

On 12 March, the royal family left for the Crimea. There were few at the station to see them off. One of them was Kokovtsov. He recalled the tsar was in his "usual mood" and said to him, jokingly, "You likely envy me, and I only pity you having to remain in this swamp." A stony Alexandra boarded the train without exchanging a single word with those gathered on the platform.[29] As for Rasputin, the press was full of contradictory reports—some stating he was due to arrive in Petersburg any day, others that he was on his way to the Crimea, or that he had traveled there with the tsar and tsaritsa themselves and had already checked in to the Hotel Russia in Yalta.[30] So intense was the coverage of Rasputin's whereabouts, that some were becoming fed up. The *New Sunday Evening Newspaper* captured the mood in a piece titled "Rasputiniana:"

> It seems there's no getting rid of this story.
> There are some diseases you just catch, like eczema. A man catches this filth and can't get rid of it for years.
> Rasputiniana has lasted way too long. We're already tired of it, but there's no way to get rid of it.
> —Rasputin has left . . .
> —Rasputin has arrived . . .
> —Rasputin has gone here . . .
> —Rasputin has gone there . . .
> Haven't we had enough of Rasputin?
> The yellow press has even turned hunting Rasputin into a kind of sport—a competition in malice . . .[31]

But the question of Rasputin's whereabouts was important, for the reigning impression in society was that he had been officially exiled to Pokrovskoe, thus the notion that he had either returned to the capital or traveled to the Crimea was interpreted (even if incorrectly) not simply as a sign of his power, but of his being permitted to thumb his nose at state authority.

Rasputin, in fact, did not remain in Pokrovskoe for long before returning to Petersburg in the middle of March, but only briefly before leaving for the Crimea, as many had speculated.[32] The royal family's embrace of him after all the scandals of the first three months of the year was an unmistakable statement that they would not allow anyone to tell them who they might receive.

*

On 16 March, Xenia, the tsar's sister, met Princess Zinaida Yusupova for tea. The conversation, not surprisingly, focused on Rasputin.[33] The princess had been obsessed with Rasputin for some time. On 12 February, she had written to her son, Felix, warning him about the danger of Rasputin and the Black Princesses allied with him. It is a "difficult time," she noted, and then urged him not to put anything secret or compromising in his letters since the Okhrana was reading everyone's mail.[34] Felix had telegraphed Munya Golovina for her view on the scandal. She wrote back to him on 14 February not to believe all the gossip and stories in the press. She insisted all the noise was nothing more than a manufactured scandal intended to damage the throne.

> People have so much anger, and most importantly envy! How they try to destroy and blacken everything beautiful and bright. Of course, he has been set upon out of envy and he bears his cross and these sufferings for Christ. If you could only see how far he is from all this swirling around him—he's in an entirely different sphere, the sphere of the spirit and far from our understanding and suffering, and we judge him according to our everyday world in which we are all immersed in sin and temptation, and so we cannot fathom the true purity he preaches and brings into life. [. . .]
>
> You do not know him well enough or have seen him enough to understand his character and that power that leads him. But I have known him for more than two years and I am certain that he is carrying God's cross and is suffering for the truth that we don't understand and if you are somewhat acquainted with the occult, then you know that great things are hidden under a certain cloud that closes off to the profane the path to the truth. [. . .]
>
> Write me everything you think of this, for your opinion is most valuable to me and I want to feel you with me, but do be honest, for I love you dearly, with a pure, clean love to the grave, and I hope no dirty tricks can undo our friendship.[35]

Felix did not bother to reply.

Not long after the Duma inquiry into Rasputin in late January, a distraught empress wrote a pained eight-page letter to Princess Yusupova bemoaning the injustice of the act. "No one loves us," she cried, "everyone is trying to do us harm. This inquiry was a revolutionary act."[36] Committed foe of Rasputin though she was, the princess still felt pity for the empress. At the urging of Ella, she tried to talk to

Alexandra about Rasputin following Guchkov's speech, but it did not go well. Alexandra was particularly upset. Along with the nasty public scandal she had also just received a disturbing document. It was an anonymous report, dated 7 March, titled "Concerning the starets Grigory Rasputin" claiming to be based on information gathered from followers of Rasputin at Vyritsa south of Petersburg and in the suburb of Okhta. It noted that although everyone the author had spoken to only confessed to the humanity and brotherly love of Rasputin, their "mentor" and "protector," some in Vyritsa had shared darker stories with him. "The pilgrim <u>Grigory was a terrible reprobate who acts in great secrecy</u>," the report read, "and at the same time makes his male and female followers engage in all sorts of khlyst rituals, pretending this is necessary to save their souls and to express their love for their neighbor, and the majority of the women try to please the pilgrim Grigory, and receive in return his affectionate admonitions."[37]

Princess Yusupova, to her credit, tried to calm her down and at the same time to open her eyes to the dangers that both Rodzianko and Guchkov had highlighted. But the empress would not listen. "No, no!" she cried. "Hanging is too good for men like Rodzianko and Guchkov!" The princess objected, insisting they were honest men trying to open her eyes, but Alexandra would have none of it.[38] The princess left knowing she had failed.

And still the opponents of Rasputin kept working. It was soon learned that Alexandra's brother Ernst Ludwig, grand duke of Hesse, and his family would be visiting. Ella was glad of the news, and she wrote to the Dowager Empress asking her to pray that "with the help of God he might bring light to that blindness that has cast a shadow on their house and the country and on all of us who love them so much."[39]

31. The Investigation II:
Was Rasputin a Khlyst?

Rasputin returned to Petersburg from the Crimea on 29 June and went straight to the apartment of Pyotr Damansky at 34 Liteiny Prospect, followed the entire way by agents of the Okhrana and hounded by reporters eager to talk to him and take his photograph. The press reported his return elicited a "sensation"; a crowd of curious St. Petersburgers waited outside the building to catch a glimpse of him. *Capital Rumor* asked how was it possible that a man who had been declared a khlyst and exiled from Petersburg could be allowed to stay at the apartment of a top Synod official? Some said he was soon to leave on another pilgrimage to Jerusalem; others, that he was to take up orders and enter a monastery.[1]

Rasputin remained only until 3 July when he returned to Pokrovskoe, staying there until the end of the month. Police agents in Tyumen recorded how "The Russian"—his Okhrana code name—boarded train No. 3 on 31 July at 11:40 in the morning with an unknown gentleman and a priest by the name of Vasilev, an assistant of Archpriest Ioann Vostorgov, and left for Petersburg. They arrived at 6:10 p.m. on 3 August and Rasputin went directly to Damansky's. The press, as always, was there to meet him at the Nikolaevsky Station. The *Stock Exchange Gazette* wrote the next day: "His appearance is tormented. He has gotten even more emaciated. He's literally skin and bone. His eyes are now more sunken. But his gaze remains the same—tense and penetrating. He was dressed in a German-style coat over a typical Russian shirt and in a soft hat. No one was at the station to meet the 'starets.'" Agents followed him over the next several days, noting his visits to the home of the Golovins on the Winter Canal, to the baths, to a few churches, a wine cellar, and the "Hotel D." on Suvorovsky Lane, with a prostitute, where he spent thirty minutes and then returned home alone. "'The Russian,'" an agent's report read, "when he is walking alone, particularly in the evening, talks to himself, waves his arms around, and slaps himself about the torso, which attracts the attention of passers-by."[2]

If these details are indeed accurate it should not be too surprising, for the pressure on Rasputin continued to mount and the scandals continued to grow throughout the first half of 1912. First had been the matter of Germogen and Iliodor; then the Duma inquiry, followed by the meetings of Kokovtsov and Rodzianko with the tsar; next came Guchkov's attack in March in the Duma. Throughout it all the press and the police had never left him alone. Rasputin was being hunted like an animal. Stories began to appear that he could no longer handle it and was trying to obtain a foreign passport to leave the country; so prevalent did the idea become that Andrei Stankevich, the governor of Tobolsk as of February 1912, felt compelled to wire the head of the department of police back in Petersburg that this was nothing but a lie.[3] If the strain was getting to him, no one could be surprised. And then, to add to his troubles, the long-dormant khlyst investigation was given new life.

Why and by whom the investigation was revived is not clear. It seems that more than one source might have been responsible. In Petersburg, Rodzianko and Guchkov were trying to revive it, and it was reported in the press that the Holy Synod was preparing to take action as well given all the renewed talk about Rasputin's links to the khlysty.[4] In February, the office of the Chief Procurator of the Synod, under Sabler, did request the file on Rasputin be sent from the Tobolsk Ecclesiastical Consistory, apparently upon the order of the tsar. According to Kokovtsov, Nicholas believed once Rodzianko had read the file he would also be convinced of the baselessness of the talk about Rasputin's links to the khlysty and so would help put an end to the rumors.[5] While all of this was going on, Yevsevy, who replaced Antony (Karzhavin) as the bishop of Tobolsk in March 1910, had ordered monthly reports compiled on Rasputin detailing his whereabouts and activities, including any information on possible links to the khlysty. All this was to be done in the greatest secrecy. Yevsevy had been the rector at the Yaroslavl Theological Seminary in 1905 where he had clashed with the young Iliodor over the new monk's promotion of the Black Hundreds. He most likely assumed the worst about Iliodor's famous friend (though now enemy), and the bishop was supposedly completing a damning report on Rasputin when he was unexpectedly transferred to the eparchy of Pskov on 17 April 1912. An interim bishop—Dionisy (Pavel

Sosnovsky)—took Yevsevy's seat until his replacement, Alexei (Alexei Molchanov), arrived in June. Dionisy was not content just to keep the bishop's seat warm, and on 14 May he instructed the Tobolsk Consistory to continue collecting information on Rasputin. Before Alexei departed Petersburg for Siberia, Damansky presented him with the consistory's secret file on the khlyst case of Rasputin so that he could be fully informed of the matter.[6]

On 21 May, Father Pyotr Ostroumov reported to Dionisy from Pokrovskoe that Rasputin had been regularly attending church and working in the fields the entire spring. He continued to fast on the holidays and undertake pilgrimages to the Abalak Monastery. The only unusual activity involved Olga Lokhtina. She had been living at the Rasputins' since January and had begun acting strangely. Ostroumov believed that her religious mania had become unhealthy, even dangerous. She had taken to calling Rasputin "God" and telling others to either acknowledge his holiness or risk God's punishment. Lokhtina was indeed not well. Her obsession with Rasputin had led to the breakup of her family; she had left her husband and children to live with Rasputin after her husband refused to accept him into their house any more. For a time she was kept in a hospital for the unbalanced, but then wandered off. Her family continued to support her financially, but she never went back to them, living alternately with Rasputin or Iliodor.[7]

Sometime around 23 April she left Pokrovskoe, apparently after an argument with Rasputin's wife. Lokhtina had been seen running away from the Rasputin home barefoot with nothing but a pillow in her hands. Rasputin ran after her, and led her back to his house, where she was heard to say that she could no longer live in his home. Rasputin managed to find a local peasant willing to conduct her to Tyumen, after which she disappeared for a time. The police had been monitoring the situation and noted she was clearly "emotionally ill."[8] The *Western Siberian Herald* reported on 9 May that Lokhtina had been seen by the villagers of Borki outside Tyumen wandering about in a strange way, barefoot and half dressed.[9] Later that month she appeared not far from the Florishchev Monastery where Iliodor was being held. What little clothing she had on was now nothing but rags, and she was threatening to kill herself.[10] The *Evening Times* ran a long story on her plight on the eighteenth titled "One of Rasputin's Victims" that presented Lokhtina as a once beautiful and loving mother who had been seduced by the fad for mysticism and then fell into the clutches of Rasputin. This formerly strong-willed woman had become "an obedient plaything in the hands of an illiterate Siberian peasant." He had destroyed her soul, ruined her home life, and even raped a young female ward of the family, the article stated with disgust.[11] A similar article appeared around this time in the *Western Siberian Herald* asserting Rasputin's wife and his other followers had mocked and terrorized the poor Lokhtina, once the beautiful "society lioness," and so she had fled the Rasputin home to save her life.[12] In his report dated 21 May, Father Ostroumov wrote that what prompted Lokhtina to flee was Praskovya's refusal to accept that her husband was in fact God. She loved her husband, but that was obviously more than she (or any wife) could take.

After Lokhtina's departure, Rasputin visited the monastery at Abalak. Throughout the month of May he was seen handing out "in massive quantities" copies of his booklets *Great Days of Celebration in Kiev!* and *Pious Meditations* at home in Pokrovskoe and across the province as well. It seems fair to say he was not terribly worried about what had become of Lokhtina. Ostroumov reported in July that Rasputin had remained at home all of June, visited by Zinaida Manshtedt and Akilina Laptinskaya, and, for two days, Bishop Varnava.[13] There was nothing about Rasputin's behavior deserving comment.

That spring Yevsevy had apparently also asked Father Alexander Yurevsky, first connected with Rasputin's possible links to the khlysty in 1907, to compile a report on Rasputin. Yurevsky told a group of pupils at the Tobolsk Theological Academy in May 1913 how he had spent three months gathering information, much of which was most sensational. Rasputin, Yurevsky said, had been a horse thief in his youth for which he had often been punished. Typically, the village elders would beat him for his crimes or have some of the younger men toss him up into the air and let him fall to the hard earth on his back until he could take no more. The punishment was harsh and painful, and once he nearly crushed his genitals upon hitting the ground. But this fall induced a mysterious change in Rasputin: he could now keep an erection for as long as he liked. Once he realized this, Rasputin used it as his ticket to win over the bored, sexually starved society ladies. He could please them like no one else, and they could not get enough of him. Rasputin told them that none of this gave him pleasure, for what he was really doing was driving the Devil from them. "You demon of the flesh, be gone!" Yurevsky said Rasputin would scream as he mounted his victims.

Yurevsky proposed sending Rasputin away to the Solovetsky Monastery in the Far North as punishment for his sins, but just then, Yevsevy was replaced by Alexei. Yurevsky said that the new bishop was a supporter of Rasputin. He took Yurevsky's two-hundred-page report and tossed it into the fire.[14] Rasputin had been saved. If Alexei did throw any such document into the fire it was probably because he could tell it was full of lies, which it most certainly was. (The story about his penis was clearly too much.) But if Alexei had been a supporter of Rasputin, then why would he have ordered Fyodor Kungurov, a new priest in Pokrovskoe, to try "in complete secrecy" to find answers to the many questions Dmitry Berezkin had raised in his report of 1908 after the initial investigation, answers that he believed would at long last determine whether or not Rasputin was a khlyst?

Father Kungurov, however, wanted nothing to do with it. He replied to the bishop that he had known Rasputin only since July when the priest first arrived in the village; moreover, it took a specialist with a good deal of expertise in sects to uncover these secret groups and he was utterly lacking in this knowledge. Twice Kungurov wrote to get out of the assignment, and twice he was ignored. It was only after Alexei threatened to demote him to a smaller, more remote village that Kungurov finally acquiesced. And so, in October 1912, Kungurov, along with Father Ostroumov and Deacon Vladimir Bryantsev, carried out a search of Rasputin's home and entire property trying to find anything suspicious. But nothing even remotely incriminating turned up. As far as they could tell, Rasputin was not a khlyst.

Alexei agreed. In June, on his way to take up the bishop's seat in Tobolsk, he had stopped in Pokrovskoe. He visited Rasputin and spoke at length with him about his religious beliefs and hopes and also talked with people who knew him well. After that, he had Rasputin visit him twice in Tobolsk, where he tested his "religious convictions." Nothing in these conversations ever gave Alexei a reason to think Rasputin was a khlyst. Everything he had learned contradicted the negative opinion he had formed about Rasputin based on what he had read in the press. No, Alexei asserted, Rasputin was an "Orthodox Christian, a very intelligent man, spiritual in nature, who was searching for Christ's truth and was capable of giving good advice to those in need." The only reason for any investigation in the first place, Alexei stated, was his predecessors' "gross ignorance of sects and sectarians."

Alexei went further in this report on the matter on 3 November:

I cannot add my support to what the Tobolsk eparchial power has done with regard to this matter, for through this investigation it has played into the hands of every enemy of the Throne of our Russian Tsar and His Most August Family. This is how the investigation has been understood by the enemies of Russian Autocracy, by various Misters Guchkov et tutti quanti [. . .] Before starting the investigation, thought should have been given to its possible consequences.

On 29 November 1912, five years after it had begun, the investigation into Rasputin and his connection to the khlysty was finally closed.[15]

But not everyone was convinced of the investigation's findings. Some had doubts about Alexei and his role in the affair. First of all, Alexei had known Rasputin well before their meeting in Pokrovskoe in June of that year, a fact that he glossed over in the letter he wrote to Damansky on 12 December 1912 saying the investigation should be put to rest. Indeed, Alexei had first met Rasputin possibly as early as 1904 in Kazan, where he had served as the rector of the local theological academy. Why he failed to mention their history to the head of the Orthodox Church is not clear.[16]

It has been suggested that Alexei had been greatly upset by his move to Tobolsk, an act of punishment by the Synod for his having kept a mistress (a school teacher by the name of Yelizaveta Kosheva) and for supposedly protecting a group of followers of the late John of Kronstadt while serving as the bishop of Pskov. Rasputin apparently learned of all this from Alexei's son, Leonid Molchanov, a secretary in the Pskov District Court, who passed through Pokrovskoe to visit his father in July 1912. Upon hearing this, so the story goes, Rasputin knew just what to do to clear his name. He went to Alexei in Tobolsk and offered him a deal: stop the investigation and he would see to it that Alexei was transferred from cold Siberia (which exacerbated his nephritis) to the warm south, and indeed, in October 1913 the tsar did appoint Alexei to be the exarch of Georgia—the fourth highest bishop in the Russian Orthodox Church—raising his status to that of archbishop and making him a member of the Holy Synod. It was then widely rumored that Rasputin had intervened to win the post for Alexei, as Alexei's son insisted had been the case, although Rasputin denied it on the pages of the *Petersburg Newspaper* in October 1913. Chief Procurator Sabler believed the stories about Rasputin's shady role in Alexei's promotion to be true.[17] Whether this was indeed what happened cannot be proven, and belongs more to the realm of gossip than fact. And it is a bit rich coming from Sabler, about whom it was said he had demeaned himself before Rasputin to win the office of Chief Procurator in 1911 and was widely believed to be Rasputin's man.

It is quite possible Alexei and Rasputin found some modus vivendi. Both saw themselves as victims of forces within the church, and so, perhaps, they made common cause to support and protect each other. In March 1913, Alexei appointed his own brother Nikolai Molchanov to be a priest in Pokrovskoe, and one of the deacons in the village was Vladimir Selivanovsky, the husband of Alexei's niece.[18] Was Alexei putting "his" people in the village to safeguard Rasputin? It is possible, although none of the other clergy in Pokrovskoe had said one negative thing about Rasputin in 1912, a fact that implies he had no such need of it.

There is the curious letter (overlooked by Rasputin's previous biographers) in St. Petersburg's Russian State Historical Archive from one Yakov Afanasev, a secretary in the office of the Tobolsk Consistory, to Viktor Yatskevich, director of the chancery of the chief procurator of the Synod, dated 8 November 1912. With a good deal of caution and indirect language, Afanasev informs Yatskevich that Alexei has concluded the Rasputin investigation in a hurried and not entirely proper fashion, without, he implies, full proof of Rasputin's innocence. He is not sure this has been communicated to the chief procurator, and asks what he ought to do: say nothing, and so risk the displeasure of the procurator, or pass this information along, and so risk the displeasure of his immediate superior, Bishop Alexei? Afanasev ends his letter by requesting that their communication remain "secret." Afanasev, it seems, had nothing to fear, for the chief procurator himself replied the following month that he had already been fully informed of Alexei and the consistory's final decision and was satisfied with the result.[19]

And then there was the opinion of Vladimir Bonch-Bruevich, an expert in Russian sectarianism. It had been Guchkov's idea to engage Bonch-Bruevich to interview Rasputin and give his opinion on the matter. An introduction was made by Baroness Varvara Iskul von Gildebrand, at whose home Bonch-Bruevich had first seen Rasputin, and the two men met several times for conversations on a range of topics, both with observers and alone. After many hours of careful examination, it was Bonch-Bruevich's opinion that Rasputin was indeed an observant and faithful Orthodox Christian and not a sectarian, and definitely not a khlyst, views that he expressed to a select gathering of members of the Octobrist party. (Bonch-Bruevich liked to tell the story of how when Rasputin arrived at his apartment, he was transfixed by a large portrait on the wall—"And who is that? Tell me, who is that? [...] Now that's a man ... Oh, you, my God! Samson, my friend, he's a regular Samson ... You must introduce him to me! Who is he? Where does he live? Let's go visit him straightaway. Now that's the kind of man the people will follow in masses." A bemused Bonch-Bruevich proceeded to explain it was a long-dead, famous thinker by the name of Karl Marx. It was clear to Bonch-Bruevich that Rasputin was hearing the name for the first time.)[20]

Not everyone, however, was ready to accept Bonch-Bruevich's professional assessment. Guchkov later came to wonder whether Bonch-Bruevich, the Bolshevik, had purposely lied to them since he knew the value Rasputin represented to the revolutionary movement.[21] It is an intriguing thought, but unlikely.

Officially, the question of Rasputin's links to the khlysty was closed. But in the end, the determination of the church meant nothing to the popular perception of Rasputin, and when he returned to Petersburg on 15 November of that year, *Evening Times* was quick to announce that the "Famous khlyst Grigory Rasputin arrived yesterday evening."[22] He took up residence at 70 Nikolaevsky Street in the apartment of a teacher named Ivan Zeiman. The police were unusually busy tracking his every move. Indeed, in the final two months of the year the Okhrana field agents filed over 140 pages of surveillance reports. This one, for example, was from 18 November. It noted that Rasputin (aka *Russky*, "The Russian") went out that evening with "Jackdaw" and "Crow." The agent made certain to catch every detail: "Jackdaw was carrying a small basket wrapped in yellow paper." The agents remarked his movements on the streets on the twenty-fifth and twenty-sixth were "Extremely cautious and slow." And it was not just Rasputin they were tracking, but everyone he came in contact with as well. For several days he had been driving around in an automobile with the license plate number 15. Agents checked into the vehicle; it belonged to Grand Duke Georgy Mikhailovich, Sandro's brother.

A *spravka*—a document containing key physical and biographical information—was completed for every person Rasputin met. Typical was this one from 1 December 1912:

Spravka on the c[ase] of "The Russian"

Unknown lady in a queer costume staying at No. 10 on the Moika, does not reside here, but has been visiting the well-known apartment No. 2, in which live Golovina, Lyubov Valeryevna, 59 yrs., widow of Chamberlain OF HIS MAJESTY Actual Priv. Counselor, and her daughters: Olga Yevgenyevna, 37 yrs., and Maria Yevgenyevna, 25 yrs.

The queer lady was here today too, based on her costume one can assume that she belongs to the educated class of khlysts.

Police Insp. Ivanov

The "queer lady," it turned out, was none other than Olga Lokhtina.[23] The agents found her particularly suspect. In another report she is described so: "Wife of actu[al] st[ate] counselor, head of communications for the Kazan district, O. Vlad. LOKHTINA, 50 yrs., apparently a religious psychopath-sectarian who calls herself 'The Virgin.' Lokhtina's costume draws special attention—a red bonnet and white dress with bows of red ribbon."[24] Lokhtina, the agents were certain, was a khlyst, just like Rasputin.

But was he? After the February Revolution, the Provisional Government took up the matter for a third time. The man in charge of the investigation was Professor Gromoglasov, an academic specialist in sectarianism at the Moscow Theological Academy. Looking over all the evidence, including reports of his bathing with women—a practice fairly common in parts of Siberia—and all of Rasputin's writings on religion, Gromoglasov found no evidence that Rasputin had been a khlyst.[25] Vladimir Rudnev, a member of the Commission following the revolution who had been given full access to the files on Rasputin, came to the same conclusion.[26] With attempts by some contemporary Russian nationalists to canonize Rasputin, the Russian Orthodox Church recently examined the question for a fifth time. In 2004, Metropolitan Juvenaly issued a statement at a major church council that not enough evidence had come forward to warrant rehabilitating, much less canonizing, Rasputin. According to the official line of the church, the question of Rasputin and the khlysts remains unanswered.[27]

The church may be undecided, but most historians are not, and the general consensus is that Rasputin had not been a khlyst.[28] Perhaps the most convincing case was made by the famous dissident and writer Andrei Amalrik in his unfinished biography. Amalrik noted Rasputin's regular and faithful church attendance; his obvious love and respect for the rites and rituals of the Russian Orthodox Church; his commitment (in his own way, of course) to marriage and parenthood; his prayers for all believers and his faith that everyone could be saved, and not just members of his "sect." Rasputin's approach to religion, Amalrik persuasively argued, was essentially ecumenical, and he was not someone to be constrained by the strictures of any one sect or that of the official church itself.[29]

Was Rasputin a khlyst? The answer is no.

32. The Miracle at Spała

In the middle of September, after marking the centenary of the Battle of Borodino in Moscow, the royal family traveled west by train for some relaxation to the Polish hunting lodge of Białowieża and then two weeks later on to Spała, a wooden villa nestled amidst a dense forest once home to the kings of Poland. One day, Alexandra took Alexei for a ride in her carriage together with Anna Vyrubova. As they drove over the bumpy road, the little boy, not fully recovered from a recent injury, began to complain of pain in his leg and abdomen. Worried, Alexandra ordered the coachman to turn around and take them back. With each bounce of the carriage, eight-year-old Alexei cried out in agony. Vyrubova later recalled the ride as "an experience in horror." By the time they returned to Spała, Alexei was nearly unconscious.

He was immediately examined by Dr. Eugene Botkin, who found a severe hemorrhage in the boy's upper leg and groin. The bleeding would not stop, and a massive hematoma began to form as the blood sought its way through the body. His groin and abdomen began to swell and tighten. Alexei was in misery. Additional medical help was summoned from Petersburg: the pediatrician Sergei Ostrogorsky, Dr. Rauchfuss, and the imperial surgeon Sergei Fyodorov along with his assistant Dr. Vladimir Derevenko. None of them, however, could do a thing to help the boy. His screams became so loud, the servants and staff stuffed their ears with cotton. The torture went on for over ten days. Alexandra, distraught, remained at his bedside. As he lay wailing in unbearable pain, she held his hand, stroked his forehead, prayed, and cried. "Mama," he moaned, "help me. Won't you help me." As for Nicholas, he did not have the strength to stay in the boy's room. At the mere sight of his poor son, Nicholas would flee the house in tears. "She bore the ordeal better than I did," he later confessed to his mother. Nicholas and Alexandra became certain their son was dying. Alexei, too, knew it was coming, but this brought him some measure of comfort. "When I am dead, it will not hurt anymore, will it, Mama?"[1]

Once it became known that gossip had begun to appear in the capital about something being terribly wrong with the tsarevich, it was decided to publish official bulletins of the boy's illness, although the precise cause was left unstated. There were references to an "abdominal hemorrhage," to "widespread hemorrhaging," and to "hematomas," but nowhere did the word "hemophilia" appear. The gossip and talk swirled and all manner of speculation seized the country. The French ambassador, Georges Louis, passed on to Paris the story that Alexei had been the victim of an assassination attempt and that Alexandra was so overwrought she had to be restrained by the doctors from throwing herself out of a window.[2] Prayer services were held in churches across the empire. Still the boy's condition worsened. Alexei was administered the last sacrament. Preparations were being made to announce the death of the heir to the throne.[3]

It was at this point Alexandra looked to Rasputin as her final hope. After the last sacrament had been administered, she asked Vyrubova shortly before midnight to telegraph Rasputin in Pokrovskoe and ask him to pray for Alexei. Rasputin sent a reply almost immediately. The original telegram has been lost, and several versions of what Rasputin responded have been printed, all of them roughly of the same content. "God has seen Your tears and heard Your prayers. Do not be sad. The little boy will not die. Do not let the doctors torment him too much."[4] The next morning there was no change in Alexei's condition. Regardless, Alexandra already felt relief. "The doctors notice no improvement," she said, "but I am not a bit anxious myself now. During the night I received a telegram from Father Grigory and he has reassured me completely." And indeed so did it come to pass. The following day, the bleeding stopped. Alexei would live.

As the historian Robert K. Massie wrote, "The part played by Rasputin's telegram in Alexis's recovery at Spała remains one of the most mysterious episodes in the whole Rasputin legend." Those most closely connected to the event—Alexandra, Vyrubova, Alexei himself—said little or nothing about Rasputin's influence; Nicholas, in a long letter to his mother dated 20 October, wrote about the role of the doctors and Father Vasilev, who gave the boy communion on the tenth, but makes no mention of Rasputin or his telegram. Nor did Rasputin ever discuss the episode.[5] So just what part did Rasputin play in the boy's recovery?

The question has no obvious answer. The medical profession had no way of treating hemophilia in the early part of the twentieth century, and it seems reasonable to assume that the doctors' persistent examinations of the boy only served to worsen the internal bleeding since this inhibited the formation of the necessary clots. In hindsight, the best thing they could have done for Alexei was to simply leave him alone— the only hope for someone with the disease in those days was that the bleeding would stop on its own, which was just what had happened to Alexei on previous occasions.

Alexei's seemingly miraculous recovery at Spała and Rasputin's murky role in it raises the larger question of his oft-noted though still poorly understood, and heavily mythologized, healing powers. The conception of Rasputin as a powerful faith healer remains one of the most salient aspects of his enduring persona. But did he truly possess the power to heal? And if so, how? Where exactly did his unusual power lie, and how did it operate?

Of course, many at the time did not believe that Rasputin possessed any such power. Some claimed that any connection between Rasputin's words and the boy's recoveries was nothing more than coincidence. Rasputin, in other words, was just lucky, happening to turn up at the sick bed or say a prayer or send a consoling telegram at the opportune time when the bleeding was stopping of its own accord, regardless of any intervention on Rasputin's part. Such was the opinion of Lily Dehn, one of the people closest to Alexandra and so in a good position to know.[6]

Others perceived something more sinister at work. Vyrubova, it was said, was not the innocent friend of the empress she pretended to be, but was in fact in league with Rasputin and Dr. Badmaev to gain control of Alexandra by playing on her fear for her son's health. The scheme worked liked this. Badmaev, drawing on his knowledge of esoteric Chinese medicine, would create a powder out of the antlers of young Siberian stags and ginseng root that in small doses would revive the flagging sex drive of old men, but in high doses could cause internal bleeding. This he gave to Vyrubova, who would surreptitiously slip it into Alexei's food and drink. Soon, the boy would begin to hemorrhage and become deathly ill. The doctors would try everything to help him, but it was all in vain because Vyrubova continued poisoning the tsarevich, and only once Rasputin had been called for would she stop.

Rasputin would appear at the sick boy's bed, and soon thereafter he was well again, all the proof Alexandra needed of his remarkable powers.

It appears the story originated with Iliodor; the source, among other things, proves its absurdity.[7] The story became quite widely held, so it would appear, by the number of times it has been repeated by a variety of people including Prince Felix Yusupov, Nikolai Sokolov, who investigated the murder of the Romanovs at the hands of the Bolsheviks, and the popular writer and journalist William Le Queux. A similar tale was passed on to an official of the German foreign office in Lucerne in early 1916 by one "Madame N.," a Russian with connections at court.[8] Sokolov took the story one step further to its logical, evil conclusion, writing that Rasputin, having proved his worth to Alexandra, next threatened her, saying that the heir would live only as long as he were alive. Soon after, Rasputin raised the threat, now asserting that were he to die, they all would perish.[9]

Despite Rasputin's well-known reputation as a healer there are only a handful of instances when it is claimed he actually cured someone. One was the son of his secretary Aaron Simanovich, who was supposedly cured by Rasputin of Saint Vitus' Dance (Sydenham's chorea). Another involves Olga Lokhtina, who told the Commission that he cured her from "neurasthenia of the intestines" from which she suffered for five years and of which no doctors, even Western European specialists, were able to cure her. Both of these instances, however, must be looked at with extreme skepticism: Simanovich's memoirs are notoriously unreliable and Lokhtina clearly suffered from mental illness, which was likely the basis for her mysterious-sounding illness.[10] The German ambassador reported in early 1916 that Rasputin had healed the tsar's daughters when they were younger, hinting that he had been allowed questionable access to the young females as well.[11] This, of course, was nothing but society gossip.

And then there is the episode with Vyrubova, also mentioned as proof of Rasputin's healing power. On 2 January 1915, Vyrubova was riding on a train that crashed between Petrograd and Tsarskoe Selo. She was nearly killed in the accident and lay pinned under the wreckage in the cold snow for hours, both her legs crushed, before being brought to the hospital. She was in a horrible condition, unconscious, and it seemed that she would likely not survive more than a few hours. A priest read her the last rites. And then Rasputin arrived. He went to her bedside, took her by the hand, and said in a loud voice: "Annushka, wake up. Look at me." With that she opened her eyes and, seeing Rasputin, smiled, and said: "Grigory, is that you? Thank God." Stroking her hand, he said so others could hear: "She'll live, but will remain a cripple."[12]

Rasputin proved to be right. She did live, but she never walked again without crutches. The story has been repeated many times by various people, but mostly persons who were not even there, which raises questions about its veracity.

Valentina Chebotaryova, a senior nurse at Alexandra's war hospital at Tsarskoe Selo, was later told about the incident from the attending doctor, Princess Vera Gedroits. "They sent for Grigory. I couldn't stand it, but I couldn't blame anyone. The woman was dying, she believed in Grigory, in his holiness, his prayers. He arrived frightened out of his wits, his beard quivering, his mouse eyes scurrying about." He took Dr. Gedroits by the hand, "She'll live, she'll live [. . .] For I shall save her." According to Gedroits, the tsar found this bit amusing and fought back a smile, saying: "Everyone heals in their own way." Chebotaryova was convinced Nicholas did not believe in Rasputin's holiness or power, but was willing to accept others did believe.[13]

Vyrubova herself did not recall the episode as signifying any great power on Rasputin's behalf. She remembered Rasputin entering her room (and so was not unconscious upon his arrival, as others have claimed) and telling those gathered around her bed that she would live, though would forever be a cripple. Then, she recalled, he approached her bed and she asked him why he was not praying to lessen her pain. And that was it. Nothing more.[14] It is difficult to know what exactly to make of this incident. What, if anything, did Rasputin do for Anna, other than to come to her bedside, stroke her hand, and say that she would live? Or perhaps it was his mere presence that was enough to save her life.

Alexandra believed beyond any doubt that Rasputin, as an instrument of God, had the power to heal her son, but it is often forgotten that Rasputin never did heal the tsarevich: he remained afflicted with hemophilia throughout his lifetime. What mattered was that Alexei did not die while Rasputin was alive, and this was enough for the anxious mother. (Although Alexei did not die from his illness after Rasputin's death either, it deserves noting.) Alexandra was convinced that it was faith—both hers and Rasputin's—that safeguarded her son's life. And it was through the lens of faith that Rasputin's acts took on the aura of miracles. Dostoevsky captured this worldview in *The Brothers Karamazov*: "Faith does not, in the realist," he wrote, "spring from the miracle but the miracle from the faith."[15] Only with faith are miracles possible.

Rasputin's power extended beyond his prayers and animated objects he had touched. When Vyrubova fell ill in early 1916, Alexandra instructed her to stay in bed and to drink hot red wine blessed by Rasputin. Alexandra made sure to drink some herself and sent the rest to Nicholas at army headquarters. And there were other talismans as well. During the war Alexandra liked to send Nicholas flowers and crusts of his bread, so-called "Rasputin rusks," to keep Nicholas safe and bring victory to the troops.[16] Society had an idea about the importance of Rasputin's charms and spun a number of myths around it. One of the more popular such tales had it that during a medical procedure doctors found under the sheets next to Alexei's body a dirty waistcoat. When they expressed shock, Nicholas told them not to worry, it belonged to Rasputin and would only help with the doctors' efforts.[17] Iliodor claimed Rasputin boasted of curing the tsar of a sore throat by sending him a shirt collar to wrap around his neck before going to bed. The next morning the pain was gone; Nicholas described it as a miracle.[18]

Strangely, Alexandra apparently did not turn to Rasputin for the myriad health problems (real and imagined) that plagued her. This is not to say he did not comfort her at times. In November 1916, for example, she wrote Nicholas that it was thanks to Rasputin's help that she had finally been able to get several nights of good sleep.[19] What exactly Rasputin did for her she never mentioned. The writer Nadezhda Lokhvitskaya, better known as Teffi, wrote that at a dinner party in April 1915 Rasputin spoke of how he helped the empress: "She is sick. Her chest hurts very much. I place my hand on it and pray. I pray well. And she is always better after my prayers. She's sick. One must pray for her and the children. It's bad . . . bad . . ."[20] Alexandra liked to instruct others at court to seek out Rasputin's help when they or their loved ones fell ill, but she seems never to have asked Rasputin to cure her of the neuralgia and neurasthenia that kept her bedridden so much of the time.[21] Rather, what Rasputin appears to have given the empress was occasional relief from her symptoms—irritability, discomfort, insomnia.[22]

The tsarevich's doctors—Fyodorov and Ostrogorsky, both of whom loathed Rasputin—stated openly and more than once that they had witnessed incidents in which Rasputin had managed to bring relief to the tsarevich and actually make his bleeding stop. The tsar's sister Grand Duchess Olga said the same thing of Rasputin's power over the boy, and she too was no supporter of Rasputin.[23]

One theory, proposed by Veniamin, about Rasputin's power traces it back to some peasants' ability to "speak the blood," that is the power to stop bleeding simply through the use of words.[24] Baroness Sophie Buexhoeveden recalled in her memoirs witnessing such an event as a child on her grandfather's estate after his favorite stallion cut its leg. The veterinary surgeon was called, but he could do nothing to stop the bleeding and so he told the old man of a local peasant named Alexander who was said to know "a mysterious word that will stop any kind of bleeding." The doctor thought this was nothing but peasant superstition, but the desperate grandfather sent for Alexander. Little Sophie was taken by the man's strange and sinister eyes: "Their hard stare seemed to pierce one through and through." Alexander slowly took the horse's leg and placed his hands gently on the wound, now gushing with blood. Quietly, he began to mutter under his breath, so softly no one could make out what he was saying, as he fingered the wound. Then, to everyone's amazement, the blood stopped flowing. Those who were there and had seen it with their own eyes could not explain it.

Later, her grandfather told Sophie that he had heard of such "horse-leeches," peasants who lived so closely to them that they had developed a deep, intimate knowledge of their animals and had discovered how to gently apply pressure to stop all manner of bleeding. Their secrets were closely guarded, passed down from father to son; some believed they possessed supernatural powers. And at times, they had even used their skill on humans. Sophie wondered whether Rasputin was such a horse-leech.[25] A corollary to this notion was that Rasputin possessed some rare power of touch, which Iliodor claimed he boasted of. Indeed, the myth of the sheer magnetic power of Rasputin's touch, supposedly strong enough to heal with the slightest contact, is still made even today.[26]

Some have suggested that Rasputin relied on hypnotism. Rasputin's daughter Maria, however, insisted that her father never resorted to hypnotism and that he did not have any idea about how it worked or was practiced. Veniamin concurred with Maria.[27] Yet many of Rasputin's contemporaries disagreed. Iliodor believed Rasputin relied on hypnotic powers (as well as "electricity" emanating through his hands and eyes), as did Charles Sydney Gibbes, English tutor to the Romanov children, Palace Commandant Voeikov, and several ministers. The Russian press printed a photograph of Rasputin hypnotizing Olga Lokhtina, which he quickly and publicly described as a fake, insisting on the pages of the *Petersburg Newspaper* in January 1914 that he had never studied hypnotism and had no ability for it at all.[28]

The belief that Rasputin used hypnotism both to heal and to gain control over people was widely held.[29] Kokovtsov wrote in his memoirs that he believed Rasputin may well have tried to hypnotize him at his office (or, he added, perhaps Rasputin was merely studying him closely, this being their first meeting—Kokovtsov could not be certain), and Stolypin, according to Rodzianko, felt a similar "great hypnotic power" during his meeting with Rasputin, a power that he managed to resist.[30] This was a common claim by Rasputin's government foes: namely, that Rasputin possessed inordinate hypnotic powers, but they (men of great will themselves) had been strong enough to resist his energy. The assertion was made by Felix Yusupov and Alexander Rimsky-Korsakov, Imperial Master of the Stables, as well as Minister of the Interior Alexei Khvostov, who also noted that most of his agents monitoring Rasputin were not so strong and quickly fell under Rasputin's power and so had to be frequently changed.[31] (Nevertheless, Khvostov told the publisher Sergei Melgunov in the autumn of 1915 that he had finally been able to break his habit of nail biting thanks to Rasputin's powers of suggestion.)[32] Some, like Nikolai Yevreinov, popular playwright and theatrical figure, in *The Mystery of Rasputin* (1924), argued that Rasputin's power came not just from "ordinary hypnotism," but his special "sexual hypnotism" that made him so successful with women.[33] Teffi claimed Rasputin tried to hypnotize her and spoke of how he used his touch in an effort to subjugate her with the current of his intense will. A magnetizer, a mesmerist, she called him, although one not powerful enough to take control of her.[34] William Le Queux claimed that he had been told by a famous Russian alienist how, along with his natural hypnotic influence, Rasputin had the rare ability to contract the pupils of his eyes at will, regardless of the amount of light in a room, a feature that gave him extraordinary power over his subjects and was, so this purported alienist claimed, the unmistakable sign of a "criminal degenerate."[35]

The police files contain some suggestive but vague reports on how in early February 1914 Rasputin was taking hypnotism lessons from "a certain Gerasim Dionisievich PAPNADATO" at an apartment on

St. Petersburg's Maly Prospect. Papnadato ("The Musician" in the files) is described as twenty-five years old, thin, "an Armenian type, dark complexion," with black hair and a black walking stick. The police tailed him for a while that month, but apparently stopped after their few meetings ended, a fact which suggests Papnadato may have been as interested in learning the secrets of Rasputin's power as Rasputin might have been in the hypnotist Papnadato.[36]

This Papnadato is likely the man Stepan Beletsky refers to in his memoirs as one of the "Petrograd magnetizers" with ties to Rasputin he was monitoring as head of the police at the end of 1913. Beletsky intercepted a letter from the man to his mistress in Samara in which he wrote of his hope for material gain thanks to his connection to Rasputin. He also mentioned his pupil's prospects as a hypnotist given his strong will as well his rare gift to concentrate this will inside him. Beletsky sent his men to learn more about this shadowy figure, but he got wind of the surveillance and disappeared from the city before they could catch him. Beletsky had no idea whether or not Rasputin continued his studies of hypnotism.[37] Regardless, neither "blood-stilling" nor hypnotism can be used as explanations for what happened at Spała, for the simple reason Rasputin was not there.

To Alexandra, the answer was simple: Rasputin was a man of God, and God manifested His power through him. A true holy man, Rasputin's prayers had the power to heal her ill son. Before dismissing the notion out of hand, it should be pointed out that the belief in the efficacy of intercessory prayer to heal is still widely held today. Take the United States, for example. According to a 1996 Gallup Poll, 82 percent of Americans affirmed "the healing power of personal prayer" and 77 percent agreed with the statement that "God sometimes intervenes to cure people who have a serious illness." Doctors appear to share these widely held beliefs. A 2004 survey of 1,100 U.S. physicians found that 73 percent believe that miraculous healings do happen. So pervasive is the belief in the efficacy of prayer in healing, that scientists and researchers at major universities have been compelled to examine the subject and the most prestigious academic presses publish monographs on the question.[38] Between 2000 and 2005, the US federal government spent over $2 million to fund research into the healing potential of prayer. For proponents of prayer, the results, however, have not been encouraging. In 2006, the largest study, led by Dr. Herbert Benson, a cardiologist at the Harvard University School of Medicine and founder of the Mind/Body Institute at Massachusetts General Hospital in Boston, found that intercessory prayer had no noticeable effect on 1,802 patients who underwent coronary bypass surgery. Indeed, those patients in the study who had been informed that strangers were praying for them (as part of the study, some were informed, others were not) actually experienced higher rates of complications after surgery. The results echoed that of a 1997 study at the University of New Mexico that found alcoholics in rehabilitation fared worse if they knew others were praying for them.[39]

Nonetheless, even as some researchers themselves admit, the connections among prayer, religious faith, and health are not just notoriously complex, but may well lie beyond the ability to be measured in any scientific manner. As for Rasputin, he never claimed to be a miracle worker, insisting that if his words ever played any role in healing then this was nothing more than the manifestation of God's will, an expression of Divine grace.[40] Vyrubova recalled that Rasputin was usually hesitant to pray for the sick. "I know of many cases of illness where the prayers of Rasputin were asked for," she wrote, "and had he been so minded he might have demanded and been given vast sums of money. But the fact is he often showed himself extremely reluctant to exert whatever strange power he possessed. In some instances where sick children were involved he would even object, saying: 'If God takes him now it is perhaps to save him from future sins.'"[41]

Did Rasputin's prayers save the life of Alexei at Spała? Possibly, although it cannot be said for certain that he prayed for him as Alexandra asked. Based on what we know, he cabled back to say that the doctors should leave the boy alone and that he would live, nothing more: nothing about whether or not he had prayed or what God had possibly communicated to him. This was, in fact, typical for Rasputin. He did not pray for Vyrubova in 1915, and there is no proof he prayed for Alexei but simply told Alexandra that the boy would live. It was not Rasputin's prayers that mattered, but merely his words—assured, confident, authoritative. And it is in his words, or rather Alexandra's reaction to them, that the clue to Rasputin's strange power over the sick little boy is to be found.

All medical evidence to the contrary, Alexandra believed Rasputin entirely when he told her Alexei would recover in October 1912. Rasputin's assurances calmed the anxious, fretful mother and filled her with unshakeable confidence, and she, in turn, transferred this confidence to her ailing son, literally willing him back to health.

At first glance the notion may seem farfetched, but this has less to do with the fallacy of such an idea and more to do with our limited understanding of the role of the mind in human health. It is only in the last fifty years that the connection between stress and physical health has been established, and researchers at institutions such as the above-mentioned Mind/Body Institute and the Cousins Center for Psychoneuroimmunology at UCLA have only begun to explore the ways in which the body and brain interact and the power of the latter in mitigating and recovering from illness. Simple relaxation via a number of techniques (meditation, repetitive prayer, yoga, diaphragmatic breathing) has been shown not just to lower blood pressure, but to ease insomnia, cardiac arrhythmias, allergies, and severe pain.[42] For decades the power of anxiety and negative emotions to worsen the effects of hemophilia, and, conversely, of relaxation and calm to decrease capillary blood flow and aid the healing process has been well known.[43]

A related aspect of the mind/body equation is the placebo effect. Harvard University Medical School, together with Boston's Beth Israel Deaconess Medical Center, recently established the Program in Placebo Studies and Therapeutic Encounter to study the role of medical ritual, cultural context, and the power of imagination in the healing process. Much more than a sugar pill, the placebo effect has come to be seen as central to the entire web of interactions that take place between doctors and patients, and the latest research is beginning to show just how vital the culture of medicine—from the doctor's white coat, to her diplomas on the examination room wall, her tone of voice, and even the strength of her eye contact—is in helping sick patients to recover. And the scope of the placebo effect is proving to be astounding, from changes in heart rates and chemical activity in the brain to lessening the symptoms of Parkinson's disease.[44]

At a time when the medical profession had no way to treat hemophilia, and the fussings of the doctors only served to exacerbate Alexei's suffering, Rasputin's instruction to leave him in peace was vital to his recovery, especially when considered together with his words of hope and assurance that all would be well. Alexei fed off the calm of his mother, he relaxed, his blood pressure most likely dropped, his pain eased, and his body mended. Alexandra, it must be recognized, was doing just the right thing for Alexei by putting her faith in Rasputin, for there was no other option. Ultimately, only belief could stop the bleeding, and this is what Rasputin gave to Alexandra and she, to her sick boy. This explanation for Rasputin's power not only makes sense medically, but was attested to by contemporaries, who expressed astonishment at the power of Rasputin's words to ease Alexei's pain, to lessen his suffering, and make him relaxed and calm, full of hope when he had earlier had none.[45]

If the court had managed to keep the chronic illness of the heir a secret for so many years, with the crisis at Spała it became public knowledge, even if the exact nature of the disease and the gravity of the danger were not. It has been suggested that had Nicholas and Alexandra only been open about the heir's ill health and Rasputin's role as a healer, the mystery of his influence would have been solved and so along with it the entire scandal of his relationship with the royal family. It is an intriguing notion, although most likely misguided. The tsar's sister Olga called such talk "calumny," and she was right.[46] More thorough, accurate knowledge of the relationship did not necessarily lead to understanding or approval. "The fact is, the heir to the throne is fatally ill," the deputy minister of the interior once told Vasily Shulgin. "Constant fear forces the Empress to throw herself on the mercy of this man. She believes that the heir is still alive thanks only to him. And in the meantime everything is turned into a pigsty. I tell you, Shulgin, he's a scoundrel."[47]

The miracle at Spała greatly solidified the "scoundrel's" place alongside the royal couple. If the scandals of the past two years had presented moments of tension between them, this swept everything aside and assured Rasputin's favored status. Society talk had it that Prime Minister Kokovtsov had managed to remove Rasputin from court and that his strange career was at its end, but then the miraculous healing of the heir had brought his return.[48] Rasputin was back for good. But he was never the prophet Nicholas and Alexandra thought they saw standing before their sick boy. Vyrubova recalled years later how he had assured their majesties that from the age of twelve Alexei would begin to get better and would eventually become strong and well.[49] At the age of twelve, Alexei had but two years to live.

33. War and Celebration

While Alexei lay recovering in Spała that October, the *Russian Word* reported that in recent days Rasputin had been experiencing strange, mystical dreams, dreams that had become a source of intense interest in influential circles in the capital. One involved an enormous woman, a symbol of Russia, over whose head a mighty sword burned violently with great flames. The woman reached up, grabbed the sword, and then gently slid it into a scabbard, extinguishing the flames. There was talk that Rasputin was soon to leave Siberia and "once more return to the stage."[1]

The dream (most assuredly the product of an overly imaginative Petersburg reporter) was a reference to the tensions mounting in the Balkans that threatened to bring Russia to war. In the spring of 1912, Bulgaria, Serbia, Greece, and Montenegro concluded an alliance, supported by Russia, that contained a secret clause according to which they agreed to consider joint military action against Turkey should disturbances threaten the status quo in the region. After an uprising against the Turks in Albania led to a number of bloody reprisals, Montenegro declared war on the Ottoman Empire on 8 October 1912 (NS), and days later the other members of the Balkan League joined the war against Turkey, launching the First Balkan War, which would last until May 1913. The Balkan allies routed Ottoman forces on the peninsula, and by early November it seemed as if victory over the Turks was assured.

Russia was swept up in war fever. The streets were thronged with crowds excitedly demanding war in defense of Russia's Slavic brethren against the Ottoman infidels. There were calls for placing a Christian cross back on the top of the Hagia Sophia in Constantinople. Others stressed the need to defend Russian interests in the Balkans against Germany and Austria as well. Among the loudest voices calling for war was Duma President Mikhail Rodzianko.

Rasputin, however, was dreaming of peace. His was one of the loudest voices against the war hysteria that autumn. He told the *Petersburg Newspaper* on 13 October 1912:

> What have our "little brothers," about whom our writers screamed, whom they defended, shown us? [. . .] We have seen the deeds of our little brothers and now we understand [. . .] Everything [. . .] Yes [. . .] As concerns all those various alliances there, well, alliances are good, as long as there's no war, but once war heats up, where are all these allies? They're invisible.
>
> So, fine, dear man, you, by way of example say, but look! There's war there in the Balkans. And so writers begin to shout in all those newspapers: Let us have war, let us have war! So we, naturally, must fight [. . .] And they have been calling everyone to war and stoking the fire [. . .] So I then would ask them [. . .] I'd ask those writers: "Gentlemen! Why are you doing this? Do you think this is right? One must try to dampen passions if there are tensions, or it'll lead to a big war, and not enflame people's anger and hatred."[2]

He told the same newspaper in December when asked about the danger of Russia being dragged into war: "Lord preserve us and save us from this. God grant ancient Russia avoid this threat. Every war, even a successful one, is fatal for matters of love and peace, for God's grace. God grant Russia, and all other states as well, manages to avoid war. All our minds must be devoted to this one problem."[3] In January 1913, Rasputin had this to say to *Smoke of the Fatherland*:

> Christians are preparing for war, they are proselytizing for it, torturing themselves and torturing everyone else. War is a bad business, and Christians, instead of practicing humility, are marching straight toward it. Let's say it won't happen, at least for us. One can't say this. It never pays to go to war, to take each other's life and life's blessings, to break Christ's testament and kill your own soul before its time. What happens to me if I do beat you into submission, for after that I must keep watch over you and fear you, but regardless you'll be against me. That's if by the sword. But if I take you by Christ's love then I need fear nothing. Let the others go at it, the Germans, the Turks—that's their misfortune and blindness. They'll find nothing and will only quickly finish each other off. And we, quietly and with love, looking into our selves, will once more stand above all others.[4]

Even abroad Rasputin became known as the man who was keeping Russia from war. The *Frankfurter Zeitung* in a story titled "Russia and the Balkans" (1 March 1913 [NS]) quoted the words of "The starets, who is still in contact with powerful men" that "the Bulgarians have repaid the Russians' love with ingratitude and hatred—we must think of ourselves now instead of being concerned with the affairs of the unworthy."[5] In May 1914, the *Vossische Zeitung* published an interview with Sergei Witte (reprinted in the Russian press soon after) in which he stated how Rasputin had saved Russia from war during the Balkan crisis with his decisive words at the key moment. "The entire world damns Rasputin," he said, "but did you know that Rasputin saved us from war?"[6] The *Odessa News* stated the same thing that July, noting that it was thanks only to Rasputin that Russia managed to avoid war with Austria over the Balkans.[7]

Here is how Vyrubova recalled it: "It was in 1912 when Nikolai Nikolaevich and his wife tried to convince the Emperor to take part in the Balkan war. Rasputin begged the Emperor practically on his knees not to do this, saying that the enemies of Russia were just waiting for Russia to involve itself in the war and then Russia would meet with inescapable misfortune."[8]

That Rasputin kept Russia from going to war in the Balkans has become part of his mythology, and although it is beyond any doubt that Rasputin was against the war and let everyone know he was—a fact much to his credit—it is less clear that his was the determining voice for peace.[9] Indeed, other, more powerful figures were saying the same thing. Foreign Minister Sergei Sazonov, for example, who was not entirely blameless in the war's outbreak, was adamant that it remain a local, Balkan matter and that neither Russia nor Austria permit themselves to be dragged into it. Even more importantly, Nicholas had told his ambassador to Bulgaria in early 1911 never to forget for an instant that Russia would not be ready for war for at least another five or six years. Pressured by the Great Powers, the Balkan League agreed to peace in May 1913, only for Bulgaria to attack Serbia and Greece less than a month later. This Second Balkan War was bloody and brief; Bulgaria was defeated and sued for peace by August. "The first round is won," a radiant and emboldened Serbian prime minister crowed, "now we must prepare for the second against Austria." Nicholas, however, was left with dark thoughts, writing to his mother: "There is no such thing as European unity—merely Great Powers distrusting each other."[10]

*

Rasputin returned to the capital in January 1913. Nicholas recorded in his diary on the eighteenth: "At 4 o'clock we received good old Grigory, who stayed with us for an hour and a quarter."[11] It was the first time they had seen each other since June 1912 in the Crimea. The court was then busy preparing for the celebrations to mark the tercentenary of Romanov rule. The celebrations began on the morning of 21 February with a twenty-one-gun salute by the cannons of the Peter and Paul Fortress. That same morning Nicholas led a procession from the Winter Palace to the Cathedral of our Lady of Kazan on Nevsky Prospect for a Te Deum at noon. The church was packed with courtiers, foreign dignitaries, and high officials. Rodzianko was also there, in a foul mood after learning that members of the Duma had been given seats in the back of the cathedral.[12]

But what really set him off was the sight of Rasputin, dressed in expensive silk and his glistening bottle boots, a large gold cross hanging across his chest, standing in front of the Duma members. According to his memoirs, Rodzianko confronted Rasputin, demanding to know how he came to be there, to which Rasputin pulled a printed invitation out of his pocket, replying he had been invited by personages much loftier than the president of the Duma. Rasputin acted impudently, showing Rodzianko no respect and even trying to hypnotize him, but Rodzianko refused to be either intimidated or swayed by Rasputin's powers, and he ordered Rasputin to leave the church immediately, which he did, followed by Rodzianko, who saw him don an exquisite sable-lined coat, climb into a waiting automobile, and drive off.[13]

This is one of the oft-mentioned episodes in Rasputin's biography, but it is difficult to know whether such an encounter ever happened and if it did, whether it was anything like Rodzianko recounted in his memoirs. He did report it to Major General Vladimir Dzhunkovsky, deputy minister of the interior as of January, on 23 February, two days after the event. Yet, interestingly, either Dzhunkovsky, or someone in his office, wrote in heavy blue pencil next to Rodzianko's description of the incident with Rasputin: "Not true."[14] What can be said with certainty is that Rodzianko liked to present himself in his memoirs as the only one who knew how to deal with Rasputin—with the firm, unyielding hand of the master—which, had Nicholas followed his example, would have meant the end of Rasputin's career at court and the likely salvation of the monarchy itself.[15] But this was not to be from a weak ruler such as Nicholas.

Rasputin may have been ejected from the celebration at Our Lady of Kazan (although probably not), but he was not silent about his impressions of the tercentenary. *Smoke of the Fatherland* carried an interview with Rasputin in which he praised the celebrations and the Romanov family. He took issue with those critical voices that had suggested the celebrations would be an occasion for unrest or even murder and would prove just how unstable the monarchy had become. Quite the contrary, Rasputin asserted. The events had shown just how much the people loved their tsar and the young heir. "He has a rare mind," Rasputin said of the tsarevich. "He's beautiful and wise, and, most importantly, he has a strong character." Alexei's illness he characterized as "God's trial and a trial for the nation," but then added that his illness had almost completely disappeared. Alexei, Rasputin told the reporter, was "our hope."[16]

Munya Golovina visited the small house of Peter the Great in the Summer Gardens together with Rasputin, Nicholas, and Alexei during the festivities. The tsar and tsarevich had come to pray before the icon of Christ in the tsar's modest bedroom that had been converted into a chapel. As they knelt down and bent their heads in prayer, Rasputin whispered to Munya: "Poor little boy, what does life hold in store for you!"

Munya asked: "Grigory Yefimovich, will there be a revolution?"

"Why do you ask? How would I know?" he shot back, with a suspicious look. "Just a little one," he replied, his eyes narrowing, "if I am here to stop it."[17] It is a moving vignette, though it feels as false as Rodzianko's.

The police had Rasputin under close surveillance at the time. All agents tasked to trail Rasputin were given this description:

Characteristics of "THE RUSSIAN"—

About 35–40 years old, above average height, medium build, type—Russian, hair: long, light-brown, a blunt-edged beard with shades of reddish-brown, average mustache, with hints of red, a thin face, eyes—sunken; dressed in a beaver hat of the kind worn by priests, his coat—black with brown trim, velvet upper, beaver collar, Russian boots, tall, with brown rubber galoshes.

"The Russian," the Okhrana's anodyne code name for Rasputin, would soon be changed under Dzhunkovsky to the ominous *Tyomny*,

"The Dark One." The agents followed Rasputin during the celebrations in St. Petersburg every day from 9 a.m. to 7 p.m. Attention was paid to his associates as well, who were also given code names: there was "The Crow," Georgy Sazonov; "The Jackdaw," Lily Dehn; "The Dove," Zinaida Manshtedt; "The Owl," Akilina Laptinskaya; "The Bird," Munya Golovina; "Winter," Lyubov Golovina; "Summer," Nadezhda Taneeva; "Masquerade," Olga Lokhtina; "The Monk," Bishop Varnava.[18]

It should be noted that it was not just the police who exhibited a fondness for code names. In her correspondence, the empress called Bishop Varnava "the gopher" (Rasputin called him "the moth") and the ministers Boris Stürmer and Alexei Khvostov were "Old Chap" and "The Tail," or "Fat Belly," respectively.[19] Princess Zinaida Yusupova, Felix's mother, littered her letters with code names too: Valida, for the empress, the Book for Rasputin, Bonheur for Nikolasha. The practice was evidence of the degree to which the police intercepted and read a great amount of the mail in the country, and particularly that of important persons, including members of the Romanov family. People knew they were being watched, which bred an atmosphere of caution, secrecy, and distrust. No one, not even the empress, felt they were safe from prying eyes.

Rasputin joined the Romanovs for more celebrations on 19 May in Kostroma, home of the Ipatiev Monastery where Mikhail Romanov had received a delegation from Moscow informing him that he had been elected tsar in 1613. General Dzhunkovsky, one of Rasputin's greatest enemies, claimed in his memoirs that he tried to keep Rasputin away from the official ceremonies there, but the empress overruled him and made sure an Okhrana agent was attached to Rasputin to see he was allowed near her and the family. Dzhunkovsky was outraged to have been overruled, and he would later attempt his revenge.[20] Rasputin was there too for the Romanovs' triumphant arrival in Moscow on 24 May, the culmination of the tercentenary celebrations. According to the tsar's sister Xenia, Rasputin was standing by the Cathedral of the Archangel in the Kremlin where Nicholas went to light a candle by the tomb of Mikhail Romanov. To her dismay she did not see him, but everyone else did. "Rasputin is once again in evidence all over the place," she wrote in her diary, "there is such discontent and protest among the clergy! They say Maklakov* is preparing a report for Nicky! How unfortunate it all is—certainly if he were a minister, he would not dare show himself."[21]

Father Georgy Shavelsky, protopresbyter of the Russian army and navy, tried to bring up the matter of Rasputin with Nicholas's sister Olga later that year. "We all know that," she told him. "It is our family grief, which we are not strong enough to do anything about." He tried to convince Olga of the need to talk to the emperor. Their mother already had, she replied, and it had done no good. He insisted she too had to speak up, for her brother loved and trusted her profoundly. "Yes, I am ready, father, to say something, but I know nothing will come of it. I'm not good at speaking. He'll say a word or two and destroy all my arguments, and then I'll get flustered and completely lose my way."[22]

Rasputin met Nicholas and Alexandra back at Tsarskoe Selo after tea on 1 June and then departed for Pokrovskoe.[23] While he was away, both Alexei and Alexandra fell ill. Vyrubova asked that he pray for them, which he did. Rasputin was back at court on the evening of 17 July and spent some time with Alexandra and Alexei, who had hurt his arm the day before. Nicholas noted in his diary that soon after Rasputin left, his son's arm started to feel better, he calmed down, and was able to fall asleep.[24] On the thirtieth, Rasputin sent Alexei birthday greetings: "Happy holiday, [be] strong in spirit and wise in your mind, for the victory over the enemy, everyone and everything loves you from the bottom of their heart, sometimes crying about the health of the amazing and radiant young man Ts. Al. Nikolaevich."[25]

---

* Nikolai Maklakov, in charge of the ministry of the interior as of 16 December 1912, officially confirmed as minister on 21 February 1913.

34. Gutter Talk, Name-Glorifiers, and Murder Plots

Rasputin's return to the capital in January 1913 was marked by a long and overwhelmingly positive article in *Smoke of the Fatherland* on the twenty-fourth. Under the title "With Grigory Rasputin," the reporter D. Razumovsky purported to recount a chance meeting with Rasputin in a second-class compartment of a train four days earlier. At first Razumovsky did not know who the man was, sitting quietly and a bit shyly next to him: "Long brown hair, without a hint of gray, a disheveled beard that he scratched with his hand, his fingers nervous and a bit neglected, and deep-set eyes, heavy wrinkles around his eyelids—all of this recalled Repin's portrait of the peasant-sectarian Syutaev of Tver, that same Syutaev whose sermon so utterly changed the soul of Lev Tolstoy."[*]

They fell into talking, about the peasantry, about foreigners and their influence on Russia, about the Russian soul, about Orthodoxy. Razumovsky was impressed by this stranger. He told Razumovsky of the superiority of the Russian "spirit"—"The very worst person here has a better spirit than any foreigner. They have the machine. They sense this and so come here themselves to get this spirit. You can't live just by the machine. It seems everything around them is good, but they having nothing inside them. And that's what's most important." He told Razumovsky of the importance of peace and the need to stay out of the war in the Balkans. He told him he was no sectarian, but that he judged the clergy for its "indolence and lack of beauty in its churchly habits." He said too many people tried to oppose evil, when what they really needed to do was not to oppose good, which was much harder to do. And he told the reporter that many people said all manner of bad things about him, none of which was true, but he took none of it to heart and there

---

[*] Vasily Syutaev (1819–92), the creator of his own brand of moral-religious teaching based on brotherly love, greatly admired by Tolstoy and painted by Ilya Repin in 1882.

was nothing he could do about it: "The blind can't see colors, and the Kingdom of God will open only to those who approach each other as children. I have and keep no other commandment."

And then the stranger said to his traveling companion: "And so it's clear to you who I am, I'll tell you: I am Rasputin."

Razumovsky was shocked. This was the man about whom so many horrible things had been written, about whom so many legends swirled? It simply could not be, for this man was so calm, so sincere, so pure —"almost childlike." He was too simple, too humble, too honest for this to be any sort of act either. No, the key to the popular perception of Rasputin lay less in the man himself, and more in the times: "He is not even any sort of riddle for our days, but simply the victim of the vulgarity of this pathetic century without heroes or righteous men, when nothing remains but worm holes, a time when horses, their ancestors, their mood and their posterity warrant a million times more attention than the human soul, now worthless, of no interest, having been turned into a machine."

In fact, Razumovsky continued, there was something remarkable about this man Rasputin:

> Perhaps he is the only one who is correct in saying that the recep-
> tive and gentle Russian soul, the easily enamored and artistic
> Russian spirit, and the powerful and unique Russian culture, with
> all their estrangement from life's narrow practicalities, open new
> horizons onto life, possess an irresistible attraction, and any
> attempts by other nations to enslave us by their very nature lead to
> the opposite: to our spiritual victory over them.[1]

The weekly *Smoke of the Fatherland* was a broadly nationalist publication launched in 1912 by Alexander Garyazin, entrepreneur, publicist, and founder of both the Russian National Club and Russian National Union. He was no Black Hundred in the manner of Iliodor, but nevertheless insisted on Russians being first among all peoples of the empire. "Only with the triumph of Russian self-consciousness and a place of leadership for the Russian people across the territory of the empire and at all levels of state power is the peaceful progress of hundreds of nationalities possible," Garyazin remarked. He was one of the few men in Russia willing to openly embrace Rasputin, even publicly attacking foes of Rasputin such as Archpriest Ioann Vostorgov and refusing to march in step with other monarchists.[2] Did Razumovsky really encounter Rasputin on the train, and did they really have such a conversation? This is not known, but no one seemed to care, for what mattered was the very fact that there were influential men now ready to stand squarely behind Rasputin in public.

The article in Garyazin's weekly represented a preemptive strike against Rasputin's enemies. There was talk that members of left-wing parties in the Duma were again wishing to raise the question of Rasputin. Rasputin himself got wind of this and sent an angry note to Olga Lokhtina, claiming that the main person behind this was none other than Iliodor and his allies in Tsaritsyn. Nicholas learned of the planned actions in the Duma and instructed Minister of the Interior Maklakov to put an immediate stop to the matter, an order he in turn passed on to Rodzianko who gave his word that Rasputin would not be mentioned in the Duma and if anyone told him anything to the contrary, then he was simply lying.[3]

The anti-Rasputin forces hit back in March with an article called "Our Time" in the moral-religious journal *Responses to Life*. The author, and the journal's publisher, was the Moscow priest Vladimir Vostokov, the very same Vostokov possibly behind a series of anti-Rasputin articles three years earlier. That spring Vostokov met Princess Obolenskaya, maid-of-honor to the empress, in Moscow at the apartment of the Tyutchev family, descendants of the great nineteenth-century poet. Talk naturally turned to Rasputin. "Pity the Tsar," Vostokov said to the princess, "pity Russia, pity our entire future. Chase that khlyst, tramp, and conman from the capital and send him back to his native land without the right to leave it. Recall God's Words of warning: Remove the unclean from the Tsar and His Throne will be saved." Obolenskaya told him they had been trying, but that nothing was working. Just the other day a group had begged the same of Prime Minister Kokovtsov, but he told them it was pointless and simply shrugged his shoulders.

It was around this time that Vostokov learned his journal had been approved for the religious instruction of the Grand Duchesses Olga and Maria. This gave him an idea: Why not try to speak directly to the royal family through the pages of *Responses to Life*? "Our Time" is an allegory set on a beautiful and wealthy Russian noble estate, where there lived a good but naive master and his wife. So trusting was the master that he let all manner of dishonest men take advantage of him, and the master's wife had fallen under the sway of a passing tramp, who was in fact a khlyst. This deceiver forced himself on all the female servants; on his visits to the local tavern he would brag about his powers and drink and dance to excess. Some of the master's trusted men tried to convince him of this interloper's true nature, but he was too naive, too passive, too weak to act, and he feared upsetting his wife, even when they pleaded with him to send the man away. Over time all the good and honest men were forced off the estate, and the interloper saw that conniving, deceitful men took their place. Everyone with a conscience eventually departed, leaving behind only weak cowards and flatterers, and their days were numbered too. The long-suffering simple people were growing impatient and began to look askance at the Lord and the age-old truths that were the foundation of their world. "Why was this rogue given power?" the article asked. "Oh, we are lost and so too is the estate."

The meaning of Vostokov's story was inescapable, and for his confrontational act Vostokov was punished. On 1 May, Chief Procurator Sabler convinced the Synod to strip the journal of official church sanction, to see all future issues were subjected to pre-publication censorship, and to transfer Vostokov from his Moscow parish. His parishioners were outraged and turned to Ella, a supporter of Vostokov, for help, and she promised to do whatever possible to overturn the decision. Ella spoke to Sabler on 11 May in Moscow and she gave him a petition not to send Vostokov away. Her request, however, was denied. Later that month, as the emperor was passing through Moscow, a group of the city's church leaders presented him with a similar appeal. Nicholas read the request and then handed it to Sabler, saying: "Tell the petitioners, that Father Vostokov touched upon my family life in his magazine." Again, the petition was denied. In August, the decision came down to transfer Vostokov to a church in Kolomna outside Moscow. On 1 September, Vostokov set out on foot accompanied by a mass of his followers and members of his parish. With the permission of Moscow Metropolitan Makary (Mikhail Nevsky), they presented Vostokov with a large gold pectoral cross inscribed with the words: "The Blessed One, banished for the sake of truth, and for them there is the Heavenly Kingdom. September 1913." The meaning of the inscription was lost on no one. But there was more to it than just the words, for even the granting of the cross amounted to an act of rebellion: priests could only wear a gold pectoral cross with the sanction of the Holy Synod, something clearly not granted in this instance. When asked about this, the aged, and often befuddled, Makary replied that he had permitted Vostokov's followers to present the cross, but had never said anything about Vostokov's right to wear it.[4]

With this act Makary appeared to be siding with the foes of Rasputin, but the metropolitan would come to be seen in the eyes of some as one of his trusted allies. It was rumored that he owed his appointment as metropolitan in November 1912 to Rasputin's influence even though the two had never met. Makary's only sin was having received a congratulatory telegram from him. To many this was enough in the agitated climate to make one a "Rasputinist." Indeed, Makary never washed off the stain: he lost his post soon after the February Revolution due to his purely mythical links to Rasputin, such was the witch-hunt atmosphere.[5]

In the midst of the Vostokov scandal, *Smoke of the Fatherland* continued its defense of Rasputin. It covered in rapt tones his visit to a foundling hospital in May, quoting Rasputin's words that these unwanted babies were "Our national strength and our spiritual beauty [...] There is no sin in them."[6] The monarchist Vasily Skvortsov responded on the pages of the *Bell*, claiming (with no proof at all) that Garyazin's weekly was secretly funded by Count Witte and the Freemasons and the publication was simply a tool to help Rasputin wield influence at court and the upper reaches of the government.[7]

The press war raged throughout spring and summer. Another lengthy defense of Rasputin appeared in *Smoke of the Fatherland* on 20 June written by Alexei Filippov. He had studied law at Moscow University and then gone on to publish a number of periodicals (*Black Sea Coast*, *Russian Review*) before writing for Garyazin's weekly. In 1912, Filippov moved to Petersburg and took up an interest in financial matters and launched the newspaper *Money*. His reputation by then was less than solid. He collected compromising information on banks and other financial institutions that he would "sell" back to them for a hefty price; they could choose whether to do business or wait and see whether he would make good on his threat to publicize the information. He later married the sister of Felix Dzerzhinsky, future head of the feared Cheka.[8] It was apparently also in 1912 he first met Rasputin on a train outside Moscow and was immediately impressed by what Filippov called "his profound faith in the Russian people and by his thoughtful rather than subservient attitude toward autocratic power. He stood for the unity of the tsar and the people without an intermediary bureaucracy."[9] Their paths would cross many times in the coming years.

Filippov took issue with the mass of stories about Rasputin as "the arbiter of fates at the top." Such talk by the day's newspapers and Duma's "romantics" was nothing more than "fantasies" that served as advertisements, of a sort, for the very man these stories were intending to bring down. No, Filippov insisted, the truth was much more prosaic: Rasputin was simply a "normal Russian peasant," albeit an intelligent, decent, and hardworking one who had maintained his connections with the common people, and it was this that made him so well regarded by both the people and "in those upper spheres that were still close to and valued the people." This was the reason for such great interest in the man, nothing more. Rasputin personified the "heightened ardor and culture of the good old days that gave us the peasant."

Instead, Filippov noted that all one heard these days was "gutter talk" fueled by the "dirt, envy, gossip, and intrigue" that had infected so much of Russian society, and particularly the clergy, people who could only imagine Rasputin's attractiveness to those at court as being "religio-sexual in nature." By explaining his rise in the vilest of terms, and then attributing to him, with no basis in fact, the transfer of Feofan, the fall of Germogen, and the confinement of Iliodor was not only to exaggerate his influence, but also to make much grander, more serious claims about Russia itself:

> They ought to be reminded that by making such claims in public they are doing something bad: one might think that Russia now lacks any rule of law, common sense, and the most primitive integrity. Can it be that the Misters Milyukov* don't realize that by devoting their speeches to Rasputin they are ultimately acknowledging their own complete insignificance, and newspapers, such as *Evening Times*, are in fact acting as tools for increased advertising for Rasputin, a truly modest man with quite limited influence and power.

Six days later the newspaper published a letter by one A. K. Gavrilov, who claimed to have known Rasputin for two years. Addressed to the editors of the *Petersburg Courier*, *Kievan Thought*, *Russian Word*, *Day*, and *New Link*, the letter criticized them for their attempts to depict Rasputin as some sort of "sorcerer." Echoing the sentiments of Filippov as to the

---

* Pavel Milyukov, historian, founder and leading member of the liberal Constitutional Democrat (Kadet) party. He became a fierce enemy of Rasputin and the regime.

inaccuracy of the mountain of reports on Rasputin's character and influence, he called out the press and politicians like Milyukov and Guchkov for what it was they were really after:

> It is more than obvious at whom all these base shots intended to prove the omnipotence of Rasputin are aimed. But besides this, such a method of attack is morally dishonorable and leads to the cheap bravery of making a fist in your pocket. It's naive and intended only for the broad and gullible dark masses. It's not hard to get them to believe the fairytale about Rasputin's influence: in the imagination of the typical man in the street the government is transformed from an enormous, elemental, self-sufficient power into a small company of people, accidentally brought together, that can easily be manipulated by any nobodies for any matter and for any reason. In this manner, by focusing all of society's attention on one individual, they leave in the shadows all those persons truly guilty for Russia's troubles.

The editors of *Smoke of the Fatherland* appended their own comment to Gavrilov's letter, opining that by spreading such horrific rumors these publications were discrediting the Holy Synod, Russian Orthodoxy, and the government. Their words about the all-powerful Rasputin under whose wicked influence these institutions had supposedly fallen equaled a torrent of water poured onto the "anti-government mill."

As for Rasputin, he appeared not to let the campaign get to him. "All these hateful words about me float over just like clouds, and I don't fear them," he told Razumovsky. His daughter Maria often asked her father about the press attacks and why he did not do more to fight back. He would always say to her: "I know who I am. And so do those close to me. As for the others, we'll settle this in the next life."[10] Other reports in the press, however, insisted he followed all the press coverage with great interest, having Akilina Laptinskaya clip and save every story about him, muttering that he would be avenged on all his critics.[11] *Evening Times* ran a story on Rasputin in May 1914 in which he spoke about the media coverage: "What do they want from me?" he asked the reporter.

> Do they really not want to understand that I am a small fly, and that I need no one and nothing? Do they really have nothing better to write and talk about than me? My every step is discussed [. . .] they turn over and examine every last thing [. . .] It's clear that someone really has need of dragging me all over the place and scoffing [. . .]

I say to you, I don't lay a finger on anyone [. . .] I do my small deeds, as best I know how [. . .] Some praise me, some curse me [. . .] But no one wants to leave me in peace [. . .] Everyone busies himself with me and nothing but me.

The debate about whether or not to publicly discuss Rasputin did not die, not even with his death. Whether to denounce Rasputin or pass over him in silence remained a fiercely contested matter in the final years of the Romanov dynasty. In June 1914, one M. Lyubimov addressed the matter at length in an article titled "Topic of the Day" for the *Voice of Moscow*. He insisted Rasputin had to be attacked, and there was no reason to fear this only helped to publicize him. Publicity Rasputin had no need of, he wrote, for he did not seek great popular support à la Iliodor, but a few powerful people in high places. And for this reason he had to be exposed for the "adventurer" he was, along with those individuals enthralled by the words of this "bogus wise man." Could Russia continue to be silent about this scandal? he asked. No:

> One had to shout about it day and night, one had to shout on every street corner, and point one's fingers at that "starets," who had landed in another's chambers and made himself comfortable with exceptional familiarity.
>
> No Iliodor could cause so much evil and so much misfortune as this "humble starets" as he travels about Russia [. . .]
>
> Rasputin together with his entire "mind" is a terrible ulcer, festering on our sick social organism. [. . .] To advertise him? Therein lies the biggest tragedy, namely that we were much too late to notice this shameful figure and much too late to start talking about him.[12]

Much of the noise swirling around Rasputin that spring and summer had to do with a scandal among a group of Russian monks living at the Panteleimonov Monastery on Mt. Athos. The origins of the scandal can be traced back to a book by the starets Ilarion titled *In the Mountains of the Caucasus* published in 1907 in which he described a rare spiritual experience in connection with the name of Jesus Christ. The Savior's name, he proposed, was not just a word, but something much greater: in the very name was "The Savior Himself." Ilarion wrote: "In The Name of God, God Himself is present—in all His essence and with all His infinite qualities."[13]

Ilarion came to this discovery not through some sanctioned

religious education (which he never received), nor through rigorous study or research (he penned no scholarly works), but through his own personal experience, a fact which was to be crucial in the coming crisis. His book, reissued in 1912, became popular among a range of religious figures, including Feofan, Veniamin, the philosopher Alexei Losev, theologians Sergei Bulgakov and Mikhail Novoselov, and even Ella. The followers of Ilarion at Mt. Athos became known as the *imiaslavtsy* (or *imiabozhtsy*)—literally, the "Name-Glorifiers."

The Athos Sedition, as the affair would be called, was sparked by Archbishop Antony's (Khrapovitsky) virulent attack on the Name-Glorifiers in the pages of the *Russian Monk* in 1912, the same year as the republication of Ilarion's influential book. Antony was soon joined by other prominent church hierarchs, including fellow members of the Holy Synod and the Constantinople Patriarch Michael III. These opponents of what they claimed was a new heresy were called the *imiabortsy*, the "Name-Fighters." The depth of emotion on both sides was extreme. To show his disdain for the Name-Glorifiers, Sergei, archbishop of Finland and Vyborg (born Ivan Stragorodsky, later Patriarch of the Russian Orthodox Church under Stalin), wrote the word "God" on a piece of paper and then trampled on it with his feet. The Name-Glorifiers on Mt. Athos, led by a former guards officer and now monk by the name of Antony (Bulatovich), refused to back down and continued to propagandize their beliefs. The Russian Orthodox Church launched a campaign of intimidation. In May 1913, the Synod declared the teaching of the Name-Glorifiers "blasphemous and heretical" and ordered all of its followers to desist in their beliefs and practices and humbly submit to the head of the church.

When it became clear the Name-Glorifiers would not submit, church leaders turned to Nicholas for his support. It was decided in May 1913 to send Archbishop Nikon (Rozhdestvensky), formerly archbishop of Vologda and a member of both the Synod and State Council, along with a Russian naval vessel to Mt. Athos to force an end to the controversy. Together with a detachment of more than one hundred soldiers and officers, Nikon arrived at the monastery on 11 June. Facing a row of guns, the monks were forced to state in writing whether they were loyal subjects of the Russian Orthodox Church or members of the "heretical" sect of the Name-Glorifiers. Openly declaring one's beliefs was not enough, and the soldiers marched all the Name-Glorifiers—833 in all, well over half the Russian monks on the mountain—from the monastery and onto the warship *Kherson* for repatriation to Russia; in the process, as many as twenty-five monks were injured.

The official Church press declared a great victory over heresy, whose followers they now branded "revolutionaries and sectarians."[14] Their fate was pitiful. Handled roughly by the sailors on the *Kherson*, upon their arrival in Odessa on 13 July matters got even worse. They were broken up into groups, some imprisoned, and others sent to distant monasteries. Many were hounded into signing humiliating documents renouncing their faith. There were instances of monks being denied last rites in the final minutes of their lives.[15]

On 17 July, Chief Procurator Sabler met with Nicholas to inform him of the successful conclusion of the "Mt. Athos Sedition." Later that evening Nicholas and Alexandra received Rasputin, and it appears Rasputin used the meeting to defend the Name-Glorifiers and to criticize the harsh measures against them. We know that Rasputin was a defender of the Name-Glorifiers from a number of sources, including Director of the Police Stepan Beletsky, who told the Commission in 1917 that Rasputin had wholeheartedly supported the monks "out of completely disinterested convictions." Indeed, Rasputin told Beletsky that he sympathized with the Name-Glorifiers and that he had met a great many monks in monasteries across Russia who did as well.[16] And Rasputin was not alone. Even some of his enemies, such as Feofan, Germogen, and Mikhail Novoselov, supported the disgraced monks. The press was not sure what to make of this strange alliance of foes and claimed that any talk that Feofan supported the Name-Glorifiers could only be explained as lies being spread by Rasputin's acolytes to further damage Feofan.[17] Mikhail Zaozersky, a former priest, progressive journalist, and confidant of Vladimir (Bogoyavlensky), the metropolitan of St. Petersburg as of November 1912, went even further in *Evening Times*, writing that the entire scandal had been manufactured by Rasputin for the sole purpose of destroying Feofan.[18] The notion was ridiculous, but many believed it, for by that time many Russians thought Rasputin truly possessed both such remarkable power and such evil hatred.

Rasputin was apparently drawn to the Name-Glorifiers for a number of reasons beyond an inclination to their beliefs. In his public attack Antony (Khrapovitsky) had likened them to the khlysts, implying they were a grave danger to Russia's religious and social life just like that most notorious of sectarians, Rasputin. Antony was a committed foe of

Rasputin, and so there may well have been an element of "my enemy's enemy" in Rasputin's embrace of the beleaguered monks. There was a strictly personal reason as well. Among the monks taken away from Mt. Athos was Dmitry Pecherkin, Rasputin's friend and fellow pilgrim of years past. From Mt. Athos Pecherkin came to live with Rasputin at Pokrovskoe and must have told him how they had suffered at the hands of the religious and secular authorities.[19] Finally, there was Rasputin's propensity to side with minorities and underdogs, to resist the dictates of the high and mighty, be they of the church or state. He sympathized with these poor, honest believers, hounded, harassed, imprisoned, and exiled, all for their ideas. He too knew what it meant to suffer for one's beliefs, to be singled out by the church, labeled a heretic and a dangerous sectarian.

Rasputin never forgot their plight. He organized an audience with the emperor for some of the Name-Glorifiers on 13 February 1914. Nicholas listened sympathetically to their tales of having been driven away from the monastery and even allowed them the honor of meeting the tsarevich. At the same time, Nicholas, likely under Rasputin's influence, distanced himself from the harsh position of the Synod, which had singled out twenty of the former monks for trial that same month. During the Easter celebrations, on 30 April, Nicholas tried to end the controversy and asked the Synod to show Christian mercy by dropping the charges, reinstating the monks, and permitting them to conduct services again. Some members of the Synod saw in Nicholas's forgiveness of the Name-Glorifiers a repeat of his capitulation to Iliodor three years earlier, and his appeal did nothing but anger the Synod and drive a deeper wedge between the church and the throne.[20]

Naturally, the press did not fail to mention Rasputin in all this. On 1 July 1914, *Russian Word* published what it said were Rasputin's words on the affair:

> It's a sin, of course, that they [the Name-Glorifiers] made so much noise. They should have prayed to themselves and not made a fuss. Father Misail [rector of the monastery on Mt. Athos, born Mikhail Sopegin] arrived and said to them, sign this. We're talking about matters of faith here, and he says "sign"? How's it possible to sign something that has to do with faith! This is Mt. Athos, not some ministry. Yet they came and told them: sign, sign! So I made sure to tell Vladimir Karlovich [Sabler] that this is a sin! I told everyone

who needed to know that this is wrong. Well, they've finally realized that I was right.[21]

The newspaper had this to say as well: "It is well known that Rasputin played a most decisive role in the affair of the 'Name-Glorifiers.' Having been thoroughly informed of the entire Athos saga by Garyazin, the publisher of *Smoke of the Fatherland*, Rasputin undertook energetic efforts to ease the lot of the monks from Mt. Athos. After his intervention on behalf of the 'Name-Glorifiers' the repression was lifted."[22] The story was correct: Rasputin had come to the defense of this small religious minority, but the press saw nothing noble in this, rather more meddling in high places by the khlyst interloper.

Although the outbreak of World War I would push the Mt. Athos Sedition off the front pages of the press, the scandal never fully died out and remained an open wound within the church. Rasputin never forgot the monks, and he continued to speak about their plight to Alexandra, who came to share his concern over the injustice under which they still suffered. Years later, during the scandal over the canonization of Ioann Maximovich of Tobolsk, Alexandra spoke out harshly against Nikon— then against canonizing Maximovich—noting his shameful role in the Name-Glorifiers' affair, calling him "that villain from Athos." On 15 September 1916, she wrote to Nicholas to say that Rasputin had asked her to speak to the new Chief Procurator Nikolai Raev about the poor monks from Mt. Athos still being denied the right to conduct services and to receive communion.[23]

It is not known whether or not Alexandra ever did bring up the matter with Raev, but what is beyond a doubt is the fact that the affair served to further worsen the relations between the crown and the church and to create a schism within the upper ranks of the church. No clergyman could remain neutral on the subject of Rasputin by now, and one had to choose one of two hostile camps: the Rasputinists or the Anti-Rasputinists. A sense of crisis settled over the church. Those in the Anti-Rasputin camp felt the church had fallen under Rasputin's control. Many believed the entire church had been profoundly degraded and had lost its independence and true Christian spirit.[24] The Synod, for its part, placed the blame elsewhere. Much of the problem, it argued, lay with the press. At a meeting in 1910, one Synod member remarked that the rise of sects and various "false prophets such as Rasputin-Novykh" was entirely the fault of the press, which, he said, had written a great deal about the church of late, but chose to focus only on its negative sides. As a result of this anti-religious propaganda, "those persons of weak faith have come to doubt and to listen to the lessons of sectarians and false teachers."[25]

If not everyone could agree on the cause, everyone could agree that there was a crisis of faith—in the institutions of the church and state and in religion itself—that was deepening across Russia.

In September, Rasputin left for the Crimea, where he stayed until the middle of October. According to the *Southern Gazette*, he arrived with nothing but one small suitcase and checked into a comfortable room—complete with balcony and view of the sea—at the Hotel Yalta for which he paid five rubles a day. He led a quiet life there, seeing only his friends and followers and members of high society, and treated all the staff with kindness; he was a generous tipper. He went to bed early and enjoyed walks through the city. At times Rasputin was seen being ferried by a palace automobile to and from Livadia to visit the royal family.[26] Despite reports that during his stay Rasputin was "gloomy and in low spirits," the *Southern Gazette* assured its readers that the entire time he had been nothing but "happy and full of life."[27]

If Rasputin had been gloomy he would have had good reason, and not just because of the year's press campaign against him. There was an even greater danger waiting for him in Yalta. General Ivan Dumbadze was the governor-general of Yalta, a harsh, decisive man, ardent Black Hundred, and committed foe of Rasputin. For quite some time Dumbadze had been thinking about just what was to be done about Rasputin and had shared this obsession with his friend General Yevgeny Bogdanovich, who exerted considerable influence over Dumbadze. Back in February 1912, Bogdanovich had called dozens of Duma members, State Councilors, mayors, and representatives of the nobility to his home for what Lev Tikhomirov described as an "États Généraux," a reference to the gathering of the Estates General in France in 1789 on the eve of the revolution, to try to find the answer to a single question: What were they going to do to physically get rid of Rasputin? Those gathered at the Bogdanoviches' could not believe their ears. Was the general really talking about murder? His question went unanswered. Soon after, Bogdanovich met Dumbadze. Their conversation turned to Rasputin, and Dumbadze told him that if Rasputin dared show his face in Yalta, he would have him drowned in the Black Sea. Bogdanovich was thrilled, though he had to admit it would not be easy.[28]

Beletsky wrote that after Rasputin's arrival that autumn in Yalta he received an encrypted telegram marked "Personal" from Dumbadze that read: "Permit me to get rid of Rasputin during his boat trip from Sevastopol to Yalta." A shocked Beletsky immediately sent the telegram to his superior, Minister of the Interior Nikolai Maklakov, and then telephoned the minister on a secure line to ask whether he ought to reply to Dumbadze; Maklakov told him no, he would handle the matter himself, although Beletsky never did learn whether Maklakov kept his word. Beletsky wrote in his memoirs that Maklakov got on well with Rasputin, so it seems likely he put Dumbadze in his place. (In June of that year, Maklakov put a halt to police surveillance of Rasputin and instructed all agents in the Tobolsk province back to Petersburg. The reasons for this are unclear, although it may well have been on the orders of the tsar.)[29]

Regardless, Rasputin, accompanied by a number of police agents, completed the trip over the water to Yalta without incident. A few years later, after Beletsky's fall from grace following a much more serious plot on Rasputin's life, he spoke to a Colonel Trotsky in Yalta about Dumbadze's plan. Trotsky told Beletsky that Dumbadze had never mentioned his intention of drowning Rasputin, but he had talked of other schemes, one involving luring Rasputin to a small castle on a cliff overlooking the Black Sea and pushing him to his death and another plot in which Rasputin would be killed in a fake attack by bandits. All of this talk, however, Trotsky described as nothing more than "plans of a fanciful nature."[30] It is worth pointing out that Nicholas thought highly of Dumbadze and was well inclined toward him. The emperor's favor appears to have meant little to the governor-general, who was convinced that the way to safeguard the monarchy was to ignore the personal feelings of the tsar and contemplate murdering a loyal subject with whom the royal family had unusually warm relations.

In the end, nothing happened to Rasputin during his visit to Yalta, and around 12 October he arrived back in Petersburg.[31] He stayed at the luxurious apartment of retired Major General Alexei Veretennikov and his wife, Vera, on the fashionable English Prospect. The Veretennikovs' home would be Rasputin's base while in Petersburg until April 1914.[32] Earlier that spring Rasputin had, as in years past, contented himself with a small, simple room. The famous wrestler Ivan Zaikin (aka "The King of Iron") visited him and described Rasputin's living quarters to *Early*

Morning as nothing but a table, chair, and bed. There were a few icons hanging in the corner and a portrait of Tsar Alexander II, before which a small lamp was always kept burning. "Rasputin lives simply," Zaikin said.[33] The newspaper *Capital Talk* ran a story (of questionable reliability) in August that Rasputin had set up a quasi "military headquarters" in an apartment at 63 Kamennoostrovsky Prospect. Intent on expanding his power and influence, he was said to be holding gatherings here practically daily attended by "chic ladies," while a large crowd waited their turn outside his door. The entire scene was worthy of the great operatic bass Fyodor Chaliapin himself, the paper commented.[34]

By November, Rasputin was back in Pokrovskoe. Vyrubova wrote to inform him that Alexei's leg was hurting and asked him to pray for the boy. Rasputin replied directly to the tsarevich: "My dear Little Boy! Look at our dear God, see what tender wounds he has. He suffered once, but then become so strong and all-powerful—just like you, my dear boy, just like you will be happy and we'll live together and I'll come visit. We'll see each other soon."[35]

On 31 December, Rasputin returned to Petersburg having been followed the entire way by reporters and police agents. The press reported enormous crowds had greeted Rasputin along the trip, something the police categorically denied. Director of the Administration of the Perm Provincial Gendarmes Yevgeny Florinsky did note, however, in a secret report to Beletsky, that joining Rasputin in Perm had been Nikolai Ordovsky-Tanaevsky, director of the Perm Revenue Department, and that the two departed alone together in Rasputin's compartment. What Florinsky apparently did not know was that earlier that year Ordovsky had secretly been instructed to travel to Tobolsk to investigate Rasputin, specifically his relations with female convents in Tobolsk and Yekaterinburg. In his memoirs, Ordovsky wrote that his assignment had come from right-wing members of the Duma then contemplating drafting another official inquiry into the activities of Rasputin. Apparently, his investigations turned up nothing negative, and his assignment ended there.[36] Florinsky believed Ordovsky was simply trying to curry favor with Rasputin. There was talk he believed Rasputin could help make him governor of Tobolsk. The gossip, it turned out, had some foundation, and in November 1915, he would indeed be appointed governor, many believed, not without justification, thanks to Rasputin's help.[37]

35. On the Edge of a Precipice

"We had the joy of seeing Grigory in the evening. It was quiet and peaceful," Nicholas wrote in his diary on 2 January 1914. Rasputin returned to Tsarskoe Selo on the evening of the twentieth, when they all sat together, drank tea, and talked. The Court Journal, which almost never mentioned Rasputin's visits, noted that Alexandra received "the pilgrim Rosputin [sic]" at 10:30 p.m. on 18 February.[1] This visit is worth noting not only since it was recorded officially, but also given the late hour and the fact that Rasputin met Alexandra alone without Nicholas present. Such meetings, needless to say, gave suspicious minds reason to talk. On the twentieth, he was back at the palace to attend an evening service with the royal couple.

On 30 January, Kokovtsov was relieved of his posts as prime minister and minister of finance. The fact that Rasputin was in Petersburg at the time led some to assume that he was the one responsible for the move. Sergei Witte so much as said so to the German *Vossische Zeitung* that spring, and the story was picked up and reprinted in the Russian press.[2] The day after Kokovtsov's dismissal the Austrian ambassador wrote that everyone was talking about it in St. Petersburg, especially how poorly he had been dismissed. He overheard one of the grand dukes at the Yacht Club say, "He was let go like a servant." The ambassador did not mention Rasputin, but characterized the firing as a "triumph of the rightist parties and the secretive, and women-dominated, court camarilla." There was no confusion about the women he meant: Alexandra and Vyrubova. He ended his dispatch on a note of foreboding, commenting that with Kokovtsov gone, the warmongers would be that much stronger: "Fire is glimmering beneath a relatively calm surface. A clumsy hand could set things ablaze."[3] Little did the ambassador realize at the time how prescient he was.

In his memoirs Kokovtsov wrote that after speaking to the emperor about Rasputin in 1910, his dismissal was only a matter of time. As far as he knew, Rasputin never once called for his being replaced, and there is no evidence to suggest he did. Rather, what sealed his fate was the fact that Kokovtsov had not been able to silence the talk about Rasputin in the press and the Duma, as Alexandra expected him to. No one could have done this, yet the empress came to believe Kokovtsov had simply been unwilling, and so he passed from being a servant of the tsar to, in her mind, a weapon in the hands of their enemies. The only option was for him to go.[4]

And there were plenty of stories. On 9 January, for example, *Day* published a short piece describing an incident at Petersburg's Kazan Cathedral two days earlier when Rasputin slapped a woman hard across the face after she came up to kiss his hand. So shocking was his behavior that all the women in the cathedral screamed and ran out.[5] The Okhrana immediately investigated the story, only to find it had been fabricated.[6] Newspapers such as *Day* were not concerned about getting their facts right, however, since Rasputin sold newspapers, regardless of the truth. Alexandra knew this, and she quite rightly wanted something done to stop it. In this, however, she was to be constantly disappointed.

On 25 February, the press announced that Rasputin was leaving Petersburg for Moscow and from there would be departing for an extended stay in Siberia.[7] Rasputin's comings and goings were by now reported in the newspapers as if they concerned the movements of the tsar himself. On 9 March, Rasputin returned to the capital with his father, Yefim. This would be his only visit. He stayed for less than two weeks, just long enough to have his photograph taken with his son surrounded by his followers.[8] One can read Yefim's discomfort on his face. He did not care for all the noise, dirt, and crowds of the great metropolis and could not wait to go home. Rasputin took his father back to Pokrovskoe and stayed there with his family through the Easter holidays.[9]

Even before Rasputin left Petersburg in February a new wave of attacks was beginning. The opening shot was fired by Andrei, bishop of Ufa (born Prince Alexander Ukhtomsky), on the pages of *Dawn*. Rejecting the notion prevalent among the right that Russia was under attack by foreign influences, Andrei insisted that the true danger was domestic and that it was coming from the most primitive elements of the Russian narod. Russia had entered a new era, he wrote, that of "false prophets and prophecies," an era characterized by the decay of the narod itself, even if the country's leaders, who had fallen under the "hypnosis" of these dangerous figures, had so far failed to recognize the decay. The blind were leading the blind, he warned, straight off "a precipice." The latest of such false prophets Andrei called "The Traitor." He never gave his name, but then there was no need: everyone knew who he was. Andrei wrote he had known the man a long time (since Rasputin's arrival in Kazan, in fact). He was a "criminal," a wolf in sheep's clothing, and "big-time charlatan." This "Mister Traitor" offered him a high position if he would just answer correctly one simple question: "Do you believe in me?" Andrei refused to answer. Russia was facing a "spiritual catastrophe." No one would escape unpunished. The coming "dark epoch" would be marked in the pages of history, and their only hope was to pray to God it would not last long.[10]

Bishop Andrei's article exploded like a bomb, especially in higher church circles. It was reprinted and commented upon in other newspapers. Should anyone have been unable to identify him, these stories made sure to mention Rasputin by name. One newspaper averred that after such an attack, Andrei's career was over.[11] Rasputin would have him destroyed. In fact, nothing happened to Andrei—he remained bishop of Ufa until 1921, ultimately becoming a victim of Stalin's Great Terror in 1937. As for Rasputin, he never raised a finger against Andrei, although the *Sunday Evening Newspaper* reported in mid-March that Rasputin was preparing to launch his own weekly magazine—*Life of the Russian Man*—which might be interpreted as a warning he was preparing to take on his enemies in print.[12] The campaign carried on throughout March and April. The old rumor that Rasputin had taken holy orders was dusted off and brought out again as further evidence of the debased nature of the church. It was said he had divorced his wife and that his powerful friends were working to grant his wish to become a bishop.[13]

The Duma took up the matter in April. Father Fyodor Filonenko got up to bemoan the sorry state of the church brought low by the enormous influence of "certain rogues" from the khlyst sect known as "the Elders." (A voice in the hall rang out, "Rasputin!") He was followed by the Kadet party leader Pavel Milyukov, who repeated the gossip of Rasputin's having been made a priest as if it were fact. Then he held up Iliodor's notorious letter from 1912, waving it about, and saying he was not permitted to read it, but then proceeded to do so anyway. He said Sabler was "Rasputin's puppet" and he owed his job to him. Milyukov went further than Filonenko, stating that not just the church, but the state itself had fallen under the sway of "the rogue" Rasputin.[14] Next,

Prince Serafim Mansyrev approached the rostrum. Rasputin, he told the Duma, had become so all-powerful that he "terrorized" anyone who dared to criticize the current direction of the church and its administration. The church hierarchs prostrated themselves before "this individual" and "our unfortunate nymphomaniacs, young ladies from high society" pray to him as if he were some sort of god. "Where can we possibly go after all this?" he asked. The Duma erupted with wild applause.[15]

All of these speeches were reprinted in the newspapers, assuring the Duma attacks became well known across the country. "The newspapers are full of the description of the scandalous meeting of the St[ate] Duma during its discussion of the church budget," Lev Tikhomirov wrote in his diary on 29 April 1914.

> The maliciously abused Sabler was overwhelmed by the protests against his church politics, with their furious references to Rasputin. [. . .] Overall, an unbelievable scandal [. . .] I think the story of Rasputin is beyond repair. Without a doubt that rogue is himself responsible for starting the rumors of his exaggerated influence. It's quite natural that all the enemies of the Throne are joyfully exploiting this dreadful weapon.[16]

It warrants noting that the press did follow up on some of these accusations. The *Petersburg Courier* inquired into the rumors that Rasputin had divorced his wife and become a priest, and it ran a story on 7 May stating it had received convincing proof from Siberia that neither statement was true.[17] Corrections, however, made no difference. The gossip was too good not to believe.

Finally in May, another Rasputin story gripped the public's attention. It was reported that Rasputin was trying to get his daughter Maria enrolled in the Smolny Institute for Noble Maidens, a prestigious finishing school for Russia's elite established in the reign of Catherine the Great. The school's director, Princess Yelena Lieven, told the *Petersburg Courier* that this was nothing more than gossip, and under no circumstances would the daughter of a commoner, much less that of a man like Grigory Rasputin, ever be admitted to the Smolny Institute.[18] She could be counted on to protect the reputation of her school, even if their tsar could not be counted on to protect the reputation of the throne, the princess implied.

Around this the time the director of Kazan's Rodionovsky Institute of Noble Maidens (which did accept commoners), Olga Yermolaeva, received a curious and vaguely threatening letter. Signed by the "Union of St. Michael the Archangel and the Filaret Society," it made reference to Princess Lieven's refusal to admit Rasputin's daughter to the Smolny Institute and then went on to praise, in evidently mocking fashion, Yermolaeva's decision to accept Maria, whose father, the anonymous author(s) noted, was known to all true patriots, "for more than a decade now as the secret spouse of Her Majesty the Empress Alexandra Fyodorovna and the father of His Highness the heir-tsarevich Alexei Nikolaevich, the future autocrat of All the Russias." No doubt terrified, Yermolaeva took the letter to the Kazan department of the gendarmes, assuring them that she had not divulged the contents to a soul.[19] By then Maria had long since left Kazan for the capital and if she ever had attended that school, it would have been several years earlier. The quality of Maria's education, and her commitment to it, is not known. Vera Zhukovskaya claimed she once heard Maria complain that learning history was pointless, but she enjoyed mathematics, which at least helped teach you to count money.[20] Zhukovskaya's anecdote sounds as if it were invented.

Rasputin left Siberia for Russia in early May. While in Tyumen, he allowed himself to be filmed for a moving picture by a "Mr. Shuster." (He had also apparently been filmed one more time, in Pokrovskoe, although neither film seems to have survived.)[21] A few days later he made brief visits to Moscow and Petersburg before heading south to Yalta to visit the royal family. He saw them on three occasions—15, 16, and 21 May—and then boarded the train for Petersburg.[22] As always, Rasputin's travels were covered by the press and he was greeted upon his arrival in Petersburg by a flock of journalists. By now, however, Rasputin was growing tired of all the attention, and particularly the negative public campaign being waged against him. He reportedly complained about the harassment to the Petersburg police, noting the constant throng of reporters outside his apartment, who, he said, "were making him nervous," and requested their help in keeping them away. It was also said he changed his telephone number as well.[23] Rasputin was quick to deny these stories. He told a reporter from the *Stock Exchange Gazette* the following month: "Tell them that I never went to the police to ask they keep the journalists from visiting me. [. . .] I'm always happy to welcome anyone. [. . .] Everyone is equally pleasant in my eyes."[24]

But this was a lie: Rasputin did not find everyone equally pleasant. Back in March, Mikhail Novoselov, the *Bell*'s Vasily Skvortsov, and Archbishop Antony (Khrapovitsky) had called Rasputin a "khlyst and a sex-maniac" and even the "servant of the Antichrist" on the pages of the *Sum of Life* and the *Voice of Moscow*.[25] An angry Rasputin immediately sent off two telegrams: one to Minister of the Interior Maklakov asking that he be protected against such "illegal" attacks and a second to Sabler asking that he defend Rasputin against "my enemies" and their "abuse."[26] This was a different Rasputin. The man who had viewed public attacks as nothing more than "clouds" was now feeling under siege and in search of defense from those in positions of authority.

The campaigns against Rasputin that spring were being waged in private as well. In the second half of May, Protopresbyter Shavelsky was visited by Prince Vladimir Volkonsky, deputy president of the Duma and deputy minister of the interior (from July 1915 to December 1916), and Prince Vladimir Nikolaevich Orlov, head of the emperor's retinue and His Majesty's Military-Campaign Chancery (from 1906 to August 1915) and one of the men closest to the tsar. They told Shavelsky they had come to talk with him in "absolute secrecy," and he showed them to a back room where no one might overhear them. They said that Rasputin's influence on the emperor and empress was fast becoming as real as the talk about it in the press. And this talk, the two men gravely asserted, was now no longer taking place just within educated society, but among the narod as well. Russia, they believed, was on the verge of open revolt. Many people were helping Rasputin, few resisted him, and some, who should know better, were doing nothing, they said. One such man was Father Vasilev, who had become the personal confessor of the royal couple that year. They all agreed that he was an unimpeachable man—good, honest, kind—but he was on the wrong path, being friendly with Rasputin and showing him respect. Orlov had already talked to him of the error of his ways, but to no effect. So they had come to ask Shavelsky to speak to Vasilev.

Shavelsky agreed to meet with him and they laid out a plan, shrouded in the utmost secrecy to ensure no one at court would discover what they were up to. Shavelsky would seek out Vasilev and meet with him, alone, casually, as if he had no particular agenda other than to become better acquainted. He invited Vasilev to his home and they met there over the course of several evenings. Shavelsky was cautious. He was not sure how Vasilev felt about Rasputin, so he did not bring the matter up and only slowly brought their conversations around to the Siberian. Shavelsky was relieved to hear Vasilev say that he shared the fears of the three men. He too believed that Rasputin presented a true danger to the dynasty and the country, and told Shavelsky that they must both work to paralyze his influence by any possible means. Shavelsky was optimistic Vasilev's role as confessor made him the best weapon they had to rid the palace of Rasputin. Their meetings ended with that, and the two men did not see each other for a year and a half. Rasputin, of course, never did leave, and Shavelsky never did learn whether Vasilev ever brought up the matter with their majesties.[27]

As for Vasilev, he never said whether he acted as the two men had agreed. He did sometime later tell Beletsky that the tsarevich once asked him in front of his parents whether it was true that Rasputin was a holy man. An awkward pause followed. Vasilev was not certain what to do, and Nicholas looked at him and asked him to answer the boy. Alexandra stared intently at her confessor anxious to hear how he would answer. Careful not to make a wrong move, Vasilev did not answer the question directly, but proceeded to explain to Alexei what the Holy Scriptures required of each of us who wished to please God. With that, the tsar stood up from the table, and the conversation ended.[28]

36. The Attack

Nicholas and Alexandra saw Rasputin on the evening of 17 June 1914. Four days later, he was shown off by friends at Petersburg's Nikolaevsky Station. Everyone at the station noted he was in good spirits, happy to be heading home to Pokrovskoe, and talking of returning to the capital reinvigorated later that summer. No one would later recall him giving the slightest hint of worry or foreboding.[1]

Rasputin arrived in Pokrovskoe via the steamer *Sokolovsky* around eight o'clock on the evening of the twenty-eighth. The next morning he attended services at the village church with his family, and that afternoon the entire household gathered for a large midday meal.[2] It was a busy time. Rasputin's friend Nikolai Solovyov had come for a visit, as had a sculptor by the name of Stepan Erzy. Rasputin's old friend, fellow pilgrim, and recent exile from Mt. Athos Dmitry Pecherkin was also at the family table. Two carpenters, Andrei and Dmitry Tupitsyn, then installing new windows at the house, were dining with the family as well. They were all still eating when, around 2 p.m., the postman, Mikhail Rasputin, stopped by with a telegram for Rasputin from Iosef Shuster in Tyumen, enquiring whether he could come to take photographs of Rasputin's family and their home. Rasputin penned a quick reply telling him yes, do come, and then ran out to catch up with Mikhail. "Stop, take this telegram!" he called, waving the slip in his hand.

As he passed the gates of his yard, Rasputin suddenly came upon a strange figure. It was a woman in black, her head fully covered and her face shrouded by a white kerchief so that only her eyes were visible. She bowed before Rasputin, and he told her to stop, this was not necessary, and then reached for his wallet, assuming the poor creature was seeking alms. She made a sudden movement, Rasputin saw a flash of metal and then felt a stabbing pain just above his navel. His hand reflexively reached for his stomach and felt blood. He let out a yell: "I'm hurt! I'm hurt! She stabbed me!" He began to run away from his attacker down the road toward the church. He got about twenty paces and then turned to look back. She was chasing him with a large, bloody dagger in her right hand. He kept running. Spying a large stick on the ground, Rasputin stopped and picked it up, when she came near he hit her hard over the head and she fell down, cutting her left wrist with the dagger. From the window Pecherkin had seen the woman run after Rasputin. He and Praskovya dashed out into the street, Rasputin's wife screaming, "She stabbed him! She stabbed him!" A crowd quickly appeared and surrounded the attacker lying in the dust. Some screamed for justice on the spot; others, so it was said, seemed pleased by what she had done. They grabbed the woman and led her back up the street, followed by a mob of screaming villagers, to the Pokrovskoe district administration building, where she was locked in the cell.

Rasputin was helped to the house and laid down on a bench. His family was in hysterics. A local medical orderly was fetched, and he bandaged the wound to stop the bleeding. Not long after a doctor, Veniamin Vysotsky, from the village of Ievlovo just a few miles north of Pokrovskoe, arrived to tend to Rasputin. For two hours Rasputin lay unconscious. It seemed to everyone gathered around him that he would die.[3]

Solovyov recalled:

When I entered the darkened room in which Rasputin lay, having earlier been bandaged by the orderly, something unimaginable was taking place. Rasputin's children were crying [. . .] and there was talk about which doctors to summon from Tyumen. [. . .] After about 2½ hours he came to. "How do you feel?" I asked. "Bad . . ." Rasputin replied. "Some woman thrust her knife in me. This . . . is the underhanded doing of that damned Iliodor . . . Unbelievable . . . Oh, why such terrible luck? God willing, I'll survive . . . I'll get well."[4]

A telegram was sent to Alexander Vladimirov, the senior doctor of the Tyumen city hospital. He told his chief nurse, Praskovya Kuznetsova, to pack everything necessary to operate and to follow him as fast as possible. Their carriage raced along the post road to Pokrovskoe, the surgeon promising the drivers extra money "for vodka" if they could drive the horses any faster. It was only on the way that Vladimirov told Praskovya what had happened and where they were going. They arrived in the early hours of the thirtieth. "It was dark when we arrived," Praskovya said later.

Somewhere in the middle of the village we pulled up at a large, two-story house. Rasputin was lying on the first floor, on a bench covered with sheepskin. The wound was bound up with a towel. His body was shaking. We did the operation right there in the house. We had to heat up the stove to boil some water. The women in the house, one of whom was his wife, helped out.[5]

Dr. Vladimirov took off the towel and examined the wound. It was serious. Rasputin would bleed to death before they could get him to the Tyumen hospital if they did not operate immediately. The conditions, however, were horrendous. The house was dirty from the remodeling, they had only minimal light from a few stearin candles. The likelihood of infection was great. But they had no choice. Vladimirov administered chloroform and put Rasputin under. He performed a laparotomy along the midline of 3.46 inches (8.8 cm) from the wound to the patient's navel and began to inspect the damage more closely. Parts of the small intestine had become twisted, and so the doctor began removing sections from the abdominal cavity to repair the damage and look for any signs of further injury. The bladder was not harmed, but the knife had nicked the intestines in a number of places and penetrated the peritoneum. He sutured the tear in the peritoneum and sewed up other lacerations with knotted silk. The doctor then closed the incision site with medicated gauze and Michel clamps and covered the entire area with an antiseptic bandage. Vladimirov and Kuznetsova returned to Tyumen and left Rasputin in the care of the orderly.[6] For the next two days Rasputin drifted in and out of consciousness. A priest was called to the home to deliver the last rites.[7]

Her name was Khionya Guseva. She was thirty-three years old, single, and a resident of Tsaritsyn, where she worked as a seamstress with her sister. She had a fleshy, round face, dark scraggly hair, parted down the center, and powerful hands. Where her nose should have been was a deep, diagonal gash; her nostrils had somehow been transformed into a jagged triangular hole. On her blouse she wore a round button depicting Jesus with a crown of thorns.

She was questioned on the twenty-ninth and thirtieth in the administration building's file room. She immediately confessed to stabbing Rasputin with a dagger, saying that he was "a false prophet, slanderer, a violator of women, and a seducer of honest maidens." Guseva told the police that she had first met Rasputin four years earlier in Tsaritsyn, when he had been received there by Iliodor, whose follower she was, "with glory" as a great man of God. But then, she said, Rasputin turned against Iliodor and Germogen, and Iliodor told her that Rasputin had admitted to being a vile creature and false prophet. In May 1914, she read an article by the writer and critic Alexander Amfiteatrov titled "Iliodor and Grisha" in the newspaper *Light* that convinced her to kill Rasputin. Her hope, so she told the police, was to follow the example of the Prophet Elijah who had killed with a knife 450 false prophets, followers of Baal, the Canaanite god (1 Kings 18:40). Amfiteatrov's article contained a variety of charges against Rasputin, but most importantly it included Iliodor's notorious 1912 letter denouncing Rasputin and the story that he had once raped a nun in Tsaritsyn

Guseva went to a local market in Tsaritsyn and purchased a fifteen-inch dagger for three rubles. Then she went to find Rasputin. First she made for Yalta, but not finding him there, headed north to Petersburg. She failed once more to locate him (even though Rasputin was in the city at the time), and so she set out for Pokrovskoe. She claimed to have had less than forty rubles with her when she first left home. Along the entire route she ate as little as possible, spending not a kopeck of her own money on food, but begging for her bread. Subjecting herself to such hardship lent an air of righteous suffering (in Guseva's mind) to her murderous exploit. To earn a bit of money, she darned the clothes of the sailors on the steamer.

She arrived in Pokrovskoe on 22 June—the day after Rasputin left Petersburg. Using a false name, she told a peasant family that she had come to meet Rasputin, and they took her in. Then she waited. No one had put her up to the murder, she stated, and she had acted alone.[8]

News of the attack filled the front page of the *Petersburg Courier* on the thirtieth. Under the headline "An Attempt on the Life of Gr. Rasputin," the newspaper carried details (many of them erroneous) on the stabbing, the mysterious noseless attacker, and Rasputin's condition. "It has been learned," one story read, "that the unknown woman arrived from Tsaritsyn and, as is being reported, had been bribed into her act by none other than the former monk Iliodor. Rasputin is in his death-throes."[9]

No one could be certain just what had happened in distant Siberia. Rumor filled the drawing rooms of St. Petersburg and Moscow, and peopled talked of nothing else. The news quickly swept across Europe, Britain, and even the United States, making the front-page headlines of the *New York Times*, which covered the story for several days. The Okhrana clipped, translated, and filed practically every one of these articles from around the world.[10] At first it was believed Rasputin had died. On 1 July, the *Petersburg Courier* wrote that Rasputin was failing. His temperature was dangerously high, he was tossing about in bed and rambling, his breathing was labored. "The patient is delirious, he recognizes no one. The death-throes have begun. Other than the doctors, no one is admitted to him. There's practically no hope left of survival."[11]

One of the first to learn Rasputin was dead was Alexei Filippov, Rasputin's champion on the pages of *Smoke of the Fatherland*. He immediately wired a friend to share the news: "Recall Pushkin: 'Fateful passions besiege us from everywhere, And there's no defense against one's fate.' Rasputin has been killed."[12] Grand Duke Konstantin Konstantinovich ("K. R.") was taking the cure in Germany when he got the news. He noted in his diary on 1 July: "He lies dying. One is caught feeling joy over the death of another and tries to suppress this sinful joy."[13]

Epitaphs began appearing in the press. Vladimir Bonch-Bruevich wrote for *Day* on 1 July: "The tragic dénouement, that overtook him so unexpectedly, will of course remove that unending anger and envy that has been boiling around him for many years and will force many to gather materials on the undeniably remarkable life of this man who so brightly highlighted the contradictions and intricacies that characterized our strange era."[14] Two days later *Smoke of the Fatherland* sought to remind its readers that Rasputin, despite all the rumor of his "hypnotic powers," had never been a political figure, but a simple man of God who had always loved to say, "One must live for the common people, one must think of them."[15] The *Russian Word* saw something darker: "Rasputin—that was a characteristic leftover of the 'old order' of the state when politics was practiced not in state institutions, not under the control of civil rights, but through personal schemes. Rasputin—he was a tragic victim of our sad current existence outside of time marked by all those attempts to return Russia to the path it has already abandoned."[16] The *Odessa Leaflet* expressed the fear that certain individuals would wish to make a martyr of the murdered Rasputin.[17]

But then, just as suddenly, it all turned out to be wrong. "We learned from the newspapers that Grigory Rasputin had been killed on the thirtieth," Alexander Blok noted in his diary on 2 July. "But no, he's alive."[18] Nikolai Dobrovolsky, the last tsarist minister of justice, was with a group of Russians in London when they got the news Rasputin had survived. In one voice they all cried out, "What a disaster!"[19] Later that summer the British press reported that Alexandra had rushed to Rasputin's hospital bed and personally nursed him back to health. She brought the knife used in the assault back with her, sleeping with it under her pillow as a holy relic.[20]

Maria Rasputina telegraphed Nicholas and Alexandra almost immediately after the attack: "A woman has inflicted a serious wound to his stomach, but somehow, by a miracle, he was saved and still lives for us, for everyone, thanks to the tears of the Mother of God. The doctor has been sent for. Matryosha Novaya."[21]

The royal family was sailing on the *Standart* in the Finnish skerries when the news arrived. The children's tutor, Pierre Gilliard, noticed that the entourage was strangely and suddenly "prey to unwonted excitement." He asked a "Colonel D" just what was happening and was told about the attack and that Rasputin's life was in danger. "There was great excitement on board, whisperings and mysterious confabulations which suddenly stopped whenever anyone suspected of being an adherent of Rasputin came near. Everyone else was inspired by a lively hope of being at last delivered from that baneful influence, but no one dared reveal his joy too openly."[22]

Exactly how the royal family reacted is not known. Strangely, Nicholas makes no reference to learning of the assault in his diary, noting, however, how on the thirtieth he played tennis (he lost), swam, and went for a motor boat ride; in fact, his diary is devoid of the least comment about Rasputin during these days.[23] Yet Nicholas had definitely been informed of the assault, for on the thirtieth he wrote to Minister of the Interior Maklakov:

Nikolai Alexeevich.

I learned yesterday that in the village of Pokrovskoe in the Tobolsk province an attempt was made on the life of the starets Grigory Yefimovich Rasputin, a man much honored by Us, and he was wounded in the abdomen by a woman.

Fearful that this attack was the doing of a clique of foul people

with evil intentions, I hereby instruct you to keep a vigilant watch
over this matter and to protect him from any further such attacks.

[. . .]

NICHOLAS[24]

Maklakov immediately ordered General Dzhunkovsky, the deputy
minister of the interior, to investigate the matter fully: to gather all
necessary details from Pokrovskoe, assume control over the investigation, and, most importantly for Dzhunkovsky, set up clandestine
protection of Rasputin and surveillance of everyone he came in contact
with and everyone petitioning him for help.[25] The order gave Dzhunkovsky, a long time enemy of Rasputin, just what he wanted: official
sanction to monitor every aspect of Rasputin's life. On 2 July he ordered
four agents to watch him—two openly, two secretly—and record every
last bit of information on Rasputin, his contacts, visitors, and activities.[26] Nothing was too insignificant.

A guard of armed peasants was set up around Rasputin's home for
protection. The police confiscated the villagers' internal passports and
began questioning everyone in the village. One person stood out from
the rest. Veniamin Borisovich Davidson (also Duvidson or Duvidzon)
was a baptized Jew from the Ukrainian town of Lypovets; a reporter
for the *Petersburg Courier*, he frequently went by the name Veniamin
Arnoldov Paganini. The fact that a reporter for a major newspaper just
happened to be in Pokrovskoe at the time of the attack immediately
raised suspicions. He was called in for questioning and several of his
documents were taken, but the police found nothing to link him to the
crime and so ordered him and his secretary, one Nikolai Levakovsky
(also given as Levanovsky), to leave Pokrovskoe. The order, however,
was ignored, and Davidson remained in the village from where he sent
a constant stream of telegrams back to his editors.[27]

To this day Davidson remains a shadowy figure and the reasons for
his presence in Pokrovskoe have never been convincingly explained.
Maria Rasputina gave one account in her memoirs.

In the spring of 1914, Maria and her friend Maria Sazonova liked to
amuse themselves by making prank phone calls. Then, one day, some-
one played the same trick on them, and a man's voice asked to speak to
Maria Rasputina. He said that he had followed her twice up and down
Nevsky Prospect and fallen in love with her. He wanted to meet her.
Maria put him off, but he did not go away. He called a few more times,

telling her exactly where she had been that day to prove he was watching her. The stalker insisted on a meeting, but again Maria refused. Then, in June, Maria, her father and sister left Petersburg for home. On the train they met a "a dark young man, rather short, with a Jewish profile and very talkative and witty." He was a reporter, he told Maria, from St. Petersburg heading in the same direction. At Tyumen, he got off the train with them and then boarded their steamer. Maria began to grow suspicious. As they floated down the Tura, he approached Maria and confessed that he was her secret admirer. She admitted to being "not a little flattered by the adventure and the sentiments I had inspired," but her feelings quickly shifted to alarm when he got off the boat in Pokrovskoe. Fearful he might tell her father of their interaction, she tried to dissuade him from staying, but he refused to get back on the boat.[28]

Maria never saw Davidson again until just after the assault when she found him lurking by the door of the family home. "Get away," she shouted. "It's you who have brought this on my father, it's because of you." Soon after, at 3:45 p.m. that very day, Maria sent a cable to Vyrubova in which she mentioned "the suspicious Paganini editors [who] have been upsetting our domestics," a fact substantiated by the police. Was this Davidson and his secretary? The following day, 30 June, a telegram in the name of Grigory Rasputin (who was still unconscious) reached Governor of Tobolsk Stankevich asking that he invest the district police superintendent N. E. Skatov with the authority to arrest these suspicious journalists. Stankevich immediately granted the request. Skatov called Davidson (aka Paganini) in for questioning, but did not find anything suspicious about him or his secretary. Nonetheless, Skatov ordered Davidson to leave Pokrovskoe, which he did on 2 July.[29]

Was Davidson involved in the attack? Was there a larger conspiracy? Her accusatory words notwithstanding, Maria Rasputina did not think Davidson was part of any plot, but she did think he knew of it in advance and thus followed the family out to Pokrovskoe.[30] A few nationalist historians have recently argued that Davidson had indeed been part of a larger conspiracy that reached all the way into the upper ministerial ranks back in Petersburg. They point to his well-informed knowledge of Guseva's interrogation record and that despite being told to leave the village he was permitted to remain for several days as proof that events in Pokrovskoe were being directed by a powerful hidden hand from the center. Crucial to this (unconvincing) interpretation is the fact of Davidson's Jewishness, an element that fits nicely into their paranoid, anti-Semitic interpretation according to which Rasputin was the victim of an international Jewish-Masonic conspiracy aimed not only at the starets but at Russia herself.[31]

Any serious proof linking Davidson to the assault is missing, and it seems his presence in Pokrovskoe at the time was nothing more than coincidence. It was not any larger plot against Rasputin that brought Davidson to Pokrovskoe. Rather, it was money, for Rasputin sold newspapers, and Davidson had followed Rasputin in search of a story.[32] And the *Petersburg Courier* had a major scoop on its hands. The rest of the press found this suspicious. The far-right newspaper *Zemshchina** asked why the "Yid-Banker" *Courier* was the only publication to have a correspondent at the scene of the crime. Did this not afford it, and the other "yid and 'progressive'" publications citing its reports, an excellent opportunity to publish all sorts of "slander" that could not be checked by the rest of the press? *Zemshchina* implied some sort of dark conspiracy was at work.[33]

Davidson arrived in Tyumen on 2 July and told his story to the *Western Siberian Herald*. He gave his name as "V. A. Paganini" and claimed to have just arrived from Pokrovskoe after having suffered "a great many trials." He was a journalist from Petersburg writing a story on the life of Rasputin and had gone to gather information. He said he happened to meet Rasputin on his way there, and the two men hit it off. He had nothing but the best to say about Rasputin and commented that all the villagers spoke of his goodness and generosity. He was there during the assault, and was the one, so said Davidson, who helped Rasputin back to his home. After this he hurried off to get some "eau de cologne and liquid ammonia" for Rasputin and when he returned he noticed Rasputin's wife was looking at him with suspicion, as if he were somehow responsible, and she insisted he was now trying to give her husband poison. The telegrams he was busy sending back to his editors aroused the suspicions of the locals, and he began to fear for his life. They even threatened him with "mob law." By a miracle, he managed to escape Pokrovskoe alive.

Much of this is, of course, pure fabrication, but one thing does seem

---

* A historical term referring to the boyar domains, as opposed to the oprichnina, in the reign of Tsar Ivan IV (the Terrible).

to be true: namely, that Davidson was there, along with his secretary Levakovsky, to dig up information on Rasputin for a story. Indeed, it had been Davidson and Levakovsky who, a day or two before the attack, approached the clerk Nalobin at the Pokrovskoe district administration building posing as agents of the St. Petersburg governor-general seeking proof of Rasputin's arrest as a horse thief.[34] The two men hid this fact from Skatov when questioned just after Guseva's attempt on Rasputin's life, and Nalobin apparently was never brought before the police. If he had been, he would have had a curious story to tell about the two journalists from the capital. (This would not be Davidson's only brush with the police over his writing on Rasputin. On 16 August 1916, *Early Morning* published a small notice stating that the reporter Davidson had been arrested for "his book on Rasputin." Within days the Okhrana began to look into the story, for they knew nothing about any such arrest or any such book. The source of the notice was "a certain Weinstein," who worked for the *Petrograd Newspaper* and the *Petrograd Kopeck*. This was all the police were able to uncover, and it seems the notice was either an error or some sort of provocation.)[35]

What had started with the *Courier's* coverage of the murder attempt quickly became a national debate about the wisdom of even following the story. Writing in *Speech* on 5 July, Alexander Stakhovich expressed disbelief that anyone would be interested in reading about such a "nothing" as Rasputin. The fascination with the story, and with Rasputin himself, was but a product of the "yellow press" that had whipped up a meaningless event that could be of concern only to his following of female hysterics.[36] Other papers, however, argued the opposite. To write about Rasputin, regardless of the pretext, was of vital importance for it brought to light the true meaning of Rasputin and his significance for Russia. *Our Workers' Newspaper* noted on 2 July when many still believed Rasputin had died:

> Behind him hid those secret forces that, given our lack of true European freedom and our lack of a constitution, carry out their work behind the scenes, secretly running the state and directing its ministers, removing them and putting others in their place, and preparing all sorts of reactionary surprises for the country.
>
> These secret forces are capable of anything, they can even turn a shameless rogue into a court favorite, to endow him with extraordinary power. [. . .] So to expose Rasputin under such

conditions is to expose the rot and filth of these dark reactionary forces threatening the country and holding it in its grasp.[37]

Hours after this story ran, the authorities shut down the newspaper.

It was not just the country's intellectuals and the urban elite who obsessed over all this talk of Rasputin. The State Archive of the Russian Federation in Moscow contains a remarkable letter sent to the police from an unnamed provincial official:

> I request your attention. 10 years ago I wrote to the State Gazette, and I zealously tried to convince the government to use every means possible to avoid a war with Japan. [. . .]
>
> Now I write to you again, but what is to be done when an honest official must write the truth in pencil and dares not sign his name . . . Out of love for the Motherland, I must say to you that which no one apparently wants to see. At this difficult time, when given the high price of goods people are forced to work twice as much as before, when this difficult year forces one to consider what the consequences of these troubles will be, Our Government is openly concerning itself with . . . the health of Grigory Rasputin!!?—Come to your senses! Come now, this Rasputin is nothing but a giant trump card in the hands of the revolutionaries, and you must know that the provinces are no worse informed than Petersb.[urg] workers about the role of Rasputin, and the provinces are seriously upset. Not a single governor has the possibility to give you such truthful information about the state of affairs in the provinces as I do, out of my love and desire for peace for our misfortunate Motherland, for not a single governor can hear what is being said in the intimate circles across the provinces, and they are all saying something quite bad: "We have 2 emperors," "we are now seeing the rebirth of the Potemkins, Orlovs, and Zubovs . . ." Have I said enough so you will change course? Have I said enough for you to understand that the provinces are in a state of unrest and that every time the ministers show "concern" for "the dear injured one" it sends the population into a frenzy.
>
> I am a poor man. I may have wasted my last kopeck on this letter, but at least give me the assurance that your babying of Rasputin will no longer be mentioned in the press.[38]

37. "This time it didn't work . . ."

Late on 2 July, Rasputin was carried from his home down to the river and placed on the steamer *Sukhotin*. A large crowd of villagers followed behind, some of the women letting out hysterical cries. In the early morning hours of the third, the steamer arrived in Tyumen, and he was transferred to the city's main hospital.[1] According to the *Petersburg Courier*, as they carried him from the pier a priest by the name of Ketov walked in front of the stricken Rasputin, crying, "Grigory is no more! Grigory is no more!"[2]

The hospital was overrun by family, friends, reporters, and the merely curious. Police had to be stationed outside to keep the crowds away. As for Rasputin, he loved the attention, and as soon as he was well enough he had Akilina Laptinskaya read to him all the news reports of the event. On the fourth, photographers captured Rasputin in his bed. He signed some of the photographs and added various captions, such as "What of tomorrow? You are our guide, Lord. How many Calvaries must we cross in Life?"[3] Dr. Vladimirov continued to tend to Rasputin and his efforts saved Rasputin's life, although he was modest about it all, saying later: "I did not do anything special. Every year I'm forced to do dozens of operations like this on Tyumen's hooligans."[4] In the first days of July, the tsar sent the honorary imperial surgeon Roman Vreden to oversee Rasputin's care and work alongside Vladimirov. For his efforts, Vreden was rewarded with 1,000 rubles.[5]

Rasputin sent regular telegrams to Vyrubova for Nicholas and Alexandra, assuring them that he was doing well and recovering.[6] The day after the stabbing, Alexandra sent a cable to Maria for her father: "We are deeply disturbed. We suffer with you, praying with all our hearts." She wrote again on 2 July: "Thoughts and prayers surround you. Our suffering is indescribable, hoping for God's mercy."[7]

Rasputin wrote to Vyrubova with a vague message for Nicholas that implied a larger conspiracy: "My dear and darling, she is not alone, there are others behind her. Just look around carefully. They are making trouble because of their pride. Don't give them a chance to quarrel." In a telegram on the sixth he admitted to his fear that this was not to be the last attempt on his life: "My health is getting slightly better, don't fantasize, don't be afraid, I was not scared too much; this time it didn't work, next time—whatever God orders."[8]

From across the country, Russians inundated Rasputin with letters and telegrams, expressing their sympathies, wishing him a speedy recovery, and offering their ideas on the people behind the murderous act.[9] Typical was this letter from an admirer in Tiflis:

Dear, dear Uncle Grisha!

I was doubly happy to receive word from you: first of all, I learned that the Lord had spared you from the knife of that crazy wench, let loose on you by Iliodor, now impotent in his hatred; second, it meant that you had not forgotten me and that though in Tiflis I am nonetheless not alone and am connected to you at least in spirit.

For truth you have experienced a miracle of miracles. How you survived, only the Lord himself knows. Your debt to Him truly is without limit and can never be repaid. I hope you are soon well, to the anger and fright of your enemies and the comfort of those who love you. I have not the slightest doubt that the attempt on your life was organized by the hands of Iliodor and you will have to be extremely careful and wary. Don't go out alone and always be aware of your surroundings when out on the street. There's no doubt your enemies will not leave you in peace, but no one other than God Himself saved you when you should have died, and now, as you recover and after you have regained your health, those murderers lurking behind the corner will not frighten you.

And then there is this curious letter from Munya Golovina:

Dear, dear Grigory Yefimovich.

This is my first letter after that terrible villainy that undid my soul and forced me to become even more convinced that you, like the sun, lighten our lives and dispel the gloom that comes from the mere thought that you could be taken from us—that gloom began to encroach on us from all corners and the light grew dim. But you, praise be to God, are alive, you are with us, and this is such a joy that one must thank all day and night God and the Virgin Mary, she protected you and knew that a blow against you was being prepared. Of course, complete joy is not possible, we must somehow earn our joy—just to know you are alive, I am gladly ready to kiss each word of yours, as long as it comes from you, yet it pains me to the point of tears that you do not believe me. But this I never expected—I was so furious at those who dared to raise a hand against you that I could not understand how you could call them my friends . . . Your friends are my friends and your enemies are my enemies! You know this, and if there is another feeling in me, then it belongs to you, but I give you my word never to write to any of your known enemies where you are, how you are feeling, what you are doing, and shall never even mention your name should it bring you the least possible harm. Is it at all possible that I, who love you so much, could cause you the least harm! All I do is ask God to instruct me how to help you, how to serve and to show you everything I feel! You will always mean more to me than Everyone and I shall tell <u>no one</u> when you visit us!! I prayed today and am wearing your portrait in an open locket—I put it on the day before the atrocity. I kiss your hands and ask for your blessing.

Your Munya.[10]

What had Rasputin said to Munya? What had he accused her of? And who were the particular enemies Rasputin had in mind? Regrettably, the archives do not have the answers to these questions, but Munya's memoir does offer some clues. After abandoning the Rasputin home two years earlier, Olga Lokhtina settled near Iliodor's New Galilee, building a small house for herself in the village of Morozovsky. To Rasputin, and others close to him, it was clear that Olga had sided with Iliodor against Rasputin. After the assault, Rasputin came to the conclusion that Olga must have been part of the plot and either assisted, or at least endorsed, Iliodor's plan to have him killed. It was at this time that Munya had been planning to visit Olga, and when Rasputin and his family and friends learned of this, they assumed that Munya had betrayed him. Munya was devastated by their suspicions and pleaded with Rasputin that she was entirely innocent. She begged to be permitted to come to Tyumen and help care for him, but was told to stay away.[11]

Munya spoke the truth. She had had nothing to do with the attempt on Rasputin's life. The irony was, however, that two years later she would lead the man who was to kill Rasputin to his door. Rasputin had been wrong not to trust Munya this time, and he would be wrong to trust her the next time.

Davidson reported that he had managed to sneak into Guseva's cell in Pokrovskoe and take down her story. "I decided to kill him long ago and put an end to this terrible evil and deception that he has spread across all of Russia. Behind the mask of a prophet, he has undermined Christianity, sown temptation, and seduced the narod, blasphemously mocking the most sacred feelings of true Christians." She talked of how he lived openly with other women, how he had seduced her good friend Xenia right in front of her own eyes, how he had destroyed "the pious Iliodor." Guseva said she was terminally ill, her life meant nothing to her, so she made up her mind to sacrifice herself. She had tried to kill him a year earlier. She went to track him down in Yalta, but his followers kept her from getting close. She would have killed him this time, but her hand shook and she was not able to stab him a second time. "Nevertheless he won't live! The Russian people won't stand for such disgrace!" she screamed.[12]

Rumors were swirling about the would-be assassin and her motives. According to one story, she was avenging her two beautiful daughters—Anastasia and Natalya—whom Rasputin had taken advantage of one night at Guseva's home in Tsaritsyn.[13] There was talk she was a follower of Darya Smirnova, the khlyst known as the "Okhtinskaya Virgin," and that she had put Guseva up to the murder. There was also a rumor that she had attacked Rasputin to test his holiness, supposedly saying that only if he were a true prophet would he survive her knife.[14]

There was a good deal of talk about accomplices too. Baron Eduard von der Ropp, a Baltic German and Catholic prelate, told the press he was convinced Rasputin had been attacked by certain individuals envious of his quick rise to notoriety who had become angry at him for not fulfilling their requests for his help. There were allegations that members of the police had known of the attack in advance but did nothing to prevent it. Others insisted this was all nonsense. Dr. Kulnev, a professor at the Institute of Female Medicine, told the Petersburg Courier that the underlying reason for the assault was to be found in Rasputin's "sexual psychosis." Rasputin, the doctor averred, was "not a normal person as regards his sexual relations," and although such cases of sexual "frustration" were most often found in women, men too, espe-

cially around the age of forty, were not immune from it. Kulnev stated
that the problem was not only difficult to cure, but caused the sufferer
to become dangerous, warranting "strict isolation." Rasputin's sexual
deviance had produced a string of abused women, and so it had been
only a matter of time until one of his victims struck back. Nonsense,
Garyazin, editor of *Smoke of the Fatherland*, shot back: there is no plot
here, nor is Rasputin in any way to blame. The attack was simply the act
of a lone "female hysteric."[15]

Guseva was taken by boat from Pokrovskoe to Tyumen and locked
up in the city jail. The police questioned her numerous times throughout the rest of the year. Slowly, a clearer picture of the attacker began to
emerge. She told the police that she had known Rasputin since 1910
when he came to Tsaritsyn to visit Iliodor. His "dissolute life" convinced
her that he was a false prophet. She tried to raise the matter with Iliodor,
but he told her not to speak of it. Later, after his downfall, Iliodor confessed to her that Rasputin was indeed a rogue and false prophet.
Guseva went even further now, telling her interrogators in September
1914 that she considered Rasputin to be the Antichrist. She believed
Iliodor to be holy, a miracle worker, but she maintained that no one
had talked her into killing Rasputin. The idea had been hers, and she
had acted alone.[16]

The police and doctors had concerns about Guseva's mental state.
Central to the case was the question of her sanity. She told the doctors
that she had been in the habit of fasting for long periods accompanied
by intense praying. Once the Devil came to her dressed as a monk;
another time the icon before which she was praying began sending her
secret messages. Invariably, her prayer sessions ended with vivid hallucinations.[17] They asked whether the rumor that she had lost her nose
from syphilis was true, but Guseva insisted it was not. The disease did
not run in her family, she told them. She fell ill with a strange, undiagnosed illness around the age of thirteen and the medicine she was
given caused her nose to fall away. She admitted, however, that madness
did run in the family. Her late brother Simeon went crazy, and he and
their father had a habit of cutting themselves on their legs.[18]

The investigators looked into Guseva's testimony. They learned that
Simeon had been held for a time in an insane asylum, and after being
released he walked out into the woods in the dead of winter with no
warm clothing on and froze to death. An interview with Guseva's sister
Pelageya Zavorotkova uncovered that in the past Guseva had talked

about being surrounded by unnamed "enemies" and she had refused to drink from anyone's cup but her own, convinced that people were trying to poison her. Family members said she suffered from scrofula, and this is what caused her facial disfigurement. After this, she was never the same again. Guseva experienced strange fits when she would talk gibberish; after such episodes she would claim it had not been her who had spoken, but Satan.[19]

In November, the investigators tracked down Xenia, the nun Guseva said Rasputin had molested before her eyes, at a convent in Zhirovits alongside Germogen's monastery. Her full name was Xenia Goncharenkova and she told the police that she had been a follower of Iliodor for eighteen years. She admitted that she had met Rasputin together with Iliodor in Tsaritsyn, in 1909 or 1910, but stated that she had never been alone with Rasputin and that he had never behaved improperly with her, much less raped her. As for Guseva, Xenia said that she knew her, although not well, and that around 1912 she noticed a change in Guseva's behavior. She began acting strangely, her speech was often disjointed, and she made no sense.[20]

Agents were sent to Tsaritsyn to uncover details about Guseva's life there, and particularly her connections with Iliodor. They learned that she had visited Iliodor just weeks before beginning her hunt for Rasputin. They corroborated her testimony about heading first to Yalta, and then to Petersburg before finally traveling to Pokrovskoe and waiting for him there. For his efforts, Nicholas awarded district police superintendent Skatov the Order of St. Anne, 2nd class.[21] After a year-long investigation Guseva was found non compos mentis and no charges were filed. It was determined that at the time of the assault Guseva had been "in a state of insanity influenced by her growing nervous excitement of a religious-political nature." She was placed in the Tomsk Regional Clinic for the Insane where she was to be held until such time as she was deemed well enough to be released.[22] Word of the decision not to press charges was interpreted as a cover-up. It was rumored that Rasputin or some of his powerful followers had something to hide and feared what might be revealed at a public trial. By putting her away, everything could be quietly buried.[23]

A report by the director of the Tomsk clinic from July 1916 noted that even though Guseva no longer showed symptoms of a distinct "emotional illness," there still were clear signs of "hysterical degradation and symptoms of a hysterical nature." Since her arrival she had been getting into fights with the other female patients, throwing things out of her room, hitting, swearing and cursing. At times she had to be placed in a special observation ward. She could not stop flirting with the male patients, trying to act the lady, and even organize dances. She went around with a permanent smile on her face and loved to talk about her crime to anyone who would listen. She called herself "the heroine of all Russia," and said that were she released she would not try again: the fact Rasputin survived showed that this was God's will. The clinic's official medical report stated she was suffering from "lues cerebri," cerebral syphilis.[24]

Rasputin was questioned four times: 30 June, 6 and 22 July, and 9 August. From the beginning, Rasputin insisted that Iliodor was behind the assault and he was certain he had sent Guseva to kill him. Among Iliodor's motives, Rasputin highlighted his stopping Iliodor from undertaking another trip along the Volga River with his army of followers and the fact that he had been against the tsar's giving Iliodor money to launch a newspaper called *Thunder and Lightning*.[25] Thinking back, Rasputin now realized he had been warned. Two weeks before he left Petersburg, he received an anonymous letter from Kharkov telling him his days were numbered. He did not recognize the handwriting and simply tore the letter up, thinking nothing more of it.[26]

From the beginning, the role of Iliodor in the attack had been the cause of great speculation. The press reported that shortly before leaving Petersburg Rasputin had been visited by two followers of Iliodor—a woman with her face covered by a kerchief and a man wearing a fake beard. They did not find him home, but left a letter for Rasputin that frightened him and convinced him to leave the city immediately. As he was boarding the train, so the story went, the two mysterious figures showed up at the station and followed him to Siberia.[27] Rasputin's acolytes were convinced Iliodor was involved, although the disgraced monk's brother, Apollon, told the *Petersburg Courier* there was little chance of this and that if anything, it was his brother whose life was in danger from Rasputin's followers.[28]

While recuperating in Tyumen, Rasputin received an anonymous letter mailed from Petersburg on 2 July: "I have come out the victor in this battle, not you, Grigory! Your hypnosis has been dispersed, like mist before the face of the sun. I say to you that you will die no matter what. I am your avenger!"[29] Rasputin gave the letter to the police and told them he recognized the handwriting as Iliodor's. The police hired two graphologists to study the handwriting. After examining the letter alongside others known to be written by Iliodor they concurred: the distinctive pressure of the pen on certain Russian letters left no doubt he was the author. In May the *Stock Exchange Gazette* published a letter purportedly from Iliodor to Rasputin calling him a heretic and threatening to hunt him down like a wolf.[30]

At the time, Iliodor insisted he had had nothing to do with the assault, a statement he contradicted later in two of his books. In *The Mad Monk* he wrote that he had known Guseva for a number of years. He was extremely close to her, even calling her his "spiritual daughter." She came to be near him at New Galilee and told him of her plan to kill the "devil Grishka" and asked for Iliodor's blessing. "I joined my will with hers," he wrote. "You must follow Rasputin, no matter where he may go, and kill him." Before she left, Iliodor claimed to have given her the knife.[31]

In an obscure booklet published in New York in 1943, Iliodor gave a different version. A group of his female followers came to New Galilee and decided one night to execute Rasputin as the man responsible for Iliodor's downfall. They selected three of the most beautiful women among them: two young widows—Maria Zavertkina, Pelageya Zavorotkova (Guseva's sister), and the young maiden Nadezhda Perfileva, who was to become Iliodor's wife. The three thanked the other women for bestowing such an "honor" upon them and swore an oath to carry out their task in the most effective way possible, not sparing their own lives. They decided to sew white silk dresses covered with designs and decorations for themselves, and so attired they would present themselves to Rasputin, thus attracting his attention, and murder him. A few days later, they appeared once more before the gathering in their new dresses and once more they swore their oath to kill Rasputin. In their honor, a large banquet was held. It was then that Khionya Guseva got up and spoke. Why, she asked the gathering, should they sacrifice the most beautiful young women among them; would it not be better to send her, ugly and poor and desired by no one? She turned to Iliodor: "I alone shall execute Rasputin! Permit me to do this! Father, bless me, for the sake of saving Russia, to stab Rasputin just as the ancient prophet stabbed the false prophets." Iliodor gave her his blessing.[32]

This tale is, no doubt, pure fiction. Guseva was more than willing to kill Rasputin, but Iliodor most likely played a much more important role in the plot than merely blessing it or giving Guseva the murder weapon.

In the first two months of 1914, police questioned a former disciple of Iliodor, a Cossack by the name of Ivan Sinitsyn. It was Sinitsyn who told them of Iliodor's plans to launch terrorist attacks against the state, including how a woman by the name of Maria Kistanova had been sent out to raise 2,000 rubles under the guise of charity that was to be used to purchase a large quantity of explosives. Sinitsyn also provided evidence of a proposed attack on Rasputin. He gave the police two letters from Iliodor to Guseva and her sister, and another to a female follower in which he mentioned their plan "to do the first job, baptize Grishka." In the language of the skoptsy, to baptize meant "to castrate." They must stick to this plan and not waver, Iliodor instructed his three disciples. Another former follower of Iliodor also spoke of plans he had been making to kill Rasputin. As part of the plot, they had gathered 150 rubles and given it to Guseva.[33] A twenty-eight-year-old peasant from the Tambov province named Ivan Nemkov corroborated the information about the money. He told investigators on 13 October 1914 that a member of the local police, acting on instructions from Iliodor, had helped collect this money for Guseva. Nemkov stated that it was known among Iliodor's followers that the funds were for her plot to kill Rasputin. The police also came across a letter from Iliodor to Guseva and her sister Pelageya in which he praised them for their "efforts" and told them to remain true to their "task."

On 2 February 1914, the informer Sinitsyn told the police that he feared for his life. He was convinced Iliodor and his disciples were trying to kill him for having talked to the authorities. Not long after he died from eating poisoned fish.[34] The press reported in April of that year that this same Sinitsyn had helped Iliodor to escape to the Don, but then later sold him out to the police.[35] Had Iliodor murdered Sinitsyn? Given what is known of Iliodor's violent nature, the possibility cannot be ruled out.

On 12 October 1914, the chief investigator of the Tyumen district issued a decree stating that based on the evidence gathered in the investigation into the assault on Rasputin there were persuasive grounds to suspect Iliodor of incitement to commit murder. Although he had not taken direct part in planning the attack, the decree read, Iliodor had convinced Guseva to kill Rasputin when she visited his home on or around 18 May of that year. The chief investigator ordered Iliodor apprehended and brought to justice.[36] Little did he know, however, that Iliodor was by then well beyond the reach of the police.

38. Iliodor's Flight

Late on the night of 2 July, Iliodor shaved off his beard and mustache, rouged his cheeks, put on women's clothing, a white scarf over his head, and then fled his home of New Galilee via an underground tunnel. Several accomplices were waiting for him, and together they made their way down to the rushes of the River Don to hide. When the steamer *Venera* pulled up to the wharf, Iliodor calmly boarded and sailed off to Rostov-on-Don along the northern shore of the Sea of Azov.[1]

Arriving on the fourth, Iliodor, still in drag (oddly, the man who would succeed where Iliodor had failed in killing Rasputin, Prince Yusupov, was also a cross-dresser), was met by an acquaintance and taken to the editorial offices of the *Morning of the South* newspaper. He laughed and joked with the newspaper men, who noted his happy, elevated mood, and posed for photographs, for which Iliodor was paid forty rubles. Among the many newspapers that printed the images was *Early Morning*, along with a copy of a telegram from Iliodor with the words, "In this world anything's possible." Iliodor also sold a journalist for ten rubles a photograph of one of Rasputin's notes denouncing Iliodor. He offered the newspaper a story about Rasputin and said he had had nothing to do with Guseva's attack, although, he added, Rasputin had so insulted Russians' moral and religious feelings that only his death could bring them any comfort.[2] Iliodor did not stay in Rostov long, and soon boarded a train (now dressed as a man) and left. No one knew where he had gone, and the press began excitedly speculating about Iliodor's flight. It is possible he traveled to Odessa. Some claimed he had escaped into the Caucasus or even gone as far as Constantinople. Where, precisely, Iliodor went is not known, but by the middle of July he was most certainly in St. Petersburg.[3]

Iliodor had to run, for the police were right behind him. They had arrived at New Galilee hoping to interrogate him only to find he had just escaped. They noticed fresh carriage tracks in the dirt near the tunnel's exit and began to follow them, but then it started to rain and the tracks

were lost. The Okhrana put all of his relatives under surveillance thinking Iliodor might go to one of them to hide. There were so many
reported sightings of Iliodor that the Okhrana could not even begin to
follow them up.[4] Heading the search was Colonel Mikhail Komissarov,
a man who would come to play an important role in another plot to
kill Rasputin a year later. Komissarov arrived in Tsaritsyn on 5 July
and began questioning Iliodor's associates for information on his
whereabouts. House searches were conducted as well for anything
incriminating on the fugitive Iliodor. Among those he questioned was
one Molchanov, a local reporter for the newspaper the *Russian Word*. As
soon as Molchanov had gotten word of the attack, he had raced to
Iliodor to bring him the news. In Molchanov's apartment Komissarov's
men found evidence that he had warned Iliodor the police were on their
way, thus allowing him to get away. They also discovered a letter from
Iliodor to a disciple by the name of Yevdokia Skudneva, directing her to
give a hundred rubles to Guseva and her sister to finance their attack on
Rasputin.[5] According to sources in Tsaritsyn, Guseva had visited Iliodor
as late as early June, just weeks before arriving in Pokrovskoe.[6] Two days
later, the director of the department of the police cabled to the head
of the Don region gendarmes ordering him to find Iliodor no matter
what.[7]

In Petersburg, Iliodor went straight to his friend Alexander Prugavin.
Realizing the danger he was in, Prugavin took him to the writer Maxim
Gorky, then in the Grand Duchy of Finland, part of the Russian empire.
It was not a coincidence that Prugavin led him to the great writer. Gorky
had heard of Iliodor's intention to write a book about Rasputin back in
1912, and he wanted to help. Gorky received him warmly and promised
to get in touch with Ivan Ladyzhnikov, his publisher in Berlin, to begin
negotiations for Iliodor's book. Gorky even supplied Iliodor with
money and made arrangements for him to escape to Sweden.[8] Iliodor,
the Black Hundred scourge of the left, now embraced Marxist revolutionaries as allies in the battle against the monarchy.

The meeting with Iliodor turned Gorky's thoughts to Rasputin,
which he recorded in a letter around this time:

> "Society" is extremely interested in the starets Grigory Rasputin
> [. . .] The most curious legend about the starets is taking shape: first

of all, informed people are saying that the starets is the son of the starets Fyodor Kuzmich, and second, that he gave the throne an heir. A curious situation and one that elicits great hopes: having plunged himself into the sea of the narod, the tsar-starets drew certain new powers there and through his son transmitted them to his grandson, so we can most certainly await all manner of blessings from this grandson, who amounts to a merging of the tsar with the narod. But was it clean?[9]

The hermit Fyodor Kuzmich, according to popular legend, was none other than Tsar Alexander I, who was said to have faked his death and slipped away to live the life of a humble elder. In the summer of 1914, talk began to spread that Rasputin was the son of Kuzmich, a rumor some believed had been created by powerful persons in the capital as a means to counter all the talk of him as a khlyst and rogue. Gorky's letter points to the merger of the Kuzmich-Rasputin myth with that of Rasputin's being the true father of the tsarevich Alexei. The notion that Kuzmich might have been Rasputin's father is, of course, absurd and physically impossible: the elder died five years before Rasputin was born.[10]

Gorky introduced Iliodor to his colleague Yevgeny Chirikov to be his guide across the border. A leftist journalist and writer arrested several times and often under police surveillance, Chirikov was already well acquainted with the former monk: he had been one of the journalists chronicling Iliodor's 1911 boat pilgrimage that he reported on in especially dark tones.[11] Like everyone who came in close contact with Iliodor, Chirikov was left with a strong impression, later calling him "a precursor of the future Lenin! A harbinger of our Bolshevism in a monk's cassock. Both were adventurers, visionaries, fanatics, mad with ambition and hungry for power—one, however, was a success, the other, a loser."[12]

On 19 July, Iliodor and Chirikov crossed the River Torneo into Sweden several kilometers upstream from the official border crossing. Stepping from stone to stone, Iliodor claimed to have lost a boot and then took off the other and tossed it back onto Russian soil, crying out: "I cast off the dust from my legs and the dust of that country that so tormented and mocked me." (Iliodor gave another version to the press of his words at the time: "Farewell, cursed Russia. Farewell, poor suffering Russia. I've been tormented on your breast by aggressors, obscurantists, traitors, and incompetent disciples and worshippers.")[13] Iliodor traveled on to Kristiania (Oslo), where his wife, Nadezhda, and their young child joined him three months later. They settled in a simple apartment at 73 Bogstadveien. He adopted the name Mr. Perfilieff (his wife's maiden name) and got a job sweeping the floors in a factory.[14]

From the safety of Kristiania, Iliodor sent off an angry article to the Tsaritsyn newspaper *Land of the Volga-Don* titled "The Sufferings of an Abused Refugee" in which he informed readers he would give them the true story of why he had abandoned Russia. He admitted to having learned of the desire among some of his followers to kill this "state and church criminal," and even hearing the talk of some wanting to cut off his genitals, but denied having had anything to do with the attack. He called Guseva a "true hero" who deserved to be rewarded for her deed. Should she end up on trial, Iliodor offered to act as her attorney, and he was prepared to show the entire world the true evil of Rasputin, a man deserving "the highest measure of punishment"—aka death. The attempt on his life would have been a success had the plot not been exposed ahead of time by the "traitorous tramp I.[van] Sinitsyn." As for himself, Iliodor had been forced to escape Russia since he was about to be arrested for insulting the honor of their majesties and for running an underground terrorist organization. He stated, with false nobility, that he would have remained to face the charges but he knew this act, while selfless, would only worsen the plight of his followers, and so, for their sake, he had to leave.[15]

Iliodor now threw himself into writing the book that would show to the world the true Rasputin, as well as the sordid life of the Russian court. Both Prugavin and Gorky encouraged him to work as fast as possible. On 29 July, Gorky wrote Amfiteatrov, the author of the article Guseva said had inspired her to kill Rasputin, that he would soon be visited by a "rather interesting fellow, in the possession of some documents that are even more interesting. It would be marvelous if you could help him make sense of the chaos in his soul and everything he knows." Iliodor also sent a letter to Amfiteatrov, then living near Genoa, to tell him that Gorky had fully endorsed the plan for his book and had offered to help him in any way possible. Gorky instructed Iliodor to settle somewhere near Amfiteatrov so they could work together, but then the war broke out and Iliodor was stuck in Kristiania. Plans to work with Ladyzhnikov in Berlin fell through as well. Later that summer

Iliodor wrote to the publisher of the *Russian Worker* based in London to say that the book was almost done.

> The book is called "The Holy Devil"—(based on the celebrated "starets of the Russian Court"—Rasputin). [...] I have told the awful and interesting truth about Rasputin in this book, the truth that even abroad is not known. On the basis of documentary evidence, I, as much as possible, have proven that Rasputin is a debauched peasant, a wretch, that he sleeps with the Tsaritsa Alexandra and is the father of the heir Alexei, and that Rasputin is the unofficial Emperor of Russia and Patriarch of the Russian Church.[16]

Amazing claims, all of them lies.

The Russian press followed the entire bizarre story. "What is Iliodor doing?" the *Petrograd Courier* asked on 13 October. "In Petrograd a letter has been received from S. M. Trufanov, the former hieromonk Iliodor, in which he reports that he has completed a book on G. Rasputin. The book, so Iliodor writes, is enormous and most interesting. In his words, this book will be of historical significance."[17]

The day before the authorities officially accused Iliodor of incitement to commit murder.[10] At the end of December, the chief investigator of the Tyumen district repeated his order from October that all possible means be used to find Iliodor, wherever he may be. In the end, however, the authorities were forced to give up, and on 6 July 1915 attempts to either find Iliodor or bring him to justice were discontinued.[19] Iliodor remained a free man.

Part Five

WAR

July 1914–1915

39. A Menacing Cloud

As Rasputin lay recuperating in a Siberian hospital, Europe was racing toward war. On 28 June 1914 (NS), Archduke Franz Ferdinand was murdered in Sarajevo by the Serbian nationalist Gavrilo Princip. It was the shot that unleashed World War I and would lead to Rasputin's own murder two and a half years later and the downfall of the Romanov dynasty soon thereafter.

The closeness of the attacks on Rasputin and the archduke has been the cause for a good deal of regrettable confusion and outright mendacity among historians and biographers. At first glance it does seem odd that both men were attacked only a day apart: 28 and 29 June. But any chronological (or other) connection is a mirage, the result of confusion over the differences between the Gregorian calendar then used in the West and the Julian calendar used in Russia. According to the Julian calendar, Franz Ferdinand was assassinated on 15 June, exactly two weeks before Guseva's attack.

This obvious fact has, unfortunately, not stopped conspiracy theorists from seeing some larger international plot. To contemporary Russian nationalist historians the attacks were part of a conspiracy by Jew-Masonry to kill the only two men who could have prevented war, the goal being to push the world into a bloody conflict that would destroy the Christian empires of Europe and Russia and ignite world revolution. (The assassination of the French socialist and leading anti-militarist Jean Jaurès, in Paris at the Café du Croissant on 31 July [NS], has also been mentioned as proof of the conspiracy.)[1] Indeed, some of the more extreme proponents of this notion go so far as to claim (against all reason and evidence) that the two attempts on the men's lives happened not only on the same day but even at the same hour. In his 1964 biography of Rasputin, Colin Wilson, who claims to have been the first person to notice the exact timing of the events, wrote: "Ferdinand's death made war probable; Rasputin's injury made it certain, for he was the only man in Russia capable of averting it."[2]

In fact, Rasputin was still in Petersburg at the time of the assassination. Asked his thoughts about it by a reporter for the *Stock Exchange Gazette*, he replied:

> Well, brothers, what can Grigory Yefimovich say? He's dead. Cry and shout as much as you want, it won't bring him back. Do what you will—the result will always be the same. It's fate. But our English guests in Petersburg can't help but be glad. It's good [for them]. My peasant mind tells me it's a big event—the beginning of friendship between the Russian and the English people. It's a union, my dear, of England with Russia, and if we find friendship with France as well, that's no trifle but a powerful force, really good.

To an Italian reporter he was less sanguine: "Yes, they say there will be war, and they are getting ready for it. May God grant that there will be no war. This troubles me."[3]

Rasputin was a man of peace, a man with an innate antipathy to bloodshed whose devout Christian faith taught him that war was a sin. His enemies, now filled with bloodlust, returned to Rasputin's pronouncements against war from the previous years when war raged in the Balkans. He was attacked in the pages of Father Vostokov's *Responses to Life*:

> Gr. Rasputin, judging from his publication *Smoke of the Fatherland*, is the worst enemy of Christ's holy Church, the Orthodox faith, and the Russian state. We don't know what influence this traitor of Christ's teaching has on Russia's foreign policy, but during the war of liberation of the Balkan Christians against Turkey (in 1912) he did not support Christ but instead the pseudo-prophet Mohammed. [...] He preaches non-resistance to evil, advises Russian diplomacy to make concessions in every issue, being fully convinced, as a revolutionary, that the lost prestige of Russia and the refusal to perform her age-old tasks will cause the destruction and decay of our country. [...] He does not care about Russia's glory and might, but aims to diminish its dignity and honor; he is fine with betraying our spiritual comrades and leaving them to the Turks and Swabians. He is prepared to welcome various misfortunes brought upon our fatherland through the disposition of Godly Providence because of the betrayal of our ancestor's legacy. And yet this enemy of God's ultimate truth is hailed as a saint by some of his followers.[4]

Here was Vostokov, an immensely popular priest, a pillar of the church, a publisher and writer whose journal had been chosen to help instruct the Romanov children in the teachings of Christ, publicly attacking Rasputin in the ugliest of terms as a traitor to both Christianity and the state for his tolerance of other faiths and his hatred of war. It is a stunning, and profoundly disturbing, indictment of the moral bankruptcy that lurked in the hearts of a good many clergymen within the Russian Orthodox Church at the turn of the century.

In the days before Guseva's assault, Vyrubova telegraphed Rasputin, then on his way to Pokrovskoe, to keep him abreast of the feelings of Nicholas and Alexandra on the international situation.[5] And then, after he had been moved to Tyumen, Rasputin tried to follow the unfolding events from his hospital bed and to offer his advice to the emperor. The reporters crowding around the hospital sought out his opinion about the grave situation in the Balkans.[6] According to his daughter Maria, Rasputin was beside himself with worry that Nicholas would go to war. He supposedly said as he lay recovering: "I'm coming, I'm coming, and don't try to stop me. [...] Oh, Lord, what have they done? Mother Russia will perish!"[7] Rasputin wrote to Nicholas telling him to "stay strong" and to ignore the voices calling for war. Such was his worry that his wound opened up and began to bleed again.[8]

On 12 July, Rasputin wired Vyrubova: "A serious moment, there's a threat of war."[9] The next day he cabled again, urging her to tell the tsar to avoid war at any cost.[10] On the following day, 14 July, he received an unsigned telegram from Peterhof most likely from Vyrubova, asking him to change his mind and support the calls for war: "You are aware that our eternal enemy Austria is preparing to attack little Serbia. That country is almost entirely made up of peasants, utterly devoted to Russia. We shall be covered in infamy should we permit this shameless reprisal. If the occasion arises, use your influence to support this just cause. Get well soon."

More pleading telegrams followed:

16 July 1914. From Peterhof to Tyumen. Rasputin.
    Bad news. Terrible moments. Pray for him. No more strength
to fight the others.

17 July 1914. From Peterhof to Tyumen. Rasputin.
    The clouds threaten ever more. For our defense we must
openly prepare ourselves, suffering terribly.

From Petersburg to Rasputin's secretary Laptinskaya.*

Should the health of the starets allow, immediate arrival is necessary to help Papa in light of imminent events, his loving friends advise and fervently request. Kisses. Awaiting your answer.[11]

Not surprisingly, by now, when Rasputin was assumed to be responsible for every last problem, some dared to lay the blame for the threat of war at his feet. Guchkov wrote a stinging letter to Minister of Foreign Affairs Sergei Sazonov on 14 July commenting that Austria's ultimatum against Serbia was the direct result of perceived Russian weakness on the part of Vienna. He concluded: "So now we have fatally sunk down to the final step of humiliation (is it really the final one?) thanks to the faint-heartedness of the emperor, the state leadership of Rasputin, and your connivance."[12] A stunning and utterly wrong-headed interpretation of events.

It was during these days Rasputin sent a pleading telegram to Nicholas, urging him not to go to war. The telegram has been lost, but Vyrubova, who claimed to have seen it, said it read: "Let Papa not plan for war, for war will mean the end of Russia and yourselves, and you will lose to the last man." Nicholas was reportedly furious at the telegram and resented Rasputin's interference in affairs of state that did not concern him.[13] Rasputin told an Okhrana agent in the summer of 1915 that while he lay in the hospital he sent the emperor approximately twenty telegrams begging him not to go to war. One of these was so strongly worded, he claimed, that some of the emperor's men wanted to bring charges against Rasputin, but Nicholas disagreed, saying, "This is Our private matter, it does not concern anyone at court."[14]

Then Rasputin made one last attempt to sway Nicholas and keep Russia from going to war. He requested pen and paper and wrote what must be considered the most remarkable and prophetic letter ever written to a Russian monarch by one of his subjects:

*

Dear friend I'll say again a menacing cloud is over Russia, lots of sorrow and grief, it's dark and there's not a ray of hope. A sea of tears, immeasurable, and as to blood? What can I say? There are no words, indescribable horror. I know they all want war from you,

---

* Akilina Laptinskaya, at Rasputin's bedside in the hospital.

evidently not realizing that this means ruin. Hard is God's punishment when he takes away reason, it's the beginning of the end. You are the Tsar Father of the people, don't allow the madmen to triumph and destroy themselves and the people. Yes, they'll conquer Germany, but what of Russia? If one thinks then truly never for all of time has one suffered like Russia, drowned in her own blood. Great will be the ruin, grief without end.

Grigory[15]

Remarkably, the letter has survived. Although it may well not be true that Nicholas carried the letter on his person through the war, as has been asserted, nonetheless he definitely placed great value on it, and for this reason took it with him into exile in August 1917 when the entire family was sent away from Tsarskoe Selo. It was while the Romanovs were being held in Tobolsk in early 1918 that Nicholas managed to secretly pass the letter on to Maria Rasputina's husband, Boris Solovyov, then in Siberia trying to organize a plot to save the family. Later, after fleeing Russia, Maria ended up in Vienna, where she apparently sold the letter to Prince Nikolai Orlov in 1922. It then changed hands at least two more times before coming into the possession of one Robert D. Brewster, who donated it to Yale University in 1951.[16]

Rasputin's letter makes for one of those powerful "What if . . . ?" moments. What if Nicholas had heeded Rasputin's words, what if the image Rasputin presented with these few charged words had opened the tsar's eyes to the horror and great danger facing Russia in the summer of 1914? Had Nicholas followed Rasputin's advice, the course not only of Russian history, but indeed world history would have been radically different. Had Russia stayed out of the war, it is hard to imagine there would have been a revolution or at least one so violent and catastrophic. The suffering that would have been avoided is unimaginable. And without the Russian revolutions of 1917, it is difficult to conceive of the rise of Nazi Germany. But again, Nicholas ignored Rasputin's words, words that would have saved his reign, and his life and those of his family, and words that more than compensated for the harm Rasputin had caused, and would later cause, the prestige of the throne.

Later, once he was healed and back in Petersburg, Rasputin liked to say that had he been in the capital at the tsar's side he would have been able to convince him not to go to war.[17] Count Witte, repeating his comments on the Balkan Crisis, said nearly the same thing.[18] It is impossible to know whether this was indeed the truth. It makes for a nice story, but ultimately it does not seem convincing, for as of 1914 Nicholas had rarely ever taken Rasputin's advice on important matters and when he did, it was restricted to religious affairs. It was not until a year later after Nicholas had assumed supreme command of the armed forces in 1915 and was away at general headquarters (Stavka)* that he showed any willingness, and then reluctantly and rarely, to follow Rasputin's advice.

It must also not be forgotten that Rasputin's was not the lone voice for peace. The former ambassador to the U.S., Baron Roman Rosen, Prince Vladimir Meshchersky (publisher of *The Citizen* and a longtime friend of both Alexander III and Nicholas), and Count Witte all spoke out against the war. After Rasputin, no one was as explicit with the tsar about the catastrophes certain to befall Russia should she go to war as Pyotr Durnovo, former minister of the interior, which he laid out in a famous memorandum in February 1914.[19]

While Rasputin was writing to Nicholas, the press was speculating on just what the starets was making of the international situation. The *Petersburg Courier*, for example, noted on 16 July how Rasputin was "extremely depressed" upon receiving a telegram from the capital about Austria's declaration of war against Serbia the day before.[20] As it had during the Balkan crisis, the European press, too, ruminated on just what Rasputin was thinking. Axel Schmidt of the *Hamburger Fremdenblatt* wrote on 21 June (NS) that the "former apostle of peace" was now supposedly speaking the language of the Panslavists and calling for the unification of all Slavs and Orthodox believers under the Russian scepter. If this were indeed true, he noted, this would present a great danger to peace in Europe, for it was only religion that could get the Russian masses to go to war. "Whatever the case," he concluded, "it is simply ridiculous to think that peace in Europe now depends on the murky wishes and the will of a cunning mystic or a simple adventurer. But in the land of unlimited impossibilities all is possible."[21]

The speculation ran wild. A newspaper in Toulouse expressed the view that Witte had been able to use Rasputin to convince the tsar to align Russia with Germany against France, that "godless country." German papers (*Vossische Zeitung*, *Berliner Tageblatt*) observed that whereas in the past Rasputin had been powerful enough to keep the tsar

---

* Stavka was located at Baranovichi (Belorussia) until August 1915 when it was moved to Mogilyov.

from going to war, he could just as easily now use this same power to make him go to war. Another German paper—*Deutsche Warte*—wondered (when in the first days after Guseva's attack it was believed Rasputin had been killed) whether he had been assassinated by those very forces in Russia that had opposed his politics of peace and now wanted to push Russia to war.[22]

On 17 July, Nicholas, under great pressure from his military command, ordered full mobilization of the Russian army for the following day. War was now inevitable. When Alexandra learned of this she rushed to Nicholas's office, where they argued for half an hour. The empress had been caught off guard by the move and was beside herself. She raced back to her room, threw herself onto her couch and started to cry. "It's all over," she said to Vyrubova, "we are now at war." As for Nicholas, Vyrubova noticed he seemed at peace. The agonizing question that had been hanging in the air had now been answered.[23]

On 19 July/1 August, Germany declared war on Russia. Rasputin telegraphed Vyrubova a message for Nicholas and Alexandra: "My dear darling ones! Don't despair!"[24] The following day he sent a cable directly to Nicholas: "My dear and darling, we treated them with love while they were preparing their swords and misdeeds for us for years, I am convinced: everyone who has experienced such evil and cunningness will get a hundredfold punishment; God's mercy is powerful, we will remain under Its cover."

On 24 July/6 August, Austria-Hungary declared war on Russia. Rasputin wired a message of hope to Alexandra: "God will never take His hand from your head, He will give you consolation and strength."[25] As insistent as Rasputin had been for peace, now that war had begun he committed himself to victory and never again questioned the righteousness of Russia's cause or wavered about the need to fight her enemies.[26] He wired Vyrubova on 26 July: "Everyone, from the east to the west, has come together with the same spirit for the Motherland, this is a great joy."

Rasputin wrote to Nicholas of his confidence in a Russian victory in the middle of August: "God is wise and shows us glory through the cross, you will win with this cross. The time will come. God is with us, the enemies will tremble with fear."[27]

A week later Rasputin was released from the hospital and left straightaway for the capital. In the early evening of 22 August, he was received by Nicholas at Tsarskoe Selo.[28] With his return came the usual salon gossip. Maurice Paléologue, recently appointed French ambassador to Russia, recorded that Rasputin had told the empress how his miraculous survival was further proof of God's care for him. And there was a good deal of speculation on what stance Rasputin had taken with regard to the war. Paléologue for one thought Rasputin had been urging Nicholas to seek an alliance with Germany, although like a good many members of the upper classes at the time who could not imagine a peasant having his own ideas the ambassador was certain that Rasputin had not come to this notion on his own, but was simply repeating the phrases fed to him by Prince Meshchersky.[29]

As for the press, the *Petersburg Courier* now reported that Rasputin not only endorsed the war, but was planning on enlisting himself and heading to the front. Such was the word at the salon of Countess Sofia Ignatieva, and when Rasputin's female followers heard of this they raised a cry of worry, insisting he not place himself in any danger.[30] The story in the *Courier* so upset one government official, a certain I. A. Karev serving in Dagestan, that he felt he had to write to Rasputin himself:

> I learned from the newspapers the other day that you are planning on leaving for the field of battle, and as every Russian must sacrifice himself for the defense of the Fatherland, so is your intention of the greatest merit, but please stop and think—this terrible war and its horrors have already devoured a great many lives and you too shall not escape this fate, yet by remaining where you are, so shall you still bring a great benefit to humanity. If your wish to leave for the war is steadfast and you nonetheless want to go there, then go with God, many will be praying to God for you [. . .].[31]

Needless to say, Rasputin never did go off to war, nor did he ever have any intention to. Regardless, not to be outdone, Iliodor's remaining followers jumped into action at word of Rasputin's martial patriotism. They contacted the *Courier* and informed its editor that Iliodor had already left for the Serbian front lines carrying a large cross in his hands and inspiring Slavic warriors to fall in behind him along his route.[32]

*

Rasputin returned to Petersburg on 20 August. He was still weak and in considerable pain, although Dr. Vladimirov recorded around this time that Rasputin's wound was draining with no signs of infection. He considered his recovery nothing short of a miracle. It was not until the first week of September that he was able to eat any solid food—a bit of bread and a fish cutlet.[33]

If Nicholas was angry about Rasputin's telegrams and letter from Tyumen he did not show it. The emperor saw Rasputin after his main meal on the twenty-second and then again on the twenty-fifth and met with him for over two hours on the evening of 5 September. And then on the fourteenth: "We waited a long time this evening for the arrival of Grigory. We sat with him for a long time," Nicholas recorded in his diary.[34] In light of the attack, Rasputin no longer took the train out to Tsarskoe Selo, but was driven in a motorcar by an agent of the Okhrana.[35] The meetings at the palace continued with regularity throughout October and November.[36]

With the war, the relationship among the three changed profoundly. Nicholas was now often away from home and, from the late summer of 1915, almost permanently at Stavka, and so Alexandra increasingly looked to Rasputin for guidance on matters both personal and political. He was more than ready to help. That September Rasputin began to show concern about the ambitions of Grand Duke Nikolai Nikolaevich (Nikolasha), his former patron and now commander-in-chief of the Russian army. Alexandra wrote Nicholas on 19 September to convey to him Rasputin's concern that "Bonheur," as she called the grand duke, with the encouragement of the Black Princesses, had designs on the throne, a thought neither Alexandra nor Rasputin could bear to imagine.[37] As part of his strategy, Nikolasha was being fed damaging information on Rasputin by chief of police Stepan Beletsky.[38] An anecdote began to circulate that Rasputin asked Nikolasha for permission to visit Stavka, saying this had been the desire of the Virgin herself, who had appeared before him in a vision. Nikolasha was said to have replied that she had appeared to him as well just the day before and said: "If that bastard dares to weasel his way to Stavka, hang him from the first lamppost. And believe me: I will execute the Virgin's order to the letter." Rasputin never did visit Stavka.[39]

Nicholas, on the other hand, welcomed Rasputin's visits to the palace. In a rare moment of candor, Nicholas admitted in his diary on 17 October to having been in a "beastly mood" all day due to the actions of the Germans and Turks on the Black Sea. But that evening Rasputin came and all was better: "Only under the influence of Grigory's calming talk did my soul return to its normal balance!"[40] At the same time Rasputin was counseling Alexandra and her daughters to get out of the palace and attend to the wounded soldiers. The sight of them, dressed as nurses, would do wonders for the troops' morale, he insisted. "When you comfort the wounded, God makes his name famous through your affection and glorious work," Rasputin told her. She found his words "touching," and tried to find in them the "strength to get over my shyness." When the soldiers she nursed died, he made certain to write her comforting words and urged her not to grow despondent and discontinue her important work.[41] To prepare herself for these visits, Alexandra tried to fill her soul with Rasputin, and she wrote to Nicholas that she was certain this was evident to the poor soldiers: "I think it's natural, why those who are so very ill feel calmer & better when I am there, as I always think of our Friend & pray whilst sitting quietly near them or stroking them—the soul must prepare itself when with the ill if one wishes to help—one must try & put oneself into the same plan & help oneself to rise through them, or help them to rise through being a follower of our Friend."[42]

Grand Duchess Maria Pavlovna gave a different assessment of the effect the empress had on the wounded:

> No matter how sincerely the Empress sympathized with the men's suffering, no matter how she tried to express it, there was something in her, eluding definition, that prevented her from communicating her own genuine feelings and from comforting the persons she addressed. [...] They watched her move about the ward with eyes that were anxious and frightened, and their expressions did not change after she had approached and spoken.[43]

By the end of October Rasputin was in a hurry to return home, but Nicholas was away and so he waited, eager to speak with the emperor before his departure. They met, together with Alexandra, on 4 November, a meeting which the emperor said gave him "comfort."[44] The reason Rasputin had wanted to talk to the emperor had to do with the actions of Nikolai Lavrinovsky, the governor of Tauride. Rasputin had recently met with a certain "Madame Muftizde" from the Crimea who had told him of the terribly harsh actions Lavrinovsky—a Russian nationalist with connections to the Black Hundreds—had undertaken in his lands against the Tatars there, even forcibly exiling some of them to Turkey. Rasputin was so upset by what he had been told that he talked to Alexandra about the matter, insisting Lavrinovsky be removed immediately and replaced by Nikolai Knyazevich. He leaned on Alexandra to talk to Minister of the Interior Maklakov about the matter at once and not bother to wait for Nicholas's return or his approval. Alexandra listened: Lavrinovsky was made the governor of Chernigov and Knyazevich took his place. It warrants noting that Knyazevich was an excellent man for the position, with an outstanding service record and deep family connections to the territory. Nevertheless, a dangerous precedent had been set: Alexandra, in consort with Rasputin, had usurped power that belonged solely to the emperor. Alexandra knew what she had done and wrote to Nicholas: "Please don't be angry with me & give me some sort of answer by wire—that you 'approve', or 'regret' my mixing in [. . .]." Nicholas, however, was not angry and approved of her actions.[45]

On 17 November, Nicholas set off again for the front. Alexandra's only consolation at his leaving was a telegram she had just received from Rasputin informing her that he had prayed God to protect the emperor on his travels. Rasputin wrote to the emperor as well, offering encouragement and predicting victory: "My dear, don't be upset by their evil cunning, wise God shows the way to glory with his cross, and with this cross you shall be victorious. That time will come. God is with us, our enemies are afraid."[46] On 14 December Alexandra wrote Nicholas to say that Rasputin had told her to expect good news from the front. Two days later Rasputin telephoned Alexandra to say that the Russian people expected Nicholas to be "a fortress of the spirit," something she made sure to mention more than once to her husband.[47] When Nicholas was away Alexandra and Rasputin worried that he would be swayed by others, that he would not be strong and play the role of the tsar that others wanted and expected of him. They made sure to remind him of just what he had to do to lead Russia at this critical time.

Rasputin returned to the palace to see the entire family at Christmas. Together, they gathered around the lit tree. He acknowledged it had been "the most difficult year of all times," but assured Alexandra that "God is with us, the enemy is nothing, the lovers' tears surround the throne."[48]

40. The Incident at the Yar

On 10 January 1915, Rasputin sent a telegram to Vyrubova, then recuperating in the Palace Hospital at Tsarskoe Selo after her near fatal train accident eight days earlier: "Although I was not present in body, in spirit I rejoice with you. My feelings are the feelings of God. I send an Angel to console and calm you. Call a doctor."[1]

It is possible that Rasputin had not been to visit since he was home recovering from his own injuries at the time. The press carried a story two days earlier that while on his way to visit the Vladimirsky Cathedral Rasputin's sledge had been overtaken and then cut off by a speeding automobile, causing the sledge to crash and sending Rasputin flying onto the pavement. A large crowd gathered and carried the unconscious Rasputin to a nearby pharmacy, and from there he was transferred to a hospital, although he awoke en route and insisted he be taken home instead. The doctors, according to the report, described his condition as quite serious.[2]

If the accident did indeed happen (which seems doubtful), Rasputin's injuries could not have been as serious as the doctors initially thought, for on 17 January Rasputin was back visiting Tsarskoe Selo with his wife and daughter Maria.[3] These trips to and from the palace continued to be made in a chauffeured car provided by the Okhrana. The automobile was old and small and nothing special, although legends about it persisted in Petrograd. It was widely believed to be especially outfitted with two machine guns in the doors for Rasputin's protection. People that spring claimed to have seen this black automobile racing through the night streets and firing at pedestrians, leaving them wounded and bleeding on the sidewalks, the car disappearing into the night.[4]

Rasputin was again at the palace on 26 January to present Alexandra with a large stack of petitions for the emperor.[5] He next saw the tsar on 27 February at Vyrubova's, where they spent an hour and a half talking before Nicholas left again for the front. After he had gone, Alexandra wrote Nicholas: "My very own deeply beloved One, [. . .] Our Friend's blessing and prayers will help. Such a comfort for me that you saw Him and were blessed by Him this evening! [. . .] I press you tenderly to my old loving heart and remain your very own Wify."[6]

Throughout the first three months of 1915 the police reported Rasputin had been drinking heavily and throwing wild parties late into the night. In late February, he was observed visiting for nearly two hours a young "courtesan" by the name of Yevgenia Terekhova-Miklashevskaya at the Great Northern Hotel on Nevsky Prospect.[7] Assignations like this were no longer something out of the ordinary for Rasputin. None of these episodes, however, would compare with the scandal that was soon to explode.

The tale of the debauchery that took place at Moscow's Yar restaurant in the spring of 1915 is one of the most notorious episodes in the life of Rasputin. Every biographer discusses it, and practically everyone who knows anything about Rasputin has heard of it.

It was late March and Rasputin had just arrived in Moscow by train from Petrograd, the new, more Slavic-friendly name for St. Petersburg. Together with a group of friends, Rasputin visited the popular nightspot called the Yar for drinks, dinner, and some entertainment. Things, however, quickly got out of hand. Rasputin drank heavily, he lost control and began grabbing at the girls in the Gypsy chorus. He started to brag loudly in obscene terms about his relations with the empress, he danced wildly, making a spectacle of himself. Then, when it seemed his outlandish behavior could go no further, he undid his pants and pulled out his penis for all to see, as if to prove the source of his hold over the empress and society women. Finally, the police arrived, arrested Rasputin and, as British diplomat Robert Bruce Lockhart saw with his own eyes that night, dragged him cursing and snarling out of the Yar. He was jailed and then freed by imperial order the next day, hurrying straight back to Petrograd. The incident became a huge public scandal that was splashed about in all the newspapers to universal outcry.[8]

The incident at the Yar offers some of the best proof of Rasputin's foul character and the base way he used his relations with the imperial couple for his own vanity. That night Rasputin showed himself for who he really was. Or did he? Can we be certain that the story of the Yar happened as it has been told and retold for a century now? Perhaps the truth of that night is not at all as it seems.

Indeed, in recent years some biographers have posited that the scandal is a good deal more complicated than has been assumed. Edvard Radzinsky has argued that Rasputin knew just what he was doing that night. Rasputin was never out of control, and his actions were part of a plan to bring down Vladimir Dzhunkovsky, deputy minister of the interior and a well-known foe of Rasputin. By creating a scandal that Dzhunkovsky could not ignore and would be certain to report to the emperor, Rasputin, according to Radzinsky, would force his enemy's hand, bringing upon Dzhunkovsky the displeasure of the royal couple and so his fall from power. Rasputin set up Dzhunkovsky and brought him down with devilish cunning.[9]

Then there is the curious theory of one contemporary Russian scholar according to which the bacchanalia was carried out not by Rasputin, but a double. This Rasputin Doppelgänger, so the idea goes, was sent out to create scandals just like the one at the Yar as a means to destroy the reputation of the ruling family. The man behind this provocation was (not surprisingly, given the nationalist source) a Jew by the name of Semyon Kugulsky. A reporter, Kugulsky put together the sham incident in order to create a public furor and give the Duma cause to bring up the scandal and tarnish the regime.[10] It is an outlandish idea, but not exactly new. According to Alexei Sukhanov, a Duma deputy, some members of the Duma at the time actually thought there might be something to the tales that the wild, drunken Rasputin was actually a revolutionary dressed as the Siberian starets. Yet in the end, Sukhanov recalled, everyone came to see the foolishness of such a notion.[11]

Finally, there is the argument proposed by other current biographers that Rasputin was not even at the Yar that night and nothing ever happened. As proof, they point to the fact that the police files for that night have mysteriously disappeared, thus making it impossible to say for certain where Rasputin was at the time and just what he was up to. There are no files, they insist, since there was no scandal.[12] But this is wrong. There are files and they have not disappeared and are safely stored in the State Archive of the Russian Federation in Moscow. It is there that the key to the mystery of the Yar scandal is to be found.

*

On 25 March, Colonel Konstantin Globachev, head of the Petrograd Okhrana, sent a telegram to his counterpart in Moscow, Colonel Alexander Martynov, informing him that "The Dark One" had departed that evening for Moscow on express train No. 1 and instructing him "to establish persistent and utterly secret surveillance and to follow [him] wherever he goes. Telegraph me at No. 139." The police were waiting the next day when at noon Rasputin's train arrived at the Nikolaevsky Station. Several policemen quietly followed him into the city, all of which one inspector Glazunov dutifully communicated to Globachev.[13] Eight Okhrana agents (Yevgenev, Yushchenko, Bychkov, Deryabin, Freer, Pakhomov, Leonov, Osminin) tracked him for the next four days. They noted everywhere he went and everyone he had contact with and telephoned Rasputin's whereabouts back to headquarters sometimes as often as every five minutes. The agents investigated every one of these individuals and sought out where they lived and every possible personal detail.[14]

The agents recorded that the Dark One had been greeted at the station by Yevgenia Terekhova-Miklashevskaya, the same "courtesan" he had met the previous month at Petrograd's Great Northern Hotel. The Moscow Okhrana, however, were unaware of this fact, and in their report she is described simply as a forty-three-year-old peasant widow. Perhaps the Petrograd Okhrana had been too quick in their assumption about the character of Rasputin's friend. Together the two of them drove to Terekhova's apartment on the corner of Bolshaya Lubyanka and Kuznetsky Bridge. Rasputin stayed there until 2 p.m., then went out on his own, returning two hours later. At 7 p.m., an automobile arrived with "a certain Yezhova," and the two of them drove off. Around midnight, the automobile returned to the apartment, now carrying a second man, apparently Yezhova's husband. An hour later—at 1 a.m. on the twenty-seventh—they came back out into the street, and the three drove together to the "suburban restaurant 'Yar'" where they stayed "until late at night."

This is the full extent of the police report for the night of 26–27 March. Not one word about Rasputin being drunk, about any insulted Gypsy chorus girls, about indecent language, public exhibitionism, and, most critically, about any arrest.

The agents spent most of the twenty-seventh gathering information on Rasputin's companions from the day before. They learned that Yevgenia and Ivan Yezhov, both peasants aged forty, lived with Ivan's sixty-five-year-old mother in an apartment building belonging to Count Sheremetev at Bolshoy Kislovsky Lane.[15]

Rasputin did not appear back on the street until noon of the twenty-seventh, when he was collected by an unknown woman and deposited at the apartment of Anisya Reshetnikova. Rasputin had known Reshetnikova for some time and had even stayed with her on at least one visit to Moscow in May. She was a wealthy widow in her mid-seventies and lived with her two grown sons: Nikolai and Vladimir.[16] According to one source, Nikolai, thanks to Rasputin, was hired as Vyrubova's private secretary and received the rank of State Councilor; Vladimir served as a church warden, a position also apparently arranged by Rasputin.[17] Their Moscow home was a popular gathering spot for members of the high clergy, including Metropolitan of Moscow Makary.

After a twenty-minute visit, Rasputin was off again with Terekhova, this time to a hospital of which she was manager, to go see some wounded soldiers. He too talked to the injured men and handed out notes in his own hand (e.g., "God loves you and will reward you"— "Don't worry, God sees, Grigory"). From there he went to the Fisher Studio and had his photograph taken in three different poses, after which he returned to Terekhova's apartment. He remained there until 6 p.m., the police noting that by now he was "drunk" and was trying to get Terekhova's chambermaid, Alexandra Slepova, aged seventeen, to kiss him. (How the agents could have known this was taking place inside the apartment is never explained in the police reports.) At 6 p.m., Yezhov picked up Rasputin, "in an intoxicated state," and they left with two unknown individuals for the Yezhovs'. At 9 p.m., Rasputin, now very drunk, was led out of the apartment, placed in a cab, and driven around the neighborhood, apparently, the agents remarked, in an attempt to sober him up, before returning a while later to the Yezhovs' home. This scenario was repeated for several hours: Rasputin being taken out and driven around, and then returned, as more men and women came to join the party at the apartment. Late that night a group of women that appeared to the agents to be singers arrived. Dancing and wild carousing ensued. The noise got so bad the downstairs' neighbor complained to the house administrator, who broke up the party in the early hours of the twenty-eighth. All the guests left, except for Rasputin, who stayed the night.[18] Parties like this were nothing rare for the Yezhovs. Ivan had supposedly turned to Rasputin for money once after losing a large sum at cards. Rasputin gave him and his wife assignments as "intermediaries" to help him earn the money back. As part of the arrangement, the couple would be sure to entertain Rasputin in Moscow with plenty of female singers.[19]

The agents recorded similar movements on the twenty-eighth, although no wild partying. (They also noted he drove off late that night with the maid Slepova for a long while. Perhaps she had finally succumbed to his advances?)[20] They checked into the identities of the party guests. They even made sure to record the license plates of the automobiles Rasputin rode in: "No. 1592," "No. 727," "No. 840." Once the identities of the owners had been established, the police then dug deeper into their personal life. And this did not stop after Rasputin left, but was still going on into the second week of April.[21]

On the evening of 29 March, agents Leonov and Osminin followed Rasputin to the Kursky Station. He boarded a separate compartment in a first class car (No. 2249) of train No. 6, departing for Petrograd at 6 p.m. With him was an unknown woman. The agents communicated that they would find out who she was, as well as the identities of all other persons of interest as yet unknown.[22] The next day Rasputin arrived in Petrograd. He immediately cabled Yelena Dzhanumova, one of his many female friends: "My gratifying treasure, I'm with you in spirit, my kisses."[23]

On 1 April, Colonel Alexander Martynov compiled a detailed report of Rasputin's visit based on the records of his agents and sent it to Moscow Governor-General Alexander Adrianov. Martynov's report corresponded exactly with what his agents had reported from the field, and he also included a list of sixteen persons Rasputin had contact with during his visit. Neither the names Kugulsky nor Soedov were on this list, a fact which will become important later.[24] Adrianov sent the report on to Deputy Minister Vladimir Dzhunkovsky.

With that the business of Rasputin's visit to Moscow came to end. But then, at the end of May, nearly two months after Martynov's report was forwarded to Petrograd, Dzhunkovsky sent a wire back to Martynov marked "Urgent" and ordering him to report in detail on just what had happened during Rasputin's visit to the Yar.[25]

Martynov knew just what his superior was asking of him, for Dzhunkovsky's hatred of Rasputin and his links to the anti-Rasputinists were no secret. Indeed, Dzhunkovsky visited Moscow in late May and it is likely he used the occasion to meet with Martynov and Adrianov and tell them just what he expected of them.[26] Dzhunkovsky's sister, Yevdokia, was close to Ella and a good friend of Sofiya Tyutcheva. Dzhunkovsky had also apparently allowed Iliodor's wife to escape Russia with her husband's archive on Rasputin, hoping, no doubt, Iliodor would use the material to ruin their common foe.[27] Dzhunkovsky was gathering his own dossier on Rasputin, hoping to use it when the time was right.[28] Indeed, on a visit to Berlin in 1913, according to Dzhunkovsky's memoirs, the empress's own family pulled him aside and urged him to do everything possible to convince Alexandra to get rid of Rasputin given the danger he posed to the throne.[29] And Dzhunkovsky had received word that some of his gendarmes agents were trying to curry favor with Rasputin. One had gone so far as to offer his wife to Rasputin in order to ingratiate himself.[30] The notion that his men, who should be trying to bring Rasputin down, might be siding with him was an outrage. Adrianov communicated to Dzhunkovsky that Rasputin did not commit "the slightest impropriety" that night at the Yar, but it did not matter. Dzhunkovsky wanted something he could add to his files, and he would get it.[31]

On 5 June, Martynov replied to Dzhunkovsky, sending along a report from a Lieutenant-Colonel Semyonov. The report stated Rasputin arrived at the Yar on 26 March around 11 p.m. with Anisya Reshetnikova, an unknown woman, and a Mr. Soedov. From the restaurant they telephoned a certain figure named Kugulsky to come join them. Next, the report states that Rasputin began to dance the "'matt-chiche' and the 'cake walk'" and talk to the girls in the choir about how his caftan was a gift from the "ol' lady," who had sewn it for him herself. "After that, RASPUTIN'S behavior took on the utterly outrageous character of some sexual psychopath: he, allegedly, revealed his sexual organs and in this fashion he continued to hold a conversation with the singers, giving some of them his handwritten notes," Semyonov wrote. When the singers said this was no way to behave, Rasputin replied that "he always behaves like this in the company of women, and continued to sit there in this same fashion." The unknown woman paid the party's bill, and then around 2 a.m. on the twenty-seventh they all departed.[32] A second report dated 6 June by a police inspector Yakovlev also purported to record the night's events, although this report did not even get the date right (28 March) and repeated the same errors in Semyonov's report about who Rasputin had visited the Yar with.

The inclusion of Soedov and Kugulsky—again, men Rasputin did not see at all during the trip—was made for a specific purpose. The police records identify Nikolai Soedov, aged fifty-four, as an employee of the *St. Petersburg Gazette* and Semyon Kugulsky, fifty-one, as the editor and publisher of the theatrical newspaper *News of the Season*. Martynov, in a report to Dzhunkovsky dated 29 July, wrote that through "secret methods" he had uncovered the nature of these two men's relations with Rasputin and just what they were up to that night. He painted Soedov in the worst possible light as a spendthrift noble, part-time reporter, and a man with a reputation of "a dark character" involved in various shady deals. He had gone to Petrograd earlier in the year to seek out Rasputin's help in setting up a corrupt deal involving a large allocation of soldiers' undergarments from which they both stood to profit handsomely. Rasputin was receptive to the idea, and promised to use his connections "to High Personages" to see it happened. They brought in Kugulsky to help with the deal, and it was their great success that they had been celebrating that night at the Yar. The party got out of hand, and when the other patrons began to inquire whether the drunken man was indeed Rasputin, the owner of the Yar, Mr. Sudakov, tried to convince them they were mistaken, that it was someone else just claiming to be him. It was at this point that Rasputin, "in the most cynical manner," got up and undid his pants to prove that he was indeed that very same Rasputin.[33]

And so, what began as simply a story about moral depravity had been elevated into a tale of political corruption in the highest places.

Late one June evening at one of his regular audiences with the tsar, Dzhunkovsky summarized the Yar incident while Nicholas listened in silence.[34] When he had finished, Nicholas then asked if he had this all written down, to which Dzhunkovsky said yes, and handed him a sheet of paper, which the tsar took and placed in his desk drawer. Dzhunkovsky later claimed that he felt it had been his duty to inform the tsar of exactly what Rasputin was doing and the danger this represented to the crown. In fact, it was Dzhunkovsky, in this instance, who was causing the greatest harm by concocting this outlandish story in the hope of destroying Rasputin once and for all. Dzhunkovsky ventured even further that night. He told the tsar that Rasputin was the weapon of some secret society (he was most likely implying the Freemasons) bent on the destruction of Russia. He spoke at length for some two hours. Nicholas, according to Dzhunkovsky, thanked him for his candor and asked that he keep him informed and that they not divulge any of this information to anyone else. Dzhunkovsky gave the tsar his word and left the palace feeling "happy and satisfied."[35]

But neither man kept his word. Nicholas informed Alexandra of the matter and Dzhunkovsky shared it with Grand Duke Dmitry and others, apparently making copies of his ministry files and showing them to his fellow anti-Rasputinists. A livid Alexandra wrote Nicholas on 22 June calling Dzhunkovsky a "liar" and "a traitor" and one of their "enemies" and insisting that he be punished for spreading lies about their friend. She warned her husband that were they to allow "our Friend" to be persecuted, Russia itself would suffer. The attacks on Rasputin were ruining her health, causing her heart pain. "If we let our Friend be persecuted we and our country shall suffer for it—once a year ago one tried to kill him and one has slandered him enough. As if they would not have called the police straight in to catch him in the act*—such a horror!"

And from the same date (22 June):

Ah, my Love, when at last will you thump them with your hand upon the table & scream at Dzh. & others when they act wrongly?—one does not fear you—& one must—they must be frightened of you, otherwise all sit upon us, & its enough Deary—don't let me speak in vain. If Dzh. is with you, call him, tell him to tear it up & not to dare to speak of Gr. as he does & that he acts as a traitor & not as a devoted subject, who ought to stand up for the Friends of his Sovereign, as one does in every other country. Oh my Boy, make one tremble before you—to love you is not enough, one must be affraid [. . .]![36]

Alexandra saw right through Dzhunkovsky, and the attempt to demolish Rasputin backfired: the empress now became more convinced than ever that all reports of Rasputin's bad behavior—his drinking, womanizing, immodest boasting—were nothing but lies concocted to keep him away from her. The unintended consequence of the Yar incident was to immunize Rasputin from all criticism in the eyes of the empress. Rasputin's enemies had actually made him stronger and his position more secure. Dzhunkovsky did not realize this at the time, and he characterized Alexandra's reaction as "psychosis on the basis of hysteria."[37] If it was indeed hysteria, she was, of course, justified in this

---

* At the Yar, that is.

instance, for it seems she knew better than her husband that the stories Dzhunkovsky was telling were pure lies, lies that everyone around them was eager to believe.

The stories grew with each retelling. It was said that Rasputin had stripped naked, that there had been an orgy, that it had been photographed by the police with special "magnesium lamps," but then some of Rasputin's followers managed to doctor the photographs to hide his identity, thus subverting Dzhunkovsky's valiant efforts to expose him.[38] Part of the myth of the Yar was that Dzhunkovsky was fired for daring to report the matter to Nicholas: Rasputin, with the support of Alexandra, insisted he be sacked immediately. But this was not the case. Dzhunkovsky held on to his post until the middle of August—a full two months after his report—before being relieved by the tsar. The reasons for his dismissal remain murky and varied and no single explanation can be given. Yet this did not matter to Dzhunkovsky and his supporters: he presented himself as a victim of Rasputin and a martyr, and Rasputin's foes were more than ready to see him in this sanctified light.[39]

Dzhunkovsky was let go along with Prince Vladimir Nikolaevich Orlov and ADC Colonel Alexander Drenteln. The empress made mention of it to Valentina Chebotaryova on 22 August: "Both of them worked against me. The ministers are cowards. When the Emperor must make some sort of decision, they immediately object, bringing up all sorts of imagined dangers. And as for me, I feel that I am wearing pants under my skirt."[40]

It was said Nicholas was so angry at Rasputin over the Yar scandal that he summoned him to demand an explanation. Rasputin admitted his transgressions, and an outraged tsar ordered him to leave immediately for Siberia and refused to see him for months.[41] This, too, is false. Rasputin visited Tsarskoe Selo more than a dozen times in April. He saw Nicholas on the evening of the first and on the twenty-seventh after the tsar had returned from his travels, and then again after the evening meal on 4 May when the tsar recorded in his diary that "Grigory blessed me before my departure" before Nicholas set out on another trip.[42] Nicholas returned to Tsarskoe Selo on 14 May, and he and Alexandra spent the evening with Rasputin on 31 May and again on 9 June. On the tenth Nicholas departed for Stavka, and he was still there when Rasputin left Petrograd for home five days later.[43] There is nothing at all to suggest that the tsar even questioned Rasputin over the story, much less that he was upset with him.

An Englishman by the name of Gerard Shelley visited the Yar not long after word of the scandal broke. He came with a friend to find out what they could from the staff, offering a bribe to one of the waiters to tell them all about what the notorious starets had gotten up to. To their astonishment, the waiter had nothing to tell. He could not even say whether Rasputin had been there. "The Devil knows who comes here," he said. "Rasputin or any other, it is all the same to us. Here we get all sorts of phizzes, red, white, black and green. But Rasputin, that's *yerunda!*"[44] Yerunda, nonsense.

But what then is to be made of Lockhart's claim that he was at the Yar that night and saw it all with his own eyes? Surely his testimony cannot be ignored. A closer look at his description, however, suggests he too may have been less than truthful. Lockhart writes the incident took place on "a summer evening" and that within twenty-four hours of Rasputin's "arrest" Dzhunkovsky was relieved of his post. Perhaps the diplomat had just grown fuzzy on some of the particulars in the years before he set down his experiences in his memoirs. Fortunately, his diaries have survived and are now kept in the Parliamentary Archives in London's Palace of Westminster. These documents provide the final nail in the coffin. During Rasputin's visit to Moscow, Lockhart, it turns out, was not even there, but was away in Kiev. What is more, nowhere in his diaries does he make any mention of any scandal at the Yar.[45] Why? Because it never happened. Just like Dzhunkovsky, Lockhart lied.

41. Rasputin's Women

Rasputin's sex life is legendary, both in the sense of being remarkably famous and of being unauthenticated, the stuff of legend. His appetite is said to have been insatiable, his stamina stupendous, his prowess unmatched. "Rasputin is incomparable," Vasily Shulgin quoted the daughter of a Russian senator after experiencing Rasputin for herself. "He is a unique man, he gives such sensations. All our other men are good for nothing," she purportedly sighed.[1] The legend of Rasputin as "a demon of the flesh, an erotomaniac, a satyr cravacheur and chief of a mystico-erotic sect," to quote his daughter Maria, was created largely by men. In his memoirs Mikhail Rodzianko wrote that Rasputin engaged in orgies in the apartments of the capital during which he ravished young maidens. He claimed to have an enormous pile of letters from mothers whose daughters had been disgraced by this "disgusting libertine" and a photograph of Rasputin surrounded by hundreds of his female devotees.[2] At the height of his fame stories of Rasputin, the deflowerer of young virgins, often appeared in the Russian press.[3]

Although talk of frenzied orgies and scores of corrupted girls is fanciful, it is beyond doubt that Rasputin took lovers. Even his daughter Maria, a defender of her father's legacy, had to admit this was true. In his early years in Petersburg, she wrote, he had tried to resist temptation. Women came to him for help, men sent women to him either as gifts or honey traps, and for a time he generally kept himself in check, but then in his later years he gave in. He would meet women in restaurants like the Villa Rode outside St. Petersburg and retreat with them to private rooms.

"No doubt they drank and danced with some exuberance. My father with his great vitality, the spontaneity of a man brought up in the country and his absolute frankness in these things as in all others, would retain his usual freedom of bearing and allow himself to be carried away by pleasure with the same passion as by prayer." And in a more candid moment she confessed: "I do not by any means claim to deny that during his life in St. Petersburg my father had mistresses, and at certain periods led a rather fast life. Surrounded by women as he was, a man of natural instincts, robust and virile, he may certainly have yielded to many temptations. Furthermore, most persistent efforts were made by those around him to loose those instincts and to multiply temptations and opportunities."[4]

The women around Rasputin tended to be emotionally fraught figures, suffering in some way. They were drawn to his inner strength and powers of perception, to the degree to which he seemed to know them even better than they knew themselves. So many of the society ladies had sad lives—husbands who cheated on or ignored them. They were lonely, their emotional lives, empty. Rasputin would listen to them, show them attention, stroke and kiss them—some found this attention just what was missing in their lives. If in the early years, this may have been chaste—a shoulder to lean on, someone to talk to and draw hope from—in later years it was not.

Although many women came and went in his life, over time there developed a small group around him that came to be known as his "little ladies." They helped take care of him, of his Petersburg household and schedule, gave him gifts and money, noted down with feverish devotion his sayings and teachings, they collected his food scraps and dirty undergarments.[5] One female follower told the Commission how they were all nervous women, with broken souls and a large, inner sorrow. They sought spiritual solace of the kind official representatives of the church were unable to understand, much less offer. Rasputin was their comfort. Time spent with him filled their unhappy souls with renewed life and hope and even joy. He knew how to divine another's suffering and, with just a few words, how to ease the pain and at times remove it entirely. They came to believe in his holiness with a mystical adoration, and entrusted him with their souls and, quite often, their bodies as well.

Here is how one married votary expressed her feelings in a letter to Rasputin:

Dear Grigory Yefimovich!
     I feel, feel so <u>painfully</u>, that I am not worthy of your holy words of comfort and joy. I was endlessly overjoyed by your letter. [...] You found me, a lost lamb, and I shall never find my way if you don't lead me, if you don't prepare my soul for Christ. I am so weak, so unsure of myself! And the further I go, the more certain

I am that there is no true joy other than the spiritual life in Christ. I cannot forget the minutes spent in conversation with you, even if it would please Our Lord God to take them from me for my sins. For I am not worthy of them. Forgive me, Grigory Yefimovich, I suffer so terribly, and I feel terrible because I have not yet found the true light.

Your forever sinful and unworthy sister Alexandra[6]

Vladimir Dzhunkovsky placed much of the blame for the Rasputin phenomenon on such women: "If in our society there had been a bit fewer hysterical and unsatisfied women seeking special sensations [. . .] then the Rasputins would not have had any influence."[7] He failed to add, however, that if the women of Petersburg were forced to leave home for "special sensations," then their husbands must accept some of the blame. In a conversation with Shulgin, one Duma deputy explained Rasputin's attraction as a natural response of society women who were in search of feelings that their "drab" husbands were incapable of providing. So they go in search of a lover, but these men tend to be of the same social class as their husbands, and so are no more able to satisfy them than their spouses. And so they must look for men from other social classes. They begin to disdain the prejudice of class, of their inherited biases, and even the demands of "aesthetics and decency." In the end, they descend to Rasputin, but by then they are utterly corrupted, having gone through a "very long path of high-society prostitution."[8]

Shulgin called this "The round dance of 'lost souls,' unsatisfied with life and love. In their search for the secret of happiness, some fall into mysticism, others into debauchery, some into both."[9] None of these souls was more lost than Olga Lokhtina. Suffering from mental illness she allowed herself to be abused at the hands of Rasputin, who was troubled by her complete self-abasement but had no idea how to deal with her in a caring way. Her frenzied worship of him put Rasputin on edge. She would kneel before him and lovingly remove his boots, kissing them before placing them by his chair. She reportedly stole his spoon and coat and would pray before them as if they were holy relics. There are reports of Rasputin beating her with a shoe or whatever was at hand as she begged forgiveness for her strange behavior. He saw in Lokhtina's oddness not, of course, an illness, but the work of the Devil, which he had failed to exorcize.[10] Rasputin's journalist friend Filippov told the Commission how he once arrived at Rasputin's apartment to find him beating Lokhtina in his bedroom. She was grabbing for Rasputin's shoulders, crying the whole time, "You are God," while he yelled back, "You're a bitch." Filippov shouted at Rasputin, upbraiding him for beating a woman. "She won't leave me alone, the bitch," Rasputin replied, "she's begging to sin," while she kept shouting out: "I'm your lamb, and you're Christ!"[11] Maria confirmed that her father had a temper and was at times angry and argumentative.[12]

The pathetic relationship between Rasputin and Lokhtina was not approved of by the other women. Akilina Laptinskaya, one of his most devoted acolytes, could not stand Olga and was terribly jealous of her. Munya Golovina called Akilina an ugly shrew and someone none of the other women could stand. The only thing she had going for her was a lovely voice, and Rasputin was always calmed by her singing.[13] Munya and her mother, Lyubov, for example, loved Lokhtina, but neither could understand nor condone what went on between her and Rasputin. Lyubov once said Lokhtina took from Rasputin all of his remarkable gifts—his power to console, his insightfulness, his mind—while closing her eyes to his improper comportment with women. Munya tried to explain Lokhtina's behavior to one outsider as a misguided attempt to put Rasputin's words of "abasement is joy to the soul" into practice. Mother and daughter never became his mistresses, but it seems likely they too were subjected to his creepy petting so often commented upon.

Lyubov said that Rasputin's spirit could be transferred to others through physical contact, and contact was something he could not do without. Rasputin never learned to keep his hands to himself and was forever stroking women's shoulders, thighs, and backsides, groping their breasts, and smothering them with wet kisses. It was worse when he had been drinking. At such times he would take whoever caught his fancy off to his bedroom, leaving his guests behind to drink their tea to the sounds of lovemaking coming from behind the door. Rasputin was especially drawn to newcomers, and he found the chase exhilarating. Once he had had a woman, his interest usually cooled. Not that this was disagreeable to the women around him. And it was never just *his* lust at work: there were typically women around him who were happy to initiate these trysts.[14]

Munya believed in Rasputin's powers from the moment they met and never doubted him for the rest of her life. "There is a man who lives among us," she wrote, who has voluntarily taken upon himself all of our burdens and carries the responsibility for them before God, giving Him all of himself, and receiving in return from God all those rich spiritual gifts with which he nourishes us, and from people, for whose benefit he is forever offering up himself as a victim, he receives only taunts, lack of understanding, coldness, ingratitude, and malice! For his boundless love and compassion for people, he is repaid with suspicion that touches upon the basest feelings, feelings that for him—God's servant and chosen one—have not existed for a long time! Slander has always pursued him and always will, for in this is his great exploit and all of God's true holy men have always been persecuted, hunted, judged, and condemned![15]

Of course, not everyone could perceive Rasputin's gifts. Olga Golovina, Munya's sister, for example, felt a certain disappointment in herself for being indifferent to Rasputin. This introduced a painful emotional distance between Olga and her sister and mother. "Look at Munya," she told the writer Vera Zhukovskaya, "she's so calm and happy, and I race about and cannot find any moral support for myself anywhere."

Zhukovskaya, a recent gymnasium graduate, met Rasputin several times for her own literary-sociological research as well as her interest in collecting erotic and other experiences deemed taboo for a young lady of her class. Rasputin, so she wrote later, was smitten with her and tried to get her into his bed. "I cannot do a thing without caresses," he told her, "because one gets to know the soul through the body."[16] She claimed she resisted all his advances, although not everyone has been willing to take her at her word.[17] The Commission went so far as to characterize Zhukovskaya as "a sex-maniac and Satanist."[18]

Zhukovskaya got to know the women of Rasputin's circle and observed their interactions. Rasputin told her that Lokhtina was his "heavy cross." He had taken away all her sin and now she was clean, yet all those sins he had taken upon himself. It was the sacrifice he made to save her. She watched how he groped the ladies gathered around his table; how his indecipherable words were met with cries of "Oh, father, father, your words are holy!"; and how they trembled with anticipation to receive from his hand the sugar for their tea. Once, Sana Pistolkors, Anna Vyrubova's sister, insisted she needed to talk to Rasputin in private, and he followed her into his room, his hand on her bottom. The rest of them continued conversing as sounds of Sana's embarrassed laughter wafted out of his bedroom, followed by soft moans and the creaking of a bed. The cheeks of the women around Zhukovskaya turned red. Zhukovskaya could not begin to fathom why they all went along with such things.[19] She said he had as many as four women at a time in bed with him. He would send his women out in the daytime to confession, and then have them come to him at night. Those who refused to come to his bed were forced to pray with him until they were convinced of the holiness of his actions. Zhukovskaya said she purposely tried to arouse Rasputin to see what he was capable of doing. Once, he grabbed her and dragged her into his bedroom and tried to force her to lie down in his bed. She refused, and he did not insist. Just in case, however, she kept a dagger on her person.

Zhukovskaya's words are evocative, but are they to be believed? Sergei Melgunov, no defender of Rasputin, met Zhukovskaya through Prugavin and came to the conclusion that, "She is a proper hysteric, one must approach her words with great skepticism."[20] Her descriptions of Rasputin's debauchery appear greatly exaggerated. One point in her discussion that warrants highlighting, however, is how Rasputin stopped trying to seduce her when Zhukovskaya resisted. Other women have made similar comments. Their testimony casts doubt on the allegations of Rasputin's violence against women and sexual assault, charges that, though they cannot be disproven, do not seem to have any basis. Another point worth mentioning is that not a single woman ever came forward as being pregnant with Rasputin's child. It is a startling fact. If he did indeed have the dozens of lovers attributed to him, it seems unlikely that none of them would have gotten pregnant. And it is also curious that his enemies never accused Rasputin of siring illegitimate children. Had this been the case, they most certainly would have publicized it.

Thirty-two-year-old Yelena Dzhanumova, the wife of a Moscow merchant, turned to Rasputin in the spring of 1915 to help her German-born mother, exiled by the state at the outbreak of the war. At their first meeting he fell for her, which the other women in their company noticed with a touch of jealousy. He called her the "black beauty." In one of his notes, he wrote to her: "Don't flee love—it's your mother."[21] That autumn she visited Petrograd without telling Rasputin. When he found out he was furious. "When he is angry, his face gets a predatory expression, his facial features become cragged. His eyes grow dark with dilated pupils, which seem to be bordered with a light rim. His mood, however, got better little by little. His wrinkles smoothed and his eyes began shining with sly kindness and care. He has a surprisingly changeable and expressive face."

At table, she was stopped from putting sugar in her cup by Akilina Laptinskaya, who took her hand and then turned to Rasputin: "Bless it, father." He put his fingers in the sugar bowl and then dropped a cube in her tea. "That's God's grace when father himself gives you sugar with his own hands," Akilina told her, upon which all the other women extended their cups to him. When the women got up to leave, they all kissed his hand and he kissed them on the lips. They requested bits of his dried bread, which they carefully wrapped in paper or handkerchiefs and tucked in their handbags. A few of the women asked Dunya Pecherkina in advance for special mementos—some of his dirty underclothes: "A bit dirtier, the most worn-out things, Dunyasha, the ones with his sweat on them," they instructed. Dunya handed them each an item of clothing wrapped in paper. "I felt as if I'd escaped a madhouse. I don't understand a thing, my head's spinning," Dzhanumova confessed.

For months Dzhanumova visited Rasputin in the hope he would help her mother, but in the end nothing came of it. Rasputin, she later wrote, made efforts to get her into his bed, but she resisted and he did not press the matter, but turned his amorous attentions to her friend Lelya. But strangely, even once she knew there was no good reason to keep seeing him, she and Lelya found it hard to stop. She had to admit that she was fascinated by his perspicacity. He could read her mind, just as people had said, and he often knew just what to say. Even when she told herself she was not going to see him, she would find herself at his door. It was bizarre, something she could not explain. "It was as if my will was paralyzed. What was really strange: both of us don't believe in him and are very critical but in his presence we both feel an acute interest to everything that happens around him. This is very unusual and attractive."[22]

Dzhanumova did not include everything about her relationship with Rasputin in her memoirs. On 8 December 1915, Okhrana agents observed Dzhanumova dining with Rasputin, the publisher Filippov, and several others at the Petrograd restaurant Donon. From there, Rasputin, Dzhanumova, and a few other ladies returned to Dzhanumova's hotel.[23] The police report is silent about how long Rasputin stayed that night.

There was another class of women Rasputin came to know during his years in the capital as well. The following report is based on police surveillance of Rasputin between January 1912 and January 1913: "Rasputin did not often go out alone, but when he did, he usually made his way to the Nevsky Prospect or other streets where there are prostitutes, and accosted them, then took one of them and went with her to a hotel or bath. During Rasputin's first trip in 1912, surveillance of him revealed six such incidents, whose particular characteristics are as follows [. . .]"

The report then gives a long list of Rasputin's debauched habits:

On 4 February [1912], on leaving the prostitutes Botvinkina and Kozlova /house no. 11, Sviechny Lane/ Rasputin went straight to the Golovins' in the company of some others. He left there after two hours and went to the Nevsky Prospect, where he again picked up a prostitute and went with her to the baths on Konyushennaya Street.

On 6 February, Rasputin left Zinaida Manshtedt, with whom he spent an hour and a half, and went straight to the Nevsky Prospect, where he picked up the prostitute Petrova and went with her to the baths at house no. 26 on the Moika.

Another report from 1912 states that on 21 November Rasputin picked up two different prostitutes in less than hour. The police apparently interrogated the first of them, who told the police that Rasputin bought her two bottles of beer, asked her to undress, and then looked at her naked body for a short while before paying her two rubles and leaving. By January 1913, the police were reporting that Rasputin was no longer trying to be cautious about his acts, but was soliciting prostitutes openly and was at times drunk on the streets, going so far once as "to answer a call of nature on the porch of the church."[24]

The spiritual advisor to the Romanovs soliciting prostitutes on the capital's main thoroughfare. Is it possible? Indeed, some historians have recently begun to insist that it is not and that the police records in the archives are not as straightforward as historians have thought. The police surveillance documents comprise two types: the hand-written notes of the agents engaged in the actual surveillance of Rasputin on the street, and the typed, redacted reports created later based on these original notes. The redacted reports were drafted by officials within the police apparatus for their bosses at the Okhrana and the ministry of the interior, and it is precisely only these reports that have been published and cited in almost every biography of Rasputin as proof of his frequenting prostitutes.[25]

Rasputin's defenders assert that these reports are mendacious fakes, pure fabrication, and are to be seen as just another instance of the scurrilous campaign to destroy Rasputin in the eyes of the tsar. As proof, they point to the fact that none of the original hand-written agent notes have survived, which, according to them, proves they were all destroyed since they would have proven the baselessness of the reports.[26] It is a bold but false notion, for hundreds of pages of the original notes *have* in fact survived in the police files in the State Archive of the Russian Federation.[27] And these notes show that Rasputin did indeed visit prostitutes. One example: police inspector Shilnikov recorded observing Rasputin pick up two prostitutes on 9 January 1913 "in the courtyard of house No. 14 on Yamskaya Street." Immediately after, the identities of the two women were established—one Maria Lysoeva and Nadezhda Lashkova. Shilnikov wrote in his note that the police would investigate the two women's backgrounds.[28]

Another report from 1914:

Glazovaya St., h. No. 2, apt. 5.
        On 5th October Rasputin came here with a prostitute he picked up on the corner of Nevsky Prosp. and Sadovaya St. and spent 30 min. here with her, was very cautious. /Identity of prostitute is being looked into/.[29]

One could produce many more agent reports documenting Rasputin's visiting prostitutes. Based on one police file in the manuscript division of the Russian National Library, in 1913 Rasputin visited the following prostitutes: Anna Petrova, Natalya Safronova, Maria Voronina, Maria Trusova, Maria Lysoeva, Yelizaveta Galkina, and Nadezhda Lashkova.[30]

Another name that comes up in the reports is Vera Tregubova. One agent recorded observing Rasputin paying a call to the prostitute Tregubova at 8 Pushkinskaya Street at 10:15 a.m. on 11 March 1915.[31] Another report referred to her as a twenty-six-year-old "heavily made-up Jewess," married, although she does not live with her husband, and a woman of "loose morals." We know that Rasputin saw Tregubova often, but was she a prostitute? Tregubova was apparently a classically trained singer seeking Rasputin's help in landing a position with the Imperial theater, which was loath to hire Jews. She told the Commission Rasputin agreed to help her, but only if she would come to him at night. She knew what he was after and claimed that she refused his offer. The police, however, reported that on 26 May 1915 she was seen arriving in an automobile at Rasputin's house. Before exiting the vehicle, Rasputin, who appeared to be drunk, "Kissed Tregubova passionately upon parting and patted her on the cheek." (The report goes on to say that Rasputin next told the wife of the building custodian to send the dressmaker Katya in apartment 31 to his place. Katya, however, was not home.)[32] And at least one woman who saw Rasputin and Tregubova together was convinced by their behavior that they were lovers.[33]

Sergei Melgunov described Tregubova as Rasputin's "secretary," and there is other evidence to suggest that this, and not sex-for-favors, was the basis of their relationship.[34] The police reported that Tregubova had no official employment, but used her connections to Rasputin to sell introductions to wealthy people, chiefly other Jews, for which she made about three hundred rubles a month. This was the reason for her almost daily visits to his apartment.[35] In the end, Rasputin turned on Tregubova. She informed the Commission that in January 1916 after refusing to agree to "intimate relations with him," an angry Rasputin told Stepan Beletsky, then deputy minister of the interior, to have her sent away from the capital, which he did. It is also possible that she had given herself to him, and once the chase was over Rasputin grew bored and wanted her gone.[36] The ultimate truth lies beyond what the documentary evidence allows us to reconstruct. Similar questions might be asked about other women in Rasputin's orbit. Take, for example, Yevfrosinya Dolina (aka Dlin or Dlin-Dolina). Rasputin met her in November 1915 at Petrograd's Hotel Select and she is described in the agents' reports as not only a con artist and prostitute, but someone involved in child sex-trafficking. There is no solid evidence in the police files, however, to substantiate these charges.[37] The police called Yevgenia Terekhova a "courtesan," yet it stretches credibility to imagine a Petersburg prostitute was also responsible for establishing and then managing her own hospital for wounded soldiers in Moscow. Clearly, the Okhrana agents were too quick to affix labels to the women around Rasputin, although the fault lay less with them and more with their superiors intent on digging up as much dirt on Rasputin as possible, generally with little regard for the truth.

The agent reports also document Rasputin's frequent trips with women to the city's baths, something Rasputin himself freely admitted to, unlike his picking up streetwalkers. Georgy Sazonov, with whose wife Rasputin apparently visited the baths, once asked him whether these stories were true, to which he replied yes, "'I don't go with them on my own, but we go as an entire group.' In response to my persistent questions as to why he did this, Rasputin told me he considered pride the greatest sin; society ladies were, without a doubt, overflowing with this sin and so to strip them of this sin one had to humble them by forcing them to go to the baths with a dirty peasant."[38]

Did Rasputin go to the baths for sex? Quite possibly. But if he did, he was not alone. Grand Duke Konstantin Konstantinovich (aka K. R.), a closeted homosexual with a wife and nine children, liked to cruise for men at the baths, taking them into one of the private cubicles for anonymous sex.[39] Konstantin also kept a steam bath in his home and would force the young male attendants there to have sex with him as well. It is clear from the grand duke's diary that their feelings on the matter were secondary to his pleasure. He especially enjoyed sex with men of a much lower social rank, which was nothing new: for centuries aristocratic men in Russia had used their serfs, male and female, for their own physical pleasure. It was seen as their birthright. It was an entirely different matter, however, to switch these roles, and this helps explain much of the anger directed at Rasputin. Here was a male peasant fondling (and a good deal more) aristocratic women in the salons of the imperial capital. It was an outrage, an inversion of the natural order of things, a sign of utter social collapse. Rasputin's critics were universally blind to the social prejudice that shaped their attitude to his relations with women.

Rasputin's long-suffering wife seems never to have complained about any of her husband's behavior. Aaron Simanovich, one of Rasputin's secretaries, maintains the couple got on well throughout their entire marriage. Praskovya never became jealous or angry at her husband, even when he would grope other women in front of her. She accepted it all. Such was her man. "He can do what he wants," she supposedly told Simanovich, "he's got enough in him for everyone."[40] The artist Theodora Krarup, who had nothing but respect for Rasputin and insisted he never once behaved inappropriately toward her, said something similar. She knew Praskovya well, describing her as "a plain and quiet peasant woman, whose being and attitude toward life had not altered under the unusual circumstances" of her husband's life. As Krarup saw matters, it was the women who chased after Rasputin more than the other way around, a fact that at times became something of a burden for him, although one, it would seem, he did not mind all that much.[41]

He did indeed have enough for everyone, of this it seems there is little doubt. But did this spring from his own desire for pleasure or from something else? In her confession presented by Feofan to the emperor as proof of Rasputin's evil debauchery, Khionya Berladskaya said something startling. After forcing her to lie with him as only a wife should, she asked Rasputin if there were not some other way to free herself from passion, to which he replied no. And then she realized that he had not done this for himself, that he did not even enjoy it, but her sin had brought it out of him, that it was his duty to act this way with her until she had freed herself entirely of the passion of the flesh.[42] Did she really mean this or was this a case of blaming the victim? It is hard to know. Once while walking with the wife of a clergyman in Pokrovskoe, Praskovya came upon her husband in the embrace of another woman. The clergyman's wife was shocked, though Praskovya purportedly was not, saying with quiet resignation: "Each must bear his cross, and this is his."[43]

42. Dinner with Rasputin

The Okhrana noted that upon Rasputin's return to Petrograd from Moscow at the end of March 1915 he began spending a good deal of time with his friend Alexei Filippov. The two men were then preparing for publication a collection of Rasputin's writings documenting his trip to the Holy Land under the title *My Thoughts and Reflections*.[1] (In connection with this event Rasputin was also sitting for the sculptor Naum Aronson, who was preparing a bust of the author.)[2] About the time Rasputin's book appeared, Filippov organized a dinner party at his home for Rasputin and a select gathering of journalists and writers. Among the guests were Vasily Rozanov, acquainted with Rasputin since their first meeting in 1906 at the Medveds; Alexander Izmailov, literary critic for the *Stock Exchange Gazette*; the playwright Anatoly Kamensky; and Nadezhda Lokhvitskaya, better known by her nom de plume, "Teffi," from the *Russian Word*. The guests, who included the heads of a few large cinematographic companies and a major publishing house, as well as four beautiful women "of a Balzacian age," to quote Izmailov, arrived at Filippov's home at 18 Sadovaya Street around 9:45 p.m. on the evening of 9 April.[3]

Teffi later set down a detailed account of that evening.[4] The idea for the party, she wrote, belonged to Ivan Manasevich-Manuilov (aka the Russian Rocambole), long Rasputin's foe and now on the edge of his circle with designs about moving to the center. At first Teffi was reluctant to attend; she had little interest in meeting Rasputin but in the end she let Izmailov talk her into it. The night before the party she had been invited to dine with a group of acquaintances. While at table she was surprised by a sign hanging over the dining room fireplace that read "Rasputin Is Not Discussed Here." She had seen such signs in other homes, but wanted to discuss Rasputin, whom she was to meet the next day, and so decided to break protocol, reading the sign aloud in a slow, steady tone: "Ras—pu—tin is not dis—cuss—ed he—re." Her attempt to open up the topic fell flat, however, and no one dared break the rule.

Later, once they had withdrawn from the dining room, a young "Lady E" approached Teffi and began to tell her of her experiences with Rasputin. She was a maid-of-honor at court, she said, and had met him two or three times. She was entranced by the man, his gaze gave her "heart palpitations," and he had invited her, insistently, to come to see him, but she did not dare. Talking about Rasputin, Lady E became terribly agitated, all of which Teffi found quite bizarre and hard to understand.

When Teffi arrived at Filippov's, the others were already there seated in a small, smoky room. She had put on her finest clothes and jewelry, per Rozanov's request, so she would appear like a society lady and not a writer, the goal being not to frighten Rasputin in front of a gathering of journalists. (Filippov had apparently not been completely forthcoming with Rasputin about his guests.) Rasputin, too, had already arrived, wearing a black cloth Russian caftan and his trademark tall glossy boots. Like everyone else, she could not help noticing his eyes: they shined so intently she could not even be sure of their color. He seemed agitated and nervous, his gaze taking everyone in and trying to gauge their reaction to him. He began to speak what she called "ceremonial words."

> "Yes, yes. I want to leave as soon as possible for home, to Tobolsk. I want to pray. One can pray well at home in my village, and there God hears your prayers. [. . .] And here's nothing but sin. You can't pray here. It's hard when you can't pray. Oh, it's hard. Nothing but vanity here. I don't like it. It's always the same. You come here from the village and everything you've accumulated you waste."
>
> "You mean in the spiritual sense, of course?" Izmailov asked.
>
> "Of course, in the spiritual," he confirmed emphatically, dismissing the mere thought of material want. "I love the village. I love the simple life of the village. You're a learned man, have read the Psalms, there it's all said quite well. There, in the village, I have the forest, and my own livestock, and birds. Good for the soul. And here one's always around people."

The way he looked at them Teffi had the suspicion that he was on to them and knew they were all journalists. She began to feel uncomfortable and wanted to leave. They moved to the dining room and sat down to fish soup and white wine. Rasputin was served first. They all raised their glasses and politely said cheers. Izmailov wrote: "He suddenly became lively, simple, gay, his eyes began to laugh and shine. His big rough peasant hands patted his sides and shoulders a bit nervously, just as if he were cold. There wasn't the least attitude or grandeur about him—he was just himself, a savage, who was happy, and he had turned to his interesting female neighbor, next to whom he had purposely been seated."

The neighbor was Teffi, no longer young, but still quite pretty. She, Filippov figured, had the best chance to get Rasputin talking. Rozanov, on her other side, kept whispering in her ear to move the conversation toward "erotic topics." He told Teffi, "He'll be interesting on such things. Now *that* we'll want to listen to." Filippov came around and filled their glasses with wine and offered hors d'oeuvres. At the far end of the table sat a few musicians. "Grisha likes to dance sometimes, especially when there's music," the host explained to his guests. "These musicians have even played for Yusupov. They're excellent musicians." Teffi noticed Rasputin began to drink a lot and fast. He leaned over and whispered: "Why aren't you drinking? Go on, drink. God'll forgive you. Go on, drink." Teffi told him she did not like wine, but Rasputin kept on encouraging, or rather instructing, her to drink. Curious, Rozanov leaned over and asked what Rasputin was saying. He wanted Teffi to tell Rasputin to speak louder since he could not hear him. When she told him his words were not worth hearing, an exasperated Rozanov replied: "Get him on to erotica. Lord! Do you really not know how to lead a conversation?"

Teffi turned back toward Rasputin.

. . . two sharp Rasputin eyes, cutting me off, pierced me.

"What, you don't want to drink? Oh, how stubborn you are. You won't drink when I tell you."

Then, with a fast, apparently habitual, movement he gently touched my shoulder. In a word, he's a hypnotist and was trying to transfer by touch the power of his will.

And this was not by accident.

Teffi remained unresponsive. Lady E had already described his particular method to her. She simply raised her eyebrows and smiled back at him, calmly. Rasputin fell silent and looked away, offended and angry, as if he were done with her. But then he turned back: "Ah, so you laugh, but your eyes are, do you know what? Your eyes are sad. Listen, tell me, does he torment you? Well, why are you silent? Ah, we all love little tears, we love women's tears. Understand? I know everything." Teffi asked him what it was he knew, loudly, hoping it would prompt Rasputin to reply at the same volume and so please her other neighbor. But he kept on in almost a whisper: "How we are tormented by love. And how we must torment each other, I know all that. But I don't want your suffering. Understand?" An angry Rozanov grumbled in Teffi's ear: "I can't hear a thing!" Rasputin went on: "When you come to me, I'll tell you much you didn't even know." Teffi told him she would not be coming. His method for luring her to his apartment echoed the same tricks he had tried with Lady E, and Teffi was not going to fall for it. But Rasputin did not give up, telling Teffi she was certain to come.[5]

The party raised their glasses and drank a toast, after which Rasputin handed out printed copies of his poetry. Teffi called them "verses in prose in the style of 'Song of Songs,' vague love poetry." She could later only recall one phrase: "The mountains are beautiful and high, but my love is higher and more beautiful, for love is God." She told Rasputin she liked them, and he was visibly pleased. He wrote the poem out for her on a fresh piece of paper and then signed it. He told her to save it, and she did, later taking it with her into exile in Paris. Rozanov saved one of Rasputin's verses titled "On Love":

> My love—is bright like the sun, and my friend, whom I love, for whom I've long been dying, is greater than the sun: the sun warms, but the love for my friend, it caresses and cuddles.
> Marvellous mountains and marvellous places—are they not created by love.
> Still, my love is brighter and higher than the mountains.
> Upon your word, Lord, You gave them out of love.
> I am certain, by my singular joy from the love of the Lord, that despite all this height and all this truth
> Love is greater than everything.[6]

"Well, he's another Knut Hamsun!" one of the women exclaimed, to which came a reply from another: "Or Rabindranath Tagore!"* Izmailov noticed the praise made Rasputin as happy as a little child.

Rasputin flirted with Teffi the entire evening. At one point he put his hand on hers and slipped off her ring. He teased her, saying he would not give it back unless she came to see him the next day. Teffi was not

---

* The Bengali poet, writer, and composer was the first non-European to win the Nobel Prize for Literature, in 1913.

playing, however, and told him to hand it over, for there was no chance of her coming to see him, whatever he might take from her.

An upset Filippov hurried into the room and told Rasputin there was a telephone call for him from Tsarskoe Selo. Rasputin went out. As they waited, Rozanov kept giving instructions to the others; he especially wanted them to ask about the rituals of the khlysty. But Rasputin did not return to the table and departed directly for the palace. However, before he left he gave Filippov a message: "Don't let her go. Have her wait. I'll be back." Teffi and the others, however, did not stay once Rasputin had gone.

Teffi told her friends about the strange evening, and they were all fascinated and full of questions. They were shocked to hear her impression of him was so negative and urged her to be cautious, noting how powerful and important he was and that it would not be wise to upset him in any way.[7]

Someone (Manuilov, perhaps) gave an account of the party to the *Petrograd Courier* that ran the very next day. The article—"Gr. Rasputin Among the Journalists"—named some of those in attendance and gave a generally positive, though largely erroneous, characterization of the proceedings.[8] Anatoly Kamensky used the material gathered that evening for a new play titled *Maybe Tomorrow*. It was set to premiere on 8 December 1915 at Petrograd's Yarovskaya Theater, but the production was stopped by order of Deputy Minister of the Interior Stepan Beletsky, apparently after hearing about it from an irate Rasputin. Changes were made to the script (the lead was changed from a Russian to a Swede), and the play was permitted to go ahead, but the public saw right through the changes and no one was fooled as to the identity of the hero. Eventually, the play was banned throughout Russia, supposedly at the insistence of Rasputin and Vyrubova.[9]

On the night of 10–11 April, agents of the Petrograd Okhrana carried out a search of Filippov's apartment, confiscating letters and photographs and questioning Filippov about just what had taken place during his party. Filippov admitted to hosting the event, but insisted nothing illegal or immoral had taken place and that he was a loyal subject of the emperor.[10] The reasons for the search are not exactly clear, although it appears the Okhrana was chiefly interested, as was described in one of the files on the incident, in finding "a gramophone record made on a 'Dictaphone' of an account by Grigory RASPUTIN-NOVY about how he visits and is received at the IMPERIAL Court." No such record was ever found, and in the end the Okhrana let Filippov go.[11]

Three or four days later Izmailov called Teffi. The evening had been a flop, he said, but they wanted to do it again since Rasputin had had to leave so suddenly. Teffi agreed to come. This time there were more people. Rasputin was glad to see Teffi, though he scolded her for not waiting for him the other night. As they sat chatting, the musicians began to play—"And at that very moment Rasputin leapt up," Teffi wrote.

> He leapt up so fast he knocked over his chair (it was a large room), and suddenly he began to jump and dance, he bent his knees and began to kick his legs out, his beard shook, and around and around he went . . . His face was contorted, tense, he hurried and his jumping was out of time with the music, as if he was not ruled by his own will, frenzied, he was unable to stop . . .
> Yet still he leapt, twirled, and we all watched . . .
> [. . .]
> No one laughed. We all watched, practically frightfully, and, at least, with the utmost seriousness.
> The sight was so awe-inspiring, so wild, that gazing upon him, one wanted to come alive and throw oneself into the circle, and to leap and twirl just like him, as long as one's energy could last.[12]

Rozanov, seated behind Teffi, said: "Well, can there be any doubt after this? He's a khlyst!" And as suddenly as he started, Rasputin stopped and fell exhausted into a chair. He drained a glass of wine as he circled the room with his "crazed eyes."

Rasputin had always loved to dance. "When the infectious melody of a gypsy band, accompanied by the shrill voices of a women's chorus, drove him into a paroxysm of excitement," his daughter Maria recalled, "he would dance with that frenzy, that ardour, that poignant joy that today is only found in the dances of the Cossacks and gypsies."[13]

The singer Alexandra Belling recalled the same thing. "I played and watched Rasputin. He could not sit quietly and watch people dance. He had trouble controlling himself, and his knees jerked, his hands jumped up from his body, which was ready to twirl in a demon's dance. [. . .] When he danced his face was inspired; one sensed that this was not just dancing for him, but some sort of prayerful ecstasy. He moved about the room with an elemental force, waving his arms and infecting the choir with his indefatigability."[14]

Dance went together with drink for Rasputin, chiefly wine, Madeira in particular. "I love wine," he admitted in 1916, and he never hid his fondness for the bottle.[15] But he was not the typical Russian drunk. Maria noted how he loved to dance when he was drunk and did it exceptionally well. He never lost his senses when inebriated, and drink did not make him crude or angry, but seemed to inspire him. Indeed, she noticed how he never spoke so beautifully about God as when he was drunk. She noted that her father had quit drinking as a pilgrim, but then started again once he began visiting St. Petersburg. There is evidence to suggest that his drinking grew following Guseva's attack. Part of this can be explained as a way of coping with the lingering pain of his wound, part as a way of coping with the stress of knowing he was a marked man. Rasputin fell deep into dipsomania in the last two years of his life, chiefly in an attempt to numb, if only briefly, the fear growing inside him as the voices calling for his destruction grew ever more intense and urgent. Most of the time he drank in restaurants and when at friends', although he also drank at home on occasion. Maria wrote that the tsarist family knew about his drinking, but never judged him for it and, it seems, never even spoke to him about it. His family, on the other hand, did, but he would always brush off their concerns. His daughter was convinced part of his excessive drinking in his later years was connected to a foreboding sense of looming catastrophe.[16]

Others confirm Maria's words about her father's drinking. Prince Mikhail Andronikov told the Commission that Rasputin could down a bottle of Madeira and show no signs of being intoxicated and would behave quite properly, never losing any control over himself. He said he never once saw the least thing "foul" in Rasputin's relations with alcohol.[17] Petrograd Okhrana chief Konstantin Globachev, on the other hand, insisted that Rasputin in fact did lose his senses and become helplessly drunk, although he did note that he had seen with his own eyes how a drunk Rasputin could miraculously sober up in minutes, something he had no way of explaining. And even after a night of wild partying, Rasputin could visit the baths first thing in the morning, go home to sleep no more than two hours, and be completely refreshed and full of vigor for the day.[18] Filippov commented on how by 1914 Rasputin was drinking heavily—and for a time turned Filippov's apartment into "a virtual bar room"—but he too remarked with amazement how when drunk Rasputin was never loutish, rude, or violent, and how following a night of carousing he was his usual, energetic self the next day despite having had almost no sleep.[19]

Drink, dance, and God went hand in hand for Rasputin. To lose himself in movement and intoxication was similar to losing himself in prayer. "He would be driven on in the dance by the surge of feeling that the music awakened in him," Maria remembered,

> and this intoxication of rhythm in his spirit was not very far removed from the religious transports which at other times he was capable of feeling. In the same way my father did not separate religion from joy: his transports of exaltation often developed from pleasures of the most temporal kind, and when others thought him clumsy or ridiculous he felt rising in his soul an irresistible buoyancy hardly distinguished from the fervour of prayer.[20]

Rasputin's love of drink is a well-known side of his biography. Rarely commented upon, however, was his involvement in Russia's temperance movement. On more than one occasion Rasputin spoke out on the dangers of vodka and the need to fight against the age-old Russian scourge of drunkenness.[21] As early as 1907, Rasputin lent support to the establishment of a "Sobriety Society" in Pokrovskoe. In May 1914, the newspaper *Virgin Soil* reported that Rasputin and the Russian Monarchist Union had decided to launch a large temperance campaign, part of which would include its own daily newspaper and the creation of various temperance societies across Russia.[22] Rasputin responded to the stories then in the press in late May, stating: "As for the rumors you are talking about, I'll only say: where there's smoke, there's fire."[23] Ivan Churikov (aka Brother Ivanushka), a peasant from eastern Russia who in the 1890s began a temperance movement among the St. Petersburg poor, praised Rasputin's efforts against the scourge of the bottle in the pages of the *Petersburg Courier* that summer.[24] Interestingly, Churikov, like Rasputin, was no stranger to scandal. More than once he had been attacked in the press and the Duma as a dangerous sectarian, and quite possibly a khlyst, who hid behind the banner of temperance and healthy living to lead simple people into dangerous heresy.[25]

*

Rasputin stuck to Teffi the rest of the evening. He would not leave her alone and insisted, repeatedly, that she come see him, alone, not with Rozanov or the others. He promised to build her "a palace of stone."

I can do that. Palaces of stone. You'll see. I can do a great deal. Just come, for God's sake, and quickly. We'll pray together. Why wait! Everyone wants to kill me. When I go out on the street now, I look all around just to make sure I'm not being followed by some mug. Yes. They want me dead. Well so what! The fools don't understand who I am. A sorcerer? Well, perhaps. They burn sorcerers, so let 'em go ahead and burn me. One thing they don't understand: if they kill me, it's the end of Russia. They'll bury us together.

Teffi rode home with Rozanov. As they talked Teffi came to think that Rasputin was far from stupid; no, he was quite clever, cunning even. She became certain he had been pressing himself on her not for sex (or at least not primarily) but to turn her into his "new wife and peace-bearer." She would become his mouthpiece, Rasputin would dictate to her what he wanted the world to know, and she would have it published. Teffi had to admit the idea appealed to her. But if such an idea had ever existed in Rasputin's head, he never followed up on it, and they never saw each other again.[26]

43. The Religious Faces of Rasputin

Khlyst. That, according to Teffi, is what Rozanov exclaimed upon watching Rasputin dance and twirl. It may well have been what he said, but if that was indeed the case, then it was not in the spirit in which either Teffi or most Russians would have uttered it. No, for Rozanov, it was said with a sense of wonder.

He wrote of that night at Filippov's on 15 April how they had all been sitting and listening to the French actor Dezarie sing and play the guitar. Everyone was moved, but especially Rasputin. He called out, "Give me some paper!" And then dictated to his neighbor a note for the Frenchman: "Your talent comforted us all … Your talent is from God, but you don't understand this." Next, the party cried, "Grisha, dance." He began to dance "the Russian, with an artistry I had never seen before, not in any theater. [. . .] He's profoundly free, and looked no one in the eyes." A quiet, reserved young woman in black went up to Rasputin, and they began to dance. Everyone was clapping and cheering them on; she smiled. Izmailov whispered to Rozanov that she would give herself to him that night, and that would be "a tragedy." Rozanov thought to himself: "Ah, what tragedy? Who *dares* to judge when she wants it and he wants it?"

"Grisha is a brilliant musician," Rozanov wrote two days later. "There's no way he's a khlyst." Now no khlyst, Rozanov imagined he saw in Rasputin a modern-day Ilya Muromets, greatest of the medieval knights, the *bogatyri*, a mythic figure who combined enormous physical strength and courage with profound spirituality, a defender of the Russian land later canonized by the church. Rasputin was an incarnation of Old Rus', pre-Petrine Russia, before the adoption of European ideas, habits, technology. *Shtunda*, Rozanov called this new Russia introduced by Peter the Great in the early eighteenth century. Shtunda, from the German *Stunde*, "hour," meant discipline, self-control, getting up early, working all day; it meant clean floors, well-kept children, all neat and tidy and boring and dead. The Russian bureaucracy exemplified shtunda, Count Sergei Witte personified it.

But the starets Grisha is full of artistry, interest and wisdom, though he's illiterate.

Witte is an utterly vacant, dull man, but he works brilliantly and energetically. He cannot not work. He cannot stop. He even dreams of work in his sleep.

Grisha is brilliant and picturesque. But he lounges around with maidens and other men's wives, he does not want to and cannot "achieve" anything, he's full of "divine consciousness," he's perspicacious, he understands dance, he understands the beauty of the world, and is himself beautiful.

But he doesn't have an ounce of Witte's genius. "Grisha is the entire Rus'."[1]

Rozanov, according to one scholar, was perhaps the first "Rasputin of Russian literature, its enfant terrible." Along with the poet Nikolai Klyuev, he was the only great Silver Age writer who went against public opinion and embraced Rasputin. Anna Akhmatova sensed the two as kindred spirits, writing about the famous Petersburg cafe the Stray Dog: "I cannot vouch that Rozanov's eyeglasses didn't twinkle and Rasputin's beard didn't curl somewhere in the corner."[2]

Rozanov could not stop thinking about Rasputin after Filippov's parties. He kept returning to him again and again. At the end of April he wrote to Father Pavel Florensky, the theologian and polymath: "I saw Grigory Rasp[utin] two times [. . .] a remarkable impression, and 'all's clear.' He's no khlyst, absolute darkness, but still a brilliant peasant, and, of course, at Court it's much more interesting to talk with him than with some chamberlain. I liked everything about him."[3]

Rozanov had been examining Rasputin for some time. In an essay in his volume *The Apocalyptic Sect* published in 1914, Rozanov, drawing upon a recent encounter with Rasputin, thought he saw in him the founder of a new religion. Gazing upon Rasputin across the table surrounded by his devoted followers, Rozanov was reminded of the Zaddik, the righteous man of Hasidism. The Zaddik is not a rabbi, but a profound spiritual figure who commands the devotion of his followers. He is seen as one of those rare persons with a special connection to the divine, whose prayers are uniquely powerful and efficacious. Holiness flows through the Zaddik. The scraps from his plate are snatched by his votaries, for they are charged with the sacred. Some even collect bits of his clothing to bring his blessings upon their homes. People come to him for healing or for spiritual guidance, as well as more mundane favors and requests, making sure to bring with them the "pidyon nefesh," literally "redemption of the soul," some money to help support the Zaddik.[4]

Watching Rasputin, Rozanov believed he was witnessing the mystical birth of holiness: "We have here the emergence of the phenomenon of *holiness*. But that is not enough—it is the moment at which *religion begins* [. . .] the *essence* of 'religion,' the 'mysterious electricity' that it is born from and through which it manifests itself, and this is precisely 'holy' itself; in both the Hasidic Zaddik and this 'Petersburg sorcerer' we can clearly discern the beginning of all religions . . ."

Rasputin was a true "religious individual," unlike most Russian clergymen. Like the great prophets, he had displayed the "signs" of his proximity to God (his prayers, his healing), and this, according to Rozanov, combined with Rasputin's clear disregard for "the *European type* of religion," was what so horrified others. As for the question of his mistresses, here, too, Rozanov saw parallels with the Old Testament prophets. Did not Abraham sleep with Hagar, Sarah's slave, he asked, and his grandson Jacob, did he not have two wives at the same time— Rachel and Leah—and did he not have sexual relations, and children, with their handmaids? Yet these facts were simply "unimaginable" for the Russian mind, he noted.

In Rasputin, they were beholding an epochal reshaping of Russian religion:

> There is one thing that can *objectively* be said about the Siberian Pilgrim here, said in a "*scientific*" way, without searching for the origins of the matter, that is he turns all the "piety of Russia," which has been subconsciously built since the beginnings on asceticism, "abstinence," "not touching women," and generally the separation of sexes, toward the kind of Asian religious poetry and Asian wisdom (Abraham, Isaac, David and his psalms, Solomon and the Song of Songs, Mohammed), which not only did not separate the sexes but strongly aimed to unite them.

His power as a healer was but a small aspect of his story, the "*personal* side of the matter." Much more important was his historic mission for Russia: "In *history*, the Pilgrim is clearly carrying out an upheaval of faith, where 'everything is different' . . . That is why his 'manners' have gone much further than 'our limited ones.' [. . .] what is happening before the eyes of Russia is not an 'anecdote' but a *history* of terrible seriousness."[5]

Rozanov's interpretation of Rasputin was extreme, but at least one person shared it. After reading *The Apocalyptic Sect*, archpriest Alexander Ustinsky in Novgorod wrote the author with great praise: "You have correctly and perfectly understood and defined the mission of Grig. Rasputin in your book. It really is a genuine protest against the one-sidedness of our ascetic view and a live voice in favor of the ancient Biblical concepts of the relations between the sexes. I completely agree with your views. How wonderful are the last three pages of your book! May God help you struggle and win."[6]

The empress herself saw something of the Old Testament prophet in Rasputin as well. She told Lily Dehn: "Our Lord did not choose well-born members of Jewish society for His followers."[7] Jesus, too, had been castigated and shunned by the elite of his people.

Such opinions, however, were extremely rare. An appalled Hieromonk Serapion of the Novo-Niametsky Monastery in Tiraspol (Kherson province) wrote Rozanov on 4 March 1914 to say he found his book to be "just beastly." Rozanov did not know the first thing he was talking about when it came to religion, nor did he have any inkling about the true Rasputin. For that, Serapion directed him to Feofan and Mikhail Novoselov.

> The former had first-hand information (he even revealed it to the tsar but alas!—the psychosis had already taken hold at the palace) that this dissipated pilgrim had kissed women many times, and not only the upper lips but lower ones as well. He spread his "holy energy" through his penis. The latter printed the letters of the former "spiritual" daughters of this "starets" two years ago where all his adventures in the bathhouses were described in full detail; but unfortunately for the Russian church, the brochure was confiscated in the printing house. And if you truly love the church, your duty is to protect it from all manner of scoundrels for such "holy men" have never been (and will never be) part of it.

Rozanov scribbled on Serapion's letter: "Didn't David, or especially Solomon, do those things with women that Serapion describes Rasputin doing? [. . .] Rasputin in fact breaks asceticism. It's not important (for Serapion) that he's dissipated, what he's indignant about is that he prays at the same time."[8]

Poet Nikolai Klyuev went one better than Rozanov. He not only praised Rasputin, he wanted to be him. One of the so-called peasant poets along with Sergei Yesenin, Klyuev, who had ties to both the khlysty and skoptsy (self-castrators) and loved to dress in peasant garb and exaggerate his rustic accent, wrote a fanciful autobiographical work called "The Loon's Fate" of his life "from the peasant hut to the palace" that paralleled Rasputin's own, true path. Klyuev never met Rasputin, although he liked to let others think he had. Contemporaries did take note of their similarities, from the peasant roots, to connections (real or imagined) to subversive sects, to a certain theatricality, and a fantastical way of combining Eros and religion.[9] The comparisons were not always in Klyuev's favor. "Klyuev is a failed Rasputin," the poet Mikhail Kuzmin observed. The writer Alexei Remizov commented that Klyuev, "wants to make his way to the tsar along Rasputin's road," a destination he never reached.[10]

Klyuev was not alone among the literary class in claiming some connection to Rasputin, even if he did take it to the extreme. With Rasputin on everyone's mind, what self-respecting writer would not want to boast of his or her encounter with this omnipresent figure? Anna Akhmatova, for example, claimed she saw Rasputin once on the train from Petersburg to Tsarskoe Selo. "He had the appearance of a smartly dressed peasant headman, the closely set eyes of a hypnotist bore through your skull. Someone said: 'He's all dressed up for Sasha's birthday.'"[11] And Lili Brik, muse of the poet Vladimir Mayakovsky, also said she encountered Rasputin on the train to Tsarskoe Selo. He sat down next to her and began to ask all sorts of personal questions, so she claimed in her memoirs. "You be sure to come visit me, we'll drink some tea, don't be afraid." Brik desperately wanted to go, but her husband refused to allow it.[12] The two women might be telling the truth. Regardless, they make for good stories.

Khlyst, pilgrim, starets, bogatyr, prophet, Zaddik—and *yurodivy*, holy fool. "We are fools for Christ's sake," writes the Apostle Paul in his First Letter to the Corinthians (4:10–13). "You are held in honor, but we in disrepute. To the present hour we hunger and thirst, we are ill-clad and buffeted and homeless [. . .] When reviled, we bless; when persecuted, we endure; when slandered, we try to conciliate; we have become, and are now, as the refuse of the world, the offscouring of all things." An ancient cultural-religious figure inherited from Byzantium, the holy fool has no religious equivalent in the West. The yurodivye, having voluntarily adopted the guise of madness and an extreme asceticism, lived as outcasts, purposely engaging in shocking, blasphemous behavior intended to provoke the rebuke, and even physical attacks, of the community. In so doing, the holy fool, mimicking Christ, humbled his own pride while at the same time forcing his tormentors to confront their own moral failings as manifested through their persecution of the holy fool. Barefoot and dressed in rags, or at times naked, they spoke in riddles and obscure language, they prophesied, they disrupted church services, consorted with prostitutes, practiced sexual deviance, defecated in public, and reviled the proud and vain.[13]

The holy fool was an inherently ambiguous figure, and where some perceived true holiness, others saw a con. While a number of early Russian yurodivye were canonized after their deaths, beginning with the Westernizing reign of Peter the Great holy fools and holy foolishness (iurodstvo) were officially banned. The state began arresting holy fools, exiling, torturing, and even putting them to death. But holy foolishness survived, especially among the common people, into the twentieth century, and holy fools could be found at Russia's great monasteries and holy sites, places visited by a young Rasputin, who was clearly impressed, and shaped, by them.

Alexandra was convinced Rasputin was a holy fool, proof of which she found in a book by Hieromonk Alexei (Kuznetsov) titled *Holy Foolishness and Pillar Dwelling: A Religious-Psychological Study*, published in 1913. Alexandra devoured the book, underlining with a colored pencil the sections that struck her most powerfully, such as the author's comments about how some saints' holy foolishness expressed itself through sexual dissipation. She gave copies of the book to others, who knew immediately what they were supposed to take from it. Contemporaries dubbed the author a "Rasputinist" and argued the book was flawed (a point still made by some historians today), but this was not the case; the text was accepted as Alexei's dissertation and as late as 2000 was republished by the Trinity Monastery of St. Sergius, the most esteemed monastery in Russia.[14] This incident was indicative of how Alexandra tried to explain Rasputin's actions with reference to precedence. When Rasputin's fondness for kissing women was brought to her, she commented that "all people in the bygone era kissed everyone alike. Read the Apostles—they kiss all as welcome."[15]

The question of whether Rasputin was a holy fool is a complex one, like nearly everything about his character. Alexandra and Prince Zhevakhov saw him as such, although they appear to have been the exceptions among their contemporaries. Among today's leading scholars of the subject, a few have endorsed this view and include him among the ranks of modern-day holy fools, or at least recognize that he played within this ancient tradition.[16] Most of Rasputin's contemporaries, however, saw in his iurodstvo an empty show meant only to deceive. "There was never any genuine holy foolishness in Rasputin," Zinaida Gippius remarked, "but he played the holy fool constantly and with considerable gumption, weighing in his head just how much to put on."[17]

Part of the confusion can be attributed to the fact that the holy fool was by definition a paradoxical, enigmatic figure. Also important was the fact that Rasputin drew on a variety of religious sources and traditions. Rasputin attended no theological academy, he was no rigorous student of religion, he was never interested in doctrinal purity. He was exposed to many forms of religious life, and he took from all of them. Rasputin was nothing if not ecumenical. If there is one fact that speaks most loudly against Rasputin's designation as a holy fool it is his conventionality. By the time he arrived in Petersburg, Rasputin had given up the ascetic lifestyle. He kept a home, he looked after his wife and children, he went about fully clothed, and not in some raggedy shirt, the ultimate sartorial symbol of the yurodivy, but in fine silk ones hand made by the empress. He visited prostitutes and took lovers, but this appears to have been less out of a desire to shock than from a more straightforward desire for sex.

In the end, one thing remains beyond doubt: Rasputin's belief in God. Throughout his life Rasputin remained a man of great personal belief. "He often talked to us about God," his daughter Maria recalled.

> He said that God was our consolation in life but that we need to know how to pray in order to get this consolation. For a prayer to reach God, one had to be completely dedicated to his faith and should drive away all other thoughts. He said that not everyone can pray and that it was difficult. He often fasted and made us fast. During fasting he only had rusks and followed that strictly. He said that the fasting days are set not for health, as scientists say, but for the salvation of the soul.[18]

44. A Summer of Troubles

Nicholas was away from Tsarskoe Selo much of April and May 1915, and a lonely Alexandra came to rely increasingly on Rasputin for comfort. Her letters to Nicholas from this period show just how considerable his influence had become in a short time. Alexandra worried about Nicholas constantly and looked to Rasputin to keep him safe. When Nicholas left for Stavka on 4 April without the icon of St. John the Warrior given to him by Rasputin, she made certain to send it the very next day. Along with gifts of icons and other talismans, she would ask Rasputin to pray for the emperor on his journeys. That month Nicholas visited the recently gained territories around Lvov and Peremyshl, but asked Alexandra not to mention the trip to others. She could not help herself, however, and told Vyrubova so she might ask Rasputin to bless the tsar's journey with his "special prayers." And she did this more than once. In November of that year Nicholas went on another trip he wished kept secret and again she defied his wishes and told Rasputin, so that he "might guard you everywhere." Far from displeased, Nicholas wired Rasputin himself to thank him for his prayers and to bless him in return.

Rasputin offered more than just blessings and spiritual protection; he expressed his opinion on the wisdom of the trips themselves. When Vyrubova told Rasputin of the trip to Lvov and Peremyshl, he replied that the idea did not please him for it was too soon and the tsar would be wiser to wait until after the war. Rasputin had been right, for only days after the emperor's visit the lands were retaken by the enemy along with almost a quarter of a million Russian soldiers. The Russian tsar was placed in an embarrassing light after his triumphal tour. Rasputin also did not like the fact that Nicholas had traveled along with Grand Duke Nikolai Nikolaevich, and he made sure to let this be known. Both Rasputin and Alexandra were displeased with Nikolasha, whom they saw as acting too high and mighty as commander-in-chief, as if he were trying to usurp the authority of the tsar.[1] The man who had helped introduce Rasputin to Nicholas and Alexandra was now seen as one of their greatest foes.[2] On 24 June, she reminded Nicholas that he, not Nikolasha, was the emperor and so he could do as he pleased. The main thing was that Nicholas listen only to her and to "our Friend." It was imperative he not tell Nikolasha about his movements at the front, Alexandra instructed, for Nikolasha was surrounded by German spies at Stavka. She was certain these spies would communicate this information to the Germans who were readying their "aeroplanes" to bomb the emperor's automobile. The next day she urged Nicholas to return home from Stavka or he might well fall under the harmful sway of the grand duke: "Remember our Friend begged you not to remain long—He sees & knows N. through and through & your too soft and kind heart."[3]

Earlier that month the empress wrote Nicholas at Stavka with more advice. She told him the ministers "must learn to tremble before you— you remember M. Philippe and Grigory say the same thing too. You must simply order things to be done, not asking if they are possible [. . .] You know how talented our people are, how gifted—only lazy & without initiative, start them going, & they can do anything, only dont ask, but order straight off, be energetic for yr. country's sake." She continued:

> Therefore our Friend dreads yr. being at the Headquarters as all come round with their own explanations & involuntarily you give in to them, when yr. own feeling has been the right one, but did not suit theirs. Remember you have reigned long, have far more experience than they—N. has only the army to think of and success—you carry the internal responsibilities on for years—if he makes faults (after the war he is nobody), but you have to set all straight. No, hearken unto our Friend, believe Him, He has yr. interest and Russia's at heart—it is not for nothing God sent him to us—only we must pay more attention to what He says—His words are not lightly spoken—& the gravity of having not only His prayers, but His advice—is great.

Alexandra was referring here to a specific matter. By the spring of 1915, Russia had lost 3,800,000 men killed, wounded, or captured, and Nicholas was considering taking a second round of conscripts of men between the ages of twenty-one and forty-three, something that had not been done since Napoleon's invasion in 1812 and that would signal a sense of emergency. Moreover, such a massive conscription would deprive the country's fields and factories of much-needed manpower.[4] Alexandra saw Rasputin at Vyrubova's on the evening of 14 June and they talked for an hour and a half. As soon as she returned to the Alexander Palace she wrote to Nicholas with Rasputin's advice that by not calling up the new conscripts he would save his reign. Rasputin also told the tsar that the mounting shortage of artillery supplies could be solved if he simply ordered Russia's factories to make more and stopped discussing the matter with his ministers. He presented Alexandra with another talisman for Nicholas: "I send you a stick (fish holding a bird), which was sent to Him [Rasputin] fr. New Athos to give to you—he used it first & now sends it to you as a blessing—if you can sometimes use it, wld be nice & to have it in yr. compartment near the one Mr Ph[ilippe] touched, is nice too." She encouraged Nicholas to look to Rasputin whenever he was uncertain how to act: "If you have any question for our Fr. write at once. I cover you with fondest kisses. Ever yr. own Wify."

Rasputin's, and Alexandra's, chief concern that month was the series of ministerial changes Nicholas was considering. Heeding a popular groundswell against the poor prosecution of the war and the critical voices at Stavka, led chiefly by Nikolasha, Nicholas sacked several of his most reactionary ministers in the hope of winning public support. In the span of a month four men fell: Prince Nikolai Shcherbatov replaced Nikolai Maklakov as minister of the interior; General Alexei Polivanov replaced Vladimir Sukhomlinov as minister of war; Alexander Samarin replaced Vladimir Sabler as chief procurator of the Synod; and Alexander Khvostov replaced Ivan Shcheglovitov as minister of justice. Rasputin, quite rightly it turned out, feared the new ministers would be less than friendly. He barely slept for five nights after hearing the news. On 15 June, as Rasputin was preparing to leave Petrograd for Siberia, Alexandra wrote Nicholas that she was worried these men would be hostile to Rasputin and said that the talk of the replacements had made Rasputin "most anxious to know what was true." She also passed on a message for the emperor from Rasputin,

> that you are to pay less attention to what people will say to you, not let yourself be influenced by them but use yr. own instinct & go by that, to be more sure of yourself & not listen too much nor give in

to others, who know less than you. [. . .] He regrets you did not speak to Him more about all you think & were intending to do & speak about your ministers & the changes you were thinking of making. He prays so hard for you and Russia & can help more when you speak to Him frankly.

It is a remarkable message. Rasputin was instructing the tsar to ignore his ministers for his own instinct, instinct that Rasputin wished to be one of the first to know, clearly so that Rasputin could help shape and guide it in the direction he, and Alexandra, believed best.

The first change, on 5 June, was the sacking of Maklakov for Prince Shcherbatov. The timing is important, for it was just weeks after this that Dzhunkovsky began putting together the bogus Yar campaign against Rasputin. It is quite possible Dzhunkovsky found an ally in Shcherbatov, unlike the more Rasputin-friendly Maklakov, and told him of his plan, and the new minister of the interior gave him the green light to continue.[5] The ministerial change that caused Alexandra and Rasputin the greatest concern, however, was the appointment of Alexander Samarin, a figure closely linked both to Ella and to Sofiya Tyutcheva. Alexandra wrote Nicholas that "now the Moscow set will be like a spider's web around us, our Friend's enemies are *ours*." She informed her husband that Rasputin was furious when he learned of the decision and was in "utter despair." She too felt "wretched" over the decision and said she now fully understood why Rasputin had been against the tsar's leaving for Stavka, for had he remained with her she could have helped him make the right decision, but she knew the men at Stavka feared her influence and so lured him there. She instructed Nicholas to talk to Samarin "severely, with a strong and decided voice, that you forbid any intrigues against our Friend or talks about Him, or the slightest persecution, otherwise you will not keep him. That a true Servant dare not to go against a man his Sovereign respects and venerates." God will not forgive us, she warned Nicholas, if we do not protect our friend.

Alexandra's despair made her physically ill. Nicholas's decision had given her heart pains, she wrote, and she missed him terribly and wished he would look more often to her for guidance. She told Nicholas that now, alone without him and Rasputin, she was so grateful to have with her the icon with its bell given to her years ago by "our first Friend" (Monsieur Philippe) that rings whenever an enemy approaches. That

God wanted her to be a helpmate to him, of this she was certain, and both Philippe and Rasputin had told her so. They must listen to Rasputin's words: "Think more of Gr. Sweetheart, before every difficult moment, ask Him to intercede before God to guide you aright [. . .] You remember dans 'Les Amis de Dieu' it says, a country cannot be lost whose Sovereign is guided by a man of God. Oh let Him guide you more!"[6]

Rasputin's advice had been not to replace Sabler until a suitable candidate (one, that is, not opposed to Rasputin) had been found. But Nicholas went ahead anyway. He knew and liked Samarin, he respected him and believed he could help put an end to the troubles plaguing the church. The son of a famous Slavophile, Samarin was well educated, respected, and an unimpeachable Orthodox believer. Yet he was a Muscovite, beloved by his fellow nobles, and was widely known to be an anti-Rasputinist.[7]

Samarin traveled to Stavka to discuss the appointment. On 20 June, he told the emperor that his conscience would not allow him to accept the post as long as "near You, near Your family there is an unworthy man." Samarin concurred with the emperor when he asked whether Samarin considered him and Alexandra true Orthodox believers, but then he told the emperor that they had been duped by Rasputin: "Your Majesty, he is clearly a cunning man, and when before you he is not the same man as all of Russia knows him to be." Tears, according to Samarin, appeared on the tsar's cheeks. Nicholas intimated to Samarin it might be possible to remove Rasputin from Petrograd, to which he replied that if the emperor meant what he said, then this would require decisive measures to convince everyone that Rasputin's harmful influence in church affairs was finally and irrevocably over. The tsar was quiet for a time, and then he told Samarin that having thought it all over he still wanted him to accept the post of chief procurator. Samarin believed Nicholas had accepted his condition for agreeing to his request. He would soon be proven wrong.

Word spread at Stavka of the agreement that would mean the end of Rasputin. The entire entourage was ecstatic. When Nikolasha heard it from Protopresbyter Shavelsky that day, he jumped up and hurried to kiss his icon. "I could do a somersault for joy!" he said, laughing. Samarin visited Nikolasha in his railcar. "Today you are the most fortunate man in Russia. You have saved the Tsar. You have saved Russia," Nikolasha told him. He went on:

You know, he truly is a remarkable man. I was myself under his influence and studied all his teachings and could teach the Synod what this khlystovism is. My sister-in-law is especially knowledge-able about all this. She could acquaint you with this teaching very quickly. But I figured out what sort of man this was and turned away from him. Then he began to threaten me, saying he would make the Emperor angry at me. And in fact, he did just that, and for a time we did not see each other. No, you are the most fortunate man in Russia.[8]

Father Vladimir Vostokov, who happened to be the religious precep-tor to Samarin's children, wrote to Count Sergei Sheremetev, an aging pillar of Russian conservatism, that with this change "in the life of our church light will begin to shine in those dark places in which a debauched khlyst is considered a 'holy starets' with nearly unlimited authority over church affairs."[9] Father Alexander Vasilev, too, expressed hope for the church now that it would be under the direction of "a man with a clean, independent soul."

Rasputin had no choice but to accept Samarin's appointment. According to Samarin's daughter, he even tried to meet the new procur-ator in Petrograd at the end of July. He arrived at the Hotel Europe where Samarin was staying, bringing with him his old ally Varnava, bishop of Tobolsk. Out of respect for Varnava's office, Samarin agreed to receive him and came over to greet the bishop, but when he spotted Rasputin behind Varnava's back, he stopped short, pulled his hand away, saying: "I don't know you and won't shake your hand."[10] Whether or not the incident ever happened, the story does convey Samarin's true feelings for Rasputin.

Samarin's appointment was a clear, indisputable victory for Ras-putin's foes. Nevertheless, the myth of the all-powerful Rasputin had by now become so pervasive, that every decision at the highest levels was attributed to him, even if there was no way to explain it. On 21 July, for example, the head of the Tobolsk Provincial Okhrana reported to Dzhunkovsky that Rasputin had been overheard boasting several days earlier that Samarin had been chosen thanks solely to his, Rasputin's, influence.[11] Nothing, of course, could have been further from the truth.

Rasputin arrived in Pokrovskoe on 21 June accompanied by Okhrana agents Daniil Terekhov and Pyotr Svistunov. He entertained several guests three days later. The agents noted Rasputin drank, danced to the sound of his phonograph, and talked about how he had saved three hundred Russian Baptists who refused to join the army from punishment and was expecting to receive 5,000 rubles from each of them for his intervention. He also bragged about having convinced the emperor to hold off calling a new round of conscripts until the end of the summer once the harvest had been brought in. On the last day of the month he was visited by Bishop Varnava and Father Martemian, a monastery abbot, bearing two barrels of wine for their host.[12]

Terekhov and Svistunov functioned chiefly as bodyguards for Rasputin, necessary protection after Guseva's attack the previous year, and although they filed reports on Rasputin's general activities, they clearly were not trying to collect information on him. Dzhunkovsky, however, was not content with this arrangement. He had failed to get rid of Rasputin with the Yar campaign, but was not willing to concede defeat. On 1 July, the head of the Petrograd Okhrana, acting on Dzhunkovsky's instructions, sent an order to Colonel Vladimir Dobrodeev, chief of the Tobolsk Provincial Gendarmes, to establish clandestine surveillance of Rasputin and report back directly to him all important details for Dzhunkovsky. Dobrodeev passed the order on to his subordinate, Captain Kalmykov in Tyumen. Dobrodeev informed Kalmykov that he wanted to know everyone Rasputin was meeting with and the nature of their relations. He added that he was particularly interested to know "what he 'is preaching,' and whether he is saying anything against the current European war." Kalmykov in turn ordered Junior Officer Alexei Prelin to go to Pokrovskoe to begin gathering information.[13] Dzhunkovsky was determined to find something to use against Rasputin no matter what.

In July, a Jewish merchant named Wolf Berger visited Rasputin. When this was reported to Dobrodeev in Tobolsk, he instructed Kalmykov to look into the man's identity and the purpose of his visit: "What is the precise nature of the 'starets' Rasputin's relations with this yid?" he asked. It took some doing, but Kalmykov tracked Berger down to Minsk. He wrote the local authorities there for any information on Berger that might cast a shadow on Rasputin, but word came back that he was a patriotic and politically loyal subject.[14] There were other visitors that month, including the wife of Grigory Patushinsky from Yalutorovsk. The police believed she was trying to cultivate connections with Rasputin in the hope he might advance her husband's stalled career. They observed Rasputin and Patushinskaya, together with one

Yelizaveta Solovyova, the thirty-year-old wife of a Synod official, walking arm in arm about the village, drinking wine and listening to music on his phonograph. When Patushinskaya left, she was said to be seen "sensually" kissing Rasputin on his lips, cheeks, and even his nose and hands. On another occasion they watched Rasputin pay a visit to the wife of the sexton Yermolaev, remaining with her about thirty minutes for one of their "intimate meetings."[15]

None of this information, however, was damaging enough for Dzhunkovsky's purposes. The decision was made to increase the level of surveillance and plant a full-time set of eyes in the village. Prelin suggested they recruit thirty-seven-year-old Tatyana Sergeeva. She had helped the police four years earlier in their surveillance of Rasputin and was still living in the village, where she worked in a store. She had expressed a willingness to assist them again for a modest remuneration. Prelin thought she would be perfect for the job. He noted that Rasputin and his wife had stopped registering their guests with the village authorities, as was required by law, telling officials, "We don't have any tramps staying with us." Sergeeva would be in a good position to spy on the Rasputins and find out what was going on in their home. Prelin's plan was approved and Sergeeva set to work on 1 August.

Around this time Dobrodeev visited Dzhunkovsky in the capital. In a letter to Kalmykov, Dobrodeev wrote that Dzhunkovsky insisted they do a better job of monitoring Rasputin's talk and record any mention he made about the emperor. It was Dzhunkovsky's hope that they could find some sort of compromising information that could be used not only to keep Rasputin away from Petrograd, but even to give them cause to exile him further east into more distant reaches of Siberia.[16] The police in Siberia took the matter seriously and followed up on every possible lead. Prelin, for example, met in late July an old woman named Paraskeva Kryazheva who said that while traveling recently on a steamer she had overheard Rasputin say to another passenger—a peasant, it seemed—that all he had to do to stop the war was to tell the emperor. Prelin was instructed to find this Kryazheva and take her statement. The police tracked her down in Tomsk and in an interview she repeated what she had heard, informing them that the incident had happened while traveling from Tyumen to Tobolsk on the steamer *Comet* on either 23 or 24 July. There was nothing more, however, she could add to her story. Kalmykov was not satisfied and sent a letter back to the Tomsk Provincial Gendarmes, instructing them to question Kryazheva once more. He included a list of questions: 1. When exactly did he say these words? 2. Where on the steamer did this take place? 3. Under what circumstances? 4. What exactly did Rasputin say? 5. Who else heard it? 6. Who else did she tell this to? 7. Can she say who the man was that Rasputin said this to? The questions were put to Kryazheva, but she told them she had already shared with the police everything she knew and was unable to provide any additional details. With that, the trail went cold. Still, the police refused to give up and continued to investigate the matter until finally putting the case aside in October.

In August, the police began looking into a similar case, this time involving a peasant from Pokrovskoe named Vasily Raspopov. He had purportedly overheard Rasputin on a steamer the previous month "publicly, and without embarrassment, say that he knows quite well that the war will end badly for us." As soon as the police learned of this, another investigation was begun. This one, too, led nowhere. It turned out Raspopov had actually never heard Rasputin say this and was simply repeating some second-hand gossip.[17] After months of intensive work, the police still had nothing on Rasputin.

As for Rasputin, he was facing his own, deeply personal troubles. In late June he received a telegram informing him that his son Dmitry was to be called up into the army. He was devastated. "I said in my heart," he wrote to Alexandra, "am I like Abraham, of ages past, having one son and supporter. I hope he will be allowed to rule under me as with the ancient tsars." The concern was genuine, and it was not just for himself and his family, as the advice he gave in early June against calling up the second class of draftees, which would have been detrimental to the internal peace of the country, shows. Alexandra asked Nicholas to do something for the boy, but he refused, and Dmitry was drafted into the army.[18] On 27 July, Rasputin and Dmitry, along with Terekhov and Svistunov, left Pokrovskoe on horseback for Tyumen and from there by train for the capital, arriving on the last day of the month. That night they saw Nicholas and Alexandra at Vyrubova's.[19]

They came hoping to keep Dmitry out of the army. Rasputin took Dmitry to see a medical doctor who might declare Dmitry unfit for service, but his report, Rasputin learned the next month, attested that he was perfectly healthy.[20] In August, Dmitry was called up into the 7th Company of the 35th Infantry Depot Battalion. His parents were sick with worry. Praskovya feared she would never see her son again. Alexandra wrote to Nicholas: "Our Friend is in despair his boy has to go to the war,—the only boy, who looks after all when he is away."[21] In the end, strings were pulled to assure Dmitry was not sent off to the front, and in October he was assigned to a hospital train at Tsarskoe Selo, to the immense relief of his parents.[22]

If all of this were not enough, the summer of 1915 saw a new and unprecedented press campaign against Rasputin. Never before had the coverage been so intense, widespread, or sweeping in its accusations.

It began in June when the *Siberian Trade Newspaper* charged Rasputin with horse thieving as a youth. It was the first time this claim had ever been made in public, and an outraged Rasputin fired a letter off to the paper, which it printed under the title "The Anger of the Starets" on 29 July: "Tyumen. To the editor Krylov: Provide proof immediately where, when, and from whom I stole horses, as was printed in your newspaper. You are well informed, so I will wait for your answer for three days; if you do not answer, I know to whom to complain and with whom to speak. Rasputin."[23] At the same time Rasputin wrote to the deputy governor of Tobolsk about the article, asking that he either bring charges against him for the crime or punish Krylov "to the full extent." If this were not done, Rasputin threatened that he would "complain higher up."[24] Neither Krylov nor the vice governor took Rasputin seriously, and it appears Rasputin never followed through on his threats.

This article was the opening salvo in a much larger campaign. Over five days in mid-August the *Stock Exchange Gazette* ran two lengthy articles purporting to be reliable, thoroughly researched investigations into the life of Rasputin. The first, by a reporter named Lukyan, opened with the statement that the censors would not allow him to tell the whole story of Rasputin since "the pornography" about his women, his harem, and his sexual exploits was prohibited. Lukyan attacked the government's attempts to prevent the press from writing about Rasputin, "a completely private person who does not have any official post. [. . .] And since the press has been told, whether by a hint, or by telephone, not to mention Rasputin, the press knows that to ignore this instruction will be followed by a series of harsh repressive measures." But the press, according to Lukyan, had to take this risk and speak out since those who ought to in the first instance—be it Shcheglovitov, Maklakov, or Sabler—had all remained silent, thanks to their "infinite servility," or tried to distract the public through their attacks on Jews and other non-Christians.[25]

Angry though it was, Lukyan's piece was tame compared to what followed under the title "The Life of the Starets Rasputin." The author was given as Veniamin Borisov, although there is evidence to suggest the man hiding behind this moniker was Rasputin's foe Davidson.[26] Borisov wrote that the entire Rasputin clan was "criminal," that Rasputin's father had regularly been beaten "for theft and mischief," and that in his youth Rasputin had also been beaten for drunkenness and theft. He alleged that as a man in his early twenties Rasputin had raped a seventy-year-old widow named Lekonidushka, as well as several pre-pubescent girls. After leaving home and starting to visit convents he continued his savagery, raping several nuns and lay sisters. Now when Rasputin visited nunneries, the mother superiors knew what was expected of them and made certain to present Rasputin with a quiet room and one of their prettiest girls for his special "soul-saving conversations." Rasputin supposedly organized khlyst orgies where fathers had sex with their daughters, and mothers with their sons. Borisov asserted the archives of the Tobolsk district court contained files on Rasputin's horse thieving and on providing false testimony.[27]

Borisov's article was reprinted in a number of newspapers, including the *Saratov Herald*, the *Siberian Trade Newspaper*, and *Yermak*.[28] The *Petrograd Leaflet* also published a series titled "Grishka Rasputin" over four days in the middle of the month, and *Evening Times* ran similar stories.[29] *Yermak* alleged that "this dark individual" was in league with the "German party" and was scheming to convince powerful circles of the need to make peace with Germany, a new element in the Rasputin myth—that of traitor and foreign spy—which would grow over the next year to become an accepted fact and play a key role in the final plot to kill him. *Evening Times* even called Rasputin a German spy and demanded his arrest. Upon reading this story, Grand Duke Andrei Vladimirovich recorded in his diary on 17 August:

This is an extremely dangerous attack. It may take on such proportions as cannot now be anticipated. But that the danger is not far off, that is entirely clear. [. . .] And who will write a rebuttal? The only method now is to prove their innocence in a decisive manner—be done with Rasputin, whether he be guilty or not. It doesn't matter what he's done or who he is. The only thing that matters is that thanks to him there is a person being subjected to public attacks of the most vile sort, and that is more than enough to be cautious and not to incite popular displeasure, especially at a time when things are not very well in the country.[30]

Valentina Chebotaryova was sickened by the campaign. "This is all so terrible and sad," she wrote in her diary.[31] Alexander Spiridovich, head of palace security and the personal safety of the tsar, agreed, if only in part. He described *Evening Times*' articles as "complete and vile slander" while characterizing Borisov's work in the *Stock Exchange Gazette* as "an entirely respectable biography." Worth noting, as Spiridovich pointed out, was that the two papers were quite different in orientation: the latter being under the editorship of Mikhail Gakkebush-Gorelov, a Jew, and the former that of the Russian nationalist Boris Suvorin, a man who together with Alexander Guchkov helped launch and then publicize the lie that Rasputin was a German spy. Rasputin was being attacked from all along the political spectrum. As for Nicholas, Alexandra, and Rasputin, they placed the blame squarely on the new Minister of the Interior Shcherbatov, convinced that he was being much too lenient with the press.[32]

An angry Rasputin sent telegrams to powerful friends imploring them to do whatever they could to stop the stories.[33] He wrote Vyrubova to ask Voeikov to prohibit the *Stock Exchange Gazette* from printing its "filth, they're sowing discord."[34] He moaned to her on 2 September: "Satan created the newspaper and spread fear."[35] Governor of Tobolsk Andrei Stankevich was apparently the only official to come to his public defense, writing to the editors to take issue with Borisov's many errors and insisting that neither he, nor his vice governor, had ever thrown parties for Rasputin or that he had ever received any complaints about him from his fellow villagers of Pokrovskoe, as Borisov alleged.[36] This lone voice was lost amid the howls against Rasputin.

The campaign emboldened his old foe Father Vostokov. Before a large gathering of pilgrims in Kolomna on 29 August, Vostokov railed against Rasputin. He asked all those who believed in God and loved the fatherland to sign his petition for the immediate arrest of Rasputin, a man guilty of "seducing the Russian people and pouring water on the water mill of international revolution threatening Russia." During wartime, he told the gathering, when the peace and tranquility of the country were more important than ever, the cynical influence of

Rasputin was worse than hundreds of the most extreme agitators of revolution. The failure to punish such a criminal was "a heavy sin before God, one that has robbed the country of God's grace and blessings." More hyperbolic language would be hard to imagine. Five hundred people signed the petition, which was then sent on to Minister of the Interior Shcherbatov. Rasputin did not take Vostokov's words lightly. He complained to the ministry and wanted Vostokov investigated for "profanation and abuse." But the minister chose to look the other way, ignoring both requests.[37] In the end it was Alexandra herself who dealt with "that horror Vostokov," as she called him. With the help of Metropolitan of Moscow Makary, she saw to it he was sent away from Kolomna to a more remote post in the Moscow district.[38]

45. The *Tovarpar*

After days of intense fighting, on 4 August the fortress of Kaunas in Lithuania, vital for Russia's western defenses, fell to the Germans. The Russians suffered approximately 20,000 casualties and the loss of considerable weaponry. The Russian commander, General Vladimir Grigoriev, was relieved of his duties, put on trial, and sentenced to fifteen years in prison. That evening Rasputin visited a downcast Nicholas and Alexandra at the palace. They talked, and Rasputin blessed the tsar with an icon. The next day he wrote Nicholas to lift his spirits: "Peace and grace, God is with us—be firm."[1] Later that day Rasputin and his son Dmitry departed Petrograd for home. Rasputin later informed Vyrubova that the governor of Petrograd had telegraphed Dzhunkovsky and the head of the police department to stop him from leaving, but for whatever reason no one held them up at the station. "God is always kind," he noted.[2]

The police in Tyumen were on hand to record their arrival: train no. 4 from Petrograd carrying Rasputin, Dmitry, and Okhrana agents Terekhov and Svistunov arrived at the station on 9 August at 5 a.m. Rasputin and Dmitry got a cab and went to visit Rasputin's old friend Dmitry Stryapchev at his home. Meanwhile, Terekhov and Svistunov went to the wharf to wait for their steamer to Pokrovskoe. Stryapchev and Rasputin—without Dmitry, who stayed behind in Tyumen— arrived at the wharf around 8 a.m. and Stryapchev bought Rasputin a ticket for a single-person cabin in first class on the steamer *Tovarpar*. At 11 a.m. the steamer departed Tyumen for Tobolsk, with a scheduled stop at Pokrovskoe. Before the boat pulled away, the police reported that "Neither at the station, nor on the wharf, did Rasputin say anything warranting attention."[3] That evening Rasputin arrived home. At 10:00 the next morning, according to police reports, Rasputin exited his house and came out into the yard, the entire time sighing and moaning and expressing amazement at how he had managed to drink three bottles of wine and gotten so terribly drunk the day before. "Oh, boys," he said to Terekhov and Svistunov, "that didn't go well."[4]

Others were also talking about how Rasputin's trip had not gone well. On 13 August, Governor of Tobolsk Stankevich ordered his chief of police Khrushchev to take a deposition from one of the passengers to follow up on talk that had reached him of trouble on the *Tovarpar*. His name was Wilhelm Harteveld, a fifty-six-year-old Swedish composer and pianist who had been living in Russia since 1882. He and his wife had been traveling that day on the *Tovarpar* when they first caught sight of Rasputin drinking tea in the first-class saloon. He was dressed in a shirt of pink brocade, military-style trousers, silk stockings and slippers. His overall appearance was rather disheveled: his shirt was dirty and his underpants stuck out from his trousers. Rasputin seemed rather nervous, on edge, but still he was behaving himself appropriately.

Rasputin approached Harteveld, his wife, and their acquaintance and offered them a copy of his new book *My Thoughts and Reflections*, inscribing it for them as well—"Love is higher than mountains." He focused his attention on Harteveld's wife, talking mostly about love and such matters, although he also kept looking at their companion, saying to him after some time: "Everyone says I only kiss women, but this man here's taken my fancy, and so I'd be happy to kiss him too." Rasputin kept getting up from their table to return to his cabin, and each time he reappeared in the saloon he was a bit drunker than before. By 2 p.m. he was completely drunk and had started to act like a "hooligan," bothering them during their card game and threatening to have them thrown out of the saloon when they objected to his pestering them.

Rasputin next led fifteen soldiers into the saloon and sat them around his table. The soldiers looked about nervously, for they knew that as enlisted men they were not permitted in the first-class areas of the vessel, which were reserved for officers only. He told them not to worry because he had been given the authority to do as he saw fit. Rasputin then instructed the men to sing for him, at which point several of the ladies got up and hurried out of the saloon. As a thank you, Rasputin pulled out 125 rubles and gave it to the soldiers. The disturbance brought the steamer's captain, M. K. Matveev, and he ordered the soldiers out of the saloon, and they got up and left. An argument ensued between Rasputin and Matveev, and then Rasputin, for no apparent reason, went after one of the waiters, accusing him of stealing 3,000

rubles from his cabin. Just as suddenly, he changed his attitude, gave the
man ten rubles, and tried to embrace and kiss him.

Rasputin stumbled back to his cabin and lay down. He could be
heard singing wildly, laughing one minute, then crying the next, his
emotions seesawing from one extreme to another. He had forgotten to
close the window shade and a crowd formed outside to watch his antics.
Some laughed and mocked, some uttered threatening words. Rasputin
was oblivious to it all. He passed out, vomited, came to briefly, and then
fell back to sleep. When they arrived at Pokrovskoe at 8 p.m. the crew
had to help him off the steamer. Many of the passengers watched and
laughed from the deck of the *Tovarpar*.[5]

After the revolution and his return to Sweden, Harteveld added
further details to his story. The songs Rasputin was singing, he recalled,
were a strange mix of the religious and the obscene, one of which
included the lines—often repeated—"Let me in to play for the night!/
Your bare white breast I want to caress,/ Come, accept all my charms!"
He produced a copy of a note from Rasputin addressed to "My educated
brother V. Harteveld" with the simple Biblical wisdom: "Judge not lest
you be judged."

In light of the timing of the *Tovarpar* incident, coming so closely on
the heels of the bogus Yar scandal and in the midst of the intense
anti-Rasputin press campaign, it is fair to ask whether this too was
nothing but another manufactured scandal. Was this simply one more
underhand operation by the police to take Rasputin down? What about
Terekhov and Svistunov? We know they traveled that day with Rasputin. Would they not have tried to stop him or at least pulled the curtains
in his cabin? It all seems a bit too dramatic, too neat, too simple.
Harteveld, however, insisted that the idea to go to the authorities had
been entirely his own. And it needs to be noted that he did this within
days of the trip, not months after the fact. Harteveld also stated that
Governor Stankevich was far from pleased with what he had been told,
as if it placed him in a difficult situation. Later, according to Harteveld,
the governor even insisted he retract his original deposition, perhaps
hoping he could make the whole business go away.[6] And as for Terekhov and Svistunov, they were attached to Rasputin as bodyguards.
It was not part of their writ to report on him, but to keep him from
harm's way. If he chose to make a spectacle of himself, this was not
their problem.

*

On 14 August, the day after Harteveld appeared before Khrushchev, Tyumen district police superintendent Skatov sent a "top secret" report to Governor Stankevich notifying him that officer Peshkov had gathered more information about the trip that corroborated Harteveld's account of Rasputin's drunken behavior. Two days later he wrote again to send Peshkov's reports, which, strangely, are missing from the Siberian archive in Tobolsk where this correspondence is held.[7] Then, on 21 August, Peshkov interrogated two passengers from the steamer: a lower-middle-class resident of Yekaterinburg named Nikolai Shelekhov and a peasant from the village of Sazonovskoe by the name of Alexander Klimshin, both of whom described events similar to what Harteveld had already testified.[8] The testimony of three other passengers was also gathered, and they too gave nearly the exact same account as all the others. On the twenty-third, Peshkov forwarded his final report to Colonel Dobrodeev, head of the Tobolsk Provincial gendarmes.[9]

Dobrodeev was livid when the report reached him the next day. Back in early July he had ordered his assistant Captain Kalmykov to maintain close surveillance on Rasputin while in Siberia and report back to him everything of potential interest, as had been ordered by Dzhunkovsky. Yet here he was only now learning of this incident, two weeks after the fact, and not from Kalmykov but another official.[10] A frightened Kalmykov sprang into action, sending his superior in Tobolsk his own detailed description of events, which Dobrodeev, in turn, forwarded on to Dzhunkovsky on 27 August. It is worth noting that Dobrodeev was not content to pass on the facts as they had been reported. Rather, he decided to spice them up a bit for Dzhunkovsky, adding a number of flavorful fictional twists. Rasputin had been making it impossible for Captain Matveev to do his duties, he wrote, and so the captain had been forced to threaten to stop the steamer and throw Rasputin off; Rasputin stuck to the wife of an assistant to the governor of Tobolsk and refused to leave her in peace; and, finally, Rasputin not only passed out in his cabin, but wet himself in his drunken stupor.[11] Dzhunkovsky was pleased, but he wanted more damaging detail. Dobrodeev, ever dutiful, pressed hard on his subordinates to comply, even threatening disciplinary measures against those officials who failed to exhibit adequate zeal in collecting the desired material.[12]

On 9 September, Governor Stankevich gathered the various depositions and sent them off to Minister of the Interior Shcherbatov with an accompanying letter highlighting Rasputin's "unbelievably disgraceful behavior" and the overall "picture of unacceptable public disorderliness" as depicted in the documents. He also added a note on how "the guilty party had bragged about his 'position in Petrograd.'" Based on the incontrovertible evidence, Stankevich concluded, he hoped the minister would agree that Rasputin be charged under Article 7 of the law on public drunkenness of 10 July, the first offense for which carried a jail term of seven to fourteen days or a fine of up to 50,000 rubles. Shcherbatov, however, hesitated to act on his own, choosing to forward the matter to Prime Minister Ivan Goremykin for his opinion. On 23 September, Goremykin, old and not one to rock the boat (the extravagantly whiskered prime minister referred to himself as the tsar's "valet de chambre"), informed Shcherbatov that as this matter did not belong "to those events that stand out as rising to the level of the life of the state," so it did not warrant his attention and ought to be handled by the appropriate provincial or local city authorities with the proper jurisdiction.[13] The firing of Dzhunkovsky, who had staked his career on bringing down Rasputin, on 19 August must have figured in both men's decisions not to press the matter. In short, neither Shcherbatov nor Goremykin dared touch this business that they well understood could blow up in their faces. And with that, the matter died.

Yet like so much in Rasputin's life, the story grew over time, becoming more outrageous with each retelling. Later that year *Responses to Life* published an account of the "Exploits of the 'starets' Rasputin," as the journal called it, according to which one angered merchant nearly beat Rasputin and the insulted waiter had intended to take him to court before being bought off for a hundred rubles by a Rasputinist prelate.[14] Alexei Sukhanov of the Duma wrote in the *Stock Exchange Gazette* that Rasputin had stripped naked in public on the steamer. The passengers were so incensed they demanded the incident be reported to the authorities, but the affair was hushed up, and it was only thanks to the refusal of Harteveld to remain silent that it ever came to light.[15]

Rasputin appears not to have forgotten the matter either. He told Alexandra that month that Governor Stankevich had turned against him, and she wrote of this to Nicholas, imploring him to have him replaced. Rasputin told Alexandra that the man he wanted to succeed him was Nikolai Ordovsky-Tanaevsky, the very man earlier sent to Siberia to investigate Rasputin and who was rumored to have been seeking Rasputin's help to advance his career in late 1913. Alexandra had to repeat the request more than once to Nicholas, but in the end, Rasputin got his way. In the middle of November Stankevich was transferred to the province of Samara and Ordovsky became the new governor of Tobolsk.[16]

46. Nicholas Takes Command

In the first days of August 1915, Nicholas made perhaps the most fateful decision of his reign: he would relieve Nikolasha of his post and replace him at the front as the commander-in-chief of all Russian forces. Here is how Prince Yusupov later described the decision in his memoirs:

> The news was, on the whole, badly received, for everyone knew that pressure had been brought to bear on him by Rasputin, and that this important step had been taken at his instigation. To overcome the Sovereign's irresolution the starets had appealed to his religious feeling. Although the Czar's opposition was feeble, it was in Rasputin's interest to remove him as far from St. Petersburg as possible. With the Czar at the front, he had a clear field. From then on, he made almost daily visits to Tsarskoe Selo. His opinions and advice amounted to orders, and were immediately transmitted to General Headquarters. Not a single important measure was taken at the front without his being consulted. The blind confidence which the Czarina had in him caused her unwisely to refer the most important, even the most secret matters, to him. Through her, Rasputin ruled Russia.[1]

Yusupov's interpretation of events has long held sway. Even today, historians write that the machinations of Rasputin and Alexandra determined Nicholas's sudden, and catastrophic, move: intent on running the country without the tsar's interference, they convinced him to replace Nikolasha, removing himself from the capital for Stavka and thus guaranteeing for themselves "a clear field" of action, as Yusupov so tidily put it.[2]

The truth, however, was just the opposite. As the correspondence between Nicholas and Alexandra from the first half of 1915 so eloquently shows, both she and Rasputin dreaded Nicholas's trips to Stavka for they knew just how weak and malleable he was. They wanted, if not to control Nicholas, then at least to steer him in what they considered the right direction and prevent him from making decisions they disagreed with, and both of them knew Nicholas well enough to realize that the only way to do this was to have him at their side in Tsarskoe Selo, safely shielded from the influence of others. A Nicholas away at Stavka was a Nicholas beyond their reach and surrounded by his officers and staff, "enemies" of the court camarilla certain to try to turn the emperor against them. Stepan Beletsky realized this very fact at the time. Rasputin, so Beletsky wrote, even told him that it was precisely for this very reason that Alexandra made certain to write Nicholas every day—and at times even more often—so that he would have her, and Rasputin's, voice in his ear all the time. And for this reason Rasputin encouraged Alexandra to visit Stavka and even wanted to visit himself, but was talked out of it by Beletsky and Vyrubova.[3]

Beletsky, however, was one of the few who understood the truth at the time. Maurice Paléologue, the French ambassador, wrote in his diary that Rasputin and Alexandra had been incessantly repeating to Nicholas that, "When the throne and fatherland are in danger, the place of the autocratic tsar is at the head of his armies. To offer that place to another is to violate God's will."[4] Zinaida Gippius claimed Rasputin had talked the tsar into it in large part to be avenged on Nikolasha, his erstwhile patron and now enemy. She noted in her diary that so great was the reaction to the news that everyone, even cab drivers, was talking about it as a sign of Rasputin's incredible power.[5] "Everyone's despondent," remarked Princess Yekaterina Svyatopolk-Mirskaya (née Bobrinskaya), widow of Minister of the Interior Prince Pyotr Svyatopolk-Mirsky, in her diary in the middle of August. "Yesterday no one spoke of anything but the removal of Nik. Nik. and that the Emp. will take up command himself, a catastrophe in every possible way [. . .] everyone says this is the result of the influence of Rasputin and Alexandra, and even if this isn't the truth, they'll say it's a victory for the so-called German party, and then there'll be revolution or God knows what [. . .]."[6]

The princess touched on something important. Namely, that even if Rasputin and Alexandra had not talked Nicholas into this, that was just what everyone would think, truth be damned. Minister of the Interior Shcherbatov made a similar point at a secret meeting of the Council of Ministers on 4 August, noting that revolutionaries and other anti-government agitators would not pass up the opportunities the scandal presented.[7] In fact, Nicholas had long planned to take up command. He wrote in his diary on 19 July 1914: "After lunch I summoned Nikolasha and informed him of his appointment as commander-in-chief until such time as I joined the army."[8] Two years later, on the first anniversary of his taking command, Nicholas wrote Alexandra that the decision to inform Nikolasha had come to him while standing in front of a large image of Christ in the Fyodorovsky Cathedral at Tsarskoe Selo: "I remember so well that I was standing opposite our Saviour's big picture upstairs in the big church [when] an interior voice seemed to tell me to make up my mind & write about my decision at once to Nik.[olasha]— apart from what our Friend told me."[9]

The Romanov family was aghast at the news. Grand Duke Dmitry went to Tsarskoe Selo to try to talk Nicholas out of it. It was a long and difficult conversation, but Dmitry left feeling he had succeeded. They were both moved by their talk and embraced upon parting, nearly in tears. Dmitry was shocked to read in the Petrograd papers two days later that Nicholas had gone ahead with his decision, without bothering to inform him. Grand Duchess Maria Pavlovna, Dmitry's sister, recalled that by then trying to reason with Nicholas and Alexandra was like "trying to argue with shadows." As for the emperor himself, he had become "more than ever a psychological enigma."[10] The Dowager Empress urged her son not to go through with it. When she told him everyone would see it as the work of Rasputin he blushed; she was shocked at his dangerous naivety. For two hours she pleaded with Nicholas, but he refused to reconsider, telling her that "it was his duty to save Russia."[11]

His government tried as well. At a meeting of the Council of Ministers on 16 August, Chief Procurator Samarin said that it was their "sacred duty" to convince the emperor to step back from this "ruinous decision." He said he was certain "hidden influences" (Rasputin, that is) had played the decisive role in the matter and that if they as a body were not prepared to act, he would bring up the matter with the emperor himself. Samarin told them the emperor had given his word to him before he accepted his position that he would put an end to Rasputin's influence, but Samarin now saw this was not the case. He would ask the tsar about this one last time and if it was indeed true, he would ask to be dismissed. "I am ready to serve my legitimate Tsar," he announced, "to the last drop of my blood, but not . . ."[12] Prime Minister Goremykin disagreed, insisting that the choice was solely the tsar's to make and that it came from his own inner conviction. He told the ministers how Nicholas had often said that he had never forgiven himself for not leading the army at the front in the Russo-Japanese War. He would not make the same mistake again. Samarin, however, would have none of it. "No, this is not a personal question, but one concerning all of Russia and the Monarchy."[13] Eight of the tsar's ministers signed a collective letter expressing their concerns, but still he remained firm. Those who spoke up directly to the tsar, such as Foreign Minister Sazonov, knew that in so doing they had effectively ended their careers.[14]

An agent of Alexander Helphand (aka Parvus, born Gelfand), the Russian-German socialist and ally of Lenin, then working with the German government to bring down the Russian monarchy, passed on to the German foreign ministry intelligence that Nicholas's decision had been greeted "with mockery and derision" by the officers and soldiers who had now lost all hope of victory. He added that the empress had told her personal physician that "The Tsar had had a vision of the Virgin Mother appearing before him with the cross in one hand and the sword in the other. It was a clear sign to the Tsar that he would be victorious."[15]

Grand Duke Nikolai Nikolaevich was relieved of his duties and made commander-in-chief of the Russo-Turkish Front and Viceroy of the Caucasus. He would not be the only one ordered to leave Stavka for the south. Joining him soon after was Prince Vladimir Nikolaevich Orlov, head of the emperor's entourage and His Majesty's Military-Campaign Chancery. Orlov and the tsar were extremely close and had been friends for decades. Orlov had been one of the first in Petersburg to acquire an automobile, and Nicholas had loved nothing more than sharing rides with him about the city. But of late Orlov had been spending most of his evenings in the railway carriage of Nikolasha. He still went for automobile rides, but now with Nikolasha, just the two of them at night so they might not be overheard. Their suspicious actions drew the attention of General Voeikov among others. Talk began to spread among the officers at Stavka that the two men were hatching a plot to have Alexandra confined to a convent. Orlov went so far as to say he wished he had proof that Rasputin was sleeping with the empress, although he regretfully admitted that he did not. As for Nikolasha, he laid all the blame for Russia's troubles at Alexandra's feet, insisting that "she's leading us all to ruin." His wife, Anastasia, was overheard to say the same at Stavka.[16] "Fat Orlov," as Alexandra called the prince, became ever freer with his tongue. In time the emperor's entire entourage and his personal servants began to hear talk of the empress being locked away. According to Spiridovich, it even reached the children. Imperial surgeon Fedorov supposedly came upon a crying Grand Duchess Maria in the palace. When he asked her whatever was the matter, she sobbed that "Uncle Nikolasha" wanted to send mama off to a convent. The doctor did his best to assure her such talk was not true.[17]

When, on 23 August, the Dowager Empress learned the news of Orlov's removal, she was saddened and appalled. "This is some sort of madness, to get rid of one of his truest and most loyal friends such as he. Unbelievable. So few friends, and he's throwing them away."[18] Two days later, Princess Yekaterina Svyatopolk-Mirskaya recorded in her diary: "Orlov has been removed, this is likely the doing of Anya and Voeikov, they've many sins on their souls. Orlov was the only man who told the E.[mperor] the truth and he's a loyal man."[19] Rasputin's fingerprints were once more seen on the affair. Okhrana agents in Kazan uncovered local gossip that Orlov had been let go since he was the only one at court who refused to kiss Rasputin's hand.[20]

Just as the previous year, when Rasputin begged Nicholas not to go to war, but then supported his decision wholeheartedly once it had been made, so too now Rasputin offered nothing but resolute encouragement as soon as it became clear that nothing would change Nicholas's mind. It is possible that this is what they had discussed on the evening of 4 August, when Rasputin blessed the tsar with an icon. While traveling back to Pokrovskoe, Rasputin sent a number of telegrams to Nicholas praising his strength and resolution. On 17 August he wrote: "St. Nicholas the Wonderworker will give his blessing, the stronghold of the throne, your house is indestructible, the decision and the strength of spirit and faith in God is your victory." Days later he wrote again comparing Nicholas to David, the warrior king, and assuring him that the icon of St. Nicholas Rasputin gave him would instill in the tsar the "heroism and courage" he needed to work "a miracle."[21]

Alexandra added her voice to Rasputin's, writing on 22 August to Nicholas at Stavka:

Lovy, I am here, dont laugh at silly old wify, but she has "trousers" on unseen [. . .]

Our Friend's prayers arise night & day for you to Heaven & God will hear them.

Those who fear & cannot understand your actions, will be brought by events to realise your great wisdom. It is the beginning of the glory of yr. reign, He [Rasputin] said so & I absolutely believe it. Your sun is rising—& today it shines so brightly.

[. . .] All is for the good, as our Friend says, the worst is over.[22]

Rasputin, Praskovya, and their daughters were back in Petrograd at the end of August to see Dmitry off to the army. They gathered at Vyrubova's on the evening of the twenty-eighth with Alexandra and her daughter Olga, who wrote to her father that she found Rasputin's wife "so easy to be around and nice."[23] That night Alexandra wrote Nicholas to pass along Praskovya's "love" and her prayers for the Archangel Michael to keep him safe. Praskovya told the empress that her husband had "had no peace and worried fearfully" until Nicholas arrived at Stavka.[24] After returning to Pokrovskoe days later, Rasputin shared with Nicholas his feelings at watching Dmitry leave for the army: "I have just seen off my son according to the Christian tradition with bread and salt to defend everything and all. Tears are flowing, my soul is filled with joy, radiance [. . .]."[25]

The timing of his telegram—9 September—is significant. That same day the agents in Pokrovskoe reported that Rasputin and his father had gotten into a terrible fight at the home of Nikolai Rasputin, Grigory's cousin. Friends and family had gathered to say goodbye to Dmitry when Yefim arrived, cursing his son in the most foul language. He let everyone know how little he thought of Grigory, announcing that he "can't do a thing other than grab Dunya [Pecherkina] by her soft parts." Rasputin flew upon his father in a rage. Both of the men were drunk and they began to beat each other wildly. By the time the others managed to pull them apart, Yefim's eye was bloody and swollen shut and Rasputin had hurt his hip, leaving him with a limp for some time.[26] The two seem never to have been on good terms. When Yefim died the following year, Rasputin apparently did not bother returning to Pokrovskoe for the funeral.[27]

If the incident of 9 September did indeed happen as described, knowing the context helps to make sense of Rasputin's actions. Despite his brave face for the tsar, Rasputin must have been profoundly sad, and worried, to send Dmitry off not knowing whether he would ever see him again. The stress of the day possibly got to Rasputin, which led to the drinking, the emotional outburst, and the flash of violence. Whatever lay behind this ugly scene, there is no denying Rasputin's flashes of temper.

And it was not just parting from his son that was bothering Rasputin. After the news of the tsar's taking command became public, a new round of press attacks against Rasputin appeared. Rasputin was intensely upset and felt hounded like never before. He told his Okhrana protectors a few days later how "my soul suffers" from all the nasty stories. It was wrong and bad for the entire country, he told them, "and I'll have to sue."[28] Alexandra shared his disgust, writing to Nicholas that "the papers find fault with everything—hang them!" Such was the fear that Alexandra informed Nicholas that Praskovya was "so anxious for Gr.'s life now."[29]

Nicholas took action. On 3 September, he had Count Fredericks write from Stavka to General Alexander Mosolov in the capital to take all possible measures to keep any mention of Rasputin out of the press. The matter was considered serious enough that Minister of the Interior Shcherbatov visited Stavka on 5 September to discuss it with the emperor. It was decided to follow every story about Rasputin and should anything at all negative appear, to seize the publication and lean hard on the editors to desist from any further articles. This strategy would work in Petrograd; Moscow, however, was a different situation. There the anti-Rasputin mood was so powerful that the authorities feared they might find it difficult to stop any serious press campaign.[30]

The censors themselves were not always sure how to act. In October, an official of the Military Censorship of the Petrograd Committee on Matters of the Press wrote to his superior Dmitry Strukov about a manuscript they had just received titled "The Truth about the Starets Peasant from the Tobolsk Province Grigory Yefimovich Rasputin." The censors were stymied since the text was a strong *defense* of Rasputin; however, it did so in such a way as to suggest Rasputin exercised great authority, although using it not for his benefit but that of the peasantry. The censors were concerned that any reference to Rasputin having special authority would lead to "new persecutions." Moreover, the censors were not quite certain what the official policy even was. Noting what he called "the existing directive about not permitting into print any details or articles about G. Y. Rasputin," the official asked whether this extended to manuscripts as well as newspaper articles.[31]

Russian military censors were also monitoring the foreign press. All articles mentioning Rasputin were clipped, translated, and filed. These clippings show how inaccurate the information on Rasputin was. A typical example was "Rasputin, One of the Tsar's Advisors" from an English journal called *Summer Reading* that stated Rasputin had been a monk at the St. Innokenty Monastery in Irkutsk before becoming the tsar's court priest and personal confessor.[32] While the censors were busy leafing through hundreds of European newspapers and magazines for every whisper of Rasputin, in Russia it was being said that Rasputin's power had grown to such heights that the press in France and England were now prohibited from writing about him.[33]

Back home, the authorities continued to struggle to get a handle on the public relations nightmare surrounding Rasputin. In October, the tsar was awarded the Order of St. George, 4th class. Nicholas was sincerely moved by the decoration, yet officials worried how to present the news: George, Grigory—the names were too similar and provided too much opportunity for wordplay. So in the capital the decision was taken not to permit the cinemas to show the newsreel footage of the tsar receiving the order out of fear moviegoers might snicker: "The Tsar with George, and the Tsaritsa with Grigory!"[34]

47. Rasputin, Favorite

Maria had this to say about her father's relationship with Nicholas and Alexandra:

> Father loved the tsar's family and was devoted to them. He always spoke highly of them and with love. But he saw the emperor's goodness as a failing and said of the emperor that he is "painfully good and simple." Of the empress, father would say that she told the emperor this many times. He treated the emperor and the empress exactly the same as anyone else. He used the informal "you" with the emperor and empress as with all other people, and never stood on any ceremony. Hot-tempered by nature, father would sometimes allow himself to yell at the emperor, and when angry he sometimes even stomped his feet in front of him. Once father shouted at the emperor and left without taking leave of him. All of these fights with him were the result of the emperor choosing on occasion not to listen to father's advice. [. . .] Father repeatedly told the emperor that he must be closer to the people, that the tsar was the father of the narod and the narod must see him as often as possible, and must love the tsar as a father, but the tsar kept himself aloof, the narod did not see him, it only feared his name: but if the narod saw and knew him, it would not fear but love him. The emperor said to father that were he to live as my father desired, the people would kill him. Father told the emperor, that the people would never kill the tsar, but the intellectuals would kill him.[1]

Maria's characterization of her father's relations with Nicholas and Alexandra is fair and accurate. Rasputin did indeed love the tsar, but he clearly saw his inadequacies. "You think one thing," he once said, "but can you truly count on him, for he can change at any minute, he's an unhappy man, he lacks inner strength."[2] There is indisputable evidence that Nicholas took comfort in Rasputin. Nicholas told Palace Commandant Dedyulin after he expressed a negative assessment of Rasputin: "You're wrong to think that. He's a good, simple, religious Russian man. In minutes of doubt and spiritual turmoil I love to converse with him, and after such conversations my soul is always light and calm."[3] Beletsky concurred on the differences between the two men's natures: "I wanted to talk about his immensely strong will that he developed, about how he acted upon the Emperor; I know at times he even pounded with his fist. It was a battle between a weak will and a strong will. That man walked the palace halls better than any other courtier, he understood and took into account all human frailties upon which he could play. That was a very intelligent man."[4]

This was something Russians at the time hotly debated. There were those like Beletsky who insisted Rasputin was a rare, powerful personality, with true intellectual, spiritual, psychological gifts. Vera Zhukovskaya, for example, agreed with Beletsky: "It takes courage to admit that R.[asputin] was by nature an exceptional figure and he possessed enormous power." To others, however, Rasputin was a "nothing." Nikolai Sokolov, investigator of the murder of the Romanovs, considered him powerless and devoid of will. Rasputin's sole defining characteristic Sokolov called "his colossal ignorance."[5] Zinaida Gippius expressed a similar view: "As a personality, Rasputin is paltry and common. [. . .] I insist he was an extremely ordinary, insignificant, commonplace peasant."[6] She found the idea that Rasputin might have any political ideas to be laughable. He was far too simple to rise to such a level. Gippius once shared her thoughts on Rasputin with Ivan Bunin, the writer and future Nobel Prize winner, and his wife, Vera Muromtseva. Vera could hardly believe her ears. Gippius, Vera had to admit, was a fine writer, but "she doesn't understand the first thing about people. He's no commonplace peasant, and much less a simpleton."[7]

Vera was right, and it is worth noting that the people characterizing Rasputin as a mere nothing were almost always those who did not know him and had had no personal experience of him, such as Sokolov and Gippius. Rasputin was anything but commonplace. Nor was Nicholas as weak as his critics insisted, and the record shows many instances when the tsar chose to ignore Rasputin's advice. Rasputin had his opinions of what was best for the tsar and Russia and he was never shy to express them, but he was not an evil Svengali, trying to manipulate the tsar as his puppet. This view of Rasputin needs to be seen as emblematic of a much older political discourse, namely that of the royal favorite.

The shadowy advisor with the ear of the ruler, often an outsider with no connections to the political-social elites and frequently with no official position, has been a recurring figure throughout history. In Europe, the royal favorite reached its apogee in the seventeenth century as best personified by Count-Duke of Olivares in Spain under King Philip IV and Cardinal Richelieu in the France of Louis XIII. Favorites were invariably perceived as cunning and manipulative, the wicked hidden hand behind the throne. Favorites were depicted as two-faced, deceitful, ambitious and obsequious in the self-abasing struggle for power. Olivares demonstratively kissed the king's chamber pot as proof of his undying love and devotion. Richelieu was able to summon tears on demand when he knew it would please the king. To insiders, their place alongside the ruler was seen as a usurpation of the proper state officials and institutions; to outsiders, the range of their power assumed fancifully grotesque proportions and every government mistake was laid at their feet.[8]

In Russia, the cult of the favorite flourished in the eighteenth century. Peter the Great's daughter, Empress Elizabeth (reigned 1741–61), had two favorites. The progenitor of the counts Razumovsky began life as a Ukrainian shepherd named Oleksy Rozum. Elizabeth noticed his lovely face after he joined the court choir, taking him to her bed, showering him with money, palaces, and serfs, and rebranding him as Field Marshal Alexei Razumovsky, count of the Holy Roman Emperor. Behind his back, however, the count's contemporaries snidely referred to him as "The Night Emperor." He was followed by Ivan Shuvalov, an army captain's son and later court page, who became in the later years of Elizabeth's reign a de-facto chief minister with incredible power and control over the empress. A saying was born: *Iz griazi da v kniazi*, from the grime to the sublime, or, more literally, out of the mud and into the princes.

No other ruler was more famous (or infamous) for her favorites than Catherine the Great, who reigned from 1762 to 1796. Her story is inseparable from the men who shared her bed and helped her rule: Count Grigory Orlov, Prince Grigory Potemkin, and Prince Platon Zubov. More than lovers and companions (and, in the case of Potemkin, probably her secret husband), these men helped put Catherine on the throne and remain there for a remarkable thirty-four years in what was one of the most politically and culturally dynamic periods of Russian history, and for their services she rewarded them with staggering riches.

Their coveted position meant these men were resented at court and became the object of unwarranted calumny, although none suffered so undeserved a reputation as Catherine, slandered by history as a nymphomaniacal virago.

Rasputin needs to be seen as one more in the long line of Russian royal favorites. But the changing nature of the institution, and Rasputin's own personality, made for important differences. Rasputin truly did come from the mud, but unlike his predecessors he never left it. He did not become a permanent creature of court, nervously trying to wash himself clean of his past and assimilate, with a bit too much eagerness, into the ranks of the aristocracy, grabbing at titles, orders, estates, and money. Just the opposite. Rasputin did not grow rich or acquire titles and lands, and he maintained his connections to his family, his class, and his home, but then this is what was expected of him. His royal patrons, as well as the society women in the capital, looked to him for a connection to the humble, God-bearing narod. Were he to shed his roots and get himself made a prince, he would have lost the very thing that made him attractive, and Rasputin was too smart not to realize this, although he truly had no desire to leave his roots behind. In this sense, Rasputin was no social climber. He worshipped the tsar and tsaritsa, but had little time for the nobles. The last thing he wanted was to join their ranks, a fact that only stoked their hatred of him. None of this mattered, for in the end the aura of the favorite hung over him, and thus his contemporaries could not help but assume that he was acting as the Razumovskys, Orlovs, and Potemkins before him: sleeping with the empress, emptying the state treasury, and holding in his hands the reins of power. This is not to say, however, that Rasputin was immune to the intoxication of power. He knew that his intimacy with the royal couple brought upon him the reflected glory of the throne, and he enjoyed this immensely. Rasputin became entangled in the webs of power, intrigue, and influence that no court figure could escape, and for years he managed to outplay the other participants in this game with considerable skill, suffering defeats and setbacks, but never losing his trusted place alongside the emperor and empress.

Stories of Rasputin's dictating to Russia's ministers were common. Typical was the one recorded by Nadezhda Platonova in her diary in 1916 according to which Rasputin had telephoned Minister of War Dmitry Shuvaev to say he needed to see him straightaway. Shuvaev told him, via his adjutant, that he was free to come during one of his official reception days and he would admit him immediately. This, however, was not enough and Rasputin let him know it, supposedly replying: "Let your minister know that mama and I don't need such ministers."[9]

Shuvaev, however, was still in his post as minister of war when Rasputin was murdered, and the idea of Rasputin, the wicked favorite, hiring and firing ministers as he saw fit, was a mere fiction. Rasputin's power to a large degree existed in the minds of others, where it grew with each passing year. In his play *Rasputin*, Ilya Surguchyov presents this scene between Prince Dzhunitsky, a fictional minister of the interior, and his wife who can talk of nothing but Rasputin: "Rasputin, again! Once and for all, this really is too much! As if there's nothing else to talk about. [. . .] You go on and on about him, puffing him up, and then you're shocked at how powerful he is."[10] Surguchyov succinctly captured how the popular perception of Rasputin's power came to be. Shulgin once asked the deputy minister of the interior whether it was true that Rasputin's hastily scrawled notes to various ministers were "as powerful as Holy Writ." The minister laughed at the mere suggestion, saying the only people who gave any attention to these notes were "other scoundrels" like Rasputin. And then he went a step further, telling Shulgin: "There is no such thing as Rasputin—only *rasputstvo*," debauchery.[11] This was the obverse of Rasputin the all-powerful favorite: Rasputin the phantom, Rasputin the mirage.

"What is Rasputin?" the *Astrakhan Leaflet* asked in the summer of 1914. "Rasputin is a nothing. Rasputin is an empty place. A hole! A collapse! The collapse of everything—faith, thought, politics, the state. Rasputin is nothing but a terrifying, fatal word. It is a name that if it did not exist would have to be made up, as a symbol, an emblem, a program, and a platform of the current moment."[12]

Just as the favorite's power was perceived in stark opposites—all or nothing—so too was his personality said to be split into contrasting halves. The royal favorite was by definition two-faced, showing a false, carefully guarded self to his royal patrons, and then a true, evil, cunning side to the rest of the world. The same was said, of course, about Rasputin. "He turned his 'starets' face to the family of the tsar, and the tsaritsa believed, as she gazed at this face, that the spirit of God lived in this holy man," Shulgin wrote. "But to Russia he turned his debauched mug, the drunken and lewd face of a satyr, the mug of a wood goblin from the Tobolsk taiga. [. . .] So did this messenger of death impose himself between the throne and Russia . . . He kills because he is two-faced."[13] Iliodor captured Rasputin's duality in the evocative title of his book: *Holy Devil*. This incredibly durable image did not begin with him, however. In 1910, *Speech* published the words of a woman who had allegedly lived in the Rasputin home for six months. "Now I don't know who he is," she is quoted as having said, "a saint or the greatest sinner in the world."[14] Gurko wrote there were two extremes battling inside Rasputin's soul: one seeking the monastery, the other ready to burn down the village. Kokovtsov said Rasputin could one minute make the sign of the cross and the next strangle his neighbor with a smile on his face.[15]

As was typical of his detractors (and defenders), Gurko and Kokovtsov go too far in their damnation (and praise): burning down the village or strangling his neighbor were never part of Rasputin's character. Although arresting, the image of Rasputin the devil was difficult to sustain. Even Iliodor had trouble maintaining the myth of Rasputin he had done so much to create, admitting at one point in his book that Rasputin was nothing more than "a common, pock-marked peasant."[16] Maria said the same thing (minus the pockmarks): "He was a simple peasant from birth, and so he remained until his very death."[17]

While the idea of Rasputin the arsonist and strangler can be dismissed outright, there remains the more controversial question of his sincerity. Was he sincere about his faith and his rare spiritual gifts or was it merely an act, part of a conscious strategy to deceive? Even if the face he showed the tsarist family was not the same one he showed Russia, did that mean one of them was true, the other false? On this his contemporaries disagreed. To his disciples, of course, there could be no question of his sincerity, but for most Russians it was *the* question. Beletsky spoke for the vast majority when he described Rasputin as "secretive, suspicious, and insincere," motivated only by his own personal interests, with no regard to larger ideas or values.[18] Few were willing to concur with French ambassador Paléologue's assessment of Rasputin: "I do not doubt in the least his complete sincerity. He would not possess such fascination if he were not personally convinced of his exceptional talents. His faith in his own mystical power is the main factor in his influence."[19]

There can now be little doubt that Paléologue was closer to the truth than Beletsky. This is not to say, however, that Rasputin was not at times secretive and suspicious, especially with someone like Beletsky. By

1915, Rasputin had plenty of cause not to trust the police or anyone in the ministry of the interior: he knew the security services were working to ruin, not protect, him, and it was this realization that was the main reason behind Rasputin's increasing involvement in the selection of state ministers—and high church officials—in the final years of his life. As his enemies grew in number and in their determination to crush him, Rasputin sought to place allies in positions of authority. Thus, in a tragic paradox, Rasputin's enemies pushed him further into the mold of the royal favorite, behaving just like the hidden power behind the throne they had long accused him of being. At the same time his enemies' actions strengthened the bond between Rasputin and the royal couple.

From the beginning, Alexandra had found comfort in Rasputin's directness and honesty. She once told Father Shavelsky that Russian clergymen only frustrated her, for whenever she asked them for advice they invariably answered: "'As you like, Your Majesty!' But why would I ask them to find out what I would like? Grigory Yefimovich, however, will always tell me with insistence and great authority what he thinks." And it was not just Alexandra who felt this way: Nicholas said the same thing in a letter to General Mikhail Alexeev, the chief of staff at Stavka, in 1916. In the gilded cage of the palace, Rasputin was their vox populi. At the same time, they knew that their embrace of Rasputin came with a price. After hearing some disparaging words about Rasputin as a simple, uneducated peasant from her maid-in-waiting Maria Tutelberg, Alexandra replied: "Christ chose for himself as pupils not learned men and theologians, but simple fishermen and carpenters. It is said in the Gospels that faith can move mountains. That God is alive today. [...] I know that I am considered mad given my faith. But then all believers have been martyrs."[20] In his memoirs the emperor's adjutant Semyon Fabritsky quoted Alexandra as saying she and Nicholas well knew that anyone they brought close to them would inevitably be punished with ruthless slander for this intimacy.[21]

The favorite brought comfort, but he inevitably tarnished the aura of the monarch. Although a favorite "despoils you of part of your glory," Louis XIV of France remarked, "he unburdens you at the same time of your thorniest cares."[22] In the case of the last Russian tsar, the favorite despoiled him of *all* his glory. Yet it was often not just the ruler who suffered from the relationship. Favorites frequently met violent ends. The list is long and gruesome. Sejanus, the commoner who began life as a soldier and went on to become the friend and trusted advisor of the Roman Emperor Tiberius, amassing great power and enemies along the way, fell from grace and was strangled and his body torn to pieces in AD 31. Piers Gaveston, favorite to King Edward II of England, was murdered—pierced clean through by a sword and then beheaded—by a group of vengeful aristocrats in 1312. Alvaro de Luna, the favorite of King John II of Castile, fell from grace and was beheaded in 1453 upon the urging of the king's second wife, Isabella of Portugal. Olivier Le Daim, the barber to King Louis XI of France, gained the ear and trust of the king and went on to amass titles, fortune, and power, yet upon the death of the monarch, Le Daim was executed by vengeful French magnates in 1484. By 1915, Rasputin knew well the danger that came with intimacy to the ruler.

48. Fresh Scandal

A fresh church scandal erupted in September 1915. On the evening of 27 August, the bells of Tobolsk's St. Sophia Cathedral began to ring, calling Bishop Varnava's flock to worship at the remains of Ioann Maximovich Maximovich, metropolitan of Tobolsk in the early years of the eighteenth century and an important figure in the history of Russian Orthodoxy in Siberia. That summer, Varnava, together with his friend Rasputin, had been writing to the tsar with requests that he canonize Maximovich, and in late August the tsar had agreed to their requests and allowed for the beatification—the first step toward eventual canonization—to begin. Crowds, overflowing with joy at the news, thronged to the cathedral in the Tobolsk kremlin.[1]

Word of the service in Tobolsk shocked members of the Synod back in Petrograd. Chief Procurator Samarin was outraged, for the Synod had not approved the canonization of Maximovich and it alone, not the tsar, had the authority to do so. A message was sent to Varnava summoning him to appear before the Synod and explain himself. Varnava came on 7 September. The meeting did not go well. Samarin and the other members of the Synod sat at a large table and forced Varnava to stand the entire time, a crude display of their power that made Varnava bristle. Samarin wanted to know on whose authority he had started the canonization of Maximovich, instructing the cleric that the decision belonged to the Synod. Varnava replied that he had acted on an even higher authority, namely that of the tsar, and he produced a letter from Nicholas approving the beatification. The Synod members were stunned; they could not conceive of the tsar acting without their prior consent. When it had finished, the Synod told Varnava he was not free to leave the city until it had interviewed him once more. He ignored their order and left soon after. In the end, the Synod concluded that the canonization of the metropolitan be declared invalid and that Varnava be removed as head of the eparchy.[2]

Samarin did not stop there. He criticized Varnava that day for his connections to Rasputin and insisted he inform the tsar of his friend's dissolute life. Indeed, it was through the lens of his own battle against Rasputin that Samarin viewed the matter of Maximovich's canonization. At base, Samarin saw the matter as one more instance in which the church had been degraded by its subjugation to the will of the Siberian peasant.[3] He was not alone. The gendarmes in Tobolsk had reported discovering anti-Varnava writings being spread about the town in April of that year. Copies of the text had even been posted on fences and doors. And in early September, Varnava was attacked on the pages of the *New Times* for his having denounced the Duma in sermons that summer in Tobolsk. The police began monitoring Varnava's actions.[4] Samarin contacted Governor of Tobolsk Stankevich and asked him to intercept Rasputin and Varnava's written communications and send them to him in Petrograd.[5]

Varnava had been unpopular with the Synod since it had been forced to elevate him to bishop of Kargopol back in 1911 at the tsar's insistence. As the vicar of the Olonetsk eparchy, he had greatly angered his superior, Bishop Nikanor, by ignoring his directives and humiliating the many priests with superior education. So unruly and difficult was Varnava that Nikanor had to write to the Synod for help in disciplining him, a story that ended up in the press as further proof of how Rasputin was destroying the church. Varnava's haughty, antagonizing treatment of other clergymen continued after he was appointed bishop of Tobolsk in November 1913, a position he probably received with the support of Rasputin, after Antony's transfer to the Caucasus. During his time in Tobolsk, Varnava began to set his sights even higher and contemplated supplanting Rasputin's place at court, a move that Rasputin learned of and that cooled their relations in early 1916.[6]

The rest of Russian society shared the Synod's view of the canonization scandal. The Moscow archeologist Alexei Oreshnikov, for example, noted in his diary on 19 September that Varnava had been called to the Synod and a trial of some sort had been launched, but since he was protected by Rasputin, the case had been dropped thanks to royal decree. "What lawlessness and arbitrary use of power!"[7] Oreshnikov was responding to brief reports printed on the fourteenth and nineteenth of the month in the *Moscow Leaflet* that presented the affair as a clear case of Rasputin's protégé Varnava overstepping his authority and having to be disciplined by Samarin.[8] Zinaida Gippius wrote how Varnava, "an arch little peasant of the Rasputin type," had dared to rebel against the Synod with Rasputin's protection and "demanded" the canonization of some insignificant churchman. The entire business reeked of "insolence."

The history of Ioann Maximovich's canonization was more complicated, however, than Samarin, Gippius, and others cared to recognize. First of all, the idea had not originated with Varnava but with Yevsevy, bishop of Tobolsk from 1910 to 1912, who had been no friend to Rasputin. His successor, Bishop Antony (Karzhavin), also held Maximovich in high regard and made significant improvements to his memorial in the cathedral. In 1913, a commission of local clergy sent a petition to the Synod and the tsar requesting the canonization of Maximovich in connection with the upcoming bicentenary of his death in June 1915. The Synod initially approved the request, but then for some unknown reason the matter was never officially settled. It was for this reason that Varnava and Rasputin had written that summer directly to the emperor in the hope he would give his blessing to the canonization that had been hanging in limbo for two years.[9] But after the church scandals surrounding Germogen and the Name-Glorifiers none of this mattered any more, for the facts became lost in the dark shadow of Rasputin. Samarin and the rest of the Synod either did not know that the request had been previously approved or they had willfully ignored it, intentionally creating a scandal so they could implicate Rasputin.

Before returning to Tobolsk, Varnava visited Alexandra and Vyrubova. On 8 September, Alexandra, in a letter to Nicholas, praised Varnava and how he had stood up to the Synod "for us & our Friend." She wrote that Nikolasha and the Black Princesses were likely behind the entire affair, as well as Sergei, the archbishop of Finland, Nikon (Rozhdestvensky), former archbishop of Vologda, and even Germogen and Father Vostokov. It was high time, she insisted, that the Synod "learn who is their master." Sergei and Nikon must be removed from the Synod, and Rasputin's friend Pitirim (Pavel Oknov), exarch of Georgia, ought to be added. As for Samarin, Alexandra concluded, he too must go.

Alexandra wrote again on the ninth with more details and instructions. Samarin had used "vile words" when speaking about Rasputin to Varnava, she informed Nicholas, and had claimed that the tsar was but the "servant" of the Synod. She had also learned that Stankevich, the governor of Tobolsk, was in league with them. He had been showing around Rasputin's personal telegrams and had been so brazen as to say to Varnava that "I was a crazy woman & Ania [Vryubova] a nasty woman etc.—how can he remain after that? You cannot allow such things. These are the Devil's last trials to make a mess everywhere & he shan't succeed." (It was that same day—9 September—that Stankevich wrote to Minister of the Interior Shcherbatov requesting Rasputin be arrested for his behavior on the *Tovarpar*. His joining the foes of Rasputin, and especially these cruel words about the empress, sealed his fate. He was removed from his post two months later.)

Alexandra, not unjustifiably, sensed treason all around her. Yet she told Nicholas not to worry, for she had a weapon at her disposal:

> My Image [icon] of yesterday, of 1911 with the bell has indeed helped me to "feel" the people—at first I did not pay enough attention, did not trust to my opinion, but now I see the Image & our Friend have helped me grasp people quickly. And the bell would ring if they came with bad intentions & wld. keep them fr. approaching me—there, Orlov, Dzhunkovsky, Drenteln who have that "strange" fright of me are those to have a special eye upon. And you my love, try to heed what I say, it's not my wisdom, but a certain instinct given by God beyond myself so as to be your help.

On 11 September and again on the twelfth Alexandra instructed Nicholas to fire Samarin. She now also included Minister of the Interior Shcherbatov's name among those who had to go. The empress was terribly anxious that her husband would not follow through on her wishes. As she had her icon and bell to help guide her in these difficult days, she reminded her husband of the icon and comb he had received from Rasputin. "My dear, don't forget to comb your hair with the little comb. [...] Remember to keep the Image in yr. hand again & several times to comb yr. hair with His comb before the sitting of the ministers." Rasputin was not at the tsar's side, but his power, Alexandra was convinced, could be summoned with the right grooming instrument. (Although she believed in the efficacy of such talismans herself, she scoffed at a rumor that same month that she was sending off officers to the front with Rasputin's "prayer belts" to keep them safe. "Such rot," she complained to Nicholas.)[10]

As for Rasputin, he wrote the tsar on the seventeenth encouraging him to ignore the Synod and follow his own judgment: "Your intention was blessed by God, Your word—peace and benevolence for all; Your hand—thunder and lightning; it will cover everything."[11]

Alexandra was growing increasingly worried that Nicholas would fail to act, and that there would be no "thunder and lightning" from his hand. She wrote yet again, her voice quaking with anger: "S.[amarin] and Shch.[erbatov] are selling us out—such cowards!" And again: "S. and Shch. slander Grig. so terribly. Shcherbatov showed your telegrams and those of our Friend and Varnava to many people. Just think, how vile (that about Ioann Max[imovich])! Those were personal telegrams!"

That month others were calling for the tsar to prove himself the master. Before a gathering of the Convention of the Union of Zemstvos and Cities, Vladimir Gurko proclaimed: "We need an authority with a whip and not an authority that is itself controlled by a whip." The quip was a play on words squarely aimed at Nicholas and Rasputin: "khlyst" was the word for "whip," and so instead of the tsar ruling with the whip, it was the whip—khlyst—that was ruling him and Russia too.[12] Gurko's words rang out like a shot. They were printed in the Moscow newspapers, a clipping of which Alexandra sent to Nicholas. "A slandering pun," she called it, "directed against you & our Friend (& especially against me!), God punish them for this [. . .] make them repent."[13] Still, Rasputin tried to reassure Alexandra, writing to Vyrubova on the day of Gurko's speech: "Don't fret, it won't get worse than it's been. Faith and the banner treat us with affection."[14]

Others, however, were far from affectionate. On the nineteenth Rasputin received an anonymous letter in the mail at home in Pokrovskoe:

> Grigory. Our fatherland is being destroyed, people want to conclude a shameful peace, and since you receive coded telegrams from the Tsar's Stavka, that means you have a great deal of influence, and so we chosen ones request that you act to make the ministers responsible before the narod, that the State Duma be summoned by 23 September of this year to save our fatherland, and if you do not do this, we'll kill you, there'll be no mercy, our hand will not quake as Guseva's did, no matter where you are this will be carried out.
>
> The lot has fallen to us 10 men.[15]

Rasputin was apparently unmoved by the letter; Praskovya, on the other hand, was terrified and sick with worry over her husband's safety.[16]

Days later Alexandra also received an anonymous letter titled "Vox Populi, Devoted to Your Imperial Majesty," prompted by a reading of Rasputin's *My Thoughts and Reflections* published earlier that year. The photograph of its author on the frontispiece struck the letter's author: "The portrait of Grigory Rasputin is unfortunate: his face does not elicit trust, his expression is secretive, his eyes burn with the phosphoric fires—power of the magnetizer, proof of shrewdness—of great envy, he has the nose of a predator, his eyebrows prove that he possesses material wisdom and is a rather evil man, a fact confirmed by his thin, tightly pressed lips in the portrait." The letter went on to say that this was without a doubt the portrait of a "false prophet [. . .] don't expect good from this genius, good is to be found in the narod. The spider before which you pray never has done any good and never will, but you must fear him, know that he is evil and is incapable of self-sacrifice, that is, of good." Were he the tsar, the anonymous letter writer continued, he would destroy Rasputin, but he had no illusions the tsar would do this, for he had already sold out the country to the foreigners and failed to uphold the legacy of Russia's great leaders of the past.[17]

The letter had been sent not only to the empress, but to other lofty personages and government officials across the country.[18] The Okhrana launched an immediate investigation, and in January 1916, the identity of the author was discovered: one Alexei Belyaev, a thirty-eight-year-old engraver, residing at 22–24 Nevsky Prospect. The suspect, according to the Okhrana, was "very nervous and his overall actions give the impression of someone who is not psychologically normal." In the middle of March, Belyaev was exiled from the capital to the town of Luga.[19]

Nicholas returned to Tsarskoe Selo on 23 September, and three days later both Samarin and Shcherbatov were let go.[20] Samarin's tenure as chief procurator had lasted barely two and a half months; Shcherbatov had lasted less than four months as minister of the interior. "It's terrifying to think of what's becoming of the church," remarked Nikon (Rozhdestvensky). "A khlyst is running everything."[21] Lev Tikhomirov wrote in his diary:

> Samarin has been run out [. . .] there are rumors this won't end with Samarin and all the top hierarchs are going to go. There are more rumors that, supposedly, Varnava's to be made the Metropolitan of Petrograd and that Grigory Rasputin has already divorced his wife so he can be tonsured as a monk and begin his rise up the

church hierarchy. [. . .] The credit of the Tsar is crumbling in a terrible way. Yet he, by supporting these Rasputins and Varnavas, is driving even the nobility and the clergy away from him. [. . .] I don't know how the war will end, but after it a revolution seems to be utterly unavoidable. Things are moving so fast that the only persons still loyal to the Dynasty are those with narrow personal interests, but these corrupt figures will turn out to be the first traitors when the frightful hour strikes. [. . .] I'm filled with pity for the Emperor. But I also pity Russia and the Church, both of which suffer from this drama.

The firing of Samarin inspired the philosopher Nikolai Berdyaev to pen a lengthy article titled "Dark Wine" published in October. Berdyaev perceived in this event something much grander, more profound, and more dangerous than anyone else at the time. Russia was being taken over by a "dark irrational force" as personified in the figure of Grigory Rasputin. Not only the state, but also the church had fallen under the "dominion of dark forces." Samarin had run headlong into "a mad and drunken hidden power, into the dark wine of the Russian land." Culture was being subsumed by irrational, unenlightened elements that dwelt deep inside the Russian narod. Those who had drunk of this dark wine found it nearly impossible to free themselves from its orgiastic intoxication. The dark wine was flowing across Russia now, engulfing every layer of society. "The dark irrationalism lurking on the lowest rungs of the life of the people is now seducing and swallowing up the top. Old Russia is falling into the abyss."[22]

An outraged Princess Zinaida Yusupova wrote to her son Felix on 2 October:

I must say that I am so shocked by what is happening at Ts[arskoe] S[elo] that I'd like to go somewhere far far away and never return! Gr[igory] is back yet again. It's said Varnava is to be promoted! They drove out Samarin because of those swine, on the order of that crazy V[alida],* who has also driven her spouse mad. I'm literally suffocating from indignation and think that this cannot be tolerated any longer. I disdain everyone who tolerates this and remains silent![23]

---

* Empress Alexandra.

That last sentence warrants repeating: *I disdain everyone who tolerates this and remains silent!* Could it have been at this moment, upon reading the words of the mother he so adored and wanted to please, that the idea of killing Rasputin first appeared in the head of Felix Yusupov?

49. The Troika

Even before Minister of the Interior Shcherbatov had been dismissed, Alexandra had chosen his replacement. Alexei Khvostov, a wealthy noble landowner and member of the Black Hundreds, had served in various provincial administrative posts before eventually becoming the governor of Nizhny Novgorod in 1910 and then, two years later, winning election to the Fourth Duma. Vain and ambitious, he distinguished himself in the Duma with his fierce anti-Germanism and his fondness for flaunting his right-wing attitudes and showy patriotism. He liked to call himself "a man without internal controls."[1] Fat (he might have challenged Rodzianko for the title of Russia's fattest man) with thick, meaty hands and burning eyes, Khvostov was immensely impressed with his own intelligence and liked to refer to other ministers as "that fool."[2] The opinions of his contemporaries were far from flattering. Count Witte described him as "one of the biggest hooligans [. . .] for whom there are no recognized laws."[3] Petrograd Okhrana chief Globachev said he had "a criminal nature."[4] Rasputin called him "Fat Belly" and "Tail" (*khvost*), nicknames that would send Khvostov into a rage.[5] The following year Rasputin would call Khvostov a "murderer," and with good reason.[6]

Alexandra wrote Nicholas several times in September urging him to appoint Khvostov, insisting that he was the best man to protect them and Rasputin from their enemies.[7] The idea of Khvostov, she had to admit, had not been hers, but had been suggested to her by Vyrubova, who had herself been presented with the idea by Prince Andronikov.[8] Born in 1875 to a Baltic German noblewoman and a Georgian prince, Prince Mikhail Andronikov was one of the great adventurer-schemers of the day. "Short, pudgy, neat and tidy, with a round pink face and sharp eyes that were always laughing," head of the palace Okhrana Alexander Spiridovich wrote, "a faint little voice, always with an attaché case and always intriguing against someone, Prince Andronikov knew how to worm his way if not into the drawing room, then at least into the reception room of every minister." He had a vague sinecure at the ministry of the interior until 1914, when Maklakov fired him for never bothering to show up to work, and the following year the prince was able to convince Sabler to hire him as his "Assistant for Special Assignments." Andronikov's speciality was information. By way of flattery, lavish gifts, and considerable wiles, Andronikov gathered every last bit of gossip, rumor, and slander that passed through the halls of the various Russian ministries, the palace, Duma, and salons of Petrograd. This trove of intimate knowledge, said to be kept in his ever-present yellow attaché case, which in fact held nothing but some old newspapers, combined with a good deal of secrets on a range of affairs and individuals, were the prince's currency, one that made him both unique and uniquely powerful. No minister dared not receive Andronikov out of fear for what he might well say about him behind his back.[9] Andronikov had his own secrets as well. He had attended the elite Corps des Pages, but never graduated, some said due to illness, others to his being a homosexual. At his home at 54 Fontanka he kept a large "boudoir-chapel," its walls covered by icons that kept watch over a massive bed, where he entertained many of the city's young men. Prince Felix Yusupov was supposedly no stranger to the allure of Andronikov's bedroom. The home was purportedly the setting for wild orgies. The prince later added to his collection of icons a large photograph of Rasputin.[10]

Andronikov met Rasputin in the summer of 1914. He had Rasputin over to his apartment and showed him his photograph; Rasputin was impressed. "A smart peasant, very, very smart," Andronikov supposedly said of his new acquaintance. "And cunning. Oh, so cunning. But one can do business with him, and we, we'll take him into our hands and give it a try."[11] And that is just what Andronikov set out to do in the late summer of 1915. Until then, Russia's ministers had tried to destroy Rasputin and break his influence, but the wily prince envisioned an entirely new strategy. If Rasputin could not be defeated, why not work with him, or at least through him? Why not make him an ally in the struggle for power and influence and money? But the prince knew he was in no position to do this alone. He needed help, and for this he turned to Khvostov and Stepan Beletsky.

Andronikov used Vyrubova to plant the idea in Alexandra's head. In an undated letter (most likely from the beginning of September), he wrote the empress's friend to make the case for Khvostov. To prove his allegiance to Rasputin, he began by attacking Vostokov, a man for whom "hanging upside down by his heels" would not be punishment enough. The prince added, however, that Vostokov, odious though he was, was only able to operate with the support of Samarin and Shcherbatov. None of these men believed what they wrote about Rasputin, a "simple, innocent Russian from Siberia, utterly devoted to our IMPERIAL Family," for their true intention was "to undermine the Throne, and authority of power, and to sow rebellion in the country." The tsar needed men who could stop these "evil and debauched traitors to our Fatherland"—and here he added the names of Dzhunkovsky, Guchkov, and Grand Duke Nikolai Nikolaevich—and the man to do this was Alexei Khvostov, "a strong Russian man, an experienced government figure, an energetic and adroit politician. He is, quite possibly, the only man at this moment who knows how to speak to the narod, who could calm the roiling passions, and who can break those barriers that are preventing the flood of the people's love from reaching their EMPEROR-Defender of the Motherland."

Andronikov, an expert in such matters, ended with the perfect touch. He enclosed for their majesties a copy of Vostokov's anti-Rasputin *Responses to Life*, but requested she not pass along his words about Khvostov.[12] Let that remain between them, devoted subjects that they are, he wrote, knowing full well, of course, that she would do just the opposite, and she did not let him down. Vyrubova began to praise Khvostov to Alexandra: "He's so smart, energetic, he loves Their Majesties so much. And he so loves Grigory Yefimovich." She was taken by "his naive and terribly kind bright eyes," as well as the appearance of this "good and decent fatty."[13]

Convincing the ambitious Khvostov of the plan was no problem. Indeed, he wanted to go a step further and be given the office of prime minister as well, then held by the seventy-six-year-old Goremykin (*glukhar*, the old deaf one, Rasputin affectionately called him), insisting that without both posts he would be nothing but a "cat without balls."[14] Beletsky, on the other hand, was another matter. Andronikov telephoned Beletsky and told him that big changes were afoot and that he, as a friend of Rasputin and Vyrubova, was in a good position to help Beletsky revive his career after having left the department of the police in January 1914 due to tensions with his superior, Deputy Minister of the Interior Dzhunkovsky. But Beletsky insisted he was not the right man since while head of the police he had not only refused to meet Rasputin but had even passed on damaging information about him to his enemies, including Prime Minister Kokovtsov, General Bogdanovich, and Grand Duke Nikolai Nikolaevich. Andronikov knew he needed Beletsky, despite the latter's reservations. Beletsky was smart, experienced, and had a vast knowledge of the police and its workings. Alexander Blok, who interviewed Beletsky for the Commission, called him "a man of practical work, obliging and ingratiating, who knew how 'to worm his way in everywhere.' [. . .] Does he believe in God? No, he doesn't believe in a thing."[15] If there was one thing Beletsky believed in it was work. Even his critics, including Dzhunkovsky, had to admit no one worked harder than Stepan Beletsky.

So Andronikov set up a series of clandestine meetings for Beletsky and Rasputin to get acquainted and form their own opinion of each other.[16] Rasputin was willing to give the former director of the police the benefit of the doubt, considering how terrible life had been for him under Dzhunkovsky—nearly murdered by Guseva, framed with the bogus Yar scandal, and abused in countless other ways. Moreover, Beletsky was a foe of Dzhunkovsky and had been greatly displeased with the work he had done as deputy minister of the interior. Beletsky considered him an enemy of the right and ally of the left, the very people who had set their sights on Rasputin, and he wrote up all of this in a self-published brochure, several copies of which he made sure to give to Rasputin and Vyrubova.[17] In the end, Rasputin was convinced he had no reason to fear Beletsky. "Styopa," Rasputin said, using his pet-name for Beletsky, was "a good man."[18] With that, Beletsky next met with Vyrubova and convinced her he was the man to protect Rasputin, which she dutifully passed on to the empress.

Alexandra met Khvostov on 17 September. For an hour he told her how he would run the government, making certain to criticize men like Samarin, Shcherbatov, and Guchkov and presenting himself as a supporter of Rasputin. According to Khvostov, the empress promised to support his candidacy on three conditions: 1. That he appoint Beletsky as his deputy; 2. that all matters concerning the safety of the royal family and Rasputin be placed in Beletsky's sole hands; 3. that he promise never to touch upon matters that concerned the private affairs of the family. Khvostov agreed. The empress was won over.[19] After he had left, she wrote Nicholas that she could not stop thinking about Khvostov: he was "a man, no petticoats [. . .] one who will not let anything touch us, & will do all in his power to stop the attacks upon our Friend."[20] On 23 September, Nicholas returned to Tsarskoe Selo and met with Khvostov.[21] Three days later Shcherbatov was out and Khvostov was in.

Beletsky became the new deputy minister of the interior, and so the man in charge of the various police agencies.

At their meeting on the seventeenth, Khvostov claimed Alexandra informed him she had received a telegram from Rasputin blessing his appointment. No such telegram has ever been found, and the role Rasputin played in these machinations is far from clear. There is no evidence to suggest that it had been Rasputin who had initially come up with the idea. Rather, it appears to have been Andronikov's plan all along as a way to advance himself and possibly to acquire powerful protectors given his involvement in a variety of shady business and financial dealings. Globachev remarked that Khvostov had been put forward by right-wing circles, which, given his politics and Andronikov's anti-Semitism (his foes are invariably denounced as "yids" in his letters) is quite plausible. Although he could not be certain, Globachev did hear that Khvostov had petitioned Rasputin both directly and through Beletsky for his support for the post.[22]

The plan of this "troika" was for Andronikov to act as the liaison with Rasputin. Andronikov would receive his many requests and petitions for favors for the other two while at the same time helping to shield them from having to deal directly with Rasputin. Andronikov would give Rasputin 1,500 rubles a month from a ministerial slush fund in small amounts as a way of ensuring Rasputin would not be forced to take any money from the many petitioners. This would also serve a second purpose: by having to see Rasputin frequently, Andronikov could better keep tabs on him and establish a deeper relationship. It was also decided to place someone they could trust in Rasputin's inner circle, someone who might observe him at home and perhaps try to turn him away from some of the more harmful influences. They settled on Natalya Chervinskaya, an older lady who was not swept away by Rasputin's charms, was already acquainted with Vyrubova, and, as a relation to Minister of War Sukhomlinov's wife, was a fount of information. Rasputin called her *vobla*, the popular salty, dried fish Russians liked to eat with their beer.[23]

Rasputin returned to Petrograd on 27 September, and the following day he dined at Andronikov's with the troika.[24] Beletsky later recalled how all of them, including Chervinskaya, were shocked by the change in Rasputin; he was full of even greater aplomb than they had remembered and overflowing with self-confidence. He began by telling them he was not pleased that all this maneuvering had been done without him present, directing his comments chiefly at Andronikov. He then purportedly turned to Khvostov and reminded him of their meeting in Nizhny Novgorod in 1911. Rasputin had arrived in Novgorod together with Georgy Sazonov on a mission from the emperor to meet Governor Khvostov and assess whether he might be the right man to replace Stolypin, the recently assassinated minister of the interior. Reports of what Rasputin passed on to Nicholas vary—Khvostov claimed his men intercepted that day his telegram to Vyrubova for the tsar: "The grace of God is upon him"—but in the end nothing came of the matter. At this particular meeting, however, Beletsky said Rasputin had harsh words for Khvostov, about how he had arrived in Novgorod with a mere three rubles in his pocket and the governor had received him unceremoniously and barely fed him.[25]

The troika explained to Rasputin that they would protect him with all the powers at their disposal and would support him before their majesties as a devoted subject and man of God who wanted nothing but to help them and the motherland. They would regularly give him money for his needs and would see that his choice for chief procurator would be honored. He was to communicate through Andronikov, and he would pass on everything to the others.[26]

Encouraged by Andronikov's fawning compliments and general subservience and, according to one source, Khvostov's swearing before an icon to keep him safe, Rasputin gave in and dropped whatever reservations he might have been harboring about this new arrangement. Globachev observed that Rasputin was incapable of judging people. For him, there were only two categories: *nashi i ne nashi*, ours and not-ours, friends and enemies, that is. (An attitude he shared with Alexandra.) All one needed to become one of "ours" was a recommendation from one of Rasputin's friends, and so, over time, the members of this group grew and grew to include a great many people—officials, bankers, speculators, adventurers, high society ladies, prostitutes, and clergymen. Nearly all were drawn to him for their own personal gain. Friendly to his face, many disparaged him behind his back.[27] At least two of these "friends" would try to kill him; a third would succeed.

Things went badly from the start. Rasputin refused to play along as they had agreed. He went around Andronikov directly to Khvostov and Beletsky, sending petitions to their offices and even to their wives at home. Beletsky increased the payouts to Rasputin, which he kept secret from Andronikov, and instructed Andronikov and Chervinskaya to discourage him from sending petitioners, which worked but only for a brief while.[28] Beletsky ordered Globachev to increase his agents' surveillance of Rasputin and to prepare daily reports for him. The agents were engaged in two types of surveillance: external and internal. The former involved very careful monitoring and following of Rasputin everywhere he went; the latter was carried out by special agents acting as both bodyguards and servants. They kept detailed records of Rasputin's comings and goings and the people he met.[29] Five or six agents were assigned at all times: two "agent-bodyguards" and two or three agents watching the exterior of his apartment building. Rasputin also had a dedicated Okhrana automobile and chauffeur—Yakov Grigorev—for his visits to Tsarskoe Selo and trips around the capital.[30] An agent often manned the staircase of the apartment building, and one stood by his door or, when Rasputin permitted, inside his apartment. This arrangement, much sought after by the police, broke down as Rasputin became ever more suspicious and certain that the men purportedly guarding him were spying as well. In the end, nearly five thousand police agents were involved in monitoring, protecting, following, and investigating Rasputin and the hundreds of visitors he received. Even the building's doorman and his wife were put on the Okhrana payroll.

No matter how fleeting the contact a person might have had with Rasputin, agents were ordered to "gather by secret means information on their activities, lifestyle, financial means, personal connections, behavior, moral qualities."[31] The political reliability of all Rasputin's associates, no matter how superficial the relationship, was examined. For just two months, from mid-April to mid-June 1916, agents compiled 760 pages of intelligence on Rasputin, nearly all of it written in brown ink on thin, unlined paper, approximately 7×5 inches in size. Everyone Rasputin wrote to or received a letter from was also investigated. Indeed, so wide did the net eventually extend that when a railroad engineer in the far reaches of eastern Siberia received a letter from someone in Australia that contained a few negative comments about Rasputin, the police in Vladivostok, Irkutsk, and Petrograd investigated the matter. Monitoring Rasputin demanded a staggering commitment of resources.[32]

But despite such close surveillance, Rasputin nonetheless managed to slip from view. "This morning the Dark One left home and it is not known where he went, but then returned at 10 this same morning," reads one agent report. "It is not known when the Dark One returned home from his trip yesterday," reads another.[33] He complained to Vyrubova and the empress of how oppressive this machinery was, and Alexandra complained to Khvostov to order Globachev to pull his men back. Rasputin would sneak down the back stairs and give the slip to the men on the street or he would lie to the agents, telling them he would be staying in for the night and then wait for them to go home before heading out.[34] Indeed, this is what happened on the night of 16 December 1916 when he left to visit the home of Prince Yusupov.

The troika did not trust Rasputin, and so as leverage they maintained files of what the Russians call *kompromat*, an abbreviation of "compromising material." Beletsky kept the inquest documents from the *Tovarpar* incident at the ready, along with those from another incident involving a drunken insult Rasputin had (supposedly) directed at one of the grand duchesses. Khvostov kept a special notebook in which he recorded Rasputin's numerous transgressions.[35] Nonetheless, for a while the troika tried to make their plan work. On 25 November, after a meeting with Khvostov, Rasputin told Alexandra that he was "very content" with the minister.[36] Two days later, Khvostov sent an order to the governor-general of Moscow, as well as to all the provincial governors and governors-general, to see to it that not even the name Rasputin appear in any of the local newspapers and magazines.[37] Beletsky too tried to quiet the press. After a series of attacks in the *Stock Exchange Gazette*, he met with its editor, Mikhail Gakkebush-Gorelov, and told him to stop the stories. The editor informed Beletsky that he had received the information for the articles from none other than Davidson, the very same reporter who had visited Pokrovskoe at the time of Guseva's attack. Beletsky already knew Davidson. He had met him before her assassination attempt, and later lent him 600 rubles from the police department's secret fund in an attempt to buy his silence and keep him from further written attacks on Rasputin, a strategy that had clearly failed. Beletsky now sent out his agents to gather evidence of Davidson's shady activities. Thus armed with *kompromat*, he convinced Davidson to hand over his "archive" on Rasputin for 1,200 rubles, which the reporter did. With that, the stories came to an end.

Khvostov and Beletsky also met with key Duma figures and tried to persuade them to leave Rasputin alone, explaining that this only worked against their goal by solidifying Rasputin's place with Alexandra.[38]

Khvostov came up with the idea of having the emperor award Rodzianko with a decoration of some sort for no other reason than that it would tarnish his reputation among the Duma's left-wing members. He begged Vyrubova to tell the empress about the suggestion, stressing that he had discussed it with Rasputin and he had supported it. (Indeed, this got Rasputin to thinking it might be wise to begin selling decorations for large sums as a convenient way for the state to raise funds.)[39]

On 13 November 1915, Ivan Smirnov, vice-director of the police department, wrote a top-secret letter to Alexander Martynov, the Okhrana chief in Moscow, asking him to secretly find out the actions Samarin was purportedly planning against Rasputin. Martynov replied that Samarin had been giving readings about Rasputin and the court camarilla to gatherings of the "Moscow noble intelligentsia" in private homes, including that of Prince Vladimir Golitsyn, the popular former mayor. One of the men involved was Professor Nikolai Kuznetsov of the Moscow Theological Seminary. The police had learned that Kuznetsov, together with a group of thirty-four progressive priests, was considering some sort of joint public statement against Rasputin. In October it was discovered that Kuznetsov had published articles in *Penza Country* exposing Rasputin's lascivious ways and even alleging he had raped a woman. When Beletsky learned of this, he wrote to the editor to immediately stop publishing anything on Rasputin. Kuznetsov frequented the home of Mikhail Novoselov, where Rasputin's influence over church matters was discussed. When Novoselov's mother learned what her son was up to, she became convinced Rasputin would find out and destroy him. Consumed by fear, she suffered a nervous breakdown and had to be admitted to a psychiatric hospital.[40] There were similar gatherings in Moscow devoted to discussing Rasputin, such as the one that met in the home of the Varvara Morozova, widow of the wealthy textile merchant Abram Morozov, that was frequented by Prince Yevgeny Trubetskoy (a founder of the liberal Kadet party and a religious thinker and writer), Sergei Bulgakov, and Nikolai Berdyaev.[41]

The police learned that at Morozova's Trubetskoy had read aloud a synopsis, and a few provocative extracts, from Iliodor's recently completed manuscript. From Kristiania, Iliodor had contacted the publisher and historian Sergei Melgunov and offered him the manuscript for 2,000 rubles. Melgunov turned to his friend Prugavin to help raise the money, but he failed, even after approaching several Duma members. In the end, the money was loaned by one "S. V. Peterson" and sent to Kristiania by way of London with a trusted courier. Vasily Semevsky, a work colleague of Melgunov's, was apparently the one who picked up the manuscript from Iliodor and smuggled it to Moscow at considerable risk. Prugavin confirmed receipt with a coded telegram to Iliodor: "Dear Mother has arrived successfully." Melgunov was terrified he would be discovered with the manuscript. The police had gotten wind of the deal and were searching for the manuscript all over Moscow, sparing no resources or expense. Khvostov was adamant it be found, which would seal his place as minister for good. Once the police arrived at Melgunov's office while he was reading the manuscript, but he managed to nonchalantly hide it from them under a pile of papers. Melgunov made sure not to store it at his office, and he made multiple copies of the text just in case one of them was discovered. His plan was to publish the book in his magazine *Voice of the Past* as soon as the time was right.[42]

But even before that Prugavin published a detailed discussion of the manuscript, complete with excerpts, titled "Iliodor's Book" in Vostokov's *Responses to Life*.[43] This, it seems, was the very article Trubetskoy had read at the home of Morozova that autumn. The Moscow Okhrana set to work. It learned that the article had been reprinted in the *Moscow Gazette* and that certain newspaper editors had taken to secretly duplicating the piece "on a copying apparatus." The police were now, by late November, trying to confiscate all copies of the newspaper, but despite their best efforts, reprints of Prugavin's article began appearing in publications such as *Kievan Thought* and *Kamsko-Volga Speech*.[44] Khvostov telegraphed the Tobolsk governor on 28 November to tell him to keep an especially close watch on the press and to make sure no one tried to reprint Prugavin's article. All of this, Khvostov remarked, was stirring up the populace "against the current political order."[45]

Meanwhile, Prugavin kept writing and publishing. That same year he penned a short piece called "Starets Grigory Rasputin and His Female Acolytes" that appeared in the journal *Illustrated Russia* (under the title "At the Side of the Starets") and then the following year in a separate, vaguely (and unconvincingly) disguised edition as *Leonty Yegorovich and His Female Acolytes*, drawing on information supplied by his niece Vera Zhukovskaya. The police confiscated some of the print run, but the majority of the copies had been securely stashed away at Melgunov's Zadruga publishing house and sold before the police found them.[46]

Khvostov was right that these writings had stirred people up. The

Tsarskoe Selo nurse Valentina Chebotaryova noted in her diary on 21 October how her neighbors had just returned from the provinces where everyone was talking of nothing but Rasputin. "The hatred, the insults directed at the poor family, all prove that every remote village knows about Rasputin: 'Let her live as she wishes, but why is she corrupting her daughters?' My Lord, how horrible!"[47] Chebotaryova was not exaggerating: the police were also getting reports that even in the most isolated corners of the empire, Rasputin was known and being talked about in dangerous ways.[48]

At the same time Iliodor was negotiating with Melgunov, he wrote to introduce himself to the German government. He spoke of his rise and fall in Russia, of his persecution at the hands of the tsar and his police, and of his struggle against Rasputin. He claimed that he had been declared a political criminal of the state and had been sentenced to life-long exile in Siberia, but had managed with great effort and at mortal risk to escape to Sweden. He was now an enemy of the tsar, and so had written a book that told the wicked truth about the Russian court, the royal couple, and Rasputin. As a sort of teaser, Iliodor added that among the revelations in his book was the fact that Rasputin was the real father of Alexei, that he had pushed the country into war against Germany, and that Rasputin was "the actual sole-ruler of all Russia and the head of the Russian church." He offered to sell his book to the German government so that it might be spread among all Russian soldiers and POWs, after which they would finally understand "what they were fighting for." Since he did not know German, Iliodor asked that they find a Russian-speaker to negotiate with him. He stated he was certain that what he had to say would be of great interest to "Kaiser Wilhelm." He wrote "Ja Nicht" at the bottom of his letter. All they had to do to communicate their answer was to strike out one of the words and then send the letter back to him. He looked forward to their reply.[49]

The Germans crossed out "Nicht" and began secretly monitoring Iliodor. The agents noticed "he makes an extremely suspicious impression," but after some time they set up a meeting between Iliodor and one Herr Oberndorff, fluent in Russian, on 13 February 1915. Two days later, Oberndorff wrote of this meeting in a secret, coded telegram to Reichskanzler Theobald von Bethmann Hollweg. The family lived in a little room on the courtyard, he noted, his wife was "small, retiring." As for Iliodor, he had a "not unpleasant, sympathetic appearance," with "an intelligent face and lively small black eyes." His hands and fingernails were clean, quite rare for a Russian, especially one on the run. He struck him as a man of deep feeling for his country, with great love for his suppressed countrymen, whom he hoped to save with his book. Oberndorff noted that the author had all the documents, secretly gathered while living with Rasputin for four years (so Iliodor told him), to substantiate his claims, including written evidence that Rasputin was the father of the heir and that he had had "sexual relations" with the eldest daughter, Grand Duchess Olga. "The truly hair-raising revelations contained in there," Oberndorff remarked, "would without doubt produce an immediate revolution in Russia." Iliodor requested that his book be distributed for free among all Russian POWs. As for himself, he told Oberndorff he was ready to come to Berlin to help prepare the book for publication. He asked nothing for his work, only that once it was finished he be given enough money so he might go into hiding somewhere for a long time.[50]

At the end of November, German intelligence reported that according to sources in Russia Rasputin's power was on the rise. He had been overheard to say, "I've made Khvostov a minister, and the young man will do well for me."[51] As for Khvostov, he was finding the strain of his relationship with Rasputin overwhelming. Rasputin's great force of will was, he said, getting to him. "He haunts me even in my sleep," he moaned.[52] He reportedly told Mikhail Chelnokov, the mayor of Moscow, "I have two months in which I shall be his favorite, two months in which he will suspect me, and two months during the course of which he will kick me out. I have roughly until January 1st. I must act quickly."[53]

50. Gorokhovaya, 64

On Gorokhovaya there's a building,
A place of power and evil,
And if you're not too bored
Then have a listen:

By the entrance, in a peaceful pose,
Attentive and severe,
A policeman's bowler
Is forever freezing in the cold.

He's been put there
As a deterrent to the people's justice—
For not everyone admires
The starets, this marvel of our days . . .

To achieve high rank,
And to avoid hell as well,
All of fashionable Petrograd
Makes sure to visit his five-o'-clocks.

The carriages never stop, bringing
Important personages to their rendezvous,
The favorites of Anya do hurry
To bow before the deity . . .

The starets, always composed,
Holds tight in his clutches
Not just the health of the heir,
But all the bribed ministers too.

To the sounds of Rasputin's pipe,
All of fashionable Petrograd,
Intent that everything goes smoothly,
Dances wildly, dances terrifyingly . . .

The Huns have yet to free us
From Rasputin's fetters,
Nor have Misters Purishkevich-Milyukov,
With their speeches from the rostrum . . .

And the honest courtiers,
Who still refuse to lie,
Make themselves unsuitable
And so must be exiled . . .

And as far and as quickly as possible,
As was done in days of old,
So that the inspired starets
May be free to ruin the country.[1]

"How Russia Lives" is the title of this anonymous verse dedicated to a particular Petrograd apartment house—64 Gorokhovaya Street. Rasputin moved here from English Prospect in the spring of 1914, the first apartment of his own in the city, which he would live in during his stays in the capital until his death. Rasputin leased apartment No. 20 on the third floor from the building's owner, Countess Anna de Less, for 121 rubles a month, his rent apparently paid by their majesties.[2] His next-door neighbor was a Synod official named Pavel Blagoveshchensky; directly downstairs in apartment 17 lived Maria and Stepan Gaponov.[3] It was not a fashionable part of the city, but a decidedly lower-class area, between the Fontanka River and the Obvodny Canal.

The apartment was as plain as its surrounding neighborhood. Five modestly furnished rooms: a sparse dining room with a wooden table and set of Viennese chairs; a reception room with a few simple chairs in it; Rasputin's study with an inexpensive writing desk, heavy chair and leather divan; and his bedroom furnished with an iron bed, table, wardrobe, and washstand. Only his daughters' room was well appointed with comfortable furnishings. Along with Maria and Varvara also living in the apartment was Rasputin's niece Anna Rasputina, then aged sixteen; one of the Pecherkina women (Dunya and Katya) took turns living with the Rasputins in Petrograd helping out around the apartment.[4] Akilina Laptinskaya acted as the mistress of Rasputin's home. She did the cooking, kept the rooms tidy, and served tea to his female visitors, although she expected them in return to clean up after themselves. Some—Aaron Simanovich and Alexander Spiridovich, among others—

have alleged Akilina was in fact a spy of Guchkov put there to provide him with information on Rasputin. There is, however, no proof for this.[5]

Daily life followed a fairly standard routine. Rasputin rose early and went to church before returning to eat. His table, all reliable sources agree, was both humble and consistent. The main meal was typically *ukha*, simple fish soup, accompanied by black bread, radishes, cucumbers, and onions, washed down with kvass, the traditional Russian drink made from fermented bread. Rasputin avoided most meat and dairy products. His tea he drank with rusks from black bread or pretzels. The press, however, liked to imagine his table was laden with expensive delicacies, the finest caviar, exquisite hors d'oeuvres, and rare fish.[6] Evenings were spent quietly at home, unless he was invited out, which in the last two years of his life became more frequent, and it was then that he would drink and dance and give in to sensual pleasures.[7]

The night-time carousing must have offered Rasputin a release from the demands of his days, for these no longer belonged to himself but were completely devoted to receiving the never-ending stream of petitioners that flocked to Gorokhovaya Street. Maria recalled:

From eight in the morning the ante-room was invaded by a flood of people who, seated or standing, waited until my father was able to see them. Throughout the morning, and sometimes even the afternoon as well, this procession continued, and my father, receiving them in turn, either in the dining room or his little study, never tired of questioning and listening to his visitors. [. . .] All classes were represented in this crowd of people who in their moral distress or material embarrassment resorted to the starets [. . .] he never furthered an injustice, nor did he favour the rich at the expense of the poor. On the contrary, in his dealings with the big speculators who came to solicit his intervention he always showed himself gruff, even insolent and brutal. He accepted their presents casually, and often made them wait for hours in the vestibule, while he would listen attentively to the sorrows of some obscure old woman complaining that her only son had been mobilized while her daughter-in-law was sick, or promise a delegation of peasants to hurry on the decision required for the reconstruction of a bridge. The money he received from the Emperor, he freely gave to others in need; he also helped the peasants back in Pokrovskoe with gifts—a cow or a couple of pigs or a colt. [. . .] He would listen attentively, pass from the dining-room to the study, clap one on the shoulder, embrace another boisterously, call Katia* to take to the kitchen the baskets of provisions and wines that had been placed on his table, upbraid some, comfort others, promise help and support to all.[8]

Here is how one reporter depicted a day at Rasputin's: "By the drive there are automobiles, coaches, and carriages ... In anticipation of 'The Master' liveried footman crowd around." The reception room is filled with admirers: "There are ladies here, in exquisite attire, and a respectable general, and colonels, and many civil servants' frock coats and even tailcoats. One might think this is some sort of aristocratic salon." And then Rasputin appears from his bedroom: "He is in his slippers, in a long white shirt tied with a raspberry sash. Upon his appearance, all the well-wishers respectfully rise and line up to approach him one at a time and kiss their host, many, in fact, kissing his hands and others his sleeves, and still others reverently touching the hem of his shirt."[9] In this fanciful depiction a drab apartment has become Versailles, and Rasputin, the Sun King.

Maria was in the best position to know what went on at the apartment, and other sources generally support her. Both Beletsky and Globachev concur that Rasputin spent his days largely receiving petitioners. The majority of them were women. They typically came for a few reasons: trying to get a family member in the army moved from the front to the rear, landing a government position, or securing some sort of material support. Others, typically society types, came out of boredom or curiosity, seeking some excitement, comfort, or the attention of a man with Rasputin's reputation as a lover. And then there was his group of true devotees, the ladies who worshipped him like a saint, eating the scraps from his plate and submissively accepting his occasionally rough words as some sort of special sign of his holiness.[10]

Rasputin's neighbor Blagoveshchensky recalled life at Gorokhovaya:

At the building there was always a detail of agents from the police's criminal investigation unit, a special detail set up in shifts so that 4 agents were constantly on duty—three of them on the main stairs, one by the gates. At the same time the wife of the building's porter

* Yekaterina Pecherkina.

watched over the driveway entrance, the custodian and the porter stood watch at the gates. At the entrance to the drive, the bored agents spent their time playing cards. [. . .] There were a great many visitors from morning until late in the evening, all sorts of people of different ages and conditions. The majority were ladies, young women, and nurses, and there were fewer men, although they too came in large numbers. [. . .] The ladies sat there, one might say, all very elegantly dressed, wearing the latest fashions, not exactly young, but of that Balzacian age, although there were a good many fresh and attractive ladies, all quite young, whose overly serious expression always surprised me, looking as they crossed the court-yard or climbed the stairs on their way to "him" as if they were on their way to a serious meeting, as if they were considering some-thing weighty, or were deep in concentration.[11]

Beletsky and others have written that Rasputin took advantage of the power he had over his female petitioners. As an example, he men-tions the case of a young woman desperate to have her husband returned from exile. She had come to his office with a note from Ras-putin asking Beletsky to help, which he could not since the man had been exiled by the military and not the police, and so the matter was out of his jurisdiction. The poor mother was beside herself, crying hysteric-ally. She told Beletsky she had given all her jewelry and savings to Ras-putin but this had not been enough. He had flirted with her and implied nasty things, but she had resisted. And then, before she knew what was happening, he took her into his small study and forced himself on her. She was certain the visitors in the reception room must have overheard it all. After that he kept coming to her hotel and promising to help with their majesties, but in the end did nothing for her.

Many sources talk of how Rasputin lured women to his study off the dining room where he would give them an ultimatum: give them-selves to him and he would help, or get out and never come back. Beletsky claims Rasputin had a rule that no one, not even family mem-bers, were to enter this room when he was alone with someone. The agents supposedly heard screams coming from inside and saw fright-ened women fleeing the apartment with tears in their eyes. Others told a different tale, according to which most of these physical encounters were initiated not by Rasputin, but the women themselves. It was said the leather cushions of his divan were entirely worn through from all these couplings.[12] Blagoveshchensky told the Commission that one night in July 1916 he and several others witnessed from the courtyard how Rasputin laid Laptinskaya (by then a woman of advanced years) across his kitchen table and "gave full rein to his passions, and enjoyed himself with that well-known act." After he had finished, a satisfied Rasputin walked over to the window and smiled down on the onlookers in the courtyard.[13] A racy if rather improbable tale.

Male visitors were spared their host's unwanted attentions. Okhrana head Globachev separated them into two types: those who openly frequented Rasputin's home and made no secret of their relations with him and those who sought his help but tried to hide the fact. Many of these men came to Rasputin for help with their careers, be it in the civil service, the military, or at court, or to seek his support for any number of business deals, many of them of dubious and even illegal nature. It was this activity that turned the apartment into a quasi-government office, where careers could be advanced, promotions sought, favors bartered, alliances forged.

The Russian archives are full of letters from ordinary people seeking Rasputin's assistance. Alexandra Frakman, for example, the wife of a worker at Petrograd's Putilov Factory who was about to be exiled from the city, wrote to Rasputin as her last hope. Rasputin did what he could to protect her husband, and although the man's fate is not known, Rasputin's action shows how he did try to help people even if they could do nothing for him in return.[14] "My Dear Benefactor Grigory Yefimovich," wrote Court Councilor David Shchuchkin from Novocherkassk on 17 August 1914, "God preserved Your life from the hand of a crazed murderer in His divine Providence so that You could be of use to all those who, through Your mediation, seek the monarch's blessings and truth, from which we are blocked by the higher ranks of our bureaucracy." After thirty-two years of service, Shchuchkin had been unjustly terminated from his post as a judge and his attempts to redress this wrong had been ignored. For more than ten years he and his family had struggled to survive without any regular income. Now they were on the verge of starvation. Only their "Father Tsar" could save him, he told Rasputin, but his ministers were intentionally keeping the tsar from hearing his petition. Thus, he had come to plead with Rasputin to inform the tsar of his plight and to right this wrong. In return, Shchuchkin promised to come to Rasputin, no matter where he was, prostrate himself before him, and donate five hundred rubles to the charity of his choice.

*

There were many similar requests seeking Rasputin's help from the tsar. Rasputin took them seriously, as this letter shows:

> Most Deeply Respected Father Grigory.
>   With a trembling spirit and a feeling of ineffable devotion to Your good soul, I am sending You and your wife my gratitude for the good You have shown us. You are our savior, You have given us life. You have saved us from that nightmare inflicted upon us by fate.
>   A holy, unknown power directed my sick wife to You, a man sent by God, in Yalta. You, with Your good heart, heard the cry of a woman in need, extended to her your powerful, helping hand, and did a good deed. On 30 July I was pardoned by the tsar.
>   I thank You, good man, and my wife and I bow down deeply before You, we kiss Your holy hand. Unto the grave shall we remember the salvation You brought us and we shall honor Your name that is praised by our unbounded Russia.
>   Your grateful and devoted admirers, Captain Nik. Petr. Agapev and wife.
>   25 August 1914. Petrograd.[15]

Rasputin sent the following request to Palace Commandant General Voeikov at Stavka: "My dear good man, write Rukhlov* to give tickets to the poor. My dear and I do apologize again but what am I to do—they're crying. Grigory Rasputin."[16] Rasputin's efforts were not always successful, but even then petitioners would write to thank him for his time and attention.[17] Some wrote to request prayers: "29 June 1914. To Rasputin in Pokrovskoe. Your prayer gave me great joy, all misery has passed. May Christ save you, my dear, priceless father. The Beautiful One."

A certain Rosinka wrote to Rasputin on at least three occasions:

> To Rasputin in Pokrovskoe from Petersburg. Alyosha has fallen out of love with me. I'm despondent. I'm crying, pray for me. Help, bless his love for me. I suffer. Rosinka.

> Dear Father.
>   [. . .] My Alyosha is now leaving for the front, but I am calm,

---

* Minister of Transportation Sergei Rukhlov. Rasputin was requesting free train tickets for the poor.

for I know Your prayer will save him. Preserve and bless him. I go to church and pray for You and him, for Dushka, and for Anna Alexandrovna.* For your dear and beloved ones. I sleep with the icon that You gave me and then my heart is calmer.

Don't forget Your Rosinka. The thought of You is always with me.

Rosinka loved her Alyosha, but she also loved her "Dear Father." She wrote him a plaintive note in December 1914 while he was away in Pokrovskoe: "You upset me, you've forgotten me, you don't write, I suffer, I miss you, I love you, write. Rosinka."[18]

Of course, not everyone was pleased with Rasputin. An angry woman by the name of Matusevich sent him a pointed letter from her home in Kursk on the first day of 1916:

You asked me to write straightaway and to bring you a letter or a petition for the emperor that you said you wanted to pass along that very day. I didn't write either of them, because I was angry with you; you yourself know why. I'd already given you a petition for the emperor, and you said that you had sent it to Stavka, but I made enquiries at the chancery there, and they do not have it. So for an entire month I sat around in Petrograd, believing that if you make a promise you will without a doubt fulfill it. You even swore that you would take care of my request and that my husband would be free by Christmas. I know quite well that you helped with all your heart everyone else who came to you with the same request as I. I ask you, dear Grigory Yefimovich, fulfill your promise.[19]

When letters to Rasputin went unanswered, some wrote to Maria or Dmitry asking that they bring up the matter with their father.[20] Unsure of his address, one nurse in Irkutsk sent her letter to "Grigory Yefimovich Rasputin, the Tsar's Palace, Petrograd."[21] Vyrubova saw how Rasputin would come to the palace with his pockets crammed with letters from people all over Russia. Receiving them upset Nicholas and Alexandra, but that did not bother, or stop, Rasputin. Their majesties would reluctantly accept the petitions and put them in a special envelope for Count Yakov Rostovtsev, chamberlain and the director of the

---

* Vyrubova.

empress's personal chancellery, who would read them and decide which deserved attention.[22]

Rasputin also sent many of his visitors away with notes for ministers and other officials asking for their help. The archives are full of these hastily scrawled notes from Rasputin.[23] On 1 June 1914, Rasputin wrote a note to the director of the police to help Yekaterina Smirnova, the wife of a retired Guards Hussar officer. She was stranded in the capital with no money or friends and needed a train ticket to get back home to Chernigov: "My dear good man sorry for this odd business and for the bother but what am I to do, this suffering one has approached me, calm the old woman and let her ride. Grigory Rasputin." The director denied the request.[24] Moscow mayor Mikhail Chelnokov recalled receiving a supplicant with a note addressed to him from Rasputin begging that he spare the woman's son from military service. Offended, Chelnokov pretended he had never heard of any such Rasputin and threw her out of his office.[25] This seems to have been the typical response from office holders receiving Rasputin's notes.

Those in need rarely left Gorokhovaya without money. Maria remarked that her father never refused any request for a few rubles. No sooner had Rasputin been given a packet of banknotes to help with some favor than he would hand it over to some poor soul. Money did not excite him, she wrote, and "he always scattered it around him lavishly to lighten the lot of those unfortunates who had succeeded in touching his heart, always readily moved to pity."[26] Globachev and Grand Duchess Olga, the tsar's sister, concurred with Maria on her father's generosity.[27] One of the few things that can be said without doubt about Rasputin was that he was never motivated by money. Greed was not his game. The sources of Rasputin's income are not clear. Alexei Vasilev, the last tsarist director of the police, wrote that Alexandra gave him 10,000 rubles a year, money that apparently came from her personal wealth and not the state treasury.[28] Popular talk, not surprisingly, held that Rasputin, with Vyrubova's help, was wheedling a large amount of money from the empress.[29] The press reported that Rasputin lived the high life in Petrograd, while his poor family back in Pokrovskoe went wanting for a single kopeck.[30] But Rasputin purportedly complained about the empress's stinginess, a trait mentioned by the empress's sister-in-law as well. Alexandra gave him clothes and items for his home in Pokrovskoe, but it seems did not help pay for his constant travels and daily expenditures. The tsar's sister Olga noted that she never once heard Rasputin beg for favors from Nicholas and Alexandra, and the requests he did make were only for others.[31] It appears he lived off the largesse of his wealthy friends, benefactors, and circle of devotees. They brought him expensive gifts, as well as food and wine. He would often borrow from friends, like Alexei Filippov, but what he did borrow he just as quickly gave away. His door was always open, and a great many people ate and drank at his expense, both at home and in the city's restaurants and clubs. Those who knew him recognized his generosity, and he took no small pride in his reputation as a host and benefactor.[32]

Life on Gorokhovaya was a whirlwind. Maria recalled that their telephone was forever ringing with invitations to go to the theater or Villa Rode or another hot nightspot. Rasputin rarely said no.[33] By the final two years of his life, many people had memorized Rasputin's phone number: 646 46. Next to the telephone, on a white sheet of paper, Rasputin kept the numbers of the people he called most frequently—Sabler, Minister of War Sukhomlinov, Munya Golovina.[34] Also on the list was "The Beautiful One" (telephone number 69–51) that supposedly belonged to a masseuse frequented by Rasputin, and possibly the very same woman who thanked him for his prayers in the letter quoted earlier.[35] Sometimes Vyrubova would call; Alexandra called rarely, and then only to ask him to come see her. After such calls, a motorcar would appear outside the house to collect him.

Rasputin enjoyed afternoon tea at home in the company of close friends. "My father would chat, laugh, grow animated, wander off absently into vague religious talk," Maria recalled, "soften as he spoke of Siberia, break into enthusiasm and announce that he would go back, that he had had enough of St. Petersburg and the spies by whom he was surrounded; then grow calm again and relapse into a long silence, lost in thought." He enjoyed listening to the gramophone or the singing of his friend Derevensky. Most nights he was out very late, returning long after his daughters had gone to bed. Sometimes they waited up for him, and would jump into bed and pretend to be asleep when they heard him bounding up the stairs. He would always come in and make the sign of the cross over the girls before retiring.[36] Some nights there were parties at the apartment. Blagoveshchensky remembered being kept up late one summer night by the noise.[37] From his study he could hear the sounds of people laughing and musicians playing operetta numbers and Georgian folk tunes. There was loud, drunken singing and dancing. It seemed to Blagoveshchensky as if the partying would never stop.

51. Dark Forces and Mad Chauffeurs

Vladimir Purishkevich dubbed it "ministerial leapfrog." Between June and November 1915, eight ministers and other key figures in the armed forces and church were let go: Maklakov, Sukhomlinov, Sabler, Shcheglovitov, Grand Duke Nikolai Nikolaevich, Samarin, Shcherbatov, and Krivoshein (the minister of agriculture). The pace of turnover would pick up in the final months of the regime. By the time Nicholas abdicated in March 1917, Russia would have had four prime ministers, five ministers of the interior, and four ministers of agriculture. The ever-changing roster looked a bit like musical chairs. Ministers were being hired and fired and moved about with no apparent logic or reason. Moreover, the quality and qualifications of a good many of these men were often lacking.[1]

"Ministers flew like autumn leaves from the trees, according to Rasputin's whim," Gippius wrote. "And according to his same whim new ones were appointed."[2] The notion that one man was responsible for ministerial leapfrog was widespread. How else could it be explained? people asked. Who, if not Rasputin, had the power to make such changes? Globachev wrote that every new minister knew that one of the first things he had to do was to decide his relationship to Rasputin: friend or foe? It was imperative he choose, for one could not hope to remain neutral.[3] Commonsense had it that only those in the first category had any chance of staying in office for long. That ministerial leapfrog was placed at the feet of Rasputin proves how by the autumn of 1915 for most Russians he had become the true tsar. In fact, Rasputin's role in these changes was minor, and the musical chairs was chiefly a by-product of the decrepit political-bureaucratic machine of tsarist Russia that was breaking down with ever greater speed under the strain of the war.[4]

Rasputin was not hiring and firing Russia's ministers, but this did not mean that he had no opinion on the matter. Indeed, he did, and he made sure to let it be known. In early May 1915, Rasputin met with

Minister of Finance Pyotr Bark for two hours, and came away pleased with their conversation.[5] But a few months later, Rasputin was trying to have him fired and replaced by Count Vladimir Tatishchev, a wealthy nobleman, ministry official, and chairman of the United Bank of Moscow. Tatishchev was also the head of Bogatyr: The Society for the Production and Trade of Rubber Products, founded in Moscow in 1910 with capital from Tatishchev's bank. Among Bogatyr's shareholders were the empress, former Prime Minister and Minister of Finance Kokovtsov, and Rasputin. Thanks to these connections, Bogatyr managed to win the designation of purveyor to the imperial court in 1912, an honor that greatly enhanced its position in the market.[6] Prince Andronikov was also trying to bring down Bark that autumn. In letters to Prime Minister Goremykin and Count Fredericks he alluded to questionable financial dealings by Bark and called him "a mix of German colonialist and Jew." (Andronikov's preferred method of attack was ad hominem, the worst sin being a Jew.)[7] It is not clear to what extent, if any, the assaults on Bark by Rasputin and Andronikov were co-ordinated.

On 13 November 1915, Alexandra wrote to Nicholas to broach the idea of Tatishchev as a replacement for Bark, noting he was most devoted to Nicholas, and liked Rasputin very much and disapproved of the Moscow nobility. Tatishchev had told Vyrubova that Bark had made a number of errors, and he would like to be of help and offer advice. "Our Friend says Tatishchev is a man to be trusted, very rich & knows the bank world very well—would be good, if you could have seen him & heard his opinion—says he is most sympathetic." She informed Nicholas that she would like to introduce the two of them.[8] But Rasputin's, and Andronikov's, advice went ignored; Bark remained in office until the end of February 1917.

Other ministerial suggestions from Rasputin were also passed over. In January 1916, he proposed General Nikolai Ivanov as minister of war and in November a certain Valuev, apparently the chief of the Russian railroads in the entire northwest, as minister of transportation. Neither candidate was chosen, and Nicholas simply acted as if he had never even heard their names, which was his usual passive aggressive way of saying no to Alexandra and Rasputin. And it warrants remembering that Rasputin had been against the appointment of Samarin in June 1915, but Nicholas went ahead with his selection anyway. More such instances could be cited.[9]

The correspondence of Alexandra and Nicholas offers the best evidence of Rasputin's political role in the last two years of his life. As their letters make clear, Rasputin was deeply involved in a wide range of affairs and he was constantly offering advice and at times practically insisting it be followed. In late August 1915, he suggested that prisoners serving time for minor crimes be released and sent off to the front, an idea that was adopted the following February. On 6 November, Alexandra wrote Nicholas that Rasputin was worried about the talk of sending troops into Romania, fearful that if their numbers were not sufficiently large they might be trapped there. Not content to let Alexandra pass along his worries, Rasputin made certain to send a telegram about the matter to the tsar himself. On the fifteenth of that month, Alexandra passed on another message from Rasputin that Russian forces must immediately attack the Germans near Riga, after having been stopped in their march on the city the previous month. Alexandra did her best to convey the urgency of Rasputin's words: "[...] he says this is just now the most essential thing & begs you seriously to order ours to advance, he says we can & we must, and I was to write it to you at once." What makes this piece of advice particularly noteworthy is that it was "prompted by what He saw in the night." Russia's war strategy, in other words, was being influenced by Rasputin's dreams. Not only did Rasputin communicate his ideas to Nicholas, but he also wrote to General Mikhail Alexeev, the tsar's chief of staff at Stavka. Neither Nicholas nor Alexeev responded to Rasputin's letters; no Russian troops were sent to attack near Riga, and the city remained in Russian hands until after the collapse of the monarchy.

Rasputin was frequently worried about the conduct of the war, but he remained an optimist. In November he told Alexandra that the war would be over in a few months and spoke with excitement about the day Russian troops would march into Constantinople.[10] After Nicholas declared war on Bulgaria on 5 October, Rasputin wrote to praise his decision: "Powerful might emanates from Your heart, the veil of the Mother of God is helping You and an invisible veil is helping the whole army of Yours [...] God is with us and we fear no one."[11] On 9 October, he saw Alexandra and Vyrubova and told them that while he was now less worried about the war, he had had another terrible dream, and he could talk of nothing else for two hours. Alexandra conveyed his concerns to Nicholas: "You must give an order that waggons with flour, butter & sugar should be obliged to pass. He saw the whole thing in the night like a vision, all the towns, railway lines etc. It's difficult to give over fr. his words, but he says it is very serious & that then we shall have no strikes. [. . .] He wishes me to speak to you about all this earnestly, severely even [. . .]."

Rasputin told Alexandra that for three days no trains except those carrying flour, butter, and sugar should be permitted to move.[12] The Russian people were growing hungry, and Rasputin, who moved and lived among them and saw with his own eyes what was happening across the country, knew of what he spoke. His advice in this instance was correct. It was, however, never followed. Life on the home front grew increasingly difficult throughout 1915 and into the following year. Higher wages for workers were eaten up by inflation. For lower-skilled workers, compulsory overtime became the norm; women and children were frequently required to work nights, consumer goods grew scarce, rents spiked, there were long lines for fuel. As peasants flocked to the cities to work in the factories supplying the army, the working-class neighborhoods experienced horrendous overcrowding. Living conditions were appalling.

Rasputin was right to worry about the food crisis and the other problems the average Russian was facing, but was utterly blind when speaking about the impending defeat of the Central Powers. Indeed, it is remarkable that he could have even made such a statement in the autumn of 1915. Following offensives begun by the Central Powers in April, the Russians retreated until September, having given up not only their gains of the previous year (Galicia and Bukovina), but even having been forced to withdraw from Poland, Lithuania, and a good deal of White Russia. During this so-called Great Retreat of 1915, the Russians lost about a million men dead and wounded and another million taken prisoner. During the three years of the war, Russia lost approximately 7 million men to the enemy, whether killed, wounded, or taken prisoner—half of the 15 million who served in the armed forces. The causes for such horrific human losses were many, from lack of training, to poor logistics, to incompetent military command, to a shortage of weapons and ammunition, to breakdowns in an over-strained transportation network. Indeed, so severe was the lack of materiel that for a time in 1915 as many as one in four of all soldiers sent off to the front arrived without any weapon and with instructions to take one off a dead comrade. Adding insult to injury, the western territories of the empire were overrun by well over 3 million refugees by the end of the year.[13]

Minister of Agriculture Alexander Krivoshein commented at a secret meeting of the Council of Ministers in July 1915 that they had been living through a time of "unending retreats and incomprehensible defeats." Incomprehensible. Krivoshein was too well informed of the realities facing Russia not to have some idea of why the country had been so thoroughly routed that year by the Central Powers. It should not have been incomprehensible to any of the ministers, yet still he managed to wail: "Why is poor Russia fated to live through such a tragedy?"[14]

The rest of the country was asking the same thing. What was happening to Russia? The answer that made the most sense to nearly everyone was simple: treason. The honest answer would have required looking too closely at the morass of problems at the heart of the Romanov regime—its inefficiencies, corruption, underdevelopment, and antiquated political system that blocked nearly every effort of the educated classes to come together as a civil society to support the war. No, it was much easier, and more gratifying, for Russians to see themselves as victims, as having been stabbed in the back, sold out. As one historian accurately remarked, "Treason was the supreme and comprehensive excuse for everything."

Russians became convinced they must be the victim of a grand conspiracy. Shadowy actors, hidden from view, were the ones truly in charge of the situation. *Tyomnye sily*, they were called, "Dark Forces." They could be different things to different people—Jews, Germans, Freemasons, Alexandra, Rasputin, and the court camarilla—but it was taken on faith that they were the true masters of Russia.[15] Although the obsession with dark forces took off during the war, it did not begin then. In July 1914, for example, Mitrofan Lodyzhensky published a novel titled *Dark Forces*, part of his "Mystical Trilogy" that examined the dark side of human existence, from passion and perversion to the occult and the Antichrist. A nobleman who had studied in St. Petersburg before embarking on a successful career in the provincial civil service, Lodyzhensky was at the same time a Theosophist fascinated by a range of mystical philosophies and traditions. He embodied the preoccupation of his generation with the occult, secret wisdom, and the hidden forces of history.[16] The *zeitgeist* of fin-de-siècle Russia is important for understanding why so many Russians, and especially well-educated, intellectually sophisticated men and women, could have been so receptive to the mass hysteria of the "dark forces" that seized Russia in the final years of the dynasty.

Fear about dark forces fed anti-Semitism and Germanophobia, both of which surged in 1915. The authorities played a significant part in this. The military command avoided taking responsibility for Russia's defeats, claiming instead it was the fault of traitors and spies. The government cracked down on ethnic German subjects of the empire both to suggest that they represented a perfidious Fifth Column attacking Russia from within and to deflect any blame for the worsening state of affairs in the country. The regime sought to use anti-German feeling to unite the people behind the crown and maintain support for the war, but in effect it led many to believe the state was not doing enough to root out internal enemies. And the press, too, bore responsibility, by whipping up their readers with exaggerated stories intended to highlight the purportedly criminal incompetence of the government. The unintended consequence of these maneuvers was to undermine faith in the monarchy and to promote a sense of cynicism and paranoia. In the coming years, nearly all Russians would be convinced that treason had fully infected the imperial elite and the country was being sold out to its enemies.[17]

In March 1915, Colonel Sergei Myasoedov, a protégé of Minister of War Vladimir Sukhomlinov, was arrested, tried, and executed as a spy in a rushed affair that took no more than a matter of days. Myasoedov had been under suspicion before, although the evidence against him was shaky at best. In the past, Sukhomlinov had managed to protect Myasoedov, but by early 1915, following the scandals over the lack of shells and defeats at the front, the cry for the blood of Russia's traitors became too great. Among those who gloated at the news of Myasoedov was Alexander Guchkov. Guchkov had been publicly attacking Myasoedov as a spy for years, and he now felt vindicated and basked in the praise heaped upon him, even though by then Guchkov knew himself that the charges were baseless and that an innocent man had been executed. This was immaterial for Guchkov. What mattered was scoring points against the regime, not the life of one minor officer. Far from calming the waters, the scandal fueled the hunt for traitors higher up in the officer ranks. The Okhrana began raiding the apartments of nearly anyone connected with Myasoedov in cities across Russia. By the end of April, thirty people had been arrested. Several were sentenced to hard labor and four were hanged. All of those executed were likely innocent.[18] The following spring Sukhomlinov as well would be arrested on charges of treason. Bruce Lockhart recorded in his diary in March

1915 a popular anecdote going around Moscow: "Tsarevich crying. Nurse says: Why are you crying, little man? Well, when our soldiers get beaten, papa cries, and when the Germans get beaten, mama cries. So when am I supposed to cry?"[19] The empress, most Russians believed, had to be working for her German countrymen.

In May 1915, anti-German riots broke out in Moscow. To cries of "Beat the German," mobs looted stores and factories and private homes. A seventy-two-year-old woman was beaten to death in her apartment just because she had a German surname; when they had finished with her, the murderers took two other women out into the street and drowned them in a nearby canal. Crowds threw rocks at the carriage of the German-born Grand Duchess Ella as it drove through the streets. Prince Felix Yusupov père, father of Rasputin's murderer, the city's military governor, sympathized with the rioters and took his time calling out the troops. When it was all over, more than fifteen people had been killed and several hundred businesses and homes torched. From Moscow the anti-German anger spread to other towns later that year. Government offices and private businesses, even orchestras and theater groups, began purging persons with German or even foreign sounding names. The state got in on the act as well, forcibly moving approximately a million Russian citizens of German ethnicity, along with Jews and Muslims too, nationalizing their property, and handing it over to so-called "favored groups."[20]

It became accepted as fact that Rasputin was at the center of the dark forces. "Tsar, I beg You: disperse the rebellious Duma, make peace with Wilhelm and you'll reign in peace." So read a phony letter purportedly written by Rasputin that was copied over and over and handed out throughout Russia.[21] Colonel Alexander Rezanov, part of a commission investigating espionage on the home front, claimed Rasputin liked to say, "Enough blood's been spilled already. The German's no threat any more; he's too weak."[22] Not surprisingly, the Central Powers followed such talk closely. On 29 June 1915, the *Wiener Allgemeine Zeitung* published an article stating it was well known that "the farmer Rasputin" was a supporter of peace and had been doing everything in his power to convince the top men in the government to take his side. As for Nicholas, he did not dare act against Rasputin, for he fully believed Rasputin's prophecy that should something happen to him, the Romanov dynasty would fall. The following month, the *Neues Wiener Journal* reported that according to "trusted circles" Nicholas and top officials in Russia's foreign ministry had been complaining that their allies were forcing Russia to carry too heavy a burden in the war and were showing signs of being willing to explore the idea of a separate peace.[23]

A large collection of documents in the Political Archive of the German foreign ministry in Berlin offers rich evidence of just how keen the government was to learn where Rasputin stood on the question of war and his influence on the tsar. In Geneva in early September 1915, a German official by the name of Einsiedel met a contact referred to as "the old Russian" then traveling through Switzerland. The unnamed source, who claimed to have close contacts at the Russian court, told Einsiedel that Nicholas was increasingly embittered with the British government, yet his personal friendship with his cousin King George V kept him in the war. "The Tsar desperately wishes for peace," the old Russian informed his German contact, "and will eventually accept the loss of Poland and Courland [. . .]." He recommended that Graf Eulenburg write to his old friend Count Fredericks and without mentioning peace directly tell him that the German Kaiser bore the tsar no ill will, as the tsar seemed to believe. Einsiedel's coded telegram was sent to Gottlieb von Jagow, the German foreign minister, and then passed on to Kaiser Wilhelm. The Kaiser endorsed the idea, but the archive contains no further documents on the matter.[24]

Another report on the situation in Russia was submitted in September, apparently again from Einsiedel after further conversations with "the old Russian." It states that the "peace party" in Russia, which included the court, was again ascendant and that even the tsar was trying to find a way to make peace. There was supposedly talk then in Petrograd, according to the report, of having the tsar step down from the throne for a time in favor of a regency, which would allow for peace without Nicholas losing face with the Allies. "Rasputin is pushing hard for this Jesuit suggestion," Einsiedel wrote. The old Russian said he was on his way home, where he planned to bring together those persons in the Duma and the "Court Party" (i.e. Baron Fredericks, Russian ambassador to Great Britain Count Alexander Benkendorf, Alexandra, Rasputin) inclined toward a separate peace and convinced of the need for immediate action.[25]

The correspondence between Rasputin and their majesties shows no evidence that Rasputin ever proposed a separate peace with the Central Powers. The costs, in human and material terms, were not lost on him, but he never wavered in his support once the war had begun.

"Dear me, what losses," Alexandra wrote to Nicholas late in the summer of 1915, "ones heart bleeds—but our Friend says they are torches burning before God's throne, & that is lovely."[26] The department of the police saw matters differently, however. In February 1915, it concluded that certain Germans with links to the Russian court had joined with Rasputin in an attempt to pressure rightist forces in the Duma to accept the necessity of ending the war. Among the deputies working with Rasputin and the Germans was, according to police sources, none other than Vladimir Purishkevich. The members of this cabal were planning to create some sort of new political organization whose members would propagandize the need for peace first among wounded officers in the country's military hospitals and then among soldiers in the active army.[27]

The linking of Rasputin with one of his murderers is striking, and clearly mistaken. Rasputin and Purishkevich were foes, not friends by 1915. Also striking is the idea that Rasputin was working with members of the Duma. The Fourth Duma, which lasted from November 1912 to October 1917, headed the entire time by Mikhail Rodzianko, had been at loggerheads with Nicholas's government since the final months of 1914 over its role in helping to mobilize and direct the efforts of the nation in the struggle against the enemy. Nicholas had never trusted the Duma and regretted ever having consented to its creation. The tsar tried to keep the Duma at arm's length and to restrict its charter, and he continually rebuffed its genuine attempts to be of use to the government. As the war progressed, relations between the crown and the Duma sank ever lower.[28]

Rasputin's views on the Duma were complex and never straightforward. In June 1915, for example, he told Alexandra that he was against the plan for the Duma to reconvene in August, insisting that it would only meddle in matters that did not concern it and cause trouble. He told Nicholas that if the Duma were to meet, he should delay its opening as long as possible.[29] Nicholas, once more, ignored Rasputin, and the Duma met for a new session in the middle of July. The following month, a grand coalition that included all the members—except those from the parties of the far left and right—was formed under the name of the Progressive Bloc. Born out of the disgust at the Great Retreat and the growing preoccupation with the "Dark Forces," the bloc announced that it was willing to work with the government if Nicholas would appoint ministers that enjoyed true popular support. The idea that bound the Progressive Bloc together was that the war could be won only if the throne was committed to working with the Duma and engaging the productive efforts of society via a new government that enjoyed the confidence of all Russians.

But Nicholas rebuffed the bloc and its modest program for co-operation. As the government and the Duma faced off, Rodzianko informed Minister of Justice Alexander Khvostov, the uncle of Alexei Khvostov, that if the Duma were dismissed ahead of time, some of the deputies were prepared to launch an inquiry into Rasputin and the only way to stop them would be for Khvostov to initiate his own criminal investigation and have Rasputin arrested and incarcerated. Prime Minister Goremykin, however, was convinced Rodzianko was bluffing and that the Duma would never go through with it.[30] Indeed, it was against Goremykin, the old "fur coat in mothballs," as Princess Yusupova called him, that the Duma was then chiefly aiming its threat. He knew that one of the first demands of the bloc was that he be fired as prime minister, and so he convinced Nicholas to prorogue the Duma on 3 September.[31]

The Kadet deputy Vasily Maklakov, outraged by the situation, let fly with a provocative article titled "A Tragic Situation" in the Moscow Gazette on 27 September. He asked his readers to imagine a situation in which they find themselves hurtling downhill in an automobile along a steep, treacherous road. They are being driven by a mad chauffeur who refuses to give up the wheel or to even listen to the advice of the fellow passengers who do know how to drive. Why is he doing this, they wonder, what are they to do? Should they grab for the wheel, or will this lead to a crash that will kill them all, including the passengers' mother, riding along with them? The driver laughs at their conundrum, mocking their indecision, certain they will not dare to act. Maklakov's parable was not lost on anyone: the mad chauffeur was Nicholas, the mother, Russia, and the fellow passengers, the educated, enlightened forces as personified by the Progressive Bloc.[32]

Goremykin continued his opposition to allowing the Duma to meet for its autumn session.[33] By now, however, Rasputin had changed his mind, and he began to try to convince Nicholas, by way of Alexandra, to permit the Duma to meet in November, even if this meant trouble for Goremykin. He purportedly said, in defense of his position: "When a Russian man yells, he won't do anything evil, but it's when he's quiet, when he has something on his chest, then watch out!"[34] Alexandra was not quite certain what to think. On 15 November, she wrote to Nicholas that the Duma had no real work to do and so, "If they sit idle, they will begin talks about Varnava & our Friend & mix into government questions, which they have not the right [. . .]." She added that she would first talk to Rasputin about the matter and ask "what He would bless." But before she could even send her letter, Alexandra heard from Vyrubova that Rasputin was sad and upset by Goremykin's attempts to block the Duma from meeting. Rasputin was now convinced the Duma must meet, even if only for a short while, and that it would be wise for Nicholas to appear before it, unannounced, as this would have a marvelous effect on the deputies. As for the potential of any scandals, Rasputin also told Vyrubova that he had the word of both Alexei Khvostov and Stepan Beletsky that no one would dare mention his name. It was most important, Rasputin believed, that the government and the Duma now try to work together and that the Tsar "must show them a little confidence." All of this Alexandra relayed to Nicholas.

Again Nicholas sided with Goremykin against the advice of his wife and Rasputin. Alexandra told Nicholas that Rasputin "venerates the Old Man," and he knew convening the Duma would mean Goremykin's downfall, yet despite his warm personal feelings for him, Rasputin sensed his time was up and he had to go. First, however, he asked that the tsar wait, and hold off getting rid of Goremykin until Rasputin could find a worthy successor.[35] Nicholas kept Goremykin on until 20 January 1916, although whether this had anything at all to do with Rasputin's influence is impossible to say. As for the Duma, it did not meet again until 22 February 1916. By then the Progressive Bloc had retracted its offer of support and become an implacable force of opposition. Nicholas's refusal to listen to Rasputin's advice caused what might be considered irreparable damage in the throne's relations with the Duma. As with the decision to go to war, one cannot help wondering what might have been, had the emperor listened to Rasputin and accepted the Progressive Bloc's offer of cooperation.

52. Another Miracle

On the afternoon of 3 December the emperor and Alexei left Stavka by train to inspect the troops. The tsarevich was ill with a head cold and was coughing and sneezing terribly. Soon he was bleeding from his nose. The imperial surgeon Sergei Fyodorov attended to the boy and found his condition serious. He recommended to the emperor late that evening that they return to Stavka. A telegram was sent to Alexandra that she come join them. The following morning, the emperor's train returned to Mogilyov. Alexei was extremely weak, his temperature had spiked. Alexandra sent Nicholas a telegram at 10:35 that morning suggesting the doctors should cauterize their son's nose, as Dr. Polyakov recommended in such instances. As for her, she wrote Nicholas that she was not worried for our "Friend says all this comes from weariness and will now pass."[1]

But Alexei's condition continued to worsen during the afternoon of the fourth. Upon the advice of Fyodorov, it was decided that they should return to Tsarskoe Selo that afternoon. Alexei seemed to revive as they rode, but only briefly. The blood continued to flow and his temperature rose during the evening. He was losing strength. The train had to be stopped several times so the doctor could change the dressing in the boy's nostrils. That night Alexei twice lost consciousness. Those attending to him feared he might die. Nicholas wired Alexandra that no one should meet them at the station.

The train pulled into Tsarskoe Selo at 11 a.m. on the fifth. Alexandra was waiting. Nicholas told her Alexei was feeling better and that the bleeding had stopped. She turned to Pierre Gilliard, the children's tutor, and asked when this had happened. At 6:20 a.m. that morning, he replied. I knew it, she said, for at that precise moment Rasputin had sent her a telegram: "God will help, He'll be fine." Alexei was carefully removed from the train and taken into the Alexander Palace. This bit of movement reopened the wounds in the boy's nose, and once more the bleeding began. They cauterized the veins in his nostrils, but to no effect. The bleeding continued. Now, Alexandra was beside herself with worry.[2]

In her memoirs, Vyrubova writes that she too was there that day (5 December) when Alexei arrived from Stavka. She witnessed how as the doctors helplessly fussed over the tsarevich, Alexandra kneeled by his bedside desperate that something be done to save her son. After returning home, Vyrubova received a note from the empress instructing her to call for Rasputin. He came immediately and went with Nicholas and Alexandra to see the boy. He approached the bed and made the sign of the cross over him. He told them not to worry, for it was not serious, Alexei would be fine. With that, he turned and left. Soon after, the bleeding stopped. Just like at Spała three years before, the doctors were at a loss to explain what had happened. Such was Alexei's recovery that Nicholas, according to Vyrubova, was able to return to Stavka the next day.[3]

It appears, however, that Vyrubova's memory is not to be trusted in this instance. Nicholas did not leave for Stavka until 12 December, a full week after his arrival in Tsarskoe Selo. More importantly, it does not seem that Rasputin came to see Alexei at the palace on 5 December, the critical day of his return, but only the following day. Nicholas wrote in his diary on the sixth that the entire family gathered after breakfast and then went in to see Alexei. He was doing much better, his fever had come down, and, most importantly, "the bleeding had stopped after the second cauterization." It was only later in the day, after dinner, that Rasputin came and they went in to sit with Alexei.[4] It would appear, then, that Rasputin did not visit the palace on the fifth at all. Beletsky told the Commission that Rasputin did not come on the fifth when summoned, but waited until the next day.[5] The police files offer little help, for they show Rasputin visiting the palace only on the eleventh, twenty-sixth, and twenty-ninth of the month.

The files do contain, however, a telegram intercepted by the police from Rasputin to the emperor sent on the sixth at 1:20 p.m.: "Your honored day has been much glorified with miracle-making, a lot of patience; this is an example of the great miracle worker. He will give us consolation and stay with us forever. There is no one to fear. Grigory Novy."[6] It was the emperor's name day, and Rasputin had written to congratulate him. It was a time of "miracle-making," indeed, for Alexei had once more been saved from what seemed certain death. For Rasputin, this had been the work of God, not medical science. It is not clear just what Nicholas attributed his son's recovery to, but as for Alexandra, this latest incident proved once more the infinite powers of their Friend.

Part Six

THE FINAL YEAR

1916

53. Revolution in the Air

"I returned in 1916," Princess Lucien Murat recalled after a three-year absence from Russia, "and the peasant was thriving. One thought of nothing but Rasputin, he occupied every mind. In the trains, in the trams, in the Duma, in the street, at the Grand Dukes', everywhere, like a refrain, the name of that man kept being repeated without end, and upon him, this scapegoat, fell all the faults of a rotten regime."[1]

A French diplomat recently arrived in Russia in January 1916 made a similar remark, noting how every conversation "always ends up leading to Rasputin." He concluded his report with the prophetic words: "*La révolution est dans l'air.*"[2]

It was not just that Rasputin was practically the only thing Russians were talking about, it was what they were saying that was so shocking. In early January the Moscow Okhrana discovered that several local newspaper editors had been circulating by post a scurrilous doggerel against Rasputin, reproduced on a hectograph machine, titled "Sick-Quarters Leisure Time: Who Rules Russia:"

> A sailor tells a soldier:
> Brother, no matter what you say
> Russia is ruled by the cock today.
> The cock appoints ministers,
> The cock makes policy,
> It confers archbishops,
> And presents medals and positions.
> The cock commands the troops,
> It steers the ships.
> Having sold our motherland to the Yids,
> The cock has raised all the prices.
> So the cock is mighty and powerful,
> And rich with talents.
> Clearly, this is no ordinary cock,
> They say it's fourteen inches long [. . .]

And the cock had been quite busy.

> Peasant women enjoyed the cock,
> And those in town as well,
> Once the merchant wives had tried it
> They had to tell the noble ladies too.
> Thus the holy man's cock gained so much power
> It might well have been made a field marshal.
> Soon it reached the Tsar's palace
> Where it fucked all the ladies-in-waiting,
> And the Tsar's maiden daughter too,
> But it fucked the Tsaritsa most of all [. . .]

The authors, given as "The Forgotten Ones," concluded with a plea to their readers to copy their words and help spread them across Russia.[3]

Rasputin's member figured in other satires. A foreign caricature popular among officers in early 1916 contrasted an image of Kaiser Wilhelm measuring a meter-long projectile with one of Nicholas, on his knees, measuring the impressive length of Rasputin's penis. That spring the Germans dropped copies of this drawing over the front lines from their zeppelins. By then Russian officers shared such things openly, laughing with no embarrassment or shame.[4] A caricature of Rasputin's penis with the caption "the rudder that rules Russia" was also a hit.[5] Soldiers gossiped that it was his large penis that had secured Rasputin his place at court. The Dowager Empress was said to be the one responsible, for she "needed a big member."[6] To some of the soldiers, it was common sense that Rasputin was sleeping with the empress. A peasant-soldier by the name of Larkin explained it so: "They say he's good with the women, and the tsaritsa, she's a woman too, she needs it, but her man is away at the front. And our women back home, you know, they've been having fun with those Austrians."[7]

Another rumor that appeared in January was that Rasputin had been designated the Tsar's *lampadnik*, the lighter of the icon lamps in the Fyodorovsky Cathedral at Tsarskoe Selo. That no such position existed was irrelevant, for it fit so naturally into the popular perception that Rasputin was forever at the side of the royal family. Some alleged that with the new title came unfettered access to the palace and, by extension, to the empress. Deputy Vasily Maklakov, author of "A Tragic Situation," mentioned it in a speech before the Duma. He said he was not certain whether the rumor was true or some kind of joke, at which point a voice rang out from the hall: *"Pravda!"*, the truth.[8] Alexandra mentioned the rumor, and the darker suggestions behind it, in a letter to Nicholas on 7 January. She called such talk "idiotic" and insisted she laughed at it as any "sensible person" would. Nevertheless, she also mentioned that though she longed to see Rasputin, she did not call for him when Nicholas was away, "as people are so nasty."[9]

Alexandra, so it seems, had no idea just how nasty people could be. That same month people were saying in the capital that some right-wing politicians had begun discussing historical precedents for tsarist divorce. It was said Alexandra had agreed to a divorce, but then went back on her word when she learned it meant she would have to go to a convent. Nicholas, so the talk went, was furious with Alexandra for changing her mind. In the trams of the capital, people were openly saying that it was high time the empress removed herself to a convent. Even Valentina Chebotaryova, who knew the empress from her work at the Palace Hospital and felt great respect for her, thought it was the right thing: "It would be such a beautiful gesture—to go off to a convent," she wrote in her diary on 27 January. "Immediately all the charges of Germanophilia would disappear, all the ugly talk about Rasputin would end, and, perhaps, the Children and the Throne itself would be saved from great danger."[10] There was also gossip it was Nicholas who was to be sent away, not Alexandra, after which she would become regent and rule alongside Rasputin.[11] The common folk began to say that Nicholas had already left for a monastery after he "gave Grishka the deed to the kingdom."[12]

It was taken as fact that Rasputin was now spending nearly every day at the palace, but the police watching Rasputin recorded only eight visits in the first three months of 1916, and from April until the beginning of October, Rasputin was at Tsarskoe Selo only six times.[13] Vyrubova, however, was a frequent guest at Rasputin's Gorokhovaya apartment throughout January and the first half of February, acting as a go-between for him and Alexandra.[14] The police files show that unlike in years past Rasputin rarely visited churches any more, about once a month, and sometimes even less. Rather, he was spending a good deal of his time drinking and carousing.[15]

He threw a large party for his name day on 10 January. Alexandra sent her best wishes from the family. "Inexpressibly overjoyed," he wrote back, "God's light shines on you, we will fear nothing."[16] Khvostov and

Beletsky used money from their secret fund to buy expensive gifts not only for Rasputin, but for his entire family, all of whom had come for what would prove to be his final birthday. The party lasted all day and into the night, guests coming in waves to congratulate Rasputin and bearing presents—works of silver and gold, furnishings, rugs, paintings, objets d'art—all of which was later brought back to the family home in Pokrovskoe by Praskovya and Dmitry. Munya Golovina came and was shocked by the number of guests, the gifts, the baskets of fruit and cakes. She gave Rasputin a white silk shirt embroidered with silver thread. At one point Pyotr Mudrolyubov, chief secretary of the Synod, gave a long toast praising Rasputin and his importance for the state as "a simple man who brought the painful needs of the people to the foot of the throne."

Having had too much to drink, Rasputin lay down for a late afternoon nap and then rejoined his guests. An intimate group remained to drink and dance to the music of a small Gypsy choir. By the end of the night everyone was drunk. Munya did not like the crowd. There were people there who came to force Rasputin to drink and dance, as if he was their entertainment. He was too simple and good natured, she commented, to realize it. Several guests slept over, too far gone to make their way home. According to the police, the next day two jealous husbands showed up with revolvers looking for their wives. The agents held them off just long enough for the women to pull themselves together and leave by the back door before the police let the men in to search for their wives. A chastened Rasputin curtailed his socializing for a time, and promised never again to let married women spend the night, but before too long he was apparently back at it.[17]

A story circulated in mid-February that a group of officers led by Count Orlov-Davydov had nearly killed Rasputin after an orgy at the suburban Villa Rode. Rasputin was said to have been so badly beaten he spent two weeks in the hospital; others claimed he had been killed.[18] None of it, however, was true, and Rasputin was at home on Gorokhovaya all of February. It was perhaps this story that prompted Purishkevich to hand out at the Duma on the sixteenth of the month copies of a photograph of Rasputin surrounded by his female votaries with Purishkevich's own caption scribbled in ink along the bottom: "Grigory Rasputin and the high-society wh—es."[19] His stunt was wildly successful.

54. The Minister Plots Murder

Even before the end of 1915, Khvostov had begun to plot Rasputin's murder. The man he had been entrusted with protecting, he now sought to do away with. The troika's plans to control Rasputin had fallen apart from the start. The money handed over to Prince Andronikov for Rasputin frequently went straight into his own pocket, and Khvostov and Beletsky realized they had to cut him out of their operation. The troika became a duo. The two men came to understand how extensive Rasputin's influence and network of contacts were as well as the man's own intelligence and natural abilities. They had underestimated him and admitted they would have no more success neutralizing him than the others before them. Moreover, Khvostov had hoped Rasputin would push his candidacy for prime minister, but Goremykin remained in place, much to Khvostov's displeasure. He was tired of Rasputin's endless notes from his petitioners, nor did he care for Rasputin's overly familiar manner.[1]

Unlike his predecessors, however, Khvostov was not willing to admit defeat, and he put every option on the table for consideration. "It's all the same to me," he told Alexander Spiridovich, "to go with Grishka to a brothel or to throw him from the buffer under a train." Spiridovich could hardly believe his ears. "It appeared that this well-fed, pinkish fatty with passionate, happy eyes was not a minister but some sort of rough bandit."[2] When asked by the Commission whether he had had other means at his disposal apart from murder to combat Rasputin's influence, Khvostov replied: "Not in the slightest. I saw when giving my reports how powerful his influence was. I tried to open their eyes about him, but encountered such resistance that I stopped and came to the conclusion that the only way to get rid of him was murder."[3] Deputy Minister Beletsky went along with his boss's plans.

In December, Khvostov and Beletsky came up with the idea of sending Rasputin on a pilgrimage to a few of the country's northern monasteries accompanied by Father Martemian, Rasputin's acquaintance. Khvostov gave Rasputin 5,000 rubles for the trip, and the two men began to prepare for their journey. Initially, Rasputin seemed to like the idea. Little did he know, however, that Martemian had been recruited to throw Rasputin from the train in some remote area. At the last minute the trip was cancelled. It is possible that Rasputin changed his mind and refused to go, perhaps because, as Beletsky later wrote, he grew suspicious of the ministers' unmistakable nervousness. Or perhaps it was due to Martemian's last minute change of mind: the clergyman may well have decided he did not want to have anything to do with murder after all.[4]

Killing Rasputin became an idée fixe for Khvostov, and he was soon looking for other possibilities. Part of the problem was that Rasputin was by now so well guarded. There were three separate groups involved: the agents of Spiridovich, in charge of the court secret police that safeguarded the royal family; the agents of the ministry of the interior; and finally, a select group of agents chosen by Khvostov himself.[5] None of these agents trusted each other, nor did they work in any coordinated fashion. Gippius captured the absurd nature of Rasputin's guards in her diary on 24 November 1915: "Khvostov, clenching his teeth, 'guards' Grishka. But who can really say who is guarding whom? Grishka has his guards, Khvostov has his own, the Khvostov agents keep their eyes on Grishka's, while Grishka's are on Khvostov's."[6]

Khvostov's agents were led by Colonel Mikhail Komissarov, former head of the gendarmes in the city of Perm, recommended by Beletsky for his rare skills in "secret services." Komissarov put together his own team of agents, complete with a dedicated automobile and driver. Officially, Komissarov's job was to prevent Rasputin from getting drunk and guard him from bad influences; in fact, however, he got Rasputin drunk as often as he could and introduced him to all manner of dubious individuals. He began visiting Rasputin, often several times a day, and would report back to Khvostov and Beletsky everything he witnessed. Globachev described Komissarov as quite intelligent and capable, but a "big intriguer willing to work with anyone if it would serve his own personal interests."[7]

Together with Komissarov, Khvostov and Beletsky began exploring new ideas about how to do Rasputin in. For a man like Komissarov, killing Rasputin was no less complicated than protecting him. He would do what his superiors told him to if he felt it would further his career. One day at the dacha of Dr. Badmaev, he said calmly as he cleaned his piece of smoked whitefish, "This is how I intend to peel the skin off Grishka."[8] A number of ideas were discussed. One was to lure Rasputin to a rendezvous with a fictitious lady and then strangle him in the automobile in a deserted part of the city. They would then dump the body in a hole in the ice of the Neva River and it would be carried out to sea come the spring melt. Another option was to have him murdered by some of Komissarov's men in disguise, claiming to be cuckolded husbands seeking revenge. And at one meeting Khvostov said he would kill Rasputin himself and pulled out his Browning pistol to prove he meant it.

Beletsky began to have doubts. Khvostov's obsession with killing Rasputin and his utter lack of principles, which Beletsky was by now well aware of, led to a change of heart.[9] He told the Commission: "The government can't start behaving like the mafia."[10] Beletsky also came to see the futility of killing Rasputin, for he realized that some other figure would simply take his place and nothing would change. But he kept these doubts to himself for the time being. As for Khvostov, he was beginning to question Beletsky's commitment to their plan and started to meet alone with Komissarov, offering him at one point 200,000 rubles from his secret fund to organize the killing on his own. During one of their conversations Khvostov pulled several large stacks of banknotes out of his safe and laid them on his desk for Komissarov to see that he was serious. Khvostov told him that he had nothing to worry about, for he gave his word as a tsarist minister to protect Komissarov and make sure nothing happened to him. But Komissarov knew Khvostov well enough not to trust him, and so he told Beletsky everything, who, in turn, passed this information on to Rasputin. There, the matter ended, for Rasputin never bothered to do anything about it.[11]

Komissarov and Beletsky joined forces and decided to come up with a plan to forestall Khvostov. At their next meeting, Beletsky proposed that they poison Rasputin. Khvostov liked the idea, so Komissarov was sent to off to obtain some sort of toxin capable of doing the job. Soon after, they met in Khvostov's office where he showed them the various drugs he had collected and how they all worked. He had experimented with one of them on a cat and explained with delight how the unfortunate feline had spun and twirled in agony before falling down dead. The plan was to kill Rasputin by putting the noxious powder into his beloved Madeira. Khvostov was delighted by the idea; little did he know, however, that the powder was innocuous. Komissarov had made up the whole story about the cat and told Khvostov of the poison's chemical makeup and effects based on what he had gleaned from a pharmacological textbook.[12] The substance was suspended in a solution and then injected into the bottles of a case of Madeira and sent to Rasputin as a gift from his friend the banker Dmitry Rubinshtein. And then they waited. Nothing, of course, happened. Khvostov sensed something was amiss, and he began to suspect he was being played by Beletsky and Komissarov.[13] Khvostov now decided he needed to find a new accomplice for his plan. He quickly settled on Rasputin's greatest enemy, the man who had already tried to kill Rasputin: Iliodor. Since the disgraced former monk had fled the country, Khvostov realized he needed to bring in one more person, someone he could send to Iliodor to help arrange the killing.

Boris Rzhevsky had served under Khvostov in Nizhny Novgorod as an official for "special assignments" and later helped his boss win election to the Duma. More recently, Rzhevsky had worked as a reporter for such papers as the *Voice of Moscow* and *Evening Times*. After Iliodor had been locked up in the Florishchev Monastery, Rzhevsky had managed to disguise himself with actor's makeup and talk his way into Iliodor's cell for an interview. Short and thin with a vulpine appearance, Boris, according to Zinaida Rzhevskaya (née Zazulina), his common-law wife, was a man "ready for any adventure."[14] Globachev called him "an unbalanced, hysterical and completely unprincipled person."[15]

Rzhevsky appeared in Petrograd in December now working for the Red Cross and living well: he had a lavish apartment, an automobile, horses, and his wife went about in diamonds and furs.[16] He looked up his former boss, and Khvostov decided to put Rzhevsky to use. He instructed Beletsky to hire Rzhevsky and give him some money from the ministry to open a journalists' club so that Rzhevsky could keep tabs on the city's leftist reporters. Beletsky interviewed Rzhevsky and found him "extremely unsympathetic" and "a vapid, arrogant braggart," but he did as ordered and hired him with a salary of 500 rubles a month. Knowing that Rzhevsky was Khvostov's man, Beletsky, much too experienced not to be suspicious, sent out some of his agents to follow him and see what they could dig up. They came back and told Beletsky there was no way Rzhevsky's official salary from the Red Cross, or the money he had from the ministry, could support his luxurious lifestyle, so he had the agents dig deeper to find out just where the money was coming from. They discovered that Rzhevsky had been using his position at the Red Cross to engage in extortion and racketeering.[17] Beletsky now had the *kompromat* he needed on Rzhevsky. He chose not to use it just yet, however; he would wait until the right moment.

What Beletsky did not know at the time was that Khvostov had even bigger plans for Rzhevsky. He informed Rzhevsky of his plan to murder Rasputin with the help of Iliodor and asked whether he might be open to working along with them in this vitally important, top secret mission. Rzhevsky said yes, for 5,000 rubles, he was their man.[18] On 8 January, Rzhevsky and Zinaida departed Petrograd for Kristiania, but before they left, Boris made sure to provide himself some cover in case Khvostov tried to double-cross him. He wrote a detailed letter describing how Khvostov had masterminded the plot and recruited him for his trip. He left the letter with a friend from the journalists' club, an engineer named Vladimir Heine, with instructions to see it got to the empress should anything go wrong. This would prove to be the undoing of Rzhevsky, as well as Khvostov, for Heine panicked and went straight to the police with the information. (According to another version of events, Zinaida told Heine about the plot after she and Boris had had a terrible fight.) Thus, soon after the couple's departure, Beletsky was already in on the secret.[19]

The Rzhevskys arrived in Kristiania on 12 January and checked into the Hotel Scandinavia under the name of Artemieff. Later that same day, Boris went to visit Iliodor on his own. He found him at home with his wife and another Russian woman. Rzhevsky introduced himself with his real name, stating that he was the personal secretary of Minister of the Interior Khvostov and had been sent on a special mission. Suspicious, Iliodor asked for proof of identification. Once he was satisfied, the men sat down to talk. Iliodor asked what Rzhevsky wanted. "Together we will carry out a great deed, which will go down in history," Rzhevsky told him. "I was sent here by Khvostov to ask you to kill Rasputin."[20]

Iliodor was not sure just what to think. He asked Rzhevsky why Khvostov, a minister, would be plotting murder. Rzhevsky told him that Rasputin had sold himself to the Jews and was working behind the scenes for a separate peace with Germany. He had become all powerful and was blocking Khvostov's important work. "He plays with the ministers like chess pieces," Rzhevsky said. "He makes life unbearable for the members of the government." He told Iliodor that Khvostov had no one he could trust to carry out the job, thus he had turned to him. In a later interview with the Swedish press, Iliodor stated he played along with Rzhevsky just to get to the bottom of the matter, promising to help by recruiting some of his people back in Tsaritsyn. In return, he wanted 60,000 rubles. Rzhevsky knew that Khvostov had set aside 100,000 for the operation. "That's a trifle," he replied. Iliodor took out pen and paper and wrote: "I agree. Need 60,000. Iliodor."[21]

Rzhevsky described their plan. A lady-in-waiting working with them would telephone Rasputin and tell him that he must appear at court at once. A car would come and pick him up. Rzhevsky, disguised as the chauffeur, would drive Rasputin to a prearranged place outside Petrograd, where their accomplices would assassinate him. Once Rasputin was dead, Khvostov would see to it that Iliodor was given amnesty so that he could return to Russia without fear of arrest. Rzhevsky and Iliodor next discussed the logistics of the operation: how the money was to be paid out and how their accomplices, five individuals from Tsaritsyn recruited by Iliodor, were to receive passports so they could come to Kristiania for further instructions. The Scandinavian press could not help but notice how Iliodor's story had all the elements of "a true crime novel." Nor could it fail to comment on what the story said about their Eastern neighbor: "The entire business appears much too insane to be possible, even in Russia."[22]

After two days in Kristiania, Boris and Zinaida left for Petrograd. Beletsky was ready for them. He had alerted the border guards to stop the couple and create an incident as they tried to reenter the country. The guards got Boris to confess to his true identity, wrote up a report on the manufactured incident, and informed Rzhevsky that upon returning to the capital he was required to appear before Beletsky for further questioning.[23] A nervous Rzhevsky turned up at Beletsky's office. The deputy minister did not dive straight into the murder plot, but began by asking how an official of the Red Cross living on only 500 rubles a month could afford such a grand lifestyle. Rzhevsky tried to tell Beletsky that he was mistaken, but Beletsky shut him down, informing him he knew all about his corrupt dealings and threatening him with exile to Siberia. Rzhevsky began to quake. He then told Rzhevsky there was only one thing that could possibly save him: he was to write down everything he knew about the plot to kill Rasputin, being certain to highlight Khvostov's role.[24] Beletsky now had all he needed to take down his boss and, with a bit of luck, make himself the next minister of the interior.

Rzhevsky apparently turned to his friend Vladimir Heine for advice on what to do. Events began to accelerate. On 4 February, Heine went to tell Rasputin's secretary Aaron Simanovich about the plot, and together they went to inform Rasputin at his home that same day. Rasputin did nothing, but asked that Heine keep Simanovich informed should he hear any more news. The following day Rasputin invited Simanovich and Vyrubova to his apartment. He proceeded to tell Vyrubova what he knew of the plot and handed her a letter for the empress with all the details. Rasputin appeared to take the matter seriously, but was not overly concerned. Realizing the game was over and he had to change course, Khvostov contacted Rasputin and urged him to leave the city, saying he had just learned that his life was in danger. Rasputin ignored the warning and remained calm until, however, Skvortsov, editor of the *Bell*, called Gorokhovaya on the sixth to ask whether the news that Rasputin had been murdered was true. Now Rasputin began to worry. His daughter Maria wrote that day in her diary that "everyone is in a terrible mood, everyone is waiting for something terrible to happen." A "black cloud" hung over the family. Maria went to church to pray and light a candle for her father's safety. He was giving everyone "black looks," yet her father refused to be cowed and kept up his visits. "How fearless he is . . . God help us."[25]

Rasputin wrote Vyrubova for help, sending Simanovich to deliver the letter. She told Simanovich to take it immediately to General Mikhail Belyaev, assistant to the Minister of War Alexei Polivanov, and inform him of everything. On the evening of the sixth, Alexandra met Vyrubova and Belyaev at the palace and learned of the threat to Rasputin. Alexandra was terrified and afraid that the Okhrana agents hired to protect Rasputin might well kill him. The empress asked the general whether he could do something to help protect Rasputin, but he insisted the matter was well outside his sphere of duties and declined to get involved.[26] Late that night back in Petrograd, Rzhevsky got word that the authorities were on their way to search his apartment. He quickly wrote another letter to Rasputin telling him everything about the plot and gave it to Heine for Rasputin should he be arrested and Khvostov not come to his defense. The police failed to find any correspondence with Iliodor at the apartment—Rzhevsky had had just enough time to hide it—but they did discover five revolvers as well as the receipt for 60,000 rubles from the ministry of the interior intended for Iliodor. They took Rzhevsky into custody.[27]

Heine and Simanovich visited General Belyaev and he assured them he was already investigating the matter. From there, they went to give Rzhevsky's letter to Rasputin:

> With this I attest that one highly placed individual commissioned me to organize the murder of G. Ye. Rasputin and at the present moment I cannot be certain that this evil deed will not be carried out.
>
> I can communicate the details only to G. Ye. Rasputin personally. My arrest took place because the organizers of the murder, seeing my disapproval and fearing that I was going to divulge everything to G. Ye. Rasputin, distorted the facts of the case in order to render me harmless.
>
> Boris Rzhevsky
> 7 February 1916.
> P.S. The documents that prove all this are in my possession.

Despite what he wrote Rasputin, Rzhevsky had not yet given up on his boss, and he sent a telegram to Khvostov that reached him on the eighth: "Urgent. Petrograd. Minister of the Interior. I've been arrested. The business you commissioned me with needs to be liquidated. The people have been summoned. They're waiting, and grumbling, they're not being given the daily money promised them. Send instructions. Rzhevsky." Someone scrawled across the telegram in blue pencil: "The blackmail begins, or continues." This may well have been the point of Rzhevsky's communication to Khvostov: If you want my silence it will cost you, otherwise I am going to tell the police everything.

Khvostov tried to get his hands on Rzhevsky's letter to Rasputin but it was too late. Rasputin had already sent it to the empress. Nicholas returned from Stavka on the eighth and Alexandra informed him of everything, as she understood it at the time. Later that day the emperor met with the new Prime Minister Boris Stürmer (he replaced Goremykin in late January) and ordered him to get to the bottom of the matter and report back to him. He also instructed Stürmer to notify both Khvostov and Beletsky of the threat against Rasputin and instruct them to use every possible measure to protect his life.[28] Clearly, the tsar, like Alexandra, was still in the dark about the main culprits in the affair.

Around 1 a.m. on the tenth, Okhrana agents arrived at Simanovich's apartment and demanded he hand over all documents in his possession on the matter. Then they arrested him on a trumped-up charge and brought him in for questioning.[29] Later that same day Khvostov appeared before the emperor and insisted he was innocent of the entire affair and that he would help get to the bottom of it. With that, Nicholas left Tsarskoe Selo for Stavka.[30] Rasputin was now in a panic. On the eleventh he received a telegram from Iliodor: "Send someone immediately, I'll show all the proofs of the plots of highly placed persons to kill you, telegraph your approval."[31] At the same time as he was warning Rasputin, Iliodor, one of the most dishonest men ever to come into Rasputin's life, was cabling Rzhevsky with updates on the situation with the would-be assassins: "the brothers say yes," he wrote, referring to their agreeing to take part in the plot, and then, "the brothers have been summoned," and finally, "the brothers have arrived."[32]

These were the very same persons grumbling about not receiving their per diem that Rzhevsky referred to in his cable to Khvostov. The Petrograd Okhrana picked up five individuals—four men and one woman from Tsaritsyn, all with ties to Iliodor— for questioning on 20 February. The leader of the group was a forty-two-year-old peasant by the name of Romanenko. In January he had contacted the others about visiting Iliodor, who asked that they come see him in Kristiania about an important matter. The plan was to travel first to Petrograd where a certain "brother Mikhail," according to Iliodor, would meet them with further instructions and money.[33] The archives are silent on whatever became of Iliodor's accomplices.

Also on the eleventh Alexandra wrote Nicholas: "Tuesday brought splendid good—and then that wretched story about our Friend. She [Vyrubova] will try her best with him—tho' in his present humour he screams at her and is so awfully nervous. But it's sunny weather and so, I hope, he will have changed again into what he always was. He is frightened to leave, he says one will kill him—well, we shall see how God turns all!"[34]

Zinaida Rzhevskaya was brought in to police headquarters and questioned on the thirteenth and fourteenth. She told them that Khvostov had twice proposed the idea of murdering Rasputin to her husband and confirmed all the details about their trip to Kristiania. She told the police that Iliodor had indeed arranged for five of his followers from Tsaritsyn to come to him to discuss the details of the killing. During his first interrogation, Boris told the police that Khvostov had first proposed the idea of killing Rasputin a full two years earlier at a meeting in Petersburg's Palkin restaurant. Rzhevsky had refused, and Khvostov brought it up again at the end of October 1915; once more Rzhevsky declined. But Khvostov kept at it and would not let the matter die. In the end, Rzhevsky agreed to do it, but, he told the investigators, he never had any intention of going through with it and was only planning to find a way to make some money on the 60,000 intended for Iliodor by a currency exchange rate scheme he had devised. Rzhevsky was under so much pressure during this interrogation he suffered a nervous attack and the questioning had to be interrupted.

When the interrogators returned the next day they were shocked to hear Rzhevsky take back everything he had said earlier. There had never been any plot, he now insisted, and Khvostov had never spoken to him about murdering Rasputin. The truth of the matter was Khvostov had sent him to Iliodor to try to acquire his manuscript in a sincere attempt to protect the throne and Rasputin. When questioned about the letter he had sent Rasputin warning him of the threats against his life, he stated that this had been a lie and he had just been trying to win Rasputin's favor.[35] Clearly, Khvostov had managed to get to Rzhevsky that night in his cell. An offer of money had likely been enough to buy Rzhevsky's cooperation.

Scrambling to save himself, Khvostov invented the tale that he was not trying to kill Rasputin, but to save him by buying Iliodor's explosive book. He went to the empress with this story and told her that the plot to kill Rasputin had been the doing of Beletsky and Rzhevsky without his knowledge. He told Prime Minister Stürmer that Beletsky had not only plotted Rasputin's murder but had been involved in intrigues against the emperor.[36] Amazingly, just when it appeared he had been cornered, Khvostov managed to outplay Beletsky. On the thirteenth, Beletsky was fired as deputy minister of the interior. He was made a senator, given a yearly salary of 18,000 rubles, and appointed governor of Irkutsk, a form of ministerial exile.[37] It was a remarkably gentle form of punishment for a high-ranking official suspected of plotting the murder of the emperor and empress's closest friend, but this was the norm at the court of Nicholas and the very thing that emboldened criminal action under his reign. In this atmosphere of moral hazard, even attempted murderers could become well-remunerated senators and governors.

At the end of February, Simanovich was banished to Tver for two years and Rzhevsky was exiled to Siberia.[38] Khvostov was tying up the loose ends. On the evening of the twenty-eighth, Stürmer met Rasputin and Ivan Manasevich-Manuilov at the Alexander Nevsky Lavra. The prime minister tried to convince Rasputin to leave the city for a while, just to be safe. Rasputin, his nerves shattered by recent events, screamed: "You're something, you're really something. Papa and Mama ordered me to stay here, ordered me themselves, and you want to run me out . . . You're in league with the murderers . . . I'm not going . . . Hear me, not going!" He ran around the room like a madman. "They want to kill me on the way. They want to arrest all my friends. I'm not going . . . Papa and Mama ordered me to stay and I'll stay. And you, old man, listen, you'll be gone yourself come spring . . . I'll show you, old man."[39]

And then, at the moment of his triumph, Khvostov fell. The truth of the entire affair, and of Khvostov's base character, finally reached Alexandra in the first days of March. On the second, she wrote to Nicholas: "Am so wretched that we, through Gregory recommended Khvostov to you—it leaves me no peace—you were against it & I let myself be imposed upon by them [. . .] the Devil got hold of him, one cannot call it otherwise. [. . .] As long as Khvostov is in power and has money & police in his hands—I honestly am not quiet for Gregory & Ania.* Dear me, how weary one is!"[40] The following day Khvostov was sacked. Beletsky ordered a cake from the popular Balle pastry shop sent to Khvostov. On top, in chocolate icing, were the words: "Don't lay traps for others."[41] Khvostov told everyone who would listen that he had been fired because he had dared to tell the emperor the truth about the German spies surrounding Rasputin and how he was selling secrets to the enemy.[42] When Rasputin learned what Khvostov had been saying, he told Alexandra that people who talk like that ought to be punished. As for Beletsky, Rasputin was forgiving and did not blame him for his role in the affair.[43] He also did what he could to help Simanovich, writing to Vyrubova after his friend's exile: "I hope no one is forced to suffer because of me."[44] Komissarov, meanwhile, had been appointed governor of the city of Rostov-on-Don in January and was then fired by order of the emperor six months later. Unlike Beletsky, he received no pension and was even denied the right to wear his uniform.[45]

Rasputin sought Spiridovich's help. "They're all killers," he

---

* Vyrubova.

grumbled, "all killers." As for Khvostov, he was "a bad man. A deceiver. He took everything and then deceived us. He's got no conscience. He's a little cheat. Just a cheat. Well, he's done for. Done for!" Spiridovich tried to calm Rasputin down, assuring him that he was safe and that the Petrograd Okhrana would never let anything happen to him.[46]

Even with Khvostov gone, Alexandra worried. Vyrubova and her father began receiving anonymous death threats. The empress was convinced it was Khvostov, seeking revenge for her role in opening Alexandra's eyes to the minister's murderous intentions. She prevented Vyrubova from visiting Rasputin in the city out of fear for her safety. This made Rasputin furious and caused a terrible row. But Alexandra stood her ground, noting in a letter to Nicholas that Rasputin too "predicts something is going to happen to her."[47]

Beletsky added fuel to the fire by sharing the details of the entire affair with his acquaintance Mikhail Gakkebush-Gorelov, chief editor of the *Stock Exchange Gazette*. Beletsky had been under the impression their conversation was off the record, only to see it splashed across the pages of the newspaper on 6 and 7 March. Nowhere was Rasputin's name mentioned, but everyone knew who the "individual" at the center of the tale was. Nicholas was so outraged by Beletsky's indiscretion that he took away from him the post of governorship of Irkutsk. With that, Beletsky's government career came to an end. He spent the rest of the war supplying clothing to low-ranking army officers.[48] "It was an enormous sensation," Spiridovich wrote, "and the public lapped up the scandal and the details about the murder as if it were some dime-store novel. There's no further to go. The entire affair of Khvostov and Co. has been tossed out into the street. The crowd has gone wild."[49]

"It would take Sherlock Holmes to get to the truth of the matter," Tikhomirov wrote in his diary. He noted he could not be certain what he had read in the press, for Milyukov was insistent that Khvostov fell only because he had wanted to replace Rasputin with another. It was said that when he learned the full truth, Yevgeny Klimovich, director of the department of the police as of the middle of February 1916, went blind and his hair turned white overnight.[50] Klimovich could not have been too surprised, however. In late 1915, he himself had told Father Vostokov that Khvostov "will get rid of Rasputin" and that it was possible he would be murdered. Vostokov must have been pleasantly surprised, for that was just what he had been hoping for. Not long thereafter he told Sergei Melgunov that what Russia needed was a coup like the ones that overthrew Tsars Peter III and Paul I, both of whom had been murdered. Melgunov could hardly believe his ears: an Orthodox priest was proposing regicide.[51] Rasputin had been utterly shaken by the affair. He knew they would eventually kill him. "I pushed death away once more. But she'll come again for me . . . Like a hungry virgin she'll find me," he purportedly said.[52]

In the middle of March, Rasputin left for home. Zinaida Rzhevskaya, on her way to see her husband in Siberia, happened to be on the same train. After Boris had been exiled, Zinaida visited Rasputin and begged him to do something. He gave her a note to give to Stürmer asking him to help her get her husband back (quite generous, considering that her husband had been willing to murder Rasputin), but what Rasputin seemed most interested in was making love to her, if one can trust her memoirs. On the train he seemed somehow distant, formal, although he did invite her to come dine with him in his compartment. Zinaida came and knocked on his door. Not hearing anything over the rumble of the tracks she opened it, only to find Rasputin making love to the young Princess Tatyana Shakhovskaya. They did not notice Zinaida, and she quickly closed the door and hurried away.[53]

It makes for a juicy tale, this unlikely meeting on the train, but like so much that has been said about Rasputin it has an odor of pure fantasy about it. What were the odds that Rzhevskaya would have ended up on the same train as Rasputin? Amazingly, a forgotten letter in the Russian archives offers evidence that Rzhevskaya may well have been telling the truth. Alexei Tatishchev, a thirty-year-old official in the ministry of agriculture, wrote his mother a letter from Siberia to tell her how he ended up in the same railcar with Rasputin as well as the wife of the official Khvostov had sent to Iliodor. "This very lady, as fate would have it, is one of R.'s followers and assures us that he is a ve[ry] nice, good, and intelligent man, although he does use his position for financial gain," he wrote. "As does, according to her, Anya Vyr."[54] Zinaida's encounters with Rasputin did not end with that train trip. The Petrograd Okhrana recorded two assignations she had with Rasputin at the city's Hotel Select in August.[55] She chose not to mention either of these meetings in her memoirs.

*

The fallout from the minister's plot to kill Rasputin reverberated throughout the spring of 1916. In the middle of May, the Duma sent an appeal to the prime minister and minister of justice demanding a full account of the scandal. The entire sordid affair gave the deputies one more opportunity to keep Rasputin in the headlines and so further their attack on the throne. There was no shortage of stories in the press. "A Byzantine Fairytale on the Banks of the Neva," *L'Echo de Russie* announced on 15 April:

> The affair Rzhevsky has already been dubbed a novel in feuilletons. In our opinion this expression is too weak. Before our eyes, as if peering into a kaleidoscope, scoundrels, officials, private citizens, adventurers and their lovers, engineers, etc. take each other's place in rapid succession. The actions move from one setting to another with remarkable speed. We are suddenly taken from Petrograd to Norway, from the apartment of an adventurer's mistress to a meeting with some highly placed personage, from some government office to a prison cell. Politics is transformed into a novel, and a novel is transformed into politics. [. . .] One cannot help but shudder when confronted with this grievous picture, when you think about all the enormous historic tasks and difficulties now facing our government.[56]

55. Iliodor in America

There was at least one person who was happy with the Khvostov affair. Sergei Melgunov had already announced the forthcoming publication of Iliodor's book in the coming year in his magazine *Voice of the Past*, and he realized that the scandal would only help to raise interest, as well as sales. The publisher planned to make a tidy sum off Iliodor's revelations.[1] But if Melgunov thought that since he had acquired a copy of the manuscript Iliodor would sit quietly and wait for him to publish it, and reap all the financial reward, he was mistaken. Iliodor, too, knew the scandal could be used to his advantage, and he did his best to play his hand.

In the beginning of 1916, Iliodor was in negotiations to sell the manuscript to a reporter for the *Russian Word* and had also received expressions of interest from the Germans.[2] According to Russian police reports, Iliodor had been receiving regular visitors from the German Reichstag and had been offered as much as 10,000 rubles for the work. The Americans showed up on Iliodor's doorstep as well. On 4 December 1915 (NS), the Henry Ford Peace Expedition sailed from Hoboken, New Jersey on the steamship *Oscar II* to bring together pacifists from the U.S. and non-combatant countries in Europe. Traveling with the delegates were a number of reporters, including Herman Bernstein, a German-born journalist, translator (of Tolstoy and Chekhov, among others), and advocate for Jewish rights. The first stop was Kristiania in late December, and it was here that Bernstein met with Iliodor to discuss the situation in Russia and also the possibility of acquiring his manuscript, which Bernstein saw as a useful tool in the struggle to bring down the oppressive, anti-Semitic Russian regime. The violent Russian anti-Semite and the American fighter for Jewish freedom and equality, one who thought the tsars were too soft on the Jews, the other, too hard—a curious pair of allies. Bernstein offered Iliodor $8,000 and promised to publish it in America, but, according to Iliodor's wife, he was rebuffed. Iliodor said he would not take anything less than $15,000.

Bernstein left without the manuscript, but their dealings with each other were far from over.[3] Indeed, Iliodor told the *Aftenposten* in March that he had already sold the rights to an American publisher, which could only have been Bernstein.[4] At about the same time, Iliodor was also corresponding with Russian exiles in England about the possibility of publishing the book there.

The Okhrana knew of Bernstein's activities, for they had been trying to acquire the book as well. Acting on the order of Beletsky, Ivan Smirnov, vice-director of the police, wrote to all the Russian embassies and consulates to find out who had the manuscript and try to acquire it by posing as an interested publisher. They were to be certain "to follow all conspiratorial methods and use extreme caution." Special agent Krasilnikov in Paris recommended sending an agent acting as a French publisher to Kristiania. But then, before anything could be undertaken, Smirnov called off the entire campaign on 24 March, stating there was now no more need to acquire the manuscript.[5]

The Okhrana may have backed off since by then another, much more powerful party had begun negotiations with Iliodor, none other than the empress herself. On 1 March (OS), Iliodor sent his wife Nadezhda to Petrograd with letters for the empress informing her of Rzhevsky's visit and the plot to murder Rasputin. Iliodor later insisted that he had never intended to assist in the plot, but had just played along until the right moment to bring it to light. Once again, Iliodor was lying. The date of his wife's departure says it all: namely, weeks after the arrest of Rzhevsky and the discovery of the conspiracy by the police.[6] Iliodor was notifying the empress about something she was already well aware of. Nevertheless, Alexandra seemed glad to have Iliodor's letters, which she believed "truthful," and handed them over to Stürmer for his investigation.[7]

The contents of the letters are not known, but it seems that as well as informing her of Rzhevsky's visit, Iliodor also offered his manuscript to the empress. In the middle of April, a man appeared at Iliodor's apartment. He said his name was Roman Ivan Petrov and that he worked for the Russian government. He had come to Kristiania with a man named Sergei Chicherin, who was waiting back at the Grand Hotel, Room 345. Their real names were Richard Perang, a lieutenant-colonel in the gendarmes who had been involved in the investigation of Stolypin's assassination, and Count Boris Borkh, actual state councilor and long-time assistant in various capacities to Prime Minister Stürmer.

According to Khvostov, Borkh had offered his apartment on occasion to Stürmer and Rasputin for their private meetings. He characterized him as "a dark figure."[8] Perang told Iliodor that they had been sent by the empress to buy Iliodor's manuscript and other documents and bring them to Russia where they would be destroyed. In return, Iliodor would receive 100,000 rubles and be granted full amnesty. Iliodor, however, smelled a rat and feared it was a trap to lure him back to Russia. He turned down the offer.[9] This, at least, is how Iliodor described it. Other sources state it was Iliodor who reached out and tried to sell his manuscript to Alexandra and she had turned him down. "You can't make something white black, and you can't sully a clean man," she supposedly said.[10]

Nevertheless, Iliodor did not give up. Agent Krasilnikov wired Director of the Police Klimovich on 8 June to report that Iliodor had apparently sold the letters from a "very highly placed individual" (i.e., Alexandra) addressed to Rasputin* to an American buyer for $30,000.[11] Perhaps this was one reason why in June Iliodor embarked on the steamer *Bergensfjord* and left Norway for America.[12] He arrived in New York City on the eighteenth and settled in the Bronx. His main objective in coming to America was to find a publisher for his book, which he did rather quickly, signing a contract for $5,000 with *Metropolitan* magazine to publish the manuscripts in several installments starting that October.[13] The Russian ambassador, Georgy Bakhmetev, charged his general counsel in New York, Mikhail Ustinov, and Archbishop Yevdokim to get in contact with Iliodor and see whether they might make some sort of deal. From Petrograd, Prime Minister Stürmer wired Bakhmetev 50,000 rubles to acquire the manuscript and documents. In the meantime, Ambassador Bakhmetev contacted British agents in New York to place Iliodor under surveillance and managed to convince the editors of *Metropolitan* not to publish Iliodor's book. Soon after, Iliodor's wife met with Father Yevdokim and informed him her husband was willing to sell everything but needed 50,000. Even though Bakhmetev had the money, Yevdokim told Nadezhda this was too much. The government was willing to offer 25,000 along with a guarantee of amnesty, but no more. Iliodor was tempted, but just then he got an especially lucrative

---

* Could these have been the same letters Minister of the Interior Makarov supposedly presented to the tsar, and that Mikhail Rodzianko claimed he took with him abroad after the revolution?

offer from a new American publisher: $50,000 for five articles combined with a promotional speaking tour to ten US cities. In addition to this, the publisher would help see a moving picture was made from the material and would cooperate in developing a theater piece on the Romanov family.

Back in Russia, Alexandra, Vyrubova, and Maid-of-Honor Lydia Nikitina, whose father had been promoted by Stürmer and was herself an important liaison between the prime minister and Rasputin, were still debating how much to pay Iliodor. On 31 August, Nikitina wired Vyrubova that the question of paying Iliodor had to be decided within twenty-four hours. The next day, Vyrubova cabled from Stavka to inform Nikitina that Alexandra had decided to hold off on paying Iliodor.[14] The empress would not be blackmailed. Stürmer wired Bakhmetev on 6 September instructing him to break off all negotiations with Iliodor. The ambassador wrote back to inform Stürmer that the matter had become moot, for the manuscript had already fallen "into the hands of local Jews," namely the "Yid" Herman Bernstein, and given America's "completely unlimited" freedom of the press, there was nothing they could do to stop Bernstein from publishing it. Were this to happen, the only remaining option would be to publicly attack Iliodor's words as nothing but "meaningless fabrications and ravings."[15]

Iliodor was quickly becoming Americanized. After *Metropolitan* reneged on their contract, he sued for damages in the New York Supreme Court and won.[16] In late December, Iliodor held a small press conference at Carnegie Hall. Among other things, he told a reporter from the *New York Times* that he had been the target of an assassination attempt while in Norway—that Generals Petrov and Chicherin tried to lure him back to Russia, steal his manuscript, and then kill him. He peddled some of his same old lies: that he had been the court chaplain and personal confessor to Nicholas and Alexandra and that Rasputin was the real father of Alexei. And he told some new ones. Iliodor stated that he had been with the tsar in the Crimea when the Archduke Franz Ferdinand was killed. Nicholas had Iliodor bless the troops, and they both hoped this would mean war between Russia and Germany. Rasputin, on the other hand, had been working behind their backs, trying to negotiate a separate peace with Germany. He told the reporters that all of this and much more would soon appear in print in his book. As part of the marketing campaign, he was planning an extended book tour across America.[17] When he was not suing in court or courting the press, Iliodor was developing his entertainment career. Early in the following year he began consulting for, and even acting in, Herbert Brenon's film *The Fall of the Romanoffs*, which debuted at New York's Broadway Theatre in late September 1917 for a two-week engagement, and also in Maurice B. Blumenthal's *The Tyranny of the Romanoffs*.[18] Iliodor had been blinded by the bright lights of Fort Lee, New Jersey, America's original Hollywood.

The Mad Monk of Russia, Iliodor. Life, Memoirs, and Confessions of Sergei Michailovich Trufanoff was finally published in New York in 1918. A year earlier, Melgunov published the original in Russia under the title *Sviatoi chert*, Holy Devil. Iliodor dedicated the book to "my good friend" Herbert Brenon, his new patron in the entertainment business. For many years *The Mad Monk* was *the* source for the story of Rasputin and his life. Along with the memoirs of Felix Yusupov, Rasputin's killer, it has done more to shape the public perception of Rasputin than any other work. Yet Iliodor's book, to quote Alexander Blok, no apologist for Rasputin, was nothing but "loathsome." Reading it left him feeling ill. The Commission deemed the work to be overflowing with "flights of imagination."[19] For Maria Rasputina, Iliodor's book amounted to "a tissue of the most outrageous slanders that have ever been conceived."[20] A fair assessment.

56. With Us or With Them

As the Khvostov scandal was erupting, the Duma turned its attention once more to troubles within the church. At the end of February, deputy Matvei Skobelev asked from the rostrum why neither the government nor the Synod had yet dealt with the appeal put forward four years earlier following the controversy surrounding Mikhail Novoselov. He then proceeded to read at length from Novoselov's "*Quousque tandem abutere patientia nostra*" that had appeared in the *Voice of Moscow* in January 1912. Skobelev repeated as well the words Guchkov had spoken before the Duma at the time: "Russia is going through dark, difficult days. [. . .] Danger threatens our sacred things. And why are the bishops' voices silent, why are the government authorities inactive?"[1]

The Duma's return to the matter of the church was prompted by a number of events. First, there had been the immensely unpopular firing of Chief Procurator Samarin, followed by the tepid response to his successor, the bland and uninspiring Alexander Volzhin, a provincial nobleman, chamberlain, and former governor. It was taken for granted that Rasputin had been behind the appointment of Volzhin, although Beletsky told the Commission Khvostov and Prince Nikolai Zhevakhov were the ones responsible.[2] It seems Volzhin knew his selection would be viewed as the work of Rasputin and so even before the news was made public he typed a short statement outlining his understanding of Rasputin's place at court and positioning himself as independent of any outside forces, which he sent to the editors of the main newspapers in Petrograd and Moscow. He began by noting that Nicholas was at last ready to get rid of Rasputin, although it was a difficult matter since "the magnetic powers, peculiar to Rasputin, are very beneficial to the Empress, who is suffering from a disease of the spine." Thus, it was not possible to remove him immediately without first finding "a suitable masseur or masseuse," after which Rasputin would disappear for good. It was the desire to limit Rasputin's influence on Alexei, according to

53. Prince Nikolai Zhevakhov, follower of Rasputin and deputy chief procurator of the Holy Synod (1916).

54. The Russian Rocambole. Ivan Manasevich-Manuilov (center) at a banquet with editors of the main Petersburg newspapers and political figures. Front row left: the editor of the *New Times*, Mikhail Suvorin; front row right: the Turkish ambassador, Turkhan Pasha.

55. Rasputin's handler-secretary, Aaron Simanovich, a man responsible for creating many of the myths about his employer.

56. Rasputin in the years following Guseva's attack.

57. Rasputin posing for the sculptor Naum Aronson in 1915.

58. Announcement for Aronson's new bust in *Sparks*, noting the work was made in connection with the publication of Rasputin's *My Thoughts and Reflections* in light of his "new role as a writer."

Новая скульптура Аронсона.

Григорій Распутинъ пишетъ и готовитъ къ выпуску въ свѣтъ книгу «Мои мысли и размышленія». Скульпторъ Н. Л. Аронсонъ сдѣлалъ бюстъ «старца» въ новой для него роли писателя.

Гр. Распутинъ-Новыхъ.
Скульптура Н. Л. Аронсона.

59. Illustrator and portraitist Yury Annenkov's sketch of Rasputin, 1915.

ю. А. 1915.

60. Rasputin the Swine. A caricature accompanying the article "The Swine" published in the Petrograd journal *Rudin* in February 1915 that presents the story of Rasputin through the allegory of the boar Vanka, a "porcine Don Juan," who mysteriously takes control of the estate of a noble family, creating a harem with the daughters.

61. A rare photograph taken of Rasputin in the last year of his life by the portraitist Theodora Krarup in her Petrograd studio.

62. Krarup's final portrait of Rasputin, dated 13 December 1916, just four days before his murder.

63. Minister of the Interior
Alexei Khvostov (1915–16).

64. Stepan Beletsky, deputy
minister of the interior (1915–16).

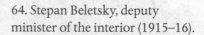

65. Prince Mikhail Andronikov.

66. Iliodor's note agreeing
to join Khvostov's plot to
murder Rasputin in return
for 60,000 rubles.

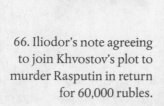

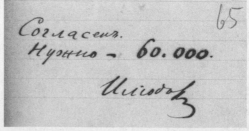

67. Prince Felix Yusupov and his bride, Irina.

68. Princess Zinaida Yusupova.

69. Grand Duke Dmitry Pavlovich.

70. Vladimir Purishkevich.

71. Dr. Stanisław Lazovert.

72. Lieutenant Sergei Sukhotin.

73 and 74. The dancer Vera Karalli and Marianna Derfelden, Dmitry's step-sister, were both possibly at the Yusupov palace the night of the murder.

75. The murder scene. Prince Yusupov went to great lengths to create just the right mood on the day of the murder, selecting furnishings that would show off his wealth and taste and, he hoped, distract his victim.

76. The courtyard adjacent to the Yusupov palace in a police photograph taken on the morning of 17 December, only a few hours after the crime. Rasputin had apparently exited through the side door (small black rectangle to the left) and tried to flee across the courtyard. Investigators found a trail of blood in the snow that stopped just shy of the gates.

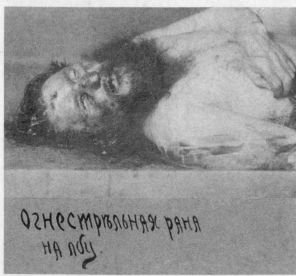

77. Rasputin's frozen corpse soon after it was retrieved from the ice of the Malaya Nevka on the morning of the 19th. The Petrovsky Bridge is visible in the background.

78. "Gunshot wound to the forehead" – the finding of the official autopsy penned below the photograph proving Rasputin's cause of death. The gruesome state of his body was largely the result of the action of the ice and river current and the grappling hooks used to pull him out of the water.

79. From the Russian headlines: "The Murder of Grigory Rasputin. New Details – Rasputin's Biography – Scenes from the Life of Rasputin." The two photographs purport to show Rasputin's final portrait soon before his murder and another, "particularly widespread among his followers."

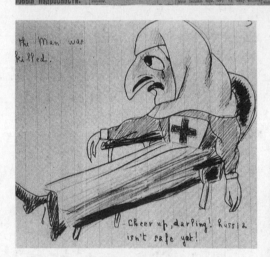

80. A caricature mocking Alexandra sketched just days after Rasputin's murder by Prince Vladimir Paley. The prince was Grand Duke Dmitry's step-brother: his father was Grand Duke Paul Alexandrovich, also Dmitry's father, and his mother was Paul's mistress, Olga Karnovich (later Princess Paley and Paul's wife). Like so many others, Prince Paley underestimated Alexandra's strength, and she did not break down with the loss of her friend.

81. Rasputin's burial site under the church then being built by Anna Vyrubova near Tsarskoe Selo.

82. The boiler house at the Petrograd Polytechnic Institute where Rasputin's body was most likely incinerated in early March 1917.

83. "The Execution of Grishka Rasputin." The cover of the *Almanac "Freedom"* published soon after the fall of the monarchy. Already shot in the head, Rasputin tries to flee but is felled from behind by Purishkevich.

Гришка Распутинъ, проснувшійся послѣ пьяной оргіи.

84. Creating the myth. The same issue of the *Almanac* contains a reproduction of a widespread image of Rasputin recuperating in the Tyumen hospital in the summer of 1914 after Guseva's attack, but now with a new caption: "Grishka Rasputin waking up after a drunken orgy."

85. "Самодержавие." A play on the Russian word for autocracy, *samoderzhavie*, which literally means "to hold in one's own hands." The image likely appeared soon after the fall of the monarchy.

„Самодержавіе."

УМЪ ХОРОШО, А ТРИ ЛУЧШЕ.

86. A play on the idiom "Two heads are better than one." The facial expressions make it clear that only two of the three heads were in use.

Сказка о Гришкѣ.

Царскосельскій павіанъ.

87. From the satirical series "The Tale of Grishka," the peacock of Tsarskoe Selo has revealed himself to be a baboon.

88. A postcard from 1917 with Rasputin, the drunken devil, and Alexandra.

89. A lecherous Rasputin having his way with the empress in the palace, from *The Tale of Grishka the Reprobate*.

90. Publicity poster for *The Firm Romanov, Rasputin, Sukhomlinov, Myasoedov, Protopopov and Co.* that appeared in the spring of 1917. The four-part film included "The Clearance Sale of Russia – Wholesale and Retail," "Butchers of the People," and "The Collapse of the Firm."

91. From the pages of *New Satyricon* in the spring of 1917: "Design for a Monument to the Main Heroes of the Russian Revolution," dedicated to Rasputin and Protopopov.

92. "*Russia's Ruling House.*" The famous cover of *New Satyricon* (April 1917) showing Rasputin, the true tsar, surrounded by Nicholas and Alexandra, Prime Minister Boris Stürmer, Minister of the Interior Alexander Protopopov, and Minister of War Vladimir Sukhomlinov. Anna Vyrubova prays at his feet.

93. A Swedish publicity poster for the 1928 film *Russia's Evil Spirit* depicts Rasputin in racialized terms as the dark beast preying on European womanhood. Ever since first attracting public attention, Rasputin has served as a convenient screen upon which to project a range of fears and preoccupations.

94. Two dwarfs depicting Minister of the Interior Protopopov and "Grishka Rasputin" ride atop a coffin emblazoned "The Old Regime" at a large workers' demonstration in Moscow during the February Revolution.

95. A blasphemous akathist devoted to "Grishka Rasputin, Honorary Member of the Tsarist House." The side panels include scenes from the life of Rasputin: "praying" with naked women in the baths, dancing with a topless woman at court, handing out medals, and being shot by Purishkevich. The lower panel depicts a man defecating on Rasputin's grave.

96. Rasputin's son-in-law, Boris Solovyov, who acted as a secret courier between the royal family and Anna Vyrubova during their captivity in Tobolsk.

97. On 27 April 1918, Grand Duchess Maria, being taken with her parents from Tobolsk to Yekaterinburg, made this sketch of the Rasputin home in Pokrovskoe after stopping there for fresh horses.

98. Iliodor, film star. Advertisement for the 1917 film *The Fall of the Romanoffs*, starring Iliodor as himself doing battle against Rasputin in his ill-fated attempt to save the monarchy.

The State Rights' Sensation That Will Make You a Fortune

HERBERT BRENON
Presents

THE FALL of the ROMANOFFS

With

ILIODOR

The Famed "Mad Monk" of Russia and an all-star cast, including NANCE O'NEIL — CONWAY TEARLE ALFRED HICKMAN—EKATERINA GALANTA and a score of others

Herbert Brenon's Screen Masterpiece Tells the Amazing Story of Rasputin and the Russian Court, of Social and Religious Intrigues and of a Nation's Dramatic Stroke for Liberty.

Personally Directed by Herbert Brenon

ILIODOR PICTURE CORPORATION

729 7th Avenue, New York City   ::   ::   Telephone: Bryant 7340

99. Iliodor, family man. Press photograph from December 1922 of Iliodor, his wife, Nadezhda, and their three children: Sergius (seven), Iliodor Jr. (four), and Hope (five) after recently returning to the United States.

100. Rasputin's family, Pokrovskoe, 1927. Dmitry Rasputin, his mother Praskovya, his wife, Feoktista, and Katya Pecherkina (in the back).

101. Maria Rasputina, circus performer and animal trainer, Paris, 1935.

102. Fiberglass statue of Rasputin erected in 2014 behind the city hospital in Tyumen where he recovered from Guseva's attack a hundred years before. Other than an informal memorial in the park at Tsarskoe Selo, it is the only such monument to Rasputin in Russia.

Volzhin, that had prompted the tsar to take the heir with him to Stavka. Once Rasputin was gone, the boy would return to live in the palace.[3]

Volzhin tried to walk a middle line, neither offending Rasputin nor giving in to all of his wishes. He did nothing to stop the canonization of Ioann Maximovich in the summer of 1916 and saw that Varnava was promoted to archbishop. One move he could not approve, however, was accepting Prince Zhevakhov as his assistant. A minor official in the Council of State, Zhevakhov was Rasputin's choice for Volzhin's deputy, as Alexandra wrote to Nicholas in November 1915, urging him to force Zhevakhov on Volzhin.[4] When it became clear Volzhin was not going to back down, Rasputin and Alexandra came up with the idea of creating a new post, a second deputy chief procurator, just for Zhevakhov. This produced howls of outrage. The Duma took up the matter, and after an examination of the legality of the idea Vasily Maklakov got up to denounce it as an "act of lawlessness" and a "crime against one of the pillars of our constitution." Maklakov insisted the proposal was not due to ignorance of the laws, but in flagrant disregard for them. He then went a step further:

> We know the author of this by what he's done: it is the manifestation of the same dark and hidden forces against which all of Russia has recently risen up. [...] Gentlemen, it's not terrifying that the man in charge of the dark forces, that the notorious Grigory Rasputin, is able to arrange matters for his own personal gain and that of his close associates and supporters; it's not important that while drunk he goes from tavern to tavern in Moscow, making a spectacle of himself in front of people and bragging the whole time of his influence; it's not important that his supporters use the myth of his omnipotence to rake in piles of money—what is terrifying and important is that none of this is a lie, that he truly does have influence on matters of state.

Maklakov ended his attack with a question for the government: "In Russia's battle against the dark forces, where is its place? With us or with them? Do the powers that be understand that it is unacceptable that we now have some hidden, undocumented deputy chief procurators, do they understand that this is shameful and a scandal?"[5] In the end, Volzhin and the Duma won. A special position for Zhevakhov was not created.[6]

There were other problems as well. Perhaps the biggest was

Archbishop Pitirim. Born Pavel Oknov in 1858, he adopted the name of Pitirim in 1883 upon being tonsured as a monk. In 1891, he was made rector of the St. Petersburg Theological Seminary, and then, in 1909, an archbishop. His rise in the church hierarchy is a bit surprising considering that while bishop of Tula he lived with his male lover and emptied the church treasury for his own personal use. Rasputin apparently first learned of Pitirim through his defense of a group of heretics, which impressed Rasputin and led him to praise Pitirim to the empress.[7] But Rasputin was not the only one impressed by Pitirim. In his younger years Pitirim was said to have been good looking, ingratiating, and known for his rather theatrical manner of conducting service, all of which caught the eye of Chief Procurator Sabler, who made sure to advance Pitirim's career. Nicholas, according to Vyrubova, first met Pitirim in the Caucasus in 1914, when he was a member of the Synod and the Exarch of Georgia, and was enchanted by him and decided he would promote Pitirim at the first possible moment.[8]

The opportunity came in the autumn of 1915 with the death of Flavian, the metropolitan of Kiev. In November, Alexandra wrote Nicholas that she wanted him to transfer Vladimir (Bogoyavlensky), the metropolitan of Petrograd, to Kiev, and give his post to Pitirim. She knew this was an obvious slap in the face to Vladimir, and so she insisted Nicholas not let Volzhin talk him out of it, but "to be firm," as Rasputin instructed. She praised Pitirim and remarked how Rasputin called him "a great Worshipper" and "the only suitable man." As for who should take Pitirim's place in Georgia, Alexandra commented that Rasputin had not settled on a candidate, but Nicholas ought to make certain it was not Archbishop Sergei (Stragorodsky), Metropolitan Antony (Khrapovitsky), or Germogen, all of them enemies of Rasputin. In the end, Nicholas chose Archbishop Platon (Rozhdestvensky), no friend of Rasputin and a figure who had opposed him in the affair of the Name-Glorifiers.[9]

The demotion of Vladimir was scandalous. No other metropolitan had ever been treated this way before. Volzhin had tried to stop Nicholas by presenting him with a report highlighting Pitirim's unacceptable behavior, but the tsar ignored it. He even overrode the established authority of the Synod to approve such decisions.[10] Nicholas chose to thumb his nose at tradition, and so provoked the anger of the very men he relied on to uphold the sanctity of his reign. The anger was such that there was talk among the clergy in Petrograd and Moscow of breaking from the Synod's authority altogether and creating what they called a "free Orthodox church." Among the supporters of the idea was Samarin, who saw it as a tragic but necessary move.[11]

The actions of Pitirim sent most churchmen into paroxysms of rage. He appointed a man by the name of Filaret father superior of the Alexander Nevsky Lavra in Petrograd. Filaret lived openly with his mistress and started demanding bribes to use the monastery. Pitirim threw wild parties at the monastery, some of which Rasputin attended; it was said Pitirim had women smuggled in through the side gates for the priests' pleasure. Even more shocking to Petrograders was Pitirim's preference in such matters. He came to the capital with a handsome young priest named Antony Guriysky, who was, like Pitirim, a homosexual, and he kept other homosexual men around him, such as Melkhizedek (Mikhail Paevsky), rector of the Tiflis Seminary and the future bishop of Kronstadt, and Ivan Osipenko, Pitirim's lover and personal secretary. There was continuing talk of financial improprieties. Rumor had it that Pitirim skimmed money off the sale of burial plots to line his pockets and pay back Rasputin for his support. The truth of such talk is difficult to ascertain.[12]

It is hard to imagine that Rasputin did not know Pitirim or these other men were homosexuals. In fact, it is well known Rasputin maintained cordial relations with Pallady (Nikolai Dobronravov), the bishop of Saratov in 1915, also homosexual, and Bishop Isidor (Pyotr Kolokolov), who had been punished by the church for his sexual relations with men. Rasputin even helped to see that Isidor was promoted, and the bishop became one of Rasputin's drinking buddies.[13] Rasputin knew, but he did not care. Nowhere in his letters or writings does he make any comment about homosexuality. It was not important to him, and in this indifference can be glimpsed a level of tolerance for what might be called outsiders—homosexuals, Jews, prostitutes, dissenters, sectarians—that was rare for Russia at the time. Rasputin did see the world as divided between "friends and enemies," but these categories did not break down along traditional Russian lines. The rich and powerful were no less likely to be friends than the marginalized and maligned were to be enemies. Indeed, it was often exactly the opposite for Rasputin. It was this way of seeing the world that allowed him to criticize fellow Orthodox Slavs and praise Muslims. Indeed, *Tsaritsyn Thought* derided Rasputin for this in 1910, calling him "the light of Islam and the right hand of Mohammed."[14]

The transfers of Vladimir and Pitirim reeked of the ministerial leap-frogging that had become an issue of contention the previous year, a problem exacerbated by the sacking of Prime Minister Goremykin on 20 January 1916. Goremykin had not been popular, but his replacement, the retired elderly statesman Boris Stürmer, was considered no improvement. A "nonentity," Shulgin called him. "While all the monarchies of Europe were mobilizing their best powers, we appointed a 'Santa Claus' as our Prime Minister."[15] Stürmer liked to think of himself as an iron fist in a velvet glove, but the consensus was he was nothing more than an empty shell. "A second-rate man" and "Too old, too selfish and too stupid for a great post"—such were the words contemporaries used to describe the new prime minister.[16] Rasputin reportedly said Stürmer would have to be kept on a string or he would break his neck.[17]

The man holding the other end of the string was Rasputin. Alexandra had pushed Nicholas to appoint Stürmer, highlighting his main qualification: his great respect for Rasputin.[18] Stürmer had originally approached Pitirim and sought his help in introducing him to Rasputin. The two men met at least twice to discuss Stürmer's candidacy, and Stürmer's cook, Anna Nechaeva, claimed she saw Rasputin come for dinner with her employer and his wife shortly before his appointment.[19] Rasputin was not terribly impressed with "Shtriter," as he called him. "He's old, but that doesn't matter. He'll do," he reportedly said. Stürmer immediately set out to prove his gratitude and his loyalty to Rasputin. He visited Rasputin secretly within twenty-four hours of his appointment, promising to be loyal and to carry out his requests.[20]

According to Globachev, no other minister ever demonstrated such concern for Rasputin's well-being, but only since he knew his position rested solely on Rasputin's favor. Stürmer demanded Globachev supply him with the most detailed reports of Rasputin's daily activities. He saw threats to Rasputin's life where none existed and would hound Globachev to do more to ensure his safety. Globachev's agents monitored Stürmer and Rasputin's regular meetings at Pitirim's office in the Alexander Nevsky Lavra and Count Boris Borkh's apartment at 18 Fontanka. Stürmer was also worried about Rasputin meeting others without his knowledge for fear he might be grooming future ministerial candidates. He was particularly concerned Rasputin was preparing Sergei Kryzhanovsky for the post of minister of the interior, but here Stürmer had no cause for concern: the post went to Stürmer after the fall of Khvostov in the first days of March, thus combining the two most powerful positions in the hands of one man, a prize Khvostov had sought from Rasputin but never won.[21] As the year went on, however, Stürmer's confidence grew and he began to adopt a more independent manner, tugging on the string in Rasputin's hand. Rasputin noticed the change, and by August he was instructing Stürmer to be sure to visit Alexandra more often and keep her (and so Rasputin as well) informed of all his plans.

"My own sweet Treasure," Alexandra wrote to Nicholas at Stavka on 14 March,

> I send you an apple & flower from our Friend—we all had fruit as a goodbye gift. He left this evening—quietly, saying better times are coming & that he leaves spring-time with us—He told her [Vyrubova] He finds Ivanov wld. be good as Minister of War on account of his great popularity not only in the army, but all over the country. In that he is certainly right—but you will do what you think best. I only asked He should pray for success in yr. choice, & He gave this answer.[22]

Rasputin was nervous about leaving, fearful someone might try to kill him along the way. Before his departure he sent this letter to Nicholas: "God's blessing is over us, your success, God's success is with us, even mountains will obey us, and our enemies will have madness in their hearts and fog in their eyes; this is joy, victory without doubt. I am hurt by a small displeasure, a little misunderstanding. Something is being plotted against me, that's not good."[23]

Regardless of his mood, Rasputin was yet again trying to shape the composition of the government. General Alexei Polivanov had been a considerable improvement as minister of war over Sukhomlinov, removed in June 1915 and arrested at the end of April the following year, and by the spring of 1916 the Russian army was in considerably better shape than it had been after the Great Retreat. But Polivanov had aroused the displeasure of Alexandra over his desire to work with the Progressive Bloc and public groups seeking to offer aid in the war effort. It is not clear whether it was Alexandra's or Rasputin's idea to propose General Nikolai Ivanov, commander-in-chief of the Southwestern Front until 17 March 1916, when he was replaced by Brusilov, but although Nicholas was willing to sack Polivanov in the middle of March, he ignored their recommendation, choosing instead the dutiful if less than competent General Dmitry Shuvaev.[24] Defeats such as these did not stop Alexandra from telling Nicholas what to do. On 17 March she wrote once more with a much more important instruction: "My beloved, For Baby's sake we must be firm as otherwise his inheritance will be awful, as with his character [we must see that] he won't bow down to others but be his own master, as one must in Russia whilst people are still so uneducated—Mr Philippe and Gr.[igory] said so too."

That same day at Stavka Nicholas received Father Georgy Shavelsky, protopresbyter of the Russian army and navy. Shavelsky had been preparing for his audience for some time. He had talked at length with both General Voeikov and General Alexeev about the need to speak to the emperor about Rasputin. Voeikov did that spring, but to no effect; still he encouraged Shavelsky to try, thinking he might have better luck. Alexeev also thought it wise and said that he would himself speak to the tsar after Shavelsky. They met in the tsar's office that evening. Shavelsky began by reminding Nicholas that the empress had welcomed his words at their first meeting in 1911 when he vowed to always speak the truth to the emperor, no matter what. He then proceeded to inform the emperor of all the talk in the army about Rasputin: how he led a life of vice, how he went out drinking with "Jews and all sorts of dark personalities;" how he was engaged in corruption and graft involving the war effort; how he was passing military secrets on to the enemy. Shavelsky told the emperor everything he had been hearing among the rank and file, keeping nothing from Nicholas.

Nicholas listened quietly. When Shavelsky had finished, Nicholas asked whether he had been afraid to come and speak to him about such matters, to which Shavelsky replied that although it was difficult for him to pass along such unpleasant truths to the emperor he had never had any fear. Whatever the emperor might do to him now, he knew he had fulfilled his duty. Shavelsky was surprised to find in the coming days and weeks that far from distancing himself, the emperor became quite attentive to Shavelsky, always sitting next to him at meals, even offering to fill his plate for him. Indeed, even though Nicholas repeated their conversation to Alexandra, and she passed it along to Pitirim, Shavelsky remained in the good graces of both their majesties.[25]

Although Alexandra remained well disposed to Shavelsky, she was distressed to hear his words about Rasputin. A few weeks later, during the Easter season, she wrote to Nicholas:

My own sweet Treasure,

[. . .]

The wickedness of the world ever increases. During the evening Bible [reading] I thought so much of our Friend, how the <u>bookworms</u> 7 pharisees persecute Christ, pretending to be such perfections (& how far they are from it now!) Yes, indeed, a prophet is never acknowledged in his own country. And how much we have to be grateful for, how many prayers of His were heard. And where there is such a Servant of Gods,—the evil crops up around Him to try & do harm & drag him away. If they but knew the harm they do!—why He lives for His Sovereign & Russia & bears all slanders for our sakes. How glad I am that we went all with Him to Holy Communion the first week in Lent. [. . .]

Our Friend writes so sadly, that as He was driven away fr. P.[etrograd] there will be many hungry ones there this Easter. He gives such a lot to the poor, every penny he receives goes to them & it brings blessings to those who brought him the money [. . .]

If Shav.[elsky] speaks about Friend or the Metropolitan [Pitirim], be <u>firm</u> & show that you appreciate them, & that when he hears stories against our Friend, he is to stand up with energy against all & forbid their talks & they dare not say he has anything to do with the Germans—& he is generous and kind to all, as Christ was, no matter what religion, as a real Christian should be. And once you find His prayers help bear one's trials, & we have had enough examples—they <u>dare not</u> speak against him, you be firm & stand up for our Friend.[26]

But they did dare speak against him. That spring Father Shavelsky attended a large celebratory luncheon for several hundred soldiers and officers on the Western Front. Much of the talk during the meal was about Rasputin. Then, to Shavelsky's shock, General Alexander Gerngross pronounced loudly enough for everyone to hear: "I'd be willing to sit for six months in the Peter and Paul fortress if they'd let me tear Rasputin apart. Oh, how I'd tear that rogue to pieces!" His words elicited laughter all around. Shavelsky could not believe his ears, especially since sitting next to Gerngross was General Alexander Ragoza, commander of the Fourth Army.[27]

Nicholas returned to Tsarskoe Selo on 13 April, around the time Rasputin arrived in the capital from Siberia. He saw their majesties at the palace on the twenty-third, the empress's name day, and the following day Nicholas returned to Stavka.[28] Rasputin was rarely at the palace during the next five months, making only six visits between the end of April and the beginning of October.[29]

Rasputin had returned to the capital in part to tend to issues with Maria. Maria had turned eighteen in March. She was tall with golden hair, striking steel-blue eyes, a lovely figure, detracted from by what one man described as "irregular facial features."[30] Boys had entered her life. She was no longer a virgin, having spent a night of lovemaking with a young lieutenant, the memory of which filled her, as she said, with "an eager desire to live more intensely." It was then that she made the acquaintance of Simoniko Pkhakadze, a Georgian "who was to set my heart aflame." She met him for the first time when one of the Princes Eristov brought him to their apartment. She recalled he was "lithe, virile, and strong," and from the moment she laid eyes on him "I felt myself conquered, at his mercy."[31] He was a captain in the cavalry, dashing and handsome, decorated with the St. George's Cross for his battle exploits, but what truly won her heart were his eyes, filled with "an indescribable fire and strength, all the ardour of love, all the vertigo of intoxication." Her father saw him often for a time and even went out with Pkhakadze and the Eristovs. A police report from 25 May described him as between the ages of twenty-five and twenty-seven, tall, medium build, dark-brown hair, a straight nose, and small dark mustache. He wore tall boots with spurs, and walked with a limp, a battle wound most likely, that only added to his dangerous allure.[32] Rasputin apparently helped get Pkhakadze transferred to the reserves in Petrograd. Vyrubova told the Commission he was nothing but "a draft-dodger who did not wish to go into the army."[33]

Maria and Pkhakadze became engaged, but Rasputin disapproved of the match. Father and daughter began to quarrel and he threatened to send her back to Pokrovskoe to get her away from her fiancé. It seemed to Maria that her father was convinced Pkhakadze was using her to curry favor with her father and that his jealous streak would make her life miserable.[34] Rasputin did what he could to keep his daughter from seeing him. She was not allowed out except in the company of her sister and Dunya Pecherkina. Her French tutor, Mme Chack, was forever inviting her to visit, and her father made sure to always include her in the tea-parties at home. At the same time, Rasputin was trying to do his own matchmaking. Nikolai Solovyov, an old friend from Kazan, now a secretary at the Holy Synod, also lived on Gorokhovaya Street, at number 69 with his wife Yelizaveta. Rasputin decided to set up Maria with Nikolai's twenty-three-year-old son, Boris, an ensign in the army.

Boris had been preparing to enter the seminary in his home town of Simbirsk when he volunteered for the army in 1914. He was wounded during the Russian retreat from the Carpathian Mountains in 1915 and brought back to Petrograd, unable to return to active duty. That year he met Rasputin and began to visit his apartment, chiefly to spend time with Maria and Varvara, whom he found unusually charming and kind. He had a few conversations with Rasputin as well, once when he was particularly downcast about the prospects for his future. Rasputin listened and then told Boris not to worry too much, to pray for God's guidance, to listen to his own heart, and all would be well in the end. Boris saw that Rasputin loved him, and he loved Rasputin in return. They met only a few times, but Boris came away with a profound respect for him. "There was so much love and goodness in the man," he told investigator Nikolai Sokolov while imprisoned in Chita in 1919, "and how clearly these qualities expressed themselves in him that he came to mean more to me, perhaps to my own shame, than my own father."[35]

According to Maria's memoirs, Boris fell in love with her at their first meeting. He was presented to the empress and she gave her approval to the union. Pkhakadze became insanely jealous and threatened to kidnap Maria and abscond with her to the Caucasus.[36] There was a rumor that Pkhakadze even tried to take his own life. After a few months of heartache and anguish, Maria broke off her engagement but she refused to marry Boris.[37]

While Rasputin was busy with Maria's love life, Russia was preparing for its greatest military campaign of the war. Former Minister of War Polivanov had done much to rebuild the army after the disastrous defeats of 1915. In the spring of 1916, plans were made for a massive surprise attack, to be led by General Alexei Brusilov, along the Southwestern Front against the Austro-Hungarian forces. The Brusilov Offensive, as it became known, was arguably the finest victory of the war and nearly achieved its goal of destroying the army of Emperor Franz Josef. Exhaustive preparations were made for months. The element of surprise was crucial to the success of the campaign, and Nicholas worried about telling Alexandra too much about it. On

9 March he wrote with details of the plan, adding: "I beg you not to tell anyone of this." It was clear to Alexandra whom he had in mind. But Rasputin already knew all about it and had even given Nicholas an icon as a "blessing" for the campaign.[38]

The assault began on 22 May (OS) with a massive artillery barrage, followed by Brusilov's 650,000 men blasting through the thick smoke and into the enemy's trenches. The Austrians were overrun. In just over a week the Russians had taken prisoner over half of the entire Austrian troops on the Eastern Front. Franz Conrad von Hötzendorff, the Habsburgs' chief of staff, quickly realized the danger of the situation, noting that they would soon have to sue for peace or risk being utterly destroyed. Crucial to the ultimate success of the Brusilov campaign were large-scale attacks against the German lines by Generals Alexei Evert and Alexei Kuropatkin, commanders of the Northwestern and Northern fronts respectively, but both men hesitated, which gave the Germans the opportunity to send reinforcements to the Austrians, thus preventing a complete rout.[39]

On 4 June, Alexandra wrote Nicholas: "[. . .] our Friend sends his blessing to the whole Orthodox army. He begs we should not yet strongly advance in the north because he says, if our successes continue being good in the south, they will themselves retreat from the north, or advance & then their losses will be very great—if we begin there, our losses will be very heavy [. . .]." In late July, after Rasputin had returned from a trip to Siberia, Alexandra wrote Nicholas to share his latest thoughts on the campaign: "He finds better one shld. not advance to [sic] obstinately as the losses will be too great—one can be patient without forcing things, as ultimately it [victory] will be ours; one can go on madly & finish the war in 2 months, but then thousands of lives will be sacrificed—& by patience the end will also be gained & one will spare much blood." Although Rasputin's concern for human life must be recognized, his advice as a strategist was worthless; he clearly knew nothing about military strategy, but his words played no role in Evert's and Kuropatkin's decision not to attack. The Brusilov campaign got bogged down as the number of dead and wounded Russian soldiers mounted.

Rasputin continued to offer his military advice to Nicholas on into September. On the twenty-second Nicholas wrote Alexandra to say the situation was "hopeless" and so he had instructed Alexeev to order Brusilov to stop his advance. Then, the next day, Nicholas changed his mind and agreed to permit Brusilov to continue his attack. A surprised Alexandra sent him a telegraph to say that "He [Rasputin] approved your original plan to halt and begin at another place. Now you write otherwise. God help us." And then, on the twenty-fourth, she wrote again that Rasputin, too, had changed his mind and was "very satisfied" with this new plan. Nicholas felt obliged to reply to Rasputin's words. He wrote back to explain why he had decided to renew the attack and gave details of the offensive, but then added: "These details are only for you—please Lovy! Tell Him only: 'Papa has ordered smart measures be taken'!" Rasputin, however, was not satisfied. On the twenty-sixth, Alexandra wrote that "Our Fr. worries that one did not listen to you (Brussilov) as your first thought was the right one & a pity you gave in, yr. spirit was right wishing the change. He took up the Virgin's Image & blessed you fr. far & said 'May the Sun rise there.'" The following day Nicholas wrote yet again to justify his decision to permit Brusilov to continue his offensive, but Alexandra, and Rasputin, refused to listen: "Our Friend says things wont go until yr. plan [to halt the Brusilov offensive] is obeyed," she remarked on the twenty-eighth.[40]

Historians now acknowledge that the failure of the Brusilov Campaign was the result of the actions taken, or avoided, by Russia's generals, particularly Alexeev and Evert.[41] Yet many at the time blamed Rasputin, who was believed to have used his influence to stop this most successful attack of the war in order to save his German masters from certain defeat. Once more, it was said, Russia had been stabbed in the back by traitors.

57. Rasputin the Spy?

On 5 June 1916 (NS), Field Marshal Earl Kitchener of Khartoum, the British secretary for war, embarked on the HMS *Hampshire* in the Orkney Islands and set off on a secret voyage. A few hours later the ship exploded and sank within a matter of minutes. Of the 655 men on board, only twelve survived. Kitchener was not among them; his body was never found. Kitchener had been on his way to Russia to reassure the tsar that Britain would provide the needed war supplies despite concerns in Britain about Russia's commitment to the war.

The loss of Kitchener was a national tragedy that gave rise to all manner of speculation about his death. From the start there was talk of conspiracy. The press wrote of German secret agents being behind the explosion. There were rumors of sabotage by either Bolshevik infiltrators or Irish nationalists, of a mysterious Boer agent disguised as a Russian nobleman, and rogue elements within the British secret service. Lord Alfred Douglas, Oscar Wilde's lover, asserted the killing had been organized by Winston Churchill and an international cabal of Jews. (Churchill sued; Douglas spent six months in prison for libel.) And some averred Kitchener had actually survived, made his way to Russia, and was now in command of the tsar's armies. The truth was somewhat more banal. Kitchener's mission was far from secret, and it would not have been difficult for German intelligence to have gotten wind of it. Not long before the *Hampshire* departed, the German submarine U-75 mined the area through which Kitchener sailed. The ship hit one of the mines and was blown to pieces.[1]

In Russia, talk quite naturally turned to Rasputin and Alexandra. People said that the empress had a special "radio-telegraph machine" in the palace that she used to transmit information on the Russian war effort to Berlin and it was via this device that she informed the enemy of the date and route of Kitchener's ship.[2] Felix Yusupov was certain the information had come from Rasputin. Convinced that Rasputin's entourage was full of German spies, he asserted they got him drunk and he told them the date of Kitchener's sailing.[3] And then there was Rasputin's odd reaction to the news. Alexandra described Kitchener's death as "awful [. . .] a real cauchemar [nightmare]" to Nicholas, whereas Rasputin told Vyrubova that it was good he had died since "later on he might have done Russia harm & that no harm papers were lost with him," as the empress put it to Nicholas in a letter of 5 June (OS).[4]

The reference to certain "papers" has kept the conspiracy theory from dying. As recently as 2004, historian Oleg Shishkin alleged that the true purpose of Kitchener's trip was to deliver to Nicholas documents gathered by British agents in Russia, as well as from other intelligence services operating across Europe, that would prove Alexandra, Rasputin, and others were secretly negotiating with the Germans. His mission was to convince Nicholas of the reality of this, and so keep Russia in the war. When Rasputin and his cohort learned of Kitchener's mission, they passed the details of the voyage to the Germans, and thus Kitchener was murdered and the German clique at court saved.[5] The notion that Rasputin was a German agent refuses to die.

The stories about Rasputin's espionage activity reached the level of comedy. It was said that Rasputin had amassed a fortune in gold from selling secrets to the Germans and that once during the war he even traveled incognito to Berlin to meet the grateful Kaiser.[6] In his 1917 biography of Rasputin the prolific Anglo-French writer William Le Queux went so far as to claim that he had discovered a "mass of documents" that Rasputin had kept in a safe in the cellar on Gorokhovaya that proved without a doubt he was a spy. Le Queux had planned to publish facsimiles of the documents, but, he regretfully informed his eager readers, "the present shortage of paper has precluded this." His fantastical work claimed that Rasputin was part of a German plot to spread cholera in Russia via poisoned apples imported from Canada.[7] Others insisted Alexandra had given Rasputin the secret password to the case holding the crown jewels, which Rasputin had stolen and sent off to Germany.[8]

Shishkin is correct that the intelligence services in cities across Europe were busily trying to divine Rasputin's position on the war, but strangely none of his biographers has taken the time to see just what the services were coming up with. The archives in Berlin offer fascinating information on just how desperate the Germans were to know Rasputin's views and just how little they did know. The reports that were coming into the ministry for foreign affairs were contradictory. A

German secret communiqué of 6 February 1916 (NS) stated that Rasputin was for peace, but that he thought it still too early.[9] And then, three weeks later, Hellmuth Lucius von Stoedten, the former German ambassador to Russia and then head of the German Legation in Stockholm, communicated to Reichskanzler Bethmann Hollweg that "Rasputin still has influence, and he has now been bought by England."[10]

On 12 May 1916 (NS), Baron Friedrich von der Ropp, a Baltic German from Lithuania and the secretary general of the League of the Non-Russian Nationalities of the Russian Empire, a group of émigrés who cooperated with Germany during the war against Russia, sent the foreign ministry a secret paper titled "On the Russian Shadow Government and its Deeds based on Reliable Reports." The central claim of the report was that Russia was secretly being ruled by an unofficial group —the Shadow Government—that essentially equaled the so-called "German party" led by Rasputin, together with Pitirim, Vyrubova, and Andronikov. Rasputin was now in control of all the major decisions of the civil government and the conduct of the war. The group had no political program, being motivated only by greed and ambition. Rasputin extorted large bribes, demanding no less than a thousand rubles for anyone wishing to meet him. The official motto of this shadow government was "Ridding the Russian State of German Influence" and the blame for all problems in the country was laid at the feet of the ethnic Germans and Jews. But it would be mistaken to think Rasputin and his clique wanted to end the war. Just the opposite. The war gave them unlimited opportunities to engage in various schemes and resort to graft and corruption on a massive scale that brought in huge amounts of money. This, in Ropp's estimation, was their chief motivation. He urged Germany not to seek peace with Russia, for no one would dare support it given the anti-German bias there, and, even more importantly, revolution and chaos were coming soon to Russia, and the monarchy was doomed. Kaiser Wilhelm himself read Ropp's report and had a copy sent to Ferdinand I, King of Bulgaria and Germany's ally as of October 1915.[11]

One Herr Junghaus, a wealthy businessman based in Paris with extensive trade contacts in Russia, informed a German official in Basel in August that "Rasputin is again in favor and is a friend of England."[12] A few months later, the ministry in Berlin was receiving reports suggesting just the opposite, that Rasputin had had enough of the war and that he and the empress were now both united in their desire for a separate peace with Germany. This confusing flow of information was being received in Berlin right up until Rasputin's death in December. Herr R. A. Ziese from the German embassy in Stockholm wrote to Bethmann Hollweg that he had information from a good source that "One seems to know little about Rasputin. It is said he is peace loving and honest, so much so that any attempt to approach him with money will not work. (One can only harm matters that way)."[13] Even after his death the Germans were still trying to figure out on whose side Rasputin had been. A report on the situation in Russia dated 6 January 1917 (NS) suggested that although Rasputin may have once been in favor of peace, more recently he had been in the pro-war camp, "because he had been afraid for his life given the many threats."[14]

Rasputin was for peace, Rasputin was for war. Rasputin had been bought by the English, Rasputin wished to make a separate peace with the Germans. Rasputin was greedy and bribable, Rasputin was honest and incorruptible. Rasputin seemed to be many things to the German government during the war. One thing he clearly was not: their spy.

The British were none the wiser. An anonymous letter from a British official dated 4 November 1916 on affairs in Russia asserted that "the governing clique is our enemy." It was clearly pro-German and was spreading all sorts of rumors against the English, so the report asserted. "Secret meetings are now being held in one of the Grand Ducal Palaces (the Constantine Palace) in which Rasputin's ladies, two or three reactionary bureaucrats and also one of the Hesse-Darmstadt princes, reputedly a prisoner of war, are said to be taking part. The situation is dangerous. The gang is certainly trying hard to betray us and betray Russia."[15]

The British certainly did fear Rasputin was trying to get Nicholas to betray England. As for Rasputin, he thought little of Russia's ally. "England has always been traitorous, and they'd sell us out now too," he liked to say, according to Governor Ordovsky-Tanaevsky.[16] Rasputin had a low opinion of the English and had suspicions about how they would treat Russia after the war. This is the sentiment that lay behind his unfeeling words about Kitchener's death, not the fear of being exposed as a spy.

If not a spy, then Rasputin was undoubtedly a tool in the hands of others, or so many have proposed. The list of culprits is long. Prince

Zhevakhov, the same man who cultivated a relationship with Rasputin in search of a high post in the Synod, wrote in his memoirs that his former patron had in fact been an unwitting weapon against the monarchy in the hands of the Jewish "International." The International sought out Rasputin before he became known and spread the word of his spiritual powers, thus preparing the ground for his appearance in Petersburg. Having paved his path into the palace, the cabal of world Jewry then proceeded to destroy its creation and, along with it, its ultimate goal, the Romanov dynasty.[17] Father Vladimir Vostokov held a similar view, although he was convinced Rasputin was no clueless tool, but an actual agent of the International chosen to destroy not just "Holy Russia," but Christianity itself.[18]

Where there is talk of Jews, there is usually talk of Freemasons, and the case of Rasputin is no exception. Among the first to make the connection was Mikhail Rodzianko. In his memoirs he recounts that in preparation for a report to the tsar on Rasputin, he came across an article from a foreign newspaper describing how, at an international congress of Freemasons in Brussels in 1909 or 1910 (he could not be sure), Rasputin was selected as the perfect instrument to introduce "the slogans of the Order" in Russia that would destabilize and bring down the dynasty in no more than two years.[19] Rodzianko's story echoes an article published in the *Voice of Moscow* on 21 February 1912, according to which Rasputin was on his way to Brussels to meet with "one not unknown titled individual" who was using Rasputin in his plans against Russia.[20] Rodzianko was correct that there had been an international Masonic convention in Brussels in 1910, but then there had also been conventions in Antwerp in 1894, Paris in 1900, and Geneva in 1902, and at none of them was Rasputin's name ever mentioned, none of which matters, of course, to minds intent on seeing hidden hands as the true motive force of history.[21]

Contemporary nationalist historians have articulated a slight twist on the Masonic conspiracy, namely that Russia's Freemasons created the myth of Rasputin the alcoholic-reprobate-khlyst-traitor as the most effective weapon in their struggle to bring down the regime. The leaders of this plot are given as the liberal Duma members, the leaders of the Kadet party such as Pavel Milyukov, and Alexander Guchkov, leader of the centrist Octobrist Party.[22] The argument has a number of serious flaws. Neither Milyukov nor Guchkov were Freemasons, for one thing, and the initial attacks against Rasputin did not come from Russia's left, but from the right. Moreover, the right never stopped attacking Rasputin and it in fact competed with the liberal and radical left to produce the most damaging attacks against Rasputin.[23] For the right, this was their duty, as they saw it, to save Russia by saving the monarchy, whereas for the left, this was their duty, as they saw it, to save Russia by either reforming the monarchy or overthrowing it. Both right and left shared in the creation of the corrosive Rasputin myth. What Rasputin managed to do, without actually trying, was to unite all of Russia against him and so, in the end, against the regime itself.

His critics projected their enemies onto the image of Rasputin. *Our Workers' Newspaper* published in Tbilisi in July 1914 saw him as the face of reaction: "Behind him hide those secret forces that carry out their work here given the lack of true European freedom and a constitution. In the dark they run the government and ministers, they choose and replace them with others, and they prepare all manner of reactionary surprises for the country."[24] The German newspaper *Volksfreund* wrote that same summer that Rasputin was a tool of the clerics working in league with a small but very powerful party of conservatives, while the Polish paper *Kurjer Poznański*, also from the summer of 1914, claimed Rasputin had been part of a secret society of "starets-miracle-workers" that wielded power over the entire Russian empire.[25] Lenin insisted Rasputin and Nicholas together created an alliance with the Anglo-French billionaires, and Sergei Melgunov had no doubt he was being blindly used by the band of court favorites and courtiers for their own selfish gain.[26] Lily Dehn wrote that Rasputin was a tool in the hands of the revolutionaries. They had originally wanted to use John of Kronstadt, but he died so they turned to Rasputin. His handler, she claims, was Akilina Laptinskaya, who under her cover as a nurse secretly worked with the revolutionaries to manipulate and control Rasputin.[27] British journalist Robert Wilton called Rasputin an agent for Ferdinand of Bulgaria.[28] Alexei Khvostov called him a weapon of Count Sergei Witte.[29]

The strangest idea belonged to Felix Yusupov. Rasputin, he wrote in his memoirs, was the tool of a group known as "the greens," who controlled him from a distance (apparently somewhere in Sweden) without his even being aware of who they were and what they were using him for. How they managed this incredible feat of mind control Yusupov never said, but he alleged it was clear to him their ultimate goal was to use Rasputin to convince Nicholas to conclude a separate peace with Germany. Once, in late 1916, Yusupov alleged to have seen four "distinctly Jewish type" men at Rasputin's apartment and three similar-looking fair men—might not these be the greens, he wondered? Investigator Nikolai Sokolov also mentioned these mysterious green men. He wrote that their center was in Stockholm and they were able to use Rasputin to control every important action of the government.

What Yusupov and Sokolov meant was that Rasputin was being used by German agents.[30] It was a common notion at the time. Alexei Khvostov and other officials believed this as well. Rasputin's apartment on Gorokhovaya was understood to be the place where spies gathered information from Rasputin's loose talk for their masters back in Germany.[31] One of these suspicious men frequenting Gorokhovaya was Arthur Gyulling. The son of a Finnish senator, Gyulling, aged forty, met Rasputin in July 1916 and saw him regularly up until his death. The exact nature of their relationship is not clear, although it seems beyond doubt that Gyulling tried to use Rasputin to help land profitable business deals, such as the sale of a number of ships for which Rasputin was to have been paid a commission of one million rubles. The Okhrana had its suspicions that Gyulling was a spy based on the fact that several officers lived and gathered at his apartment at 54 Fontanka and the fact that he claimed to have a fortune of 600,000 Finnish Marks, from which he was able to pay 600 rubles a month in rent and 300 rubles a month to his personal secretary, Leonty Voronin, who was also the chief political reporter for Skvortsov's conservative Orthodox newspaper the *Bell*. He told the Okhrana that while he invested in a number of ventures, none of them had brought him any profit. The Okhrana, however, had its doubts. They found in Voronin's address book the names of a good many persons suspected of espionage. Moreover, Voronin was married to an Austrian citizen. As for Gyulling, according to Voronin, he was a relative of the Swedish Foreign Minister Knut Wallenberg.[32]

On the night of 19 December 1916 the Petrograd Okhrana arrested Gyulling along with six other men, including Maria Rasputin's former fiancé Pkhakadze, Prince Nestor Eristov, and Voronin. The Okhrana had their concerns the men were preparing to make some sort of "demonstration" at Rasputin's burial. Voronin told the Okhrana that his employer Gyulling met with Rasputin only to help direct the latter "onto good deeds" and that their gatherings at Gyulling's apartment were purely for social entertainment and nothing more. Voronin insisted there was nothing illegal or traitorous about the activities of Gyulling and his interactions with Rasputin, adding that Gyulling's main goal was the creation of an anti-German coalition of the Scandinavian countries. The men were held for two days and then released. No proof was ever found to suggest they were spying for Germany.[33]

And then there was the odd case of one Charles Perren. No one knows who he really was. He arrived in Petrograd before the war on a U.S. passport presenting himself as a doctor. On the pages of the local newspapers he advertised his talents as a hypnotist, medium, and fortune teller, which he demonstrated in shows at the Palace Theater. He befriended Rasputin in the hopes of establishing connections with top government officials, which he in fact did, most notably in the person of Alexander Protopopov, the last minister of the interior. Russian counter-intelligence took note of Perren during the war, only to discover that his true name was Karl, not Charles, and that he was in fact Austrian, not American. On 4 July 1916, Perren was expelled from Russia on suspicion of spying for the enemy, and settled in Stockholm. Later, following Rasputin's murder, Protopopov tried to bring him back to Petrograd so he could avail himself of Perren's mystical powers. Or so some claimed. The last tsarist chief of police, Alexei Vasilev, told the Commission that it was Perren who twice wrote Protopopov requesting permission to come to Russia, but Protopopov sent him a polite telegram of refusal.[34]

It is no more likely that Gyulling, Voronin, or Perren were German spies than was David Rowland Francis, appointed the new U.S. ambassador to Russia in the spring of 1916. But this was exactly what one of the Russian grand duchesses insisted at the time. She also insisted that the American capital was completely under German influence.[35] It was not, however, only Russians who saw spies hovering around Rasputin. In early 1918, U.S. military intelligence was monitoring Baroness Ida Leonie von Seidlitz; Princess Vilma Lwoff-Parlaghy, a noted Hungarian-born portraitist who had lived for years in Germany; and Dmitry Florinsky, the former Russian vice consul in New York. The three individuals were described as "secret agents of the Russian Czarina, the monk Rasputin and former Russian premier v. Sturmer." They had purportedly been conducting secret meetings at the "apartments of a certain Mrs. Goldsmith in New York," joined by the former German ambassador Johann Heinrich von Bernstorff and Jacob Schiff, the noted millionaire, philanthropist, and German-born Jewish banker. Military intelligence was convinced they were in the U.S. trying to bring about a separate peace and, adding a new element to the Rasputin myth, were all suspected of having ties to the "Russian Bolshevik movement." By November 1918, Baroness von Seidlitz had been arrested and interned at Fort Oglethorpe, Georgia.[36]

One of the tasks the Commission set itself in 1917 was uncovering the truth about the "dark forces" under the old regime, and specifically whether Rasputin, Vyrubova, and the empress had been spies or tools of Germany. The Commission, heavily biased against the three, looked hard to find proof to substantiate the charge. In the end, they found nothing.[37] For a century, disinterested scholars have investigated the matter and have all come to the same conclusion.

58. Rasputin and the Jews

Yusupov saw "distinctly Jewish-type" men at Rasputin's in Petrograd, hence he suspected him of nefarious activities. Father Shavelsky complained to the tsar that Rasputin went out drinking with "Jews and all sorts of dark personalities." The police recorded a Jewish merchant from Minsk visiting Rasputin in Pokrovskoe and had the man thoroughly investigated. Socializing with Jews was something upper-class Russians typically did not do. It signified bad taste, or something worse.

Rasputin had shared these attitudes for most of his life. For years he had been close to prominent anti-Semitic clergymen like Germogen and Iliodor, he had written harshly about the Jews during the Beilis Affair, and he had praised the activities of the Black Hundreds, to whom it was said he belonged. But then, following his break with Germogen and Iliodor, his attitudes began to change. From the ugly prejudice of his earlier years, Rasputin grew to accept Jews, as friends and business colleagues, and even to champion liberalized state policies toward Russia's Jews that put him well ahead of the vast majority of his countrymen. Part of the reason for this was the fact that Russian nationalists had themselves turned away from Rasputin, but just as important was Rasputin's own personality, his relaxed tolerance toward other nationalities and faiths and his general live-and-let-live nature.

The artist Alexander Raevsky recalled during one of his sessions with Rasputin in 1912 how someone in his studio began to curse the Jews. In a flash, Rasputin cut the person off: "That's not true!" he yelled. "All people are equal before God ... Once I traveled from Jerusalem with a Jew. He was a kind man, a pious man. Just as among Christians, so too among them, one finds all kinds of people."[1] It may well have been comments such as this that led some Black Hundreds to turn against Rasputin. That same year they produced a satire mocking Rasputin as busy destroying Orthodox Russia for the "Yids."[2]

Best remembered of the Jews close to Rasputin was his secretary Aaron Simanovich. Originally from Kiev where he ran a small jewelry shop, Simanovich made his way to Petersburg in the early years of the century and quickly amassed a small fortune as a purveyor of diamonds to the city's well-to-do. He also opened a number of gambling parlors, being himself an inveterate gambler, known to win, and lose, big on high-stakes games at the tables. Reports as to his character diverge wildly. One Okhrana report described him as "quite a nasty man, a powerful string-puller with an insinuating manner, capable of any adventure or speculation."[3] Petrograd Okhrana head Globachev, however, noted Simanovich was an honest gambler, a man with limited education, barely able to speak or read Russian, yet quite bright and endowed with street smarts. Beletsky described him as an excellent family man and father, dedicated to his children's upbringing and education. With the money he made Simanovich managed to become a merchant of the first guild, a social designation that brought with it the right for a Jew such as himself to live permanently in the capital. He lived with his wife and six children in a spacious apartment. Many knew Simanovich as a generous man, ready to help out with a gift or loan to those in need, even if some grumbled at the high interest he charged.[4] Following the revolution, Simanovich wrote (or, more likely, dictated) a book titled *Rasputin and the Jews* that would come to exercise a strong influence on later perceptions of the man, regrettably considering the book's many errors and ridiculous notions (e.g., Rasputin healed the emperor of alcoholism, General Orlov was the true father of the tsarevich, etc.).[5]

At the time of Rasputin's murder Simanovich said the two men had met, by coincidence, in 1900 at the railway station in Kazan, and then renewed their acquaintance and began to grow close around 1911.[6] Could Simanovich's gambling addiction have played a role? The Petersburg press reported in 1914 that when the "Capital Arts and Social Club," the anodyne name behind which one of the city's larger gambling establishments operated, was on the verge of bankruptcy, Rasputin stepped in to arrange a large loan to keep it afloat. The club, according to the article, was notorious for all sorts of vice and illegality, but this never seemed to bother Rasputin, and although he did not play the tables himself, he liked to come and watch the action.[7] Like most newspaper stories about Rasputin, it is difficult to say how much, if any, of this was true.

Rasputin had had other secretaries before Simanovich. At first there was Laptinskaya, intelligent, honest, and hard-working. Next came a man by the name of Volynsky, about whom almost nothing is known, and then one Ivan Dobrovolsky. These men were less secretaries in the traditional sense and more gatekeepers between Rasputin and the endless stream of petitioners. They were the ones who collected the gifts, bribes, and other "fees" intended for their boss. Dobrovolsky, a former government school inspector, and his wife Maria, "a heavily made-up and dubious personage," in Vyrubova's words, began pocketing some of the money that was supposed merely to pass through their hands. He and Maria began to lead a luxurious lifestyle with their new-found wealth. When Rasputin found out, they were dismissed. According to the testimony of Alexander Protopopov, the last minister of the interior, Dobrovolsky was arrested in the summer of 1916. Simanovich took their place.[8]

Simanovich came to spend most of his time at the Gorokhovaya apartment in the final two years of Rasputin's life. The family grew close to him. "Simochka," Maria fondly called him. Simanovich had helped to save Rasputin's life during the Khvostov affair and had paid a heavy price for it. Rasputin did not forget, and saw to it that Simanovich was permitted to return from exile. Simanovich purportedly witnessed Rasputin's respect for Jews at Gorokhovaya. "If among the petitioners were some generals," Simanovich recalled, "then he would jokingly say to them: 'Dear Generals, you are used to always being received first. But there are Jews here, people without any rights, and I should see to them first. Jews, let us talk. I want to do everything for you.'"[9]

It is possible Simanovich opened Rasputin's eyes to the plight of the empire's Jewish subjects and introduced him to other Jews in the city.[10] One of these was Genrikh Sliozberg, a prominent lawyer and one of the leading advocates for Jewish rights in Russia. They first met in early 1914 when Rasputin came to him to request money for an almshouse back in Pokrovskoe. Rasputin treated Sliozberg over lunch as if they were old acquaintances. Sliozberg was immediately impressed. "In his eyes there was something riveting," he found. "Of course, his lack of culture seeped through every gesture and every word. But it was impossible not to listen to him. Every expression was so alive and, if nothing else, offered proof that this was an extremely intelligent man."[11]

Their conversation turned toward Jewish affairs, and Rasputin told Sliozberg it was thanks to his conversations with the tsar that a chapel had not been erected on the spot where the body of the Yushchinsky boy had been found in Kiev, the murder that set off the Beilis Affair. He had told the tsar that this would make a martyr of the boy, something to be avoided especially since his death had not been an instance of ritual murder. Rasputin made his views on the matter public around the time of his lunch with Sliozberg, telling the press that the Beilis Affair was nothing but the work of troublemakers.[12] Rasputin also spoke to Sliozberg of his role in the Affair of the Dentists, another scandal then roiling Russia. At a time when Jews were denied the right to live in Moscow, exceptions were made for dentists, and when a large number appeared with diplomas from a stomatological institution in Pskov, an investigation was launched that uncovered a diploma factory cranking out fake certificates for sale. Some involved were brought before the courts, while the Jewish dentists were banished from Moscow. Rasputin, so he told Sliozberg, had been approached by many of these men for help, and he had saved several hundred of them from having to leave the city. Rasputin was apparently telling the truth here. Other sources confirm that Rasputin had helped the Jewish "dentists" remain in Moscow. Khvostov commented that this was the truth and that all Rasputin got for his trouble was "a fur hat and coat," even though as much as 30,000 rubles in bribes had been handed out to settle the matter. As well as coming to the aid of the dentists, Rasputin also helped many Jews avoid military service during the war.[13] Before he left, Rasputin made Sliozberg an enormous promise, telling him he would see to it that the Pale of Settlement* would be done away with. "I am not Rasputin if I do not give you the pale," he informed Sliozberg.[14] He said the same thing to Vera Zhukovskaya, although he added that while he wanted Jews to be free to live anywhere in the Russian empire, he was not in favor of their having equal rights with Russians. Zhukovskaya suggested that there was nothing humanitarian about Rasputin's help for the Jews, and that he was doing it just for the money, something that does not chime with Rasputin's well-documented indifference to lucre.[15] If Rasputin did bring up the matter with the tsar, it never moved beyond the level of vague discussions. Nicholas, like Alexandra, was preternaturally anti-Semitic, and like most Russians at the time did not favor doing away with the pale or giving Jews full rights. The Pale of Settlement

---

* An area in the western part of the Russian Empire created under Catherine the Great where Jews were permitted to live. Only Jews with specific skills or wealth were allowed to live on a permanent basis in the traditional Russian areas of the empire, although there was considerable illegal immigration from the Pale. By the late summer of 1915, the Pale had in effect been largely abolished and would be legally ended by the Provisional Government in 1917.

survived Rasputin and the Romanov dynasty and was abolished by the Provisional Government in March 1917.

Dmitry Rubinshtein was born into a poor Jewish family in Kharkov, a city outside the Pale of Settlement that had allowed Jews to settle and that came to boast a wealthy and vibrant Jewish community by the end of the nineteenth century. A gifted child, he attended the lycée in Yaroslavl and went on to earn a doctorate in law and enter the world of banking, rising to the status of a first-guild merchant and director and chairman of the board of the Franco-Russian Bank in Petersburg. Rubinshtein, referred to, unaffectionately, as "Mitka," became wealthy and well connected, although resented by most of the elite, and together with his wife Stella, was intent on moving up the social ladder. Not surprisingly, he landed on philanthropy as the surest road to acceptance among the capital's elite. The Rubinshteins gave generously to the army hospital set up by the empress at Tsarskoe Selo as well as to an infirmary created by Vyrubova. In 1914, they gave 20,000 rubles to a charity of the Dowager Empress, for which Dmitry received the Order of St. Vladimir, Fourth Class. But it seemed there was only so high a Jew could ascend, and certain opportunities were closed to him. One of them involved Rubinshtein's greatest wish: to be granted the rank of actual state councilor. Every avenue, however, seemed blocked to him no matter how hard he tried. His requests were repeatedly denied.[16]

At some point Rubinshtein came to the realization he would never succeed without the help of Rasputin. He started frequenting Gorokhovaya, and by the autumn of 1915 he was on the Okhrana's radar. In November an agent reported that Rubinshtein was living at a house that belonged to Countess Sofia Ignatieva at 5 Tsaritsynskaya Street that he hoped to buy with the help of Rasputin, for which he was planning to pay him a 20 percent commission. The report added that Rubinshtein had set up with his own money an infirmary for soldiers in a rented house on Vasilevsky Island, an act of charity that had apparently gained him an audience, arranged by Rasputin, with the empress.[17]

Alexandra first mentioned Rubinshtein in a letter to Nicholas in September 1915. Either Rubinshtein himself, or Rasputin for him, had told the empress that he had donated a thousand rubles of his own money for the production of airplanes for Russia's infant air force. He was prepared to give another 500,000 if he could be made an actual state councilor. Alexandra found the request repugnant: "How ugly these requests are at such a time—charity has to be paid for—how vile!" Rasputin, the realist, told Alexandra that while she found the practice reprehensible, in such times as these, when the state was in desperate need of money, requests such as Rubinshtein's ought to be granted.[18] And he certainly was not the first. There was also the case of Ignaty Manus, a baptized Jew, wealthy banker, and industrialist. Like Rubinshtein, Manus gave a great deal to charity, and in 1915 he had been granted the rank of actual state councilor. Also like Rubinshtein, Manus cultivated a relationship with Rasputin for the same reason so many other Russians did: he was the only man in Russia by then who had the ear of the tsaritsa and, through her, of the tsar. Powerful men, or men seeking power, could not ignore Rasputin, even if they wanted to. No friends of each other, Rubinshtein and Manus competed for Rasputin's favor. According to Globachev, both men put on big parties and banquets for him and with Rasputin's help they made huge deals and gained important contracts. Rasputin got a cut of all the action. Sometimes he was content with his share, sometimes not, and then he would quarrel and demand more. The money went to maintain his apartment in Gorokhovaya and his family back in Pokrovskoe, though most of it he gave away.[19] The relationships were purely self-serving. They used Rasputin, and he used them, each for their own ends.

In the paranoid atmosphere of the time, Rasputin's relationships with men like Manus and Rubinshtein attracted attention. Two men made it their business to get to the bottom of this relationship: General Mikhail Bonch-Bruevich, the brother of the Bolshevik Vladimir and the head of the general staff of the Northern Front, and his subordinate, Colonel (later General) Nikolai Batyushin. The general was a fanatic about catching spies. Ever since the Myasoedov Affair, he had become convinced they had infiltrated every corner of the army, court, civil administration, and the home front. He made it his job to rid the country of German spies and was angered that no one took the task as seriously as he did. Batyushin shared his boss's passion. In the spring of 1916, he was ordered by General Mikhail Alexeev to head up a commission to root out military espionage. The first assignment of the "Commission to Investigate Activities Endangering the Home Front" was to investigate the financial dealings of the banker Dmitry Rubinshtein. Alexeev set one condition: Rasputin was not to know about the investigation, for he alone had the power to stop it. Even before he began, Batyushin was convinced of Rubinshtein's guilt and that his charitable efforts were nothing but a smokescreen to hide the fact. Batyushin was among those who believed Rasputin was a blind tool in the hands of spies like Dmitry Rubinshtein. He was certain Rubinshtein was feeding him bogus German military intelligence knowing he would communicate it to Alexandra and Nicholas, and so disrupt Russian military operations, causing Russian troops to move according to Berlin's plans. He was also certain Rasputin was accepting massive bribes from Rubinshtein. Batyushin's plan was to take down Rubinshtein and destroy Rasputin in the process.[20]

Others were tracking Rasputin's meetings with wealthy Jewish figures as well. In February 1916, the Okhrana noted that Rasputin had become a frequent guest of honor at the feasts put on by Abram Boberman, a Jewish merchant from Samara, in the Hotel Europe, where Boberman was living. The police reported that Boberman was involved in "large scale financial operations; the majority of BOBERMAN's undertakings are conducted with the cooperation of G. Rasputin." Boberman also happened to be a frequent guest at Gorokhovaya.[21] The press was full of stories about Rasputin's hand in business deals with a number of figures, many of them shady, some foreigners. Some of these involved state military contracts, but not all of them, like the story about how Rasputin was busy negotiating the rights to open a large cinema in Petrograd that would show off the "Kinotofon," the latest invention of Thomas Edison. Common to the stories, however, was the understanding, stated or implied, that bribery was involved and Rasputin stood to make a tidy sum.[22]

A letter from Dr. Badmaev to Rasputin dated 8 October 1916 shows how the game was played:

> My dear Grigory Yefimovich.
>
> "God is beyond the clouds, and the tsar is far away"—so do people still say who need his attention to their serious problems in life. The ministers continue to be such cowards about doing anything useful, or they do it only after having been beaten with a stick by the State Duma. Not everyone has the possibility to force them to take up matters that require immediate attention. And then there are all manner of go-betweens demanding great sums of money to influence the ministers. But not all go-betweens can be trusted, for they take the money and still the business does not get taken care of. There is one such matter, upon which its owner has

expended a great deal, that I present to You to bring to the attention of our dear tsar, who alone can see it is forwarded to the Council of Ministers. Were one to follow the usual path this would require a great deal of time to see it through to fruition, and I might add this concerns a vital branch of an industrial concern. Its owner, whose most humble petition I present to You, believes in me and General Kurlov, and is offering us 50,000 rubles if the business is successfully completed. We refused to take any money for our help with this matter, but we did tell him that we could ask You to send this request along the proper channel, for it is an entirely fair and proper matter that demands that the ministers know that the Eye of the Emperor is following it. [. . .]

With sincere love for You, Pyotr Badmaev[23]

Badmaev was, of course, being coy about his refusal to take any money for his help, and the implied message to Rasputin was that he would get his cut of this 50,000 as well.

If they were going to penetrate the secretive world of espionage, Bonch-Bruevich and Batyushin decided they needed someone well informed in counter-intelligence with connections to the key figures. They chose as their man Ivan Manasevich-Manuilov, the Russian Rocambole, albeit with reservations. His reputation for double-dealing was well known to them, as was his new role as a special secretary to Prime Minister Stürmer, seen by most as an ally of Rasputin. Bonch-Bruevich and Batyushin could not be completely certain whether Manuilov would be working with them or against them, but it was a risk they felt they had to take.[24]

Originally, the trail seemed to lead not to Rubinshtein, but to Manus as the head of the German spy-ring. General Dmitry Dubensky, a member of the tsar's entourage and the official chronicler of the Russian war effort, insisted that he had heard from a knowledgeable source in the banking world that Manus was the one responsible for controlling the flow of money being used to aid the Germans. Manus was called in for questioning on 1 March, but he vociferously rejected any suggestion that he was involved in spying for the Germans or part of any "German party" and was let go.[25]

In the meantime, Manuilov began passing along information to the commission that seemed to prove Batyushin's suspicions about Rubinshtein. On 10 July, Rubinshtein was arrested on charges of espionage and state treason and sent to the city of Pskov. When they went to search his premises for the documents that would substantiate the information Manuilov had provided them, Batyushin and his men were stunned to find none. Instead of accepting the obvious—that there never had been any documents—Batyushin assumed that someone had tipped off Rubinshtein, most likely Minister of the Interior Protopopov or Yevgeny Klimovich, director of the department of the police since March of that year, and he had managed to destroy everything.[26]

The man charged with hearing the case against Rubinshtein, Procurator Sergei Zavadsky, was stunned by the lack of evidence handed over to him by Batyushin, which he called "childish prattle: nothing but rumors and gossip." If, Zavadsky said, Rubinshtein truly was guilty, then Batyushin and his commission were his best defense; if he was innocent, then this was nothing but "a horror." Others went even further. Pavel Kurlov, reappointed deputy minister of the interior for two months in late 1916, was extremely critical of Batyushin's commission for acting well beyond its remit and in a high-handed, arbitrary way. Counter-intelligence under Batyushin, Kurlov said, had become "a form of white terror."[27]

Batyushin's work was dealt another major setback when Manuilov, the man he had chosen to work with him, was arrested in late August on charges of blackmail and extortion by Director of the Police Klimovich. The police claimed to have proof that Manuilov had, among other things, tried to extort 26,000 rubles from the United Bank (headed by Tatishchev, the same man Rasputin had recommended as minister of finance), and received illegal funds from the Franco-Russian Bank (whose chairman of the board was none other than Rubinshtein). The arrest was seen as an attack on Rasputin by targeting one of his powerful allies. Klimovich was a creature, and friend, of disgraced Minister of the Interior Alexei Khvostov, and was also close to Khvostov's uncle, Alexander Khvostov, who served as minister of the interior from early July to mid-September 1916, precisely when Manuilov was arrested.[28] Klimovich was a ruthless character. According to a document in the archives of the ministry of the interior, Klimovich, while head of the Moscow Okhrana in 1907, had been involved in plotting the murder of Grigory Iollas, Duma deputy, Kadet, and a Jew.[29] None of this was lost on either Rasputin or Alexandra.

The arrest put Batyushin in a difficult position: he could not hope to carry on his work without Manuilov's help, but to come to his defense was impossible, given the nature and severity of the charges against him. Indeed, it is possible that this, and not an attack on Rasputin and his circle, had been the true aim of Klimovich's arrest of Manuilov.[30] Either way, the result was the same. Batyushin realized his effort to catch Rasputin had failed. If Simanovich can be believed (which is doubtful), Batyushin now swallowed his pride and went to beg for mercy from Vyrubova. Nicholas summoned Batyushin to Stavka and threatened to relieve him, but, with the help of General Alexeev, he managed to avoid being dismissed. Nonetheless, henceforth Batyushin changed his attitude to Rasputin and even tried to curry favor with him.[31] Perhaps this explains why the Commission included Batyushin's name among a list of sixty-seven "Rasputinists."[32]

In May 1916, Colonel Alexander Rezanov was added to Batyushin's commission on the order of General Alexeev. Rezanov had been charged with investigating espionage as an official of the justice ministry for years, and he was as convinced as Bonch-Bruevich and Batyushin that spying was rampant among Russia's Jewish industrialists. He told investigator Nikolai Sokolov in Paris in 1921 how it worked. Various large insurance firms engaged in reinsurance for managing foreign risk that was nothing more than a clever scheme for passing on military secrets concerning Russian military production and shipping movements to the enemy. All of the major firms were involved, according to Rezanov. One of the main actors, he told Sokolov, had been none other than Alexander Guchkov. The commission had gathered convincing proof of Guchkov's crimes, but before he could be arrested the revolution broke out and he was saved.

The other major figure was Rubinshtein. Rezanov alleged that they had confiscated coded letters at Rubinshtein's apartment proving his involvement in espionage. As for Rasputin, Rezanov, who had met him on several occasions, told Sokolov that he did not think he had been a spy, but was surrounded by spies, all under the direction of Manuilov, who used him for their own ends. The man who had been running the spy ring in Russia, he said, was none other than Hellmuth Lucius von Stoedten in Sweden. Lucius's letters in the Political Archive of the Foreign Ministry in Berlin show without any doubt that he was not running a group of agents in Russia, a fact that casts a large shadow on Rezanov's accusations against all the others in his testimony to Sokolov.[33]

*

Rasputin and Alexandra were not indifferent to the fate of Rubinshtein and Manuilov. On 26 September, she wrote to Nicholas to say that Protopopov now agreed with her and Rasputin that the entire investigation and arrest of Rubinshtein had been carried out solely for the purpose of damaging "our Friend," and the man behind it must have been Guchkov. Alexandra did not think Rubinshtein was a model of propriety ("Certainly he had ugly money affairs—but not he alone," she commented to Nicholas), but the actions against him were biased from the beginning, and she either wanted him freed or at least quietly moved from Pskov to Siberia, and "not left here to aggravate the Jews."[34] She, and Rasputin too, wrote again to the tsar asking him to ease the plight of Rubinshtein. He was eventually freed on 6 December, but the charges against him were not dropped, and he was arrested a second time, before finally being freed along with many other inmates of the capital's prisons by the crowds during the February Revolution.[35]

On 10 December, Alexandra wrote Nicholas again, now begging him to stop the trial of Manuilov set for the fifteenth. She told him that Batyushin had been to see Vyrubova and had said that the trial should not be allowed to take place because now he knew that the case against Manuilov was a pure fabrication intended to harm Rasputin. The man behind it all, according to Batyushin, was Alexei Khvostov, who had been saying to people that he was sorry "Tchik"—Alexandra's (or possibly from Khvostov's) nickname for Boris Rzhevsky—had not succeeded in killing Rasputin.* A trial would simply lead to all the details of Khvostov's murderous conspiracy being dredged up again. Alexandra simply could not bear the thought of it. She instructed Nicholas to write the words "discontinue the case" on Manuilov's file and send it to Minister of Justice Alexander Makarov, and immediately, before it was too late. At the same time she implored Nicholas to fire Makarov, whom she deemed a foe of Rasputin's, and replace him with his deputy, Nikolai Dobrovolsky. The tsar obeyed. Ten days later Makarov was replaced by Dobrovolsky, and Manuilov was temporarily freed and his trial postponed until February.[36] (It was rumored Dobrovolsky was an occultist much in favor with the empress, hence his promotion.)[37] Alexandra wrote Nicholas on the fifteenth: "Thanks so

---

* Khvostov, it should be noted, had earlier wanted to murder Rasputin with poisoned wine sent (falsely) by Rubinshtein, and so kill two birds with one stone: Rasputin would be dead, Rubinshtein behind bars. See Mel'gunov, *Legenda*, 400–401.

much (& fr. Gr.[rigory] too) for Manuilov."[38] The public outrage at the tsar's decision was enormous. At his trial in mid-February, Manuilov was found guilty, stripped of all his property, and sentenced to prison. He did not stay there for long, and was freed by the very crowds that released Rubinshtein in the euphoria of late February.

Protopopov told the Commission that after being freed a grateful Rubinshtein bought 500 rubles' worth of flowers and had them sent to Rasputin's apartment. What stupidity, he added, for Rubinshtein to advertise Rasputin's power in this way.[39] Rasputin did indeed help free Rubinshtein, but, flowers or not, he turned his back on Rasputin once he no longer had need of him. After the fall of the Romanovs he gave an interview to a Polish newspaper insisting he had been Rasputin's "sworn enemy" and never his friend. He insisted he had not sought out Rasputin, rather, it had been the other way around: Rasputin and Vyrubova, on behalf of the throne and with the express backing of the minister of finance, had forced him to hand over money from his bank or else lose all of his business dealings with the state. Rasputin did, he admitted, assist him in putting together several deals, but this did not last long before Rasputin started to intrigue against him. Nevertheless, it was Rasputin, moved by an impassioned plea from Rubinshtein's wife, who won his freedom and thus saved him from "unavoidable death."[40]

"All people were created by God," Rasputin was quoted as saying with regard to the Jews by the *Odessa Times* in 1916, "no one should be oppressed."[41] It is difficult to know whether or not Rasputin actually said these words, but what does ring true is the sentiment behind them. Even if Rasputin was not a great friend to the Jews, by the later years of his life he had grown enough as a man to reject the uglier views of his past.

59. "The sun will shine . . ."

In the middle of June Rasputin left Petrograd for Tobolsk to attend the canonization ceremonies for Ioann Maximovich. Governor Ordovsky-Tanaevsky met with Rasputin in the capital before he left and tried to talk him out of coming, saying that the crowds would be much too large for the police to control and that his life would be in danger. Rasputin ignored the governor's warning. From Tobolsk, Rasputin sent a telegram to Nicholas on the last day of June: "The saint bishop Ioann Maximovich blesses with his strong, holy, and mighty hand and blinds infidelity and the enemy's army, the ungodly force. The sun will shine through over our armies, goodness will win."[1] On 2 July, he wrote to Vyrubova: "Took communion of the Holy Mysteries at the shrine with the relics. Only simple people and simplicity, not a single aristocrat in the crowd, and all the people are in God and talk to God. We're leaving for Verkhoturye."[2] Vyrubova replied that the weather at the front was not good (cold and rainy) and asked him to pray, so that "God will bless the front with Sunshine." Rasputin prayed, but it did not help. The sun refused to come out. By the end of July, Rasputin was back in Petrograd.

Rasputin had been giving a good deal of thought to a range of matters early that summer. Before leaving for Tobolsk he had Alexandra write to Nicholas with questions and advice. He wondered about what was the correct approach to the Duma, whether Governor-General of Petrograd Alexander Obolensky ought to be replaced, what should be done about the long food lines in the capital, and whether the ministry of the interior, and not the ministry of agriculture, ought to be responsible for managing the growing food and fuel crisis. Rasputin was especially vexed by the recent change in train fares, which had been raised from five to ten kopecks. He told Alexandra to let Nicholas know that this hike was "not fair upon the poor people—let the rich be taxed but not the others who daily have often more than once to go by train." Rasputin was especially upset by the law that barred enlisted men from

riding on trams and streetcars in the capital during the war, and he
made sure Vyrubova passed this on to Alexandra and Nicholas. He saw
this as senseless, unfair, and the cause of anger and resentment among
the common soldiers against the officers, who were permitted to ride.
It was, in Rasputin's opinion, a policy that had to be stopped, and in this
Rasputin was correct, for this needlessly humiliating law would become
an important factor in stoking the anger that led to the February Revolution. She instructed Nicholas to make sure to pass this along to
Stürmer, as well as Rasputin's command that Nicholas be very firm with
his ministers. Rasputin also let it be known he would like Nicholas to
return to Tsarskoe Selo for a day or two to discuss with him these
"essential" matters before he departed for Tobolsk.[3] Nicholas ignored
Rasputin's request and remained at Stavka.

On 7 July, the emperor shuffled his ministers once again in another
round of ministerial leapfrog. Stürmer maintained his office of prime
minister but was replaced as minister of the interior by Alexander
Khvostov, the former minister of justice and uncle of the would-be murderer Alexei Khvostov. Alexander Makarov was named the new minister
of justice, and Foreign Minister Sergei Sazonov was sacked and his
portfolio added to the duties of Prime Minister Stürmer.[4] Neither Rasputin nor Alexandra was pleased by the selection of Makarov. Both
were still angry at his actions during the letters scandal surrounding
Iliodor in 1912, feeling he had not done enough to protect the empress.
Nonetheless, they were able to take some comfort in the fact that he had
not been made minister of the interior, as Nicholas was considering
back in May, but the less powerful—and less dangerous—position at
the ministry of justice.[5]

But it seems Rasputin may well have already been intriguing against
the new ministers. Prince Andronikov wrote a letter to Palace Commandant Vladimir Voeikov, "under the strictest secrecy," on 2 August to
recount a visit he had had from Manuilov and Colonel Alexander
Rezanov, Batyushin's deputy. According to Andronikov, Manuilov
informed him that he was busy with a number of schemes to undermine Khvostov, Makarov, and Stürmer. "Gr. Yef. Rasputin is playing the
main role in all of this," he confessed, "for he's hypnotizing against
Khvostov, saying that he is just like Alexei Nikolaevich Khvostov." As for
Makarov, he was being attacked since he had failed to show Rasputin
the due respect.

Manuilov is loudly and cynically declaring that the Empress is stronger than everyone else and will take care of "the weak-willed Tsar." This is the end of the road! If that dark gang of Messrs. Manuilov and Co. are to rule Russia, then we must all flee Russia as quickly as possible, for the consequences will be horrifying!

No matter what, we must now support Khvostov and Makarov and strike back firmly against these scoundrels and intriguers, for whom personal gain is more important than the interests of the Dynasty and the Motherland!

This is a cry from my soul, which I hope will elicit a response in Your noble heart![6]

What was Andronikov really seeking with his letter? Was he telling the truth about his meeting with Manuilov? Had it even happened, and if so, in the way he described it in his letter? Or was this rather a bit of intriguing on the part of Prince Andronikov, seeking to curry favor with Voeikov and the new ministers? And did this letter play a role in Manuilov's arrest later that same month, as a counter-attack by the very man, Minister of the Interior Khvostov, mentioned in the letter?

Andronikov also noted in his letter that this "gang" had its sights on Chief Procurator Volzhin, in large part because he would not pay court to Vyrubova, even going so far as to refuse to visit her. Volzhin was tired of the intrigues against him, and what Andronikov apparently did not know was that Volzhin had already asked to resign the day before, on 1 August. His proposed candidates for a successor were ignored in favor of Nikolai Raev. The choice was a regrettable one. Not merely a nonentity, Raev was not even a churchman. He had studied Asian languages and then served for many years in the ministry of education, during which time he founded a women's college. Shavelsky later commented on his commonplace mind and comical appearance: painted cheeks highlighted by a shining black toupee, dyed mustache and beard. "He left the impression of a prematurely old, and indecent, man," Shavelsky noted.[7] His chief qualification was that he was the son of Pavel Raev, the former metropolitan of St. Petersburg, better known as Pallady (died in 1898). It was Pallady who had appointed Pitirim rector of the St. Petersburg Theological Seminary. Rasputin met Raev and spoke with him for over an hour. He told Alexandra the man was "a real godsend."[8] Raev knew to whom he owed his promotion and what was required of him: for his assistant he made certain to choose Prince Zhevakhov.[9] By now there was no doubt. Rasputin had gained control over the church. The defeat of his opponents was complete.

On 28 July, Alexandra and her daughters left Tsarskoe Selo for Stavka to be with Alexei on his birthday. Rasputin sent his best wishes: "The day of glory, this bell has rung from the light, and its ringing will be with us forever; what God gave enemies cannot take."[10] Rasputin had encouraged Alexandra to visit Stavka, telling her that God would look favorably upon it and thus "send his Blessing to the army."[11] While there, Alexandra spoke to General Alexeev about Rasputin. She presented the general with an icon from her friend and later told Nicholas that she hoped he had accepted it in the right spirit, for this would bring yet greater blessings to the army. Alexeev later shared Alexandra's words with Captain Dmitry Tikhobrazov, a field-staff officer at Stavka: "He is such a holy and miraculous man, unjustly slandered, and he is so devoted to our family, and he prays for us with zeal. Believe me, general, that if he could visit Stavka he would bring everyone great happiness."

Alexeev frowned and drily replied: "Your Imperial Majesty, I formed my opinion of this matter a long time ago and nothing can change it. I should add, that as soon as he appears at Stavka, I shall immediately resign my position."

"Is that your final word, general?"

"Without the slightest doubt."

With that, their conversation ended. Tikhobrazov noticed that despite these honest words, Alexeev never suffered for speaking out directly against Rasputin. He maintained not only his post, but the respect of the tsar, if not of Alexandra.[12]

After she and the girls had left for home, Alexandra wrote Nicholas to talk to Alexeev about Rasputin. "[It was] thanks to Him that you remained firm & took over the command a year ago, when all were against you," she wrote, revising what had in fact really happened, "tell him that & he will understand the wisdom then—& many wonderful escapes to those he prays for at the war who know Him—not to speak of Baby & Ania." In November, Alexeev suffered a heart attack and had to be sent to the Crimea to recover. To Alexandra, it was a sign of Divine punishment.[13] A downcast Alexeev told Shavelsky: "You know, Father Georgy, I want to quit service. There's no point in serving: one cannot do a thing, there's no way to help matters. Really, what can one do with that child! He's dancing on the edge of a precipice . . . and is completely calm. A mad woman is running the state, and around her is a lump of dirty worms: Rasputin, Vyrubova, Stürmer, Raev, Pitirim . . ."[14]

On 9 August Rasputin, along with his daughters, Vyrubova, Lily Dehn, Zinaida Rzhevskaya, two valets, and a gendarme departed the capital for Siberia. Before he left, Rasputin presented Alexandra with two roses for Alexei. The party was leaving to pray to the relics of the new St. Ioann Maximovich in Tobolsk on behalf of the empress. Vyrubova was sad and depressed and did not want to go. Getting around on her crutches was slow and painful. Rasputin, however, insisted she come, and so she did.[15] In Tobolsk they stayed in the large white house of the governor in the lower part of the town, the same building where the Romanovs would be held prisoner from late summer of 1917 until spring of the following year. The party was there for just two days to pay their respects to the shrine of the new saint, and then traveled by steamer up river to Pokrovskoe.[16] Rasputin had insisted they be his guests, and they were all received warmly by Praskovya. They spent a day there fishing and visiting Rasputin's peasant friends. Rasputin told Lily Dehn that he hoped their majesties would one day also come visit. When she said this was rather far for them to travel, Rasputin held firm, saying in a serious voice: "They must come."[17]

From Pokrovskoe they traveled to Verkhoturye. Tamara Shishkina, the daughter of the headmistress of a local girls' school, was there to witness their visit.

There was an unbelievable crush in the cathedral. Rasputin and the members of his party stood in the center of the church. Everyone was well dressed, important, many had come from all over the Yekaterinburg district, and maybe even farther. Everything in the church was shining. [. . .]

Grigory Yefimovich Rasputin stood in the place of honor on a rug laid out upon the floor. He was in a bright yellow shirt, belted with a sash and tassel, baggy velvet trousers, and polished boots. His hair was parted down the middle. He prayed fervently, making broad signs of the cross over himself. His face was beautifully calm, concentrated, and pleasant.

After the liturgy a large cross was brought out from the altar and placed on the analogion in the center of the church, so that everyone could kiss it. The first to approach and kiss the cross was Rasputin, and after him his entourage. And then, after them, a terrible crush of worshippers threw itself at the cross, trying to get close to Rasputin and catch a better glimpse of the "starets" and touch him. At that moment the crowd pushed me right into the "starets" himself, right up against his right arm, which he used to bless.

We spent three days in Verkhoturye, and this scene was played out every day, just like on the day of Grigory Yefimovich's arrival in town. There were loud gatherings of people everywhere, everyone discussing their encounters with the "starets" and solemn services in the churches.[18]

Rasputin and his party fasted during their stay and prayed before the holy relics of St. Simeon. Rasputin sent a telegram to Nicholas: "We have fulfilled the wish at the shrine of the righteous man. He will cure, will give our military commanders holy reason. Reason will be our victory over all."[19] He also wrote to congratulate the emperor on the anniversary of his taking command and it seems that the timing of the trip was meant to both mark the occasion and seek the intercession of the holy saint for his help in the war. Next, they visited the starets Makary at his modest shelter located off deep in the woods a few miles from the monastery. Vyrubova sat and listened with great interest as the two men talked.[20] Makary had known Rasputin for many years, since his days as a simple pilgrim. It would be their last meeting. From Verkhoturye, Vyrubova and Dehn returned to Petrograd, and Rasputin left for home.

60. Apotheosis

On the evening of 5 September Rasputin met Alexandra alone at the palace. He presented her with two flowers for the tsar and a note: "There is warmth after the storm, the sun will shine and bring joy to the devout heroes, light and blessing is with them."[1] The following day Alexandra wrote Nicholas to share more of Rasputin's thoughts. "He says from to-day on the news will be better. The Image in the Monastery to wh. I several times went (He knows it, years ago prayed there when He walked all over Russia), says its a very miraculous one & will save Russia.– Do go to it at once, its so close to the house—& the Virgin has such a sweet face."[2] Nicholas replied: "I kiss you tenderely, and A[nyu]* and our Friend as well."[3]

The icon of the Virgin might save Russia, but in the meantime more ministerial changes were necessary. The Rubinshtein affair and the arrest of Manuilov had proved just how dangerous Minister of the Interior Alexander Khvostov and his assistant General Klimovich were for Rasputin. A change was being sought even though the minister had been in office only two months. On the seventh, Alexandra wrote Nicholas with Rasputin's choice, Alexander Protopopov. "I think you could not do better than name him," she bubbled enthusiastically. "He likes our Friend since at least 4 years & that says much for a man. [. . .] do listen to Him who only want yr. good and whom God has given more insight, wisdom & enlightenment than all the military put together. His love for you & Russia is so intense & God has sent him to be yr. help & guide & prays so hard for you."[4]

On the ninth, Nicholas responded to thank her for the "messages from our Friend" and promised to consider the candidacy of Protopopov. "I must think that question over as it takes me quite unexpectedly," he remarked with candor. "Our Friend's ideas about men

---

* Vyrubova.

are sometimes quite queer, as you know—so one must be careful especially in nominations of high people."[5]

Born in 1866 into a noble family in Simbirsk (the birthplace of Lenin and Khionya Guseva), Protopopov, dubbed "Kalinin" by Rasputin, for no apparent reason, was bright and gifted. He learned to speak several languages as a child, studied piano under Jules Massenet, and then served in the imperial guards, before taking over the family's cotton factory. He went into politics after the 1905 Revolution and became a leading figure of the Octobrist Party, serving as the vice president of the Fourth Duma under Rodzianko. He had a distinguished appearance and a polished manner. Pyotr Bazilevsky, the court equerry, remarked that "Protopopov had a way of charming everyone he came in contact with, winning them over to his advantage by way of the sincere and heartfelt manner of his comportment."[6]

But not everything was as it appeared. There was something off about Protopopov. He acted strangely at times, talking to the icon on his desk when others were present, for example. Part of this was supposedly due to syphilitic insanity, brought on by the venereal disease he contracted while in the guards. Part was due to his drug addiction. He began seeing Dr. Badmaev and became addicted to his secret powders. He twitched, sobbed, and heard voices in his head, which he talked back to. At one point he suffered a nervous breakdown and spent six months in Badmaev's sanatorium, housed in a magnificently decorated villa south of the capital. It was said he was also a patient of the noted psychiatrist Vladimir Bekhterev, but even he could do nothing for him.[7] "Sharp-sighted when it came to the details, near-sighted when it came to the big picture," Alexander Blok noted. "Talented but unsettled and lacking restraint."[8] One thing was for certain: he loved the Romanovs, especially the empress, and he believed destiny had summoned him to save Russia.[9]

It was at Badmaev's sanatorium that Protopopov and Rasputin first met, most likely in 1913. Rasputin took to Protopopov from the start.[10] In 1916, when it had been decided to replace Alexander Khvostov, Badmaev organized a number of "try-outs" at his apartment on Liteiny Prospect for the two men to get to know each other better and so Rasputin could be won over to the idea of his candidacy. The man ultimately pushing for Protopopov was most likely Badmaev himself. Badmaev had apparently gained a good deal of control over his patient and possibly wanted to put him in a place of power where he could be of use to the doctor and his various schemes. Once he had convinced Rasputin, Badmaev was certain he would recommend Protopopov to Vyrubova and she, to the empress. For Protopopov's assistant, Badmaev suggested General Pavel Kurlov, his business partner and the former director of the police.[11] All the while, Badmaev had no doubts about the kind of man he was dealing with in Rasputin. "A khlyst, deceiver, and liar," Badmaev called Rasputin, though he was careful not to let him hear.[12]

Protopopov would be their man, according to the plan, put in power by this new troika of Badmaev, Kurlov, and Rasputin. Rasputin felt comfortable with Protopopov. He knew there was no chance of him trying to kill him as had Alexei Khvostov or scheme against him and his allies as had Alexander Khvostov and his assistant General Klimovich. Protopopov's experience in the Duma would mean he could defend Rasputin there as well. As part of the plan to install Protopopov, Badmaev wrote the empress a letter explaining how both Rasputin and Vyrubova, and even their majesties, were in great danger. He told her they were surrounded by "the followers of Azef," a reference to the notorious double agent Yevno Azef, who worked for both the Socialist Revolutionaries and the Okhrana and helped to organize the assassination of Grand Duke Sergei Alexandrovich, the tsar's uncle, in 1905. "The followers of Azef are crafty, cunning, and smart people, but their goals are often very dangerous. It seems we have been reminded of this many times. It is my opinion that the tsars ought to be surrounded by pure toilers."[13] At the same time Rasputin wrote to sell Protopopov to Nicholas. He was a "jealous man" in his love for the motherland and his heart was "simple," Rasputin told the tsar. Protopopov, Rasputin informed Alexandra, was "my surety." He will be "Your sun, and my joy."[14] Poor Protopopov was in over his head. There was little chance he could hold his own in this game. His brother described him as "an infant kidnapped by devils."[15]

On 16 September, Alexander Khvostov was fired and replaced by Protopopov. Rasputin was pleased, but he now had to make certain "Kalinin" knew his place. Alexandra wrote Nicholas on the twenty-second to say Protopopov "needs being kept in hand as our Friend says, so as that pride should not spoil all."[16] When news of the appointment was released, Purishkevich purportedly told his fellow Duma deputies that he had certainly paid Rasputin for the job.[17] French ambassador Paléologue remarked that although the selection of Protopopov was a surprise to everyone in Russia, "It has certainly been known for some time already in Berlin."[18]

Protopopov's appointment has traditionally been seen as the work of Rasputin, but the truth is a good deal more complex. Earlier in the summer of 1916, Foreign Minister Sergei Sazonov had recommended Protopopov to the tsar for a top government post and arranged a meeting between the two on 19 July, at which Nicholas was most impressed with him. Nicholas soon after latched on to the idea of Protopopov as a logical choice since it would smooth relations with the Duma, and this is exactly how news of his appointment was initially greeted by not only liberal, but even radical circles. The socialist-leaning *Day* hailed the selection of Protopopov as "the beginning of a new era of reconciliation between the government and society." A jubilant Alexander Guchkov called it "a colossal victory for the public."[19] The stock market soared on news of Protopopov's appointment. The honeymoon, however, proved to be short-lived.

Rasputin, Praskovya, and their daughter Maria met the empress at Vyrubova's home in Tsarskoe Selo on the evening of 21 September. It was probably at this meeting Rasputin gave Alexandra a list of instructions to pass along to Nicholas, which she did several days later.

> Keep my little note before you—our Friend begged for you to speak of all these things to Protopopov & its very good if you mention our Friend that he should listen to him & trust to his advice;—let him feel you dont shun his name. I very calmly spoke of him—he came to him when he was very ill, some years ago.—Badmaev called him.—Tell him to be warned against Adronnikov coming to him (Prot.) & keep him away. Forgive my bothering you, Deary—but am always affraid as you are so terribly hard worked—that you may forget something—& so [I] act as your living notebook.—Sunny.
>   Speak to Pr. about:
>   1. Sukh., order to find a way to get him out of prison.
>   2. Rubinshtein to send away
>   3. Prefect
>   4. Augment wages of the officials as your kindness to them,
> not fr. the ministers.

5. About food supplies tell him strictly, severely that all must be done to set it to rights—you order it.

6. Tell him to listen to our Friend's councils, it will bring him blessings & help his work & Yours—please say this, let him see yr. trust in him—he knows him several years already.

Keep this paper before you.[20]

The emperor and his minister fell into line.

On 12 October, former Minister of War Vladimir Sukhomlinov was freed from the Peter and Paul Fortress. His release provoked howls in Petrograd, where everyone was convinced he, like his executed protégé Myasoedov, was a traitor. The reasons for his release set off a storm of speculation, much of it focused on Sukhomlinov's gorgeous wife. Yekaterina Butovich, the third Mrs. Sukhomlinova, was a popular music hall singer and a determined social climber, thirty-four years his junior. Yekaterina knew how to get her husband out of prison. Sukhomlinov had been Rasputin's foe, but Yekaterina had a plan to win him over. She paid Rasputin a visit, and from the first time he saw Yekaterina, Rasputin was lost. "Only two women on this earth have ever managed to steal my heart," he supposedly told Manuilov, "Vyrubova and Sukhomlinova." For her part, Sukhomlinova made sure Rasputin could not forget her. During his visits to Krarup's studio, she would telephone repeatedly to ask when he would be free and able to come see her.[21]

Over the course of the summer, Rasputin visited Yekaterina sixty-nine times. Her attentions to Rasputin's needs, as well, perhaps, as a large cash payment, got Yekaterina what she wanted: first an introduction to Vyrubova and then to the empress, before whom she pleaded the innocence of her husband. Rasputin took up the cause as well and had Alexandra ask Nicholas to free the sick and aged general: "Every [person], even the vilest sinner, has moments where the soul rises & is purified through their fearful suffering—then the hand must be reached out to save them before they are lost by bitterness & despair," he told their majesties. Whatever the motives that drove Rasputin to help Sukhomlinov, the result was just, for Sukhomlinov was innocent of the charges against him. Next, Rasputin urged that Sukhomlinov's upcoming trial be dropped as well.[22] Alexandra agreed, and begged Nicholas to dismiss the entire case before the Duma reconvened on 1 November, certain the deputies would use it as just one more occasion to attack Rasputin.

"I feel cruel worrying you, my sweet, patient Angel," she wrote on

31 October, "—but all my trust lies in our Friend, who only thinks of you, Baby* & Russia.—And guided by Him we shall get through this heavy time. It will be hard fighting, but a Man of God is near to guard yr. boat safely through the reefs—& little Sunny is standing as a rock behind you, firm & unwavering with decision, faith & love to fight for her darlings and our country." Nicholas heeded her words. He also augmented the officials' wages, as instructed.

The "prefect" mentioned in Alexandra's letter referred to Prince Alexander Obolensky, the Petrograd governor-general, with whom Rasputin was not pleased and wanted replaced. His main grievance was the growing food crisis in the capital and what Rasputin saw as Obolensky's ineffectiveness in dealing with it. As early as January of that year, Rasputin had been concerned by the growing bread lines, food shortages, and high prices, problems that he quite perceptively realized were not only hard on the urban poor, but could lead to disturbances and undermine the authority of the state.[23] Rasputin's worry for the common folk was real. His daughter Maria recalled accurately:

> The thing that especially aroused his indignation was the delay to transport that was threatening to aggravate the famine already rife in the capital.
>
> "The people must eat," he would exclaim. "You must have your corn back, Little Father. We must transport more corn and less soldiers and guns. God did not make corn to rot in warehouses and barns. You will give your corn, when it arrives, to the hungry."[24]

Rasputin even had a plan for the empress herself to lead an organization that would hand out bread and flour to the poor of the capital. He talked to Alexandra about the idea and she was in favor of it. Rasputin wanted the empress to be one of those actually out in the streets giving out food as a way to show her true concern for the common folk. Nothing, however, came of the idea.[25]

That autumn he bombarded Minister of the Agriculture Count Alexei Bobrinsky with his pleading notes:

> kind dear apologies forgive me much meat is needed, let Piter† eat, listen help rosputin

---

* The Tsarevich Alexei.

† Petrograd. The notes are devoid of proper grammar and spelling, including his own

kind dear apologies for the strange trouble dear, let them eat not starve, they ask to eat rosputin

kind dear apologies allow oats taken, much woe in zalenburg province,* lots of oats, Petrograd cart drivers are worried, that's not good, siberia is full of lard please feed Petrograd and Moscow[26]

And it was not just Bobrinsky who got an ear full from Rasputin about the food crisis. He shared his concerns with many others at the time.[27]

Obolensky sought a meeting with Rasputin. He dispatched his finest automobile to collect Rasputin and ferry him to his office. Practically shaking with nerves, Obolensky greeted Rasputin and for an hour tried to defend himself, insisting he was doing the best he could and promising henceforth to be certain to always seek Rasputin's advice in the fulfillment of his duties. He pulled out a large packet of the many letters and petitions Rasputin had sent over the years and told Rasputin that he had always done his best to honor each one of them. Rasputin asked Obolensky whether he took bribes, to which he said no, but that his assistant had taken a great deal. When Rasputin left, the governor-general broke down in tears from the strain.

It is a remarkable scene. Obolensky was not just an important official, he belonged to one of Russia's oldest aristocratic families, was a court chamberlain and a member of his majesty's entourage, and here he was debasing himself before a Siberian peasant, terrified of losing his position and the favor of the emperor. Few episodes from the life of Rasputin convey so clearly just how powerful he had become. It was his apotheosis. Obolensky's humiliation did not save him. In November he was removed from office and sent to the front as a brigade commander.

Rasputin had specific suggestions for how food could be packaged and sold more quickly, which would mitigate the long lines that had become breeding grounds for angry talk. He passed all these ideas along, but nothing was done.[28] He also proposed that the provision of food be taken away from the ministries of agriculture and transport and given to the ministry of the interior. Protopopov, however, dragged his feet, which angered Rasputin, and then after the change had been made an irate Minister Bobrinsky sabotaged the new procurement system

---

surname. I have tried to capture the feel of Rasputin's Russian, while making concessions to comprehensibility.
* Likely Orenburg province.

by sending circulars to local officials across Russia to ignore all of Protopopov's instructions.[29] The change was no doubt a smart one, but even without Bobrinsky's machinations it most likely would not have worked. By the autumn of 1916, a host of intractable problems were reaching a crescendo. Among them was the collapse of the transportation system: it is quite possible Russia no longer had enough working locomotives and railcars to bring the necessary food to the hungry cities.[30] Regardless, Rasputin's great concern about the food crisis was prescient and had his concerns been heeded in January, matters might have developed differently. In the end, it was bread riots in Petrograd in February that would light the spark of revolution.

When he was not advising on the food crisis, Rasputin was busy suggesting ways to solve problems with the infant Russian air force (he had some ideas on what to do about the troublesome engines), opining on the question of Polish autonomy (he was against the idea, for the tsar must leave his empire whole to his son), offering advice on Russia's treaties with her allies (he was insistent Britain and France make public the secret agreement to give Constantinople to Russia after the war), and proposing ways to include the empire's Methodists in the war effort (put them to work digging trenches and working on the front lines as medics, he suggested).[31] There was nothing too big or too small for Rasputin's attention.

"The damage inflicted by Rasputin was enormous, but he tried to work for the benefit of Russia and the dynasty," Gurko commented, "and not to harm them. An attentive reading of the Empress's letters, which contain a great many of Rasputin's pieces of advice, leads to the conclusion that although most of his advice was simplistic and naive, nonetheless there was nothing remotely harmful to Russia."[32] It is hard not to agree with Gurko's assessment.

61. Stupidity or Treason

"How I wish you cld. have come for 2 days only," Alexandra wrote Nicholas on 12 October, "just to have got our Friend's blessing, it would have given you new strength—I know you a brave & patient [*sic*]—but human—& a touch of His on your chest would have soothed much pain & given you new wisdom & energy from Above—these are no idle words—but my firmest conviction."[1]

Just as Alexandra was extolling the power of Rasputin's very touch, his life was spinning out of control. His daughter Maria recalled:

> Towards the end he drank heavily and that made me pity him. The drunkenness was not reflected in his mental capacities. He spoke even more interestingly. [. . .] Protopopov complained in conversation with me that he was very tired, that he was in pain, and that only God could help him. And that he would go away to a small cloister somewhere, if only he could, but that he wasn't able to out of love for "them"—the sovereign and empress.

Others saw the same thing. His publisher Filippov remarked how when Rasputin would come to see him he now wanted to get drunk as quickly as possible and then demanded Gypsies and entertainment. Georgy Sazonov told the Commission:

> I remember six months before his death he came to see me drunk and, bitterly sobbing, told me that he had spent the entire night carousing with Gypsies and had squandered two thousand, and that he had to be at the tsarina's at 6:00. I took him to my daughter's room, where between his sobs Rasputin said, "I am a devil. I am a demon. I am sinful, where before I was holy. I am not worthy of staying in this pure room." I saw that his sorrow was real.[2]

Sazonov said Rasputin's drinking sprang from a tormented consciousness, an attempt to salve the pain that came from recognizing how far he had fallen. Maria attributed it to a sense of foreboding.

"Towards the end of the year 1916 it seemed as though a cloud was lowering over my father's mind. Was he beginning to be conscious of the hostility surrounding him and the attacks of which he was the target; or had he a secret presentiment of his approaching death?"[3]

Others concur that by the autumn of 1916 Rasputin believed his life was once more in danger. He felt threatened and requested that his security be increased. One day a lady showed up at Gorokhovaya. He sensed trouble and told her to show him what was in her right hand. She was holding a revolver and handed it to Rasputin, saying she had come to kill him but then realized her mistake upon seeing his eyes.[4] Perhaps Rasputin had already accepted he was soon to die. Maria recorded in her diary a year after her father's murder how he had liked to say, "Death's my little friend."[5]

On 25 October (NS), Gérard Encausse (aka Papus) died in Paris. He had supposedly told Nicholas in 1905 that he would use all his power to prevent revolution in Russia, but once he was dead his power would lose all potency. A certain Madame T. told Ambassador Paléologue that she had seen in the hands of Madame Golovina a letter from Papus to Alexandra concerning Rasputin that ended with the words: "From the cabalistic perspective, Rasputin is a vessel similar to Pandora's box, containing in it all vices, all crimes, everything bad that exists in the Russian people. Should that vessel break, we shall witness how this terrifying contents will spread across all Russia." Supposedly the empress showed this letter to Rasputin. "This is exactly what I've been saying," he replied. "When I die, Russia will perish."[6]

A group of Duma representatives summoned Protopopov to a meeting at the apartment of Rodzianko on 19 October. They were outraged by the fact that one of their own had agreed to serve alongside a man like Stürmer and that he had freed Sukhomlinov. They also wanted him to explain his relationship with Rasputin. Protopopov, in their eyes, had betrayed them to side with their enemies. They insisted he resign his post immediately. Protopopov was ambushed. He thought he had been invited for a discussion, not some sort of inquisition. He clarified to them that Sukhomlinov had not been freed, but simply released from prison and was under house arrest. As for Stürmer, Protopopov insisted his love for the tsar was what mattered most to him, and so he felt it his duty to serve, regardless of the others in the government. But he refused to answer any questions about Rasputin, particularly whether he had played any role in his being appointed minister. This, he informed Milyukov, was "a secret." The deputies told Protopopov he had brought shame on the Duma and the Octobrists. As Protopopov was leaving, Milyukov bellowed at him in front of the others, "You are leading Russia to destruction." Shulgin called him "a Judas."[7]

Protopopov described his relations with Rasputin to the Commission in the following terms:

> This is how I related to him: all that loathsomeness, all that damage that he inflicted, I could not attribute to him personally. It was that nasty circle around him, all of them hideous and immoral people seeking their own personal gain, that used him for their dirty affairs. [. . .] I did not do anything of the kind. It was my goal to liquidate the many problems, to do away with the scandals, the drinking, the number of wild parties, and, if you will, to a certain extent I was successful.[8]

The Duma men were also suspicious of Protopopov in light of reports about a trip he had made abroad in June. He had traveled through Europe with a delegation of Duma and State Council members, meeting King George V of Britain and Victor Emanuel, the king of Italy, along the way. On their return through Sweden Protopopov and two others in the delegation—Count Dmitry Olsufev and Alexander Vasilev—met with Fritz Warburg, an advisor to the German embassy and the brother of the powerful Hamburg banker Max Warburg. The nature of the meeting has long been the subject of considerable speculation. It has been suggested that Protopopov sought out Warburg to test the Germans' openness to the idea of a separate peace; others believed that although this had been the purpose of their conversation, Protopopov was not acting on his own initiative but was following the instructions of the Russian ambassador, Anatoly Neklyudov. Both notions, however, are wrong. According to Neklyudov, the idea for the meeting had been Protopopov's, although not to probe the Germans about peace, but to gain a general understanding of the mood in Germany, just as he had done with their colleagues while traveling through France and England. When word of the meeting, not surprisingly in a highly distorted form (Protopopov was reported to have met with the German ambassador, not Warburg, among other things), got out in Russia, a wave of anger welled up against Protopopov. Few could imagine how a man who had made a career in the Duma supporting the war had become a traitor-spy in league with the dark forces. The story ran in the press causing considerable anger, and upon returning home Protopopov only made matters worse by giving conflicting accounts of what had really happened in Sweden.[9]

Coded telegrams in the German archives show that Russia's enemy had been engaged in a clever campaign of disinformation. A pleased official in Stockholm wrote to the foreign ministry in Berlin that as a result of the meeting Protopopov and Olsufev "have been incorrectly accused of having taken part in peace talks" and noted how the story had been picked up in the Russian press. The Germans had skillfully planted bits of information about how Stürmer was willing to let Poland go to the Germans and that he had been complaining about how England was trying to ruin Russia. It was a coup for German propaganda.[10]

The French and British representatives in Petrograd took such stories about the possibility of a separate peace with deadly seriousness. "The danger is real," a report from the French embassy commented at the time, "and it is great." Their friends at the Russian court and in the ministry of foreign affairs were telling the French: "Be prepared, you might find yourselves presented with a surprise one of these days. Have you taken precautions? Do you have everything sorted out?"[11]

At the end of October Nicholas and Alexei visited the Dowager Empress in Kiev. For two days Nicholas's mother, together with Grand Dukes Paul and Alexander Mikhailovich (Sandro), and Nicholas's sister Olga, pleaded with him one last time to get rid of Rasputin and Stürmer. He listened, impassively, saying nothing, and then returned to Stavka.[12] Several days later Nikolasha arrived in Kiev. When Alexandra found out she was furious. She was convinced he and her mother-in-law were conspiring against them. She called them "the revolutionary party" and wrote Nicholas to say they were pushing the country into the abyss. Be careful, she instructed, "remember Gr. saved you once from him & his evel people."[13] Nicholas's strange passivity fed talk among the elite that Alexandra and Rasputin were administering Dr. Badmaev's powders to zombify the emperor, effectively making him unfit to rule and allowing them to seize the reins of power. The notion was even addressed at a meeting of the Congress of the All-Russian Nobility in November. The idea that Nicholas was on drugs is not as outlandish as it seems; he did, in fact, use cocaine during the war, although this was not considered dangerous and was not terribly uncommon at the time. Alexandra was prescribed barbiturates, opium, and cocaine by her doctor as well.[14] The degree to which drug use (or possibly even abuse) might have influenced the royal couple's thinking and behavior remains an unanswered question.

The Duma reconvened on 1 November. Milyukov took the rostrum and delivered a thundering, accusatory speech that he would later call "the opening signal of the revolution." He attacked the policies of Stürmer and Protopopov and called out Pitirim and Manuilov and Rasputin by name. This was a dangerous tactic, for the Duma was not allowed to make any pronouncements that could be seen as questioning the honor of the royal family, but Milyukov found a way to get around this. He held up a copy of the *Neue Freie Presse* and claimed that the words he had spoken did not belong to him, but the Austrian newspaper. He was walking a thin line. Referring to the appointment of Stürmer, he continued to read from the newspaper: "That is the victory of the Court party that has gathered around the young tsaritsa." As he enumerated the mistakes of the government, he kept repeating the same question: "Is this stupidity or treason?" Milyukov concluded by answering his own question: "No, gentlemen, as you wish, but there has been too much stupidity. It is too hard to describe everything as just stupidity." With that the hall erupted in applause, while one of the right-wing deputies yelled out: "Slander, Slander!"[15] He was correct, but he was ignored.

Milyukov had no proof of any treason, and he knew it. He lied intentionally. His chief motive was not to bring to light the sins of the government, but to poison the waters and so make any further cooperation between the Duma and the crown impossible.[16] He wanted to provoke a reaction, and he did. Although his words were censored in the official transcript, copies of the speech spread across the country. Purishkevich, for one, printed reams of hectographic copies and used his hospital train to distribute them to officers and soldiers along the front. Although Milyukov knew he had been lying, those reading his words did not, and they took them for the truth.[17] In the first days after the speech pirated copies were selling for twenty-five rubles; individuals with copies even charged ten rubles to read it to those without one. Russians praised Milyukov. Princess Maria Tenisheva thanked him for finally speaking "the truth we have long wished for" and called his speech "a heroic act."[18] It was only now, after his former allies in the Duma had turned against him, that the rumors of Protopopov's supposed syphilitic insanity began to appear, clearly part of the larger campaign to destroy him at any cost.[19]

Amazingly, Milyukov was not punished for accusing the government and the empress herself of treason. No one came to their defense. There was, however, a rumor that Rasputin was organizing a plot to kill Milyukov, and another that the editor of the Russian Banner had hired a hit man to do him in. But this was nothing but talk.[20]

The day of Milyukov's speech, Grand Duke Nikolai Mikhailovich met Nicholas and handed him a letter. The tsar was in thrall to the dark forces, the grand duke warned, and they were feeding lies to Alexandra that he took from her lips as the truth. The country was becoming ungovernable. "You find yourself on the eve of an era of new disturbances, and I will say even more: on the eve of an era of murder." The tsar, he said, must free himself from these forces before it was too late.[21] Nicholas showed the letter to Alexandra. She wrote back a biting reply in which she denounced the grand duke as "the incarnation of all that's evil" and admonished her husband for not defending her at their meeting. "As your chosen wife—they dare not Sweety mine, you must back me up, for your and baby's sake. Had we not got Him—all wld. long have been finished." Alexandra gave Rasputin the grand duke's letter to read. "God's goodness never appeared in a single line of his letter, only evil," he said. "As a brother of Milyukov, he is like all the brothers of evil. [. . .] He's a ruined man." Rasputin told Alexandra he had had a dream in which the Lord communicated to him that all this conflict was "worthless."[22]

It seems one family member was already contemplating moving beyond mere talk. On the afternoon of Saturday, 5 November 1916, Baron Colonel Nikolai Vrangel visited Grand Duke Mikhail Alexandrovich, the tsar's younger brother, at Gatchina to tell him the latest news from the capital. Talk turned to the recent scandals surrounding Rasputin and the government, and the grand duke said that Rasputin had to be "eliminated." He proposed to Vrangel that they hop into his automobile that very instant and go kill Rasputin. Vrangel remarked in his diary that Mikhail had uttered the words in jest, but behind the humor lurked a real desire to see it done.[23] Father Shavelsky stated in his memoirs that, on 9 November at Stavka, former Minister of Education Pyotr Kaufman actually asked the emperor whether he would give him permission to kill Rasputin. The tsar supposedly cried, hugged, and kissed Kaufman, without ever answering his question.[24]

The same day that Baron Vrangel visited Gatchina, the ceremonial cornerstone was being laid in Tsarskoe Selo for a new church being built by Vyrubova as a sign of gratitude for God's mercy in saving her life in the previous year's train crash. Among those present were Rasputin, Bishop Isidor, Melkhisedek, Father Alexander Vasilev, and Colonel Dmitry Loman. The ceremony was followed by a small reception at Vyrubova's infirmary. Rasputin, according to Alexandra, "was very gay after dinner in the ve[stry]—but not tipsy." Someone took a photograph of the party, including Rasputin along with a few of the nurses, seated at the table covered with food and wine. If looked at in a certain way it seemed as if some sort of wild party were under way. Later, someone doctored the photograph to make it appear as if a monk was embracing one of the nurses in a provocative manner. Purishkevich got hold of the photograph, identified all the participants in pen, and included an insulting inscription along the border. He had 9,000 copies of his handiwork printed and passed out at the Duma and to the editors of the newspapers.[25] The story of the photograph took on a life of its own. Soon it was being said the photograph depicted one of Rasputin's orgies that included Vyrubova, Princess Shakhovskaya, and Countess Ignatieva.[26]

Four days after the ceremony Nicholas fired Stürmer as prime minister over the objections of Alexandra. He was replaced by Alexander Trepov, the minister of transportation and a man with a long if not terribly distinguished record of service, a conservative and devoted monarchist, albeit one who realized the need for reforms. "Our Friend is very grieved at his nomination," Alexandra informed Nicholas, "as He knows he is very against him. . . . & he is sad you did not ask his advice." Nicholas had apparently given Trepov his blessing to take the fight to the dark forces and the new prime minister made no secret of his desire to have Protopopov relieved as minister of the interior. It was clear his ultimate target was Rasputin. Alexandra raced to Stavka to talk Nicholas out of this move, and Rasputin sent the emperor four telegrams urging him to reconsider.[27] In a number of remarkable letters, Alexandra warned Nicholas that they could not survive without Rasputin:

> Once more, remember that for your reign, Baby & us you need the strenght [sic] prayers & advice of our Friend. Remember, how last

year all were against us & for N. & our Friend gave you the help &
strength you took over all & saved Russia. [. . .] Ah, Lovy, I pray so
hard to God to make you feel & realize, that He is our caring, were
He not here, I dont know what might not have happened. He saves
us by His prayers & wise counsils [sic] & is our rock of faith &
help.[28]

She told him he had to have the "deepest faith in the prayers & help of
Our Friend, for it was his power that has kept you where you are."[29]

Nicholas went back on his word; Protopopov remained. But Trepov
was not ready to admit defeat. He instructed his brother-in-law General
Alexander Mosolov to offer Rasputin 200,000 rubles, a house in the
capital, a monthly allowance, and reliable bodyguards if he would give
up his meddling in government affairs. Rasputin was beside himself
with anger. "You think that Mama and Papa will allow that? I don't need
money, any old merchant will give me what I need to hand out to the
poor and needy. And I don't need some idiotic guards. Ah, so he thinks
he can run me off!"[30]

62. "Vanya has arrived."

Not to be outdone by Milyukov, Vladimir Purishkevich got up before the Duma on 19 November 1916 to deliver what has been called the angriest anti-Rasputin speech ever.

> I permit myself to say here, from this tribune of the State Duma, that all evil proceeds from those dark forces, from those influences [. . .] which are headed by Grishka Rasputin. [. . .] I turn to the Council of Ministers. If for ministers duty is above career [. . .] if you are in fact a united cabinet, then go to the Tsar and say that this can no longer be. This is not a boycott of the state, gentlemen, this is your duty before the Sovereign. [. . .] Go, go to the Tsar's Stavka, throw yourselves at the Sovereign's feet, and ask Him to permit you to open His eyes to this horrific reality, ask him to rid Russia of Rasputin and the Rasputinists, big and small, no matter how mighty they are. [. . .] Believe me, gentlemen, I know that you think as I do, I feel that all of Russia is repeating my very words before you, everyone without regard to party [. . .] May Grishka Rasputin no longer be the leader of life in Russia.[1]

With that the hall exploded with cheers and cries of "Bravo." Among those in the gallery was Prince Felix Yusupov. One eyewitness claimed he turned pale and began to tremble during the speech, as if an "uncontrollable emotion" had taken over him.[2]

It was no surprise that such a speech came from Purishkevich. He had long had a reputation for outlandishness. The descendant of a wealthy landowning family from Bessarabia, he began his public life as a member of a special commission in the ministry of the interior under Vyacheslav von Plehve in the first years of the century. He went on to serve in the Duma, though chiefly so that he could insult the institution and disrupt its proceedings. An arch reactionary, Purishkevich was against the idea of a Russian parliament on principle. He attacked its members, even its president. One of his preferred tactics was to make faces at his opponents. Shulgin commented how he had a tendency to twitch all the time from nerves; the shaking made the bracelets on his wrists rattle.[3] Once he showed up with a carnation in his fly. So bad were his antics that on several occasions he was expelled from the Duma. Maklakov called him a "troublemaker." After the war broke out, he devoted himself to obtaining medical supplies for the Russian army on the Romanian and Southern fronts, chiefly by working through the Red Cross.[4] In June 1914, a reporter asked Rasputin for his opinion of Purishkevich. "Purishkevich is sincere," he replied, "he works truthfully, but there's one thing about him that causes harm: his tongue. Thus the saying—'My tongue is my evil.'"[5] The editor of his memoirs was less gracious in his assessment, describing Purishkevich as "a buffoon whose career was both suspect and comically sordid."[6]

He was a founder of the Union of the Russian People and another right-wing, anti-Semitic organization, the Union of the Archangel Michael. In June 1914, the *Petersburg Courier* ran a story according to which Purishkevich, as the union's chairman, had decided to elect Rasputin an honorary lifetime member after he had told Purishkevich he was going to donate several thousand rubles to help fund its activities. The story was a provocation, eliciting an angry response from Purishkevich who called it "slander." Rasputin told the newspaper that Purishkevich hated him since he had come to the defense of Jews from time to time, such as once seeking permission for Jews to participate in the great market at Nizhny Novgorod. "He cannot forgive me for helping many poor Jews in Siberia," Rasputin said, "and he doesn't bother to hide this."[7]

Rasputin learned of Purishkevich's speech that very day. Judging by what he wrote the emperor, he was not terribly worried by it: "Purishkevich fought daringly but it didn't hurt. My peace remained undisturbed. God will give you strength. Your victory and your ship. Nobody has the power to get on it."[8] But Rasputin did not reveal everything he was thinking, and he was clearly trying to put on a brave face for the tsar. At the same time he wrote Palace Commandant Voeikov of the need for allies:

> Listen, my dear, even porridge is not tasty until you get used to it, not only Purishkevich with his foul mouth. Now millions of such wasps have hatched. So believe me, when it comes to matters of the spirit, we should act as consolidated friends. Though the circle is small still it contains like-minded people, and while they are

numerous their forces are scattered. They are overcome with spite
while we have the spirit of truth. Look at Annushka's face: it should
be the best appeasement for you. Grigory Novy.[9]

The telephone at the Purishkevich home rang throughout the twentieth as friends and acquaintances called to congratulate him. One of
those was Prince Yusupov. He asked if they might meet, as there were a
few items about Rasputin and his role at court he wanted to speak about
in person, it being "awkward" to do so over the telephone. Yusupov
came to see Purishkevich at 9 a.m. the next day, and they talked for over
two hours. He told Purishkevich that words alone could not solve the
problem of Rasputin, that action was needed. "But what can be done?"
asked Purishkevich. Yusupov fixed him with a stare: "Get rid of him."
When Purishkevich replied he doubted such men could be found for
this job, Yusupov told him resolutely, "Yes, I am sure of it! And one of
them stands before you."[10]

The idea to kill Rasputin began with Yusupov.[11] It began to crystal-
lize in his mind sometime around the end of October. According to his
memoirs (an admittedly unreliable document, as will be discussed
below), Yusupov first brought up the necessity of murdering Rasputin
with his wife, Irina, and "she agreed with me completely." He next spoke
about his plans to various "influential people," but none of them, he
found, had the courage to act. Among these was Rodzianko, the Duma
President, married to a relation of Yusupov's mother and close to the
family. Rodzianko told him: "The only solution is to kill the scoundrel,
but there's not a man in Russia who has the guts to do it. If I weren't so
old, I'd do it myself." This, according to Yusupov, was all he needed to
convince him he would "deliberately prepare to murder a man in cold
blood."[12]

On 3 November, Vasily Maklakov delivered a powerful speech in the
Duma attacking the government—"Either us, or them: a life together is
not possible," was its memorable refrain—that apparently set the plot
in motion.[13] Soon after, Yusupov paid Maklakov a visit. Maklakov was
appalled by the purpose of Yusupov's call. "Do you think I keep office
for assassins?" he asked. Maklakov then told Yusupov that Rasputin was
useful: it was his influence that was undermining the regime and would
lead to its downfall and the birth of a democratic Russia. What is more,
were Rasputin to be killed, Alexandra would just find another figure to
take his place. Yusupov rejected this idea. He told Maklakov this showed

he had no idea of Rasputin's "supernatural forces." He continued: "But I'm involved in the occult, so I know the truth. I assure you that Rasputin has a power you find only once in a hundred years. The Empress would land in an asylum within two weeks if Rasputin were killed today. Her spiritual equilibrium depends entirely on Rasputin; she would fall apart as soon as he toppled. And if the Emperor were freed of the influence of Rasputin and his wife, everything would change; he would be a good constitutional monarch." Murder, Yusupov, insisted, was the only answer.

The problem, Yusupov confessed, was that given his status he could not do it himself, for this would be tantamount to a revolutionary act. No, he was thinking of hiring someone to do the job for him. Maklakov cautioned against this, saying that anyone willing to agree to murder Rasputin for money would just as likely sell Yusupov out for even more. No, this was too risky. With that, the meeting ended.[14]

Yusupov began to recruit others. He first spoke to Lieutenant Sergei Sukhotin, a strongly built young officer in the Life Guards Infantry Regiment. The two men were the same age—twenty-nine—and it is possible they had met and grown close while Sukhotin was recovering from battle wounds on a hospital train at Tsarskoe Selo run by the Yusupovs. Sukhotin, as Yusupov knew, shared his views on Rasputin, and immediately signed up. His dear friend Grand Duke Dmitry Pavlovich was then away at Stavka, and so Yusupov had to wait to bring up the matter with him, which he did sometime in the middle of November. Dmitry told Yusupov that he too had been thinking about killing Rasputin for months, and so joined in the plot.[15]

A fourth figure in the conspiracy was Yusupov's mother, Zinaida, then away in the Crimea. As they did not trust the postal system, Sukhotin's brother was used as a courier for their letters. To be doubly safe, they devised a series of code names for their correspondence: the emperor was "Uncle;" the empress was "Aunt" or "Valide;" Rodzianko, "Medvedev;" Protopopov, "l'intérieur;" and Rasputin was alternately referred to as "Pontin," "the book," and "the manager." It is clear from Zinaida's letters that she not only supported the plot, but was strongly encouraging it. She wrote to Felix on 18 November: "Tell Uncle Misha [Rodzianko] that *nothing can be done* unless the book [Rasputin] be destroyed and Valide tamed. [. . .] This is imperative." On 3 December she wrote Felix again to say that killing Rasputin was both "*imperative, and most urgent.*"[16]

On 20 November, an excited Yusupov wrote to Irina in the Crimea:

I'm terribly busy working out the plan to destroy R[asputin]. It's now simply imperative, or else all is lost. [. . .] You must take part in it. Dmitry Pavlovich knows about everything and is helping. It'll all take place in the middle of December. [. . .] How I wish to see you as soon as possible, but it'd be better if you did not come any earlier, since the rooms will only be ready on the fifteenth of December, and not even all of them, and the upstairs is still not done, and you'd have nowhere to stay. Not a word to anyone about what I've written you, that is about our plans. [. . .] Tell my mother to read my letter.[17]

A shocked Irina replied: "Many thanks for your mad letter. I could not understand half of it, but I can see that you are preparing for some wild action. Please, be careful, and don't mix yourself up in some bad business." At first Irina did not even understand what Felix had written to her, but then she writes: "I have just understood what these words mean, and who the people are, this very minute while I was writing. In a word, be careful!"[18]

At a meeting with Purishkevich on the twenty-first, Yusupov recruited the fifth member of the plot. After hearing his speech, Yusupov felt certain Purishkevich would join them, and he wanted to include a politician among their members. He wrote in his memoirs that he felt it "important that members of all classes should participate in this momentous event." Dmitry was a member of the ruling family; he and his mother were nobles; Sukhotin, an officer, and so Purishkevich as a politician, Yusupov reasoned, completed the picture. Amazingly, neither the vast peasant class—the largest social group in Russia—nor the smaller, but growing middle and working classes even registered in Yusupov's mind as part of the equation.[19]

Yusupov invited Purishkevich to come to his palace on the Moika that night at eight o'clock. There he met Lieutenant Sukhotin and Dmitry, and they began discussing how to murder Rasputin. They agreed poison made the best choice, for gunshots would likely be heard and raise suspicion. Purishkevich also suggested they add Dr. Stanisław Lazovert, a Polish physician who had served under Purishkevich for two years in his military unit at the front. His medical knowledge might come in handy with administering any poison, and he was brave—wounded three times and the recipient of a number of decorations.[20]

They settled on the middle of December for the crime. Before the meeting ended, all of the men agreed on one crucial element: they would never tell anyone about their participation in Rasputin's murder. This solemn pledge would hold for no more than a few days.[21]

Rasputin's killers all shared the belief that they were preparing for an act of noble patriotism, but other motives were in play as well. Purishkevich was driven by his own ambition and vanity and the wish to prove himself a man of action. Yusupov's motives were more complicated than he had explained them to Maklakov. The desire to please his domineering mother was certainly a factor, as was his search for some sort of purpose in his aimless life. Plotting Rasputin's murder gave him a goal and an outlet for his energies beyond redecorating the family home on the Moika, his other primary preoccupation that autumn. Dmitry's participation must also be explained in part by his desire to please Ella. She was like a second mother to him, and it was only after a lengthy conversation with her that Dmitry agreed that murder was the right course of action.[22] Vainglory was present in Purishkevich's and Yusupov's thinking. They would become men of History for their part in saving Russia. What none of the killers seemed to realize was how their understanding of Rasputin and his role in Russia mirrored that of Alexandra, for they saw him just as she did, only in reverse: all of them believed Rasputin held the fate of Russia in his hands, whether to preserve or destroy it. Yusupov and his co-conspirators were as simplistic as the empress in their understanding of what it would take to save Russia.

After the meeting on the twenty-first Yusupov went back to Maklakov to see whether he would change his mind. Maklakov was more open to discussing the killing, but he told Yusupov he would be away in Moscow in December and so could not take part. Maklakov suggested they kill Rasputin in a staged automobile accident, but Yusupov told him they had settled on poison. As for the body, they wanted it to be found or else they feared Alexandra would never accept that he had been killed. There were a few more meetings between the two men to discuss details. At their last meeting Maklakov gave Yusupov a two-pound "rubber-coated dumbbell," saying it might come in handy, and, so Yusupov claimed, a box of potassium cyanide crystals, something Maklakov later denied.[23]

The five conspirators gathered on the evening of the twenty-fourth in Purishkevich's train at the Warsaw Station. At that meeting, Yusupov showed them the potassium cyanide he had been given by Maklakov. They decided they would kill Rasputin by feeding him poison-laced sweet cakes and wine. Once he was dead, Sukhotin, disguised as Rasputin, would drive off with Dmitry and Lazovert, as the chauffeur, to the Warsaw Station and Purishkevich's wife would burn Rasputin's clothes in the rail car's stove. The three men would leave the car there and go by taxi to Dmitry's palace on Nevsky Prospect, and then return to Yusupov's in Dmitry's car. They would take Rasputin's body, wrapped up like "a mummy," to a deserted spot on the river, weigh it down with chains and weights, and toss it into a hole in the ice. Purishkevich promised to get the chains and weights at the Alexandrov Market. Having all agreed to the plan, the meeting broke up around midnight. On the morning of the twenty-ninth, Purishkevich made his purchases at the market and then in the afternoon all of the men, in two separate cars, spent several hours driving along the river looking for places to dispose of the body. They found only two useful holes in the ice—the better of the two was outside the city limits on the Malaya Nevka River by the Large Petrovsky Bridge. The men gathered on the night of the thirtieth for one final planning session. The date was set for 16 December.[24]

Purishkevich ran into Vasily Shulgin about this time at the Duma. "Listen, Shulgin," he told him, "Remember the sixteenth of December." Shulgin gave him a puzzled look. "I'll tell you. You can be trusted. We're going to murder him on the sixteenth." Shulgin told Purishkevich he found the idea "repulsive" and tried to explain to him that the plan was pointless and would change nothing. Purishkevich would hear none of it. His nerves twitching, he told Shulgin that he knew the stories about Rasputin and the empress were lies, but that was immaterial at this point. "We cannot sit by, no matter what. We'll follow through to the end. It can't get worse. I'm going to kill him like a dog."[25] On 23 November he visited the home of the historian Sergei Platonov and let him and his wife know in veiled terms of what was coming.[26] Soon after, a female journalist by the name of M. I. Beker came by the office of Maklakov. She told him that Purishkevich, after arguing with a group of journalists in the Duma, announced that on 17 December he and Prince Yusupov and Grand Duke Dmitry Pavlovich were going to kill Rasputin. They thought this was a joke, and Maklakov convinced her it was. But then he called in Yusupov and warned him of Purishkevich's talking. Yusupov was aghast and complained his co-plotters had been leaving everything to him.[27] In early December Purishkevich arranged a meeting with

Samuel Hoare, head of the British Secret Intelligence Mission in Petrograd. At Hoare's office, Purishkevich matter-of-factly told him that "he and his friends had determined 'to liquidate the affair of Rasputin'" and gave him the details of their plot. Hoare put little stock in it, however. He had heard a good deal of talk about killing Rasputin, and Purishkevich's strangely casual manner made him dismiss it as more of the same.[28] Purishkevich never could keep his mouth shut. By now there was little chance they would not be identified as Rasputin's killers. Purishkevich would not be able to hold his tongue on the night of the murder either, and thus sealed their fate.

A crucial element of the plot was Irina. Rasputin had long wanted to meet Yusupov's lovely wife, and she would be the one to lure him to Yusupov's house. On the twenty-fifth, Felix, nervous and tired yet unable to sleep, wrote to her: "My head is breaking into pieces from all my thoughts, plans, etc." He told her that for the plot to work, she absolutely had to be in Petrograd in the middle of December. "The plan I'm writing you about has been worked out in detail, ¾ of it is done, all that remains is the final chord, and for that we await your arrival. This is the only and most reliable way of saving the situation, which is practically hopeless. Of course, not a word to anyone. Malanya is also involved. You'll serve as the bait. Understand? So the sooner you come the better."[29]

"Malanya" was most likely Marianna Derfelden (née Pistolkors), Grand Duke Dmitry's stepsister, and possible lover, and he no doubt mentioned her to help persuade Irina to join in. But Irina did not approve of her husband's plan. She refused to come and tried to talk him out of it and to join her in the Crimea. "I can't live without you," she wrote on 3 December, "come to me."[30] But his mind had been made up. He remained in the capital.

Felix now had to make contact with the target. He had not seen Rasputin since January 1915, and so he turned to Munya Golovina for help. Did he tell Munya the truth behind his reason for asking her to help him? It is an intriguing question. It seems unlikely he was honest with her, for had she known, she would not have been willing to do as he asked. She and her mother had been acolytes for years. They believed in Rasputin. There is no reason to think she ever would have sold him out. And so Yusupov must have lied to her. He claimed to be ill, suffering from an unexplained fatigue and a pain in his chest, and in need of Rasputin's assistance.[31] According to Munya, Felix asked her to set up a meeting, which took place on 17 November at her family's apartment on the Winter Canal. After this meeting, Munya encouraged a second, and she then later accompanied Felix to Rasputin's home.[32] They were extremely careful and their visits escaped the notice of the agents watching his address.[33] Rasputin promised to cure him, and so Felix began visiting Rasputin at his apartment.

It was here, in Rasputin's small study on Gorokhovaya, that their first session was conducted. Rasputin had him lie down on the sofa and then began to run his hands in a series of "mesmeric passes" over Felix's chest, neck, and head as he murmured a prayer. Felix later wrote that he sensed Rasputin's "tremendous hypnotic power."

> I felt as if some active energy were pouring heat, like a warm current, into my whole being. I fell into a torpor, and my body grew numb; I tried to speak, but my tongue no longer obeyed me and I gradually slipped into a drowsy state, as though a powerful narcotic had been administered to me. All I could see was Rasputin's glittering eyes: two phosphorescent beams of light melting into a great luminous ring which at times drew nearer and then moved farther away. [. . .]
>
> My mind alone was free, and I fully realized that I was gradually falling into the power of this evil man. Then I felt stirring in me the will to fight his hypnosis. Little by little the desire to resist grew stronger and stronger, forming a protective armor around me. I had the feeling that a merciless struggle was being fought out between Rasputin and me, between his personality and mine. I knew that I was preventing him from getting complete mastery over me [. . .].[34]

Felix began spending a good deal of time with Munya and Rasputin, and he wrote Irina that "they have fallen very much in love with me." Munya referred to Felix as "my little friend," and so Rasputin started to call him "the little one." Yusupov charmed the peasant who loved to belittle the aristocracy. Rasputin began inviting him out to see Gypsies perform at night.[35] Yusupov said he would like to have Rasputin over to his home to meet his wife. They agreed on the night of 16 December. On the morning of the thirteenth, Yusupov telephoned Purishkevich and uttered the code: "Vanya has arrived."[36] The operation was a go.

63. "My hour will soon strike."

The mood in Russia in December 1916 was gloomy. Despair hung in the unusually cold air. In the cities, critical food shortages loomed, labor unrest grew, yet whereas in years past the police had been willing to engage in bloody struggles against the workers, the situation had changed. Instead of firing on them, soldiers now began to join the strikers in the streets and fall in behind the banners crying "Down with the War" and add their voices to the *Marseillaise*.[1] On a dark afternoon in that last winter of the Romanov dynasty a group of boys chased the automobile of the tsar's sister Xenia through the streets of Petrograd, pelting it with snowballs and yelling "Down with the dirty bourgeoisie!"[2] When Prince Andrei Lobanov-Rostovsky arrived in Petrograd at the end of 1916, the city struck him as a "lunatic asylum," filled with a "poisonous" atmosphere and "profound despondency and fear."[3] Ambassador Neklyudov in Stockholm received a letter from a friend back home telling him, "We are not living now, we are on fire. Sugar and sensational news—panem et circenses—that is the cry that greets you on all sides."[4]

A report from the Petrograd Okhrana to the department of police marked "Top Secret" painted a frightening picture of Russia on the brink of catastrophe. The dire shortage of food and daily necessities combined with inflation of 300 percent made a dangerous rebellion on the part of the lower classes imminent. Talk throughout the city that "Russia is on the verge of a revolution" could no longer be discounted as the product of German agents but was becoming a reality. The country stood on the brink of a "hungry revolt" after which would follow "the most savage excesses."[5]

Respect for the crown had largely vanished. Another friend of Neklyudov's travelling third class by train from his estate in the provinces to Petrograd recounted the conversation he overheard by the millers, well-to-do peasants, and rural traders riding with him. He was struck by how freely they talked about the court, joking openly about Alexandra and Rasputin and exchanging "some truly filthy talk and horse-laughs without end."[6]

Ella came to Tsarskoe Selo to make one last attempt to convince her sister to send Rasputin away. She felt she had to open Alexandra's eyes to the danger of the situation and the need for quick, decisive action. But Alexandra received her coldly and would not hear a word of it. Upon parting, Ella said to her, "Remember the fate of Louis XVI and Marie Antoinette." The following day Alexandra sent Ella a note instructing her to return to Moscow. Ella tried to speak to Nicholas but he also refused to see her. Before she left Ella saw Yusupov. "She drove me away like a dog!" she told him through her tears. "Poor Nicky, poor Russia!" She never saw her sister again.[7]

On 2 December, the day after Ella departed, Nicholas, Alexandra, and their daughter Olga spent the evening at Vyrubova's with Rasputin. Vyrubova recalled he acted strangely that evening. When the emperor stood to leave, he asked that Rasputin bless them all as usual. But this time Rasputin replied: "Today you bless me." And the emperor did.[8] It was the last time the two men saw each other.

That same day at the XIIth Congress of the Union of United Nobility a resolution was passed on the danger of the "dark forces" that had taken control of the highest levels of the state and the church and called for the necessity of removing these forces once and for all. Russia, the resolution noted, was passing through "a threatening historic hour." It called for a strong, united government that enjoyed the confidence of the people and was willing to work together with all legislative bodies and at the same time recognize its responsibility to the emperor.[9] The resolution was highly significant in that it was issued by one of the main pillars of the Romanov regime. Criticism from the Duma or the press was not surprising, but that the nobility, one of the most traditional, loyal institutions of the state, was now agitating against the dark forces showed the extent to which the throne had lost all support. It was difficult to imagine how much longer the monarchy could survive.

Lev Tikhomirov accurately recorded in his diary the significance of the moment.

This resolution of the noble congress will make a much bigger impression than the comparable pronouncements of the St. Duma and St. Council. It's terrifying to think that all these dark clouds are rising over the Monarchy thanks simply to one insignificant and vile individual. For what, in fact, are these "dark forces"? At base, just Grigory Rasputin. All those stuck to him are nothing and not important. And so just because of one insignificant and vile individual the very foundations of the Monarchy are crumbling. There's never been anything like it in History. They are ready to sacrifice all the Stürmers, Kurlovs, whomever, but Grigory, the one responsible for all this ruin, he remains unshakeable. There's something fatal and mystical about this.

An even more pessimistic Tikhomirov noted a few days later on 9 December:

Yes, a revolution is developing and approaching. Now the top classes and ranks will get it started, then the workers and peasants will follow in their own way. Who will survive, only God knows. But one can imagine that the one responsible, that "dark force" represented by Grishka Rasputin, will manage to escape abroad at the critical moment.[10]

Around this time Alexandra received a letter begging her to rid the court of the dark forces. It was from Princess Sofia Vasilchikova, a maid-of-honor at court and the wife of Prince Boris Vasilchikov, a member of the Imperial Council and former minister of agriculture. "There is much You do not know, that does not reach You," Vasilchikova wrote, "but I move among various circles and I see how great is the danger, and I beg you to save Yourself and Your Family." In the letter, she told how she had heard talk of members of society wanting the empress dead. Alexandra was outraged and dug in her heels. She told Chebotaryova at the Tsarskoe Selo hospital about the letter and that the emperor would "defend Me." She showed the letter to Vyrubova, pointing out that Vasilchikova did not even have the decency to write on proper paper, but had used two small sheets torn from her notebook. This lack of etiquette seemed to upset her almost as much as the words themselves.[11] Vasilchikova was forced to leave the capital for her estate in Novgorod. The scandal was covered in several newspapers, all of which made certain to highlight the fact that before she left the princess received a great many visitors, including several members of the Imperial Council, and a huge number of letters and telegrams of support.[12]

Alexandra remained blind to the reality of the situation up until the end. On 4 December, Nicholas and Alexei returned to Stavka. "Goodbye, sweet Lovy!" she wrote:

It's great pain to let you go—worse than ever after the hard times we have been living and fighting through. But God who is all love and mercy has let the things take a change for the better, just a little more patience and deepest faith in the prayers and help of our Friend—then all will go well.

I'm fully convinced that great and beautiful times are coming for you and Russia. [...] Show to all, that you are the master and your will shall be obeyed—the time of great indulgence and gentleness is over—now comes your reign of will and power, and they shall be made to bow down before you and listen to your orders and all forgiveness.

Why do people hate me? Because they know I have a strong will and when am convinced of a thing being right (when besides blessed by Grigory), do not change my mind and that they can't bear. [...]

Remember Mr Philippe's words when he gave me the image with the bell. As you were so kind, trusting and gentle, I was to be your bell, those that came with wrong intentions would not be able to approach me and I would warn you. Those who are afraid of me don't look me in the eyes or are up to some wrong, never like me.

[...]

Sleep well, heart and soul with you, my prayers around you— God and the holy Virgin will never forsake you.

Ever your very very Own

Alexandra seemed to cling more tightly to Rasputin and his every word. She wrote Nicholas on the fifth:

To follow our Friend's councils, lovy—I assure is right—He prays so hard day & night for you—& He has kept you where you are— only be as convinced as I am & as I proved it to Ella & shall forever—then all will go well. In "les Amis de Dieux" one of the old men of God said, that a country, where a man of God helps the Sovereign, will never be lost & its true—only one must listen trust & ask advice—not think He does not know. God opens everything to Him, that is why people, who do not grasp His soul, so immensely admire His wonderful brain—ready to understand anything; & when He blesses an undertaking—it succeeds & if He advises people—one can be quiet that they are good—if they later on change that is already not His fault—but He will be less mistaken in people than we are—experience in life blessed by God.

She was becoming increasingly irritated by Nicholas's weakness and sent him hectoring letters demanding that he "bang on the table" and act like a tsar, for "Russia loves to feel the whip." She passed on Rasputin's advice that he be strong and stand up to the ministers, especially Prime Minister Trepov: "He <u>entreats</u> you to be <u>firm</u>, to be the Master & not always to give in to Tr.—you know much better than that man (still let him lead you)—& why not our Friend who leads through God?" She ordered her husband to be "a man" and confessed that "its harder keeping you firm than [enduring] the hatred of others wh. leaves me cold." In exasperation she cried, "How I wish I could pour my will into your veins!"[13] But she could not. The monarchy, as Alexandra saw it, was threatened chiefly by her husband's lack of will. In Rasputin, Alexandra had hoped to find the strength to support Nicholas and his reign. Her belief in Rasputin never wavered, but her hope for the success of his mission to guide Nicholas was fading.

On the eleventh, Alexandra and the girls visited Novgorod. They went to pray in the Znamensky Cathedral where they were met by Archbishop Arseny. He presented Alexandra with an icon of the Virgin Mary, and she gave it to Vyrubova as a gift for Rasputin. He was buried with the icon a few days later.[14] They also saw the aged staritsa Maria Mikhailovna, said to be 107 years old, at the Desyatinny Monastery. As they entered her dark room, Maria cried out, "Behold the martyred Empress Alexandra Fyodorovna!" Alexandra did not hear her words, but others in the party did and were deeply shaken by them.[15]

On the evening of the twelfth, Rasputin dined at Vyrubova's with Alexandra and her daughters Olga and Maria. It was to be their last meeting.[16] Alexandra had written to Nicholas just days before that Rasputin had been in "good, cheery spirits" of late.[17] Others claim just the opposite, and it may well be that Rasputin was putting on a good show for the empress. His secretary Aaron Simanovich (not, it needs stressing again, a reliable source) stated soon after the murder that, in the days leading up to it, Rasputin had received many warnings that an attempt on his life was imminent. Rasputin took this seriously and had the information passed along to the ministry of the interior and the palace.[18] Simanovich later told Vyrubova that in his final days Rasputin was "sad" and in a "depressed state."[19] Munya Golovina supposedly mentioned to Rasputin two days before his death that Yusupov had joined a secret English society, to which Rasputin replied: "Now he'll kill me."[20] Vasily Skvortsov echoed Simanovich and Golovina's words. He saw Rasputin just days before the murder and found him defeated, his face a sickly green, the "the mark of death" already upon him. Beletsky, on the other hand, also saw him at the time and found Rasputin lively and upbeat and full of confidence. His enemy Alexander Makarov was going to be replaced by Nikolai Dobrovolsky as minister of justice, which he counted as an important victory. In his memoirs, Beletsky claims he cautioned Rasputin nonetheless about making visits to "homes he did not know well."[21]

Rasputin's artist friend Theodora Krarup wrote in her memoirs that, in late November, "two foreign officers" visited her in her studio and offered a large sum of money to secretly let them in the next time he came so they could kill him. She went straight to Gorokhovaya to warn Rasputin, but he was not worried. "You should not be afraid, Theodora," he told her, "Our Lord is holding his hand over me."[22] A few weeks later, just days before the murder, a young officer in the Life Guards Hussar Regiment came to the residence of Palace Commandant Voeikov, then away at Stavka, and told his wife: "I know that the old man is going to be gotten rid of, he's going to be killed." The man's tone left no doubt as to the seriousness of what he said. His words were immediately communicated to Vyrubova, who put little stock in them, saying: "It's not that easy to kill people."[23] Maybe it was not, but there is evidence to suggest Rasputin was being unusually cautious. On the fifteenth, Alexandra wrote Nicholas how Rasputin "never goes out since ages, except to come here." The day before he and Munya had visited the Kazan and St. Isaac's Cathedrals, and Alexandra was happy to report there was "not one disagreeable look, people all quiet." Rasputin passed on these words to Alexandra that, in light of what was to happen, do appear to be strangely meaningful: "The path is narrow, but one must walk along it straight, in the manner of God and not of man."[24]

The police files for November and December also paint a picture of a withdrawn Rasputin. He visited the Golovins on 23 November, but for the most part he stayed at home. One rare outing was on 30 November to the Makaev wine shop at 23 Nevsky Prospect. The first eleven days of December were especially quiet. On the seventh, he paid a visit to Arthur Gyulling's at 54 Fontanka, and to Alexander Kon, a thirty-eight-year-old court councillor and member of the Petrograd Committee on Matters of the Press. On the tenth, he went out to see Simanovich on Nikolaevsky Street. But that was it. There were no parties, no social activities. All had gone quiet. The last extant police report is for the eleventh. The reports for the last five days of his life seem to have disappeared.[25]

A foundational text in the Rasputin mythology is the so-called testament published by Simanovich in his memoirs. He alleges that Rasputin dictated it to his lawyer Aronson over the course of an entire evening as Simanovich looked on in amazement. In it, Rasputin predicts that he will die before the end of the year and that if he is killed by his fellow Russian peasants, then the tsar will have nothing to fear and the monarchy will flourish for centuries, but if he is killed by the nobles, then Russia will descend into bloodshed and brother will kill brother for twenty-five years. Furthermore, should the bells tolling his death come with the news that the tsar's relatives killed Rasputin, then everyone in Nicholas's family will be dead within two years, killed by the Russian narod. Simanovich wrote that he gave this letter to Alexandra after Rasputin's death.[26] Needless to say it was not found among her papers after the revolution for a simple reason: Rasputin never wrote such a letter. But he did write another vaguely similar one addressed to his family that was found among his things by his daughter Maria:

*

My dears,

A disaster is threatening us, a great misfortune is drawing near. The face of Our Lady has darkened and the spirit is disturbed in the calm of the night. This calm will not last. Terrible will be the wrath. And whither shall we flee? It is written: Watch, for ye know neither the day nor the hour. This day has come for our country. There will be cries and blood. In the great darkness of these griefs I can now distinguish nothing. My hour will soon strike. I am not afraid, but I know it will be bitter. I shall suffer and it will be pardoned to men. I shall inherit the kingdom, but you will be saved. The road of your sufferings is known to God. Men without number will perish. Many martyrs will die. Brothers will be slain by their brothers. The earth will tremble. Famine and pestilence will reign, signs will appear to men. Pray for your salvation. And through the grace of the Saviour and of Her who intercedes with Him you will be consoled.

Grigory.[27]

Rasputin's prediction of coming disaster is not prophetic. By December 1916, many Russians could see the bloody revolution staring them in the face. But his knowledge of his approaching death is striking and cannot be argued away. Perhaps Rasputin did indeed foresee the violent end just around the corner.

64. The Last Day

Everyone who saw Rasputin on 16 December agreed he seemed nervous and agitated. It started when the telephone rang that morning. Rasputin answered and listened as an unfamiliar voice threatened to kill him.[1] The telephone call was then followed by the delivery of several anonymous death threats in the mail.[2] Next came word that Simoniko Pkhakadze had tried to kill himself with a gunshot to his chest, although he had failed, the bullet simply grazing him. The circumstances were murky, and Rasputin was concerned that it had something to do with Maria.[3]

Only a few visitors came by the Rasputin home that day. Around 11 a.m. Simanovich and Bishop Isidor arrived and stayed for three hours. Munya also paid a visit, remaining the entire afternoon and into the early evening, as did Princess Tatyana Shakhovskaya, Yekaterina Sukhomlinova, and Vyrubova, who showed up later in the afternoon for tea and to deliver the icon from the empress acquired on the trip to Novgorod days earlier. Vyrubova was surprised to hear Rasputin say he was going to visit Felix Yusupov that night to meet his wife. She found it odd that he would be going over to the Yusupovs' so late, but Rasputin told her that this had been arranged so Felix's parents would not know about his visit. She and Munya tried to talk Rasputin out of going, saying there were such ghastly stories circulating in the city and he needed to be extra careful. But he would hear none of it. "No one stops me from doing what I want. If I want to go out, I go out." Before she left, Rasputin said to her: "What else do you need from me? You've already gotten everything . . ."[4] She found this strange, but was not certain what to make of it. Later that evening in the empress's boudoir she mentioned the visit to Alexandra. "But there must be some mistake," the empress remarked. "Irina is in the Crimea, and neither of the older Yusupovs are in town." Alexandra lost herself in thought, puzzled by what Vyrubova had told her. "There is surely some mistake," she said, and with that the conversation moved on to other matters.[5]

By 11 p.m., everyone had left. The family began to get ready for bed. Maria noticed her father was smartly dressed in a light-blue embroidered silk shirt, velvet trousers, and polished black boots. "You're going out tonight?" she asked. Maria noted her father seemed impatient, absent, and for several minutes he did not reply to her question. Then he looked his daughters in the face and smiled; he stroked Varvara's forehead. "Yes, I'm going out again, my doves. Don't be anxious. I've been invited to Prince Yussupoff's and he's coming to fetch me after twelve o'clock." He asked the girls not to tell this to Munya. He then followed his daughters into their room and made the sign of the cross over them as they got into bed. Maria found her father's behavior curious. It was the last time they saw him alive.[6] Out on the street, Maria Zhuravlyova, the building's caretaker, locked the heavy iron front gate for the night.[7]

Rasputin lay down in bed, and then got up and went into the kitchen. He was having trouble with the buttons on the collar of his shirt and asked Katya Pecherkina to help him. Just then the bell for the back door rang. It was going on 1 a.m. on the seventeenth. Rasputin opened and Yusupov entered. "No one's here, right?" he asked, to which Rasputin replied everyone had gone and the children were asleep. "Let's go, little one," he said, and the two men went to Rasputin's bedroom. As they passed through the kitchen, Katya peeked out from behind the area curtained off for the servants and recognized Yusupov.[8]

Throughout the day workmen had been busy preparing the murder scene in the cellar of the Yusupov palace at 94 Moika. Carpets were being laid, curtains put up, oak chairs, tables, and various curios brought in and carefully placed. Yusupov's servants Grigory and Ivan helped their master arrange the furniture just so, and then prepared biscuits, cakes, tea, and wine. After a few hours spent with his "crammer" (Yusupov had exams the following day), supper, and a brief visit to the church of Our Lady of Kazan, Yusupov returned to survey the cellar one last time at eleven o'clock. "On the table the samovar smoked, surrounded by plates filled with the cakes and dainties that Rasputin liked so much," Yusupov wrote in his memoirs.

An array of bottles and glasses stood on a sideboard. Ancient lanterns of colored glass lighted the room from the ceiling; the heavy red damask portières were lowered. On the granite hearth, a log fire crackled and scattered sparks on the flagstones. One felt isolated from the rest of the world and it seemed as though, no matter what happened, the events of that night would remain forever buried in the silence of those thick walls.

Soon Dmitry arrived, then the others. They gathered in the cellar to examine the room. No one said a word. Felix took a box of poison from a large ebony cabinet. Donning rubber gloves, Sukhotin ground the cyanide into a powder and then sprinkled the cakes with enough poison, so the doctor said, to kill several men instantly. There were two plates of petits fours. Lazovert took all the pink pastries (there were only pink and chocolate), lifted off the top half, and sprinkled the ground cyanide on them, and then replaced the tops, and put them onto plates with the chocolate ones. Lazovert tossed the gloves into the fire and the room began to fill with smoke, so they had to open the windows to clear the room. The men went back upstairs. In the drawing room Yusupov pulled out two vials of the potassium in solution and gave one to Dmitry, the other to Purishkevich. They were to pour this into two of the four glasses behind the bottles in the dining room downstairs twenty minutes after Yusupov had left to pick up Rasputin. Everything prepared, Yusupov put on a heavy deerskin overcoat and a large fur hat that obscured his face. Dr. Lazovert, wearing a chauffeur's uniform, started up the automobile, and off they drove to Gorokhovaya.

After they had left, the others checked the gramophone to make sure it was working. The music would help set the mood and suggest to Rasputin that some sort of party was underway as a sort of diversion. Purishkevich took out a weighty Sauvage revolver from his pocket and laid it on Yusupov's desk. It was now 12:35 a.m. on the seventeenth. Ten minutes later, Purishkevich and Dmitry went downstairs and poured the vials into the glasses. They hoped Yusupov would not take the wrong one in his nervousness.

Yusupov arrived at Gorokhovaya in Purishkevich's large motorcar. The lights were off and the license had been covered up. Yusupov climbed out and went over to the caretaker and said he was on his way to see Rasputin and let himself in by the back staircase. It was pitch black, and so he had to feel his way to Rasputin's apartment. He rang the bell and was let in. Passing through the kitchen he felt a pair of eyes on him. He turned up his coat collar and pulled down his hat. "Why are you trying to hide?" asked Rasputin, and he assured Yusupov he had told no one about their arrangements and that he had sent the agents home for the night. Yusupov helped him on with his overcoat. Just then, according to Yusupov's memoirs, his conscience bit: "I was ashamed of the despicable deceit, the horrible trickery to which I was obliged to resort. At that moment I was filled with self-contempt, and wondered how I could even have thought of such a cowardly crime." Before him stood Rasputin, "quiet and trusting."[9] Rasputin had no idea that before him stood his murderer.

65. A Cowardly Crime

Rasputin was murdered early on the morning of 17 December at the home of Felix Yusupov and his dead body dumped in a branch of the Neva River. This we know for certain. What happened in the final hours of Rasputin's life remains a subject of intense curiosity and speculation a century later.

Here is the story that has most often been told.

Shortly after midnight the motorcar carrying Rasputin and Yusupov pulled into the courtyard at 92 Moika, the home of Yusupov's neighbor Prince Orlov, that afforded access to the Yusupov residence via a side door. As Rasputin and Yusupov entered, "Yankee Doodle Dandy" could be heard on a gramophone amidst the murmur of voices. Rasputin asked whether he was having a party, and Yusupov assured him it was just some of his wife's friends but that they would soon be leaving. They went down into the cellar, removed their coats, and sat down to talk, and drink some tea. Yusupov offered Rasputin the poisoned cakes, which he at first refused, but then ate, one after another. Yusupov could not believe his eyes: Rasputin showed no ill effects, the poison did nothing to him. Next, Rasputin asked for some of his beloved Madeira, which Yusupov gave him, again laced with poison. Yusupov stood and watched, waiting for him to collapse at any moment, but just as with the cakes, the poisoned wine was having no effect. Three glasses he drank, and yet nothing. Yusupov grew nervous. The two men were now sitting across from each other at the table, their eyes locked. "Now, see," an angry Rasputin suddenly let out, "you're wasting my time, you can't do anything to me." Yusupov felt certain Rasputin now knew why he had invited him to his home, but then he got up and spying Yusupov's guitar on a chair, asked him to sing him a song. Yusupov obliged, singing one, then another Russian ditty.

The time dragged on. By now it was 2:30 a.m. Nervous what his friends upstairs were thinking, Yusupov excused himself, saying he was going upstairs to check on his wife and her guests. His friends could not believe the poison had failed to act, so Yusupov took Dmitry's revolver and went back down to the cellar to finish the business. He found Rasputin drooping and breathing heavily, but after yet another glass of Madeira Rasputin revived and talked of them going to see the Gypsies. Yusupov changed the subject, and gazing at a large Italian cross of rock crystal and silver standing atop an ebony cabinet, he said: "Grigory Yefimovich, you'd far better look at the crucifix and say a prayer." With that, Yusupov raised the revolver and shot Rasputin, who screamed and collapsed onto a bearskin rug. With the sound of the gun, the other men ran downstairs. There lay Rasputin, blood spreading from a wound in his chest, his body motionless. Lazovert inspected the body and declared Rasputin dead. The men turned off the light and went back upstairs.

Dmitry, Sukhotin, and Lazovert then drove back to Rasputin's apartment, Sukhotin having put on Rasputin's overcoat and cap, to make it look to any police possibly following them that night that Rasputin had indeed been brought home safely. Then they returned to the Moika. In the meantime, Yusupov and Purishkevich waited and congratulated themselves on having saved Russia and the dynasty from "ruin and dishonor." And then a strange feeling swept over Yusupov, and he went back downstairs to make certain that Rasputin was indeed dead. He felt for a pulse. Nothing. But then, as he turned to leave, he saw something—Rasputin's left eye was quivering, his face began to twitch, and suddenly his left eye opened, then the right. "The green eyes of a viper," Yusupov wrote, "staring at me with diabolical hatred." A terrified Yusupov stood, his feet frozen to the flagstones with fear.

> With a sudden violent effort Rasputin leapt to his feet, foaming at the mouth. A wild roar echoed through the vaulted rooms [. . .] He rushed at me, trying to get at my throat, and sank his fingers into my shoulder like steel claws. [. . .]
>
> This devil who was dying of poison, who had a bullet in his heart, must have been raised from the dead by the powers of evil. There was something appalling and monstrous in his diabolical refusal to die.
>
> I realized now who Rasputin really was. It was the reincarnation of Satan himself who held me in his clutches and would never let me go till my dying day.

Yet, with "a superhuman effort," Yusupov managed to free himself from Satan's grip and charged back upstairs calling to Purishkevich for help. Before they knew what was happening, the door on the stair landing leading out to the courtyard opened and a bleeding Rasputin—"crawling on his hands and knees and roaring like a wounded animal"—slipped out into the night. They chased after him, guns drawn. Purishkevich fired off two shots, then two more just as Rasputin was about to escape out onto the Moika. Rasputin tottered and then fell next to a snow bank. Yusupov approached the body. Finally, he was dead for certain. Two servants next carried the body back inside, laying it on the stair landing by the side entrance.

After their return, Dmitry, Sukhotin, and Lazovert gathered Rasputin's body, which had been wrapped in a piece of heavy linen, shoved it into the automobile, and drove off in the direction of the Large Petrovsky Bridge. The streets were empty, and within ten minutes they had arrived. They stopped on the bridge near the railing, hauled out Rasputin's body, and tossed it into the icy water below. Yusupov, who had fainted upon seeing the corpse on the landing even before the three had returned from Rasputin's, had been put to bed by Purishkevich and a servant, Ivan, and did not awake for hours. Later, after regaining consciousness, Yusupov and a servant cleaned all the blood, tidied the cellar, and checked the yard for any damaging evidence. At 5 a.m., Yusupov left to return to his father-in-law's (Grand Duke Alexander, aka Sandro) on the Moika. "I felt full of courage and confidence," he wrote later, "at the thought that the first steps to save Russia had been taken."[1]

The story of Rasputin's death is one of the best-known moments of his life. Even people who know almost nothing about the man have heard of how he died, and his bizarre end has long since become part of global popular culture. The source of this account was Yusupov's memoirs, first published in 1927 as *Rasputin*.[2] Later, he published a revised version of the same book titled *Lost Splendor*, which appeared in 1953. The authorship of Yusupov's memoirs is open to question. It was widely assumed in émigré circles when the book appeared that Yusupov had not written it himself, and that the book was in fact ghostwritten, although by whom is not known. Similarities between the depiction of Rasputin's supernatural resistance to death and a scene from Dostoevsky's 1847 Gothic novella *The Landlady* imply a clear literary inspiration.[3] Regardless of who wrote the book, the power it has exercised in establishing the accepted view of Rasputin's death is truly remarkable, especially when one considers that Yusupov's memoir was neither an honest exploration of his own life nor a biography of the man he had killed, but a work of naked self-justification and self-glorification.

Murderers make for problematic narrators (recall Humbert Humbert), but Yusupov's relationship to his text has largely gone unexamined. The context of its composition is important. The Yusupovs lost everything in the revolution and fled to Europe with only what they could carry. Their immense fortune was gone. Felix Yusupov struggled to support his family in exile. Money was tight. The one thing he had to sell was his notoriety as the man who killed Rasputin, and this was his primary motivation for writing the book. He had to make money, and so it had to be dramatic if it were to sell, and this it most certainly was. The second edition was also written to make money. Yet Yusupov knew he could not simply retell the same story, for this would be old news. He had to make it appear fresh and new, and so he embellished, making changes to heighten the drama. To give one example. In his 1927 memoir Yusupov wrote that Rasputin seemed to be the Devil himself, while in *Lost Splendor*, Rasputin no longer has the appearance of the Devil but has grown to become "the reincarnation of Satan himself."[4]

But it was much more than money woes that shaped Yusupov's book. Although he never expressed any remorse over what he had done, there was no getting around the fact that Yusupov had invited an unarmed man to his home under false pretenses and murdered him in cold blood. This was far from a noble act. And so he had to tell a different story. In Yusupov's version of events, he had not killed a man, but Satan. When the emperor's sister Grand Duchess Olga read Yusupov's memoirs she remarked that "the murder was so staged as to present Rasputin in the guise of the devil incarnate and his killers as some fairy-tale heroes."[5] Inflating the demonic power of Rasputin's evil genius to a superhuman level, Yusupov not only tried to justify the murder and the manner in which it was carried out, but also to exaggerate his own righteous bravery and willpower. In his version of their confrontation, Yusupov casts himself as the archangel Michael, vanquishing Satan in the Book of Revelation. He is a man not to be condemned, but praised.

Two other participants had spoken of the murder even before Yusupov. In September 1918, Lazovert told the *New York Times* that they had shot Rasputin in the street near the palace of Grand Duke Dmitry while he was on his way to see the empress. Lazovert also told the newspaper that a price had been put on his head after the killing, and so he had to flee Russia.[6] Lazovert played with the truth as freely as Yusupov.

It was also in 1918 in Kiev that Purishkevich published what he called his "diary" with a detailed account of the murder.[7] A diary it was not, having been written well after the events it described. Maklakov called the work "nonsensical," and one of Rasputin's recent biographers has characterized it as "empty phraseology and demagoguery." Purishkevich's diary adds little to Yusupov's account, although in places the two differ on some minor details (e.g., whose gun was used to shoot Rasputin in the cellar, how many times Yusupov went up and down the stairs, etc.). Both accounts agree it was Purishkevich, not Dmitry or anyone else, who fired the fatal shots. One bit of detail provided by Purishkevich is how they disposed of the body. Dmitry was at the wheel of the automobile as they drove to the snowy bridge. There, they heaved the body out and flung it over the railing into the dark water. But only after they had let go did the men realize they had forgotten to attach the weights and chains Purishkevich had purchased to weigh down the corpse. After a moment of confusion, they decided to simply toss these in after the body. As they were about to leave, someone noticed one of Rasputin's boots had fallen off. This too was then tossed over the railing, but it failed to reach the water and landed on one of the piers. Finally, they drove to Dmitry's palace by the Anichkov Bridge on Nevsky Prospect. The trip took longer than expected since the car was having engine trouble and kept stalling.[8]

Maria Rasputin found Yusupov's description "all imagination and embroidery."[9] The idea that her father would have eaten all those cakes—a man who disliked sweets—she found particularly unlikely. It is possible Rasputin did not eat them, but it is also possible he did and nothing happened since they had never been poisoned. Maklakov wrote the French publisher of Purishkevich's memoirs in Paris in 1923 that he never gave Yusupov the potassium cyanide mentioned in the memoir, but merely some harmless powder. One source states this powder was just crushed aspirin.[10] This might have been nothing more than Maklakov's conscience speaking. But even if he had given the conspirators potassium cyanide, it might not have ever touched Rasputin's lips. Not long before his death Lazovert confessed that he had had second thoughts about the murder and qualms about his Hippocratic oath and so substituted some benign substance for poison.[11]

Potassium cyanide releases hydrogen cyanide gas that attacks the central nervous system by depriving it of oxygen. Serious effects are noticeable seconds after exposure. Rapid breathing and giddy sensations or dizziness are followed by confusion and anxiety. The sufferer is gripped by nausea and vomiting. The neck becomes tight and constricted and one experiences a sense of suffocation. In some cases, the back arches, muscles go into spasm, the pupils dilate and become fixed. Coma comes next or death, typically within a few minutes. No one would have survived exposure to potassium cyanide as described in Yusupov's story.[12]

Maria also did not believe that her father would have stayed so long in the cellar with Yusupov given his "strange clairvoyance, that accurate intuition of thoughts of the people he was speaking with."[13] This is an interesting point. Rasputin, many people said, did indeed possess such a clairvoyance, but by the last years of his life this gift was well in decline. He vouched for Alexei Khvostov with Alexandra and met with him often, all while the man was plotting to kill him, something Rasputin never noticed. No, by the last year of his life, Rasputin's sixth sense for people had abandoned him.

What really happened at the Yusupov home on 17 December will never be known. All that can be said is that Rasputin was killed by three bullet shots, one delivered directly into his forehead at extremely close range. He was forty-seven years old.

Yusupov's version of events has an undeniable appeal in the way it elevates a vulgar killing into an epochal struggle of good versus evil. This narrative strategy explains much of the reason for the great success of his story. Indeed, so powerful is this myth that it has been taken up and reinvented by contemporary nationalist historians intent on creating a new legend. For them, the great lengths to which Yusupov had to go to kill Rasputin (and here new, more horrific details are added) prove not that he was trying to kill the Antichrist, but just the opposite: Yusupov, the bisexual, secularized Westerner, could barely kill Rasputin because he, a true Orthodox believer, was protected by the power of the Almighty.[14] Rasputin, in this version, was martyred at the hands of an effete traitor for his faith in God and the monarchy, just as Holy Russia would be destroyed by the atheist Bolsheviks in 1917.

And it cannot be denied that the manner of Rasputin's end did foreshadow what lay ahead for the Romanovs: the early morning walk down to the basement, the confusion about what was happening followed by gunshots, the bloody murder scene, the hurried loading of the bodies onto vehicles under the cover of darkness, the drive to a remote location where they could be quickly disposed of, only for the corpses to reappear later. Nicholas and Alexandra could not have known it, but the death of their Friend presaged their own gruesome end.

66. The Investigation

Even before the sun rose on the seventeenth, news of the killing was beginning to spread. Not surprisingly, Purishkevich was chiefly to blame. No sooner had the body been driven off to the river than Purishkevich went up to two soldiers stationed at the main entrance of the Yusupov palace and informed them that he had just killed Rasputin, at which one of them kissed him and the other said, "Thank God, about time!" Before going back inside, Purishkevich instructed them not to breathe a word about it [1] Soon, Purishkevich himself would be telling the police about what he had done.

Shots had been heard in the streets near the Yusupov palace early that morning. Around 2:30 a.m., Flor Yefimov, a policeman of the 2nd station of the Admiralty Region Police Division, heard four shots and then about thirty minutes later saw an automobile driving along the Moika, which he reported to fellow policeman Stepan Vlasyuk, of the 3rd station of the Kazan Region Police Division. One of those shots had been fired by Yusupov's batman, Ivan Nefedov. Still alive but bleeding heavily, Rasputin had likely managed to get out into the yard via the side door just a few steps up from the cellar and stumbled along in a vain attempt to escape before being shot a third and final time. A long trail of Rasputin's blood stained the snow. Yusupov stared at the blood and came up with a plan on the spot. He had Nefedov shoot the family dog, Frale, kept chained up in the yard and then drag his bloody carcass over the trail left by Rasputin. This, he thought, would answer any uncomfortable questions about the blood stains. When he had finished, Nefedov tossed the dead Frale off into the garden and went back inside.

Around 4 a.m., policeman Vlasyuk ventured into the courtyard at 92 Moika to check up on Yefimov's report. He was talking to the caretaker of the neighboring house of Prince Orlov when Yusupov and his major-domo Buzhinsky came out into the yard. He asked them about the gunshots, to which both replied they had not heard a thing. Satisfied with their answers, and having not noticed the blood in the dark,

Vlasyuk went back to his post at the corner of Prachechny and Maksim-ilianovsky Lanes. He was not there long before Buzhinsky appeared and told him the prince wished to speak to him back in the palace study. Vlasyuk entered. The home was utterly silent. In the study was Yusupov and a man he did not recognize.

"You are Orthodox?" the man asked.

"Yes, sir."

"Are you a Russian?"

"Yes, sir."

"Do you love the Emperor and the motherland?"

"Yes, sir."

"Do you know me?"

"No, I do not."

"Have you ever heard of Purishkevich?" Vlasyuk replied he did not know him, but had heard of the man. Purishkevich continued:

"Listen here, he [Rasputin, that is] is dead, and if you love the Tsar and the Motherland, you'll keep this quiet and won't tell anyone a thing."

"Yes, sir."

"You can go now."

With that Vlasyuk turned, left the house, and went back to his post. He was confused. He saw no signs of any murder and the men had seemed quite calm. The man did not appear to be drunk, as Yusupov would later claim Purishkevich had been. He took the entire incident as some sort of test: maybe they wanted to see what he would now do with such information, he thought. Vlasyuk did not think long before report-ing everything to his superiors back at the station.[2] Word began to travel fast up the ranks of the Petrograd police.

Procurator of the Appellate Court Sergei Zavadsky received a tele-phone call early that morning from an official in the ministry of justice, informing him that Rasputin had likely been murdered that previous night at the Yusupov palace and to begin an investigation.[3] By 9 a.m., Zavadsky, Investigator for Extraordinary Affairs Viktor Sereda, and a police photographer were on the scene. They noticed the trail of blood in the snow that ran from the steps of the side door across the yard. It appeared that based on the pattern in the snow a badly bleeding body—possibly of someone already dead—had been carried across the yard. Sereda wanted to go into the house and see behind the small door where the blood drops led, but was not permitted inside. So, the investigator gathered some samples in a jar for analysis. The report soon came back from the laboratory: the blood was human.[4] Despite their findings, Zavadsky and Sereda were told by senior officials that there was no need to investigate. Rasputin, it was being said, had no doubt been out drinking and was sure to turn up soon. Minister of Justice Makarov, no friend of Rasputin, saw no reason to dig any further into the matter.

That morning police arrived at the Rasputin apartment on Gorokhovaya. They asked his daughters where their father was, but they had no idea and could not understand why he was not at home. Anxious, they telephoned Munya, but she assured them that if their father had gone out the night before with Prince Yusupov then he was probably still there asleep and they had nothing to worry about. Munya came over to the apartment at 11 a.m. and now she too began to worry. They called Yusupov's home, but he was not there. Meanwhile, Simanovich had been out looking for Rasputin. He arrived at Gorokhovaya with bad news for the girls: there was talk their father had been murdered at the Yusupov palace and his body driven off somewhere. At noon the telephone rang. It was Yusupov asking to speak to Munya. They talked briefly, in English for privacy, and then Munya, clearly upset, left saying she was going home to wait for Yusupov. An hour later Maria and Varvara went to Munya's, where she told them she had spoken with Yusupov and he swore that he had not come by for their father the night before and Rasputin had never been in his house.[5]

Yusupov left his family palace and arrived at his father-in-law Sandro's house, where he was staying while his family's palace was being renovated, around 5 a.m. on the seventeenth. Yusupov found his brother-in-law Fyodor still up, anxiously awaiting his return. Felix, it would seem, had told him of their plans. "Rasputin is dead," he informed Fyodor. At 10 a.m. that same day, General Georgy Grigorev, the local district police superintendent, came to Sandro's to question Yusupov about the shots. He asked whether Rasputin had been among the guests; Yusupov replied no, Rasputin had never been to his home. He then told him the story of the dead dog, and that what Purishkevich meant when he had spoken to the police earlier was that it should have been Rasputin, not a dog, who had been shot.[6] Satisfied, Grigorev left.

Next Yusupov went to see Minister of Justice Makarov, to whom he gave the same story he had just told Grigorev. Makarov was satisfied with Yusupov's account and once more Zavadsky and Sereda were instructed to stop the investigation. In the meantime, Minister of the Interior Protopopov had decided to start his own investigation, which he put in the hands of General Pyotr Popov, a former head of the St. Petersburg Security Section (part of the Okhrana), now an officer for special operations at the ministry of the interior.[7] Early that afternoon Governor-General Alexander Balk summoned Yusupov, and now for the third time that day Yusupov insisted he had been at home with some friends having a party and did not see Rasputin. The blood in the yard was from his dog, he said, shot by Grand Duke Dmitry as he left early in the morning. He informed Balk that even though he had had nothing to do with it, people were trying to link his name to Rasputin's disappearance. Balk, like General Grigorev, was convinced and let Yusupov go.[8] Yusupov had now told his version of the night's events to three authorities and all of them had believed him. He must have allowed himself the satisfaction of thinking they might just get away with murder. Later that afternoon, he went to see Dmitry at his palace on Nevsky Prospect.[9]

Purishkevich had avoided the authorities. He paid a visit to his mother, whom he told nothing, and then stopped by to see Yusupov late in the afternoon. Yusupov was then occupied writing a long letter to the empress protesting his innocence. According to his memoirs, Yusupov and Dmitry were still anxious, but Purishkevich tried to calm them. From there he left for his medical train at the Warsaw Station and departed with his wife and two sons for the Romanian front. Later, he claimed that he wrote in his diary as the train rolled away from Petrograd: "It has pleased fate that I and no other should deliver the Tsar and Russia of him, that he should fall by my hand."[10]

Earlier that day two workmen crossing the Large Petrovsky Bridge noticed blood on the railings and informed the watchman Fyodor Kuzmin. He went out to see for himself, and observed not only the blood but a rubber boot on the ice near one of the bridge's piers. He went down and fetched it; it was a man's boot, brown, size ten, manufactured by the "Treugolnik" company. Kuzmin passed on everything to the local policeman, and he informed his superiors. Soon Lieutenant General Alexander Naumov, head of the river police, arrived and ordered an investigation of the surrounding area.[11] The search for Rasputin's body now began in earnest.

The police questioned a total of fifteen persons, most of them on the eighteenth and nineteenth.[12] Yusupov was interrogated on the eighteenth. Once more he told the story about how he had had a party at his home with several friends, including Dmitry and a few ladies. At one point, he said, Rasputin called to invite him to the Gypsies, but he declined. As for Purishkevich, yes, Felix recalled he did say something to a policeman, but he could not remember, and, he added, Purishkevich had been terribly drunk. The police brought up the fact they had had the blood tested and it turned out to be human, not canine. Flustered, Yusupov told them he knew nothing about that. He surmised someone, the true killers of course, must have planted it there to cast suspicion on him. The police were not convinced. For one thing, they knew that Purishkevich was a teetotaler and so there was no way his words to the police that night had been the result of drink. Still, Yusupov kept up the charade, insisting that if Rasputin had indeed been murdered, then his killers had planned it exceedingly well to make it look as if he was responsible.[13]

Yusupov did not like where this was going. On the night of the eighteenth he headed to the station to board a train for the Crimea but was stopped by the head of the police and told to go home. He was not free to leave the city until further notice.[14]

67. The Body in the Water

Everyone in Russia was looking to the court to see how it would react. "The fate of the dynasty as well as of the country depended upon that," Grand Duchess Maria, Dmitry's sister, recalled.[1]

Alexandra had slept well on the night of 16 December and awoke to unusually cold temperatures on the morning of the seventeenth. Light snow was falling.[2] That morning one of Rasputin's daughters called Vyrubova to say their father had not come home last night. Vyrubova communicated this immediately to the empress upon arriving at the palace. Alexandra was puzzled by the news. Then, about an hour later, Protopopov called Alexandra to say that a policeman near Yusupov's palace had heard shots in the night and a drunken Purishkevich had come out to tell him that Rasputin had been murdered. They sat and waited for more news. "It's so terribly difficult," Alexandra's daughter Olga wrote in her diary that day. "Father Grigory went missing last night. They are looking for him everywhere."[3]

Alexandra wrote to Nicholas: "We are sitting together—can you image our feelings—thoughts—our Friend has disappeared. Yesterday Ania saw him & he said Felix asked him to come in the night, a motor wld. fetch him to see Irina." She related what she had heard so far, that a military car with two civilians had fetched him after which there had been a "big scandal" at Yusupov's. Dmitry and Purishkevich were there, they had been drinking, shots were fired, Purishkevich ran out screaming that Rasputin had been killed. She had already told Protopopov to stop Felix from leaving for the Crimea. She added: "Our Friend was in good spirits but nervous these days & for A. too, as Batyushin wants to catch things against Ania." Alexandra feared for them all, and asked Nicholas to send Voeikov. She added that she had brought Ania to live with them, worried that she was next in line. "I cannot & won't believe He has been killed. God have mercy. Such anguish (am calm & can't believe it). [. . .] come quickly—nobody will dare to touch her or do anything when you are here. Felix came to him lately . . ."[4]

That same day Dmitry called to request a meeting with Alexandra, but she refused to see him. Then Felix called, saying he wanted to explain everything either to her or Vyrubova, but he too was told by Alexandra to stay away and instructed to put his words in a letter. Felix did so immediately: "Your Imperial Majesty, I hasten to obey the command of Your Majesty and to report what occurred in my house last night. It will be my aim, in doing so, to clear myself of the dreadful accusation that is being made against me."

He told the empress that he had been having a small party with Grand Duke Dmitry and some lady friends when Rasputin rang and asked him to come join him to see the Gypsies. He could hear loud voices on the other end, but Rasputin would not tell him where he was. Felix wrote that the party began to wind down around 3 a.m., when a shot was heard outside. They went out to investigate, but no one knew anything about it. He then phoned Dmitry, who told him he had shot a dog that was about to set upon one of the ladies as they were leaving. Felix went out in the yard and found his dog had indeed been shot. By four o'clock in the morning the rest of the guests had left, and he then went to his father-in-law's, where he was staying. He denied in his letter any talk of his involvement in Rasputin's disappearance, which he called "a complete lie," claiming he never left his house that night and never saw Rasputin. "I assure Your Majesty that I can hardly find words to express to Your Majesty how deeply concerned I am by all these happenings and how monstrous the accusations made against me appear to be. I remain, Your Majesty's devoted and faithful servant, Felix."[5]

It is a shameful letter (practically every sentence of which is a lie) that shows Yusupov for the dishonest coward he was. A decent man, convinced of the righteousness of his actions, would have told Alexandra the truth and faced the consequences. Yusupov, however, felt no compunction about lying. Yusupov saw Munya Golovina on the seventeenth and insisted to her face that he had not seen Rasputin at all the previous night. She did not believe him and now felt such guilt over the unwitting role she had played in Rasputin's murder she could never again bring herself to go visit his bereaved family.[6]

Alexandra sent the letter on to the minister of justice, but did not bother to respond to Yusupov for several days, such was her disgust. "No one has a right to murder," she eventually wrote him. "I know very well that many people are suffering the tortures of remorse, for it is not only Dmitry Pavlovich who is involved in this affair. Your letter filled me with utter amazement."[7]

Around 5 p.m., Alexandra telephoned Lily Dehn to tell her the news and ask her to hurry to the palace. Lily came immediately and found the empress in the mauve boudoir. The room smelled of flowers and freshly cut firewood. Alexandra was lying on her couch, her daughters seated around her; Vyrubova was on a small bench next to the empress. Alexandra was pale and in tears; Lily could tell Anna had been crying as well. The empress was terribly upset, but she refused to accept that Rasputin might be dead. She told Lily that she wanted her to spend the night at Anna's for her own safety. Lily left and went to Anna's house and was shocked to find it full of agents from the secret police. They informed her that a plot to kill both Alexandra and Vyrubova had recently been uncovered. They were there for protection. As she was falling asleep in Anna's bedroom that night, an icon fell from the wall and knocked over a portrait of Rasputin.[8] She took it for a sign.

That afternoon, ignoring the risk of severe fines for even mentioning the story, the *Stock Exchange Gazette* published a short notice underneath a massive headline: "THE DEATH OF GRIGORY RASPUTIN." It read: "This morning at 6 o'clock the life of Grigory Rasputin suddenly ended after a party in one of the most aristocratic homes in the center of the city." The story was reprinted hours later in *Evening Petrograd*. There was talk the *Stock Exchange Gazette* had been fined 3,000 rubles for printing the story.[9]

The emperor was in a particularly good mood on the morning of 17 December, playful even during his morning briefings, according to Captain Dmitry Tikhobrazov, a field staff officer at Stavka. At noon, everyone was dismissed and invited to the tsar's table to dine. At 12:30 p.m., the officers lined up as usual according to rank along the wall between the emperor's personal apartments and the dining hall. Yet Nicholas, who never kept the men waiting, failed to exit his rooms at the usual time and the men began to wonder what might be the matter. Finally, the doors opened, Nicholas exited and made his way down the hall to the dining room. He approached the hors d'oeuvres table, took a few small bites and poured himself a vodka, moving away to make room for the others. After General Maurice Janin, head of the French military mission in Russia, had done the same and was bringing the vodka to his lips, his eyes sweeping the men around him, he said softly, "He's been killed." The surrounding officers knew immediately who Janin was referring to, and without saying a word they all downed their shots at the same time, a subtle way of expressing their shared joy over the news. After they all took their seats at the table, Tikhobrazov kept his eyes on the tsar. Nicholas gave nothing away: "Not his eyes, not his voice, none of his gestures suggested in the least that the Emperor was shaken by the event."

But it was an entirely different Nicholas at the afternoon meeting. He appeared tense and sat without uttering a word; his eyes roamed the room just over the heads of the officers, avoiding all eye contact. He seemed not to be listening. As General Nikolai Ruzsky described with his dry, monotone voice the terrible morale of the troops, Nicholas could not control himself any longer. "Excuse me, general," Nicholas interrupted. Ruzsky fell silent. "Gentlemen, there are moments in the life of every man when the circumstances of his private personal life take precedence over everything else. Please continue your discussions without me. I must leave you now and depart."

And with that, the officers rose. Nicholas went around the table and shook everyone's hand before leaving. An unmistakable awkwardness filled the air. After Nicholas had left the room, General Ruzsky picked up where he had left off. No one even bothered to ask what had just happened and what the tsar had meant by his words, even though not everyone had yet heard the news. It was an important meeting at which the plans for the campaign of 1917 were to be discussed. But without the emperor, no one knew how to act or what was to be done, and so in the end the meeting concluded without any decision at all. Each commander would act as he saw fit on his front, and as circumstances allowed.[10] At four o'clock on the afternoon of the seventeenth the tsar's train left Mogilyov for Tsarskoe Selo.

The morning of the eighteenth broke bright, sunny, and bitterly cold. Alexandra, her daughters, Vyrubova, and Lily spent the day together waiting for news. Alexandra still refused to believe something terrible had happened and kept insisting that he had most certainly just been driven out of the city somewhere and would return at any moment. Regardless, they all suspected Felix and Dmitry and feared more trouble. Dmitry once more requested to see Alexandra; again she refused, and she ordered Adjutant-General Konstantin Maximovich, in the name of the tsar, to prevent Dmitry from leaving his home.

Vyrubova had been receiving vague anonymous threats and Alexandra insisted she stay with them in the palace.[11] At 6:38 p.m., Nicholas wired Alexandra from the Orsha train station: "Only now read your letter. Anguished and horrified. Prayers [and] thoughts together. Arrive tomorrow at 5."[12] A rumor was by now going about Petrograd that Alexandra had offered a large reward for information on the whereabouts of Rasputin.[13]

On Monday the nineteenth, the four Romanov sisters went back to work at the royal hospital, but they found it difficult to concentrate. Alexandra, Vyrubova, and Dehn remained in the palace and were joined that day by Akilina Laptinskaya. And then, early that afternoon, news reached the palace that Rasputin's body had been found. At 1:50 p.m., Alexandra cabled Nicholas the dreaded news: "They've found him in the water."[14] Lily Dehn recalled that the news shook Alexandra profoundly, but she did not go to pieces, but somehow managed to hold herself together.[15]

Around eleven o'clock on the morning of the eighteenth, divers were brought to the Large Petrovsky Bridge to search the Malaya Nevka. By then the rubber boot had already been shown to Rasputin's daughters, and they had confirmed that it was their father's. The divers made a number of holes in the ice and then spent the day searching the waters below the surface but found nothing. The search had only resumed early on the nineteenth when a member of the river police named Andreev happened to notice a piece of frozen fabric sticking up out of the ice about two hundred meters downstream from the bridge. Divers were sent over, and with the aid of grapnels began to investigate the area below the ice. Here they came upon the body. Rasputin was frozen to the underside of the ice and his body had to be chipped away and broken free before it could be brought to the surface. A police photographer captured the scene.

Investigator Sereda arrived at the bridge at 9 a.m. He was joined there by Generals Kurlov and Popov, Procurator Zavadsky, Governor-General Balk and others. By then the corpse had been removed from the river. A crowd had gathered, including practically every state official of consequence, but everyone except for officials and police was moved off the bridge and held back by the police. Sereda could make out the tire tracks in the snow and noticed how it had pulled over to the railing. It appeared the body had been taken out of the car, leaned standing up against the rail, and then someone had lifted his feet and dumped him over the side. They had not thrown him with enough force to clear the bridge, however, and he had hit his head on the way down to the water, thus the blood splattered on the piers.

The body was wrapped in a fur coat. Around the feet the killers had tied a bag fashioned from thin blue cloth. It had been filled with something heavy, but after getting wet the material had ripped and so whatever had been in the bag fell to the bottom, and Rasputin's corpse failed to submerge along with it. This material further served to link Yusupov to the crime, for it was soon traced back to his home. The body drifted with the current under the ice. The fur coat, not fully attached, billowed out in the icy water and acted almost like a life preserver. The body slowly floated to the river's edge, where it froze. The cord tying his hands had been ripped, and his arms had become locked in a grotesque manner over his head. The corpse was first taken to the casualty ward on the Vyborg Side. Rasputin's daughters were brought in to see the body.[16]

"It was a terrible spectacle," Maria recalled, "which my nerves, stretched to the breaking point, were hardly able to stand."

> The thick matted hair was covered with clots of blood. The face was swollen and the eyes already glazed. When the pelisse had been removed the clothes looked like a hard skin which held in places and in others peeled off like mica. But the strangest thing was the position of the right arm and clenched hand, which in death still held my father's last gesture. He had succeeded in the water in untying the bonds which held his arms, and it was as though in a supreme effort to save himself he had tried to make the sign of the cross.[17]

Maria is engaging in myth-making here. The fanciful assertion that Rasputin died while making the sign of the cross began almost immediately after his murder, and Maria repeats it here in her memoirs. It is part of the Rasputin myth that lives on, refusing to die.[18]

A coffin was brought but the body, with its arms frozen over the head, would not fit inside, so a lidless wooden box was hastily nailed together instead. Throughout the day, a number of officials and journalists, as well as Simanovich, were permitted to view the corpse. The crowd along the river grew. Some began filling pails with water, convinced it was carrying the same power that had once flowed through Rasputin.

No one could decide what to do with the body. Makarov wanted it sent to the anatomical theater of the Military Medical Academy in Petrograd, but Protopopov would not hear of it, convinced that to keep Rasputin's body within the city limits would be seen as a provocation and might well lead to civil unrest. Instead he had the body placed in a Red Cross truck around 5 p.m. and sent south outside the city to the almshouse attached to the Chesmensky Palace along the road to Tsarskoe Selo. A roadblock was set up and guards placed around the almshouse.[19]

An hour after Rasputin's body was driven off to the almshouse, Nicholas and Alexei arrived at Tsarskoe Selo. The rest of the family was there to greet them when the train pulled into the station. They were overjoyed to be reunited. Nicholas said upon his return, "I am ashamed before Russia that the hands of my relatives are stained with the blood of a peasant."[20] At ten that night, Protopopov joined the grieving family at the palace.[21]

Purposely vague headlines (that fooled no one) filled the papers that day: "A Mysterious Find," "A Secret Case," "A Baffling Crime." Rasputin's name did not appear in any of the articles; there were only references to "the corpse" and "the murder victim." Specific details, however, were mentioned—that shots had been heard early on the morning of the seventeenth along the Moika, that masked men had been seen carrying something large and heavy wrapped in fabric out of a house and placing it in an automobile, that a bloody rubber boot had been found on the Large Petrovsky Bridge, and that Prince Felix Yusupov and Vladimir Purishkevich were somehow connected to the events.[22]

The autopsy was set for Wednesday the twenty-first at eleven o'clock in the morning. The body was put in the charge of a Professor I. P. Petrov, with the order to let no one in to see the corpse. The heat in the almshouse's mortuary was turned up to 20 degrees Réaumur (74 Fahrenheit) to try to thaw the body in time.[23]

But that evening of the nineteenth the tsar telephoned Minister of Justice Makarov and ordered him to begin the autopsy immediately, since he wanted to be able to hand the body over to the family the next day. Sereda was dumbfounded by the order, but was instructed such was the will of the emperor. The autopsy was to be conducted by Dr. Dmitry Kosorotov, the city's senior autopsy surgeon, but no one knew where he was or even how to find him. The police eventually located him in a local restaurant, and he was taken directly to the almshouse. The mortuary had no electricity, so police had to be sent out to collect kerosene lamps from nearby residents. With the body still frozen, and amid the dim light of four lamps, Kosorotov and his assistants set to work on the body around 10 p.m. Kosorotov later recalled of the procedure: "I often had to perform difficult and unpleasant autopsies. I have strong nerves and have seen a lot of what there is to see. But I seldom had an experience as gruesome as the one of that terrible night. The body made a terrible impression. The goat-like expression of the face and the enormous head wound were hard even on my experienced eyes."[24]

Rasputin's light-blue shirt with gold embroidery was heavily stained with blood. (The murderers had bungled their plan to burn all his clothing: many of the items had been too big to fit into the stove on Purishkevich's train.)[25] He had a chain around his neck with a large cross on it, on the back of which was written: "Save and preserve." On his wrist was a gold and platinum bracelet with a clasp bearing a double-headed eagle and Nicholas's cypher. The shirt became the subject of various myths. One claimed Alexandra later went about the wards of the military hospitals placing it on the wounded soldiers convinced it would heal the men.[26] British intelligence officer Samuel Hoare heard that not long after Rasputin's murder a surgeon operating on the leg of the tsarevich noticed Alexandra had secretly placed it under the operating table, again as a healing talisman.[27]

The official autopsy report compiled by Kosorotov disappeared from a Leningrad archive years later and has never been seen since. It is possible the report was smuggled out of the country and sold. In 1929, the Leipzig bookseller Karl W. Hiersemann offered for sale, at the price of 20,000 German marks, the "Original Documents of the Inquiry Made by the Russian Government into the Murder of Rasputin," to wit: "The whole of the authenticated legal records of one of the most far-reaching events in modern history of Russia, forming at the same time a historical source-work of outstanding and universal importance." Just how Hiersemann acquired the documents, and whether they included the original autopsy, is not known.[28]

Then, in 1998, the French writer Alain Roullier published what he claimed to be a copy of Kosorotov's report, and several subsequent books have cited this text, even though it is undoubtedly fraudulent.[29]

Kosorotov did, however, give an extended interview in 1917 to *Russian Liberty* about the autopsy, and he also discussed the results with Investigator Sereda, and these two written accounts remain the only reliable sources for what was revealed during the examination of Rasputin's body.[30]

The corpse was in horrific shape. Rasputin's face and head showed the signs of severe trauma. The right side of his head had been smashed. His nose had been battered, his right eye blackened, and his right ear had been practically ripped from his head. The left side of his torso had been sliced open, perhaps by a sword or knife. Kosorotov deemed that many of these wounds likely occurred posthumously, from hitting part of the bridge or being crushed by the heavy ice floes of the river or being pulled from the water by the grappling iron. His genitals, despite various later accounts, were intact and undamaged.

Rasputin had been shot three times. One bullet entered the left side of his chest below the heart, piercing his stomach and right kidney, and then exiting the body on the right side. Another shot caught Rasputin in the back and penetrated his right kidney, the bullet lodging in his spinal column. Kosorotov noted that either of these two shots would have weakened him immediately and led to death within twenty minutes. The third shot was delivered directly into Rasputin's forehead. The first shot had left powder traces on Rasputin's shirt, suggesting it was fired at close range. This was true of the final shot as well, fired perhaps at a distance of only eight inches from Rasputin's head. Although Kosorotov could not be sure of the sequence of the shots, he felt confident that Rasputin had first been shot in the left side, then while trying to escape was shot in the back, and then finished off with a "control shot" as he lay dying on his back. Alexander Pistolkors, however, told Maria that Grand Duke Dmitry had described the murder to him, saying that her father had first been shot in the back by Yusupov and then finished off by the others.[31]

The bullet removed from the body was badly deformed. Kosorotov stated there was no way of saying with any certainty what sort of gun had been used, for such bullets were used by a range of revolvers. As for any signs of poison, Kosorotov could find none, which suggests that either whatever poison he had ingested had broken down to the point it could no longer be detected or, as is more likely, he never consumed any.[32]

The autopsy findings found their way almost immediately into the press. The *Stock Exchange Gazette*, which, along with the other newspapers, had begun to mention Rasputin by name in its pages the previous day, carried the story on the twenty-first. The newspaper got the details right: Rasputin had been killed by a bullet fired directly into his forehead; no trace of poison was found in his body; the victim had no water in his lungs.[33] The story that Rasputin was thrown still alive into the Malaya Nevka and died of drowning (thus the water in the lungs) has had a long and tenacious history. Kosorotov found no evidence of water in Rasputin's lungs, but within days of his murder the rumor began to circulate that this was indeed what had happened. Vyrubova believed it to be true, as did his daughter Maria and Ambassador George Buchanan.[34] Most recent books on Rasputin, even those by respected scholars, have, regrettably, repeated this falsehood.[35]

After Kosorotov and his assistants had completed their work, the body was handed over to Akilina Laptinskaya on the twentieth. She washed Rasputin's corpse and dressed it in a shroud of white linen. The office of the Petrograd governor-general had purchased a zinc coffin from Martynov's Funeral Services for five hundred rubles. (Martynov, graciously, offered a 10 percent discount off the list price.) Before the lid was closed, Laptinskaya placed inside some dried flowers and an icon signed by members of the royal family and Vyrubova. Rasputin's cross and bracelet she took with her to give to the empress.[36]

There is one mystery that surrounds the events at Chesmensky almshouse on the night of 19–20 December. Both Sereda and Zavadsky claimed that a woman dressed as a nurse appeared and sat alone with the body for several hours. Neither man got a good look at her and so never learned her identity. Both could not help wondering, however, whether the mysterious visitor was none other than Alexandra.[37] It is an intriguing thought, but most unlikely.

There was some debate about where to bury Rasputin. Alexandra asked Voeikov where he thought best, and he told her that he had once heard Rasputin say he wished to be laid to rest in the church graveyard in Pokrovskoe. Protopopov, however, objected to the idea of sending the body back to Siberia, fearful that once word got out they might encounter violent demonstrations along the route. Alexandra said she wished him to be buried at Tsarskoe Selo so that his followers could be near him, to which Voeikov replied it might be difficult to keep the grave safe. In the end, Alexandra won out.[38] After further conversations with Vyrubova and Dehn, it was decided to bury Rasputin at Vyrubova's church under construction that lay just outside the Alexander Park at Tsarskoe Selo, the very church where Rasputin had participated in the laying of the cornerstone the previous month. It was argued, apparently by Vyrubova, that this would avoid the potential scandal of burying him on the grounds of the tsarist park itself.[39] Perhaps not surprisingly, no one bothered to ask the dead man's family what they thought about the matter.

A police van brought the coffin from the Chesmensky almshouse to the burial site shortly after 8 a.m. on the twenty-first. A shallow hole had been dug in the foundation and the coffin was put in place even before the burial party had arrived. Boards were laid on the ground so the mourners could approach the site through the frozen mud and debris.[40] It was a cold, gray morning. Two automobiles pulled up at the Alexander Palace to take the family the short drive through the park to the gravesite. They arrived around nine o'clock. It was a small gathering—Nicholas, Alexandra, the four grand duchesses, Vyrubova (aided by her medical orderly Akim Zhuk), Dehn, Laptinskaya, Colonel Vladimir Maltsev, commander of the Tsarskoe Selo air defenses, and one or two other persons. It seems the tsarevich did not attend due to ill health. Father Alexander Vasilev conducted the brief service. Alexandra was pale but composed, until she saw the coffin and then began to cry. She was carrying a bouquet of white flowers. She handed each daughter a flower, and then gave one to Vyrubova and Dehn, and they each gently tossed them into the grave. A few prayers were recited, and with that the service was over. By ten o'clock the family had returned to the palace.[41]

Gossipers were soon whispering that Nicholas and Alexandra's daughter Olga had refused to attend the funeral as a sign of her dislike of Rasputin. This was nothing but empty talk, although Olga did say to Valentina Chebotaryova on 5 February 1917: "Maybe he had to be killed, but not so violently. [. . .] It's shameful to admit it was our relatives."[42]

True to character, Nicholas did not let the service deter him from his routine. He went for a walk in the park, received reports from two of his ministers, and then went out for another stroll, this time accompanied by his daughters.[43] Late that afternoon they all gathered at Vyrubova's, where they were joined by Rasputin's daughters who had not been invited to their own father's funeral. Later, at 8 p.m. back at the palace, Sandro visited Nicholas and Alexandra.[44]

In the capital, rumors were swirling. Some claimed Rasputin's body had secretly been sent to Siberia, either Tobolsk or Pokrovskoe; others that he had been buried in the Fyodorovsky Cathedral at Tsarskoe Selo or somewhere nearby. It was being said that the guards at the Fyodorovsky Cathedral had refused to bury the body there, and the empress had them all arrested. There was also talk that they had had trouble finding any grave diggers willing to do the job and that Alexandra was supposedly wailing inconsolably over his grave. Alexandra, some insisted, had ordered medallions with Rasputin's portrait made and gave one to each of her children to wear. This rumor, it turned out later, was in fact true.[45]

Grand Duchess Olga wrote in her diary on 22 December: "Papa and Mama accept everything. Oh, God, how they try and how hard it is for them. Please help and bless them."[46] A confused Alexei asked his father: "Papa, surely you will give them a good punishing? The man who killed Stolypin was hanged for what he did!" Nicholas did not reply to his son.[47] To add to their pain—and fear—Protopopov handed Nicholas and Alexandra a letter his men had intercepted from Yusupov's mother to Grand Duchess Olga, the tsar's sister. In it Princess Yusupova expressed her regret that her son and the other perpetrators had not managed as they had planned "to get rid of everyone who ought to go," including Alexandra, who was to have been locked up in a convent.[48]

On one of the last days of the year an automobile was sent from the palace to fetch Rasputin's daughters. Maria and Varvara found the empress in her bedroom with Vyrubova. Nicholas and Alexandra spoke to the girls and expressed their support and protection and told them they were now to think of Nicholas as their father. He said he would never forsake them. Alexandra had Protopopov give the family 40,000 rubles.[49] They all gathered again for Christmas on Sunday the twenty-fifth at Vyrubova's. Rasputin's widow and son were also there this time. Two days later, they returned to Pokrovskoe.[50]

Among Alexandra's papers recovered after the revolution were these verses written in her own hand:

> Pursued by the wild and vulgar throng,
> By the greedy hounds, crawling around the Throne,
> His graying head has been forever laid low
> By a tool in the hands of an obscure Freemason.

Murdered. What's the use of lamentations,
Or sympathy, which are, obviously, insincere.
It's either laughter or curses over the corpse
Or a solitary, burning hot tear.

Why did he direct his righteous gaze
From the peaceful Siberian villages,
Where lowly sins have been branded
And the ultimate truth receives Pilate's verdict.

Where the trading of souls has long flourished,
Where the body is openly sold without shame
And the demon of envy flies like a spirit
And hymns to gold are sincerely sung.

He has departed to the faraway world forever
Forgiving his enemies, along the path of suffering,
A hero with a tranquil gaze during his brilliant life
And an upright, childlike, and naive soul.

May his soul find peace and heavenly paradise
And eternal memory and the kisses of angels,
For his honest and sincere earthly path,
And over his grave, the sobs of those he has left behind.[51]

It is not clear whether the empress composed these lines on the murder of Rasputin or merely copied someone else's work. Regardless, they capture both her grief and her understanding of the murder. In her eyes, Rasputin, a simple man of Godly righteousness, had been killed by lesser men envious of his gifts, and even if she did not think Freemasons had been directly responsible for his death, she would come to see the secret society as behind the revolution that swept the Romanovs from the throne. It is quite possible Alexandra, if only later once in captivity, understood the killing of their friend as an important mission in the Freemasons' broader campaign against the Christian monarchies of Europe.[52] Profoundly saddened though she was, Alexandra never succumbed to grief as Yusupov and his conspirators had assumed she would. She proved stronger than they had imagined, and so destroyed the logic at the heart of their conspiracy.

68. The Romanov Family Drama

The reaction of the extended Romanov family was mixed. For most, reports of the murder were met with glorious relief. The tsar's sister Xenia, then in Kiev, wrote in her diary on the twenty-first: "One thing can be said for certain. Thank God that he's been killed."[1] Maria, Grand Duke Dmitry's sister, was in Pskov at the time. She later recalled the joy in the streets, people embracing each other as if it were Easter. Prince Shakhovskoy arrived from Petrograd to bring her details of the killing "Rest assured the brave action of your brother arouses general admiration. The destruction of Rasputin is the greatest benefit to Russia." Maria admitted to feeling pride, but was hurt he had not confided in her. The people around her looked at Maria with "a sort of covert excitement and hidden admiration."[2] The Dowager Empress had thanked the Lord for removing Rasputin, but was deeply upset that members of the family had been involved in his murder.[3] Nicholas's sister Olga, on the other hand, wrote in her memoirs it was "a vile conspiracy. There was just nothing heroic about Rasputin's murder." She found it ironic that she had to agree with Trotsky of all people when he characterized the killing as something out of a movie for people of "bad taste."[4]

On the night of the seventeenth, Grand Duke Nikolai Mikhailovich went to the Imperial Yacht Club to learn what he could about Rasputin's disappearance. The club was crowded and abuzz with talk of nothing else. Prime Minister Trepov was insisting word of the murder was just "nonsense," another provocation by Protopopov. The grand duke spied Dmitry at another table, noticing he looked "as pale as death." They did not speak that evening, but the grand duke did overhear Dmitry say that Rasputin had either "disappeared or been killed." Soon after, Dmitry left the club for the Mikhailov Theater.[5]

Ella returned to Moscow on the evening of the seventeenth from Sarov, where she had gone to spend a week in prayer for Dmitry and

Felix, her "darlings," as she called them, on the eve of their plot. The next morning she sent two telegrams, the first to Felix's mother blessing the actions of her son and sending him and the entire family her prayers and then a second to Dmitry, asking that he send her a letter with all the details of "the patriotic deed."[6] Both telegrams were intercepted by the police, and Protopopov saw that they were delivered to the imperial palace. Later that month, Ella told Dmitry's sister on her way through Moscow how thrilled she was with Rasputin's murder and that Providence had deigned to select her brother and Felix.[7]

Maria left Pskov immediately for Petrograd. She found her brother holed up at his palace. In the days after the murder there was fear Rasputin's men would try to avenge the murder; suspicious characters had tried to talk their way into the palace, but had been kept out. Some were saying that Dmitry had in fact been killed. Plain-clothes police were stationed outside for his protection. The guards were Trepov's men, who feared Protopopov might send his own agents to harm Dmitry. It was a sad commentary on the state of the Russian government. "It's a good government when the prime minister takes actions against the minister of the interior," Grand Duke Andrei Vladimirovich noted in his diary.[8] Dmitry was tense; "his face was drawn, and he had black circles under his eyes," Maria noticed. Suddenly, overnight, "he was old." Standing by the fireplace, a chain-smoking Dmitry talked all night without stopping until the next morning. He avoided the details of that night, but swore that he personally had no blood on his hands and she believed him. He told Maria that he hoped they had not only rid Russia of a monster, but through their actions given an impetus to others to act and so put an end to the country's endless drift toward disaster. Despite such lofty sentiments, Maria sensed her brother already had misgivings about the killing.[9]

Dmitry was informed by Adjutant-General Maximovich that he was now under house arrest on the orders of the empress, even though the general had to admit that he lacked the authority to do this without the word of the emperor. Dmitry telegraphed Grand Duke Andrei Vladimirovich of the news, at the same time denying that he had played any part in Rasputin's disappearance.[10]

Felix, too, continued to lie about his involvement. After trying to leave the city on the night of the eighteenth but having been stopped by the police at the station, Yusupov moved in with Dmitry.[11] On the nineteenth, Andrei Vladimirovich and two other grand dukes went to see

Dmitry and Felix. They let them know they wanted the truth and said that regardless of their guilt, they stood behind them. Dmitry again insisted he was innocent. He had spent the night at Felix's with some ladies, leaving around 3 a.m., he told them. They were set upon by a dog in the yard, which he shot with his Browning, and then, leaving the ladies on Karavannaya Street, he went home around four o'clock in the morning. Not once during the entire evening, he assured them, did he see Rasputin. Yusupov corroborated Dmitry's story.[12] Whereas her brother anguished over what they had done, Maria noted Felix seemed intoxicated by it, particularly his role in the affair. He told her he could now foresee a "great political future" for himself.[13] Later, when Grand Duke Nikolai Mikhailovich arrived, he happily addressed the two young men as "Les messieurs assassins."[14]

Grand Duke Paul had asked his son soon after the murder whether he could swear on the name of his dead mother that he had no blood on his hands. Dmitry swore. Paul was not entirely certain what to make of the entire business, but he was certain he could blame Yusupov for dragging his son into it and that whatever had happened it would only push Alexandra further toward reaction.[15] After speaking with Dmitry, Paul went to see Nicholas at 11 p.m. on the nineteenth. He asked under what authority Alexandra had ordered Maximovich to arrest Dmitry, and Nicholas said it had been his order, but he knew that the tsar was just covering for her. He asked Nicholas to free his son, but was told he could not give him an answer now. Nicholas replied by letter the next morning, saying he could not free Dmitry while the preliminary investigation was under way. "I pray to God," the tsar added, "that Dmitry will emerge clean from this affair, into which he was drawn by his own hot temper."[16]

Early on the evening of the twenty-first members of the Romanov family met at the home of Grand Duke Andrei Mikhailovich to discuss what to do, particularly in regard to Dmitry. Paul told those gathered that his son had sworn "both on an icon and on the portrait of his mother, that he had not sullied his hands with the blood of that man." They decided that if Dmitry were not freed, Paul would go to see Nicholas and tell him that holding Dmitry would only make a hero of him. Given the nation's rejoicing at Rasputin's death, to persecute Dmitry was to elevate him to the rank of a national liberator behind whom everyone, including the army, would be ready to rally against the throne.[17]

In the end Sandro, not Paul, went to see Nicholas on the twenty-second. He tried to persuade Nicholas to drop the investigation and release Dmitry and Yusupov for the above reasons. "The whole affair should be wound up and nobody touched," he told the tsar. It is possible Sandro was chosen for this mission since he was one of the few in the family who saw the murder as wrong, if not morally then at least tactically, for it threatened to turn Rasputin into a martyr and was unlikely to break Alexandra's will. Sandro recalled that he asked Nicholas to pick up the telephone and order the investigation stopped immediately, but Nicholas refused, saying this was impossible and hinting he would not know how to handle Alexandra if he did.[18]

> I begged him not to treat Dmitri and Felix as common murderers but as misguided patriots inspired by a desire to help their country.
> "A very nice speech, Sandro," Nicholas said after a silence. "Are you aware, however, that nobody has the right to kill, be it a grand duke or a peasant?"

Nevertheless, the tsar promised to be "moderate." After he left, Sandro wired the Dowager Empress and asked her to plead with Nicholas to stop the investigation, which she did.[19] Sandro never forgave Yusupov: "I wished then and I do now that Felix would some day repent and realize that no decorous explanations and no acclaim of the masses could justify a murder in the eyes of a true Christian."[20]

Like Sandro, Grand Duke Andrei Vladimirovich wanted the investigation stopped. He was convinced Protopopov was pushing it to curry favor with Alexandra. Trepov, on the other hand, opposed Protopopov and sided with the grand dukes. If they dared put Dmitry on trial Andrei Vladimirovich predicted an "open revolt." He saw no reason for such concern over the life of a mere peasant. "War, the enemy threatens, and we're busy with this nonsense. It's most shameful to make all this noise over the murder of some dirty scoundrel. Shame on all of Russia."[21]

Although Sandro had failed in his mission with Nicholas, pressure was being applied from others in positions of authority. A battle was being waged between factions within the ministries of the interior and justice over how far the investigation should go. On 19 December, Alexei Vasilev, chief of the police department, ordered General Popov to end his investigation, which Popov did, sending the materials he had managed to collect back to Vasilev on the twenty-third. But Popov appeared to be deceiving Vasilev, for days later he was back on the trail and questioning more persons of interest in the case.[22] Popov was Protopopov's man, and so he most likely appeared only to play along with Vasilev, while continuing to follow the directives of the minister of the interior. Investigator Sereda saw his efforts blocked by Trepov at every turn. Sereda then fell ill and left for the spa town of Kislovodsk in the northern Caucasus. With this, his efforts to unravel the murder came to an end.[23]

Dmitry spent the twenty-third at home with his sister Maria, Felix, Grand Duke Nikolai Mikhailovich, Sandro, and his sons Andrei and Fyodor. As they sat quietly drinking tea and discussing matters, Sandro insisted that the investigation was sure to be closed and that Nicholas was likely to allow Dmitry to go join his father. Then the telephone rang. It was General Maximovich saying he had an order from the tsar that Dmitry was to appear before him immediately. Dmitry hurried to the general's where he learned his fate: Nicholas had ordered Dmitry to leave the city immediately and report to General Nikolai Baratov in Persia on the Caucasian Front. A special train was being made ready for the grand duke. Returning home, Dmitry told everyone the news. Some burst into tears, others became outraged at the tsar's decision. Around midnight, Governor-General Balk arrived to inform Dmitry the special train would be departing from the Nikolaevsky Station at 2 a.m. He told Dmitry no one was to know about this in order to avoid provoking any unrest. The general spoke softly and with difficulty. It appeared to Dmitry his assignment had not been an easy one. Dmitry and Felix retreated from the others for one final conversation. A year later, Dmitry wrote in his diary:

> We talked about whether I ought to submit to the emperor's order or stay in the capital and we two go to the regiments' barracks and organize a palace coup. And often after that—and even now—I ask myself, would it not have been better to have done that? Perhaps then there would have been no revolution.—Who knows, but of course I could not make such a decision, for I had only participated in the murder in order to give poor Niki one last chance—so that he could change political course. So that he could openly take on the friends of the dead Rasputin. From this it clearly follows that I took part in this affair out of my desire to help the Emperor, out of my loyalty to him, and not for the sake of my own

popularity. But many were then of the opinion that I was a candidate for the throne, they said that the Rasputin affair was a trampoline or spring that would put me on the throne.

The entire household was in tears when Dmitry left for the station. Waiting there in the bitter cold were Nikolai Mikhailovich, Sandro, and his two sons. Maria, who rode to the station with her brother, wept terribly, as did Nikolai. As Dmitry boarded the train, the grand duke shouted in an agitated voice: "God grant you a quick and triumphant return!"[24] Accompanying Dmitry were Count Konstantin Kutaisov and General Georgy Mikhailovich Laiming, Dmitry's much beloved tutor and former guardian. Kutaisov, an officer and former ADC to the tsar, was distraught over the order he had been given. He so much as told Dmitry he was on his side and felt deeply ashamed at having to act as his guard. He broke down and cried nearly the entire trip. At one point he nearly tried to kill himself, such was the shame he felt the tsar had forced upon him.[25]

Back in Petrograd, Dmitry's family worried. There was talk a group of Rasputin's supporters had followed Dmitry in the hope of killing him along the way; it was rumored the men had been caught.[26] The regime was worried too, namely that if news got out about who was on the train it would serve to rally opponents of the throne. Dmitry was forced to stay out of sight the entire way; the train was purposely routed around Moscow, the center of so much anti-Rasputin and anti-Romanov feeling. For Dmitry, the trip was excruciating. He could not stop crying and suffered a total emotional collapse. General Laiming did what he could to comfort him and the count.[27] The three men reached General Baratov on 31 December. The general was ecstatic to welcome "the hero of all Russia," as he called Dmitry in his diary, to his headquarters. By now, it seems Dmitry's mood had changed. Baratov was taken by his modesty and charm and sincerity. Dmitry confided in the general that he was proud of his act, a fact that was obvious to Baratov, adding that the revolver he carried with him was "historic," although "my hands are not stained by blood."[28] Perhaps, then, it had been his weapon that fired the fatal shot, even if Dmitry had not been the one to pull the trigger. Dmitry and his companions were treated to a large banquet during which the grand duke practically drowned himself in vodka.

After returning from the station, Grand Duke Nikolai Mikhailovich wrote in his diary:

I still cannot make sense of young people's psyche. They are without a doubt neuropaths, some sort of aesthetes, and everything they've done, which though it has cleared the air, amounts to nothing but half-measures, because one must most definitely put an end to Alexandra Fyodorovna and Protopopov. Just look, once again I'm entertaining murderous schemes, not fully defined, but logically necessary, for otherwise things will only get worse than they have been. My mind is spinning, while Countess N. A. Bobrinskaya, Misha Shakhovskoy frighten me, try to arouse me, beg me to act, but how, with whom—for one can do nothing on one's own. One could still come to an understanding with Protopopov, but how is Alexandra Fyodorovna to be rendered harmless? It's an almost impossible task. In the meanwhile, time moves forward, and with their departure, and Purishkevich's too, I don't see or know anyone to carry this out. Nonetheless, I truly am not an aesthetc by nature and a murderer much less, so I ought to break free out into some clean air. The best would be to go hunting in the woods, for here, living in this state of agitation, I am apt to do and say something stupid.[29]

It is a stunning letter that shows how wide the chasm had become between the tsar and the ruling elite. Nikolai Mikhailovich, a Romanov grand duke and first cousin to Alexander III, was beset by persistent thoughts of murdering the empress of Russia and was being goaded into action by Countess Nadezhda Bobrinskaya, wife of Count Alexei Bobrinsky, minister of agriculture, member of the Imperial Council, and marshal of the Petersburg nobility.

Maria, Dmitry's sister, recalled spending a miserable Christmas day after her brother's departure. She was at the palace of her father, Grand Duke Paul, and her stepmother, Princess Olga Paley (née Karnovich), in Tsarskoe Selo. They, together with the princess's son, Prince Vladimir Paley, now belonged not just to the anti-Rasputinists, but were related to one of his murderers. Also there were Princess Paley's children from her first marriage (to Erik Pistolkors): Marianna Derfelden and her brother Alexander Pistolkors, the brother-in-law of Anna Vyrubova. To complicate the scene even more, also joining them around the holiday table were Princess Paley's older sister, Lyubov Golovina, and her daughter, Munya. Some in the party were in tears over Dmitry's exile, others over the violent death of their beloved spiritual father at

Dmitry's hands. The mood was tense and gloomy. Princess Paley tried to keep the conversation going, being sure to stay as far away as possible from the elephant in the center of the room, but no one would play along. The tension finally became too much for the grand duke and he quietly got up and left to go light the Christmas tree.[30]

Members of the Romanov family gathered at the elder Maria Pavlovna's ("Aunt Michen," the mother of Grand Duke Andrei Vladimirovich) on the twenty-ninth to discuss Dmitry's situation. All of them deemed his punishment unacceptable. They decided to write a collective letter to Nicholas imploring him to rescind his order and to allow Dmitry to return to one of his estates in Russia, insisting that to send him to Persia would mean his "certain death." The letter was signed by sixteen members of the family. Two days later Nicholas sent it back, with his reply scrawled angrily across the top: "No one has been given the right to practice murder, and I know that many are troubled by their conscience, for Dmitry Pavlovich is not the only one involved in this. I'm surprised by your appeal to me."[31]

His answer shocked the family. In fact, however, with his firmness Nicholas saved Dmitry's life. Had he permitted Dmitry to return to Russia, he most likely would have been murdered by the Bolsheviks, as was the fate of so many in the family.

It was rumored at the time that when Nicholas refused to execute Rasputin's killers as Alexandra had demanded, she slapped him across the face.[32] One wonders what his son thought when the tsar failed to hang the murderers as Alexei had hoped he would. But no one was hanged, and the punishments, such as they were, were shockingly mild. Felix was exiled to his estate of Rakitnoe near Kursk. Neither Purishkevich, nor Lazovert, nor Sukhotin were punished at all. The only other person to be affected was Grand Duke Nikolai Mikhailovich, banished by Nicholas for two months to his estate of Grushevka. And this for a man who had made no secret of his fantasies of murdering Nicholas's wife.[33] After learning of his exile on the last day of 1916, an angry grand duke wrote in his diary: "Alexandra Fyodorovna is victorious, but will that scum hold power for long?! And what sort of man is he, he disgusts me, yet still I love him, for he does not have a bad soul [. . .]."[34]

The grand duke might have been outraged at how he and the others had been treated, but the fact was no one was ever found guilty and no one was ever punished. Rasputin's killers had gotten away with murder.

The lesson was easy for every Russian to draw: the state did not dare touch the perpetrators.

Felix and Irina enjoyed their exile at Rakitnoe. On 13 February 1917, Sandro came to visit and found them both "buoyant."[35] Protopopov had placed the estate under surveillance, and the reports coming in from his agents suggested that life at Rakitnoe was relaxed and carefree. In the middle of January a group of sixty aristocrats, including two grand dukes, arrived for several days of hunting. Their visit was an obvious signal of support for Felix and a rebuke to the throne. The Yusupovs were living in their usual splendor, and Felix had organized a special group of ten bodyguards dressed in the uniform of the Terek Cossacks with orders not to allow anyone within several miles of his house.[36] It is not entirely clear who he was protecting himself from. Most Russians viewed him as a hero. In early January he received a letter signed by the "Vox populi" promising that should the tsar dare to lay a hand on Rasputin's murderers, all of Russia would rise up and kill him.[37]

When not listening to the gramophone or entertaining guests, Felix continued with his conspiratorial plans. From Rakitnoe he wrote to Grand Duke Nikolai Mikhailovich that since the murder of Rasputin had not caused Alexandra to break down as he had hoped, another plan was necessary. He suggested that as soon as the emperor left for Stavka in late February, the Dowager Empress, and others close to her, should go to the capital and together with Generals Alexeev and Gurko demand that Protopopov, Shcheglovitov, and Vyrubova be arrested, and that the empress be sent away to Livadia. If it were not already too late, this, he insisted, was their only hope.[38]

69. Orgies, Gay Love, and the Secret Hand of the British

From the beginning, rumors swirled about what had really happened at the Yusupov palace. There was talk that after he arrived, Rasputin had been presented with a pistol and told to kill himself. Others said he had been given a choice: either drink poisoned wine or put a bullet in his own head. Yet he had resisted, and some said Rasputin even tried to use the gun against his killers, but they fired back, shooting him dead. For some time no one was sure who had been there that night and who had fired the fatal shot, but gossips mentioned, along with Yusupov, Purishkevich, and Dmitry, the tsar's brother Mikhail, Dmitry's half-brother Prince Vladimir Paley, and a number of grand dukes.[1] It was even reported the holy fool Mitya Kozelsky had been there that night. (He supposedly told the press his uncle was a cook at the Yusupovs'.)[2]

Minister of Foreign Affairs Nikolai Pokrovsky told Ambassador Paléologue in private that Rasputin had been murdered at Yusupov's during "an orgy," a rumor repeated by Samuel Hoare in a cable back to London.[3] Had there been an orgy, women would have been at the palace as well, but whether or not this was the case remains unclear. Irina, the honey used to lure Rasputin, most definitely was not there, for it is known for certain she was still in the Crimea. *Russian Morning* stated soon after the murder that several women had been at Yusupov's that night, including the adventuress Princess Catherine Radziwill, Countess Olga Kroits, a Madame von Drenteln, and the ballerina Karalli.[4]

The police looked into the ballerina's connection to the murder. A twenty-seven-year-old dancer with the Moscow Imperial Ballet, Vera Karalli had arrived in Petrograd from Moscow on 12 December, along with her servant Veronika Kukhto, and checked into the Hotel Medved. They apparently left the city on the 7:20 p.m. train to Moscow on the seventeenth, although according to another police report they remained in the capital until the nineteenth. She had been visited at the hotel during her stay by Grand Duke Dmitry, but Karalli assured the police she had spent every evening in her room.[5] General Pyotr Popov examined the evidence on Karalli and determined there was nothing linking her to the murder.[6] It would appear, however, that Popov had not done a thorough job, for Karalli visited Dmitry at his palace on the eighteenth, a little-known fact he admitted to in his diary.[7] His words imply a deep attraction to Karalli; they may well have been lovers. His diary, nonetheless, is mute as to whether she had been at Yusupov's the night of the murder.

As for the other women mentioned by the press, it appears none of them was ever questioned by the police. They did, however, interview one other woman, Marianna Derfelden, whom the Okhrana had been secretly following (code name "Thespian") since the beginning of December.[8] Grand Duke Dmitry's stepsister, and, some said, one of his lovers, Marianna told her friends she learned of the murder from the *Stock Exchange Gazette*, just like everyone else, and denied she had had anything to do with it.[9] But the police had their suspicions. General Popov and ten police officers searched her apartment on the night of the twenty-fifth, during which her correspondence was taken and handed over to the director of the police department. Derfelden was questioned, but insisted all she knew about the matter was what she had read in the newspapers, just as she had told her friends.[10] The police perused her correspondence, trying to find any clues linking her to the plot. They also placed her under house arrest. Two officers were left in the apartment to take down the name of everyone who telephoned her. She was instantly flooded with visitors, including Dmitry's sister Maria and deputies from the Duma she did not even know, since her arrest had made her into a hero. On the twenty-sixth, Protopopov summoned her to his office for questioning. "Unfortunately, I did not take part," she told the minister of the interior, "and I am deeply sorry about that. I simply don't understand why such a great fuss is being made of the murder of this peasant. Really now, if I were to kill the chief custodian in my building no one would pay the least bit of attention." Protopopov replied that she was young and ought to be more careful about what she said. (In Marianna's account of their meeting, Protopopov had fallen in love with her and was not shy about it. Marianna was, in truth, young, beautiful, and elegant, if horribly snobbish and callous toward the lives of those socially beneath her.)

In the end, Protopopov had no evidence linking Marianna to the murder and she was released. The minister may have wanted to put more pressure on her to see if she might reveal more, but the empress let him know she was against this. Alexandra had met with Marianna's brother, Alexander Pistolkors, and he had assured her that Marianna had had nothing to do with Rasputin's death. Alexandra sent him straightaway to Protopopov and telephoned the minister to receive him and listen to what he had to say. Protopopov realized what he was meant to infer, and so let Marianna go after meeting her brother.[11] This might also explain why Countess Olga Kroits was not questioned. Olga, the beautiful estranged wife of Count Alexander Kroits, happened to be Marianna and Alexander's sister. Protopopov most likely realized the empress did not wish any of the three Pistolkors siblings implicated in the murder.[12]

Even if there had been no orgy, could there have been another sexual dimension to that night's events? A few months after the murder, Grand Duke Nikolai Mikhailovich tried to make sense of why Rasputin, fearful of being killed, would have allowed himself to be taken to the Yusupov palace. The grand duke could conceive of only one explanation: Rasputin had been in love with Felix, and it was his passion that led him to his death. Nikolai was convinced that the time the two men had alone in the cellar was spent not just drinking and talking; the two men exchanged caresses and kisses and possibly more. He could not be certain of this, however, since Rasputin had taken the truth of their relationship with him to the grave.[13] The murder as sexual psychodrama has been repeated, in various forms, by others.[14] But there is a simple problem with such theories. Among the sea of lies spread about Rasputin during his lifetime, not once was he accused of having homosexual affairs. His sex life was legendary, but not that legendary. No, Rasputin was decidedly heterosexual and harbored no secret lust for Felix. It was his wife he hoped to meet that night; she was the bait, not her husband.

There is also this revealing bit of testimony Yusupov offered to the police on 18 December, in which he admitted that he had told Rasputin in November that he sought out Rasputin's help for his "unnatural" tendencies. He initially told Rasputin he was suffering from chest pain, but curiously at one of their last meetings, Rasputin said to Yusupov: "We'll fix you for good. We just need to visit the Gypsies, and there you'll see some pretty women, and your illness will disappear forever."[15] Was this an admission his ill-health sprang from his attraction to men? Or simply impotence? Regardless, it is clear Rasputin was not steering

Yusupov toward a physical relationship with him, but was trying some sort of "conversion therapy" to cure him of his attraction to men.

The sexcapades have grown in scope and complexity over time. It has been alleged that Dmitry, Karalli, and Derfelden were lovers (which is quite possible), or that Felix and Grand Duke Nikolai Mikhailovich were lovers, or Felix and Dmitry, or Felix, Dmitry, and Sukhotin (which is not at all likely). The theory has been proposed that Rasputin was killed because he had discovered the truth about Felix and Dmitry's relationship and informed the tsar.[16] The bruises on Rasputin's dead body, it has been suggested, were the result of Yusupov's blows from the club Maklakov gave him, a furious response by Yusupov to Rasputin's unwanted advances. The opposite has been suggested as well, namely that Yusupov beat Rasputin savagely for refusing him. And then there is the business of Rasputin's member, supposedly cut off by Yusupov and then gathered up and saved by one of Yusupov's servants, a secret follower of the starets. Sometime later, according to this bizarre tale, the severed penis ended up in Paris where a few of his surviving votaries kept it preserved in an icebox, taking it out only for their strange sacred rites. From there, after further adventures, it made its way into the collection of Russia's first museum of erotica in Petersburg, a hideous hunk of graying flesh suspended in a jar of formaldehyde.[17]

Even if he had not been Yusupov's lover, Grand Duke Nikolai Mikhailovich, according to some, was the mastermind behind the murder. As his diary proves, the grand duke did harbor thoughts of murdering Rasputin (as well as the empress), but then such fantasies were common. The diary also proves that he did not have the stomach for murder. The grand duke's latest biographer finds the idea that he had been involved in the plot absurd. Nikolai Mikhailovich craved attention and it is unimaginable that had he had anything to do with the murder he would have been able to keep it a secret.[18] Procurator Zavadsky said the same thing, noting that the grand duke was known for shooting his mouth off and there was no way he would have kept quiet. Zavadsky in fact met Grand Duke Nikolai Mikhailovich soon after the murder and became quickly convinced that he knew little about the affair.[19] The diary of Grand Duke Dmitry, in which he describes Nikolai as a "tragi-comic figure," also makes clear the grand duke had had nothing to do with it.[20]

*

And then there is the matter of the English. Almost immediately after the killing, rumor began to spread that Rasputin had been murdered by an agent of the British Intelligence Mission. Such talk was common among Russians as well as their enemies. German agents in Stockholm cabled to Berlin that they had it on good authority that among the men in Yusupov's home that night was "a young Englishman." Another secret communication sent to the king of Bulgaria placed this same Englishman in the automobile that drove off with the body.[21] The reports seem compelling, except when placed in the context of the entire universe of rumors at the time. In this light, they read like just one more unsubstantiated bit of gossip. Such reports are highly unreliable. Nonetheless, stories of mysterious Englishmen gained traction and began to appear in the Russian and foreign press. The Swedish newspaper *Aftonbladet* stated in early 1917 that England "was monitoring and controlling everything" in Russia. As proof, it noted that one of the plotters in the Rasputin murder had been an Englishman. The unnamed man had purportedly been involved from the beginning and had been at the palace to make certain everything was done "thoroughly and smoothly." He even helped dump the body in the river.[22]

It makes sense that the Germans and Bulgarians would want to place an Englishman at the murder scene, for they, and a good many Russians, were convinced that Rasputin had been killed given his desire to make a separate peace with the Central Powers. The English, desperate to keep Russia in the war, had the perfect motive. As early as August of that year, a former official of the Russian ministry of foreign affairs who had served in Persia, where he had observed what he considered the perfidious machinations of the British, told Alexandra that Sir George Buchanan and the English were preparing to kill Rasputin. The empress brushed off his words as baseless.[23] Others have also implicated Buchanan, most notably Spiridovich who thought he and officials at the British embassy were decisive in convincing Yusupov to act.[24]

The communiqués from Buchanan in the British National Archives show that the ambassador had heard of a plot not long before the murder. He commented in a secret cable on 18 December that "I was told about a week ago by a friend who is in close touch with some of the younger Grand Dukes that a number of young officers had sworn to kill him before the end of the year."[25] Was this the same group who did kill Rasputin or some other gang? This is the only evidence to show Buchanan had prior knowledge of the murder, and there is nothing in the archives to suggest that he had anything to do with any plot.

Regardless, some in Russia wanted to blame the English for Rasputin's death. On 20 December, an article appeared in *Russian Word* titled "The Story of the English Detectives." The author, a certain "Romanov," wrote that Rasputin had hired several agents from Scotland Yard to work alongside the Okhrana for his protection shortly before his death. What he did not know, however, was that these imported agents had been bought off by Yusupov and so stood by outside the palace while he was being murdered. The English in Petrograd responded to the story immediately. The Anglo-Russian Commission contacted the newspaper and the story's author to request the sources for his article. Romanov replied that "some of the people mixed up in this affair had given English names and the matter would be enquired into." As for the commission, it stated that "As the matter now stands, Sir George Buchanan has directed that unless the story is denied by Romanoff within the next few days we are to deny it officially."[26] The same day the article appeared, Samuel Hoare sent a cable to Mansfield Cumming, head of MI1(c), the branch of the Secret Service responsible for counter-espionage and intelligence gathering outside the British Empire (it would later become known as the Secret Intelligence Service [MI6]), informing him of the matter and asking whether the story was true and if so, what were the names of the agents.[27] No list of any Scotland Yard agents operating in Russia was forthcoming, however, for there had never been any.

Hoare later came to the realization that in the days after the murder, Russian "rightists" had been trying to frame the British for the crime, and him in particular. The rumor of his role as the killer, he wrote, spread so far and so quickly that Ambassador Buchanan had to have an audience with Nicholas to address it.[28] Buchanan did speak to the tsar about the matter at Tsarskoe Selo on 1 January 1917. He wrote about it that day in a secret telegram:

> At to-day's New Year's reception the Emperor spoke to me in his most gracious and friendly manner. As reports have spread, evidently by German agents, that not only had English detectives been conducting an enquiry into Rasputin's murder, but that English officers had been associated in it, I told His Majesty that as I should be deeply grieved were either he or the Empress to believe such an

infamous story, I wished to give him the most formal assurance that there was not a word of truth in it.

Nicholas was quite specific with the ambassador that day, mentioning by name the British agent he had been hearing talk about. It was not Hoare, however, but one Oswald Rayner. Buchanan offered this explanation to the emperor. As to the story's origins, he wrote, it likely had to do with the fact that Rayner, "who was temporarily employed here," had been at Oxford with Yusupov and they had seen a great deal of each other in Petrograd. "Rayner," he continued, "positively assures me that the Prince had never said a word to him about the plot, and I need hardly tell His Majesty that assassination was a crime held in abomination by British people. The Emperor, who evidently heard something about Rayner, said that he was very glad that I had told him, and expressed his warmest thanks."[29] Buchanan believed he had settled the matter with the emperor, but months later Nicholas still had his doubts about Buchanan and the British stationed in Russia.[30]

A draper's son born into modest circumstances in 1888, Oswald Rayner was unusually intelligent, with a rare knack for languages. He entered Oxford University in 1907, and two years later met and became close friends with another young student there, Prince Felix Yusupov. The two men never forgot each other, and when, in November 1915, now Lieutenant Rayner arrived in Petrograd to serve in the British Intelligence Mission he looked up his old university friend. The men became quite close over the course of the next year. They saw each other often in the autumn of 1916.[31] A letter from Rayner to Yusupov has survived in the Russian archives. Dated 9/22 November 1916, Rayner wrote to Yusupov, who was then away from the capital, to tell him that he had moved to a new apartment (14 Moika, apartment 56) and asked Yusupov to be certain to telephone him as soon as he returned to Petrograd for he wished to see him once more before leaving for England.[32] It appears that by then Rayner was no longer serving in the British Intelligence Mission in Petrograd. Buchanan's words to the emperor on New Year's Day imply this, and a list of the active agents of the mission dated 24 December 1916 (NS) does not include his name.[33]

Yusupov told Rayner of the conspiracy. In his memoirs Yusupov records that Rayner came to see him at Sandro's palace on the night of the seventeenth to learn how things had gone. "He knew of our conspiracy and had come in search of news. I hastened to set his mind at ease."[34] Yusupov, in other words, had talked to the British about their plans, but then so too had Purishkevich at his meeting with Samuel Hoare in early December. British agents knew all about the plot to kill Rasputin, but does this mean they came up with the idea, planned it, or helped carry it out? For this there is no incontrovertible proof. But there is one intriguing letter dated 25 December 1916/7 January 1917 sent from Captain Stephen Alley, then with the British Military Control Department in Petrograd, to Captain John Scale, an officer with the British Intelligence Mission there, away from Russia at the time on a secret mission to Romania:

> Dear Scale,
>   [. . .]
>   Although matters here have not proceeded entirely to plan, our objective has clearly been achieved. Reaction to the demise of "Dark Forces" has been well received, although a few awkward questions have already been asked about wider involvement.
>   Rayner is attending to loose ends and will no doubt brief you on your return.[35]

If the letter is authentic (and this is far from certain)[36] it would offer the best proof of British involvement in Rasputin's murder. Involvement, yes, but of what sort and to what extent is not clear. Since Hoare and Rayner, and presumably the rest of the mission, knew of the plot, and most likely would have endorsed it, it does seem likely they would have offered advice on how to kill Rasputin, but this does not mean they set it in motion or were there at Yusupov's the night he was killed.

Even though there is no convincing evidence that places any British agents at the murder scene, this has not stopped those who continue to insist Rasputin was killed by the English, and by Rayner in particular.[37] The latest attempt to make the case has centered on the gun that delivered the fatal shot to Rasputin's head. Neither Kosorotov who conducted the autopsy, nor the chief prosecutor of Petrograd at the time, nor the case investigator at the autopsy, nor Dr. Vladimir Zharov, a Russian forensic expert who in 1993 reexamined the surviving evidence, could say with any accuracy the caliber or make of gun that had been used in the murder.[38] Yet two recent studies of the evidence claim to have come to a startling conclusion. Based on the (supposedly) distinctive markings around the bullet wound on Rasputin's head as shown in the autopsy photographs, Rasputin must have been shot by a .455 caliber

Webley revolver. Manufactured by Webley and Scott in the London borough of Enfield, the .455 Webley was the standard-issue sidearm for all British troops during the First World War (the Russians used the Nagant revolver), and so, it must follow, it had been an Englishman who killed Rasputin.[39]

The theory suffers from a number of problems, however. First, the photographic evidence is grainy and does not convincingly show the type of markings left by a .455 Webley. Second, a number of different makes and calibers of guns have been referred to by the killers. To cite but one example, Lazovert told a reporter from the New York Times in September 1918 that Purishkevich had fired the two fatal shots into Rasputin while in the yard outside the palace using "an automatic American-made revolver."[40] Third, and most importantly, not only Englishmen carried Webleys during the war. Among the voluminous police files on Rasputin in the State Archive of the Russian Federation is a receipt, dated 27 January 1916, issued to a Lieutenant-Colonel Polyakov for a Webley-Scott revolver, serial number 26313.[41] Perhaps it was the barrel of a .455 Webley that Rasputin was staring down in the final seconds of his life, but only he, and his killers, could say who had his finger on the trigger.

The archives of the British intelligence service (MI6) do not hold a single document linking Rayner, Hoare, or any other British agent or diplomat to the murder.[42] This has not stopped some Englishmen from asserting they played a part. In 1934, Commander Oliver Locker-Lampson, a British MP who had served for a time in Russia during the war, told the press that Purishkevich had asked him to kill Rasputin. His claim was laughed off. The commander, the Church Times noted, "has a genius for getting into the news."[43]

The amateurish and bungling manner in which the crime was plotted and carried out also speaks against the involvement of professional intelligence operatives. It is hard to imagine that had British agents been running the show things would have been conducted with such utter incompetence from beginning to end. Procurator Sereda told Grand Duke Andrei Vladimirovich in Kislovodsk in early 1917 that "he had seen many crimes, both intelligent and stupid, but such incompetent action on the part of the perpetrators as in this instance he had never seen in his entire career."[44] But this did not matter to a country that had come to see its ally in a critical light. Many Russians, tiring of the war, shared the opinion expressed in the diary of a regimental doctor named

Vasily Kravkov that "the English, having grabbed us by the neck, are forcing us to fight the war until the very end."[45] It was widely held that the British were dictating to the Russians and exerting pressure on the tsar to stay in the war, no matter the cost.

The situation recalled the atmosphere surrounding another momentous political murder from Russia's past. In March 1801, Emperor Paul I, the son of Catherine the Great, was strangled in his bedroom by a clique of aristocrats and officers of the imperial guards. Paul had recently broken Russia's alliance with Britain in favor of Napoleon's France. He turned on his former ally with a plan to challenge British supremacy on the seas and began seizing their ships in Russian waters and imprisoning their sailors. The emperor even ordered Russian forces to attack the British in India. The British fought back. Just days before Paul's murder, a British fleet sailed into the Baltic Sea heading for St. Petersburg. Only after learning of the regicide, and the new emperor Alexander's pledge of renewed friendship, did the ships turn around. Napoleon, and many Russians at the time, was certain the British government was responsible for Paul's murder. There was talk in Petersburg that Charles Whitworth, Britain's ambassador to Russia, had had a hand in the affair. But all of this was mere gossip, and any British involvement in the murder of the tsar was a mirage.[46] It is an important fact to remember when considering the case of Rasputin. Indeed, the (supposed) historical parallels were noticed at the time. There was talk in Russia that Yusupov and the others had had nothing at all to do with the murder. Rather, they had been cunningly framed by English agents, who had planned and carried out the murder for their own country's benefit, just as they had done a century earlier.[47]

In the end whether the fatal bullet was fired by Yusupov, Purishkevich, Dmitry, or even some British agent is beside the point, for what really killed Rasputin was the mass hysteria that had seized Russia by the end of 1916. Nearly every Russian had become delusional in his understanding of what had happened to his country, who was to blame, and how Russia could be saved. The Italian newspaper *La Stampa* accurately captured the mentality at the time: "For the entire Russian people Rasputin had become the symbol of an omnipotent and irresponsible government that had led Russia to ruin. The blind, mortal hatred of Rasputin seized the entire Russian people. [...] The symbol of inert power that had been blocking the road of the Russian people to renewal has at last left the stage."[48] To most people, Rasputin had to die for Russia to live. They would soon realize just how mistaken they had been.

70. The End of the Tobolsk Yoke

Russia received the news of Rasputin's murder with near universal rejoicing. Samuel Hoare noted on 19 December: "The feeling in Petrograd is most remarkable. All classes speak and act as if some great weight had been taken from their shoulders. Servants, *isvostchiks* [cab drivers], working men, all freely discuss the event. Many say that it is better than the greatest Russian victory in the field."[1]

No one could talk of anything else. It was the only story that mattered. Nadezhda Platonova, the wife of a noted historian, recorded with dismay in her diary on the twenty-second how even the cashier at her local Petrograd fish market was openly offering her opinion on the matter, even daring to denounce the tsar for his role in Rasputin's sordid career.[2] In Moscow, when the news was announced, the audience at the Imperial Theater demanded the production be stopped and the band play "God Save the Tsar" as they all rose and sang along.[3] The same thing happened in other cities across the empire.

The murderers were hailed as heroes. *The Times* of London reported that while at a party in the home of a wealthy banker Yusupov was received with an exultant ovation and then showered with flowers and carried about on the men's shoulders.[4] The All-Russian Zemstvo Union was reportedly setting up a fund in Yusupov's name to help wounded soldiers. Donations were said to be pouring in.[5] Felix was inundated by congratulatory letters from well-wishers across Russia.[6] A congress of three hundred medical doctors in Moscow voted to present Dmitry with a laurel wreath as a sign of the country's gratitude.[7] The English war correspondent Henry Hamilton Fyfe reported that future generations in Russia would erect a monument to the killers.[8]

There was no discernible talk of revenge. The Petrograd Okhrana did, however, arrest seven men with close ties to Rasputin on the nineteenth out of concern they might cause trouble. Among them were Pkhakadze, Prince Nestor Eristov, and the merchant Sergei Vitkun. Vitkun told the authorities that he was prepared to strangle the murderers himself and blamed Munya Golovina for having sold out Rasputin to his killers. There was talk among the men that Pkhakadze would not rest until he had exacted vengeance for the murder of Rasputin.[9] Such attitudes, however, were extremely rare.

To most, it was as if Russia had woken up from a long and terrible night into the bright sunlight of a new day filled with hope and possibility. The profound sense of optimism that seemed to emerge from the death of Rasputin was captured by *Russian Morning* on the twentieth:

> One wants to believe that this "dark" death of a dark man will not fail to leave traces for Russia, that the cleansing power of death will appear like never before, that this death will open, finally, the eyes of those who still insist on keeping them shut. [. . .] Let this dark blood, washing clean with the dead water of historic redemption, bring the country closer to radiant deeds. Let the dark forces of Russia atone with this blood their fatal sin before our beloved country.[10]

Russian Word declared that the death of Rasputin marked the end of the "Tobolsk Yoke"—a play on the "Mongol Yoke" of the Middle Ages. The epoch of Rasputin had so humiliated the country it had managed to unite all Russians into a single, undivided "society of citizens."[11] The life of Rasputin was, then, truly historic in that it had meant the birth of Russian citizenship. But there were voices in the press that dared to raise uncomfortable, and unpopular, questions.

The same *Russian Morning* that praised the murder also ran an article that asked what could be said about a country that rejoiced in death. This strange reaction signified "the true spirit of Russian history," a land in which "every joy of the narod demanded death and every step forward was taken on the backs of corpses." This was not an occasion for joy, but despair for the notion that life would be made better through murder; this was only a sign of just how retarded Russia's political and cultural life was. It was as if they were taking pride in reaching a point in their country's development that the rest of Europe had passed through back in the Dark Ages. People reacted to the news as if they had won the lottery. Luck, fate—this is what determined life in Russia, not the people themselves through their own hard work, initiative, and responsibility. No, they were no different than "Roman slaves," the newspaper regretfully admitted, hoping that the gods might take pity and smile down upon them. The murder of Rasputin will change nothing, for he was never the reason for Russia's problems, only one of the symptoms. The reason lay in Russia's eternal "darkness born of irresponsibility and political arbitrariness."

The newspaper *Day* made a similar point: "'Dark forces'—this became a pseudonym for Rasputin, but in reality among the dark forces Rasputin was an enormous nothing, and the dark forces have remained just as they were before. Rasputin gave us the chance not to notice them. That is why Russia is not exhaling more freely with the death of Rasputin and nothing will change. Only the breakdown will increase."[12] *Russian Liberty* likened the murder to cutting off the "head of the hydra:" Rasputin was gone, but the system that created him was not, and it would be certain to create another to take his place. Rasputin's murder meant nothing.[13]

Shulgin, writing in *Kievlyanin* on the twenty-third, opined that while the motives of these "voluntary executioners" were "pure," still they had set out on a "false path, which could well bring us many troubles." Later, he quite accurately likened the murder to the "secret violence" of the eighteenth and early nineteenth centuries, when small groups of rebellious courtiers unseated and killed tsars in ruthless fashion—Peter III in 1762 and Paul I in 1801 being the most notorious examples.[14]

Governor of Tobolsk Ordovsky-Tanaevsky was possibly the only tsarist official to openly denounce the killing. The governor had known Rasputin longer than most. As early as 1900, he had spent the night in the Rasputin home in Pokrovskoe. He knew the entire family well, and though not blind to Rasputin's vices, he was able to see him for the man he was, not the myth others took for the real thing. Before a large gathering in Tobolsk, Ordovsky-Tanaevsky got up and announced that "A peasant from our province, from the village of Pokrovskoe, Grigory Yefimovich Rasputin, has died a martyr's death. I say 'martyr's' since he was hunted down like a rabbit. [. . .] Dear Lord, forgive God's martyred slave Grigory all his intentional and unintentional transgressions, and forgive us our transgressions in connection with his name, for no one is without sin, this we pray with fervor, for he perished without penance."[15]

It says much about Russia in 1916 that many Russian Orthodox clergy not only approved of the murder, but actually blessed it. Sergei Bulgakov was on a pilgrimage to the Zosimov Monastery outside Moscow when the news arrived. Bulgakov was stunned to see how all the monks celebrated the news of Rasputin's murder.[16] Metropolitan

Yevlogy noted that he let out "a sigh of relief" upon reading about it in the papers. Even years later not a single twinge of sadness, regret, or the slightest misgiving clouded the soul of this leader of the Russian Orthodox Church. A fellow Russian Christian and a friend of the tsar, a man innocent of the crimes he was supposed to have committed, had been killed in cold blood, and still the only emotion the metropolitan felt was relief.[17]

Germogen claimed he heard Rasputin's loud voice behind him only minutes after hearing of his death: "What's there to rejoice in?" the familiar voice asked. "One shouldn't be rejoicing, one needs to be crying! Look what is coming toward you!" Germogen could not believe his ears. It was real, the voice had been real. He did not dare turn around. He crossed himself, frozen to the spot. Finally, he drew up courage and looked behind him: there was no one else in his cell. He opened his door, but the hallway too was empty.[18]

Pavel Zavarzin was reading the news along with his fellow travelers in the restaurant car of a train heading through central Russia when one man, a middle-aged Siberian merchant, broke the silence: "Thank God they've done away with that bastard." With that, everyone began to speak out at once. The passengers' opinions varied. "A dog's death for a dog," some muttered, while others saw something wrong in the affair. One man was heard to say a true nobleman does not invite a man into his home to kill him, another that the murder by men so close to the throne amounted to a knife in the back of the Russian sovereign. "It's a sign of collapse and inescapable revolution," said one bearded Siberian man in glasses.[19]

The fact that Rasputin's murderers were aristocrats was not lost on the common folk. A society lady in Petrograd overheard wounded soldiers in a military hospital complaining, "Yep, only one peasant managed to reach the tsar and so the masters killed him." It was a fairly common opinion among the masses and helped fuel the hatred of Russia's upper classes that was soon to erupt with white hot fury.[20] A peasant from Pokrovskoe told Sergei Markov while he was traveling through the village in early 1918 that the "Burschujs" had killed Rasputin since he had defended the interests of the poor folk before the tsar.[21]

And, of course, the murder was a painful blow to Rasputin's followers. The Golovins, it was said, were hysterical when they heard the news.[22] But it appears Lyubov Golovina came to terms with it fairly quickly. Beletsky wrote that he saw her early the next spring at Vyrubova's, where she told him that the fact of Rasputin's death proved to her that he had actually not been prophetic, for otherwise he would have spoken to them of this coming tragedy. Beletsky agreed. He had heard Rasputin himself say one Sunday evening in June 1916 at his Gorokhovaya apartment that he would be with his followers for another five years, after which he would leave them, his family, and the world behind and withdraw to live according to the ways of the ancient holy men.[23]

Yusupov and his fellow conspirators had hoped to free Nicholas from the influence of Rasputin and Alexandra and so save the monarchy. They not only failed to save the monarchy, but helped to hasten its demise. As Alexander Blok famously, and correctly, noted, the bullet that killed Rasputin "struck the very heart of the reigning dynasty."[24]

Though the bullet had already hit its target, still the authorities sought to maintain their vigilance. Indeed, the Moscow Okhrana noted with surprise at the end of December that far from diminishing the talk about Rasputin, his murder had in fact given a boost to it, and they had uncovered various efforts to publish damning material. It was becoming clear that the ultimate point of interest had been not Rasputin, but those circles under his influence, at which his enemies continued to take aim. Alexander Prugavin had been giving readings full of "sensational material" discrediting a number of the loftiest personages to groups around Moscow. Much of this material he had received from Iliodor's manuscript, portions of which Prugavin had already published in the *Russian Gazette*. He was also negotiating the rights to Iliodor's book with publishers in England, France, and Germany, and at the same time Sergei Melgunov was making plans to publish it in Russia. Alexander Kerensky, lawyer, Duma politician, and future head of the Provisional Government, was said to be preparing a work that would contain new and startling information on Rasputin. He had used the simplest language to assure it would reach the largest possible audience.

Vasily Maklakov was busy giving talks to groups in Moscow as well. He told audiences that Rasputin's evil influence had been much greater than anyone had realized. If this had once been known only in the major capitals, now it had penetrated all of Russia, even the humblest peasant huts of the most remote villages. Were the country's rulers to hear what was being said in these poor huts, Maklakov said, they would be horrified. It was too late to turn back. A revolution was under way in the minds and souls of the Russian people, the likes of which had never before been seen in history. The narod's centuries-old faith in the tsar, in the God-given nature of his authority, was collapsing. More than a revolution, Russia now stood face to face with utter catastrophe. "Russia," he wrote after learning of the murder, "has become a cupola without a cross."[25] Sandro had tried to open Nicholas's and Alexandra's eyes to this fact of revolution, telling them on Christmas day that they were living through the most dangerous moment in the history of Russia.[26] His words were dismissed as baseless paranoia.

George Buchanan had an audience with Nicholas at Tsarskoe Selo on 31 December. It was a terribly difficult meeting. The tsar acted aloof, and it was clear he did not want Buchanan to touch on uncomfortable subjects, but the ambassador felt he had no choice. He stressed the danger of the situation and "the necessity of his regaining the confidence of his people," to which Nicholas replied, "Do you mean that I am to regain my people's confidence, or that they are to regain mine?" Buchanan kept on. He tried to convey to Nicholas his fear of the danger hanging over the emperor and his family. Buchanan left Tsarskoe Selo with little hope. "It is impossible to say how this crisis will end," he observed, "but both the Emperor and Empress would seem possessed with madness and to be wantonly courting disaster."[27]

Once Buchanan had gone, Nicholas went for a walk and then attended a midnight church service. "I prayed fervently that God will have mercy on Russia!" he wrote in his diary.[28]

Part Seven

THE AFTERMATH

1917–1918

71. A Time for Dominoes

In early January 1917, Hellmuth Lucius von Stoedten, the German representative in Stockholm, met with a Swedish diplomat recently returned from Russia, where he had attended the New Year's Day reception at the palace. He told Lucius that the tsar's face was quite red and that there was talk he had been drinking heavily of late. No one spoke of anything but Rasputin's murder and everyone was in agreement that grand dukes from every branch of the family had been involved. It was also being said that an attempt had been made on the life of the empress, but the assassin had been caught before he could act and was immediately hanged, thus keeping it out of the public eye. More assassinations, however, were certain to follow. The next in line was Vyrubova, followed by Protopopov, Prince Andronikov, and General Voeikov.[1]

In late December, Vyrubova received a threatening letter:

> Finally, that vile creature, that villain Rasputin has been wiped from the face of the earth. Have no hope that his rotten body will bring you and Alexandra Fyodorovna any joy—you traitors, they'll get to you and her yet, and the Imperial Fyodorovsky cathedral will be blown to pieces so that the remains of that scoundrel, who mocked all Russia and Europe, do not sully the holy altar, under which you and that Hessian fool managed to bury him. Cry, howl along with that reigning hysteric, Russia's misfortune. We rejoice that the great sons of Russia have put an end to him at the right hour.[2]

Buchanan was sending dispatches with similar information about assassinations back to London. Even before the beginning of the year, he communicated that based on conversations he had had with Grand Duke Nikolai Mikhailovich more assassinations were certain to follow, beginning with Protopopov.[3] Prime Minister Trepov, he reported, was so frightened of being killed, he was considering resigning. There was talk of assassination of the empress as well.[4] On 3 January, he wrote that the general expectation in Petrograd was "that if the Emperor does not yield something will happen in the course of the next fortnight either in the shape of Palace Revolution or of attempted assassinations. The latter are believed to be the more probable and though all this talk may be exaggerated I have heard ex-Ministers and high officials discussing questions whether the Emperor will be killed as well as the Empress."[5]

Army doctor Vasily Kravkov noted in his diary in January how upon arriving from the front in Petrograd he was taken aback by the revolutionary atmosphere in the city. There was a great expectation of a palace coup and constant talk of political murder. He even heard talk that General Brusilov had tried to shoot the emperor.[6] In early February, the German foreign ministry received a cable from Copenhagen stating that a Guards officer with ties to Prince Yusupov purportedly shot at the emperor but missed. The fate of the officer was unknown.[7] A secret report on conditions in Russia was sent to Chief of the German General Staff Field Marshal Paul von Hindenburg on 24 January (NS) that detailed the revolutionary mood taking over the country. Ninety Guards officers had sworn to kill Protopopov and Vyrubova and then the emperor and empress. Hindenburg sent the document on to Kaiser Wilhelm, who wrote down his reaction at the bottom of the report:

> If the Tsar wants to survive, then he must hang the Grand Dukes, those murderers, including, quite naturally, Nikolai, and he must neutralize as quickly as possible Lady Buchanan—that female Satan—or else he is utterly lost and England will do away with him like Tsar Paul, Pollio, Jaurès, Casement, Witte, Rasputin! Whoever means well by him must tell him that straight to his face.[8]

The German government received information in January that suggested the Russian government did have at least one plan: namely, for the dynasty to try to divert the hatred against it by shifting anger onto the Jews and inciting anti-Jewish pogroms. Underneath the plan was the notion that the Jews had to pay for Rasputin's death. "The Jews will pay for the blood of Rasputin with their own blood."[9]

People had, of course, being trying to open Nicholas's eyes to the situation but he refused to recognize it. Sandro wrote him at the end of January that the country was experiencing the most dangerous moment in its history and they were heading toward inescapable ruin. The tsar had to act, he had to listen to the voice of the people, to bridge the ever widening gap between the throne and its subjects. Sandro next visited

Nicholas and Alexandra to warn them to their faces of the danger. Alexandra received him coldly. Nicholas sat quietly smoking and adjusting the folds on his circassian coat, not saying a word. "I refuse to continue this dispute," Alexandra snapped. "You are exaggerating the danger. Some day, when you are less excited, you will admit I knew better."[10] It was the last time they saw each other. Around this time she had a dream: there was Rasputin, up in Heaven, with his arms outstretched blessing Russia.[11] All would be well. Her Friend had told her so from beyond the grave.

Buchanan had had a talk similar to Sandro's a month earlier alone with the emperor. "I asked the Emperor whether he fully realized the gravity of the situation and revolutionary language that was being heard not only in Petrograd," he wrote in a secret communiqué,

> but throughout Russia. His Majesty said he was quite (aware) people were indulging in such talk but that I must not take it too seriously. I replied that a week before Rasputin was murdered I had been told that an attempt was about to be made on his life but I had paid no attention to it. I could not therefore disregard reports which were now reaching me from all sides of other assassinations that were contemplated. There was no saying where they would stop. [. . .]
>
> In conclusion I begged His Majesty to forgive my frankness and to believe that it had been inspired by my warm feelings of devotion to His Majesty and the Empress and my fear that without a reconciliation between him and his people the war would be lost. His Majesty was at a parting of the ways. One road led to victory and a glorious peace—the other to revolution and disaster.

Nicholas thanked Buchanan for his frankness and said that he agreed with him. But the ambassador left convinced that in the end the emperor would ignore his advice, and do nothing.[12]

It was being said that Nicholas and Alexandra were now listening only to Protopopov and that he had gone completely mad. On 29 January, the U.S. ambassador, David Francis, wrote to the State Department that he had been told Protopopov had fallen into a trance while talking to the empress, after which he told her that he had spoken to Jesus Christ, who had instructed him to follow the teachings of "Saint Rasputin."[13] Rumors were widespread that Protopopov was holding séances with Nicholas and Alexandra at which they would call forth the spirit of

Rasputin and seek his advice. Others claimed Protopopov had been telling their majesties that Rasputin's soul had left his dead body and now resided in him. One Russian diplomat even claimed Protopopov had taken to trying to mimic Rasputin's manner of speech.[14] The German foreign ministry received information from a source in Sweden that Protopopov often went to pray with Alexandra at Rasputin's grave and that the minister was in desperate need of money, thus offering a possible opening for talks of a separate peace with Russia.[15]

At the same time as Protopopov was believed to be assuming the place of favorite, there were reports of other contenders. One report had it that Rasputin's former rival Mitya the Nasal Voice had returned and was vying for the position.[16] Another candidate was a monk by the name of Mardary. Father Mardary, later bishop (born Uskoković), a Montenegrin and graduate of the Petersburg Theological Seminary, had been spoken of as a potential substitute since early 1916. He was known as an inspired preacher, a man with the gift of prophecy, and, like Rasputin, someone with burning, intense eyes. He was also young—only twenty-seven—and handsome.[17] The press reported soon after Rasputin's death that Rasputin had feared losing his place to Mardary for the past three years and had tried to have him expelled from Russia. He had grown increasingly angry over the good-looking monk's growing popularity in the capital's salons.[18] According to Rodzianko, Alexei Khvostov had had plans to replace Rasputin with Mardary as his own tool at court.[19]

Mardary himself clearly had ideas about improving his status. He apparently wanted to give a talk to the Duma on 22 December titled "The Mystery of Russia" that would include his thoughts on Rasputin's murder.[20] Indeed, he did give a talk on the twenty-second in Petrograd—though not before the Duma—that attracted an enormous crowd. Many of Rasputin's followers arrived and offered him 4,000 rubles not to mention Rasputin in his speech, which he refused to accept; but then the deputy minister of the interior appeared and ordered him in the strictest terms not to dare to mention Rasputin's name or the talk would be stopped immediately. This order he did listen to. Mardary was overrun by young women all asking for his phone number and address. One of his male followers there that night wrote how Mardary was different, and indeed superior to Rasputin: "Mardary is an entirely different species: a fervent Russian patriot and a warrior for Slavic unity. He is himself from Montenegro—very handsome, brown haired, and looks like Christ. If he were blond the similarity would be even more striking."[21]

No one it seemed could take Rasputin's place for the tsarevich Alexei. He fell ill in February, and when the sailor Derevenko, whose job was to look after the tsarevich, told him he had just been to pray to the saints for Alexei to get better, the boy would hear none of it. "There are no more saints! There was a saint—Grigory Yefimovich, but they killed him. Now there's no point in prayers or trying to heal me. If he were here, he would bring me an apple, stroke me where it hurts, and I'd feel better that instant."[22]

On 22 February Alexandra wrote Nicholas from Tsarskoe Selo:

> My very Own precious one,
>
> With anguish & deep pain I let you go—alone, without sweet Baby's* tender, warming, sunny companionship! And such a hard time as the one we are going through now. Being apart makes everything so much harder to bear [. . .] I can do nothing but pray & pray & Our dear Friend does so in yonder world for you—there he is yet nearer to us—Tho' one longs to hear his voice of comfort and encouragement. [. . .] Christ be near you, & the sweet Virgin never fail you—our Friend left us to [join] her.[23]

The following day she sent Nicholas the cross Rasputin had been wearing when he was murdered, telling him to wear it for it would help when making difficult decisions.[24] As for Nicholas, he felt no need of any cross since he did not foresee any difficult decisions. He wrote her from the train on the way back to Stavka that he was thinking of taking up dominoes since, in his own words, "there is no work for me" there.

As she had done many times in the previous two months, Alexandra, accompanied by her daughter Maria, went to pray at Rasputin's grave on 26 February. She was pleased that the construction of the church had progressed far enough so the walls protected her from view when she knelt down to pray. She felt such profound peace there. "He died to save us," she wrote Nicholas later that day.[25] The following day, the twenty-seventh, the empress visited the grave again with Vyrubova and Lily Dehn.[26] It would be the last time. Two days earlier disturbances had broken out in Petrograd. The February Revolution had begun.

On the morning of the twenty-third, thousands of female workers

---

* The tsarevich.

took to the streets chanting for bread. As they marched they were joined by other workers, streaming out of the city's factories. By noon, more than 50,000 had flooded the streets, and by nightfall their numbers had grown to 90,000. Their cries had now grown to "Down with the War!" and "Down with the Tsar!" Windows were smashed, shops were broken into, the shelves of the city's bakeries were stripped bare. The authorities managed to restore order, but the next day the numbers grew to as many as 200,000. The striking workers marched into the very heart of the capital, down Nevsky Prospect. The police, overwhelmed by the situation, looked on in confusion. On 24 February, all the top ministers, president of the Duma Rodzianko, and the mayor of Petrograd met to discuss the crisis. Only Protopopov was not there. Paléologue wrote on the twenty-fifth that during the crisis he "was no doubt conferring with the astral spirit of Rasputin."[27] By the twenty-fifth, the number of protesters had reached 300,000, an outpouring of anger not seen since the Revolution of 1905. Soldiers sent to quell the people starting going over to them. Cries of "Long Live the Revolution!" now supplanted "Down with the War!" The situation was spinning out of control. On the twenty-sixth, dozens of protesters were shot and killed, but instead of breaking the spirit of the people, it gave them strength. Soldiers began to join them. They turned their guns on their commanders, and mutiny spread through the garrisons. The authorities had lost all control of the capital. On the twenty-seventh, workers and soldiers opened the city's prisons, next they raided the police stations, courthouses, the ministry of the interior, and the headquarters of the Okhrana, burning its files. Mob violence ruled. Policemen were hunted down and killed in the streets. Well-dressed persons were set upon. The city was looted. That evening the tsar's ministers met at the Mariinsky Palace to tender their resignations and then slip away into the darkness, hoping to make it home safely. Over the Winter Palace flew the red flag.

Early on the morning of the twenty-eighth, Nicholas left Stavka for Tsarskoe Selo, but his train was stopped some one hundred miles away when reports of mutinous troops in the vicinity were received. From there, the imperial train headed west to Pskov, headquarters of the Northern Front, where it arrived on the evening of 1 March. "Look what you have done," General Ruzsky, commander of the Northern Front, told Voeikov on their arrival, "all your Rasputin clique . . . What have you got Russia into now?"[28] Alexandra was desperate with worry, not sure what had happened to Nicholas. On the second, she sent him a letter reminding him to wear Rasputin's cross even if it were uncomfortable, for this alone would bring her some peace of mind.[29]

Events had moved quickly during the two days Nicholas was on the train. Back in Petrograd, a group of Duma members had set up a Provisional Committee—soon to become the Provisional Government that would (nominally) rule Russia for eight months—to try to restore order and to thwart the rising power of a competing body, the Soviet of Workers' and Soldiers' Deputies. Pressured by Rodzianko, as well as Ruzsky and the other generals who had no desire to quell the uprising with troops from the front, a move that might have worked but risked igniting civil war, Nicholas decided that the only option left for him was to abdicate. Late on the night of 2 March 1917, the reign of Nicholas II came to an end, and with it, three centuries of Romanov rule. Nicholas marked the occasion with a single line in his diary: "Treachery, cowardice, and deceit all around!"[30] Nicholas finally arrived at Tsarskoe Selo on the ninth, joining his family at the Alexander Palace where they now resided under house arrest.

News of the abdication was met with an explosion of joy. There was a surge of optimism and hope that things would finally improve now that the nightmare of Nicholas's reign and the Romanov dynasty was over. A new era of freedom seemed to be at hand. A peasant was recorded as saying how "the people's soul could put up with anything other than Grishka on the throne." The common folk joked that instead of the royal flag a pair of Rasputin's trousers was now flying over the imperial palace.[31]

72. Here Lies the Dog

Rasputin's grave had been discovered within days of the collapse of the monarchy. The circumstances surrounding the discovery are confused and contradictory. Alexander Kerensky, minister of justice of the new Provisional Government, is said to have met with a group of journalists in Petrograd's Tauride Palace in the first days of March to discuss a "most delicate matter." It was imperative that the final resting place of Grigory Rasputin be found, he told them, lest it become a shrine for the murdered holy man's many followers and possibly a rallying point for adherents of the old regime. At the time, no one seemed to know where his body had been buried. There were rumors it had been sent home to Siberia or secretly buried in one of the capital's cemeteries. Wherever it lay, he told the reporters, the body "must be found and destroyed without any noise."[1]

According to a different version, Captain Klimov, head of the aerial battery stationed at Tsarskoe Selo, had heard tales of Rasputin being buried in the area and decided to task his men with finding the grave on 1 March. He tried to locate the gravediggers, but was told they had all been sent off to Siberia directly after the burial. They had not been trusted to keep their mouths shut. Locals talked of a service in the woods held in late December near where a church was being built for Vyrubova. He had spied Alexandra and her daughter Olga walking in the area more than once and had also heard of people going to the building site and surreptitiously gathering up clumps of snow and sawdust, which was said to possess rare healing powers. He directed his attentions to this spot and ordered his men to begin digging beneath the chapel. Here, where the future altar was to be, they came across a metal coffin buried under about three meters of earth.

The discovery was reported in the press on 9 March. Rasputin's head, resting on a pillow of white silk lace, had turned black, the stories read, and the fatal bullet wound to the forehead was stuffed with cotton wool. His eyes had sunk into his skull. The coffin was lifted out of the ground, placed on a truck and driven off to the local town hall. The commandant of Tsarskoe Selo telephoned the leaders of the new government in Petrograd for further instructions.[2]

After local officials had inspected the body, Rasputin's coffin was loaded onto a truck and driven to the Tsarskoe Selo rail station. Here the coffin was put into a wooden box and moved to a freight car, which was then sealed and placed under guard to await orders from the Provisional Government.[3] Back in the capital, Prince Georgy Lvov, head of the Provisional Government, had already decided that Rasputin's body had to disappear for good. He called in journalist Filipp Kupchinsky and entrusted the job to him. They discussed how to dispose of Rasputin's remains and decided that the best thing to do was to burn them. As Kupchinsky was leaving for Tsarskoe Selo, Lvov said: "Of course, if it is destroyed then we will put an end to any worshipping of the corpse or any other trouble with his remains, which will be beneficial for all of Russia. [. . .] I entrust you to do whatever you think necessary, but remember: be careful."

By the time Kupchinsky had arrived at the station on the night of the ninth a large crowd, responding to the rumors about Rasputin's body, had already gathered. Worried about being followed if he tried to move the coffin, Kupchinsky decided to leave it and ordered the train to depart the station quietly for the southeast toward Pavlovsk. There, in the empty station, Kupchinsky was waiting with a truck to bring the body to Petrograd. They drove back in the dark of night through heavy snow and wind to the old Imperial Stables building on Konyushennaya Square, arriving around 1 a.m. on the tenth. They parked the truck, locked the door to the stables, and left. It was later said the truck was parked next to the royal nuptial carriage. Kupchinsky went back later that morning. He opened the coffin; there before his eyes lay Rasputin. He then met with Lvov to inform him that the body was now in the city. Lvov instructed him to finish the job that night. Late that evening, Kupchinsky, along with a few trusted hands, filled the truck with gasoline and told the driver to get ready. Shortly before midnight on the tenth the truck rolled out of the stables and slowly worked its way through the empty streets toward the edge of the city. The driver had been given a special pass by the new authorities to make sure he would not be detained by any of the militia along the way. After leaving the city, the truck headed northeast in the direction of Lesnoi.

Where the truck went after that has remained a mystery for a hundred years. According to an account left by Kupchinsky, before reaching Lesnoi the truck got stuck in heavy snow and could not go any farther. After talking it over, the men decided they would have to dispose of Rasputin there. They opened the truck's back doors, pulled out the zinc coffin from the wooden box, and headed off into some woods by the side of the road. The coffin was heavy, and the men sank into the snow, making it hard to walk. They trudged on, deeper into the woods. It was now early on the morning of the eleventh.

A few of the men prepared a fire and then fed it with gasoline, while the others opened the coffin and pulled back the lid. Despite the deep frost, the smell of rotting flesh hit them in the face. Kupchinsky looked down into the open coffin: "In the rays of the fire I glimpsed the completely exposed and still preserved face of Grigory Rasputin. The well-groomed, somewhat straggly beard, one eye knocked out, the bashed-in head. Everything else was preserved. His hands looked like those of someone still alive. His colored silk shirt seemed to be perfectly fresh and clean."

They lifted the body out of the coffin and heaved it into the fire with the use of several boards. Then they poured on more gasoline. Soon Rasputin was engulfed in flames. Bluish-green sparks flew from the body. Kupchinsky recalled:

> Suffocating smoke and the most distinctive stench, nightmarish and strange.
>   We stood around the bonfire in a tight group and did not take our eyes off the dead man's face. Rasputin's beard was long gone, but his embalmed cheeks stubbornly resisted the flames for a long time. Accompanied by hisses and sputtering, trails of vile yellow smoke escaped from the depths of the corpse.[4]

Mikhail Shabalin was one of the men standing around the fire. He remembered how the body burned for hours. It began to get light in the sky, and they worried about being discovered. Passersby had noticed the fire and a few men in uniform had to be sent to keep them back by the road. By seven o'clock in the morning all that remained was Rasputin's chest, which for some reason refused to burn. Suddenly, one of them grabbed a shovel and slammed it down into the charred mass of flesh and bone. Over and over he hacked into Rasputin's torso. Slowly, it began to break apart into pieces, giving off a horrible smell. "Forgive us, Grigory Yefimovich," someone whispered.[5] They put out the fire, scattered the ashes and bits of bone, and covered over the ground with fresh snow and branches. They arrived back in the city before noon. Not long after, Kupchinsky returned to the site. He found someone had hung a crude sign on a nearby birch tree: "The dog lies buried here."[6]

News of the cremation was carried in the newspapers. "His ashes were scattered across the field and covered with snow," the *Stock Exchange Gazette* solemnly recorded. "When spring finally arrives, the vernal waters will wash away the ashes and the filth, and, just maybe, the luxuriant shoots of new life will crowd out from our memory the very name of Rasputin." Nicholas and Alexandra read the newspaper account of Kupchinsky's expedition in the day's papers. One of them underlined the most horrific parts of the story in red pencil. Zinaida Gippius noted in her diary after reading the story: "Psychologically it's understandable, however, there's something dirty here from a Russian way of thinking."[7]

Dirty, yes, but is this what really happened?

Kupchinsky published his account in May of that year, and it became the basis for the accepted story of the fate of Rasputin's body. But recently his story has been reexamined, and it now appears that he was perhaps not telling the truth about what happened in those early morning hours.

In his narrative Kupchinsky mentions stopping at the Petrograd Polytechnic Institute in Lesnoi both before and after the body of Rasputin was burned. Indeed, the official document testifying to the destruction of Rasputin's corpse drafted immediately after the event is signed by six students of the institute who helped Kupchinsky dispose of the body. Kupchinsky, it turns out, was not just a journalist, but several years before the revolution had also led an effort to organize the first crematorium in Petrograd. As part of this project, he had visited the institute to consult with experts there on the matter. As someone with an understanding of the enormous fire it takes to completely destroy a human corpse, it stands to reason Kupchinsky would have known the near impossibility of burning Rasputin's body in a hastily constructed bonfire in the snowy woods. And during his visit to the institute, he most likely would have been shown its vast boiler house, whose gigantic cauldrons could easily have consumed Rasputin's body in complete secrecy. Lvov called Kupchinsky to get rid of the body since he knew of his interest in human cremation. In all likelihood, there never was any truck stuck in the snow or improvised bonfire. Rather, Kupchinsky drove the body straight to the institute in Lesnoi, where it was unloaded, tossed into the cauldrons, and incinerated. Indeed, years later two former students of the institute, including the noted Soviet chemist Ivan Bashilov, confirmed that Kupchinsky arrived at the institute on the night of 10 March to destroy the body of Grigory Rasputin.[8]

Kupchinsky most likely lied to please the Provisional Government. By fabricating a tale about burning Rasputin in some vaguely identified woods, Kupchinsky fulfilled his orders to make the body of Rasputin disappear without a trace. He had covered their tracks. No one would ever find Rasputin's final resting place.

73. The Myth

The collapse of the monarchy unleashed an explosion of anti-Rasputin propaganda, and it was then that the myth of Rasputin took on its ultimate shape. The process had actually begun two months earlier in the days following his murder, but now, with the regime and any restraints on free speech gone, the pamphlets, broadsheets, theater plays, films, cartoons, and satires devoted to Rasputin turned into a tidal wave. After a decade of playing cat-and-mouse, everyone was free to say whatever they wanted, and they did.

The *"Freedom" Almanac* devoted all of its first edition to Rasputin. "An entire epoch of Russian life has been tied to that name," it began. "A shameful epoch, an epoch of rumors passed about by whispers, an epoch of slavish silence and universal trembling before the omnipotent favorite, lover of the tsaritsa and a host of other court ladies." The magazine told his life's story, as it was interpreted in the first weeks of freedom—this was Rasputin the rapacious, Satanic sex fiend, the evil sorcerer, the German agent. It is not the portrait of a real man, but a caricature. Rasputin the harem master holds young women under his sway and against their will. They want to run but know they are helpless for his power is infinite. Even if they were to flee thousands of miles, Rasputin is still there, controlling, dominating them. There is no escape. He does not just drink, but holds epic bacchanalias that last for days at the Villa Rode. Here he proclaims himself "Tsar Grigory I," brags of his hold over "Sashka," and waves about his "passports"—pornographic photographs of a naked Alexandra in his lecherous embrace and all manner of poses—that guarantee his immunity. There is Rasputin the wizard, having tricked the tsar to drink magical wine that makes him a hostage to Rasputin's will. His sexual appetite knows no limits. He takes one woman after another for hours on end, all of them dropping to the floor in somnolent ecstasy as he greedily moves on to the next.[1]

In the magazine's second installment, Rasputin is referred to as Russia's "complete master, what he wanted, he did."[2] There were reports in the press that Rasputin had been part of a "Black Cabinet" set up by members of the ministry of the interior that carried out surveillance on top court and government figures, a sort of shadow government.[3] The *Petrograd Leaflet* called Rasputin "the true tsar and patriarch of all Russia."[4]

His family's history and biography were distorted beyond recognition. *Russian Liberty* informed its readers that the Rasputins had been drunks for generations, that Rasputin had been tried in court for horse theft and bearing false witness and beaten with sticks for his crimes. Fanciful versions of the bogus Yar scandal of 1915 were printed in large numbers. Rasputin was said to have amassed an enormous fortune through theft and graft and corruption and to be the owner of large holdings in the fishing industry and the rubber concern "Bogatyr" in Moscow.[5] "Money, vodka, food, and women—that's what the horse thief of Tobolsk craved," wrote one P. Kovalevsky in his pamphlet *Grishka Rasputin.*[6]

He was cast as something more than human. The London *Times* claimed Rasputin had possessed "colossal animal vitality" and had been "a man with something of the gorilla in his composition."[7] All of this fed his extraordinary power. In his 1917 biography, William Le Queux wrote that this "fiendish satyr" had held such power that "even at his word men in high position did not hesitate to cast off their brilliant uniforms and decorations and mortify their flesh." His "hypnotic influence was irresistible, no woman, however high born, or highly religious, was safe."[8] American Ambassador Francis repeated the same claim in a letter to Washington from February 1917, writing "He had been a man of extraordinary if not unprecedented sexual passion and it is claimed no woman was ever able to resist his advances."[9]

In an article titled "The Secret of Rasputin's Deadly Eyes," the medical correspondent for London's *Daily Express* studied photographs of Rasputin and said he had located the source of Rasputin's power in the special squint of his eyes. This characteristic allows the hypnotizer "to fix the gaze of the person to be hypnotised for he, or she, is caught by the unusual quality of the squinting eye and stares at it with the pertinacity necessary to produce the hypnotic state."[10]

Others located the source of his power further down on his anatomy. In his *Why Rasputin Had to Appear*, the writer and lawyer (and future SS officer in Nazi Germany) Grigory Bostunich alleged that "Rasputin was the kind of man who makes his career thanks solely to sexual anomaly, what the doctors call priapism, and what the common folk call 'the wolf's disease.'" Rasputin, according to Bostunich, possessed the same sexual stamina found among the Crimean Tatars, which allowed him to satisfy the most insatiable desires of his female followers, including the empress.[11] An English biography published in 1920 claimed that Rasputin "certainly suffered from what is variously described as praepotentia, priapism, satyriasis, and could prolong a woman's pleasure indefinitely without any specific satisfaction to himself."[12] The number of his conquests was now given as in the thousands.[13]

One Russian booklet at the time stated Rasputin had cured Alexandra of all her ailments through a course of sexual healing. The same source presented his paternity of Alexei as a known "fact."[14] Another publication reported Rasputin had taken as his lovers not only the empress and her eldest daughter Olga, but in fact all four of the girls, even Anastasia, just fifteen at the time of his murder.[15] It was reported Alexandra had been so distraught at Rasputin's death she had his corpse brought to her bedroom and lay down upon it. She insisted he be buried at Tsarskoe Selo, and after all the other mourners at his funeral had left, she collapsed and put her ear to the freshly dug earth—from deep inside the coffin she could hear Rasputin's voice. A great mound of flowers was placed around the gravesite. The next morning they were all gone, mysteriously transformed into a thick layer of fetid yellow slime. This was cleared away and fresh flowers laid down again. But the following day, the slime reappeared. This went on for days, until it was decided the best thing to do was to dig up the body and send it back to Pokrovskoe. It was said the same strange thing happened there as well, and no one could explain it or much less make it stop.[16]

A number of theatrical pieces played on the stages of the capital that spring and summer: *Rasputin's Happy Days*, *Rasputin's Nightly Orgies*, and *Grishka's Harem*. The stage play *Tea at Vyrubova's*, also premiering in 1917, featured all the stars of the old regime, including Rasputin, whose miraculous "male attributes" helped win over Alexandra and convinced her to make him her true husband. *Rasputin's Nightly Orgies* presented Alexandra and Vyrubova kneeling before Rasputin as they kissed his hands. "Do you feel me?" Rasputin asks. Alexandra, "in ecstasy," moans in reply: "Oh, papa, I feel you . . . How I feel you." In a later scene, Rasputin is heard off stage driving the demons out of the empress in one of the Villa Rode's private rooms:

Protopopov (drunk): Now that's talent. Enormous talent. You
know he has an enormous talent?

Vyrubova (languidly): Oh, I know, he's got an enormous, an
enormous talent . . .[17]

One can imagine the cascade of laughter and guffaws that greeted
such broad humor. So great was the demand for tickets that the plays
often ran twice a day for months at a stretch. Playbills were plastered
around the city: "A Sensational Play: Rasputin and Alexandra in Intimate Relations." Not just for hoi polloi, even Alexander Blok went and
admitted that if exaggerated, the plays did contain "an element of
truth."[18]

Within two weeks of the tsar's abdication the first moving pictures
appeared in cinemas with titles like *People of Sin and Blood*, *The Holy
Devil*, *The Mysterious Murder in Petrograd on the 16th of December*, *The Firm
Romanov, Rasputin, Sukhomlinov, Myasoedov, Protopopov and Co.*, and *Rasputin's Burial*. They were all wildly popular. The first to appear, and
apparently the most successful, was *Dark Forces: Grigory Rasputin and His
Associates*, advertised as "A Sensational Drama in 2 Parts." And sensational it was, with scenes that even by today's standards would be
considered pornographic.[19] At the end of March, *The Life of Grigory Rasputin* came to the screen of Tyumen's "Gigant" cinema. The local press
described the crowd outside the cinema as huge and threatening, as
people pushed and shoved feverishly to get tickets before it sold out.
The scene of Rasputin's murder in the Yusupov cellar elicited frantic
applause.[20]

Broadsides, pamphlets, postcards, and other ephemera promising
to expose the lurid, behind-the-scenes workings of the old regime were
printed in huge numbers and distributed across Russia.[21] Photographs
of Rasputin taking tea with his followers were endlessly published by
various photography studios. Russians loved collecting these and liked
to see if they could name the women seated around him. Many mistook
Vyrubova or Munya Golovina for the empress.[22] There were satirical
imperial manifestoes issued in the name of "We Grigory the 1st and
Last, Horse Thief and Former ALL-RUSSIAN Autocrat who now reigns
in Hell."[23] Especially widespread were a number of blasphemous
akathists, special hymns in the Eastern Orthodox Church dedicated to
various saints and members of the Holy Trinity:

AKATHIST

To The Newly Appeared Saint Grigory "The Horse Thief" Novy
Oh, Grigory Novy, Satan's saint, to you, blasphemer of the Christian faith, destroyer of the Russian land, defiler of women and girls, for which you have accepted death, we pay our respects, we praise you [. . .][24]

These parodies, sold by street vendors, were particularly well received by the common masses. The authorities seized copies of this akathist from some soldiers of the Moscow garrison in January 1917, and in February, police collected a similar one that someone was illegally posting on fences in the Siberian town of Novo-Nikolaevsk.[25]

So great was the demand for Rasputiniana the market became saturated by publishers and printers seeking to make a quick ruble.[26] Eventually, Russians began to tire of it all. A reporter recorded this interaction with a soldier on a Petrograd tram:

"Do you like what's being written now?" I asked.

"Sure I do, of course. Now they write about the narod. About liberty. I just don't like how they write about that Rasputin. What he'd been doing at the imperial court. It's useless."

"Really?"

"What's the point? All the talk now is about the republic. You'd think you could pick up a newspaper and read how it works in other places, in other countries, you know, with foreigners, it came from over there. But instead whenever you see some leaflet it's got nothing but Grishka, well enough of him already!"[27]

74. Unsettled Business

The Provisional Government had no interest in punishing Rasputin's murderers, and so the fall of the monarchy meant Yusupov was a free man. The press covered his return to Petrograd on 12 March 1917. Two days later he gave an interview to the *New Times*. He told a story about how Rasputin and Dr. Badmaev had given the tsar special Oriental drugs that had turned him into a useless idiot with no will of his own. As for the empress, she had long suffered from a "mania of greatness," thinking she was a second Catherine the Great, sent from Germany to save Russia. Vyrubova, Rasputin, and Protopopov fed this self-deception. The court clique had led the country to ruin, from which there had been no exit. He made certain everyone understood the danger he had willingly accepted, telling the paper how upon returning to his room after the murder he found a mysterious woman dressed all in black who warned him that twenty of Rasputin's followers were already plotting to kill him.[1]

Yusupov relished his new identity as Rasputin's murderer. His life had acquired meaning. He began hosting dinner parties in the now famous cellar, which he kept exactly as it had been that night. He delighted in recounting the grisly story to young ladies and watching them tremble as he showed them the white bearskin rug that, he said, had once been soaked in Rasputin's blood. Grand Duchess Maria, Dmitry's sister, was a guest at one such soirée. She examined the rug closely, but could not detect the slightest trace of any blood.[2]

That spring, Yusupov visited Ella in Moscow to tell her the entire story in person. "It was no crime to kill Rasputin," said the future saint of the Russian Orthodox Church, "you destroyed a fiend who was the incarnation of evil."[3] Her words pleased him, but he did not need anyone to help him with his conscience. When asked by Sergei Kostritsky, a dentist who traveled to Tobolsk to tend to the royal family later that year, whether he ever felt any guilt over taking the life of another human being, Yusupov said, with a smile: "Never. I killed a dog." Not only his words, but the cold, cynical tone in which Yusupov uttered them filled Kostritsky with disgust.[4] "I have never had the slightest qualms of conscience," Yusupov nonchalantly acknowledged in his memoirs. "The thought of Rasputin never troubled my sleep."[5]

The same could not be said of Grand Duke Dmitry. He wrote his father from the Russian army headquarters at Qazvin in Persia in January that the recent days had been "terribly difficult" and it had taken all of his inner strength not to break down and cry like a child on the train. It is possible these words were intended for Nicholas and Alexandra. In the same letter he wrote that he did not know who had killed Rasputin, but whoever it was they clearly were "people who love Russia, their motherland, sincerely, fervently, passionately [. . .] and are zealously devoted to their Emperor." Dmitry knew the Okhrana was reading his mail, and he hoped these words would reach the emperor. In late April, Dmitry wrote of matters to his father in a more honest light, admitting he had taken part in the murder after giving the matter a great deal of thought, although he now admitted killing Rasputin had only made matters worse. Kerensky had by then let it be known Dmitry should not be arrested, for he had played his part in the fight against the old regime. But Dmitry wavered about whether or not to return to Russia. He wrote his father that had he returned immediately after the abdication, this would have amounted to "terrible boorishness" toward "poor Niki." What is more, he was wary of coming back since he feared that Kerensky's words might well not be enough to keep him out of jail. He was, after all, a Romanov, whatever his role in Rasputin's murder.[6] As late as September, he was still desperate to return, but remained in Persia due to what he called in his diary "the Yusupovs' categorical and repeated instruction" that he not come back. In the end, Dmitry chose to stay away, a decision that most likely saved his life.

On the first anniversary of the murder, Dmitry, now living at the British Mission in Tehran, woke to find the city covered in snow. The unexpected sight brought him back to Petrograd and events of the previous year.

> Today is the sixteenth of December. One year since that unforgettable day. And here, on the pages of my diary, where some of my soul is reflected, I must openly declare that I would give much not to be filled with such memories. Can it truly be that I took part, in the true meaning of the word, in the killing of another man? Of

course, for others, for the people en large, I did this, with the loftiest patriotic scentiments. Still, I cannot adopt some knightly pose
on these pages. Now I must say unequivocally my soul constantly
suffers from a heavy burden. What happiness, that the Lord did not
allow me to actually kill. There is no blood on my hands and the
memory of my mother has not been sullied by the oath I swore
before Papa. [. . .]

Only one thing will forever torment me, that is poor Niki's
feelings. I'm constantly beset by the difficult thought that he probably still hates me and considers me a simple criminal and a
murderer! And perhaps he even thinks that the death of Rasputin
is the main cause of all that is happening now in Russia. Alix! Perhaps she thinks the very same thing and supports her husband in
this! [. . .]

Poor Niki. How much I would give now to speak with him. To
dissuade him of the notion that I am some simple murderer. [. . .]
I will never believe that Alix purposely carried out her politics of
turning society against Niki and her. That can't be. I am firmly
convinced that she fatally lost her way. The entire time she thought
that only with such politics could Niki maintain power and order
in the country. And she was not that far from the truth.[7]

Anna Vyrubova was arrested at Tsarskoe Selo on 21 March and
imprisoned in the Trubetskoy Bastion of the Peter and Paul Fortress. She
was placed in cell 70. On one side of her was Yekaterina Sukhomlinova
(cell 71), and on the other, Ivan Manasevich-Manuilov (cell 69). The
Provisional Government was busy filling the prison with key figures of
the old regime: General Voeikov, General Sukhomlinov, Boris Stürmer,
Ivan Shcheglovitov, Stepan Beletsky, among others. Even Olga Lokhtina
had been arrested. Beletsky was on the verge of a nervous breakdown.
He was weak and distraught and terrified. He had trouble sleeping: Rasputin haunted his dreams.[8] They were questioned at length by the newly
created Extraordinary Commission of Inquiry. The Commission was
eager to prove that Vyrubova, together with the empress, Rasputin, and
others, had held secret meetings at her home where they plotted their
traitorous campaign against Russia.[9] She was subjected to harsh treatment. The guards spat on her, beat her about the face and body, and
stripped her naked. At times, they threatened to kill her. She never complained, later saying to a member of the Commission: "They are not
guilty, for they do not know what they are doing."[10] The most humiliat-

ing moment during her months in the bastion came when the prison doctor was brought in for a special examination. Her investigators did not believe her when she said that she had not been Rasputin's mistress, and so they sought definitive proof. Anna was lifted up onto a table and her legs were spread open. After a thorough examination, the doctor confirmed her story. Anna was a virgin.[11]

Vyrubova defended Rasputin and their majesties before the Commission. Not so Protopopov. After his arrest, he claimed to have evidence that proved treason had been committed at the highest levels. He wondered whether Rasputin had not been delivering counterfeit money to the empress, which he received from either Manuilov or Simanovich. He also implicated Alexei Khvostov, Manuilov, Stürmer, and Andronikov as traitors. Clearly, Protopopov was trying to save his own skin. "A two-faced Janus," Alexander Blok called him. Simanovich behaved little better, telling the Commission he never knew Rasputin and had had nothing to do with him.[12]

The Commission did not concern itself with matters related to the church, which was busy settling its own affairs. Neither the Holy Synod nor the Russian Orthodox Church condemned Rasputin's murder or the desecration of his grave. Instead, they busied themselves rehabilitating those clergymen who had suffered in recent years and preparing purges against all real, and supposed, Rasputinists in their ranks. Father Vostokov was returned to Moscow, where, on 8 March, he demanded that everyone who had dirtied themselves with Rasputin be removed from their positions. The newly elected Chief Procurator of the Synod, Vladimir Lvov, former Duma deputy and devoted enemy of Rasputin, was relentless in his war against the Rasputinists. One of his first acts was to expel Pitirim and Makary, the metropolitan of Moscow, from the Synod. In April he put together an investigative committee, chaired by himself, to examine the role of Rasputin in the church administration and, according to the *New Times*, "take every possible measure to liquidate his influence."[13] In an article on the fight against Rasputinism in the church, the *Petrograd Leaflet* wrote that Serafim (Sergei Golubyatnikov), the bishop of Yekaterinburg and Irbit, had been removed from office and forced into retirement due to his relations with Rasputin. His chief sin had been going to comfort Rasputin in Tyumen after Guseva's attack and helping see to his medical care.[14]

Bishop Varnava, fearing the rough justice of the mob, left Tobolsk for the safety of the Abalak Monastery. The authorities searched his residence, confiscating his correspondence with Rasputin, Nicholas and Alexandra, and others and shipping it to the Provisional Government as proof of his crimes.[15] Back in the capital, Pitirim was grabbed and hauled out of his residence, placed on a throne, and paraded up and down Nevsky Prospect as passersby mocked and jeered.[16]

The hierarchs of the church were convinced of Rasputin's evil influence, as were the members of the Commission, yet search though the commissioners did for damaging evidence against Rasputin and the party clique, in the end they could find nothing but lies, rumor, and mass hysteria. After examining the volumes of press coverage on Rasputin carefully clipped and filed by the Okhrana, the Commission noted how little public perception of Rasputin matched the reality of the man, his life, and his influence. The Rasputin Russians thought they knew had been nothing but a "fantasy," yet a dangerous fantasy that proved poisonous to the throne.

> If a military revolt in Petrograd launched the Russian Revolution, if not one man in the army or the narod bothered to come to the defense of the former emperor, then this was due not only to the proletariat and the revolutionary army, but also to the Tyumen peasant Grigory Yefimovich Rasputin, the saint of the last days of the monarchy, whose "deeds" destroyed the narod's faith in the divine authority of the autocracy and in the last bearer of tsarist power. It is not known whether a grateful Russia will ever erect a monument to Rasputin, but there is something mystically providential in the fact that it was a Russian peasant who saved the first Romanov and then another peasant, 300 hundred years later, who destroyed the last representative of that dynasty.[17]

That earlier peasant was Ivan Susanin, the subject of Mikhail Glinka's 1836 opera *A Life for the Tsar*. In the early years of the seventeenth century, during the so-called Time of Troubles, Susanin was captured and tortured to death by a group of Poles after he refused to divulge the hiding place of Mikhail Romanov. The facts behind Susanin's heroic self-sacrifice on behalf of the tsar are shrouded by the past, but nineteenth-century Romantics turned the legend into truth. The myth of Susanin was created to prove the holy bond between the tsar and the people. The myth of Rasputin was created to destroy that bond.

*

That spring, while suffering from the measles, Vyrubova had a dream. She was in Tobolsk, walking down a street when she came upon Rasputin. He was angry and his appearance frightened her. He told her, "Go and tell Papa and Mama that I've come to say farewell." She tried to tell him this would be difficult for they were far away in Tsarskoe Selo, but then he interrupted her, saying, "They are in Tobolsk," as he pointed to the tsar's blue train.[18]

On 1 August, the Romanovs, along with thirty-nine servants and retainers and an armed guard of over three hundred, were put on a train at Tsarskoe Selo. For their own safety, the train was adorned with the insignia of the Red Cross and flew the Japanese flag. The family had not been told where they were being taken, but Alexandra had a premonition. She wrote to Vyrubova that they were heading to the homeland of "our Friend—wonderful is it not."[19] At Tyumen the Romanovs left the train and were taken down to the wharf on the Tura River and placed on a steamer for the trip to Tobolsk. Around dinner time on the fifth, they reached Pokrovskoe. The boat stopped, and Alexei and Tatyana went ashore on the far side of the river to collect flowers along the banks. The others, except Alexandra who was sick in bed, went out on the deck to take a look at Rasputin's home.[20] The empress said to her valet Alexei Volkov: "Grigory Yefimovich lived here. He caught fish in this river and would bring it to us in Tsarskoe Selo." Volkov noted she had tears in her eyes.[21] The entire party took this stop at Pokrovskoe for a good omen. "Rasputin had foretold that it would be so," the tutor Pierre Gilliard recalled, "and chance once more seemed to confirm his prophetic words." On the evening of the sixth, they reached Tobolsk.[22]

Rasputin's family was at home the day the Romanovs sailed through. It had been a difficult period for them as well. Maria and Varvara had continued to visit Alexandra and Vyrubova twice a week until the violence at the end of February made this impossible. After the revolution, it had been too dangerous to remain at Gorokhovaya—the new authorities frequently came by to search the premises—so the family had moved in with Simanovich at 8 Nikolaevsky Street. The three siblings were arrested in Petrograd in the middle of March and taken to the Tauride Palace for questioning and then released a short time later. Praskovya had left for Pokrovskoe not long before, and so avoided arrest.[23] After this, the family were reunited in Pokrovskoe for the rest of the spring and summer. In early September, Maria and Varvara returned to Petrograd and moved in with their French tutor, the Jewish Madame Tatyana Chack.[24]

Rasputin had left no will. An inventory of his property dated 24 March 1917 shows he was not poor, but far from the rich man many people had believed. He had his home in Pokrovskoe, along with its four stables, three barns, and one bathhouse (valued at 10,000 rubles), some livestock (a bull and two cows, and eight foals and horses, and the same number of sheep), furniture (including twenty Viennese chairs, a gramophone and fifty records, and an Offenbach piano—valued at 900 rubles), some fine silver and jewelry (including a man's gold watch and chain by the famous firm of Pavel Buré worth 700 rubles), and a few items of clothing (one gray overcoat, one fur coat with a beaver collar, one pair of leather boots, and a few bolts of black cloth).[25] In total, Rasputin left behind property worth 18,415 rubles and cash and savings worth 5,092.66 in the Tyumen branch of the State Bank. Given the hyperinflation of the time, it amounted to little. Almost all of his property was awarded to his two daughters in December 1917; smaller shares went to his widow and son.[26]

It filled Maria with joy to be back in Pokrovskoe during the spring and summer of 1917. "How nice it is here," Maria wrote in her diary, "every little thing reminds me of dear papa."[27] Life at home was not easy, however. On 22 April, a steamer carrying a large group of soldiers passed through Pokrovskoe. When they learned they had stopped in the village of Rasputin, the men went ashore to have a look around. Led by Sergei Kochurov, a warrant officer in one of the Siberian rifle regiments, and accompanied by the sounds of a squeeze box, they made their way to Rasputin's house. They began pounding on the door and demanding to be let in, saying they would not hurt anyone and just wanted to look around. The two sisters were home at the time, along with their cousin Anna Rasputina and Katya Pecherkina. Terrified, they refused to open the door. The men threatened to knock it down and set the house on fire if they did not let them in. They unlocked the door. The soldiers immediately set about ransacking the house. They tore photographs of Rasputin off the walls and pocketed a gold clock and other mementoes. Tables were tipped over, cupboards emptied onto the floor, clothes inspected and strewn about. Stumbling upon a pile of hundreds of postcards with Rasputin's image, they began ripping them up before the women's eyes. Next, they grabbed two portraits—one by Krarup and Raevsky's large full-length portrait that had hung at the 1912 exhibit.

Kochurov cut the Raevsky portrait from its frame, rolled it up, and tucked it under his arm, all while Maria begged him not to take it. As Kochurov and his men were leaving, he yelled out: "Greetings to Grishka Rasputin!" Back on the steamer they handed out the postcards to the other soldiers and bragged of their exploits. Kochurov hung the Krarup portrait on the door to the head, below which he wrote: "Grigory Rasputin, Holy Man of Pokrovskoe." It hung there only a short while before someone ripped it down and tossed it in the river. Kochurov kept the Raevsky portrait for himself. Its subsequent fate is unknown.[28]

Throughout the summer Maria had been receiving letters from Boris Solovyov begging her to marry him. Her heart was not in it, but Praskovya worked to convince her daughter it was the right thing to do given their situation. In the end, Maria gave in, largely since she knew this had been the wish of her late father. They were married in Petrograd on 22 September. Alexander Pistolkors gave away the bride. After a brief honeymoon in Pokrovskoe and Simbirsk, where Boris's family was from, the couple returned to Petrograd.[29] At the end of October, Lenin and the Bolsheviks overthrew the Provisional Government. The country was plunged into civil war. From Tobolsk, Alexandra sent letters to Vyrubova moaning that Russia was suffering because of Rasputin's murder.[30] On the first anniversary of his death, Alexandra wrote Vyrubova to say that though they were separated by a vast distance, their thoughts of that horrible day united them. "We are reliving it all over again," Alexandra confessed. That night the family prayed for his soul before a cross he had given them.[31]

Back in Petrograd, Maria and Boris took refuge on the edge of the city. Vyrubova would come and visit them in secret, at great risk to her own safety.[32] Meanwhile, Alexandra was sending distressing letters to Vyrubova, begging for help with money, clothing and other personal items. It was decided that these would be delivered by Solovyov. He made his first trip to Tobolsk in October and then returned in January 1918. On this second trip Boris came in contact with a small group of monarchists and decided to join their plot to save the Romanovs.[33] He arrived in Tobolsk late that month, disguised as a fishmonger, carrying money and small gifts—chocolate for Alexei, books and eau de Cologne for the girls—that he passed along by way of Alexandra's valet Volkov and her maid Anna Romanova. From a window in the governor's house, the family spied Boris waiting a safe distance away. When he saw them, he made the sign of the cross and bowed down to the ground.

Alexandra wrote to thank him and bless his marriage to Maria. His coming she described as a miracle from God.[34] Boris appears to have given the family unwarranted hope for their escape, implying the secret monarchist cells intent on saving them were larger than they really were. Alexandra took heart, convinced that they would soon be rescued.[35]

Boris stayed in Tobolsk two weeks. There, he met Rasputin's old foe Germogen, elected bishop of Tobolsk in March. He confessed to Boris, saying about Rasputin:

> I loved him and believed in him, or rather in his mission to introduce something new into Russian life, which should have helped strengthen the weakened bonds between the Tsar and the narod to the benefit and blessing of the latter. But his smug turning away from our program, the path he then chose to tread, against my wishes, his attacks on the aristocracy and on such people as Grand Duke Nikolai Nikolaevich, whom I always considered the foundation of the throne, forced me at first to break from him and then, upon seeing how his influence was growing at court and recognizing that this would make his ideas that much more dangerous, I began an energetic campaign against him.

Germogen went on to say that at the time he did not realize how his battle against Rasputin served to help the anti-dynastic elements in the Duma, or how the true Devil all along had been Iliodor, not Rasputin.[36] Finally, before Boris left, Germogen blessed his marriage to Maria: "I know you have willingly accepted a very heavy cross in marrying the daughter of Rasputin in this difficult time." He wished them both health and happiness.[37]

Maria's diary for 1918 chronicles a year of pain and heartache. Money was forever short, as were the basic necessities of life. She loved Boris, but he treated her poorly. He flirted shamelessly with other women, made fun of her looks, abused and at times even hit her. She was torn between her love for him and her desire to flee his cruelty. But she felt herself not only a defenseless orphan, but the child of the second-most hated man in Russia, and so in need of protection. She could not convince herself to leave. "Such is the cross God gave me—to suffer," she wrote on 11 January. She would recall her father's words to her: "Well, Matryoshka, you are my ill-fated one." She had remained behind in Petrograd, spending her days with Vyrubova, Olga Lokhtina, and Munya Golovina. She enjoyed visiting Krarup's studio since her father had always felt so welcome and relaxed there. In the first days of March, her father's spirit came to her: "Blessed are the ways of the Lord! . . . For the first time I felt our dear papa so close to me, it was so good and yet so bitter and sad that I could not hear papa's words from his own mouth, but our minds clearly felt that he's with us." He started visiting Maria in her dreams. "I'm so happy, so happy, he has been with us recently, I feel it." Lokhtina told her that she had been to Gorokhovaya and stood for a while in the courtyard. Rasputin's spirit was unmistakably present, she said.[38]

That month Red Army soldiers arrived in Pokrovskoe. They smashed up the family home and arrested Boris, taking him to Tyumen. Maria hurried to be near him.[39] With a bribe of 2,000 rubles, Maria managed to free Boris in late April, two days before Easter. The holiday unleashed thoughts of her father. "Why, O Lord, did you take him from us so soon? We've been left like leaves without a tree. Papa, dear papa, be with us when we break the fast, precisely with us—with Borya and me; I'm a sinner, and so perhaps you don't want to be with me, but do forgive me."[40]

While Maria had been seeking Boris's release in Tyumen, a detachment of Red Guards seized Tobolsk. The Romanovs were now their prisoners. Early on 26 April, Nicholas, Alexandra, their daughter Maria, and a few others in their party were taken from Tobolsk. Alexei, then ill, stayed behind in the governor's house with the other girls. There was too much ice on the river to travel by boat, so they rode overland— Alexandra and Maria in a hooded tarantass, Nicholas in a crude cart—on the post road to Tyumen. Around noon on the twenty-seventh they stopped opposite Rasputin's house in Pokrovskoe to change horses. "We saw his whole family looking through the window," Nicholas recorded in his diary.[41] Maria took out pencil and paper and made a sketch of the Rasputin home. One of the guards noticed Alexandra making gestures toward an upstairs window. "Get away from the window!" he yelled, pointing his gun at them, "or I'll shoot!" Praskovya and the rest of them retreated out of sight.[42] From Tyumen, they journeyed to the Ural town of Yekaterinburg, where they arrived on 30 April and were imprisoned in the Ipatiev House, or, as it was called by the Soviets, the House of Special Purpose.[43]

On 20 May, the tsarevich and his three sisters left Tobolsk. Two days later Maria went down to the pier in Tyumen to purchase tickets for a trip to the Abalak Monastery. She was struck by the sight of a steamer at the dock under heavy guard. People were being kept away, but Maria managed to sneak close, and through one of its windows she saw Alexei and Anastasia Gendrikova, a lady-in-waiting to the empress. And they saw her too. "They were terribly happy," she wrote in her diary, "[St.] Nicholas the Miracle Worker arranged this. [. . .] What a pity I couldn't say a word to them! They were like angels."[44] The following day, the family was reunited in Yekaterinburg. The mood in the town was hostile. The local Soviet leaders had been flooding the town with anti-Rasputin propaganda—obscene pamphlets and broadsheets depicting Rasputin and the empress were being sold on every street corner, and the local cinema was presenting a film showing Rasputin having sex with Alexandra and her daughters.[45]

The Romanovs had taken mementoes of Rasputin with them into exile. They had four icons he had given them over the years and a small box filled with Rasputin's letters, "the most precious thing we have," Nicholas said.[46] Before they left Tsarskoe Selo, the four sisters and their mother sewed into their dresses and undergarments eleven topaz stones, gifts from Rasputin. They would be wearing them at the time of their murder.[47]

The guards at the House of Special Purpose offered up their own reminders. They covered the walls with crude graffiti in places their prisoners could not avoid. A favorite subject was Rasputin having sex with Alexandra or the two of them in lewd poses, Nicholas usually depicted sitting nearby and drinking. They scratched sexually graphic doggerels into the walls about "Grishka and Sashura." No opportunity to make reference to the size of Rasputin's phallus was ever passed up.[48] It was past such grotesque pornography that the family descended, for the last time, the twenty-three wooden steps to the basement of the Ipatiev house in the early morning hours of 17 July 1918.

Epilogue

The fortunate ones escaped Russia, the rest did not. It is true a few individuals who remained behind managed to avoid a violent death—Dr. Badmaev, Alexander Samarin, as well as Purishkevich, Pitirim, Varnava, and Sabler—but they were the exceptions. Many more were killed by the Bolsheviks. The list is long: Beletsky, Protopopov, Shcheglovitov, Dzhunkovsky, Menshikov, Novoselov, Manasevich-Manuilov, Prince Andronikov, Nikolai Maklakov, Alexander Makarov, Alexei Khvostov, Yekaterina Sukhomlinova, Grand Dukes Paul and Nikolai Mikhailovich, Ella, Bishop Isidor, Father Alexander Vasilev, Ioann Vostorgov. Even the holy fool Mitya Kozelsky was put to death. One could cite still more names.[1]

Boris Rzhevsky joined the Cheka, the Bolshevik political police, in Moscow and gained a reputation for his sadistic cruelty. He then double-crossed his new masters, stealing a large sum of money and fleeing with Zazulina to the Whites in Odessa, where he resumed his high living and shady deals in the criminal underworld. Early on a February morning in 1919 his body was found in the street outside the Artists' Club. Reports of the exact cause of death vary. Zazulina said he had been shot twice and stabbed seventeen times in the head, while other sources state he had been pumped with fifteen bullets.[2] Either way, Boris's life ended in a spectacularly bloody fashion.

Germogen also came to a cruel end. Arrested by the Bolsheviks in March 1918, he was imprisoned in Yekaterinburg and then moved to Tyumen and from there taken by steamer to Tobolsk in June. As the boat approached Pokrovskoe, Germogen was brought out onto the front deck in his underwear. His captors tied his hands behind his back, affixed a heavy stone to his waist, and then shoved him into the river. The villagers found his body several weeks later. It bore the marks of torture. They buried him in the Pokrovskoe church cemetery. He was later moved to Tobolsk and laid to rest next to the remains of St. Ioann Maksimovich. In 1991, Germogen was canonized by the church.[3]

Maria and the rest of her family were at home in Pokrovskoe when they found Germogen's body. Praskovya, Dmitry and his new wife, Feoktista, had remained in the family home. In 1920, after having been stripped of most of their possessions, the family was forced to move to make room for a hospital. Drifting from one house to another, they eventually built a small place for themselves on the edge of the village where they remained until 1930. Then, in May of that year, they were designated as kulaks, class enemies of the Soviet state, and banished to the far northern reaches of the Ob River and put to work constructing a large fish cannery. Conditions were harsh. On 5 September 1933, Feoktista died of tuberculosis, followed a few days later by six-year-old Yelizaveta, her daughter with Dmitry, Rasputin's grandchild. Three months later Dmitry died of dysentery, and four days after him, on 20 December, Praskovya's heart gave out.[4]

Varvara ended up in Tyumen working as a stenographer in a government office. She was all alone, short of money, and miserable. There were men in town willing to offer help, but only in return for sex. She declined their offers. "Lord, it's so hard," she wrote her sister, "my soul is breaking into pieces, why was I born?" Sometime after February 1924, she left for Moscow in the hope of leaving Russia and joining Maria, who had managed to get to Europe. She died of typhus not long after arriving in the capital. Maria was convinced her sister had been poisoned by the Soviet authorities. She was buried at Novodevichy cemetery, but then, in 1927, after the government decided to make the cemetery a place only for persons it deemed important, her coffin was dug up and discarded.[5]

In early December 1919, Boris Solovyov was arrested in Vladivostok on suspicion of espionage and sent under guard to Chita for questioning by Nikolai Sokolov, the man in charge of the investigation into the murder of the Romanovs. Maria followed after her husband, only to be arrested as well. Sokolov was convinced Boris was a Bolshevik agent and that his claim of being part of a monarchist plot to rescue the tsar and his family had been a lie. The accusation would haunt Boris for the rest of his life. Many in the White Russian emigration were convinced he had been secretly working for either the Communists or the Germans. There never was any evidence for these suspicions, and now it is widely agreed that Rasputin's son-in-law was who he claimed. Attempts by the likes of Sokolov and Felix Yusupov to frame Boris as responsible for the fate of the Romanovs were at base nothing more than one last attempt to blame Russia's misery on Rasputin and those connected to him. If Rasputin was the scapegoat for the fall of the monarchy, Boris was to be the scapegoat for the murder of the tsarist family.[6] Boris and Maria were interrogated at length by Sokolov. He apparently had become convinced Boris had stolen the tsarist jewels and also money intended for the royal family during their captivity, and he offered to let them go if they confessed. But they could not confess to something they knew nothing about. In the end, Maria Mikhailovna Sharaban, a gorgeous cabaret artist and the favorite mistress of the local warlord Ataman Semenov, intervened and convinced Sokolov to let them go free in the first days of 1920.[7]

The couple separated in Vladivostok, Maria traveling to Berlin by way of Trieste and Prague. She was now the mother of two little girls, Tatyana and Maria, named after the daughters of the tsar. They lived with Aaron Simanovich for a time and then moved to Paris, where they were reunited with Boris. They found themselves broke and living hard in Montmartre. Boris brought in a few francs washing cars. They opened a restaurant, but it went bust. In 1926, Boris died of tuberculosis. Alone with the girls, Maria used her famous name to find work as a cabaret performer, having inherited her father's talent for dance. As of 1932, she was performing with a Cossack choir and her trained pony in Paris's "Cirque d'hiver," having begun her new career as a performer back in Berlin upon the urging of Simanovich.[8] Her reputation quickly spread. By the next year she was performing with a circus in Latvia, and then in December 1934 she appeared as a lion tamer in Islington, England.[9] Three months later Maria crossed the Atlantic to become part of the Hagenbeck-Wallace Circus, billed as "Europe's Most Sensational Arenic Star." She was to be the main attraction of the 1935 season, but while in Peru, Indiana she was mauled by a bear and nearly killed. After five weeks in hospital, Maria returned to Europe in November 1935, now taking the safer job of an equestrienne, returning to perform with Ringling Brothers at Madison Square Garden in 1937.

In 1940 in Miami, she married Gregory Bern, described in the press as a childhood friend from Russia, but she filed for divorce six years later citing unspeakable cruelty on the part of her husband.[10] Maria eventually settled in the Silver Lake area of Los Angeles, surviving on private language lessons and various editions of her memoirs and surrounded by photographs of her past life in Russia. She died at home in September 1977 at the age of seventy-nine and was laid to rest under the palm trees of the Angelus-Rosedale Cemetery just off Venice Boulevard.[11]

From Berlin Simanovich also traveled to America and tried to earn a living by selling his "secrets," as he called them, about Rasputin, but he failed to attract any offers. He left for France where he was arrested in a counterfeiting scam and spent some time in jail. From a hotel in Paris, sick with tuberculosis, he wrote to a Jewish acquaintance for money, claiming that he had been the only Jew in Russia who "held in his hands all the political reins" and had exercised "unlimited power" under the last tsar. He insisted he had used his influence as Rasputin's secretary to help the Jewish people, at considerable risk to himself and his family. No one, he boasted, did as much for Russia's Jews as he. No money, however, was forthcoming. Simanovich ended up in a Nazi concentration camp, but somehow managed to survive. After the war he made his way to Liberia and opened a restaurant, Atlantik chez Rasputin.[12]

After the Bolshevik Revolution Grand Duke Dmitry left for Tehran and was taken in by the British ambassador, Sir Charles Marling. He lived with Marling for nearly two years before moving to London. There, he was reunited with his sister Maria. Dmitry strayed about across the Continent, mostly in France, living a life of what he himself called "feverish idleness." He spent his days playing golf and seeing friends at his club, his nights drinking and frequenting the casinos though he had little money with which to gamble. He married an American heiress from Cincinnati, had a son, and moved to America, but the marriage fell apart and before long he was back in Europe. He dabbled in émigré politics and became the lover of Coco Chanel, though nothing seemed to cure an aching ennui. He died of tuberculosis in a Davos sanatorium in 1942, aged fifty.[13]

Dmitry had kept true to his word never to speak of the murder of Rasputin, unlike his friend Felix. The two men were reunited in London, but Dmitry avoided Felix, upset at how casually his co-conspirator talked about what they had sworn never to mention. According to Maria, her brother was revolted by Felix's nonchalant attitude to the murder and could never forgive his constant chatter about it.[14] On 27 February 1920, Dmitry wrote to Felix to tell him their different views on the matter threatened to destroy their friendship. For Dmitry, it would forever be a "stain on my conscience," for "a murder is a murder and will be forever."[15] Maria shared her brother's opinion of Felix, noticing with a mix of pity and disdain how he had mistaken notoriety for popularity and deluded himself into thinking he was a person of great historical importance.[16]

In 1927, Yusupov, short of money, published a book on the killing that upset many in the émigré community. Felix, however, remained unrepentant: "Even now I don't have the least regrets about that murder," he told the press. Scandals seemed to follow Felix wherever he went. The French press and the Russian émigré newspaper *Days*, edited by Alexander Kerensky, reported that Yusupov was forced to leave France in early 1928 after seducing the underage son of a prominent French politician. The father caught the two of them in flagrante delicto and beat them both, his son so badly he had to be taken to the hospital. The father did not want to take the matter to court, and Yusupov offered him some money to hush up the affair. After the story broke in *Days*, Yusupov sued the newspaper and complained that for the past eight years he had been the target of an unremitting campaign of rumor and slander. Yusupov won, although a French court rejected his demand for 500,000 francs in damages, ordering *Days* to pay him a symbolic fine of one franc.[17]

Lawsuits would become a theme in Yusupov's life. In 1932, upset with his depiction in the German film *Rasputin*, he sued the film's makers, insisting they either edit him out (impossible to do as it had already been released) or pay him an indemnity of 50,000 marks.[18] Two years later he sued Metro-Goldwyn-Mayer for libel over its *Rasputin the Mad Monk* starring Ethel, John, and Lionel Barrymore. The basis of the suit centered on the film's depiction of Rasputin's seduction of Irina that Yusupov called libelous. The Yusupovs won an amazingly large judgment of £25,000 against MGM. A triumphant Felix crowed to reporters after the verdict was announced:

> You cannot image the torture I went through reliving the killing of Rasputin [. . .] The incident is especially harrowing to me as I believe my well-intentioned efforts to save my country by destroying the monk only released the devils concentrated in him. These were broadcast and resulted in the Revolution, causing the downfall of Imperial Russia. Then the defense had the audacity to suggest that I, Prince Youssoupoff, did not kill Rasputin, when I have suffered ever since for doing so. No one can calculate the damage of that.[19]

Yusupov tried his luck one more time in 1965, bringing a case in New York state against Columbia Broadcasting System demanding

$1.5 million in damages for its portrayal of Rasputin's murder. He claimed the television program had invaded his privacy by suggesting he had used his wife as bait to get Rasputin to come to his house and then shocked the court by stating that he had not killed Rasputin for any political motive, but solely over the repugnance he felt for Rasputin's debauchery. The trial lasted for weeks, but in the end the New York State Supreme Court rejected the suit.[20] Felix died in Paris in 1967, followed by Irina three years later.

The other killers left little trace after the revolution. Sukhotin married Tolstoy's granddaughter Sophia in 1921, although the marriage did not last long. In 1926, he fell ill and Yusupov generously brought him to Paris, although he died soon thereafter.[21] Lazovert found himself in Paris in the summer of 1918. He used his fame as one of Rasputin's killers to acquire a transit visa from Great Britain, saying at the time he wished to make his way to the Russian Far East and join the White Army fighting the Bolsheviks.[22] He arrived in New York City on 22 September and told the press that he had come to meet with President Woodrow Wilson and inform him of conditions in Russia. Two days later he gave a brief interview to the *New York Times*. In his statement, Lazovert affirmed that it had been Purishkevich, not Yusupov, who fired the fatal shot that night in the yard outside the palace. No one other than he, Yusupov, Grand Duke Dmitry, Sukhotin, and Purishkevich had been involved in plotting and carrying out Rasputin's murder, he told the paper.[23]

Guchkov, Kokovtsov, Milyukov, and Rodzianko all left Russia with the revolution and died in exile. Feofan ended up in Sofia, where, in 1931 it was reported he had gone mad and had to be confined to a lunatic asylum. Overcome with guilt for having introduced Rasputin to the royal family, he was said to be convinced he had caused the collapse of the monarchy. For many nights, beset by this growing obsession, he had been seen lying prostrate before the altar of Sofia's Nevsky Cathedral, wailing about his guilt. He died in France in 1940.[24] Father Vostokov moved to the United States and spent the next forty years trying to alert the world to the danger of "kikes and Freemasons" to Christian civilization.[25] He had an ally in Prince Zhevakhov. The prince worked tirelessly to promote the anti-Semitic fraud *Elders of Zion* and hailed the rise of Mussolini and Hitler. His ultimate fate is unknown.[26]

Iliodor's life after the revolution was, not surprisingly, one of the more colorful ones. In May 1918, he returned to Tsaritsyn telling everyone he had made his fortune in the United States and bearing gifts from Macy's department store for some of his remaining followers.[27] In 1921, as the patriarch of the Russian People's Universal Christian Church, he wrote to Lenin to offer his help in building communism. Lenin did not bother to reply. The following year, after his attempts to revive his fortunes in Tsaritsyn faltered, Iliodor returned to New York. He told wild tales of his times in Bolshevik Russia. He claimed to have visited the Romanovs at the Ipatiev House during Easter in 1918, that he had been embraced by Lenin and other Bolshevik leaders, and that once while touring the Kremlin he was shown the head of Nicholas II, brought to Moscow in a suitcase, he claimed, by none other than Khionya Guseva. It was preserved in a large glass jar, the dead tsar's left eye wide open. Iliodor's imagination knew no bounds. [28]

He threw himself into a number of projects. He tried to work with the Soviet government to recover the lost gold of the tsars, he sent screenplays to directors in Fort Lee. One, based on his life, Iliodor called *Five Years in Hell*. He planned to star in the film himself. After negotiations with Rising Sun Productions for this biopic fell through, he sued for fraud and created his own production company. He dreamed up various get-rich-quick schemes and had plans to use his millions to construct a massive Cathedral of Eternal Truth where he would preach a new gospel. What little money Iliodor did manage to make he lost in the Crash of 1929. With that, his wife left him, taking the children with her.[29] In 1936, he filed a $100,000 defamation suit against the Viking Press and Garden City Publishing Company over statements made in René Fülöp-Miller's *Rasputin: The Holy Devil* that described Iliodor as an anti-Semite and the mastermind of a plot to kill Rasputin. The jury was shown translations of Iliodor's vulgar anti-Jewish writings and sermons from his past in Russia. It took the jurors only forty minutes to rule against him.[30] Defeated in America, in 1947 Iliodor wrote to Stalin asking for permission to move to the Soviet Union. It is not known whether the Soviet leader ever replied.[31] Iliodor died in Manhattan's Bellevue Hospital on 27 January 1952, aged seventy-two, having spent the final years of his life working as a porter at the offices of the Metropolitan Life Insurance Company on Madison Avenue.[32]

The Provisional Government released Khionya Guseva from the Tomsk insane asylum on 27 March 1917. Despite the mass of problems facing the new regime, it made time to see that Rasputin's failed assassin went free. Guseva disappeared for two years, before she turned up in

Moscow, where, on 29 June 1919, exactly five years to the day after her attack on Rasputin, she tried to stab to death Patriarch Tikhon on the steps of Moscow's Cathedral of Christ the Savior. Yet again, she failed. The Soviet government declared her innocent due to mental incompetence and took a lenient stance given her earlier attack on Rasputin. With that, Guseva disappeared from history.[33]

Olga Lokhtina was among those arrested by the Provisional Government and held at the Peter and Paul Fortress before being freed by the Bolsheviks. As late as 1923 she was seen begging for alms at a Petrograd rail station, after which all record of her is lost.[34] Nothing is known about most of Rasputin's other female disciples. Zinaida Manshtedt managed to stay in contact with Alexandra, exchanging letters and even sending her a copy of *The Protocols of the Elders of Zion*. She was captured carrying letters from the former empress and shot together with her husband.[35] Vyrubova remained behind in Petrograd and was arrested on several occasions by the Bolshevik government and threatened with execution. Destitute, cold, and hungry, she managed to escape with her mother to Finland in December 1920. In 1923, she took holy vows as Sister Maria at the Valaamsky Monastery. She died in July 1964, aged seventy. Alexandra's other close friend, Lily Dehn, bounced from Russia to England to Poland to Venezuela. In 1957, she came back to Europe to meet a woman named Anna Anderson, claiming to be Anastasia, the youngest daughter of the last tsar. The two met for a week and after that Lily swore in a Hamburg court that she truly was the lost daughter of the tsar. The woman had told her things, she stated, that no one but a member of the family ever could have known. (She was wrong. Anastasia was actually a mentally unbalanced Polish factory worker named Franziska Schanzkowska.) Dehn died in Rome in 1963 at the age of seventy-eight.[36]

Theodora Krarup remained in Russia until 1938 when she returned to her native Denmark. For over two decades she had kept safe in her apartment a number of mementoes of her relationship with Rasputin—some of his furniture, a lock of his hair, and several of the portraits she had painted of him. Not long before his murder, Rasputin had visited her studio one last time and presented her with a large album of photographs and a manuscript of his aphorisms and thoughts on the state of Russia that he had dictated over the years to Munya Golovina. He told Krarup to publish it someday, promising it would make the poor artist he so admired a lot of money. In the years following the revolution it had not been possible to publish the manuscript and so it sat in her desk drawer. Upon leaving Soviet Russia, she was not permitted to bring most of her personal possessions with her, so with great regret she burned the manuscript as well as the album and her remaining portraits.[37]

A few of the Romanovs managed to escape Russia during the civil war and survive, mostly in rather modest circumstances, for several decades. The Dowager Empress Maria Fyodorovna died in Copenhagen in 1928. Sandro, Felix Yusupov's father-in-law, died in France in 1933. Nikolasha died in Antibes on the French Riviera in 1929, the same place where two years later his brother, Grand Duke Pyotr, would end his days, and, in 1935, Nikolasha's widow, Stana. Her sister, the other Black Crow, Militsa, survived her late husband by twenty years, dying in Alexandria, Egypt in 1951. Tsar Nicholas's two sisters, Olga and Xenia, both passed away in 1960, in Canada and England respectively.

After Yakov Yurovsky, commandant of the House of Special Purpose, and his men had executed the Romanov family and their few remaining servants, they moved the corpses to a truck and drove out of Yekaterinburg in the dark. They headed north about twelve miles to an area of abandoned coal mines known as the Four Brothers near the village of Koptyaki. Here, amidst the pines, birch, and bogs, they transferred their victims to carts and carried them deeper into the woods. Finally, they reached the Four Brothers and placed the bodies on the ground. Two fires were lit. Yurovsky ordered the men to strip the bodies. Undressing Alexandra and her daughters, they discovered their clothing had been lined with diamonds and jewels, including the topaz stones Rasputin had given them. Yurovsky had to maintain order as the men grew excited by the find and the sight of the naked bodies. One of the men took liberties with the corpse of the empress. They burned the clothes and then dumped the bodies into a muddy nine-foot-deep shaft known as Ganin's Pit. Yurovsky threw in a few hand grenades in an attempt to close the pit and hide the bodies.

By ten o'clock on the morning of 17 July 1918 Yurovsky and his men had finished the job. Walking back to their truck they carried a few sacks with the jewels they had taken off the bodies. Along with the diamonds and pearls were four amulets the daughters had been wearing around their necks when they were killed—each bore a portrait of Rasputin and the words from one of his prayers.[38] Up until the end the Romanovs never lost faith in their Friend.

Acknowledgments

It is a pleasure to thank the many people who have offered help and support in the writing of this book: Robert K. Massie, Helen Rappaport, Daniel Beer, Jeremy Bigwood, Rudy de Casseres, Dr. William Lee, Peter Basilevsky, Denise Youngblood, Nikita Sokolov, Alexander Bobosov, Anya Babenko, Pavel Shevyakov, Boris Ilyin, Jonathan Daly, William Pomeranz, David Myers, Keith Jeffrey, Rachel Polonsky, Mel Bach, Aurelia van Moere, Beatrice Benech, Kim Kraft, Britt Lewis, Paul Norlen, Melissa Lucas, Dr. Maria Mileeva, Vladimir von Tsurikov, Dr. Anne Turner, Brian Perry, Dr. Merrell Wiseman, Frances Asquith, Charlotte Miller, Selby Kiffer, RD Zimmerman, Sarah Gordon, Derek Butler, Andrew Jack, and Jo-Anne Birnie Danzker. I thank Kevin McKenna, Wolfgang Mieder, and Denis Mahoney of the University of Vermont for their support and encouragement over the years.

I have had the good fortune to work with dozens of excellent librarians and archivists and am especially grateful to Carol Leadenham, Stephanie Stewart, Vishnu Jani, and Rachel Bauer at the Hoover Institution Archive. Anatol Shmelev, curator of the Hoover's Russia and Eurasian Collection, has helped me enormously for many years on this and my previous book. I wish to thank Prince Andrew Andreevich Romanoff for permission to quote from the papers of Grand Duchess Ksenia Alexandrovna in the Hoover Archive. At Yale University: Tatjana Lorkovic, William Massa, Stephen Jones, Anne Marie Menta, and helpful staff of the Beinecke Rare Book and Manuscript Library and the Sterling Memorial Library. At Harvard University: Anna Rakityanskaya and Hugh Truslow. Tanya Chebotarev and the staff of the Bakhmeteff Archive at Columbia University. Catherine Miller at the National Archives in Atlanta and Charliann Becker at the archive's Seattle satellite. Solveig Nestler and Dr. Gerhard Keiper at the Bundesarchiv and Politische Arkhiv des Auswärtigen Amts in Berlin. Lena Ånimmer and Kerstin Söderman at the Swedish National Archives. Thomas Just of the Haus-, Hof- und Staatsarchiv in Vienna. In Moscow, I am particularly grateful to Sergei Mironenko, former director of the State Archive of the Russian Federation, for permitting me to read the extensive police files on Rasputin, and also to Viktor Neustroev of the Russian State Archive of Literature and Art. In St. Petersburg, Alexei Kulegin, Valentina Ushakova, and Svetlana Khodakovskaya of the State Museum of the Political History of Russia provided considerable assistance.

In Siberia, I wish to thank Olga Tarasova, Natalya Galian, and Anna Miachenskaya of the State Archive of the Tyumen Oblast and Tatiana Kokliagina, Liubov Zhuchkova, Olga Iuzeeva, and Dinara Akberdeeva of the Tobolsk archive. Vladimir Smirnov and Marina Smirnova gave me a private tour of the Rasputin Museum they have established in Pokrovskoe and graciously answered my many questions. Sergei Rasskazov of Tyumen State University was especially welcoming and helpful, as were Natalya Karmanova and Vlad Urban.

Natalya Bolotina, Svetlana Dolgova, Yelena Matveeva, and Yelena Mikhailova provided invaluable help in locating and transcribing hundreds of documents from a number of archives in Russia, and Tatiana Safronova offered great assistance in accessing materials held in the State Historical Museum. My debt to them is enormous. Mariana Markova helped in a number of important ways, especially in making sense of Rasputin's often impenetrable Russian and transcribing documents whose handwriting resisted my best attempts at decipherment. My colleagues Willard Sunderland, Nadieszda Kizenko, Melissa Stockdale, and Peter Pozefsky read the book at various stages, offering helpful comments and catching a number of errors.

I am fortunate to have excellent agents in Melissa Chinchillo and Peter Robinson, whose support, advice, and encouragement have been indispensable. I would also like to acknowledge the work done by their colleagues on my behalf at Fletcher and Company and Rogers, Coleridge & White. Thank you to my publishers Farrar, Straus and Giroux and Macmillan, including Jonathan Galassi, Jeff Seroy, Devon Mazzone, Laird Gallagher, Amber Hoover, Steven Pfau, Robin Harvie, Nicholas Blake, Philippa McEwan, Charlotte Wright, Jo Gledhill, Douglas Matthews, Fergus Edmondson, Caitriona Row, John English, and especially my marvelous editors Eric Chinski and Georgina Morley.

My largest debt is to my family—to Annette Smith, Emma and Andrew, and, most importantly, Stephanie, for everything.

Bibliography

Note on Sources

The literature on Rasputin is not only vast, it is also characterized by works of widely divergent reliability, usefulness, and authorial intent. It must be pointed out that the earliest, and most influential, writings on Rasputin were undertaken not to shed light on the complex truth of the man, but to publicly destroy him, as is particularly evident in the works of Iliodor and Prince Felix Yusupov.

Dozens of biographies have appeared in the hundred years since Rasputin's death. Each biographer has sought in his own way to make sense of this mysterious figure, and I have had the advantage of benefiting from a century's worth of investigation, study, and reflection. The most honest, reliable single-volume work in Russian is Alexei Varlamov's *Grigorii Rasputin-Novyi* (2008). I have drawn heavily on the work of Oleg Platonov and especially Sergei Fomin, whose books are full of new and important information, while being careful to filter out their anti-Semitism and preoccupation with various Russophobic conspiracies. The best biographies in English have both been written by Joseph Fuhrmann: *Rasputin: A Life* (1990) and *Rasputin: The Untold Story* (2013). I have also made extensive use of Fuhrmann's magisterial *Complete Wartime Correspondence of Tsar Nicholas II and the Empress Alexandra* (1999). Although it contains much valuable testimony from Rasputin's acolytes, Edvard Radzinsky's *The Rasputin File* is to be approached with caution.

There have been a number of literary fakes connected with the life of Rasputin. Perhaps best known among them is the diary of Anna Vyrubova, written by Alexei Tolstoy and Pavel Shchegolev, historian and member of the Provisional Government's Extraordinary Commission, and published more than once in Russia. More recently, a purported diary of Rasputin was published in Moscow in 2008. Based on my reading of the text, this is also a forgery, as the editors themselves admit may well be the case. A memoir by Maria Rasputina (*Rasputin: Pochemu?: Vospominaniia docheri*) published in Russia in 2000 does not appear genuine, and, as with the previous forgeries, I have avoided using it in my biography. Maria published a number of books on her father, and their reliability decreased with each subsequent edition. For that reason I have generally avoided *Rasputin: The Man Behind the Myth* (1977) and limited myself to her first two books.

The memoir literature concerning Rasputin is enormous and also of varied reliability. I have tried to maintain a skeptical approach and to use it with a clear eye to each author's particular biases. This body of work, however flawed, cannot be ignored for the wealth of information it contains, and these works can yield a great deal of insight into Rasputin and his times depending on the kinds of questions one puts to them.

It has been my intention during the six years of research and writing of *Rasputin* to seek out every last possible primary documentary source and to rely on published secondary sources as little as possible. Without wishing to fetishize the archives, the inaccessibility of the documents on Rasputin in Russian archives for many decades has hampered our knowledge of the man and at the same time helped to perpetuate many of the lies, distortions, and errors that have passed for the truth for much too long.

Abbreviations

AD: Archives diplomatiques (La Courneuve)

BA: Bakhmeteff Archive, Columbia University

BV: *Birzhevye vedomosti*

Commission: *Chrezvychainaia sledstvennaia komissiia dlia rassledovaniia byvshikh ministrov i prochikh dolzhnostnykh lits*

CUL: Cambridge University Library, Department of Manuscripts

FA: S. V. Fomin, *"A krugom shirokaia Rossiia—"*

FB: S. V. Fomin, *Bozhe! Khrani svoikh*

FDNO: S. V. Fomin, *Dorogoi nash otets*

FN: S. V. Fomin, *Nakazanie pravdoi*

FR: Joseph T. Fuhrmann, *Rasputin: The Untold Story*

FSA: S. V. Fomin, *Skorbnyi angel*

FStr: S. V. Fomin, *"Strast' kak bol'no, a vyzhivu—"*

FSu: S. V. Fomin, *Sud'ia zhe mne Gospod'!*

GARF: Gosudarstvennyi arkhiv Rossiiskoi Federatsii

GATO: Gosudarstvennyi arkhiv Tiumenskoi oblasti

GAUKTO/TIAMZ: Gosudarstvennoe avtonomnoe uchrezhdenie kul'tury Tiumenskoi oblasti: Tobol'skii istoriko-arkhitekturnyi muzei-zapovednik

GBUTO/GAGT: Gosudarstvennoe biudzhetnoe uchrezhdenie Tiumenskoi oblasti "Gosudarstvennyi arkhiv v g. Tobol'sk"

GRS: Kriukov, *Grigorii Rasputin: sbornik istoricheskikh materialov*

HHStA: Haus-, Hof- und Staatsarchiv

HIA: Hoover Institution Archives, Stanford University

HL/DiaryDP: Houghton Library, Diaries of Grand Duke Dmitry Pavlovich

HL/Sokolov: Houghton Library, Documents Concerning the
   Investigation into the Death of Nicholas II, 1918–1920. (Nikolai
   Sokolov Investigation)
IMM: Iliodor (Trufanov), *The Mad Monk*
KVD: Rassulin, et al., *Khronika velikoi druzhby*
LP: Maylunas and Mironenko, *A Lifelong Passion*
NA: National Archives (Kew)
NA/US: National Archives (College Park, MD)
NIOR/RGB: Rossiiskaia gosudarstvennaia biblioteka, nauchno-
   issledovatel'skii otdel rukopisei
OPI/GIM: Gosudarstvennyi istoricheskii muzei, otdel pis'mennykh
   istochnikov
OR/RNB: Rossiiskaia natsional'naia biblioteka, otdel rukopisei
PA: Parliamentary Archives
PAAA: Das Politische Archiv des Auswärtigen Amts
PK: *Peterburgskii [Petrogradskii] kur'er*
PZ: Oleg Platonov, *Zhizn' za tsaria*
RGADA: Rossiiskii gosudarstvennyi arkhiv drevnikh aktov
RGALI: Rossiiskii gosudarstvennyi arkhiv literatury i iskusstva
RGIA: Rossiiskii gosudarstvennyi istoricheskii arkhiv
RR: Edvard Radzinsky, *The Rasputin File*
RRR: Marie Rasputin, *The Real Rasputin*
SML: Sterling Memorial Library, Yale University
TsM: *Tsaritsynskaia mysl'*
TsV: *Tsaritsynskii vestnik*
VR: Aleksei Varlamov, *Rasputin*
VV: *Vechernee vremia*
VVFR: Spiridovich, *Velikaia voina i fevral'skaia revoliutsiia*
WC: Fuhrmann, ed., *The Complete Wartime Correspondence*
YLS: Felix Yusupov, *Lost Splendor*

Archives

Austria
Haus-, Hof- und Staatsarchiv (Vienna)

France
Archives diplomatiques, Ministère des Affaires étrangères et
   européennes (La Courneuve)

Germany
Das Politische Archiv des Auswärtigen Amts (Berlin)

Russia
Gosudarstvennoe avtonomnoe uchrezhdenie kul'tury Tiumenskoi

oblasti, Tobol'skii istoriko-arkhitekturnyi muzei-zapovednik
(Tobolsk)
Gosudarstvennoe biudzhetnoe uchrezhdenie Tiumenskoi oblasti
"Gosudarstvennyi arkhiv v g. Tobol'sk" (Tobolsk)
Gosudarstvennyi arkhiv Rossiiskoi Federatsii (Moscow)
Gosudarstvennyi arkhiv Tiumenskoi oblasti (Tyumen)
Gosudarstvennyi istoricheskii muzei, otdel pis'mennykh istochnikov
(Moscow)
Gosudarstvennyi muzei politicheskoi istorii Rossii (St. Petersburg)
Rossiiskaia gosudarstvennaia biblioteka, nauchno-issledovatel'skii otdel
rukopisei (Moscow)
Rossiiskaia natsional'naia biblioteka, otdel rukopisei (St. Petersburg)
Rossiiskii gosudarstvennyi arkhiv drevnikh aktov (Moscow)
Rossiiskii gosudarstvennyi arkhiv literatury i iskusstva (Moscow)
Rossiiskii gosudarstvennyi istoricheskii arkhiv (St. Petersburg)

Sweden
Riksarkivet (Stockholm)

United Kingdom
Cambridge University Library, Department of Manuscripts (Cambridge)
National Archives (Kew)
Parliamentary Archives (London)

United States
Bakhmeteff Archive, Columbia University (New York)
Beinecke Rare Book and Manuscript Library and Sterling Memorial
Library, Yale University (New Haven, CT)
Holy Trinity Orthodox Seminary, Archives and Library (Jordanville, NY)
Hoover Institution Archives (Stanford, CA)
Houghton Library, Harvard University (Cambridge, MA)
National Archives (College Park, MD)

Newspapers and Journals (Contemporary)

Aftenposten
Aftonbladet
Al'manakh "Svoboda"
Astrakhanskii listok
Avanti!
Badische Landes-Zeitung
Berliner Allgemeine Zeitung
Berliner Morgenpost

Berliner Tageblatt
Berliner Zeit
Bich
Birzhevye vedomosti
Byloe
Chertenok
Church Times
Dagens Nyheter
Daily Express
Daily Mail
Daily Mirror
Den'
Dépêche de Toulouse
Deutsche Warte
Dni
Donetskaia zhizn'
Drug
Dsihwe
Dsihwes Spehks
Dym otechestva
Dziennik Polski
L'Echo de Russie
L'Eclair
Ekaterinburgskie eparkhial'nye vedomosti
Ermak
Frankfurter Zeitung
Gazeta-kopeika
Gazette de Lausanne
Golos minuvshego
Golos Moskvy
Golos naroda
Golos Rossii
Golos Rusi
Groza
La Guerre Sociale
Hamburger Fremdenblatt
L'Homme libre
L'Humanité
Iskry
Iuzhnaia zaria
Iuzhnye vedomosti
Iuzhnyi krai
Jauna Dienas Lapa

Le Journal
Journal de Genève
Kamsko-volzhskaia rech'
Kazanskii telegraf
Kievliane
Kölnische Volks-Zeitung
Kolokol
Köslinger Zeitung
Kurjer Poznański
La Lanterne
Le Matin
Morning Post
Moskovskie vedomosti
Moskovskii listok
Nasha rabochaia gazeta
Nationalzeitung
Neue Freie Presse
Neues Wiener Journal
New Statesman
New York Times
Norske Intelligenz-Seddeler
Nov'
Novaia voskresnaia vecherniaia gazeta
Novoe vremia
Novosti dnia
Novyi satirikon
Nya Dagligt Allehanda
Ob"edinenie
Odesskie novosti
Odesskii listok
Orenburgskaia gazeta
Otklik na zhizn'
Penzenskii krai
Peterburgskaia gazeta
Peterburgskii kur'er
Peterburgskii listok
Petit Parisien
Petrogradskaia gazeta
Petrogradskaia listovka
Petrogradskii listok
Petrogradskii vesel'chak
Post-och Inrikes Tidningar
Priazovskii krai

Pridneprovskii krai
Przegląd Codzienny
Rannee utro
Rassvet
Rech'
Reichspost
Revel'skii vestnik
Rheinisch-Westfälische Zeitung
Rostovskii listok
Rudin
Rul'
Russkaia pravda
Russkaia riv'era
Russkaia volia
Russkie novosti
Russkie vedomosti
Russkoe slovo
St. *Peterburger Herald*
Saratovskii listok
Saratovskii vestnik
Sibirskaia nov'
Sibirskaia torgovaia gazeta
Sibirskie voprosy
Smekh dlia vsekh
Solntse Rossii
Sovremennoe slovo
Sovremennyi mir
La Stampa
Step'
Stolichnaia molva
Strannik
Svet
Le Temps
The Times (London)
Tobol
Trepach
Tsaritsynskaia mysl'
Tsaritsynskii vestnik
Tserkov'
Ufimskii vestnik
Ural'skaia zhizn'
Utro luga
Utro Rossii

Vechernee vremia

Vechernie izvestiia

Vechernii Petrograd

Vestnik Zapadnoi Sibiri

Volksfreund

Volzhskii vestnik

Volzhsko-Donskoi krai

Voskresnaia vecherniaia gazeta

Vossische Zeitung

Wiener Allgemeine Zeitung

Yorkshire Post

Za narod!

Zaural'skii krai

Zemshchina

Zhemchuzhina

Zhivoe slovo

Zhurnal zhurnalov

Primary Sources

Al'bionov. "Zhitie nepodobnogo startsa Grigoriia Rasputina." In *Smekh dlia vsekh.* Petrograd, 1917.

Alexander, Grand Duke of Russia. *Once a Grand Duke.* New York, 1932.

———. "Pis'mo k Nikolaiu ot 25 dekabria 1916 g.–4 fevralia 1917 g." *Arkhiv russkoi revoliutsii* 5 (1922).

"Aleksandro-Nevskaia Lavra nakanune sverzheniia samoderzhaviia." *Krasnyi arkhiv* 77 (1936).

Aleksin, S. *Sviatoi chert. (Blagodat' Grishki Rasputina.).* Moscow, 1917.

Alfer'ev, E. E. *Pis'ma tsarskoi sem'i iz zatocheniia.* Jordanville, NY, 1974.

Al'manakh "Svoboda" 1 ("Kazn' Griskhi Rasputina.") (1917).

Andrei Mikhailovich, Velikii kniaz'. "Iz dnevnika velikogo kniazia Andreia Vladimirovicha za 1916–1917 gg." *Krasnyi arkhiv* 26 (1928).

Arbatskii, F. P. *Tsarstvovanie Nikolaia II.* Moscow, 1917.

Badmaev, P. *Za kulisami tsarizma. (Arkhiv tibetskogo vracha Badmaeva).* Leningrad, 1925.

Bashkiroff, Z. *The Sickle and the Harvest.* London, 1960.

Basily, Nicholas de. *Nicolas de Basily, Diplomat of Russia, 1903–1917: Memoirs.* Stanford, 1973.

Belaia, S. [Markiza Dliaokon']. "Rasputinskaia blagodat'." *Teatral'nye novinki* (1917).

Beletskii, S. P. *Grigorii Rasputin. (Iz zapisok).* Petrograd, 1923.

———. "Vospominaniia." *Arkhiv russkoi revoliutsii.* Vol. 12. Berlin, 1923.

Bel'gard, A. V. "Pechat' i Rasputin." *Mosty* 9 (1962).

Beliaev, A. I. "Dnevnik protoiereia A. I. Beliaeva, nastoiatelia Fedorovskogo sobora v Tsarskom Sele." *Dvorianskoe sobranie* 5 (1996).

[Belling, A. A.]. *Iz nedavnego proshlogo: Vstrechi s Grigoriem Rasputinym.* Petrograd, 1917.

Benckendorff, Count Paul. *Last Days at Tsarskoe Selo.* London, 1927.

Berberova, N. *Kursiv moi.* Moscow, 1999.

Blok, A. A. *Poslednie dni imperatorskoi vlasti.* Moscow, 2005.

———. *Sobranie sochinenii.* Vols. 5, 6. Compiled by V. Orlov. Moscow, 1982–83.

———. *Sobranie sochinenii.* Moscow-Leningrad, 1962–63.

———. *Zapisnye knizhki, 1901–1920.* Moscow, 1965.

Bobrinskii, A. A. "Dnevnik A. A. Bobrinskogo (1910–1911)." *Krasnyi arkhiv* 1 (26) (1928).

Bogdanovich, A. V. *Tri poslednikh samoderzhtsa: Dnevnik.* Moscow-Leningrad, 1924.

Bogoslovskii, Mikhail. *Dnevniki (1913–1919).* Edited by Tat'iana Timakova. Moscow, 2011.

Bok, M. P. (Stolypina). *Vospominaniia o moem ottse P. A. Stolypine.* Moscow, 1992.

Bonch-Bruevich, M. D. *Vsia vlast' sovetam. Vospominaniia.* Moscow, 1958.

Botkin, Gleb. *The Real Romanovs.* New York, 1931.

Bricaud, Joanny. "Un mage à la Cour de Russie." *La Revue* 16–17 (1918).

Buchanan, Sir George William. *My Mission to Russia and Other Diplomatic Memories.* 2 Vols. London, 1923.

Buchanan, Meriel. *The Dissolution of Russia.* London, 1932.

Bulanov, L. P. *Skol'ko stoilo narodu tsar' i ego sem'ia.* Petrograd, 1917.

Bulgakov, M. A. *Dnevnik. Pis'ma. 1914–1940.* Moscow, 1997.

Bulgakov, S. N. *Avtobiograficheskie zametki.* 2nd edn. Paris, 1991.

———. *Khristianskii sotsializm.* Novosibirsk, 1991.

———. "Na piru bogov." In *Iz glubiny.* Moscow, 1991.

Buranov, Iu., comp. "Strannik iz sela Pokrovskogo." *Rodina* 3 (1992).

Burtsev, V. L. "Delo ob ubiistve Rasputina. Rasputin v 1916 godu." *Illiustrirovannaia Rossiia* 17 (363) (23 April 1932).

Buxhoevden, Sophie. *Before the Storm.* London, 1938.

Cantacuzène, Julia, Princess. *Revolutionary Days; Recollections of Romanoffs and Bolsheviki, 1914–1917.* Boston, [1919].

Chebotaryova, Valentina. "V dvortsovom lazarete v Tsarskom Sele: Dnevnik 14 iiulia 1915–5 ianvaria 1918." *Novyi zhurnal* 181, 182 (1990).

Chernyshev, A. V., and N. S. Polovinkin, editors and compilers. *Grigorii Rasputin v vospominaniiakh sovremennikov: sbornik.* Moscow-Tiumen', 1990.

Cockfield, Jamie H, ed. *Dollars and Diplomacy. Ambassador David Rowland Francis and the Fall of Tsarism, 1916–1917.* Durham, NC, 1981.

Collection du Prince et de la Princesse Félix Youssoupoff. Auction Catalogue. Olivier Coutau-Bégarie. Paris, 2014.

Damer, Aleksandr. "Rasputin vo dvortse." *Illiustrirovannaia Rossiia* 16 (362) (16 April 1932).

Den, Iuliia. *Podlinnaia tsaritsa: Vospominaniia.* Moscow, 1998.

Diterikhs, M. *Ubiistvo Tsarskoi Sem'i i chlenov Doma Romanovykh na Urale*. Pt. 1. Vladivostok, 1922. Reprint, Moscow, 1991.

"Dnevnik Andreia Vladimirovicha za 1916–1917 gg." *Istochnik* 3 (1998).

Dnevnik krest'ianina A. A. Zamaraeva, 1906–1922. Edited by V. V. Morozov and N. I. Reshetnikov. Moscow, 1995.

Dolgova, S. R. *Nakanune svad'by*. Moscow, 2012.

Dorr, Rheta Childe. *Inside the Russian Revolution*. New York, 1918; 1970 reprint.

Dostoevsky, Fyodor. *The Brothers Karamazov*. Translated by Constance Garnett. New York, 1950.

Durnovo, A. "Kto etot krest'ianin Grigorii Rasputin." *Otkliki na zhizn'* 11–12 (1917).

Dzhanumova, E. F. *Moi vstrechi s Rasputinym*. Petrograd-Moscow, 1923.

Dzhunkovskii, V. *Vospominaniia*. Moscow, 1997.

Eager, M. *Six Years at the Russian Court*. London, 1906.

Elizaveta Fedorovna, velikaia kniaginia. "Pis'ma k imperatritse Marii Fedorovne, 1883–1916 gg." *Rossiiskii arkhiv* 11 (2001).

Engel'gardt, Nikolai. "Iz Batishcheva. Epizody moei zhizni. (Vospominaniia)." *Minuvshee* 24 (1998).

Epanchin, N. A. *Na sluzhbe trekh imperatorov. Vospominaniia*. Edited by A. Kavtaradze. Moscow, 1996.

Evlogii, Mitropolit (Georgievskii). *Put' moei zhizni: vospominaniia*. Moscow, 1994.

Fabritskii, S. S. *Iz proshlogo. Vospominaniia fligel'-ad"iutanta gosudaria imperatora Nikolaia II*. Berlin, 1926.

Feoktistov, E. M., V. Novitskii, F. Lir, F., and M. Kleinmikhel'. *Za kulisami politiki. 1848–1914*. Moscow, 2001.

Fetisenko, O. "Iz dnevnika 'peterburgskogo mistika' (Evgenii Ivanov i ego eskhatologicheskie vozzreniia." *Eskhatologicheskii sbornik*. St. Petersburg, 2006.

Francis, David. *Russia from the American Embassy, April 1916–November 1918*. New York, 1921.

———. *Russia in Transition. The Diplomatic Papers of David R. Francis, Ambassador to Russia*. Frederick, MD, 1985.

Fuhrmann, Joseph T., ed., *The Complete Wartime Correspondence of Tsar Nicholas II and the Empress Alexandra. April 1914–March 1917*. Greenwood, CT, 1999.

"G. E. Rasputin glazami ofitsial'nykh vlastei." Edited by S. L. Firsov. *Russkoe proshloe* 6 (1996).

Gaiderova, Z. N. . . . *Tsarstvovanie Nikolaia II. (Ocherk obshchestvennogo i revoliutsionnogo dvizheniia)*. Moscow, 1917.

Gavriil Konstantinovich. *V mramornom dvortse. Iz khroniki nashei sem'i*. St. Petersburg-Düsseldorf, 1993.

———. *Velikii kniaz' Gavriil Konstantinovich v Mramornom dvortse*. Moscow, 2001.

[Gibbs, Philip]. *The Russian Diary of An Englishman, Petrograd, 1915–1917*. New York, 1919.

Gilliard, Pierre. *Thirteen Years at the Russian Court*. Translated by F. Appleby Holt. London, 1921.

Gippius, Z. N. *Dmitrii Merezhkovskii. Vospominaniia*. Moscow, 1991.

———. *Dnevniki*. Moscow, 1999.

———. *Vospominaniia*. Moscow, 2001.

Glinka, Ia. V. *Odinnadtsat' let v Gosudarstvennoi dume*. Moscow, 2001.

Globachev, K. N. "Pravda o russkoi revoliutsii. Vospominaniia byvshego nachal'nika petrogradskogo okhrannogo otdeleniia." *Voprosy istorii* 7–8 (2002).

———. *Pravda o russkoi revoliutsii. Vospominaniia byvshego nachal'nika petrogradskogo okhrannogo otdeleniia*. Moscow, 2009.

Golder, Frank. *War, Revolution, and Peace in Russia. The Passages of Frank Golder, 1914–1927*. Stanford, 1992.

"Gor'kii i russkaia zhurnalistika nachala XX veka. Perepiska." *Literaturnoe nasledstvo* 95 (1988).

Gorodtsov, P. A. *Pis'ma k bratu Vasiliiu. Iz bumag P. A. Gorodtsova, sudebnogo sledovatelia, advokata i sobiratelia sibirskogo fol'klora*. Supplement to *Iskateli prikliucheniia*. Accessed online on 28 January 2015: http://magru.net/pubs/1819/Pisma_bratu_Vasiliyu?view_mode=slider#1

Gosudarstvennaia Duma. *Stenograficheskie otchety, 1912–1916*. Vol. 4. Moscow, 1995.

Grabbe, P. *Okna na Nevu. (Moi iunye gody v Rossii)*. St. Petersburg, 1995.

Graham, Stephen. *With the Russian Pilgrims to Jerusalem*. London, 1914.

Grigorii Rasputin. Iz ego zhizni i pokhozhdenii. Iliodor i V. M. Purishkevich o Rasputine. Kiev, 1917.

Grigorii Rasputin: Iz ego zhizni i pokhozhdenii. Kiev, 1917.

Grigorii Rasputin v vospominaniiakh uchastnikov i ochevidtsev. (Iz materialov Chrezvychainoi komissii Vremennogo Pravitel'stva). Moscow, 1990.

Guchkov, A. I. *Guchkov rasskazyvaet*. Moscow, 1993.

Gul', R. B. *Ia unes Rossiiu*. 3 Vols. Moscow, 2001.

Gumilev, N. S. *Selected Works*. Translated by Burton Raffel and Alla Burago. Albany, 1972.

Gurko, V. I. *Cherty i siluety proshlogo: Pravitel'stvo i obshchestvennost' v tsarstovanie Nikolaia II v izobrazhenii sovremennika*. Edited by N. P. Sokolov. Moscow, 2000.

———. *Tsar i tsaritsa. O tsarstvovanii Nikolaia II*. Moscow, 2008.

Iakhontov, A. N. *Prologue to Revolution. Notes of A. N. Iakhontov on the Secret Meetings of the Council of Ministers, 1915*. Edited by Michael Cherniavsky. Englewood Cliffs, NJ, 1967.

Ilarion (Alfeev), episkop, comp. *Spory ob imeni Bozhiem. Arkhivnye dokumenty 1912–1938 godov*. St. Petersburg, 2007.

Iliodor (Trufanov, Sergei). *Kogda-zhe konets?* Moscow, [1906].

———. *Pamiatka o vechnoi istine*. New York, 1947.

———. "Pis'mo ieromonakha Iliodora V. I. Leninu." *Otechestvennye arkhivy* 4 (2005).

———. *The Mad Monk of Russia, Iliodor. Life, Memoirs, and Confessions of Sergei Michailovich Trufanoff.* New York, 1918.

———. "The Mystery of the Head in the Kremlin." *Liberty*, 18 February 1933.

———. "Sviatoi chert. (Zapiski o Rasputine)." *Golos minuvshego* 3 (1917).

———. *Sviatoi chert. (Zapiski o Rasputine).* Introduction by S. P. Mel'gunov. Moscow, 1917.

———. *Tainy doma Romanovykh.* Moscow, 1917.

———. *Velikaia stalingradskaia marfa.* New York, 1943.

Ilyin, Olga. "The Court and I." Unpublished manuscript.

Ioffe, G. Z. "'Rasputiniada', bol'shaia politicheskaia igra." *Otechestvennaia istoriia* 3 (1998).

Istoriia tsarstvovaniia Nikolaia II. Vols. 1–2. Moscow, 1917–18.

Istratova, S. P., comp. *Zhitie bludnogo startsa Grishki Rasputina.* Moscow, 1990.

Ivnev, R. *Neschastnyi angel.* Petrograd, 1917.

"Iz dnevnika A. V. Romanova za 1916–1917 gg." *Krasnyi arkhiv* 26 (1928).

"Iz semeinoi perepiski Iusupovykh." *Reka vremen* 2 (1995).

"K istorii poslednikh dnei tsarskogo rezhima (1916–1917)." *Krasnyi arkhiv* 1 (14) 1926.

"K istorii ubiistva Grigoriia Rasputina." *Krasnyi arkhiv* 4 (1923).

Kafafov, K. D. "Vospominaniia o vnutrennikh delakh Rossiiskoi Imperii." *Voprosy istorii* 7 (2005).

Kak khoronili Rasputina. Za velikokniazheskimi kulisami. N.p., n.d.

Kakurin, N. "Iz dnevnika generala V. I. Selivacha." *Krasnyi arkhiv* 2 (9) (1925).

Kalpaschikoff, Andrew. *A Prisoner of Trotsky's.* Garden City, NY, 1920.

Karrik, V. "Voina i revoliutsiia: Zapiski, 1914–1917 gg." *Golos minuvshego* 7/9 (1918).

Kazn' Grishki Rasputina. Compiled by E. Sno. Petrograd, [1917].

Kerensky, Alexander. *The Catastrophe; Kerensky's Own Story of the Russian Revolution.* New York, 1927.

———. *Russia and History's Turning Point.* New York, [1965].

Khersonskii. *Akafist Grishke Rasputinu.* Petrograd, [1917].

———. *Skazka o tsare-durake, o tsaritse-bludnitse i o Grishke Rasputinoi shishke.* Petrograd, [1917].

Khvostov, A. N. "Iz vospominanii." *Golos minuvshego* 2 (1923).

Kireev, A. A. *Dnevnik, 1905–1910.* Edited by K. A. Solov'ev. Moscow, 2010.

Kir'ianov, Iu. I., comp. "Pravye v 1915-m–fevrale 1917go. (Po perliustrirovannym departamentom politsii pis'mam)." *Minuvshee* 14 (1993).

Klaving, V. V., comp. *Ia szheg Grigoriia Rasputina.* St. Petersburg, 2001.

Kleinpennig, Petra H., ed. *The Correspondence of Empress Alexandra of Russia with Ernst Ludwig and Eleonore, Grand Duke and Grand Duchess of Hesse, 1878–1916.* Norderstedt, Germany, 2010.

Kliachko, L. M. . . . *Za kulisami starogo rezhima.* *(Vospominaniia zhurnalista)*. Vol. 1. Leningrad, 1926.

Kliuev, N. *Slovesnoe drevo.* St. Petersburg, 2003.

Kokovtsov, V. *Iz moego proshlogo.* Moscow, 1991.

———. *Out of My Past: The Memoirs of Count Kokovtsov.* Edited by H. H. Fisher. Translated by Laura Matveev. Stanford, 1935.

Koni, A. F. *Nikolai II: Vospominaniia,* Vol. 2. Moscow, 1966.

Korostovetz, Vladimir. *Seed and Harvest.* Translated by Dorothy Lumby. London, 1931.

Korovin, Konstantin. "Sviataia Rus', Vospominaniia." *Illiustrirovannaia Rossiia* (2 April 1932).

Kovalevskii, P. *Grishka Rasputin.* Moscow, 1917.

Kovyl'-Bobyl', I. I. *Tsaritsa i Rasputin.* Petrograd, [1917].

———. *Vsia pravda o Rasputine.* Petrograd, 1917.

Krarup, Theodora. *42 Aar i Czarriget og Sovjet.* Copenhagen, 1941.

Kriukov, V., comp. *Grigorii Rasputin: sbornik istoricheskikh materialov.* 4 Vols. Moscow, 1997.

Kshesinskaia, M. *Vospominaniia.* Moscow, 1992.

Kshesinskii, S. *Sviatoi chert. (Imperatritsa Aleksandra i Grigorii Rasputin): Istoricheskii roman v 2 chastiakh.* Moscow, 1917.

Kulikov, S. V., ed. "'Uspokoeniia nichego ozhidat': pis'ma kniazia M. M. Andronikova Nikolaiu II, Aleksandre Feodorovnoi, A. A. Vyrubovoi i V. N. Voeikovu." *Istochnik* 1 (1999).

Kupchinskii, F. P. "Kak ia szhigal Grigoriia Rasputina." *Solntse Rossii* 369 (1917).

Kurlov, P. G. *Konets russkogo tsarizma: Vospominaniia byvshego komandira korpusa zhandarmov.* Moscow-Petrograd, 1923.

Kuz'min, M. A. *Dnevnik, 1908–1915.* Edited by N. A. Bogomolov and S. V. Shumikhin. St. Petersburg, 2009.

Laganskii, E. "Kak szhigali Rasputina." *Ogonek* 52 (1926); 1 (1927).

Lamzdorf, V. N. *Dnevnik.* Moscow, 1926; 1934; 1991.

Lazovert, Stanislaus. "An Account of Rasputin's Assassination." In Charles F. Horne and Walter F. Austin, eds. *Source Records of the Great War.* Vol. 5. Alabama, 1923.

Lemke, M. K. *250 dnei v tsarskoi stavke, 1914–1916.* 2 Vols. Minsk, 2003.

The Letters of Tsar Nicholas and Empress Marie, Being the Confidential Correspondence Between Nicholas II, the Last of the Tsars, and His Mother, Dowager Empress Maria Feodorovna. Edited by Edward J. Bing. London, 1937.

Lettres des Grands-Ducs à Nicolas II. Translated by M. Lichnevsky. Paris, 1926.

Levin, K. N. *Poslednii russkii tsar' Nikolai II.* Moscow, 1918.

Liberman, Anatoly. *On the Heights of Creation. The Lyrics of Fedor Tyutchev.* Greenwich, CT, 1992.

"Lichnost' Nikolaia II i Aleksandry Fedorovny po svidetel'stvam ikh rodnykh i blizkikh (gazetnye materialy)." *Istoricheskii arkhiv* (April 1917).

Lockhart, Sir Robert Bruce. *The Diaries of Sir Robert Bruce Lockhart*. Vol. 1: 1915–1938. Edited by Kenneth Young. London, 1973.

———. *Memoirs of a British Agent*. London, 1932.

Lodyzhenskii, M. V. *Misticheskaia trilogiia. Temnaia sila*. Moscow, 1998.

Lopukhin, V. B. *Zapiski byvshego direktora departamenta Ministerstva inostrannykh del*. St. Petersburg, 2008.

Lukomskii, A. S. *Vospominaniia*. 2 Vols. Berlin, 1922.

Lunin, S. *Rasputin. P'esa v 4 deistviiakh*. Leningrad, 1927.

L'vov, L. *Za kulisami starogo rezhima. (Vospominaniia zhurnalista)*. Vol. 1. Leningrad, 1926.

Makhetov, A., ed. "'Starets' Grishka Rasputin v vospominaniiakh sovremennikov." *Pravoslavnyi khristianin* 3 (2003).

Maklakov, V. A. "Nekotorye dopolneniia k vospominaniiam Purishkevicha i kniazia Iusupova ob ubiistve Rasputina." *Sovremennye zapiski* 34 (Paris, 1928).

Marie, Grand Duchess of Russia. *Education of a Princess. A Memoir*. New York, 1931.

———. *A Princess in Exile*. New York, 1931.

Marie, Queen of Romania. *The Story of My Life*. New York, 1934.

Mariia Fedorovna, Empress of Russia. *Dnevniki*. Moscow, 2006.

Mariia Fedorovna. *Dnevniki imperatritsy Marii Fedorovny (1914–1920, 1923 gody)*. Moscow, 2005.

Markow, Sergey von. *Wie ich die Zarin befreien wollte*. Zürich, 1929.

Martynov, A. P. *Moia sluzhba v otdel'nom korpuse zhandarmov. Vospominaniia*. Edited by Richard Wragi. Stanford, 1972.

Materialy k zhitiiu prepodobnomuchenitsy Velikoi Kniagini Elizavety Feodorovny. Pis'ma, dnevniki, vospominaniia, dokumenty. Moscow, 1996.

Maud, Renée Elton. *One Year at the Russian Court: 1904–1905*. London, 1918.

Maylunas, Andrei, and Sergei Mironenko. *A Lifelong Passion: Nicholas and Alexandra, Their Own Story*. Translated by Darya Galy. New York, 1997.

Mech (Mendelev), R. *Golos s togo sveta, ili Grishka Rasputin v gostiakh u satany*. Moscow, 1917.

Mel'gunov, S. P. *Poslednii samoderzhets. Cherty dlia kharakteristiki Nikolaia II*. Moscow, 1917.

———. *Vospominaniia i dnevniki*. 2 Pts. Paris, 1964.

Mel'nik (Botkina), T. *Vospominaniia o Tsarskoi Sem'e i ee zhizni do i posle revoliutsii*. Moscow, 1993.

Men'shikov, M. O. "Dnevnik 1918 goda." *Rossiiskii arkhiv* 4 (1993).

Mikhail Aleksandrovich, Velikii kniaz'. *Dnevnik i perepiska, 1915–1918*. Edited by V. M. Khrustalev. Moscow, 2012.

Mikhailov, A. *Temnye sily*. Moscow, 1917.

Miliukov, P. N. *Political Memoirs, 1905–1917*. Edited by Arthur P. Mendel. Translated by Carl Goldberg. Ann Arbor, MI, 1967.

———. *Vospominaniia*. Moscow, 1991.

Miule-Vasil'ev, V. K. *Grishka Rasputin u tsygan. Byl' v litsakh s peniem v 1-m deistvii.* Petrograd, 1917.

Moe, Ronald C. *Prelude to Revolution: The Murder of Rasputin.* Chula Vista, CA, 2011.

Monarkhiia pered krusheniem (1914–1917 gg.): Bumagi Nikolaia II i drugie dokumenty. Edited by V. P. Semennikov. Moscow-Leningrad, 1927.

Mordvinov, A. A. "Poslednii imperator, vospominaniia fligel'-ad'iutanta A. Mordvinova." *Otechestvennye arkhivy* 3–4 (1993).

Mosolov, A. A. *Pri dvore poslednego imperatora: zapiski nachal'nika kantseliarii ministra dvora.* St. Petersburg, 1992.

Naryshkin-Kurakin, Elizabeth. *Under Three Tsars.* Edited by René Fülöp-Miller. Translated by Julia E. Loesser. New York, 1931.

Naumov, A. N. *Iz utselevshikh vospominanii, 1868–1917.* 2 Vols. New York, 1954–55.

Nekludoff, A. V. *Diplomatic Reminiscences, Before and During the World War, 1911–1917.* Translated by Alexandra Paget. London, 1920.

New York Times Current History, The. Vol. 17. New York, 1919.

Nicholas II, emperor of Russia [Nikolai II]. *Dnevniki imperatora Nikolaia II (1894–1918).* Edited by S. V. Mironenko. Vol. 1. Moscow, 2011; Vol. 2, Pt. 2 (1914–1918). Moscow, 2013.

————. *Letters of the Tsar to the Tsaritsa, 1914–1917.* Translated by A. L. Hynes. Commentary by C. E. Vulliamy. London, 1929.

————. *The Secret Letters of the Last Tsar.* Edited by Edward J. Bing. New York, 1938.

Nikolai II Romanov: ego zhizn' i "deiatel'nost'", 1894–1917 gg. Po inostrannym i russkim istochnikam. Petrograd, 1917.

Nikolai II. Materialy dlia kharakteristiki lichnosti i tsarstvovaniia. Moscow, 1917.

Nikolai II. Semeinyi al'bom. Katalog vystavki. Moscow, 1998.

Nikolai i Aleksandra: Dvor poslednikh russkikh imperatorov. Katalog vystavki. St. Petersburg, 1994.

Nikolai II i velikie kniaz'ia: Rodstvennye pis'ma k poslednemu tsariu. Moscow-Leningrad, 1924.

Nikolai Mikhailovich, Velikii kniaz'. "Zapiski N. M. Romanova." *Krasnyi arkhiv* 47–49 (1931).

Nikol'skii, B. V. "Vyderzhki iz dnevnika." *Krasnyi arkhiv* 1 (1935)

Nikon (Rklitskii), archbishop. *Zhizneopisanie blazhenneishego Antoniia, mitropolita Kievskogo i Galitskogo.* 10 Vols. New York, 1956–63.

Nikulin, L. V. *O startse Grigorii i russkoi istorii . . . : Skazka nashikh dnei.* Moscow, 1917.

Novaia knizhka ob sviatom cherte Grishke, ob Nikolae bezgolovom, glupom i bestolkovom, ob Alise-nemke, chto snimala s russkikh penki, o ministrakh-predateliakh i obo vsekh pridvornykh obirateliakh. Moscow, 1917.

Novoselov, M. A. *Grigorii Rasputin i misticheskoe rasputstvo.* Moscow, 1917.

Obninskii, V. P. *Nikolai II—poslednii samoderzhets. Ocherki iz zhizni i tsarstvovaniia.* Moscow, 1992; orig. 1917.

Ol'ga Aleksandrovna, velikaia kniaginia. *Memuary.* Moscow, 2003.

Ordovskii-Tanaevskii, N. A. *Vospominaniia.* Caracus, St. Petersburg, Moscow, 1993.

Oreshnikov, A. V. *Dnevnik, 1915–1933.* Book 1. Edited by P. G. Gaidukov. Moscow, 2010.

Originalakten zum Mord an Rasputin. (Original Legal Documents Concerning the Murder of Rasputine.) With a Description in English. Offered for Sale by Karl W. Hiersemann. Leipzig, [1929].

Padenie tsarskogo rezhima. Stenograficheskie otchety doprosov i pokazanii, dannykh v 1917 g. v Chrezvychainoi sledstvennoi komissii Vremennogo pravitel'stva. 7 Vols. Edited by P. E. Shchegolev. Moscow-Leningrad, 1924–27.

Paléologue, Maurice. *An Ambassador's Memoirs.* Translated by F. A. Holt. 3 Vols. London, 1923–25.

Peregudova, Z. I., ed. *"Okhranka": vospominaniia rukovoditelei politicheskogo syska.* 2 Vols. Moscow, 2004.

Perepiska sviashchennika Pavla Florenskogo i Mikhaila Aleksandrovicha Novoselova. Tomsk, 1998.

"Podrobnosti ubiistva Rasputina." *Krasnyi arkhiv* 6 (1931).

Pokrovskii, M., ed. "Politicheskoe polozhenie Rossii nakanune Fevral'skoi revoliutsii v zhandarmskom osveshchenii." *Krasnyi arkhiv* 17 (1926).

Polivanov, A. A. *Iz dnevnikov i vospominanii po dolzhnosti voennogo ministra i ego pomoshchnika. 1906–1916.* Moscow, 1924.

Polovtsev, A. A. "Dnevnik." *Krasnyi arkhiv* 3–4 (1923).

Portugalov, V. V. *Tsarstvovanie poslednego Romanova.* Petrograd, 1917.

Poslednie dnevniki Imperatritsy Aleksandry Fedorovny Romanovoi. Fevral' 1917 g.–16 iiulia 1918 g. Sbornik dokumentov. Edited by V. A. Kozlov and V. M. Khrustalev. Novosibirsk, 1999.

Poslednie dni Rasputina. Arkhangel'sk, 1917.

"Poslednii vremenshchik poslednego tsaria." *Voprosy istorii* 10, 12 (1964); 1–3 (1965).

Pourtalès, Friedrich. *Am Scheidewege zwischen Krieg und Frieden. Meine Letzten Verhandlungen in St. Petersburg, Ende Juli 1914: Tagesaufzeichnung und Dokumente.* Berlin, 1927.

Preston, Thomas. *Before the Curtain.* London, 1950.

Priadilov, A. N. *Krakh Rossiiskoi imperii: Svidetel'stva i suzhdeniia uchastnikov i ochevidtsev.* Moscow, 2005.

Prishvin, M. M. *Dnevnik, 1918–1919.* St. Petersburg, 1991.

———. *Dnevniki, 1914–1917.* St. Petersburg, 2007.

"Protokol doprosa M. G. Solov'evoi (Rasputinoi) sledovatelem po osobovazhnym delam N. A. Sokolovym, 26–27 dekabria 1919 g. v Chite. (Iz arkhiva Sokolova)." *Rodina* 3 (1992).

"Protokoly doprosa admirala Kolchaka chrezvychainoi sledstvennoi komissiei v Irkutske v ianv.–fevr. 1920 g." *Arkhiv russkoi revoliutsi.* 10 (1991).

Prugavin, A. S. *Leontii Egorovich i ego poklonnitsy.* Moscow, 1916.

Purishkevich, V. M. *The Murder of Rasputin*. Edited by M. E. Shaw. Translated by Bella Costello. Ann Arbor, MI, 1980.

Raitblat, A. I., ed. *"Okhranka". Vospominaniia rukovoditelei politicheskogo syska*. Moscow, 2004.

"Rasputin as Known to the Secret Police (Ochrana)." In C. E. Vulliamy, ed. *The Red Archives: Russian State Papers and Other Documents Relating to the Years 1915–1918*. London, 1929.

"Rasputin v osveshchenii 'okhranki.'" *Krasnyi arkhiv* 5 (1924).

Rasputin v vospominaniiakh sovremennikov. Moscow, 1990.

Rasputin, Grigorii. *Blagochestivye razmyshleniia*. St. Petersburg, 1912.

———. *Dnevnik Rasputina*. Edited by D. A. Kotsiubinskii and I. V. Lukoianov. Moscow, 2008.

———. *Dukhovnoe nasledie. Izbrannye stat'i, besedy, mysli i izrecheniia*. N.p., 1994.

———. *Moi mysli i razmyshleniia*. Moscow, 1991.

———. *Moi mysli i razmyshleniia. Zhitie opytnogo strannika. Pis'ma*. Moscow, 2001.

———. *Velikie torzhestva v Kieve. Poseshchenie Vysochaishei Sem'i. Angel'skii privet*. St. Petersburg, 1911.

———. *Zhitie opytnogo strannika*, in Platonov, *Zhizn' za tsaria*.

Rasputin, Marie [M. G. Rasputina]. "Dnevnik Matreny Grigor'evny Rasputinoi." Edited by L. A. Lykova. *Rossiiskii arkhiv* 11 (2001).

———. [Solovieff-Raspoutine, Marie]. *Mon père Grigory Raspoutine*. Paris, 1925.

———. *My Father*. London, 1934.

———. *Rasputin: Pochemu?: Vospominaniia docheri*. Moscow, 2000.

———. *The Real Rasputin*. Translated by Arthur Chambers. London, 1929.

———, and Patte Barham. *Rasputin: The Man Behind the Myth: A Personal Memoir*. Englewood Cliffs, NJ, 1977.

Rassledovanie tsareubiistva. Sekretnye dokumenty. Moscow, 1993.

Rassulin, Iurii, Sergei Astakhov, and Elena Dushenova, comps. *Khronika velikoi druzhby. Tsarstvennye mucheniki i chelovek Bozhii Grigorii Rasputin-Novyi*. St. Petersburg, 2007.

Raupakh, R. R., von. *Facies Hippocratica (Lik umiraiushchego): Vospominaniia chlena Chrezvychainoi Sledstvennoi Komissii 1917 goda*. Edited by S. A. Man'kov. St. Petersburg, 2007.

Remizov, A. M. "Dnevnik, 1917–1921." *Minuvshee* 16 (1994).

Rodzianko, M. V. *The Reign of Rasputin: An Empire's Collapse*. Introductions by Sir Bernard Pares and David R. Jones. Translated by Catherine Zvegintzoff. Gulf Breeze, FL, 1973.

Rom-Lebedev, Ivan. "Zapiski moskovskogo tsygana." *Teatr* 3–6 (1985).

Romanov, A. V. *Dnevnik velikogo kniazia Andreia Vladimirovicha*. Leningrad, 1925.

———. "Pozornoe vremia perezhivaem." Iz dnevnika Velikogo Kniazia Andreia Vladimirovicha Romanova. *Istochnik* 3 (34) (1998).

———. *Voennyi dnevnik velikogo kniazia Andreia Vladimirovicha Romanova (1914–*

1917). Edited and compiled by V. M. Osin and V. M. Khrustalev. Moscow, 2008.

Romanov, D. P. "Pis'ma k ottsu." *Krasnyi arkhiv* 30 (1928).

Romanov, K. K. *Dnevniki. Vospominaniia. Stikhi. Pis'ma.* Edited by E. Matonina. Moscow, 1998.

Romanov, N. M. "Dnevnik velikogo kniazia Nikolaia Mikhailovicha." *Krasnyi arkhiv* 4, 6, 9 (1931).

———. "Zapiski." in *Gibel' monarkhii.* Moscow, 2000.

Romanova, A. F. (imperatritsa Aleksandra Fedorovna). *Divnyi svet. Dnevnikovye zapisi, perepiska, zhizneopisanie.* Moscow, 1999.

Rozanov, V. V. *Apokalipticheskaia sekta (khlysty i skoptsy).* St. Petersburg, 1914.

———. *Listva. Iz rukopisnogo naslediia.* Moscow, 2001.

———. *Mimoletnoe.* Moscow, 1994.

———. *O sebe i zhizni svoei.* Moscow, 1990.

———. *V nashei smute. Stat'i 1908 g. Pis'ma k E. F. Gollerbakhu.* Moscow, 2004.

———. *Vozrozhdaiushchiisia Egipet.* Moscow, 2002.

Rozanova, Tat'iana. *"Bud'te svetly dukhom." (Vospominaniia o V. V. Rozanove).* Moscow, 1999.

Rudnev, V. [V. M. Roudnieff]. *La vérité sur la Famille Impériale Russe et les Influences occultes.* Paris, 1920.

———. *Pravda o tsarskoi sem'e i temnykh silakh.* Ekaterinodar, 1919.

———. "Vospominaniia." *Russkaia letopis'.* Vypusk 2. Paris, 1922.

Sablin, N. V. *Desiat' let na imperatorskoi iakhte "Shtandart."* St. Petersburg, 2008.

Sadovskii, B. "Zapiski (1881–1916)." *Rossiiskii arkhiv* 1 (1991).

Saf'ianova, A. *O startse Grigorii i russkoi istorii . . . Skazka nashikh dnei.* Moscow, [1917].

Savich, N. V. *Vospominaniia.* St. Petersburg, 1993.

Sazonov, S. D. *Fateful Years, 1909–1916: The Reminiscences of Serge Sazonov, Russia's Minister for Foreign Affairs.* London, 1928.

Schelking, Eugene de. *Recollections of a Russian Diplomat.* New York, 1918.

Semennikov, V. P. *Monarkhiia pered krusheniem. 1914–1917 gg. Bumagi Nikolaia II i drugie dokumenty.* Moscow-Leningrad, 1927.

"Sem'ia Romanovykh—Nikolai i Aleksandra: Svidetel'stvuiut rodnye i blizkie." *Neva* 8 (1997).

Sh. P. *Grigorii Rasputin. Ego zhizn', rol' pri dvore imperatora Nikolaia II i ego vliianie na sud'bu Rossii.* Moscow, 1917.

Shaika shpionov Rossii i gnusnye dela Grishki Rasputina. Moscow, 1917.

Shakhovskoi, Prince Vsevolod. *Sic Transit Gloria Mundi (Tak prokhodit mirskaia slava), 1893–1917.* Paris, 1952.

Shavel'skii, Georgii. *Russkaia tserkov' pered revoliutsiei.* Moscow, 2005.

———. *Vospominaniia poslednego protopresvitera russkoi armii i flota.* New York, 1954.

Shelley, Gerard. *The Blue Steppes. Adventures Among the Russians.* London, [1925].

———. *The Speckled Domes: Episodes of an Englishman's Life in Russia.* New York, 1925.

Shkulev, F. S. *Nikolai v adu: Rasskaz o tom, kak Nikolai Romanov v ad popal, gde Rasputina Grishku uvidal.* [Moscow, 1917].

Shtiurmer [Stürmer], B. V. "Vsepoddanneishie zapiski B. V. Shtiurmera, 1916 g." *Istoricheskii arkhiv* 6 (1994).

Shulenberg, V. *Vospominaniia ob imperatritse Aleksandre Fedorovne.* Paris, 1928.

Shul'gin, V. V. *Dni. (Zapiski).* Belgrade, 1925.

———. *Poslednii ochevidets.* Moscow, 2002.

———. *The Years. Memoirs of a Member of the Russian Duma, 1906–1917.* Edited by Jonathan E. Sanders. Translated by Tanya Davis. New York, 1984.

Simanovich, Aron. *Rasputin i evrei.* Moscow, n.d. [1991?].

——— [Simanowitsch]. *Rasputin, der allmächtige Bauer.* Munich, 1928.

Sliozberg, G. B. *Dela minuvshikh dnei, zapiski russkogo evreia.* 3 Vols. Paris, 1934.

Smitten, B. N. "Poslednii vremenshchik poslednego tsaria. (Materialy chrezvychainoi sledstvennoi komissii o Rasputine i razlozhenii samoderzhaviia)." Edited by A. L. Sidorov. *Voprosy istorii* 10, 12 (1964); 1, 2 (1965).

Sokolov, N. A. "Predvaritel'noe sledstvie. 1919–1922 gg." Compiled by L. A. Lykov. *Rossiiskii arkhiv* 8 (1998).

———. *Ubiistvo tsarskoi sem'i.* Berlin, 1922; reprint, Moscow, 1990.

Sokolov, V. *Temnye sily Rossiiskoi Imperii.* Moscow, 1917.

Sotheby's, Auction Catalogue, 2 June 2006.

Spiridovich, Alexander I. *Last Years of the Court at Tsarksoe Selo.* Vol. 1. Translated by Emily Plank. Fremantle, Western Australia, 2009.

———. *Les dernières années de la cour de Tzarskoïé-Sélo.* Paris, 1928.

———. *Zapiski zhandarma.* Moscow, 1991.

Stenograficheskie otchety zasedanii Gosudarstvennoi Dumy. St. Petersburg, 1906–17.

Stoeckl, Baroness de. *Not All Vanity.* Edited by George Kinnaird. London, 1950.

Stolypin, P. A. "Iz perepiski P. A. Stolypina s Nikolaem II." *Krasnyi arkhiv* 5 (30) (1928).

[Stopford, Albert]. *The Russian Diary of an Englishman, 1915–1917.* London, 1919.

Stremoukhov, P. P. "Moia bor'ba s episkopom Germogenom i Iliodorom. Iz vospominanii senatora P. P. Stremoukhova." *Arkhiv russkoi revoliutsii* 16 (Berlin, 1925).

Sukhomlinov, V. A. *Erinnerungen.* Berlin, 1924.

"Sviatoi chert." Rasputin Grishka, zloi genii Doma Romanovykh. Moscow, [1917].

"Svidanie dolzhno byt' obstavleno tainoi (novye materialy ob ubiistve Rasputina)." *Istochnik* 3 (1993).

Syroechkovskii, B. E. *Nikolai II i ego tsarstvovanie.* Moscow, 1917.

Taina Doma Romanovykh. Vol. 1. Petrograd, 1917.

Taina Doma Romanovykh ili pokhozhdeniia Grigoriia Rasputina. [Kiev, 1917].

Taina vliianiia Grishki Rasputina. Grishka i zhenshchiny. Grishka politik. Grishka i "Sashka". Grishka spirit. Petrograd, [1917].

Tainy tsarskogo dvora i Grishka Rasputin. Moscow, 1917.

Tainy Tsarskosel'skogo Dvortsa. Tainy kartiny i grammofonnoi plastinki. Petrograd, 1917.

Teliakovskii, V. A. *Dnevniki direktora Imperatorskikh teatrov.* Vol. 4. Edited by M. G. Svetaeva. Moscow, 2001.

——. *Vospominaniia.* Moscow-Leningrad, 1965.

Temnye sily. Tainy Rasputnogo dvora. "Rasputin". Petrograd, 1917.

Templewood, Samuel John Gurney Hoare. *The Fourth Seal. The End of a Russian Chapter.* London, [1930].

Tenisheva, M. K. *Vpechatleniia moei zhizni.* Leningrad, 1991.

Tikhomirov, L. A. *Dnevnik L. A. Tikhomirova, 1915–1917 gg.* Edited by A. V. Repnikov. Moscow, 2008.

——. "Iz dnevnika." *Krasnyi arkhiv* 3 (1930); 6 (1935); 1 (1936).

——. *Vospominaniia.* Moscow-Leningrad, 1927.

——. "25 let nazad. (Iz dnevnikov L. Tikhomirova)." *Krasnyi arkhiv* 1–5 (1930).

Tkhorzhevskii, I. I. *Poslednii Peterburg: Vospominaniia kamergera.* St. Petersburg, 1999.

Tolstoi, A., and P. Shchegolev. *Zagovor imperatritsy (p'esa).* Moscow, 1926.

Tomskii, O. *Skazka o Grishke Rasputnom, glupykh ministrakh i Dvore Vysochaishem. [V stikhakh].* Petrograd, 1917.

Trewin, J. C. *House of Special Purpose: An Intimate Portrait of the Last Days of the Imperial Russian Family Compiled from the Papers of their English Tutor, Charles Sydney Gibbes.* New York, 1975.

Trotsky, Leon. *History of the Russian Revolution.* Vol. 1. Translated by Max Eastman. Chicago, 2008.

Tsesarevich. Dokumenty. Vospominaniia. Fotografii. Moscow, 1998.

Tumanskii, A. "Zlobodnevnye p'esy." *Teatr i iskusstvo* 20, 21 (1917).

Uspenskii, K. "Ocherk tsarstvovaniia Nikolaia II." *Golos minuvshego* 4 (1917).

"V tserkovnykh krugakh pered revoliutsiei. Iz pisem arkhiepiskopa Antoniia Volynskogo k mitropolitu Kievskomu Flavianu." *Krasnyi arkhiv* 6 (31) (1928).

Vasilevskii, I. M. *Belye memuary.* Petrograd, 1923.

Vasil'chikova, L. L. *Ischeznuvshaia Rossiia. Vospominaniia kniagini Lidii Leonidovny Vasil'chikovoi. 1886–1919.* St. Petersburg, 1995.

Vasil'ev, A. T. *The Ochrana, the Russian Secret Police.* Edited and with an Introduction by René Fülöp-Miller. Philadelphia, 1930.

Vatala, El'vira. *Grigorii Rasputin bez mifov i legenda. Roman v dokumentakh.* Moscow, 2000.

Vecchi, Joseph. *The Tavern is My Drum. My Autobiography.* London, 1948.

Veniamin (Fedchenkov), Metropolitan. *Na rubezhe dvukh epokh.* Edited by A. K. Svetozarskii. Moscow, 1994.

Vershinin, A. P. *Sviatoi chert (Grigorii Rasputin). P'esa v 1-m deistvii (repertuara mosk. i petrogr. teatrov).* Viatka, 1917.

Vetukhov, A. *"Mikroby zla"*. (*Zametki po povodu knigi M. Lodyzhenskogo "Temnaia sila"*). Khar'kov, 1916.

Vinberg, F. *Krestnyi put'. Chast' 1: Korni zla*. Munich, 1922.

Vinogradov, Igor. "Nicholas II, Stolypin, and Rasputin: Letter of 16 October 1916." *Oxford Slavonic Papers* 12 (1965).

Vitte, S. Iu. *Vospominaniia*. 3 Vols. Moscow, 1994.

———. *Iz arkhiva S. Iu. Vitte: Vospominaniia*. Edited by B. B. Anan'ich, et al. 2 Vols. St. Petersburg, 2003.

Vladykin, Akim. *Taina rozhdeniia b. naslednika i pridvornaia kamaril'ia*. Petrograd, 1917.

Voeikov, V. N. *S tsarem i bez tsaria. Vospominaniia poslednego dvortsovogo komendanta Gosudaria Nikolaia II*. Moscow, 1995.

Volkov, A. A. *Okolo tsarskoi sem'i*. Paris, 1928 [Moscow 1993].

Vonliarliarskii, V. *Moi vospominaniia*. Berlin, n.d.

Vrangel', N. N. *Dni skorbi. Dnevnik 1914–1915 godov*. St. Petersburg, 2001.

"Vsepoddanneishie zapiski B. V. Shtiurmera. 1916 g." *Istoricheskii arkhiv* 6 (1994).

"Vstrecha v stavke. Nikolai II i A. D. Samarin." *Istoricheskii arkhiv* 2 (1996).

Vulliamy, C. E., and A. L. Hynes, eds. *The Red Archives: Russian State Papers and Other Documents Relating to the Years 1915–1918*. London, 1929.

Vyrubova (Taneeva), A. A. "Dnevnik A. A. Vyrubovoi." *Minuvshie dni* 1, 2 (1927); 3 (1928).

———. "Neizvestnye fragmenty 'Vospominanii' Anny Vyrubovoi." *Rodina* 2 (1988).

———. *Rasputin*. Moscow, 1990.

———. *Stranitsy moei zhizni*, in *Vernaia Bogu, Tsariu i Otechestvu. Anna Aleksandrovna Taneeva (Vyrubova)—monakhinia Mariia*. Edited and compiled by Iurii Rassulin. St. Petersburg, 2005.

Woytinskii, W. S. *Stormy Passage*. New York, 1961.

[Yusupov, Felix]. "Kak my ubivali Rasputina." *Ogonek* 50, 52 (1927).

———. *Lost Splendor: The Amazing Memoirs of the Man Who Killed Rasputin*. Translated by Ann Green and Nicholas Katkoff. New York, 2003.

——— [Iusupov, F. F., kniaz']. *Pered izgnaniem, 1887–1919: memuary*. Edited by N. Strizhova. Moscow, 1993.

——— [Youssoupoff, Prince Felix]. *Rasputin*. NY, 1927.

Yusupova, Princess Zinaida Nikolaevna. "Diary, January 1–April 25, 1919." Translated by Christine Galitzine. Unpublished ms.

Zancke, H. Th. v. *Rasputin. Russische Sittenbilder nach den Erinnerungen eines Okhrana Agenten*. Berlin, 1917.

Zavarzin, P. P. *Zhandarmy i revoliutsiia*. Paris, 1930.

Zhdanov, Lev. *Nikolai "Romanov." Poslednii Tsar': Istoricheskie nabroski*. Petrograd, 1917.

———. *Sud nad Nikolaem II. Stranitsy istorii proshlykh i nashikh dnei*. Petrograd, n.d.

Zhevakhov, N. D. *La Verità su Rasputin*. Bari, 1930.

————. *Vospominaniia tovarishcha ober-prokurora Sviashchennogo Sinoda.* 2 Vols. Moscow, 1993.

Zhizn' i pokhozhdenie Grigoriia Rasputina. Kiev, 1917.

Zhukovskaia, V. A. "Moi vospominaniia o Grigorii Efimoviche Rasputine, 1914–1916 gg." *Rossiiskii arkhiv* 2–3 (1992).

Zotov, M. *Grishka Rasputin (muzhik vserossiiskii). P'esa v 1-m deistvii.* Petrograd, 1917.

Secondary Sources

Alberg, V. L. "Grigori Efimovich Rasputin, 1871–1916." *Social Studies* 47, no. 8 (1956).

Almazov, Boris. *Rasputin i Rossiia. (Istoricheskaia spravka).* Prague, 1922.

Amal'rik, A. *Rasputin. Dokumental'naia povest'.* Moscow, 1992.

Antrick, O. *Rasputin und die politische Hintergründe seiner Ermordung.* Braunschweig, 1938.

Arkhipenko, V. "Zagovor Iliodora." *Nauka i religiia* 9 (1969).

Aronson, G. *Rossiia nakanune revoliutsii.* New York, 1962.

Ashton, Janet. "'God in All Things': The Religious Beliefs of Russia's Last Empress and Their Personal and Political Context." *British Library Journal* 6 (2006).

Avrekh, A. Ia. *Masony i revoliutsiia.* Moscow, 1990.

Bariatinskii, V. V. "Oshibka istorii." *Illiustrirovannaia Rossiia* 16 (362) (16 April 1932).

Bartlett, Rosamund. *Tolstoy. A Russian Life.* New York, 2001.

Batyushin, N. S. *Tainaia voennaia razvedka i bor'ba s nei.* Edited by I. I. Vasil'ev and A. A. Zdanovich. Moscow, 2002.

————. *U istokov russkoi kontrrazvedki: sbornik dokumentov i materialov.* Moscow, 2007.

Bennett, J. D. C. "Princess Vera Gedroits: Military Surgeon, Poet and Author." *British Medical Journal* 305 (19–26 December 1992).

Berberova, Nina. *Kursiv moi: avtobiografiia.* Moscow, 1999.

————. *Liudi i lozhi. Russkie masony XX stoletiia.* New York, 1986.

Berdiaev, N. *Sud'ba Rossii.* Moscow, 1990.

Berger, Joachim. "European Freemasonries, 1850–1935: Networks and Transnational Movements." In *European History Online (EGO)* by the Institut für europäische Geschichte, Mainz, 2010. Accessed at: http://www.ieg-ego. eu/bergerj-2010-en.

————. "Local–National–Transnational Heroes? Hero-worship in Western European Freemasonries (c. 1870–1914)." In *Hinter den Kulissen. Beiträge zur historischen Mythenforschung.* Edited by Claus Oberhauser and Wolfgang Knapp. Innsbruck, 2012.

Berry, Thomas E. "Séances for the Tsar: Spiritualism in Tsarist Society and

Literature." *Journal of Religion and Psychical Research* (January 1984–January 1986).

Betskii, K., and P. Pavlov. *Russkii Rokambol' (prikliucheniia I. F. Manasevicha-Manuilova)*. Leningrad, 1925.

Betts, Richard. *Pshenitsa i plevely: bespristrastno o G. E. Rasputine*. Moscow, 1997.

———, V. Marchenko. *Dukhovnik tsarskoi sem'i. Sviatitel' Feofan Poltavskii (1873–1940)*. 2nd edn. Moscow, 1996.

Bienstock, J. W. *Raspoutine. La fin d'un régime*. Paris, 1917.

Billington, James. *The Icon and the Axe. An Interpretive History of Russian Culture*. New York, 1970.

Bisher, Jamie. *White Terror: Cossack Warlords of the Trans-Siberian*. Abingdon, 2009.

Blok, A. *Poslednie dni imperatorskoi vlasti*. Moscow, 2005.

Bokhanov, A. N. *Delovaia elita Rossii, 1914 g.* Moscow, 1994.

———. *Pravda o Grigorii Rasputine. Ostorozhno: fal'sifikatsiia*. Moscow, 2011.

———. *Rasputin: Anatomiia mifa*. Moscow, 2000.

———. *Rasputin: Byl' i ne byl'*. Moscow, 2006.

———, et al. *The Romanovs: Love, Power and Tragedy*. London, 1993.

Borisov, D. *Vlastiteli i chudotvortsy. (Iliodor, Germogen i Rasputin)*. Saratov, 1926.

Bostunich, G. *Masonstvo i russkaia revoliutsiia: pravda misticheskaia i pravda real'naia*. Moscow, 1993.

———. *Otchego Rasputin dolzhen byl poiavit'sia. (Obosnovaniia psikhologicheskoi neizbezhnosti)*. Petrograd, 1917.

Botsianovskii, B. F. "Karikatura i tsenzura v nachale XX v." *Byloe* 4 (1925).

Brown, Candy Gunther. *Testing Prayer: Science and Healing*. Cambridge, MA, 2012.

Budnitskii, O. V. *Russian Jews between the Reds and the Whites, 1917–1920*. Philadelphia, 2012.

Bukharkina, Ol'ga. "Tak pisal Rasputin." *Diletant* 10 (22) (October 2013).

Buksgevden, S. K. *Ventsenosnaia muchenitsa. Zhizn' i tragediia Aleksandry Feodorovny, imperatritsy vserossiiskoi*. Moscow, 2006.

Carey, Benedict. "Long-Awaited Medical Study Questions the Power of Prayer." *New York Times*, 31 March 2006.

Carlson, Maria. *"No Religion Higher Than Truth:" A History of the Theosophical Movement in Russia, 1875–1922*. Princeton, 1993.

Chambrun, Charles. *Lettres à Marie, Pétersbourg-Pétrograd, 1914–1917*. Paris, 1941.

Chambrun, Marie, Princesse Lucien [Marie] Murat. *Raspoutine et l'aube sanglante*. Paris, 1917.

Cherepakhov, M. S., and E. M. Fingerit, compilers. *Russkaia periodicheskaia pechat' (1895–oktiabr' 1917)*. Moscow, 1957.

Chernow, Ron. *The Warburgs: The Twentieth-Century Odyssey of a Remarkable Jewish Family*. New York, 1993.

Chernyshev, A. V. "O vozraste Grigoriia Rasputina i drugikh biograficheskikh detaliakh." *Otechestvennye arkhivy* 1 (1992).

———. "Rasputinskaia tema na stranitsakh izdanii nashikh dnei (1988–2005)." Tiumen', 1996.

———. *Religiia i Tserkov' v Tiumenskom krae. Opyt bibliografii.* Pt. 2. Tiumen', 2004.

———. "Vybor puti (Shtrikhi k religiozno-filosofskomu portretu G. E. Rasputina)." In *Religiia i tserkov' v Sibiri. Sbornik nauchnykh statei i dokumental'nykh materialov.* No. 11. Tiumen', 1998.

Cockfield, Jamie H. *White Crow: The Life and Times of Grand Duke Nicholas Mikhailovich Romanov, 1859–1919.* Westport, CT, 2002.

Coleman, Heather J. *Russian Baptists and Spiritual Revolution, 1905–1929.* Bloomington, IN, 2006.

Cook, Andrew. *To Kill Rasputin. The Life and Death of Grigori Rasputin.* Stroud, 2007.

Coonrod, Robert Wingate. "The Fourth Duma and the War, 1914–1917." Ph.D. Dissertation. Stanford University, 1950.

Crummey, Robert. O. *The Formation of Muscovy, 1304–1613.* New York, 1987.

Cullen, Richard. *Rasputin: The Role of Britain's Secret Service in his Torture and Murder.* London. 2010.

Curtiss, John Shelton. *Church and State in Russia, The Last Years of the Empire: 1900–1917.* New York, 1940.

Daly, Jonathan W. *The Watchful State: Security Police and Opposition in Russia, 1906–1917.* DeKalb, IL, 2004.

———, and Leonid Trofimov, eds. *Russia in War and Revolution, 1914–1922: A Documentary History.* Indianapolis, IN, 2009.

Danilov, Iu. N. *Na puti k krusheniiu: ocherki iz poslednego perioda russkoi monarkhii.* Moscow, 1992.

de Enden, M. *Raspoutine et le crépuscule de la monarchie en Russie.* Paris, 1991.

De Jonge, Alex. *The Life and Times of Grigorii Rasputin.* New York, 1982.

"Delo ob ubiistve Rasputina." *Illiustrirovannaia Rossiia* 28 (374) (9 July 1932).

Dionisii (Alferov), ieromonakh. "Rasputin i pravoslavnaia asketika." Accessed at: http://catacomb.org.ua/modules.php?name=Pages&go=print_page&pid=270.

Dixon, Simon. "The 'Mad Monk' Iliodor in Tsaritsyn." *Slavonic and East European Review* 88, nos. 1/2 (January/April 2010).

———. "Superstition in Imperial Russia." *Past and Present* (2008): 199 (Supplement 3).

Dobson, Christopher. *Prince Felix Yusupov. The Man Who Murdered Rasputin.* London, 1989.

Dowling, Timothy C. *The Brusilov Offensive.* Bloomington, IN, 2008.

Dresner, Samuel H. *The Zaddik.* New York, 1960.

Dudakov, S. *Etiudy liubvi i nenavisti.* Moscow, 2003.

Elliott, J. H., and L. W. B. Brockliss, eds. *The World of the Favourite.* New Haven, 1999.

Erdmann-Pandžić, Elisabeth von. *"Poéma bez geroja" von Anna A. Achmatova.* Cologne, 1987.

Essaulov, Captain A., and G. P. Malone. "Rasputin: A Vindication." *Contemporary Review* 211, No. 1221 (1967).

Etkind, Alexander. *Eros of the Impossible: The History of Psychoanalysis in Russia.* Translated by Noah and Maria Rubins. Boulder, CO, 1997.

———. *Internal Colonization. Russia's Imperial Experience.* Malden, MA, 2011.

———. *Khlyst: Sekty, literatura i revoliutsiia.* Moscow, 1998.

Evreinov, N. N. *Taina Rasputina.* Leningrad, 1924.

Evsin, I. V., comp. *Oklevetannyi starets: Istoricheskie svidetel'stva o G. E. Rasputine.* Riazan', 2001.

Faitel'berg-Blank, Viktor, and Viktor Savchenko. *Odessa v epokhu voin i revoliutsii. 1914–1920.* Odessa, 2008.

Faleev, V., and V. Raikov. *Grigorii Rasputin bez grima i dorisovok.* N.p., 2007.

———. "Za chto ubili Grigoriia? (Novye materialy k biografii G. E. Rasputina)." *Dorogami tysiacheletii* 4 (1991).

Feinberg, Carla. "The Placebo Phenomenon." *Harvard Magazine.* January–February 2013.

Ferro, Marc. *Nicholas II. The Last of the Tsars.* Oxford, 1995.

Figes, Orlando. *A People's Tragedy. The Russian Revolution, 1891–1924.* New York, 1996.

Firsov, S. L. *Pravoslavnaia Tserkov' i gosudarstvo v poslednee desiatiletie sushchestvovaniia samoderzhaviia v Rossii.* St. Petersburg, 1996.

———. *Russkaia Tserkov' nakanune peremen (Konets 1890-kh–1918 g.).* Moscow, 2002.

Fomin, S. V. "A krugom shirokaia Rossiia—". Moscow, 2008.

———. *Bozhe! Khrani svoikh.* Moscow, 2009.

———. *Dorogoi nash otets: G. E. Rasputin-Novyi glazami ego docheri i dukhovnykh chad.* Moscow, 2012.

———. "Lozh' velika, no pravda bol'she—". Moscow, 2010.

———. *Nakazanie pravdoi.* Moscow, 2007.

———. *Poslednii Tsarskii Sviatoi.* St. Petersburg, 2003.

———. *Skorbnyi angel. Tsaristsa-Muchenitsa Aleksandra Novaia v pis'makh, dnevnikakh i vospominaniiakh.* St. Petersburg, 2006.

———. "Strast' kak bol'no, a vyzhivu—". Moscow, 2011.

———. *Sud'ia zhe mne Gospod'!* Moscow, 2010.

Fuhrmann, Joseph T. *Rasputin: A Life.* New York, 1990.

———. *Rasputin: The Untold Story.* Hoboken, NJ, 2013.

Fuller, William C., Jr. *The Foe Within: Fantasies of Treason and the End of Imperial Russia.* Ithaca, NY, 2006.

Fülöp-Miller, René. *Rasputin: The Holy Devil.* New York, 1928.

Gatrell, Peter. *Russia's First World War. A Social and Economic History.* New York, 2005.

Geifman, Anna. *Russia Under the Last Tsar: Opposition and Subversion, 1894–1917.* Malden, MA, 1999.

Gerasimov, A. V. *Na lezvii s terroristami*. Paris, 1985.

Gessen, V. Iu. "Ignatii Porfir'evich Manus—promyshlennik, bankovskii i birzhevoi deiatel'." Accessed at: http://www.hist.msu.ru/Banks/sources/gessen/gessen.htm. 22 September 2015.

Ginzburg, S. S. *Kinematografiia dorevoliutsionnoi Rossii*. Moscow, 2007.

Girchich, G. "Tol'ko pravda." *Vechernee vremia* (Paris) 119 (30 August/12 September 1924).

Giroud, Vincent. *Nicolas Nabokov: A Life in Freedom and Music*. New York, 2015.

Goldberg, Harvey. *The Life of Jean Jaurès*. Madison, WI, 1962.

Gosudarstvennaia Duma Rossiiskoi Imperii. Vol. 1: 1906–1917. Moscow, 2006.

Grashchenkova, I. N. *Kino Serebrianogo veka*. Moscow, 2005.

Groian, T. *Muchenik za Khrista i za Tsaria. Chelovek Bozhii Grigorii. Molitvennik za Sviatuiu Rus' i Eia Presvetlogo Otroka*. Moscow, 2001.

Guess, Harry, Linda Engel, Arthur Kleinman, and John Kusek, eds. *Science of the Placebo: Toward an Interdisciplinary Agenda*. London, 2002.

Gusev, B. *Petr Badmaev. (Krestnik imperatora. Tselitel'. Diplomat)*. Moscow, 2000.

———, and T. I. Grekova. *Doktor Badmaev: Tibetskaia meditsina, tsarskii dvor, sovetskaia vlast'*. Moscow, 1995.

Hall, Coryne. *Little Mother of Russia. A Biography of the Empress Marie Feodorovna (1847–1928)*. New York, 2001.

Halliday, E. M. "Rasputin Reconsidered." *Horizon* 9, No. 4 (1967).

Hanbury-Williams, John. *The Emperor Nicholas II, as I Knew Him*. London, 1922.

Hantsch, Hugo. *Leopold Graf Berchtold, Grand-seigneur und Staatsmann*. Graz, 1963.

Harcave, Sidney. *Count Sergei Witte and the Twilight of Imperial Russia. A Biography*. Armonk, NY, 2004.

Harmer, Michael. *The Forgotten Hospital*. Chichester, West Sussex, 1982.

Haurani, Farid I. "Rasputin Used Hypnosis: Reply to 'Russia's Imperial Blood.'" *American Journal of Hematology* 80:4 (2005).

Haywood, A. J. *Siberia. A Cultural History*. New York, 2010.

Heresch, Elisabeth. *Rasputin. Das Geheimnis seiner Macht*. Munich, 1995.

Heretz, Leonid. *Russia on the Eve of Modernity: Popular Religion and Traditional Culture Under the Last Tsars*. Cambridge, 2008.

Hunt, Priscilla Hart, and Svitlana Kobets, eds. *Holy Foolishness in Russia: New Perspectives*. Bloomington, IN, 2001.

Iakobii, I. P. *Imperator Nikolai II i revoliutsiia*. St. Petersburg, 2005.

Idel, Moshe. *Hasidism: Between Ecstasy and Magic*. Albany, NY, 1995.

Ioffe, G. Z. "'Rasputiniada': Bol'shaia politicheskaia igra." *Otechestvennaia istoriia* 3 (1998).

Iskenderov, A. A. *Zakat Imperii*. Moscow, 2001.

Iurkin konduit. Tiumenskie familii v pis'mennykh istochnikakh. Compiled by Iurii Zotin. 5 bks. Tiumen', 2009.

Ivanov, Sergey A. *Holy Fools in Byzantium and Beyond*. Translated by Simon Franklin. Oxford, 2006.

Izmozik, V. S., comp. *Zhandarmy Rossii: politicheskii rozysk v Rossii, XV–XX vek.* St. Petersburg, 2002.

Jeffrey, Keith. *The Secret History of MI6.* London, 2010.

Judas, Elizabeth. *Rasputin: Neither Devil nor Saint.* Los Angeles, 1942.

Kazarinov, M. G. "Rasputinskii schet." *Illiustrirovannaia Rossiia* 22 (368) (28 May 1932); 24 (370) (11 June 1932).

Kendrick, John. "Rasputin Didn't Hypnotize Alexei." *American Journal of Hematology* 80:4 (2005).

———. "Russia's Imperial Blood: Was Rasputin Not the Healer of Legend?" *American Journal of Hematology* 77:1 (2004).

Kilcoyne, Martin. "The Political Influence of Rasputin." Ph.D. dissertation. University of Washington, 1961.

King, Greg. *The Court of the Last Tsar. Pomp, Power, and Pageantry in the Reign of Nicholas II.* Hoboken, NJ, 2006.

———. *The Man Who Killed Rasputin: Prince Youssoupov and the Murder that Helped Bring Down the Russian Empire.* Secaucus, NJ, 1995.

Kizenko, Nadieszda. *A Prodigal Saint: Father John of Kronstadt and the Russian People.* University Park, PA, 2000.

Kniazev, S. "Rasputiny iz sela Pokrovskogo i ikh korni v Komi krae." *Genealogicheskii vestnik* 5 (2001). Accessed at: http://www.vgd.ru/VESTNIK/5vest3.htm#.

Kniaz'kin, Igor'. *Bol'shaia kniga o Rasputine.* St. Petersburg, 2007.

Kolonitskii, B. I. "Evrei i antisemitizm v delakh po oskorbleniiu Chlenov Rossiiskogo Imperatorskogo Doma (1914–1916)." In *Mirovoi krizis 1914–1920 godov i sud'ba vostochnoevropeiskogo evreistva.* Moscow, 2005.

———. "K izucheniiu mekhanizmov desakralizatsii Monarkhii (slukhi i 'politicheskaia pornografiia' v gody pervoi mirovoi voiny)." *Istorik i revoliutsiia: sbornik statei k 70-letiiu so dnia rozhdeniia O. N. Znamenskogo.* Edited by O. N. Znamenskii, et al. (1999).

———. *Simvoly vlasti i bor'ba za vlast'. K izucheniiu politicheskoi kul'tury rossiiskoi revoliutsii 1917 goda.* St. Petersburg, 2001.

———. *"Tragicheskaia erotica": obrazy imperatorskoi sem'i v gody pervoi mirovoi voiny.* Moscow, 2010.

Koshko, A. *Ocherki ugolovnogo mira tsarskoi Rossii.* Vol. 2. Paris, 1929.

Kotsiubinskii, A. P., and D. A. Kotsiubinskii. *Rasputin: tainyi i iavnyi.* St. Petersburg-Moscow, 2003.

Kozlov, N. *Drug tsarei.* Moscow, 1994.

———. *Ubiistvo Rasputina.* Moscow, 1990.

Kozyrev, F. N. *Rasputin, kotorogo my poteriali.* St. Petersburg, 2000.

Kraft, Barbara S. *The Peace Ship: Henry Ford's Pacifist Adventure in the First World War.* New York, 1978.

Krivorotov, V. *Pridvornyi iuvelir. (Strashnoe igo. Rasputiniada i ee sekretar').* Madrid, 1975.

Krivoshein, K. A. *A. V. Krivoshein (1857–1921 g.). Ego znachenie v istorii Rossii nachala XX veka.* Paris, 1973.

Kulegin, A. M. *Kto ubil Rasputina? Versii i fakty o pokusheniiakh na "sviatogo cherta."* (Seriia "Legendy politicheskoi istorii"). St. Petersburg, 2011.

———. *Zagrobnye prikliucheniia "sviatogo cherta."* St. Petersburg, n.d.

Kulikov, Sergei. "Chisto politicheskoe ubiistvo." *Rodina* 3 (2007).

Kulikowskii, Mark. "Rethinking the Origins of the Rasputin Legend." In *Modernization and Revolution. Dilemmas of Progress in Late Imperial Russia.* Edited by Edward H. Judge and James Y. Simms, Jr. New York, 1992.

———. "Rasputin and the Fall of the Romanovs." Ph.D. dissertation. SUNY Binghamton, 1982.

Kurlov, P. G. *Gibel' Imperatorskoi Rossii.* Moscow, 1992.

Lachapelle, Sofie. *Investigating the Supernatural: From Spiritism and Occultism to Psychical Research and Metaphysics in France, 1853–1931.* Baltimore, 2011.

Le Queux, W. *Le Ministre du Mal: mémoires de Feodor Rajevski, secrétaire privé de Raspoutine.* Paris, 1921.

———. *Rasputin the Rascal Monk: Disclosing the Secret Scandal of the Betrayal of Russia by the Mock-Monk "Grichka" and the Consequent Ruin of the Romanoffs, with Official Documents Revealed and Recorded.* London, 1917.

Leskin, Dimitrii. *Spor ob imeni Bozhiem. Filosofiia imeni v Rossii v kontekste afonskikh sobytii 1910-kh gg.* St. Petersburg, 2004.

Levin, Edmund. *A Child of Christian Blood. Murder and Conspiracy in Tsarist Russia: The Beilis Blood Libel.* New York, 2014.

Levin, K. N. *Poslednii russkii tsar' Nikolai II.* Khar'kov, 1919.

Liepman, Heinz. *Rasputin: A New Judgment.* Translated by Edward Fitzgerald. London, 1959.

Lieven, Dominic. *Nicholas II: Emperor of All the Russias.* London, 1993.

Lincoln, W. Bruce. *The Conquest of a Continent. Siberia and the Russians.* New York, 1994.

———. *Passage Through Armageddon. The Russians in War and Revolution, 1914–1918.* New York, 1986.

Livchak, B. "Chrezvychainaia sledstvennaia komissiia Vremennogo pravitel'stva glazami A. A. Bloka." *Voprosy istorii* 2 (1977).

Lohr, Eric. *Nationalizing the Russian Empire: The Campaign against Enemy Aliens during World War I.* Cambridge, MA, 2003.

Loks, K. "Povest' ob odnom desiatiletii (1907–1917)." *Minuvshee: istoricheskii al'manakh* 15 (1993).

Lopukhin, V. B. "Liudi i politika (konets XIX–nachalo XX v.)." *Voprosy istorii* 10 (1966).

Lyandres, Semion. "Progressive Bloc Politics on the Eve of the Revolution: Revisiting P. N. Miliukov's 'Stupidity or Treason' Speech of November 1, 1916." *Russian History/Histoire Russe.* 31, No. 4 (Winter 2004).

McKee, W. Arthur. "Sobering up the Soul of the People: The Politics of Popular

Temperance in Late Imperial Russia." *Russian Review*. Vol. 58, No. 2 (April 1999).

McMeekin, Sean. *The Russian Origins of the First World War*. Cambridge, MA, 2011.

McReynolds, Louise. *The News Under Russia's Old Regime. The Development of a Mass-Circulation Press*. Princeton, 1991.

Maevskii, Vl. *Na grani dvukh vekov*. Madrid, 1963.

Mager, Hugo. *Elizabeth: Grand Duchess of Russia*. New York, 1999.

Marchant, Jo. *Cure: A Journey into the Science of Mind Over Body*. London, 2016.

Markov, S. *Pokinutaia Tsarskaia Sem'ia*. Vienna, 1928; Moscow, 2002.

Marsden, Victor. *Rasputin and Russia: The Tragedy of a Throne*. London, 1920.

Massie, Robert K. *Nicholas and Alexandra*. New York, 1967.

———. *The Romanovs. The Final Chapter*. New York, 1995.

Mel'gunov, S. P. "Kak my priobretali zapiski Iliodora." *Na chuzhoi storone* 2 (1923).

———. *Legenda o separatnom mire*. Paris, 1957.

———. *Na putiakh k dvortsovomu perevorotu. (Zagovory pered revoliutsiei 1917 goda)*. Paris, 1931; Moscow, 2003.

Mille, Pierre. "Esquisses d'après Nature. Philippe de Lyon." *Le Temps* (23 November 1904).

Minney, R. J. *Rasputin*. London, 1972.

Mironova, Tat'iana. *Iz-pod lzhi. Gosudar' Nikolai II i Grigorii Rasputin*. Krasnodar, 2004.

Montefiore, Simon Sebag. *Jerusalem: The Biography*. 2011.

———. *Young Stalin*. New York, 2007.

Moorehead, Alan. *The Russian Revolution*. New York, 1958.

Moynahan, Brian. *Rasputin: The Saint Who Sinned*. London, 1998.

Mramornov, A. I. "'Delo' saratovskogo episkopa Germogena 1912 g. i sinodal'naia sistema upravleniia Russkoi tserkov'iu v nachale XX v." *Klio*. No. 3/34 (2006).

———. *Tserkovnaia i obshchestvenno-politicheskaia deiatel'nost' episkopa Germogena (Dolganova, 1858–1918)*. Saratov, 2006.

Mstislavskii, S. *Gibel' tsarizma. Nakanune 1917 goda*. Leningrad, 1927.

Myles, Douglas. *Rasputin: Satyr, Saint, or Satan*. New York, 1990.

Napley, Sir David. *Rasputin in Hollywood*. London, 1989.

Nazanskii, V. *Krushenie velikoi Rossii i doma Romanovykh*. Paris, 1930.

Nelipa, Margarita. *The Murder of Grigorii Rasputin, a Conspiracy that Brought Down the Russian Empire*. Pickering, Ontario, 2010.

Niemi, Maj-Britt. "Placebo Effect: A Cure in the Mind." *Scientific American*. February–March 2009.

Nikolaevskii, B. I. *Russkie masony i revoliutsiia*. Moscow, 1990.

Nikoliukin, Aleksandr. *Rozanov*. Moscow, 2001.

Oakley, Jane. *Rasputin: Rascal Master*. New York, 1989.

Obolenskii, D. *Imperator Nikolai II i ego tsarstvovanie*. Nice, 1928.

Ofri, Danielle, M.D. "A Powerful Tool in the Doctor's Toolkit." *New York Times*,

15 August 2013. Accessed at: http://well.blogs.nytimes.com/2013/08/15/a-powerful-tool-in-the-doctors-toolkit/?_r=0 on 4 January 2015.

"Okhota za masonami, ili pokhozhdeniia asessora Alekseeva." *Byloe* 4 (1917).

Ol'denburg, S. S. *Tsarstvovanie imperatora Nikolaia II.* St. Petersburg, 1991.

Omessa, Charles. *Rasputin and the Russian Court.* Translated by Frances Keyzer. London, 1918.

Onchukov, N. E. "P. A. Gorodtsov. (Zapadno-sibirskii etnograf)." *Sibirskaia zhivaia starina* 7 (1928).

Paert, Irina. *Spiritual Elders: Charisma and Tradition in Russian Orthodoxy.* DeKalb, IL, 2010.

Pares, Sir Bernard. *The Fall of the Russian Monarchy.* New York, 1939.

———. "Rasputin and the Empress: Authors of the Russian Collapse." *Foreign Affairs* 6 (1927).

Pavlov, N. *Ego Velichestvo Gosudar' Nikolai II.* Paris, 1927.

Paxman, Jeremy. "The Strange Death of Lord Kitchener." *FT Magazine,* 7 November 2014.

Peregudova, Z. I. *Politicheskii sysk v Rossii. 1880–1917.* 2 Vols. Moscow, 2000.

Pereverzev, P. N. "Ubiistvo Rasputina." *Illiustrirovannaia Rossiia* 21 (367) (21 May 1932).

Pipes, Richard. *The Russian Revolution.* New York, 1990.

Platonov, Oleg. *Rasputin i "deti d'iavola."* Moscow, 2005.

———. *Ternovyi venets Rossii. Nikolai II v sekretnoi perepiske.* Moscow, 1996.

———. *Ternovyi venets Rossii. Prolog tsareubiistva. Zhizn' i smert' Grigoriia Rasputina.* Moscow, 2001.

———. *Zhizn' za tsaria. Pravda o Grigorii Rasputine.* St. Petersburg, 1996.

Poliakoff, Vladimir. *The Empress Marie of Russia and Her Times.* London, 1926.

Pomeranz, William. "The Provisional Government and the Law-Based State." Unpublished ms. Forthcoming in *Russia's Great War and Revolution.*

Powell, Anne. *Women in the War Zone: Hospital Service in the First World War.* Stroud, 2009.

Radzinsky, Edvard. *The Rasputin File.* New York, 2000.

Radziwill, Catherine, Princess. *Rasputin and the Russian Revolution.* New York, 1918.

Ragsdale, Hugh, ed. *Paul I: A Reassessment of His Life and Reign.* Pittsburgh, 1979.

Rappaport, Helen. *Four Sisters. The Lost Lives of the Russian Grand Duchesses.* London, 2014.

Raskin, D. I. "Dnevnik 'Sviatogo cherta.'" *Rodina* 10 (1993).

Rassulin, Iurii, ed. and comp. *Vernaia Bogu, Tsariu i Otechestvu. Anna Aleksandrovna Taneeva (Vyrubova)—monakhinia Mariia.* St. Petersburg, 2005.

Rogger, Hans. *Russia in the Age of Modernization and Revolution, 1881–1917.* New York, 1983.

Rosenthal, Bernice Glatzer, ed. *The Occult in Russian and Soviet Culture.* Ithaca, NY, 1997.

"Rossiia epokhi gosudaria imperatora Nikolaia II." *Dvorianskoe sobranie* 2 (1995).

Rossiia v sviatoi zemle. Dokumenty i materialy. 2 Vols. Moscow, 2000.

Roullier, Alain. *Raspoutine est innocent.* Nice, 1998.

Rylkova, Galina. *The Archeology of Anxiety: The Russian Silver Age and Its Legacy.* Pittsburgh, 2007.

Sava, George. *Rasputin Speaks.* London, 1941.

Savchenko, V. A. *Avantiuristy grazhdanskoi voiny: istoricheskoe rassledovanie.* Moscow, 2000.

Schewäbel, Joseph. "Un précurseur de Raspoutine. La mage Philippe." *Mercure de France* (6 June 1918).

Semennikov, V. P. *Politika Romanovykh nakanune Revoliutsii.* Moscow-Leningrad, 1926.

———. *Romanovy i germanskie vliianiia, 1914–1917 gg.* Leningrad, 1929.

Serkov, A. I. *Istoriia russkogo masonstva XX veka.* Vol. 1. St. Petersburg, 2009.

———. *Russkoe masonstvo. 1731–2000. Entsiklopedicheskii slovar'.* Moscow, 2001.

Service, Robert. *Spies and Commissars. Bolshevik Russia and the West.* London, 2011.

Shargunov, A. "G. Rasputin: opasnost' razdeleniia v Tserkvi." *Radonezh* 1 (130) (Moscow, 2003).

Shemanskii, A., and S. Geichenko. *Poslednie Romanovy v Petergofe. Putevoditel' po nizhnei dache.* Moscow-Leningrad, 1931.

Shevzov, Vera. *Russian Orthodoxy on the Eve of Revolution.* New York, 2004.

Shishkin, Oleg. *Rasputin: istoriia prestupleniia.* Moscow, 2004.

Sh.[pitsberg], I. "Delo episkopa Palladiia." *Revoliutsiia i tserkov'* 3–5 (1919).

Smirnov, V. L, and M. Iu. Smirnova. *Neizvestnoe o Rasputine P.S.* Tiumen', 2010.

Smith, Michael. *Six: The Complete History of the Secret Intelligence Service.* London, 2007.

Smyslov, I. V. *Znamenie pogibshego tsarstva.* Moscow, 2002.

Solov'ev, M. E. "Kak i kem byl ubit Rasputin?" *Voprosy istorii* 3 (1965).

Solov'ev, V. "Ziat' Rasputina u episkopa Germogena v Tobol'ske." *Nashi vesti* 10–11 (1988).

Spiridovich, A. E. "Nachalo Rasputina." *Illiustrirovannaia Rossiia* 15 (361) (9 April 1932).

———. *Raspoutine, 1863–1916, d'après les documents russes et les archives privées de l'auteur.* Paris, 1935.

———. *Velikaia voina i Fevral'skaia revoliutsiia, 1914–1917 gg.* New York, 1960.

Startsev, V. I. *Russkoe politicheskoe masonstvo nachala XX v.* St. Petersburg, 1996.

———. *Tainy russkikh masonov.* 3rd edn. St. Petersburg, 2004.

Stein, Frank N. *Rasputin: Teufel im Mönchsgewand?* Munich, 1997.

Stein, Rob. "Researchers Look at Prayer and Healing." *Washington Post,* 24 March 2006. Section A, p. 1.

Steinberg, Mark D. "Russia's *fin de siècle,* 1900–1914." In *The Cambridge History of Russia.* Volume III: *The Twentieth Century.* Edited by Ronald Grigor Suny. Cambridge, 2006.

————, and Heather J. Coleman, eds. *Sacred Stories: Religion and Spirituality in Modern Russia*. Bloomington, IN, 2007.

————, and Vladimir M. Khrustalëv, eds. *The Fall of the Romanovs: Political Dreams and Personal Struggles in a Time of Revolution*. New Haven, 1995.

Stogov, D. I. "Salon kniazia M. M. Andronikova i sistema vlasti Rossiiskoi imperii." *Klio*. No 3/34 (2006).

Svift, Entoni (Anthony Swift). "Kul'turnoe stroitel'stvo ili kul'turnaia razrukha? (Nekotorye aspekty teatral'noi zhizni Petrograda i Moskvy v 1917 g.)." In *Anatomiia revoliutsii. 1917 god v Rossii: massy, partii, vlast'*. Edited by V. Iu. Cherniaev. St. Petersburg, 1994.

Tabachnik, D. V., and V. N. Voronin. *Krestyni put' Petra Stolypina*. Khar'kov, 2011.

Tal'berg, N. D. *Nikolai II: Ocherki istorii imperatorskoi Rossii*. Moscow, 2001.

Telitsyn, V. L. *Grigorii Rasputin, zhizn' i smert' "sviatogo greshnika"*. St. Petersburg, 2004.

Tereshchuk, A. *Grigorii Rasputin: poslednii "starets" Imperii*. St. Petersburg, 2006.

Thompson, Donald. *Blood Stained Russia*. New York, 1918.

Tisdall, E. E. P. *Dowager Empress*. London, 1957.

Trotsky, Leon. *History of the Russian Revolution*. New York, 1932.

"Tsarskaia okhranka o politicheskom polozhenii v strane v kontse 1916 g." *Istoricheskii arkhiv* 1 (1960).

Tumanskii, A. "Zlobodnevnye p'esy." *Teatr i iskusstvo* 20 (1917).

"Ubiistvo Rasputina." *Byloe* 1, 23 (July 1917).

Vada, Kh. "Rasputin, tsar' i tsaritsa: Chitaia roman Valentina Pikulia." In idem, *Rossiia kak problema vsemirnoi istorii: Izbrannye trudy*. Moscow, 1999.

Van der Kiste, John, and Coryne Hall. *Once a Grand Duchess: Xenia, Sister of Nicholas II*. London, 2002.

Vance, Wilson. *René Fülöp-Miller's Search for Reality*. London, n.d.

Varlamov, A. N. *Grigorii Rasputin-Novyi*. Moscow, 2008.

Varnava (Beliaev), episkop. *Ternistym putem k Nebu. Zhizneopisanie startsa Gavriila Sedmiezernoi pustyni. (†1915)*. Moscow, 1996.

Vasil'evskii, I. M. *Nikolai II*. Petrograd, 1923.

Vishnevskii, V. E. *Khudozhestvennye fil'my dorevoliutsionnoi Rossii*. Moscow, 1945.

Vogel-Jørgensen, T. *Rasputin: Prophet, Libertine, Plotter*. New Hyde Park, NY, 1971.

von Reenen, P. "Alexandra Feodorovna's Intervention in Russian Domestic Politics during the First World War." *Slovo* 10, Nos. 1–2 (1998).

Vorres, Ian. *The Last Grand Duchess: Her Imperial Highness Grand Duchess Olga Alexandrovna*. New York, 1965.

Vozchikov, V. A., Iu. Ia. Kozlov, and K. G. Koltakov. *Koster dlia "sviatogo cherta."* Biisk, 1998.

Warth, Robert. "Before Rasputin: Piety and the Occult at the Court of Nicholas II." *The Historian* 47, No. 3 (1985).

————. *Nicholas II: The Life and Reign of Russia's Last Monarch*. Westport, CT, 1997.

Warwick, Christopher. *Ella: Princess, Saint and Martyr*. Hoboken, NJ, 2006.

Wcislo, Francis W. *Tales of Imperial Russia: The Life and Times of Sergei Witte, 1849–1915*. New York, 2011.

Wilcox, E. H. *Russia's Ruin*. London, 1919.

Wilson, Colin. *Rasputin and the Fall of the Romanovs*. New York, 1964.

Wolfe, B. D. "The Reign of Alexandra and Rasputin." In idem, ed. *Revolution and Reality: Essays on the Origin and Fate of the Soviet System*. Chapel Hill, NC, 1981.

Wood, Alan, ed. *The History of Siberia: From Russian Conquest to Revolution*. New York, 1991.

Zaslavskii, D. *Poslednii vremenshchik Protopopov*. Leningrad, n.d.

Zerman, Z. A. B., ed. *Germany and the Revolution in Russia*. Oxford, 1958.

Zetterberg, Seppo. *Die Liga der Fremdvölker Russlands, 1916–1918 : ein Beitrag zu Deutschlands antirussischem Propagandakrieg unter den Fremdvölkern Russlands im ersten Weltkrieg*. Helsinki, 1978.

Zuckerman, Fredric S. *The Tsarist Secret Police Abroad: Policing Europe in a Modernizing World*. New York, 2003.

———. *The Tsarist Secret Police in Russian Society, 1880–1917*. London, 1996.

Zvonarev, K. K. *Germanskaia agenturnaia razvedka do i vo vremia voiny, 1914–1918 gg*. Kiev, 2005.

Film/Video

Rayner, Gordon, and Muriel Harding-Newman in "Time Watch: Rasputin: Marked for Murder," aired on BBC2, 1 October 2004.

Radio

"Russkii fashist kniaz' Nikolai Zhevakhov." Radio Svoboda. Broadcast 28 November 2009. Accessed online at: http://www.svoboda.org/content/transcript/1890856.html on 3 April 2015.

Notes

Introduction: The Holy Devil?

1. Chiefly Oleg Platonov, Sergei Fomin, Alexander Bokhanov, Tatyana Gorian. Their works are listed in the bibliography.
2. VR, 443, 775–76, 768–86; Tereshchuk, *Grigorii Rasputin*, 488–98; PZ, 231–33.
3. Blok, *Sobranie sochinenii*, (1962 edn.), 6:10.
4. Tikhomirov, *Dnevnik*, 211.

1: Origins

1. Haywood, *Siberia*, xii–xv, 74; Lincoln, *Conquest*, xxi, 55.
2. Wood, *History*, 4–8, 11; Lincoln, *Conquest*, 55, 58, 81–89, 163–67.
3. Lincoln, *Conquest*, 257–62.
4. PZ, 11; FR, 4; Haywood, *Siberia*, 52–55; FStr, 52, 60.
5. On Rasputin's genealogy: FR, 4–5; Chernyshev, "O vozraste," 112; Smirnov, *Neizvestnoe*, 9–15.
6. VV, 16 December 1911. At: www.starosti.ru; RR, 26.
7. Kniazev, "Rasputiny."
8. *Iuzhnaia zaria*, 30 May 1910, p. 2. On Yefim's birth: GATO, I-205.1.1, 138; FR, 6.
9. FR, 6-7; HL/Sokolov, Vol. VII: testimony of M. Solovyova (Rasputina), undated.
10. GATO, I-177.1.109, 2ob–3; VR, 9; FR, 7; Amal'rik, *Rasputin*, 18. On Matvei Rasputin: GATO, I-205.1.1, 138; I-205.1.2, 121; I-205.1.3, 9.
11. FR, 8–10; Chernyshev, "O vozraste," 113; VR, 9–10; Birth records at GATO (I-205.1.1–3) make no mention of any Dmitry.
12. 12 June 1910. At: www.starosti.ru.
13. GARF, 1467.1.479, 1–7.
14. FR, 7, 9.66.
15. *Petrogradskii listok*, 21 December 1916, p. 66. And also *Kievlianin*, 24 December 1916, p. 75; *PK*, 7 July 1914, p. 1.
16. GARF, 1467.1.479, 1–7.

17. VR, 11–12; HIA, Nikolaevsky Papers, Series No. 74, 129-1; Smirnov, *Neizvestnoe*, 36.
18. "Min Bekantskap med Rasputin," In: Riksarkivet, Wilhelm Sarwe Papers, Svenska Missionsförbundet, Om Rasputin (Svenska Publikationer); YLS, 205.
19. Smirnov, *Neizvestnoe*, 51–52.
20. GATO, I-239.1.90, 200–200ob.
21. GBUTO/GAGT, I-331.19.809, 118–21.
22. Her birthdate, previously unknown, is given in GBUTO/GAGT, I-154.24.58, 8–9, 19ob.
23. Various dates are given for the wedding, but documents in the Tobolsk archive cite 22 February 1887. GBUTO/GAGT, I-733.1.49, 8–9.
24. FR, 12–14; Chernyshev, "O vozraste," 113; GATO, I-255.1.3, 192; I-255.1.88, 48; GBUTO/GAGT, I-733.1.49, 10–11, 12–13.
25. PZ, 13; GATO, I-205.1.1, 15, 138–39; I-205.1.2, 121.

2: The Pilgrim

1. This exceedingly rare source is reprinted in PZ, 235–47. On its history, see FB, 522; *Iuzhanaia zaria*, 2 June 1910, p. 2.
2. VR, 12–13; FR, 14.
3. *PK*, 7 July 1914, p. 1.
4. PZ, 241.
5. FR, 20; VR, 14.
6. *Iuzhnaia zaria*, 30 May 1910, pp. 2–3; VR, 14.
7. GBUTO/GAGT, 156.18.565, 7; FB, 585–86.
8. FB, 582.
9. VR, 12–13.
10. FR, 15, 21; Ware, *Orthodox Church*, 73–74; PZ, 13–14.
11. Liberman, *On the Heights*, 53.
12. Vasili'ev, *Ochrana*, 111.
13. PZ, 242–44.
14. VR, 23–24.
15. *Brothers*, 24–27.
16. Ware, *Orthodox Church*, 48, 93–95, 130–35; Crummey, *Formation*, 120–21.
17. FR, 16–18; VR, 22–26.
18. VR, 19-20; Buranov, "Strannik," 55; *Iuzhnaia zaria*, 2 June 1910, p. 2; RRR, 18–22.
19. VR, 20; FB, 590; Ware, *Orthodox Church*, 47; FStr, 33–34n2; Buranov, "Strannik," 55.
20. RRR, 8–13.
21. FB, 582; Rassulin, *Vernaia Bogu*, 321; PZ, 14.
22. RRR, 18–22; Buranova, "Strannik," 56.

23. FB, 471, 590–93; FR, 18–19; FStr, 33–34n2; VR, 20–22. On Nikolai Rasputin: GATO, I-205.1.1, 138–39; I-205.1.2, 120–21. In some sources Arapov's name is mistakenly given as "Arsenov" or "Aronov."
24. RRR, 17; FB, 471, 592. On the rumor of the women: GBUTO/GAGT, 156.18.565, 11.

3: Nicholas and Alexandra

1. Rappaport, *Four Sisters*, 9–17; Massie, *Nicholas*, 27–34.
2. Massie, *Nicholas*, 42–43; Alexander, *Once*, 168–69.
3. FR, 156—orig: Naryshkin-Kurakin, *Under Three Tsars*, 203–204; on his need: Vyrubova, *Stranitsy*, 27.

4: Monsieur Philippe

1. FA, 634; WC, 13n1; RR, 50–51; King, *Court*, 90–91; Witte, *Vospominaniia*, 91.
2. Carlson, *No Religion*, 20; HIA, Nikolaevsky Papers, Series No. 74, 129-6; FA, 682–84; Shishkin, *Rasputin*, 270–71.
3. Schewäbel, "Un précurseur," 639–43; FA, 575–77.
4. FR, 36; Schewäbel, "Un précurseur," 638; FA, 617–24. A search of the University of Cincinnati's records shows no diploma given for any such dissertation, *pace* Fomin.
5. Schewäbel, "Un précurseur," 639–43; HIA, Nikolaevsky Papers, Series No. 74, 129-6; Mille, "Esquisses."
6. HIA, Nikolaevsky Papers, Series No. 74, 129-6; Mille, "Esquisses"; FA, 565–66.
7. FA, 577–78, 631–33; Rappaport, *Four Sisters*, 61–64.
8. Shemanskii, *Poslednie Romanovy*, 85; Vyrubova, *Neizvestnye fragmenty*, 66.
9. Nicholas II, *Dnevniki*, 1:588; 1:605–09, 887; *LP*, 206; Shemanskii, *Poslednie Romanovy*, 85.
10. FA, 702.
11. Nicholas II, *Dnevniki*, 1:617, 886; FA, 701, 704.
12. HIA, Nikolaevsky Papers, Series No. 74, 129-6; Shemanskii, *Poslednie Romanovy*, 85; FA, 709; VR, 54; Rappaport, *Four Sisters*, 65.
13. Nicholas II, *Dnevniki*, 1:628–29, 633, 642, 654; FA, 709, 724; Rappaport, *Four Sisters*, 65.
14. HIA, Nikolaevsky Papers, Series No. 74, 129-6; FA, 548–51, 565; Kireev, *Dnevnik*, 241; Bricaud, "Un mage," 437–38.
15. FA, 708–709, 548–59, 565; *LP*, 208–09; Shemanskii, *Poslednie Romanovy*, 84.
16. *LP*, 216–19; Shemanskii, *Poslednie Romanovy*, 86. And FA, 546–47.
17. Nicholas II, *Dnevniki*, 1:677; FA, 702, 711–15; Shemanskii, *Poslednie Romanovy*,

88. Historian Helen Rappaport writes that Alexandra may have experienced what is known as a "Mole Carnosum" (hydatidiform mole), a fertilized egg that stopped developing after the fourth week of gestation and was expelled from the empress's body in August. Rappaport, *Four Sisters*, 66.
18. Nicholas II, *Dnevniki*, 1:677–78; *LP*, 217–19; FA, 717–19.
19. FA, 549–52.
20. *LP*, 220.
21. Elizaveta Fedorovna, "Pis'ma," 469; FA, 549–52, 565.
22. *LP*, 221.
23. Gul', *Ia unes*, 2:206; FA, 545–46.
24. FA, 553–57; 705. 722; Vyrubova, *Neizvestnye fragmenty*, 66; WC, 149.
25. Shemanskii, *Poslednie Romanovy*, 87.
26. FA, 734–35; VR, 55.
27. *LP*, 219.
28. FA, 553–54.
29. *LP*, 297.
30. *Za kulisami*, v; RR, 57–58. A police file for 1912 gives his birth name as Dmitry Andreevich Znobishin; other times it is written Oznobshin. GARF, 111.1.2974, 295; Mel'gunov, *Poslednii samoderzhets*, 10–11; *PK*, 5 July 1914, p. 2.

5: Alexei

1. *LP*, 228–30; Rappaport, *Four Sisters*, 68–70; Ware, *Orthodox Church*, 130–33; Naryshkin, *Under Three Tsars*, 175; Dixon, "Superstition."
2. *LP*, 239–43; Bokhanov, *Romanovs*, 210; Massie, *Nicholas*, 112.
3. Massie, *Nicholas*, 150–51.
4. *LP*, 248.
5. IMM, 178; Hanbury-Williams, *Emperor*, 140; Vladykin, *Taina*, 8.
6. Pares, *Fall*, 16. See also Massie, *Nicholas*, 200.

6: The Burning Torch

1. Gumilev, *Selected Works*, 98–99.
2. The date of Rasputin's visit has long been only roughly known, but can now be more precisely established. See VR, 30; FB, 20.
3. VR, 30; *Iuzhnaia zaria*, 30 May 1910, pp. 2–3; *Kievlianin*, 24 December 1916, p. 75.
4. FB, 8, 14, 25.
5. PZ, 242.
6. FR, 23–26; *Sovremennoe slovo*, 20 December 1916, p. 2; *Rech'*, 26 May 1910, No. 142.
7. VR, 28.

8. PZ, 246–47. Sergei became the first Patriarch of All Russia under Stalin in 1942.
9. VR, 27; FB, 19.
10. Various dates for his arrival have been proposed between 1902 and 1905. This dating, the most accurate, comes from the testimony of Archimandrite Feofan to the Commission. See RR, 47–48; VR, 31–33.
11. Veniamin, *Na rubezhe*, 134–37. Also: Shavel'skii, *Vospominaniia*, 1:55, incl. n. 10a.
12. Zhevakhov, *Vospominaniia*, 1:203–204, 239–40; VR, 41–42.
13. *GRS*, 4:9. See also FB, 24–25; Betts, *Dukhovnik*, 39.
14. IMM, 87–88.
15. Zhevakhov, *Vospominaniia*, 1:203–04, 239–40; RR, 49.
16. VR, 33–34.
17. SML, Spiridovich Papers, No. 359, Box 14, Folder 2, pp. 1–5.
18. PZ, 22; RR, 46; RRR, 26–36.
19. RRR, 17, 41–43.
20. FB, 216.
21. RRR, 49.
22. VR, 45, 48.
23. Witte, *Vospominaniia*, 492; Witte, *Iz arkhiva*, vol. 1, bk. 2, 841; Shishkin, *Rasputin*, 60–67; FB, 213–58 (pp. 218–23 for quote); Vladykin, *Taina*, 3. Also: Vasilevskii, *Nikolai II*, 73–74; Kovalevskii, *Grishka Rasputin*, 19–30; OR/RNB, 585.5696, 28ob.
24. Evlogii, *Put'*, 201; FB, 241–42; OR/RNB, 1000.3.439, 8.
25. GARF, 1467.1.479, 7–13.
26. Gippius, *Vospominaniia*, 371–72.
27. *Novaia voskresnaia vecherniaia gazeta*, 18 March 1912, p. 3.

7: The Mad Monk

1. VR, 247.
2. Dixon, "'Mad Monk'," 382, 389.
3. Iliodor, *Kogda-zhe konets?*, 3, 10–15.
4. Dixon, "'Mad Monk'," 384–85.
5. IMM, esp. 3, 6–7, 13, 15, 21.

8: To the Throne

1. *KVD*, 7; Nicholas II, *Dnevniki*, 1:1042. Sergeevka, also known as the Leuchtenberg Palace, at Peterhof was a gift from Nicholas I to his daughter Grand Duchesses Maria, who married Maximilian, Duke of Leuchtenberg, in 1839.

2. FB, 354. The address of the rector's wing is now Obvodny Canal, No. 10.

3. RR, 50–52. Other sources confirm Feofan's role in introducing Rasputin to the Black Princesses. See: VR, 35–36; Rassulin, *Vernaia Bogu*, 297.

4. OR/RNB, 307.80, 2; VR, 36–40; RR, 52.

5. VR, 48–49; FR, 40–41; Veniamin, *Na rubezhe*, 138; Den, *Podlinnaia tsaritsa*, 62; Amal'rik, *Rasputin*, 8; Smirnov, *Neizvestnoe*, 48; RR, 71.

6. VR, 49–50; Voeikov, *S tsarem*, 58.

7. *PK*, 5 July 1914, p. 2.

8. Betts, *Dukhovnik*, 32–33; FB, 25.

9. Vasilevskii, *Nikolai II*, 72; VR, 51–52.

10. Zhevakhov, *Vospominaniia*, 1:207. For a contemporary echo of this idea, see FB, 414–16.

11. Steinberg, "Russia's *fin de siècle*," 70–71.

12. GARF, 640.1.323, 20ob–21.

13. The letter does, however, appear in the collection of correspondence in *KVD*, 8, although without any commentary.

14. GARF, 102.316.1910.381, ch. 2, 99–102.

15. GARF, 111.1.2978, 17ob.

9: Rasputin-Novy

1. VR, 127–30; Kizenko, *Prodigal*, esp. 1–5, 114–16, 158; Dixon, "Superstition," 225–26; *PK*, 2 July 1914, p. 2; 3 July, p. 2; Nicholas, *Dnevniki*, 1:119–23.

2. FB, 9–13, 355, 560–61, 567; VR, 131–32; Vinogradoff, "Nicholas," 116n8; and, with caution, Igumen Damaskin (Orlovskii), "Sviashchennoispovednik Roman (Medved')." Accessed at http://www.fond.ru. 3 July 2013.

3. FB, 354, 571–72; GARF, 102.316.1910.381, 165; RR, 72–74.

4. RR, 72–74.

5. FB, 566–67.

6. *KVD*, 9.

7. *Iuzhnaia zaria*, 2 June 1910, p. 2. Documents in GBUTO/GAGT (I-154.24.58, 18ob) give the purchase date as 19 December 1906.

8. *KVD*, 9; FB, 560–61.

9. Rozanov, *Vozrazhdaiushchiisia Egipet*, 426–35; idem, *V nashei smute*, 373–74; FStr, 9–28; OR/RNB, 1000.1975.22, 21ob–22; VR, 219–20.

10. Rozanov, *O sebe*, 17n.

11. NIOR/RGB, 249.4213.7, 26, 29ob, 32–33ob.

12. GARF, 640.1.323, 20ob.

13. *KVD*, 10–11.

14. Damer, "Rasputin vo dvortse," 7.

15. SML, Spiridovich, No. 359, Box 6, Folder 3, pp. 50–51; *KVD*, 10–11; Vinogradoff, "Nicholas II," 116.

16. KVD, 11; LP, 296; Vinogradoff, "Nicholas," 114–16.

17. SML, Spiridovich Papers, No. 359, Box 14, Folder 2, pp. 1–5.

18. GARF, 651.1.10, 1ob–2.

19. GARF, 601.1.1088, 1–1ob.

20. IMM, 111; Rasputin, *Mon père*, 48; VR, 58–59. Rasputin usually wrote "Novy" and at other times "Novykh," the genitive plural ending. Some Siberians apparently preferred this form since it sounded grander, more dignified, and projected a feel of Old Church Slavonic. See FR, 244n43.

21. Biographies typically cite 22 December as the official date of the change, but the documents in the Russian State Historical Archive are clear that it happened later. RGIA, 1412.16.121, 1–8; FR, 59; KVD, 13; GATO, I-205.1.3, 98.

22. KVD, 13.

23. *Iuzhnaia zaria*, 2 June 1910, p. 2.

24. 15 December 1911. At: www.starosti.ru.

10: Sects and Whips

1. Unless otherwise noted, the following details are from Etkind, *Khlyst*, 4, 25–50, 72–73, 138–39, 475–79; idem, *Internal Colonization*, 194–98; Riasanovsky, *History*, 182–86.

2. FB, 502–503.

3. Amal'rik, *Rasputin*, 28; Etkind, *Khlyst*, 4, 588.

4. Etkind, *Khlyst*, 595–98.

5. Etkind, *Khlyst*, 8–10.

6. Rosenthal, *Occult in Russia*, 10.

7. Etkind, *Khlyst*, 476.

8. *Otklik na zhizn'*, No. 1, 1916, pp. 17–25.

9. VR, 119, 145.

10. Bogoslovskii, *Dnevniki*, 139–40, 281–82. Also: Zhevakhov, *Vospominaniia*, 1:203–204.

11. "Taina khlystovshchiny," *Novoe vremia*, 20 March 1912, pp. 4–5; 21 March, p. 5. Such an article coming from Gofshtetter is a bit odd, for as late as the end of 1910 he was supposedly a devoted believer in Rasputin. See Tikhomirov, "Iz dnevnika," 1:182, 184.

11: Demons of the Silver Age

1. See Steinberg, "Fin de siècle"; Carlson, *No Religion*, 3–5, 22–28; idem, "Fashionable Occultism," in Rosenthal, *Occult*; Etkind, *Eros*, 83, 115–19; Rosenthal, *Occult*, 8, 18–19; Lachapelle, *Investigating*.

2. Etkind, *Eros*, 83, 115–19; Carlson, "Fashionable Occultism," 135.

3. Shishkin, *Rasputin*, 141–48; FA, 685–86; Carlson, *No Religion*, 27–29.

4. Steinberg, "Fin de siècle," 80–81, 86–87.

5. Etkind, *Khlyst*, 125, 525–26. And discussion in Firsov, *Pravoslavnaia tserkov'*, 239–62.

6. Etkind, *Khlyst*, 527–28. The quote is from the Apostle Paul: "Unto the pure all things are pure: but unto them that are defiled and unbelieving is nothing pure; but even their mind and conscience is defiled." Titus 1:15.

7. Etkind, *Khlyst*, 143–44, 228–29, 525; Gippius, *Dnevniki*, 1:416–17.

8. Gippius, *Vospominaniia*, 373–75.

9. VR, 111–12; Etkind, *Khlyst*, 122, 143–44, 526–28.

10. NIOR/RGB, 869.86.18, 2–13.

11. Above quotes and details: Etkind, *Khlyst*, 244–46, 346–54, 468–69; FB, 5–9.

12. Rosenthal, *Occult*, 7; Carlson, *No Religion*, 22.

13. Rosenthal, *Occult*, 379–82, 392–93. Talk of "dark forces" can be found as early as 1910. See "Nechto o 'reaktsii'," *Moskovskie vedomosti*, 29 July 1910, p. 1.

14. Rosenthal, *Occult*, 102–103.

15. On Vrubel and Scriabin, see, for example, Billington, *Icon*, 474–81, 503.

16. Groberg, "Shade," 116–31, in Rosenthal, *Occult*; Lodyzhenskii, *Misticheskaia trilogiia*; Etkind, *Khlyst*, 121.

17. Georgy Chulkov called his 1914 anti-Rasputin novel *Satan*.

18. Etkind, *Khlyst*, 587, including n5.

19. *Novaia voskresnaia vecherniaia gazeta*, 18 March 1912, p. 3.

12: Anna Vyrubova

1. GARF, 602.2.62; Rudnev, "Pravda," n.p. The tsar's sister Grand Duchess Olga Nikolaevna concurs with Rudnev on the matter. Vorres, *Last*, 132–33.

2. Blok, *Sobranie sochinenii*, 5:363.

3. VR, 72.

4. Gippius, *Dnevniki*, 2:159.

5. Vorres, *Last*, 133.

6. GRS, 4:270; Shulgin, *Years*, 270.

7. RR, 78–80, 91, 93. See also VR, 73.

8. Kolonitskii, *Tragicheskaia erotika*, 320; OR/RNB, 585.5696, 21.

9. Vyrubova, *Stranitsy*, 20–21.

10. WC, 264, 698, 701.

11. GRS, 4:5–6.

12. YLS, 46.

13. RRR, 73.

14. Vyrubova, *Stranitsy*, 115.

15. VR, 71.
16. Vyrubova, *Stranitsy*, 115; GARF, 651.1.27, 35ob–38.
17. GARF, 640.1.323, 27ob.
18. GARF, 651.1.27, 35ob–37.
19. Rassulin, *Vernaia Bogu*, 359.
20. RR, 91; VR, 78–81; Vyrubova, *Stranitsy*, 34–37; OR/RNB, 585.5696, 21; FR, 74.
21. GARF, 713.1.24, 3–4ob.
22. GARF, 640.1.323, 35.
23. GARF, 1467.1.710, 251, 282, 283.
24. Marie, *Education*, 277; FDNO, 237–38n7, 8, 9. Marianna married four times. Here she is given her most widely used married name, Derfelden.
25. Belling, *Iz nedavnego*, 3, 17.
26. GARF, 612.1.61, 114ob.

13: The Eyes

1. *KVD*, 17–18.
2. Gul', *Ia unes*, 2:276. This refers to Nikolai Pavlovich (not Vasilevich) Sablin.
3. *KVD*, 23.
4. Gul', *Ia unes*, 2:276–77; on the apartment: FB, 354.
5. Belling, *Iz nedavnego*, 7; on her: RR, 370.
6. Prugavin, *Leontii*, n.p.
7. Mel'gunov, *Vospominaniia*, 1:205.
8. Voeikov, *S tsarem*, 57–58. See also Bonch-Bruevich, *Vsia vlast'*, 80.
9. RGIA, 472.50.1619, 3.
10. Dzhanumova, *Moi vstrechi*, 34–36.
11. RRR, 41.
12. Shulgin, *Years*, 264–65.
13. Dzhanumova, *Moi vstrechi*, 34–36.
14. GARF, 102.242.1912.297, ch. 2, 1. Also: *Rannee utro*, 20 December 1916, p. 2; Beletskii, *Vospominaniia*, 15–16; VR, 370; Schelking, *Recollections*, 117; Shelley, *Blue Steppes*, 83; idem, *Speckled Domes*, 35–36; Murat, *Raspoutine*, 62; Rozanov, *Mimoletnoe*, 66; Den, *Podlinnaia tsaritsa*, 62–63; GARF, 102.242.1912.297, ch. 1, 137; OR/RNB, 1000.1975.22, 50ob.
15. Dzhanumova, *Moi vstrechi*, 34–36.
16. Buchanan, *Dissolution*, 139.
17. Den, *Podlinnaia tsaritsa*, 62–63.
18. OR/RNB, 1000.1975.22, 26ob.
19. Beletskii, *Vospominaniia*, 15–16.
20. Globachev, *Pravda*, 68.
21. HIA, Batyushin, "V chem byla sila Rasputina," 5–6; Dzhanumova, *Moi vstrechi*, 19.

22. OR/RNB, 1000.1975.22, 25.
23. RR, 235.

14: ". . . prayers that purify and protect us."

1. FR, 49–50; *KVD*, 16; Den, *Podlinnaia tsaritsa*, 69.
2. *Iuzhnaia zaria*, 2 June 1910, p. 2; FB, 637; FR, 50; SML, Spiridovich Papers, No. 359, Box 14, Folder 5, pp. 1–9.
3. FB, 589–90. Quote: FDNO, 249n13.
4. GARF, 1467.1.710, 227–28. The letter may have been written after a different visit to Pokrovskoe that year. Quote on her character: SML, Spiridovich Papers, No. 359, Box 14, Folder 5, p. 8. Also: Al'ferev, *Pis'ma*, 521; OR/RNB, 1000.3.349, 6ob; FDNO, 246. A report from 1912 describes Manshtedt as the wife of a nobleman from the village of Porechye in the Smolensk province. GBUTO/GAGT, I-156.18.920, 8–9.
5. HIA, Nikolaevsky Papers, Series 74, 129-1, pp. 27–40; FB, 588.
6. Vorres, *Last*, 134–39.
7. SML, Spiridovich Papers, Box 6, Folder 3, pp. 64–65; Rasputin, *Mon père*, 47.
8. *KVD*, 20.
9. GARF, 651.1.27, 39–40ob. On Vishnyakova: SML, Spiridovich Papers, No. 349, Box 6, Folder 3, pp. 65, 80; RR, 128–29; Rappaport, *Four Sisters*, 162.
10. Ilyin, "The Court," 35–57.

15: The Investigation: Part I

1. FB, 468, 554–55, 559–61; GBUTO/GAGT, I-156.18.565, 1. Duma President Mikhail Rodzianko wrote in his memoirs that the investigation into Rasputin's connections to the khlysty was launched in 1902. This is clearly incorrect. *Reign*, 56–57.
2. FB, 556–66, 576–84.
3. Dixon, "'Mad Monk'," 412.
4. FB, 561–66.
5. GARF, 1467.1.479, 4–4ob.
6. FB, 561–66.
7. *Iuzhnaia zaria*, 4 June 1910, p. 2.
8. FB, 566–67, 587–88, 613.
9. I read the original file in Moscow in October 2013, an exact copy of which has been published by Sergei Fomin in *Bozhe! Khrani svoikh!* (Moscow, 2009), 546–645. Instead of citing the archival original, I refer here to Fomin's book to make it easier for other scholars to trace my citations.
10. For this view, see RR, 83; PZ, 397.

11. GATO, I-239.1.90, 199–200ob.
12. The point is also made in FR, 51; VR, 89–80.
13. PZ, 246–47; *KVD*, 17; FB, 554–55; FR, 52–53.
14. VR, 91; FR, 51–52; FB, 570–76; "Nepriiatnyi podarok. S. Pokrovskoe, Tiumenskogo uezda." *Tobol*, No. 30, 29 May 1907, p. 3.
15. GARF, 640.1.323, 25ob–26.
16. FB, 571–72. This last story of the girl would grow over the years, forming part of his legend. See *Kievlianin*, 24 December 1916, p. 75.
17. FB, 571–73, 593. Karneeva's words appeared in Mikhail Novoselov's *Grigorii Rasputin i misticheskoe rasputstvo* in a letter dated 13 December 1911 by one "priest of the Tobolsk eparchy." She is referred to as "E. K-va" in HIA, Nikolaevsky Papers, Series No. 74, 129-1, pp. 42–43.
18. FB, 573–75.
19. Markow, *Wie*, 145.
20. FB, 575–76.
21. Amal'rik, *Rasputin*, 109–10.
22. FB, 585–86. On the Pecherkins: HL/Sokolov, Vol. VII, Testimony of Maria Solovyova (Rasputina).
23. Above quotes and information: FB, 585–90, 595–97.
24. GBUTO/GAGT, I-156.18.565, 11ob–12.
25. GBUTO/GAGT, I-156.18.565, 12–14.
26. FB, 599–632.
27. VR, 100–101; RR, 84; Rodzianko, *Reign*, 58.
28. *Sibirskaia nov'*, No. 19, 24 January 1910, p. 4; *Iuzhnaia zaria*, 4 June 1910, p. 2.

16: The First Test

1. VR, 116–17.
2. GARF, 640.1.323, 24ob–25.
3. SML, Spiridovich Papers, Box 6, Folder 3, p. 67; FR, 60.
4. *KVD*, 23.
5. GARF, 640.1.323, 32–33; *KVD*, 19.
6. *KVD*, 24–25.
7. Zhevakhov, *Vospominaniia*, 1:212-16. On Trauenberg, FB, 246n1; Spiridovich, *Raspoutine*, ch. 6.
8. HHStA, P.A. X, Russland, Karton 138, p. 114.
9. VR, 245–46; Dixon, "'Mad Monk'," 388; FSu, 634; Montefiore, *Young Stalin*, 55, 62.
10. RGIA, 1101.1.1111, 7–7ob.
11. VR, 43; FStr, 546.
12. King, *Court*, 105.

13. Zhevakhov, *Vospominaniia*, 1:215–18. Gossip about the new mystic at court had started as early as November 1906. See Teliakovskii, *Dnevniki*, 4:68.

14. Mel'nik, *Vospominaniia*, 42–43.

15. FB, 225–26, 226n1, 227–32, including 229n1; Dzhunkovskii, *Vospominaniia*, 2:171–72; Evlogii, *Put'*, 199–200; Dixon, "'Mad Monk'," 384; VR, 158. See also on the salon of Admiral Konstantin Nilov in Sablin, *Desiat' let*, 252–54.

16. Bogdanovich, *Tri poslednikh*, 465; RR, 416.

17. Kolonitskii, *Tragicheskaia erotika*, 320.

18. FB, 233.

19. *Russkoe slovo*, 19 February 1908. At: www.starosti.ru; VR, 134; FB, 433.

20. VR, 136–37.

21. Gerasimov's memoirs in Peregudova, *Okhranka*, 2:309–13. His memoirs, especially concerning Rasputin at this time, are not terribly credible. For example, he writes Stolypin had not yet even heard of Rasputin until Gerasimov spoke to him. This is clearly incorrect. See also: VR, 136–37; FB, 346.

22. KVD, 25.

23. GARF, 640.1.323, 21ob.

24. GARF, 651.1.10, 4ob 5.

25. KVD, 28.

26. Vorres, *Once*, 135.

17: "better ten Rasputins . . ."

1. Sederkholm's reminiscences: SML, Spiridovich Papers, No. 359, Box 14, Folder 5, pp. 1–9. Iliodor claimed Vishnyakova was in love with Rasputin and engaged in orgies with him, pulling the hair of the other women who sought too much of his lovemaking. OR/RNB, 1000.3.439, 2ob.

2. Biographers have disagreed about the timing of the trip, some citing 1908 or 1910 as possible dates. But the evidence points to 1909. See VR, 156–57; RGALI, 2167.2.22, 2.

3. Vasilevskii, *Nikolai II*, 72–73. Also VR, 214; *Rech'*, 21 December 1916, p. 3.

4. RGALI, 2167.2.22, 2, 12.

5. FDNO, 258–61.

6. LP, 320.

7. Betts, *Dukhovnik*, 32–33; VR, 192–93.

8. Veniamin, *Na rubezhe*, 133–34.

9. LP, 321; VR, 193–97; RR, 119. The sources are not clear on who went to Pokrovskoe at that time.

10. VR, 195–96; RR, 119–21.

11. Veniamin, *Na rubezhe*, 141–42; RR, 117; VR, 192–93. It is not clear from the

sources, but it is possible this meeting took place before Feofan and Rasputin visited Pokrovskoe in late June.

12. VR, 198–99; RR, 127–28.
13. TsM, 29 May 1910, p. 3.
14. VR, 197–98, 236–37.
15. LP, 322–23.
16. FB, 355.
17. IMM, 105–06; FStr, 546, 574; Dixon, "'Mad Monk'," 385.
18. IMM, 52.
19. IMM, 59; VR, 253; OR/RNB, 1000.3.439, 1–1ob; Dixon, "'Mad Monk'," 391–93.
20. IMM, 103.
21. GARF, 713.1.24, 3-4ob; OR/RBN, 1000.3.439, 1ob–2.
22. IMM, 108–113; OR/RNB, 1000.3.439, 2.
23. OR/RNB, 1000.3.439, 2; IMM, 114–19.
24. IMM, 116, 120–25; GATO, I-239.1.90, 199-99ob.
25. Sibirskaia nov', 2 February 1910, p. 2; TsV, 3 January 1910, p. 3; 14 January 1911, p. 2; KVD, 39; Dixon, "'Mad Monk'," 397. Some sources report Rasputin departed on 31 December.
26. IMM, 132–33.
27. Peregudova, Okhranka, 2:320.
28. Rodzianko, Reign, 24.
29. Bok, Vospominaniia, 332–33. Other sources put the number at one hundred Rasputins. See: Istoriia tsarstvovaniia Nikolaia, Vyp. II, p. 25; Shulgin, Years, 256–60.
30. Gurko, Tsar', 226.
31. Shul'gin, Dni, 96–97, 100–101.

18: Trouble in the Nursery

1. LP, 328–30.
2. GATO, F. I-239.1. 90, 200–201.
3. LP, 330.
4. KVD, 43.
5. LP, 330–31. The Anichkov Palace was the home to the Dowager Empress Maria Fyodorovna.
6. Bogdanovich, Tri poslednikh, 484; and see Stoeckl, Not All Vanity, 133.
7. GARF, 102.316.1910.381, 2ob.
8. GARF, 713.1.24, 3–4ob.
9. LP, 331.
10. VR, 184. On Madlena Frantsevna Zanotti: Damer, "Rasputin vo dvortse," 7–8.

11. RR, 128–29.

12. Vishnyakova told the Commission the trip happened in 1910, but she appears to be mistaken.

13. RR, 126–27.

14. Bogdanovich, *Tri poslednikh*, 488.

15. VR, 184.

16. Vorres, *Last*, 137.

17. VR, 184, 187; Rappaport, *Four Sisters*, 162.

18. Chebotaryova, "V dvortsovom lazarete," 182:239.

19. GARF, 651.1.10, 6–8, 16ob–21.

20. *KVD*, 27, 29–30, 31.

21. GARF, 640.1.323, 22–22ob; *KVD*, 33–34.

22. Rasputin's letters to the children: GARF, 651.1.10, 6–8, 13–13ob, 15ob, 16ob–21.

23. GARF, 640.1.323, 44, 47ob–48.

24. GARF, 651.1.27, 26–28.

25. *LP*, 318–19.

26. *KVD*, 32, 35.

27. Globachev, *Pravda*, 5.

28. GARF, 102.316.1910.381, 3–6.

29. Kakurin, "Iz dnevnika," 116.

30. *LP*, 331–32.

31. RR, 127–28.

32. Dixon, "'Mad Monk'," 387.

33. Vyrubova, *Stranitsy*, 78–79.

34. Bogdanovich, *Tri poslednikh*, 488.

35. Den, *Podlinnaia tsaritsa*, 46.

36. RR, 127–28; VR, 199.

37. VR, 199; *KVD*, 44.

38. A copy of Berladskaya's account, titled "Confessions of N," along with Bonch-Bruevich's assessment, is in HIA, Nikolaevsky Papers, Series 74, 129-1. See also VR, 202.

39. IMM, 134, 186–87; VR, 202.

40. FDNO, 250–51, including n14; GRS, 1:362–63.

41. IMM, 218–19.

42. OR/RNB, 1000.3.439, 3.

43. *Rech'*, 30 May 1910, No. 146. No p. n.

44. Dixon, "'Mad Monk'," 395, 412; VR, 252, 254–55.

45. VR, 223, 244; FStr, 547.

46. *Rech'*, 7 June 1910, No. 154. Missing p.n.

47. VR, 230–33.

19: The Press Discovers Rasputin

1. K. K. Romanov, *Dnevniki*, 321.
2. *Moskovskie vedomosti*, 2 March 1910, pp. 2–3.
3. VR, 160–63; Dixon, "'Mad Monk'," 397.
4. Bulgakov, *Avtobiograficheskie zapiski*, 82.
5. Nikol'skii, "Vyderzhki," 159.
6. Tikhomirov, *Dnevnik*, 354.
7. VR, 164–65.
8. Tikhomirov, "Iz dnevnika," 1:171.
9. See *Moskovskie vedomosti*, 30 March 1910, p. 2.
10. Dixon, "'Mad Monk'," 397.
11. *Utro Rossii*, 23 March 1910. At: www.starosti.ru.
12. Tikhomirov, "Iz dnevnika," 1:171.
13. *Moskovskie vedomosti*, 30 March 1910, p. 2. Also: Dixon, "'Mad Monk'," 397n122.
14. *Moskovskie vedomosti*, 30 April 1910, p. 1.
15. Tikhomirov, "Iz dnevnika," 1:171–72; 3:105.
16. Quotes from *Rech'*, 26 and 28 May 1910, Nos. 144, 146, missing p.n.
17. See Budnitskii, *Russian Jews*, 211.
18. VR, 169; Amal'rik, *Rasputin*, 117–18; FSu, 550–52. See, for example, *TsM*, 6, 26 29 May; 1, 2, 3, 6, 10, 11, 13 June; 3 July; 11 August 1910; and *TsV*, 10 March 1910.
19. *Iuzhnaia zaria*, "Grigorii Rasputin," 30 May 1910, pp. 2–3; 2 June, p. 2; 4 June, p. 2. On Senin: VR, 92. Could this Senin have been the same "journalist" Alexander Senin in the *New York Times* called a new "Red Rasputin," the true power in Soviet Russia following Lenin's death? See *New York Times*, 2 August 1925, p. 1.
20. *Rech'*, 30 May 1910, No. 146, missing p.n.; 7 June 1910, No. 154, missing p.n.
21. *TsM*, 3 July 1910, p. 2; 11 August 1910, pp. 2–3.
22. HHStA, P.A. I, Karton 135, 7 April/25 March 1910.
23. *TsM*, 13 June 1910, p. 1.
24. Bel'gard, "Pechat'," 345–46; VR, 139–40, 170; Tikhomirov, "Iz dnevnika," 1:184.
25. Lauchlan, *Hide*, 309–10; Bel'gard, "Pechat'," 345–46.
26. Bel'gard, "Pechat'," 345–46.
27. GARF, 63.47.484(35), 97–98.
28. Tikhomirov, "Iz dnevnika," No. 1, 184.
29. GARF, 102.316.1910.381, 5–6, 58–59ob, 66–73, 84, 161, 169; and ch. 1, 220–32.
30. Amal'rik, *Rasputin*, 118.

20: In Search of Rasputin

1. *TsM*, 29 May 1910, p. 3; and 6 June 1910, pp. 1–2.
2. GARF, 1467.1.710, 104. This was most likely Nikolai Vasilevich Sablin, who served on the *Standart*.
3. GARF, 102.316.1910.381, 1–1ob.
4. Witte, *Iz arkhiva*, vol. 1, bk. 2, 893; idem, *Vospominaniia*, 565.
5. FB, 356.
6. RGIA, 1659.1.63, 81ob.
7. VR, 118; Gurko, *Tsar'*, 248; GARF, 111.1.2979a, 122ob.
8. Vitte, *Iz arkhiva*, vol. 1, bk. 2, 893; idem, *Vospominaniia*, 565.
9. OR/RNB, 1000.1975.22, 21ob–22.
10. Bogdanovich, *Tri poslednikh*, 504.
11. RRR, 37–38; Buranov, "Strannik," 55–56.
12. GARF, 102.316.1910.381, 1–1ob.
13. *Utro Rossii*, 14 September 1910. At: www.starosti.ru.
14. *Rul'*, 15 September 1910. At: www.starosti.ru.
15. *Stolichnaia molva*, 15 September 1910. At: www.starosti.ru.
16. GARF, 111.1.2978, 1–4.
17. GARF, 102.316.1910.381, 1–2ob.
18. GATO, I-239.1.95, 186–88.
19. GARF, 63.30.1910.1513, 1–9.
20. GATO, I-239.1.119, 52–53ob. Previous biographies mistakenly give his name as "Prilin." The documents at GATO, however, unmistakably show that it is Prelin, as confirmed by Zotin, *Iurkin*, 172.
21. GARF, 640.1.309, 25–27.
22. Tikhomirov, *Iz dnevnika*, 1:182, 184.

21: Prince Yusupov

1. YLS, 34, 66–67.
2. *Reka vremen*, 2:98–100; YLS, 28–29.
3. YLS, 102.
4. *Reka vremen*, 2:100–101; YLS, 120–23; RR, 107–108.
5. YLS, 43–44, 66, 83, 152–53.
6. YLS, 46–48, 70, 78, 83–91, 104–105, 117–21, 141, 152–59.
7. OPI/GIM, 411.47, 143–53ob.
8. YLS, 100, 124, 131–35.
9. Marie, *Education*, 19–22, 66–73, 153–54; YLS, 94, 100, 131–33.
10. *Lettres des Grands-Ducs*, 50, 52, 55–56, 60–61, 64.
11. RR, 181–82.

12. *WC*, 407.
13. YLS, 94, 154–55.
14. *LP*, 382.
15. Dolgova, *Nakanune*, 164–65.
16. YLS, 138–39, 165, 187–89.
17. NIOR/RGB, 261.20.6, 47; YLS, 200–201; Stoeckl, *Not All Vanity*, 133–34.
18. FDNO, 246–47, 296–302.
19. OR/RNB, 307.80, 10. On Felix and his brother's duel, see FDNO, 302n52.
20. Compare OPI/GIM, 411.48, 9–10ob; OR/RNB, 307.80, 10; GARF, 102.314.35, 25–27; YLS, 147.
21. YLS, 147–49.
22. OR/RNB, 307.80, 10.
23. RRR, 118.
24. OPI/GIM, 411.48, 26–27, 76–77ob.
25. YLS, 258–59. Note the translation given of Rasputin's inscription in Yusupov's memoirs is not accurate.
26. OPI/GIM, 411.48, 34.
27. OPI/GIM, 411.48, 90–93ob.
28. Undated letter. OPI/GIM, 411.48, 114–17ob.
29. OPI/GIM, 411.48, 81–82ob.
30. OR/RNB, 307.80, 10.

22: Holy Land

1. Dixon, "'Mad Monk'," 398–99.
2. GARF, 1467.1.710, 117–18, 231–32ob.
3. Dixon, "'Mad Monk'," 399.
4. *Russkoe slovo*, 29 January 1911. At: www.starosti.ru.
5. *Russkoe slovo*, 7 February 1911. At: www.starosti.ru.
6. SML, Spiridovich Papers, Box 6, Folder 3, p. 125.
7. Gurko, *Tsar'*, 230–31; FSu, 440–45.
8. VR, 261–62.
9. NIOR/RGB, 261.20.2, 10–12, 15–19, 70–72.
10. VR, 261.
11. Gurko, *Tsar'*, 231.
12. Dixon, "'Mad Monk'," 399–402.
13. VR, 140; *LP*, 342–43.
14. *LP*, 341.
15. GARF, 640.1.309, 1, 2.
16. *KVD*, 59–60.
17. FR, 72; RR, 139.

18. Gurko, *Tsar'*, 231.
19. FDNO, 250–54.
20. FR, 73; FSu, 467–68; *Rossiia v sviatoi zemle*, 1:27–31.
21. FR, 73–74; WC, 103n84; KVD, 62.
22. KVD, 59–60; PZ, 249; SML, Spiridovich Papers, Box 6, Folder 3, pp. 133–34; RGALI, 2167.2.22, 3.
23. Above quotes from: PZ, 249–57.
24. KVD, 61.
25. FDNO, 254.
26. Montefiore, *Jerusalem*, 386–88.
27. PZ, 257, 260, 263–64.
28. *LP*, 343.
29. FDNO, 255.
30. FSu, 480.

23: Rasputin in His Own Words

1. RGADA, 1290.2.4765, 3. Another panning of this book: GARF, 63.47.484(35), 57. Clipping from 4 November 1915. Also: N. Konstantinov, "Malogramotnyi favorit," *Zhurnal zhurnalov* 16 (1915).
2. VV, 16 December 1911. At: www.starosti.ru.
3. For one reference to his public preaching, see *Voskresnaia vecherniaia gazeta*, 15 September 1913, p. 2.
4. RR, 131. Metropolitan Veniamin claims he was asked by the empress to "translate" some of Rasputin's autobiographical writings he made in a yellow morocco notebook into proper literary Russian, a task he never completed. The notebook's fate is unknown. Veniamin, *Na rubezhe*, 133.
5. FB, 527–28.
6. Unless otherwise noted, all these extracts are from Alexandra's notebook: GARF, 640.1.309, 1–62ob. The document has been printed in full in PZ, 265–90.
7. GARF, 651.1.10, 95ob–99, 126ob.
8. PZ, 239.
9. Sokolov, *Ubiistvo*, 85–86, 89.
10. GARF, 651.1.27, 30–32.
11. GARF, 102.242.1912.297, ch. 1, 80.
12. *Grigorii Rasputin v vospominaniiakh*, 71–73.
13. She writes about their relationship in Krarup, *42 Aar*, 123–52. Also: Christie's, Sale 6827, 25 November 2003, Notes to Lot 164: Krarup, Portrait of Rasputin.
14. PZ, 243, 246–47.

15. *Dym otechestva*, 16 May 1913, pp. 10–11.
16. See Etkind, *Khlyst*, 594–95.
17. Kizenko, *Prodigal*, 85–86.

24: Iliodor's Triumph

1. RGALI, 2167.2.22, 1.
2. *Russkoe slovo*, 11 March 1911. At: www.starosti.ru.
3. Stremoukhov, "Moia bor'ba," 33–34; Dixon, "'Mad Monk'," 399–402.
4. RGALI, 2167.2.22, 1ob.
5. VR, 255–57, 263. For comparison, see IMM, 70–72.
6. *Russkoe slovo*, 27 March 1911. At: www.starosti.ru.
7. Gurko, *Tsar'*, 231–32.
8. IMM, 71–72; VR, 257.
9. OR/RNB, 1000.3.439, 3ob.
10. "Iz perepiski P. A. Stolypina," 85.
11. Stremoukhov, "Moia bor'ba," 39–41.
12. VR, 258; Dixon, "'Mad Monk'," 402.
13. Hall, *Little Mother*, 236–39.
14. *LP*, 342–43.
15. VR, 235–36, 267–68.
16. Dixon, "'Mad Monk'," 402–403; VR, 268.
17. See *TsM*, 21 June 1911, p. 3; and stories in 22–24, 26, 28 June; 1, 7 July.
18. *TsM*, 26 June 1911, "Khronika"; 28 June, p. 3; 1 July 1911, pp. 3–4.
19. *Tserkov'*, No. 32, 1911, pp. 779–80; *TsM*, 1 July 1911, pp. 3–4; *Utro Rossii*, 7 July 1911, No. 155 in HIA, SCAN 87162–64.
20. *TsM*, 7 July 1911, p. 3.
21. Dixon, "'Mad Monk'," 404–405, 415; FSu, 496–98.

25: Two Murders

1. *KVD*, 62.
2. FB, 522–23.
3. *KVD*, 63–66.
4. On the case, see Levin, *Child*.
5. Shul'gin, *Dni*, 105–106.
6. *KVD*, 63–66.
7. VR, 613.
8. GARF, 102.316.1910.381, 3–6; PZ, 106–107.
9. GARF, 102.OO.245.1915g.244, ch. 1, 220–21.
10. Stremoukhov, "Moia bor'ba," 34.

11. IMM, 199–200; YLS, 153.
12. Guchkov, *Guchkov*, 83–84.
13. VR, 141.
14. Shulgin, *Years*, 261–63.
15. Bogdanovich, *Tri poslednikh*, 499.
16. PAAA, 15029, R.10680.
17. Schelking, *Recollections*, 269–71.
18. Kokovtsov, *Out*, 290–91; Ioffe, "Rasputiniada," 108.
19. VR, 234–36; Betts, *Dukhovnik*, 65–68; Rasputin quote: *PK*, 3 July 1914, p. 2.

26: Confronting the "Antichrist"

1. RGALI, 2167.2.22, 1.
2. FSu, 623–27; Stremoukhov, "Moia bor'ba," 39.
3. GARF, 111.1.2974, 293, 295.
4. OR/RNB, 1000.3.439, 4.
5. IMM, 233–35.
6. Rodzianko, *Reign*, 15–17.
7. VR, 279–80; Evglogii, *Put'*, 183–84.
8. IMM, 235–36; VR, 279–80.
9. Dixon, "'Mad Monk'," 406; PZ, 133–36.
10. IMM, 83–84.
11. FR, 82–83.
12. OR/RNB, 1000.3.439, 4.
13. IMM, 219, 225; FStr, 547–48.
14. "Gor'kii i russkaia zhurnalistika," 981n8.

27: Germogen's Fall

1. VR, 281; Dixon, "'Mad Monk'," 406; Mramornov, *Tserkovnaia*, 284–85.
2. Mramornov, *Tserkovnaia*, 278–79, 285–86, 300–301; idem, "'Delo'," 211–12.
3. OR/RNB, 1000.1975.22, 21ob–22; *Ekaterinburgskie eparkhial'nye vedomosti*, No. 4, 1912, pp. 86–90; VV, 14 February 1912. At: www.starosti.ru.
4. OR/RNB, 1000.1975.22, 25ob.
5. RGIA, 1101.1.111, 8.
6. *PK*, 23 April 1914, p. 6.
7. VR, 240–43; BA, Vostokov Papers, Untitled Ms., p. 1.
8. "V tserkovnykh krugakh"; VR, 241n, 243–44; FR, 77–80; Firsov, *Pravoslavnaia tserkov'*, 234–37.
9. Vatala, *Bez mifov*, 251; VR, 281–82.

10. Kokovtsov, *Out*, 293–94; VR, 282–84, 287; Mramornov, *Tserkovnaia*, 290–92.
11. RGIA, 1101.1.1111, 10–11ob.
12. VR, 284–85; Amal'rik, *Rasputin*, 148; see also the untitled article by S. Nikitin in *Peterburgskaia gazeta*, 16 February 1912.
13. FN, 360–63; RR, 299–300; Mel'gunov, *Legenda*, 397.
14. VR, 623.
15. *Novoe vremia*, 18 February 1912, p. 3.
16. FB, 234–35, 239; "Aleksandro-Nevskaya lavra," 204–205.
17. Mramornov, *Tserkovnaia*, 316.

28: Iliodor, Apostate

1. *Novosti dnia*, 19 December 1902; *Moskovskii listok*, 3 October; 4, 14 November 1902. At: www.starosti.ru; *Za kulisami*, iii.
2. *Rech'*, 2 November 1911. At: www.starosti.ru.
3. GRS, 4:272.
4. Dixon, "'Mad Monk'," 407; *Za kulisami*, vii, 7–8; IMM, 245; VR, 282.
5. SML, Spiridovich Papers, Box 6, Folder 3, p. 186; VR, 291.
6. Copies of the letter are in RGALI, 2167.2.26; OR/RNB, 1000.3.439, 1–5. On Dedyulin's instruction: GARF, 102.242.1912.297, ch. 1, 57.
7. *Za kulisami*, vii; GARF, 102.242.1912.297, ch. 1, 57.
8. GARF, 102.242.1912.297, ch. 1, 46; 102.316.381, ch. 1, 2; 102.316.1910.381, ch. 2, 87, 89, 99–102.
9. GARF, 713.1.18, 1–1ob.
10. Dixon, "'Mad Monk'," 407.
11. GARF, 612.1.42, 5; IMM, 116.
12. Buranov, "Strannik," 56; VR, 294.
13. FStr, 595–97.
14. There is some disagreement over how many letters there were. Kokovtsov later claimed there was also one from Alexei. *Out*, 292, 299–300. Iliodor wrote there was one letter from Alexei, but Rasputin had kept it for himself. IMM, 116.
15. VR, 292–94.
16. Amal'rik, *Rasputin*, 103–106. Another (purported) letter from Alexandra was published in 1917. See Vladykin, *Taina*, 14–15.
17. OR/RNB, 1000.3.439, 2ob; GARF, 713.1.24, 5–5ob.
18. GARF, 713.1.24, 3–5ob.
19. Beletskii, *Vospominaniia*, 8; and see RR, 163. She is incorrectly called Karbovich.
20. VR, 299.
21. Bogdanovich, *Tri poslednikh*, 502.
22. On the possibility the letter was a fake, see Betts, *Pshenitsy*, 69.

23. Rodzianko, *Reign*, 35–38.
24. RR, 163–64.
25. Kokovtsov, *Out*, 299.
26. VR, 300–301; Gurko, *Cherty*, 617.
27. Dixon, "'Mad Monk'," 407.
28. "Gor'kii i russkaia zhurnalistika," 981–82; VR, 414–17; FStr, 248n2.
29. GARF, 1467.1.710, 218.
30. IMM, 264–66; Dixon, "'Mad Monk'," 409.
31. SML, Spiridovich Papers, Box 6, Folder 3, p. 186.
32. *Peterburgskaia gazeta*, 7 December 1912. Accessed at: www.starosti.ru.
33. FStr, 595-97; IMM, 203.
34. Mramornov, *Tserkovnaia*, 317.
35. OR/RNB, 1000.1975.22, 32ob.
36. IMM, 269–80; *PK*, 29 January 1914, p. 2; *Voskresnaia vecherniaia gazeta*, 12 January 1914, p. 2.

29: *Quousque tandem abutere patientia nostra?*

1. His notes on the title page to a copy of the typescript in HIΛ, Nikolaevsky Papers, Series 74, 129-1.
2. GARF, 63.32.1912.82, 1–13; RGIA, 1101.1.1111, 7ob, 11–11ob; FB, 470.
3. VR, 304, 391.
4. Bel'gard, "Pechat'," 347–48.
5. GARF, 63.32.1912.82, 9, 14.
6. RGIA, 1278.2.2641, 1–2; Dzhunkovskii, *Vospominaniia*, 1:628; FR, 91.
7. VR, 307; Guchkov, *Guchkov*, 86.
8. Shulgin, *Years*, 230–32.
9. RGIA, 1101.1.1111, 10.
10. Dzhunkovskii, *Vospominaniia*, 1:628; *Novoe vremia*, 26 January 1912, p. 2; FR, 91.
11. Shulgin, *Years*, 230–32; RGIA, 1278.2.2641, 1–3; VR, 306. On Lvov's character, Gurko, *Cherty*, 696.
12. *Novoe vremia*, 26 January 1912, p. 2.
13. RGIA, 1278.2.2641, 1–3.
14. VR, 302, 304–308.
15. Bulgakov, *Avtobiograficheskie zapiski*, 82–83.
16. VR, 303.
17. Dzhunkovskii, *Vospominaniia*, 1:628. Quoted material from a letter from one V. Berezin in the Kursk province to Stishinsky of the State Council. RGIA, 1101.1.1111, 10–11.
18. *LP*, 156.
19. VR, 309.

20. Kokovtsov, *Out*, 294–95; VR, 309–11.

21. GARF, 111.1.2978, 1–4; 111.1.2981b, 35.

22. *LP*, 350–51.

23. Kokovtsov, *Out*, 296–98.

24. HHStA, P.A. X, Karton 139, 24/11 October 1913.

25. VR, 318–19.

26. FDNO, 256–57.

27. VR, 315–18.

28. *KVD*, 82, 86.

29. GARF, 102.316.1910.381, 51.

30. OR/RNB, 1000.1975.22, 26ob; Mordvinov, "Poslednii imperator," 4:49–50; *Peterburgskaia gazeta*, 20 February 1912; VV, 23 February 1916: Both at: www.starosti.ru.

30: The Blow to the Alcove

1. VV, 18 February 1912. At: www.starosti.ru.

2. GARF, 612.1.12, 1–3.

3. See the "New Introduction" to his memoirs by David R. Jones, *Reign*, xv–xxvi. As Jones points out, Rodzianko's memory is far from reliable, and the mere title of his memoirs reflects his bias and ignorance of the true state of affairs under the last tsar.

4. Rodzianko, *Reign*, 8–21, 35–36; VR, 308–10.

5. VR, 319–20.

6. Blok, *Poslednie dni*, 10; Bogdanovich, *Tri poslednikh*, 502–503. On Nilov and Rasputin, see also: Sablin, *Desiat' let*, 252–55, 294–95, 327–29.

7. On Rasputin and the Freemasons: Rodzianko, *Reign*, 30.

8. Bogdanovich, *Tri poslednikh*, 502–503.

9. Rodzianko, *Reign*, 40–54; VR, 320.

10. RGIA, 797.82.77/3/2, 1–8.

11. VR, 321–22.

12. Voeikov, *S tsarem*, 60–61, 131.

13. VR, 322.

14. Den, *Podlinnaia tsaritsa*, 65.

15. Mordvinov, "Poslednii imperator," 54.

16. Den, *Podlinnaia tsaritsa*, 58.

17. VR, 324–26; Kokovtsov, *Out*, 302–303.

18. Bogdanovich, *Tri poslednikh*, 505, 507. The articles were likely "Taina khlystovshchiny," by Ippolit Gofshtetter, *Novoe vremia*, 20 March 1912, pp. 4–5; 21 March, p. 5.

19. Fuller, *Foe*, 83–84.

20. *Novoe vremia*, 10 March 1912, "Razdel: V Gosudarstvennoi Dume."

21. Savich, *Vospominaniia*, 83; VR, 329.

22. Savich, *Vospominaniia*, 83; Ioffe, "Rasputiniada," 107–108. See also: K. K. Romanov, *Dnevniki*, 429.

23. *Novaia voskresnaia vecherniaia gazeta*, 18 March 1912, p. 3.

24. RGIA, 1101.1.111, 1.

25. VR, 33.

26. RGALI, 2167.2.42, 18–28.

27. HHStA, P.A. X, Karton 138, 11 April /29 March 1912.

28. NA, FO 371/1467, No. 8227, Buchanan to Sir Edward Grey, 14 February 1912 (NS).

29. VR, 334.

30. *Novaia voskresnaia vecherniaia gazeta*, 11 March 1912, p. 1; *Novoe vremia*, 13 March 1912, p. 3; *Peterburgskaia gazeta*, 17 March 1912. At: www.starosti.ru; *Russkaia riv'era*, 21, 22 March 1912. At: www.starosti.ru; GARF, 102.316.1910.381, 134; Polivanov, *Iz dnevnikov*, 110–11.

31. 18 March 1912, p. 3.

32. Sablin, *Desiat' let*, 254–55.

33. *LP*, 352.

34. Iusupov, *Pered izgnaniem*, 230.

35. OPI/GIM, 411.48, 40–43.

36. Rodzianko, *Reign*, 55.

37. RGIA, 525.1 (205/2693).202, 6–7.

38. Rodzianko, *Reign*, 55–56.

39. Elizaveta Fedorovna, "Pis'ma," 482; GARF, 642.1.1584, 74–75ob.

31: The Investigation II: Was Rasputin a Khlyst?

1. *Voskresnaia vecherniaia gazeta*, 1 July 1912, p. 2; *Peterburgskaia gazeta*, 30 June 1912, n.p.; *Russkoe slovo*, 30 June 1912, n.p., *Stolichnaia molva*, 2 July 1912, n.p., and *Gazeta-kopeika*, 30 June 1912, n.p.—all at www.starosti.ru; GARF, 102.316.1910.381, 104, 108–12.

2. GARF, 102.316.1910.381, 15–20, 28, 114, 126; 111.1.2975, 43, 76; FSu, 707n2498. "Hotel D." was the Hotel Dagmar.

3. GARF, 102.316.1910.381, 90–91, 122.

4. FB, 521, 536–38; VR, 104, 346–47.

5. RGIA, 797.82.77/3/2, 1–6; Kokovtsov, *Out*, 295; Rodzianko, *Reign*, 50–51.

6. VR, 347–48; FB, 521, 643-45; RGIA, 797.82.77/3/2, 8; GBUTO/GAGT, I-156.18.920, 7.

7. VR, 348-49; FB, 521–22; GARF, 102.316.1910.381, 165.

8. GARF, 102.316.1910.381, 121.

9. *Vestnik zapadnoi Sibiri*, 9 May 1912, p. 3.

10. RGALI, 2167.2.22, 2.

11. GARF, 102.316.1910.381, 63–64.

12. *Vestnik zapadnoi Sibiri*, 9 May 1912, p. 3.

13. GBUTO/GAGT, I-156.18.920, 4–6, 8–9.

14. The details are largely in the short memoir of one of the academy pupils, M. V. Andreev, in: GAUKTO/TIAMZ: TMKP 12223. "Vospominaniia M. V. Andreeva: 'Neizvestnoe o Rasputine'." Further details: PZ, 81–83; FB, 576–84.

15. FB, 633–38, 643–45; GARF, 612.1.13, 1–2.

16. VR, 356.

17. RR, 184–86; VR, 357–59; FR, 80–81. On Sabler: VR, 309–11. On Rasputin in the press: GARF, 102.316.1910.381, 152–53, 199–199ob.

18. OR/RNB, 1000.3.439, 8.

19. RGIA, 797.82.77/3/2, 9–11.

20. Bonch-Bruevich, "O Rasputine," *Den'*, 1 July 1914.

21. Guchkov, *Guchkov*, 85.

22. VV, 16 November 1912. At: www.starosti.ru; GARF, 102.316.1910.381, 32.

23. GARF, 111.1.2976, 13, 18, 58, 64, 92–92ob, 106, 105.

24. GARF, 111.1.2978, 1–4.

25. VR, 106–107.

26. Roudnieff, "La vérité," 7; GARF, 602.2.62.

27. VR, 106.

28. The consensus unites biographers across political and national lines to include Fuhrmann, Varlamov, Fomin, Platonov, Amalrik. The one biographer who continues to insist Rasputin had been a khlyst—rather unpersuasively—is Radzinsky.

29. Amal'rik, *Rasputin*, 111.

32: The Miracle at Spała

1. Massie, *Nicholas*, 180–83; LP, 355, 357.

2. LP, 357, 359–60; AD, Correspondance politique et commerciale, Nouvelle série, 1896–1918, NS 14, Questions Dynastiques, 1896–1914, No. 309.

3. Massie, *Nicholas*, 183–85.

4. KVD, 100; Vyrubova, *Stranitsy*, 67; VR, 361–62.

5. Massie, *Nicholas*, 185–86; LP, 357–59; Bing, ed., *Secret Letters*, 275–78.

6. Den, *Podlinnaia tsaritsa*, 82. Dehn, however, did write that Rasputin cured her son of a high fever. See p. 64.

7. IMM, 181–82.

8. PAAA, AS 251, R.10694.

9. VR, 362–65; Sokolov, *Temnye sily*, 10–11; Maud, *One Year*, 196; Le Queux, *Rasputin*, 21–22; Marsden, *Rasputin*, 34–35. For other stories of Rasputin and Vyrubova's devious plots to control Alexandra by presenting themselves as

the protectors of the tsarevich, see Omessa, *Rasputin*, 65–67; and the memoirs of G. A. Benua in OR/RNB, 1000.6.4, 243.

10. GARF, 602.2.62; 1467.1.949, 2–5; Amal'rik, *Rasputin*, 45–46. See also: Shul'gin, *Dni*, 108.

11. PAAA, AS 251, R.10694.

12. Vyrubova, *Stranitsy*, 82–85; VR, 356–57; KVD, 175; *LP*, 416.

13. Chebotaryova, "V dvortsovom lazarete," 181: 181–82; FSA, 294–95. On Gedroits, Bennett, "Princess," 1532–34; Mordvinov, "Poslednii," 52–53.

14. Vyrubova, *Stranitsy*, 82–85.

15. Dostoevsky, *Brothers*, 25.

16. WC, 355, 362–63. "Crust"—rusk made from black bread, the so-called "Rasputin rusks."

17. Vasilevskii, *Nikolai II*, 93. In other versions it is a dirty shirt or hat. See OR/RNB, 585.5696, 13ob; *Golos minuvshego*, No. 4–6, 1918, p. 35.

18. IMM, 117, 120–21.

19. WC, 651. According to her long-serving maid Madeleine Zanotti, the empress never did suffer from a bad heart. Rather, her health issues were physical manifestations of psychological and emotional problems that grew into "hysteria" by her later years. See Sokolov, *Ubiistvo*, 85–86.

20. GRS, 2:236.

21. Grabbe, *Okna*, 130.

22. Vorres, *Last*, 138–40.

23. FR, 102; Vorres, *Last*, 138–40; VR, 362.

24. VR, 67.

25. Buxhoeveden, *Before*, 116–19.

26. IMM, 135–36. See also the unconvincing story in Shelley, *Blue Steppes*, 86–87. For a current example, Shishkin, *Rasputin*, 73.

27. VR, 366.

28. GARF, 102.316.1910.381, 165, 175.

29. IMM, 136, 209–10; Evreinov, *Taina*, 49-50; Mel'gunov, *Vospominaniia*, 1:207; FR, 103; HHStA, P.A. 38, Karton 364, 4 July 1914; Voeikov, *S tsarem*, 57–58; Gurko, *Tsar'*, 235.

30. Kokovtsov, *Out*, 296–97; Rodzianko, *Reign*, 24, 76.

31. YLS, 211; VR, 370; Khvostov, "Iz vospominanii," 166–67; FB, 312–13.

32. Mel'gunov, *Vospominaniia*, 1:202.

33. Evreinov, *Taina*; Etkind, *Eros*, 126–27.

34. GRS, 2:230–31, 234–35.

35. Le Queux, *Rasputin*, 4. The story is repeated in Marsden, *Rasputin*, 25.

36. GARF, 111.1.2981a, l. 9–10ob. His name is sometimes mistakenly given in biographies as "Papandato."

37. Beletskii, *Grigorii*, 21–22.

38. Brown, *Testing*, 1–2.

39. Carey, "Long-Awaited Medical Study;" Stein, "Researchers."

40. FR, 105.
41. *LP*, 444–45.
42. See http://www.massgeneral.org/bhi/about/; http://www.semel.ucla.edu/ cousins.
43. Massie, *Nicholas*, 201–202.
44. On Harvard's program, see http://www.programplacebostudies.org./ On the placebo effect, see Ofri, "A Powerful Tool;" Niemi, "Placebo;" Feinberg, "Placebo;" Guess, et al., *Science*; Marchant, *Cure*.
45. See Dzhanumova, *Moi vstrechi*, 28–29; Beletskii, *Vospominaniia*, 56; HHStA, P.A. X, Karton 139, 11/24 October 1913. Other historians have suggested, although without the benefit of the latest science, that the mind/body connection was at the heart of Rasputin's ability to help the heir. See Amal'rik, *Rasputin*, 45–46; FR, 103; Massie, *Nicholas*, 201–202.
46. Vorres, *Last*, 140; VR, 143.
47. Shulgin, *Years*, 263; VR, 61.
48. PAAA, 19432, R.10680; dispatch of Ambassador Pourtalès to Bethmann Hollweg, 4 November 1912 (NS); Voeikov, *S tsarem*, 58–59.
49. Vyrubova, *Stranitsy*, 61.

33: War and Celebration

1. *Russkoe slovo*, 18 October 1912. At: www.starosti.ru.
2. GARF, 102.316.1910.381, 152. On Rasputin's indifference to pan-Slavism of any sort: Sokolov, "Predvaritel'noe sledstvie," 284.
3. *Peterburgskaia gazeta*, 7 December 1912. At: www.starosti.ru.
4. *Dym otechestva*, 24 January 1913, pp. 6–8.
5. PAAA, R.10897.
6. *PK*, 7 May 1914, p. 1.
7. GARF, 102.242.1912.297, ch. 2, 168.
8. VR, 376.
9. RR, 190–91. He sees Rasputin as being the key reason, even giving Nicholas the strength to stay out of the fighting.
10. Lincoln, *In War's*, 408–13.
11. *LP*, 374.
12. FR, 107.
13. Rodzianko, *Reign*, 75–77.
14. GARF, 270.1.46, 3.
15. VR, 327–28; Amal'rik, *Rasputin*, 156.
16. *Dym otechestva*, 14 March 1913, p. 5.
17. FDNO, 257–58.
18. GARF, 111.1.2977, 2, 5, 32–33ob, 35–35ob; 111.1.2981b, 35–36; KVD, 82.
19. RR, 346, 410–11; GARF, 602.2.62.

20. FR, 108; Sablin, *Desiat' let*, 294; Dzhunkovskii, *Vospominaniia*, 2:201–02; OR/RNB, 585.5696, 35.

21. *LP*, 377–78.

22. VR, 61.

23. *KVD*, 111.

24. *LP*, 378–80; GARF, 1467.1.710, 288.

25. *KVD*, 114.

34: Gutter Talk, Name-Glorifiers, and Murder Plots

1. *Dym otechestva*, No. 4, 1913, pp. 6–8.

2. See: http://www.hrono.ru/biograf/bio_g/garjazin.html. Accessed on 17 August 2015.

3. VR, 338–39; FStr, 595.

4. BA, Vostokov Papers, "Tochnyia dannye," pp. 5–10, 20.

5. VR, 390–91; *Padenie*, 4:188–89.

6. *Dym otechestva*, 16 May 1913, pp. 10–11; and 11 June 1913, pp. 4–5.

7. Http://www.hrono.ru/biograf/bio_g/garjazin.html. Accessed: 17 August 2015.

8. FB, 525–26; GARF, 102.242.1912.297, ch. 2, 195; 111.1.2980, 196–96ob.

9. RR, 176–79.

10. *Dym otechestva*, 20 June 1913, pp. 7–8; 26 June 1913, pp. 2–3; 24 January 1913, pp. 6–7; Buranov, "Strannik," 57.

11. See, for example, the piece in *Volzhsko-Donskoi krai* from 1914. In: GARF, 102.242.1912.297, ch. 2, 154.

12. GARF, 102.242.1912.297, ch. 1, 50, 82.

13. The discussion of the Athos Sedition is based on Firsov, *Pravoslavnaia tserkov'*, 462–502; Leskin, *Spor*; Ilarion, *Spory*; VR, 380–81.

14. Firsov, *Pravoslavnaia tserkov'*, 475, 480–83, 493; Leskin, *Spor*, 67.

15. VR, 382–83.

16. Firsov, *Pravoslavnaia tserkov'*, 493–94, 499n65.

17. *Golos Moskvy*, 7 June 1913. At: www.starosti.ru; VV, 12 June 1913, p. 3.

18. GARF, 102.316.1910.381, 153, 190–90ob, 199–99ob. On Paozersky: Dixon, "'Mad Monk'," 398n126.

19. VR, 384; FStr, 33–34n2.

20. VR, 385-86; Leskin, *Spor*, 71–73.

21. Leskin, *Spor*, 71–72n2.

22. VR, 387.

23. Firsov, *Pravoslavnaia tserkov'*, 497–98.

24. VR, 392.

25. *Utro Rossii*, 1 July 1910. At: www.starosti.ru.

26. *KVD*, 115; GBUTO/GAGT, I-331.19.809, 34.

27. *Iuzhnye vedomosti*, 13 October 1913. At: www.starosti.ru.

28. FB, 237–39; Bogdanovich, *Tri poslednikh*, 503–504.

29. GARF, 102.316.1910.381, 36.

30. Beletskii, "Vospominaniia", 7–9; Bonch-Bruevich, *Vsia vlast'*, 78.

31. GARF, 102.316.1910.381, 198.

32. KVD, 117; FB, 426, 456–57, 357–58; GARF, 102.316.381, ch. 1, 220–32.

33. *Rannee utro*, 26 May 1913. At: www.starosti.ru.

34. *Stolichnaia molva*, 12 August 1913. At: www.starosti.ru.

35. GARF, 640.1.323, 27–27ob.

36. Ordovskii-Tanaevskii, *Vospominaniia*, 310.

37. GARF, 102.316.1910.381, 170, 172–73, 178–78ob; *Den'*, 3 January 1914, p. 5. On Ordovsky's appointment, WC, 181, 188–89; Ordovskii-Tanevskii, *Vospominaniia*, 366–69; VR, 643–44; Gurko, *Tsar'*, 241–42.

35: On the Edge of a Precipice

1. KVD, 119–21. The Court Journal recorded only three visits by Rasputin to the palace. GARF, 1467.1.479, 18ob–19.

2. *PK*, 7 May 1914, p. 1.

3. HHStA, P.A. X, Karton 140, 31 January/13 February 1914.

4. VR, 376.

5. GARF, 102.316.1910.381, 171.

6. GARF, 102.242.1912.297, ch. 1, 8.

7. *PK*, 25 February 1914, p. 4.

8. GARF, 102.242.1912.297, ch. 1, 13–14, 16, 20, 23; KVD, 121–22.

9. KVD, 122; FStr, 37, 46.

10. NIOR RGB, 249.4214.16, 11–11ob.

11. GARF, 102.242.1912.297, ch. 1, 17; *PK*, 21 March 1914, p. 2.

12. *Voskresnaia vecherniaia gazeta*, 16 March 1914, p. 3.

13. *PK*, 26 January 1914, p. 1; *Russkoe slovo*, 30 April 1914; *Svet*, 30 April 1914; *Rech'*, 23 April 1914; GARF, 102.316.1910.381, 176–77.

14. *PK*, 29 April 1914, p. 2; NA, FO 371/2093, No. 22097, Letter of 14 May 1914 (NS) to Sir Edward Gray from George Buchanan.

15. *PK*, 30 April 1914, p. 2.

16. VR, 393.

17. *PK*, 7 May 1914, p. 2.

18. *PK*, 18 May 1914, p. 4; HIA, Nikolaevsky Papers, Series No. 74, 129-6, "Pis'mo v redaktsiiu;" GARF, 102.242.1912.297, ch. 1, 67–69.

19. GARF, 102.316.381, ch. 1, 10–13ob.

20. Zhukovskaia, *Moi vospominaniia*, 305.

21. FA, 118–19n1; Grashchenkova, *Kino*, 135.

22. GARF, 102.242.1912.297, ch. 1, 44; FStr, 461–62; *PK*, 7 May 1914, p. 1; *KVD*, 123–24; Sablin, *Desiat' let*, 327–28.

23. GARF, 102.242.1912.297, ch. 1, 56; *PK*, 4 June 1914, p. 4.

24. FStr, 80.

25. GARF, 102.316.381, ch. 1, 1.

26. GARF, 102.242.1912.297, ch. 1, 21, 45–45ob, 52–52ob, 54, 61.

27. Shavel'skii, *Vospominaniia*, 1:64–68.

28. *Padenie*, 4:297.

36: The Attack

1. *KVD*, 128; FStr, 83–85.

2. PZ, 111; FStr, 85–87; Smirnov, *Neizvestnoe*, 66. The following discussion of Guseva's attack and the subsequent investigation draws chiefly on the police files in several Siberian archives: GBUTO/GAGT, 164.1.436, 437, 439; Kazennoe uchrezhdenie Omskoi oblasti "Istorichicheskii arkhiv Omskoi oblasti," 190.1.1881–1917gg.332. These important, though little-studied files, are produced in full in FStr, 378–826.

3. FStr, 101–105, 109, 117–18, 204, 385–88, 407, 486; Smirnov, *Neizvestnoe*, 66; GARF, 102.242.1912.297, ch. 2, 1.

4. GARF, 102.242.1912.297, ch. 2, 1.

5. Smirnov, *Neizvestnoe*, 66.

6. Vladimirov's description of the operation: RGIA, 472.2 (195/2683).7, 8–9.

7. FStr, 117–20.

8. GARF, 102.316.381, ch. 1, 5ob–6, 8–8ob; 102.242.1912.297, ch. 1, 162; 102.242.1912.297, ch. 2, 30–30ob; FStr, 391–93; FR, 125. The article appeared in *Svet*, No. 127, 18 May 1914, having first been published in a number of other newspapers. See PZ, 97; FStr, 95, 413–19, 426–25, 290–92; GARF, 102.242.1912.297, ch. 1, 180–81ob; Faleev, "Za chto," 180–81.

9. *PK*, 30 June 1914, p. 1.

10. See GARF, 102.242.1912, ch. 2. *New York Times*, 14 July (NS) 1914, p. 1, 3; 15 July (NS), p. 4; 16 July (NS), p. 4; 17 July (NS), p. 4.

11. *PK*, 1 July 1914, p. 2.

12. GARF, 102.242.1912.297, ch. 2, 195. The lines come from the end of Pushkin's narrative poem "The Gypsies" (published 1827).

13. PAAA, R.10684. Also: K. K. Romanov, *Dnevniki*, 440.

14. VR, 419.

15. *Dym otechestva*, 3 July 1914, p. 7.

16. VR, 419.

17. GARF, 102.242.1912.297, ch. 2, 85.

18. FN, 553.

19. VR, 419–20.

20. RGIA, 1617.1.45, 1–2.
21. FStr, 136.
22. Gilliard, *Thirteen Years*, 97–98.
23. Nicholas II, *Dnevniki*, 2(2): 42–43.
24. SML, Spiridovich Papers, Box 6, Folder 3, p. 198.
25. GARF, 612.1.21, 1.
26. Dzhunkovskii, *Vospominaniia*, 2:330–35; GARF, 102.242.1912.297, ch. 1, 172.
27. GARF, 102.242.1912.297, ch. 1, 164–65; *PK*, 30 June 1914, p. 1; 1 July 1914, p. 2; FStr, 86n1, 418, 434. Also on Davidson: GARF, 102.242.1912.297, ch. 2, 67 and Faleev, "Za chto," 181. One historian claims he is also the man hiding behind the names "V. Borisov" and "Ven. Bor." responsible for anti-Rasputin articles in the next year. FStr, 204–206. And: PZ, 148.
28. RRR, 78–82.
29. GBUTO/GAGT, I-331.19.809, 54, 77, 79–81, 95.
30. RRR, 84–85, 87. In a later bogus memoir Maria claimed Davidson was in fact a member of the conspiracy. See VR, 408–409.
31. PZ, 113; FStr, 211–18; Faleev, "Za chto," 181.
32. See FR, 125; VR, 409–410.
33. GARF, 102.242.1912.297, ch. 1, 111.
34. GBUTO/GAGT, I-331.19.809, 99–101, 118–21.
35. GARF, 102.316.1910.381, ch. 2, 76, 77, 79.
36. GARF, 102.242.1912.297, ch. 2, 2, 6, 17, 21.
37. GARF, 102.242.1912.297, ch. 1, 134. And see *PK*, "Tragediia russkogo byta," 3 July 1914, p. 2; 4 July, p. 2.
38. GARF, 102.242.1912.297 ch. 2, 108–109ob.

37: "This time it didn't work . . ."

1. FStr, 127–30, 499; RGIA, 472.2 (195/2683).7, 8–9. The papers mistakenly wrote he sailed on the *Lastochka*, which has been repeated in most biographies.
2. *PK*, 4 July 1914, p. 2.
3. FR, 120–21; FStr, 126, 131, 143; *PK*, 3 July 1914, p. 2.
4. OR/RNB, 1000.1975.22, 31ob.
5. RGIA, 472.2 (195/2683).7, 3–4, 10–14; FStr, 139.
6. *KVD*, 132–35.
7. GARF, 1467.1.710, 24–25.
8. *KVD*, 133–34.
9. See FStr, 123–24; GARF, 1467.1.710.
10. GARF, 1467.1.710, 205–205ob, 235–36ob.
11. FDNO, 261–62n30.
12. *PK*, 2 July 1914, p. 2.

13. VR, 407.

14. VR, 408; *PK*, 2 July 1914, p. 2; 5 July, p. 2.

15. *PK*, 1 July 1914, p. 2; 3 July, p. 2.

16. GARF, 102.242.1912.297, ch. 2, 30–30ob. Also, 102.242.1912.297, ch. 1, 172–73ob, 180–81ob; FStr, 455, 521, 634–35, 793–95.

17. FStr, 521, 793–95.

18. VR, 411–12; PZ, 122–23.

19. FStr, 147, 522, 553–57.

20. PZ, 95–97, 113, 128–33; FStr, 186–91, 548, 615–17.

21. GARF, 102.242.1912.297, ch. 2, 30–30ob, 168; GBUTO/GAGT, I-331.19.809, 128.

22. FR, 126; FStr, 161–62, 701–702; PZ, 136–37.

23. GARF, 102.242.1912.297, ch. 2, 196; *PK*, 3 July 1914, p. 2; 6 July, p. 2; 12 July, p. 1.

24. FStr, 710–11, 790–92, 799–800.

25. GARF, 102.316.381, ch. 1, 9; Smirnov, *Neizvestnoe*, 67–68.

26. FStr, 445–46.

27. GARF, 102.242.1912.297, ch. 2, 193.

28. *PK*, 1 July 1914, p. 2.

29. GARF, 1467.1.709, 92.

30. FStr, 231–32, 468, 471, 519–20; Smirnov, *Neizvestnoe*, 71.

31. IMM, 275–80.

32. Iliodor, *Velikaia Stalingradskaia*, 51–52.

33. PZ, 90–93, 124–25. FStr, 148–50.

34. FStr, 107, 148–50, 437–43, 550–51; VR, 405–406; PZ, 121, 124–25.

35. *Voskresnaia vecherniaia gazeta*, 20 April 1914, p. 1.

36. FStr, 535–36. Beletsky also believed Iliodor had been behind the attack. *Vospominaniia*, 48.

38: Iliodor's Flight

1. FStr, 239–42, 453; IMM, 281–84; GARF, 102.242.1912.297, ch. 2, 58, 179–89ob.

2. OR/RNB, 1000.1975.22, 32ob; FStr, 242–45; GARF, 102.242.1912.297, ch. 2, 58; *Rannee utro*, 11 July 1914.

3. FStr, 250, 256; GARF, 102.242.1912.297, ch. 2, 80, 176, 172; *PK*, 12 July 1914, pp. 1–2.

4. GARF, 102.242.1912.297, ch. 2, 36, 43.

5. GARF, 102.242.1912.297, ch. 1, 174, 176.

6. GARF, 102.242.1912.297, ch. 2, 44–44ob; GARF, 102.242.1912.297, ch. 1, 176.

7. GARF, 102.242.1912.297, ch. 2, 36, 43, 48.

8. FStr, 250, 256; IMM, 281–84; VR, 412–14, 419.

9. "Gor'kii i russkaia zhurnalistika," 452.

10. On the myth: *Rannee utro*, 20 December 1916, p. 2; GARF, 102.242.1912.297, ch. 1, 127.

11. VR, 419.

12. Dixon, "'Mad Monk'," 410; FStr, 251–54; "Gor'kii i russkaia zhurnalistika," 452n5.

13. GARF, 102.242.1912.297, ch. 2, 179–89ob.

14. IMM, 285–86; FStr, 254–55; *Aftenposten*, 29 March 1916 (NS), in RGIA, 1101.1.1073.

15. GARF, 102.242.1912.297, ch. 2, 179–89ob.

16. VR, 417–18; GARF, 102.242.1912.297, ch. 2, 179–89ob; *PK*, 13 October 1914, p. 4.

17. *PK*, 13 October 1914, p. 4.

18. FStr, 258.

19. FStr, 258, 631–32, 702.

39: A Menacing Cloud

1. On his murder, see Goldberg, *Life*, 458–74.

2. Wilson, *Rasputin*, 156; VR, 426–28; Groian, *Muchenik*, 95–96; Rassulin, *Vernaia Bogu*, 545.

3. FR, 115, 118; VR, 422–23.

4. *Otkliki na zhizn'*, No. 11–12 (1914): pp. 71–72.

5. GARF, 1467.1.710, 151–55.

6. GARF, 102.242.1912.297, ch. 1, 94.

7. KVD, 140–41.

8. Sokolov, *Ubiistvo*, 94.

9. KVD, 136.

10. GARF, 640.1.323, 2.

11. GARF, 1467.1.710, 159, 161–63.

12. GARF, 555.1.1432, 1.

13. FR, 129; *LP*, 397; Vyrubova, *Strannitsy*, 73–74.

14. GARF, 111.1.2978, 19.

15. Yale University, Beinecke Library, Romanov Collection, GEN MSS 313, Series 1, Box 1, Folder 100.

16. Yale University, Beinecke Library, Romanov Collection, GEN MSS 313, Series 1, Box 1, Folder 100; and GEN MSS 313, Box 8, Folder 111; VR, 424–25; FStr, 279–81. S. V. Markov, who was with Solovyov in Tobolsk in 1918, saw the letter then, though in his memoirs he implies the empress had given it and other letters from Rasputin to him earlier for safekeeping. *Pokinutaia*, 54.

17. [Belling], *Iz nedavnego*, 11; VR, 425–26.
18. FR, 128–29.
19. Raupakh, *Facies*, 141; FStr, 272–75, 313n1; FN, *Nakazanie*, 493; Amal'rik, *Rasputin*, 163–64, 185; Lieven, *Nicholas II*, 205.
20. *PK*, 16 July 1914, p. 1. Austria declared war on 15/28 July.
21. GARF, 102.242.1912.297, ch. 1, 69. And similar comments by *Dsihwes Spehks* of Riga. Ibid., 88–88ob.
22. GARF, 102.242.1912.297, ch. 2, 82–84, 204, 206–206ob.
23. Rassulin, *Vernaia bogu*, 73–74.
24. KVD, 141.
25. GARF, 640.1.323, 3, 3ob.
26. VR, 429–31.
27. KVD, 144, 147.
28. Nicholas II, *Dnevniki*, 2(2): 54.
29. Paléologue, *Ambassador's Memoirs*, 1:136–38.
30. *PK*, 16 August 1914, p. 4; 18 August, p. 2.
31. GARF, 1467.1.710, 208–209.
32. *PK*, 17 August 1914, p. 1.
33. KVD, 147–48; FStr, 290; RGIA, 472.2 (195/2683).7, 9ob.
34. VR, 421–22; KVD, 147–49.
35. GARF, 111.1.2979a, 19–19ob, 24, 28.
36. KVD, 155–56.
37. WC, 16–17.
38. Beletskii, *Vospominaniia*, 9–10.
39. CU, Bakhmeteff Archive, Tikhobrazov Papers, Box 3, "Rasputin i stavka," pp. 30–31.
40. Nicholas II, *Dnevniki*, 2(2): 66; KVD, 156–57.
41. WC, 39, 47–49, 57, 86, 88–90; KVD, 162–63; GARF, 640.1.323, 5ob.
42. WC, 296.
43. Marie, *Education*, 193–94.
44. KVD, 162–63.
45. WC, 35, 40.
46. WC, 41; GARF, 640.1.323, 6. Also: GARF, 640.1.323, 5–5ob; KVD, 165.
47. KVD, 170; WC, 66.
48. GARF, 640.1.323, 5ob–6.

40: The Incident at the Yar

1. GARF, 111.1.2978, 14.
2. *Moskovskii listok*, 8 January 1915, p. 3.
3. KVD, 178.
4. Globachev, *Pravda*, 73, 201; GRS, 2:226.

5. WC, 73.

6. LP, 419; WC, 82–83.

7. Vulliamy, *Red Archives*, 26–27; "Rasputin v osveshchenii 'okhranki'," 273, 275.

8. VR, 457; SML, Spiridovich Papers, Box 6, Folder 3, p. 215; FR, 138–39; RR, 293–96; Lockhart, *Memoirs*, 128–29.

9. RR, 298–99.

10. Mironova, *Iz pod lzhi*; AV, 466-68. Other right-wing biographers have endorsed this absurd notion. See PZ, 219–20; Smirnov, *Neizvestnoe*, 61.

11. OR/RNB, 1000.1975.22, 31ob.

12. See PZ, 202–204; Bokhanov, *Rasputin*, 233–34; Nelipa, *Murder*, 89–92.

13. GARF, 63.47.484(35), 1–2.

14. GARF, 63.47.484(35), 12–14ob; 63.44.6281, 2–7ob.

15. GARF, 63.47.484(35), 7–7ob, 10–11.

16. GARF, 102.242.1912.297, ch. 1, 52–52ob; PZ, 201; Tikhomirov, *Dnevnik*, 410n300.

17. RGIA, 797.86/3/5.62, 1.

18. GARF, 63.47.484(35), 7–7ob; 63.44.6281, 4–5ob.

19. Mel'gunov, *Vospominaniia*, 1:206.

20. GARF, 63.47.484(35), 8ob–9.

21. On the individuals, GARF, 63.47.484(35), 20–22ob; on the automobile owners, folios 23, 26–39.

22. GARF, 63.47.484(35), 9; 63.44.6281, 6–7ob.

23. GARF, 111.1.2978, 15–15ob.

24. GARF, 63.47.484(35), 6–9, 40–41; 102.316.381, ch. 1, 24–26.

25. GARF, 63.47.484(35), 43.

26. VR, 463.

27. FStr, 214; VR, 460–61; Beletskii, *Vospominaniia*, 7.

28. Lemke, *250 dnei*, 1:31.

29. Dzhunkovskii, *Vospominaniia*, 2:190.

30. GARF, 270.1.46, 75.

31. Amal'rik, *Rasputin*, 190–91.

32. GARF, 63.47.484(35), 50–50ob; same report in GARF, 612.1.22, 56–56ob.

33. GARF, 63.47.484(35), 46–47ob, 50–50ob, 52–53ob.

34. Dzhunkovsky told the Commission he did not recall the date of this meeting. *Padenie*, 5:100–106; VR, 461–63.

35. VR, 461-63. Shavelsky, reflecting the prevalent view, described Dzhunkovsky's report to the tsar as "honest." *Vospominaniia*, 2:23.

36. WC, 160–61; KVD, 213–15. Spelling and punctuation as in the original.

37. VR, 466.

38. BA, Vostokov Papers, "Tochnyia dannye," pp. 20–21; Lemke, *250 dnei*, 1:345; *Zhivoe slovo*, 10 March 1917, No. 3, p. 3; Mel'gunov, *Vospominaniia*, 1:205, 212.

39. VR, 472–74; Romanov, *Voennyi dnevnik*, 174; PZ, 206; Peregudova, *Okhranka*, 1:347–48; Shavel'skii, *Vospominaniia*, 2:23n7.

40. Chebotaryova, "V dvortsovom lazarete," 181:192.
41. FR, 139; Vasil'ev, Okhrana, 152; VR, 463–64; GARF, 1467.1.479, 54ob–55.
42. GARF, 111.1.2979a; KVD, 186, 194–95.
43. KVD, 196–97, 206.
44. Shelley, Blue Steppes, 89–90.
45. PA, Lockhart Papers, Diaries, LOC/1. Lockhart makes no mention of the Yar incident in his published diaries either. See Lockhart, Diaries. On the unreliability of Lockhart's memoirs in general, see Service, Spies, 347–48.

41: Rasputin's Women

1. Shulgin, Years, 264–65.
2. RRR, 59–60; Rodzianko, Reign, 7–9.
3. For example, "Iz startsev, da rannii," Nov', 11 April 1914 in GARF, 102.242.1912.297, ch. 1, 33.
4. RRR, 59–61.
5. FR, 45–46; Zhukovskaia, Moi vospominaniia, 313.
6. GARF, 1467.1.701, 233–34. It is possible the letter was from Sana Pistolkors.
7. Dzhunkovskii, Vospominaniia, 2:335.
8. Shul'gin, Dni, 111–12.
9. Shulgin, Years, 264–65.
10. GARF, 713.1.48, 7; [Belling], Iz nedavnego, 23–24, 50; RR, 400; PK, 7 July 1914, p. 1; Zhukovskaia, Moi vospominaniia, 269.
11. GARF, 1467.1.479, 5.
12. RRR, 55.
13. FDNO, 249.
14. VR, 184, 445–46; Zhukovskaia, Moi vospominaniia, 295–301, 304.
15. PZ, 177.
16. Zhukovskaia, Moi vospominaniia, 254–61, 295–310.
17. RR, 379; Etkind, Khlyst, 522–23.
18. GARF, 1467.1.479, 10–11.
19. Zhukovskaia, Moi vospominaniia, 271, 280–84.
20. Mel'gunov, Vospominaniia, 1:212.
21. Moi vstrechi, 11–12. The Okhrana was following her at the time: GARF, 63.47.484(35), 40–41ob.
22. Moi vstrechi, 14, 16-20, 30. For a similar comment, see Sablin, Desiat' let, 307.
23. GARF, 111.1.2980, 354.
24. LP, 373–74; and see PZ, 138.
25. One frequently cited example of the redacted reports: "Rasputin v osveshchenii 'okhranki'," 272–83. Also: Vulliamy, Red Archives, 25–47; LP, 373–74; Shishkin, Rasputin, 85–86. The report is in GARF, 111.1.2978, 14–28ob.

26. See PZ, 145–46, 148; Globachev, *Pravda*, 5–6; VR, 442–43. His daughter Maria made the same argument first. See RRR, 60.
27. GARF, 111.1.2975, 2976, and 2977 contain hundreds of such notes.
28. GARF, 111.1.2977, 32, 35–35ob.
29. GARF, 111.1.2979a, 22.
30. OR/RNB, 1000.3.439, 6–8.
31. GARF, 111.1.2980, 398.
32. "Rasputin v osveshchenii 'okhranki'," 273, 275.
33. RR, 292–93, 377.
34. Mel'gunov, *Vospominaniia*, 1:213–14.
35. PZ, 197.
36. RR, 377, 381.
37. GARF, 111.1.2980, 81–91ob. For more on Rasputin and prostitutes, see, with caution, RR, ch. 7, and 159–60, 236–37.
38. GARF, 1467.1.479, 5ob. Also GARF, 111.1.2981b, 35.
39. *LP*, 238, 239, 241–43.
40. Simanovich, *Rasputin*, 24.
41. Krarup, *42 Aar*, 124, 130–31.
42. HIA, Nikolaevsky Papers, Series No. 74, 129-1, pp. 27–40.
43. RR, 175.

42: Dinner with Rasputin

1. GARF, 111.1.2978; 102.242.1912.297, ch. 2, 219–19ob; Vulliamy, *Red Archives*, 28.
2. *Iskry*, No. 27, 1915, p. 215.
3. RR, 306.
4. The meeting is fully recounted by Teffi in GRS, 2:221–44. Also by Izmailov in the *Petrogradskii listok*. From: RGIA, 472.50.1619, 66.
5. *GRS*, 2:224–31.
6. RGALI, 419.1.799, 1.
7. *GRS*, 2:232–35.
8. GARF, 102.316.381, ch. 1, 30ob.
9. RR, 310; Beletskii, *Vospominaniia*, 48.
10. GARF, 102.316.381, ch. 1, 37–40.
11. GARF, 111.1.2980, 196–96ob. See also FB, 353–54.
12. *GRS*, 2:237–38.
13. RRR, 62–63.
14. [Belling], *Iz nedavnego*, 17, 35.
15. GARF, 713.1.52, 3.
16. Buranov, "Strannik," 56.

17. *Padenie*, 1:376–77.
18. Globachev, *Pravda*, 69–71.
19. RR, 271–72.
20. RRR, 62–63.
21. *KVD*, 63–66; FR, 112–13.
22. Smirnov, *Neizvestnoe*, 35–36; *PK*, 28 May 1914.
23. PZ, 106–107.
24. *PK*, 2 July 1914, p. 2. On Churikov: McKee, "Sobering."
25. *Moskovskie vedomosti*, 7 March 1910, p. 3; *PK*, 26 January 1914, p. 3; GARF, 102.242.1912.297, ch. 1, 30.
26. *GRS*, 2:239–41.

43: The Religious Faces of Rasputin

1. Rozanov, *Mimoletnoe*, 56–57, 60, 65–66; idem, *Listva*, 175–76. Rozanov does not appear to be referring with the word to the "shtundisty," peasants in Ukraine who created a religious movement after their encounter with German Baptists living in the area. See Coleman, *Russian Baptists*, 13–26.
2. Erdmann-Pandžič, *"Poema,"* lxxiv. Translation by Mariana Markova.
3. FStr, 27.
4. Rozanov, *Apokalipticheskaia sekta*, 202. On the Zaddik, Dresner, *Zaddik*; and Idel, *Hasidism*, esp. p. 201.
5. Rozanov, *Apokalipticheskaia sekta*, 202, 204, 206.
6. NIOR/RGB, 249.4209.13, 65–66.
7. FR, 65.
8. NIOR/RGB, 249.4214.16, 1–2. This letter was intercepted by the police and a copy sent to Dzhunkovsky, which he kept among his "especially secret correspondence." See GARF, 270.1.60, 42.
9. VR, 114; Etkind, *Khlyst*, 292–303.
10. VR, 114; Kuz'min, *Dnevnik*, 564.
11. VR, 342–43; FN, 645–48. Sasha, Empress Alexandra.
12. FB, 352.
13. See Hunt and Kobets, *Holy Foolishness*; Ivanov, *Holy Fools*.
14. VR, 203–205; FR, 64–65; Kobets, *Holy Foolishness*, 27–28.
15. WC, 599.
16. For example, Svitlana Kobits and Sergey Ivanov. See *Holy Foolishness*, 16; Ivanov, *Holy Fools*, 358. Ivanov, it warrants noting, bases his assessment of Rasputin on Zhevakhov's memoirs.
17. *GRS*, 4:9–10.
18. VR, 210.

44: A Summer of Troubles

1. WC, 100, 101n83, 102, 106, 111, 288; Gatrell, *Russia's First*, 19.
2. *LP*, 429; WC, 147–51, 282.
3. WC, 164–66,167.
4. WC, 134–135n93; Gatrell, *Russia's First*, 22–23.
5. WC, 140–47; VR, 481–82.
6. WC, 146–51; *LP*, 428–29.
7. VR, 482–83; FB, 231.
8. Samarin, "Vstrecha," 178–85; VR, 485–87.
9. VR, 486; BA, Vostokov Papers, "Tochnyia dannye," p. 13.
10. VR, 492–93.
11. GARF, 612.1.22, 66–66ob.
12. PZ, 207; "Rasputin v osveshchenii," 275–76.
13. GARF, 612.1.22, 66; GATO, I-239.1.183, 33–36ob, 52–53ob.
14. GATO, I-239.1.183, 40, 41, 43–45, 49, 52–53ob.
15. GARF, 612.1.22, 64–65; PZ, 208–209.
16. GATO, I-239.1.183, 35-39, 53, 64–65ob.
17. GBUTO/GAGT, I-331.19.809, 170–74; GATO, I-239.1.183, 64–65ob, 100–100ob.
18. WC, 158.
19. PZ, 209; GARF, 111.1.2978, 20–21ob; KVD, 222.
20. GARF, 612.1.61, 101.
21. GARF, 111.1.2978, 22ob; WC, 193–95, 196, 198, 223.
22. GATO, I-239.1.219, 20; I-239.1.183, 103–103ob.
23. GARF, 612.1.22, 76–76a. An article published in *Living Siberian Antiquities* in the 1920s by Pyotr Gorodtsov revived the story of Rasputin's horse-thieving. Nonetheless, there is not a single bit of archival evidence to substantiate the claim. See Onchukov, "P. A. Gorodtsov," 122–24; Gorodtsov, *Pis'ma*.
34. GARF, 612.1.57, 20.
25. *BV*, 14 August 1915, p. 2; RGADA, 1290.2.4765, 1.
26. PZ, 212–13.
27. *BV*, 15, 16, and 17 August 1915, all on p. 3.
28. GARF, 102.316.381, ch. 1, 71; 612.1.22, 81, 89, 91.
29. GARF, 102.316.381, ch. 1, 64, 66, 69, 70; Romanov, *Voennyi dnevnik*, 174.
30. Romanov, *Voennyi dnevnik*, 174; VR, 520–21.
31. Chebotaryova, "V dvortsovom lazarete," 181:190.
32. VR, 521; Polivanov, *Iz dnevnikov*, 214; WC, 155n108; GARF, 612.1.22, 87–88.
33. GARF, 612.1.57, 4, 47, 48; 612.1.61, 147.
34. GARF, 612.1.61, 81.
35. KVD, 235.

36. GARF, 612.1.22, 91.
37. GARF, 102.242.1912.297, ch. 2, 221–22; BA, Vostokov Papers, "Tochnyia dannye," pp. 13–14.
38. WC, 259–60.

45: The Tovarpar

1. KVD, 223; VR, 474.
2. GARF, 612.1.61, 59.
3. GATO, I-239.1.183, 69–71; GARF, 111.1.2978, 20–21ob.
4. "Rasputin v osveshchenii," 279.
5. RGIA, 1276.11.1484, 3–4ob.
6. "Min Bekantskap med Rasputin," in: Riksarkivet, Wilhelm Sarwe Papers, Svenska Missionsförbundet, Om Rasputin (Svenska Publikationer).
7. GBUTO/GAGT, I-331.19.809, 159–60.
8. RGIA, 1276.11.1484, 5–5ob.
9. GATO, I-239.1.183, 73–74. The testimonies of Harteveld and five other passengers are in RGIA, 1276.11.1484, 3–8ob; GBUTO/GAGT, I-331.19.809, 166–69ob.
10. GATO, I-239.1.183, 34–34ob, 72–72ob.
11. GARF, 612.1.22, 84–84ob.
12. GATO, I-239.1.183, 78–78ob, 96–97.
13. RGIA, 1276.11.1484, 1–2ob, 9–11; Schelking, Recollections, 275–76.
14. Chernyshev, Grigorii, 79–81.
15. BV, 21 December 1916, p. 3.
16. WC, 181, 188–89; Beletskii, Vospominaniia, 28; VR, 643–45.

46: Nicholas Takes Command

1. YLS, 201.
2. See, for example, Figes, Tragedy, 270; FR, 147. Also Gurko, Cherty, 678–82.
3. Beletskii, Vospominaniia, 46–47; Simpson of the Commission made the same observation, stressing Alexandra and Rasputin's interest in shielding Nicholas from the influence of the grand dukes, and thus their displeasure at his decision to take up command. GARF, 1467.1.479, 47ob.
4. VR, 510–12.
5. Gippius, Vospominaniia, 384; idem, Dnevniki, 1:414. And see Prishvin, Dnevniki, 1914–17, 221.
6. NIOR/RGB, 218.1325.2, 11ob–12.
7. Iakhontov, Prologue, 80–81.
8. LP, 394.
9. WC, 554.

10. Marie, *Education*, 223–25.
11. Hall, *Little Mother*, 264; Mariia Fedorovna, *Dnevniki imperatritsy*, 88–89.
12. Iakhontov, *Prologue*, 113–14.
13. Warth, *Nicholas*, 209; VR, 513–14.
14. Sazonov, *Fateful*, 291, 294.
15. PAAA, AS 5771, R.20992.
16. Shavel'skii, *Vospominaniia*, 1:190–92, 196–99; FB, 405–406; VR, 533.
17. VVFR, 1:260–63.
18. VR, 532.
19. NIOR/RGB, 218.1325.2, 15–15ob.
20. GARF, 102.316.381, ch. 1, 146.
21. GARF, 640.1.323, 8ob–9; KVD, 223.
22. WC, 171–73.
23. KVD, 232.
24. WC, 195.
25. GARF, 640.1.323, 10ob.
26. GARF, 111.1.2978, 22–22ob.
27. Beletskii, *Vospominaniia*, 51.
28. "Rasputin v osveshchenii," 40.
29. WC, 196, 202, 206–07, 235.
30. RGIA, 472.40 (194/2682).47, 1–4.
31. RGIA, 777.22.3, 186–86ob.
32. RGIA, 1617.1.45, 1–2.
33. Mel'gunov, *Vospominaniia*, 1:212.
34. Shulgin, *Years*, 268–69; Kolonitskii, *Tragicheskaia erotika*, 176–78.

47: Rasputin, Favorite

1. Buranov, "Strannik," 56.
2. GARF, 1467.1.479, 13–16.
3. VR, 152–53.
4. *Padenie*, 3:408.
5. VR, 46. See also Den, *Podlinnaia tsaritsa*, 80; Vasil'ev, *Ochrana*, 133.
6. GRS, 4:10–11, 21; VR, 115.
7. VR, 436.
8. Elliott, *World*, 113, 280, 290.
9. OR/RNB, 585,5696, l. 22.
10. BA, Il'ia D. Surgachev Collection. Box 7, "Rasputin," pp. 9–10.
11. Shulgin, *Years*, 263.
12. GARF, 102.242.1912.297, ch. 2, 143.
13. Shulgin, *Years*, 266–67; VR, 142–44.
14. *Rech'*, 28 May 1910, No. 144, no p.n.

15. Gurko, *Tsar'*, 235; VR, 182, 314.
16. IMM, 209.
17. Buranov, "Strannik," 56.
18. Beletskii, *Vospominaniia*, 20, 39–40.
19. VR, 372–73.
20. VR, 145, 147, 153.
21. Fabritskii, *Iz proshlogo*, 54.
22. Elliot, *World*, 219.

48: Fresh Scandal

1. WC, 211n143; GARF, 640.1.323, 9ob; VR, 494–501.
2. WC, 211n143; GARF, 102.316.381, ch. 1, 74; Shavel'skii, *Vospominaniia*, 1:370–73.
3. VR, 496–97; VVRF, 1:229–30.
4. GARF, 102.OO.245.1915.297, 1, 4–5ob, 12, 17.
5. WC, 219.
6. Firsov, *Pravoslavnaia tserkov'*, 235–36. Cites: "Stavlennik Rasputina," *Golos Moskvy*, 11 August 1913; "Iz pisem gnoma," RGIA, 796.205.809.
7. Oreshnikov, *Dnevnik*, 45–46. See also Romanov, *Voennyi dnevnik*, 183.
8. *Moskovskii listok*, 14 September 1915, pp. 1–2; 19 September, p. 2; 20 September, p. 2.
9. VR, 494–96.
10. WC, 215–22, 229–33, 237, 239, 254–55.
11. GARF, 640.1.323, 11.
12. VR, 522.
13. WC, 215–18.
14. GARF, 612.1.61, 93.
15. GARF, 111.1.2978, 22ob–23.
16. WC, 254.
17. RGIA, 525.3.529, 2–2ob.
18. RGADA, 1290.2.4765, 5–6ob; RGALI, 2167.2.30, 1–1ob.
19. GARF, 102.316.381, ch. 1, 169–69ob, 203.
20. WC, 251, 252, 254; KVD, 259.
21. VR, 205.
22. Berdiaev, *Sud'ba*, 50–55.
23. "Iz semeinoi perepiski," 2:140–41.

49: The Troika

1. VR, 539; VVFR, 1:219–20; GRS, 2:348.
2. GRS, 2:341; Mel'gunov, *Vospominaniia*, 1:202.

3. Vitte, *Iz arkhiva*, vol. 1, bk. 2, 895.

4. Globachev, *Pravda*, 82–83.

5. RR, 363.

6. *GRS*, 2:349.

7. WC, 213, 225–28, 247, 254.

8. WC, 213, 214n147.

9. VVFR, 1:217; Stogov, "Salon;" FB, 381–82, 387; WC, 454; Fuller, *Foe*, 70.

10. See Mel'gunov, *Legenda*, 407–409; *Padenie*, 4:152, 241; Smitten, "Poslednii," 12:98; VR, 538–39; FB, 384. Stogov, quite correctly, questions some of the more outlandish tales. See Stogov, "Salon," 130–31.

11. FB, 387–88.

12. RGIA, 1617.1.64, 25–27.

13. VVFR, 1:220–21.

14. RR, 368; Faleev, "Za chto," 173.

15. VR, 539–40; *GRS*, 4:276; FN, 374–75; Martynov, *Moia sluzhba*, 217.

16. Beletskii, *Vospominaniia*, 8, 12–13; VR, 540.

17. Izmozik, *Zhandarmy*, 453–54.

18. *GRS*, 2:349.

19. Khvostov, "Iz vospominanii," 163–64; VR, 543–45.

20. WC, 247.

21. KVD, 259.

22. Globachev, *Pravda*, 82–83. Andronikov's letters in Stogov, "Salon."

23. Beletskii, *Vospominaniia*, 20–22; Stogov, "Salon," 129.

24. FR, 160; VR, 537–38, 549.

25. Beletskii, *Vospominaniia*, 23–24; Khvostov, "Iz vospominanii," 160–62; VR, 537; GARF, 1467.1.479, 51; Guchkov, *Guchkov*, 87–88; Savich, *Vospominaniia*, 76. Gurko later wrote Sazonov and told him that he and Rasputin were seeking out men "who could run the country." Gurko, *Tsar'*, 248.

26. VR, 549.

27. Globachev, *Pravda*, 71, 82 83.

28. Beletskii, *Vospominaniia*, 26.

29. GARF, 602.2.62. Rudnev.

30. GARF, 111.1.2981a, 16.

31. Beletskii, *Vospominaniia*, 26; GARF, 111.1.2980 has 453 pages of such information, to cite just one file.

32. GARF, 111.1.2981a, 3–3ob; Globachev, *Pravda*, 74–75. For lists of his visitors: GARF, 102.316.381, ch. 1, 15–21ob, 27–29, 34–35, 44–54, 56–61. On the 1916 materials: GARF, 111.1.2981. On the Australian letter: GARF, 102.242.1912.297, ch. 1, 2–7, 10.

33. GARF, 111.1.2981, 92, 113.

34. Globachev, *Pravda*, 73–75; VR, 683.

35. VR, 557.

36. WC, 312.

37. GARF, 102.316.381, ch. 1, 100.
38. Beletskii, *Vospominaniia*, 26, 48.
39. *WC*, 288.
40. Tikhomirov, *Dnevnik*, 154.
41. GARF, 63.47.484(35), 65–67; 102.316.381, ch. 1, 89, 91, 149, 157–58, 161.
42. Mel'gunov, *Vospominaniia*, 1:200–201; FStr, 258; PZ, 97.
43. *Otkliki na zhizn'*, No. 1, 1915, pp. 94–96.
44. GARF, 102.316.381, ch. 1, 116, 118, 129. Copy of 25 November 1915 article of Prugavin in *Russkie vedomosti*: folio 155.
45. GBUTO/GAGT, I-733.19.809, 180.
46. Bogoslovskii, *Dnevniki*, 508n46; RGALI, 2167.2.43; Lemke, *250 dnei*, 2:299–300; FSu, 306.
47. Chebotaryova, "V dvortsovom lazarete," 181:203.
48. GARF, 102.OO.245.1915g.167, ch. 52, 8; and ch. 80, 23–23ob.
49. PAAA, R.20986; and R.9208, R.20994.
50. PAAA, 6370, R. 20987; 3657, R. 20986.
51. PAAA, AS 5771, R.20992.
52. Khvostov, "Iz vospominanii," 166–67.
53. PA, Lockhart Papers, Diaries, LOC/1. 27 October 1915.

50: Gorokhovaya, 64

1. GARF, 613.1.28, 12–13ob.
2. FStr, 457; FB, 358–59; GARF, 102.1916.246.357, 62. Other sources suggest it was paid for by Vyrubova's father or Dmitry Rubinshtein. See Amal'rik, *Rasputin*, 195; FR, 137.
3. GARF, 102.1916.246.357, 62—on Gaponovs; 1467.1.479, 11—on Blagoveshchensky.
4. Buranov, "Strannik," 55–56; Globachev, *Pravda*, 68; RRR, 99; FStr, 457; Ordovskii-Tanaevskii, *Vospominaniia*, 390–91. On Anna: GARF, 102.314.35, 13–13ob.
5. FDNO, 249, including n13.
6. OR/RNB, 1000.1975.22, 32. On his true diet: RRR, 49.
7. Buranov, "Strannik," 55; FB, 360–61; Ordovskii-Tanaevskii, *Vospominaniia*, 393.
8. RRR, 50–53.
9. *PK*, 30 January 1914, p. 3. Also: *PK*, 5 February 1914, p. 3.
10. Beletskii, *Vospominaniia*, 51–52; Globachev, *Pravda*, 69.
11. GARF, 1467.1.479, 11–12ob.
12. Beletskii, *Vospominaniia*, 51–52; Globachev, *Pravda*, 70; AV, 445–48; RR, 372–74, 378; "Rasputin v osveshchenii," 280.

13. GARF, 1467.1.479, 11ob–12.
14. GARF, 1467.1.628, 6–7. See also: GARF, 1467.1.710, 4–5ob; VR, 449–52; Amal'rik, *Rasputin*, 194; FStr, 291.
15. GARF, 1467.1.710, 1. And the letter of the disgraced official Kuzma Ustichev in GARF, 612.1.10.
16. "Poslednii vremenshchik," 12:96.
17. See, for example, the letter of archpriest Khristofor, 20 August 1914 in GARF, 1467.1.710, 203–203ob, 221.
18. GARF, 1467.1.710, 21, 26, 134, 201.
19. GARF, 102.242.1912.297, ch. 2, 229.
20. GARF, 1467.1.710, 166a–66aob.
21. GARF, 102.242.1912.297, ch. 2, 236, 240–40ob.
22. Vyrubova, *Stranitsy*, 122.
23. See, for example, OR RNB, 781.1207, 1–3; Beletskii, *Vospominaniia*, 51–52.
24. GARF, 102.OO.71.1914g.27, 361.
25. Romanov, *Voennyi dnevnik*, 208.
26. Buranov, "Strannik," 56; RRR, 52.
27. Globachev, *Pravda*, 68; LP, 455.
28. Vasil'ev, *Ochrana*, 142; FR, 137.
29. Bogdanvich, *Tri poslednikh*, 493.
30. GARF, 102.316.1910.381, ch. 2, 5.
31. LP, 455; RR, 97.
32. FR, 108–11; GARF, 97.4.118, 14–16, and 602.2.62; *GRS*, 4:24; FN, 418–29.
33. RRR, 55–56. On his phone number: Dzhanumova, *Moi vstrechi*, 23.
34. OR/RNB, 1000.1975.22, 32; *PK*, 5 February 1914, p. 3.
35. RGALI, 2167.2.43, 105.
36. RRR, 56–57.
37. GARF, 1467.1.479, 11–12ob.

51: Dark Forces and Mad Chauffeurs

1. On Purishkevich, see Coonrod, "The Fourth Duma," 4–5.
2. Gippius, *Vospominaniia*, 384.
3. Globachev, *Pravda*, 77–78.
4. FR, 177–78; Rogger, *Russia*, 262–63.
5. WC, 131.
6. After Rasputin's death, it was rumored (incorrectly) that he had acquired great wealth from his stock in Bogatyr. See: *Kazn' Grishki Rasputina, Al'manakh "Svoboda,"* 1:7; Sokolov, *Temnye sily*, 4–6. On Tatishchev: Bokhanov, *Delovaia elita*, 231.
7. Stogov, "Salon," 130.
8. WC, 304.

9. Ol'denburg, *Tsarstvovanie*, 577–78n.; GARF, 1467.1.13, 38–38ob.
10. WC, 188–89, 273–74, 292–93, 295, 307, 314.
11. GARF, 640.1.323, 12. And his letter of 7 October in GARF, 111.1.2978, 23.
12. WC, 272–73.
13. Rogger, *Russia*, 257–60; Riasanovsky, *History*, 392; Gatrell, *Russia's First*, 77.
14. Lincoln, *Passage*, 136–37.
15. Fuller, *Foe*, 109, 259–60.
16. Lodyzhenskii, *Misticheskaia trilogiia*; Vetukhov, "Mikroby."
17. Fuller, *Foe*, 182–83; Lohr, *Nationalizing*, 1–3, 18–22, 166-68; GARF, 102. OO.1915g.245.167, ch. 167, 30, 75ob.
18. Fuller, *Foe*, 1–9, 140, 141–49, 262.
19. PA, Lockhart Papers, Diaries, LOC/1, 10 March 1915.
20. Lohr, *Nationalizing*, 1–3, 31–35, 42, 53; WC, 136; Marie, *Education*, 198, 219.
21. BA, Vostokov Papers, "Tochnyia dannye," p. 23.
22. Sokolov, "Predvaritel'noe sledstvie," 284.
23. HHStA, MdÄ Zeitungsarchiv, 162–63.
24. PAAA, AS 5047, R.20457. Secret coded telegram by Staatssekretär von Jagow, dated 26 September 1915. This telegram was presented to the Kaiser and he gave it the okay on 27 September. Graf Eulenburg most likely refers to Philip of Eulenburg, diplomat and close friend of Wilhelm II.
25. PAAA, AS 5047, R.20457, Report of 27 September 1915. On the members of the "Hofpartei," see *Golos minuvshego*, No. 4–6, 1918, p. 36.
26. WC, 201.
27. GARF, 102.OO.245.1915g.244, ch. 1, 3.
28. See Coonrod, "Fourth Duma."
29. WC, 152–53.
30. VR, 517–18.
31. Coonrod, "Fourth Duma," 193; Rogger, *Russia*, 263; Ol'denburg, *Tsarstvovanie*, 573; Yusupova in RR, 339. Also: Schelking, *Recollections*, 275–76.
32. Ferro, *Nicholas II*, 171; *Gosudarstvennaia Duma*, 357–59.
33. FR, 161–62; WC, 292–93.
34. "Aleksandro-Nevskaia Lavra," 207.
35. WC, 298–300, 304–305, 309–10, 317.

52: Another Miracle

1. WC, 322–23; VVFR, 1:279–80.
2. WC, 323; Nicholas II, *Dnevniki*, 2(2): 170–71; VR, 523–24.
3. Rassulin, *Vernaia Bogu*, 124–25; Paléologue, *Ambassador's Memoirs*, 2:134–35.
4. Nicholas II, *Dnevniki*, 2(2): 170–71.
5. *Padenie*, 4:307.
6. GARF, 111.1.2979a, 146–47, 152, 161.

53: Revolution in the Air

1. Murat, *Raspoutine*, 52–53.
2. AD, Correspondance politique et commerciale, Nouvelle série, 1896–1918, "Guerre, 1914–1918:" répertoires. Dossier Général, No. 641. "Mission en Russie," pp. 56, 80–81. Also: Mel'gunov, *Vospominaniia*, 1:206.
3. GARF, 102.316.318, ch. 1, 159–60.
4. Lemke, *250 dnei*, 2:300–301, 464.
5. NIOR/RGB, 140.7.9, 11ob.
6. Kolonitskii, *Tragicheskaia erotika*, 524.
7. VR, 608–609. Austrians refers to POWs being held in Russia.
8. GARF, 613.1.40, 1–4.
9. FSA, 337; *WC*, 353–54; "Rasputin v osveshchenii," 284.
10. FSA, 337–38; Trams: Tikhomirov, *Dnevnik*, 188.
11. Bonch-Bruevich, *Vsia vlast'*, 73–74.
12. Kolonitskii, *Tragicheskaia erotika*, 318.
13. Visit information drawn from the police file: GARF, 111.1.2979a.
14. GARF, 111.1.2979a, 121, 123ob, 125, 132ob, 136, 142, 150ob, 153ob, 160, 179.
15. GARF, 111.1.2979a, 239–39ob, 250, 258; Vulliamy, *Red Archives*, 47; Shavel'skii, *Vospominaniia*, 2:11–12.
16. PZ, 188; *WC*, 362; *KVD*, 305.
17. Beletskii, *Vospominaniia*, 57–58; RR, 382–83; FDNO, 265.
18. Chebotaryova, "V dvortsovom lazarete," 181:217; Mel'gunov, *Vospominaniia*, 1:209; FSA, 339; Oreshnikov, *Dnevnik*, 59; PAAA, R.10740; CUL, Templewood Papers, II:1 (16). Which Count Orlov-Davydov this supposedly was is never stated.
19. GARF, 102.316.381, ch. 1, 175, 183.

54: The Minister Plots Murder

1. FR, 163–65; *WC*, 352, 357n201; Beletskii, *Vospominaniia*, 21; VR, 562–63; SML, Spiridovich Papers, Box 6, Folder 3, p. 320.
2. VR, 559–60.
3. *Padenie*, 6:79–80.
4. GARF, 1467.1.479, 54ob–55; "Poslednii vremenshchik," 1 (1965): 106; VR, 558–59; Beletskii, *Vospominaniia*, 27–28.
5. *GRS*, 2:345–46. On Spiridovich: Lauchlan, *Hide*, 124–25.
6. Gippius, *Dnevniki*, 1:419.
7. Globachev, *Pravda*, 83–84; Peregudova, *Okhranka*, 1:398; *New York Times*, 14 December 1924, p. 73.

8. Globachev, *Pravda*, 84.

9. Beletskii, *Vospominaniia*, 61–65.

10. *Padenie*, 4:69.

11. VR, 560–61; GARF, 1467.1.479, 58–58ob; Beletskii, *Vospominaniia*, 61–65. On Khvostov's attempts to get rid of Rasputin: *Padenie*, 1:40–43.

12. Beletskii, *Vospominaniia*, 63–65. Khvostov told the Commission a very different story about poisoned cats: *Padenie*, 1:43.

13. SML, Spiridovich Papers, Box 6, Folder 3, pp. 278–79; GARF, 1467.1.479, 58–58ob.

14. BA, Z. A. Rzhevskaia, Ms., 1965, p. 1; *Padenie*, 1:40–42.

15. Globachev, *Pravda*, 84–85. On his biography: VR, 563; SML, Spiridovich Papers, No. 359, 14/1, p. 1; GRS, 2:341–44. Visit to Iliodor: GARF, 102.316.1910.381, 199–99ob.

16. Lemke, *250 dnei*, 2:365.

17. Clipping: 1101.1.1073; BV, 7 March 1916, p. 3; "Aleksandro-Nevskaia Lavra," 205.

18. GARF, 1467.1.709, 1–5.

19. BA, Z. A. Rzhevskaia, Ms., p. 1; GARF, 1467.1.709, 43–46ob; 102.OO.1916r.246.56, ch. 2 166–66ob; BV, 6 March 1916, p. 5; "Aleksandro-Nevskaia Lavra," 206.

20. Newspaper clipping, 29 March 1916 (NS), in RGIA, 1101.1.1073.

21. GARF, 1467.1.709, 65.

22. Clipping, RGIA, 1101.1.1073.

23. Globachev, *Pravda*, 84–85; BA, Z. I. Rzhevskaia ms, p. 1. Beletsky gives a different account of how he learned of Rzhevsky's plans: BV, 7 March 1916, p. 3.

24. Lemke, *250 dnei*, 2:367–68; SML, Spiridovich Papers, Box 6, Folder 3, pp. 279–88, and Box 14/1, p. 1.

25. Sotheby's, Sale 2 June 2006, Notes to Lot 115.

26. GARF, 612.1.25, 1–5; Lemke, *250 dnei*, 2:366-67; SML, Spiridovich Papers, Box 6, Folder 3, pp. 279–88; and Box 14/1, p. 1; *Padenie*, 2:167–70.

27. GARF, 612.1.25, 1–5.

28. GARF, 1467.1.709, 6, 67, 83; 612.1.25, 1–5; Globachev, *Pravda*, 86.

29. GARF, 612.1.25, 5ob; 102.OO.1916g.246.56, ch. 2, 166–66ob.

30. *KVD*, 310–11.

31. GARF, 1467.1.709, 4–5. When Rasputin failed to respond, Iliodor sent a second cable on 17 February. GARF, 1467.1.709, 33.

32. GARF, 612.1.25, 1–5ob.

33. GARF, 1467.1.709, 54–56.

34. *LP*, 454.

35. GARF, 1467.1.709, 1–3ob, 43–46ob.

36. Lemke, *250 dnei*, 2:369–70; Globachev, *Pravda*, 86–87.

37. WC, 403n232; VR, 592–93; Izmozik, *Zhandarmy*, 455.

38. Clipping, RGIA, 1101.1.1073; GARF, 601.1.1101, 1–1ob; Lemke, *250 dnei*, 2:371; SML, Spiridovich Papers, MS 359, Box 14, Folder 4; *BV*, 6 March 1916, p. 5.

39. SML, Spiridovich Papers, Box 6, Folder 3, pp. 293–94. Ellipses in orig.

40. *WC*, 393.

41. Lemke, *250 dnei*, 371.

42. HIA, Vasily Maklakov Collection, 15–14, pp. 9–10; GARF, 1467.1.479, 61; Mel'gunov, *Vospominaniia*, 1:211.

43. *WC*, 418.

44. GARF, 612.1.61, 34.

45. *New York Times*, 14 December 1924, p. 73.

46. VVFR, 2:55–56.

47. *WC*, 399, 406. The letters may in fact have come from Prince Andronikov. See VR, 568–69.

48. *BV*, 6 March 1916, p. 6; 7 March, p. 3; *KVD*, 320; Izmozik, *Zhandarmy*, 455.

49. VVFR, 2:63–64.

50. Tikhomirov, *Dnevnik*, 212–13. Gippius, like Milyukov, refused to believe the truth about Khvostov and insisted Rasputin cooked up the scandal to bring him down. See Gippius, *Dnevniki*, 1:427–28.

51. Mel'gunov, *Vospominaniia*, 1:206–207.

52. Amal'rik, *Rasputin*, 233.

53. BA, Z. I. Rzhevskaia, Ms., pp. 2–4.

54. RGIA, 878.2.186, 158.

55. GARF, 111.1.2978a, 258.

56. GARF, 102.OO.1916g.246.56, ch. 2, 166–67ob.

55: Iliodor in America

1. Mel'gunov, *Vospominaniia*, 1:214.

2. PZ, 98–99; GARF, 102.316.381, ch. 1, 188-88ob; 1467.1.709, 31.

3. PZ, 99; GARF, 1467.1.709, 31; 102.316.1910.381, ch. 2, 109–109ob. On Bernstein and the expedition, Kraft, *Peace Ship*, 104–105, 108, 148–51.

4. *Aftenposten*, 29 March 1916, clipping in: RGIA, 1101.1.1073.

5. GARF, 102.316.381, ch. 1, 156, 164, 173, 177–77ob, 186, 197–97ob, 204–206.

6. Date of her departure: Iliodor's interview, *Aftenposten*, 29 March 1916, clipping in RGIA, 1101.1.1073. On his playing along: GARF, 1467.1.709, 41; and his words to the newspaper *Norske Intelligenz-Seddeler* in late March 1916. In: GARF, 102.316.381, ch. 1, 210–10ob.

7. *WC*, 407.

8. On Perang (also Pirang): Tabachnik, *Krestnyi put'*, 523–26; *Padenie*, 4:31, 68, 440; On Borkh: *Padenie*, 1:43, 66; 4: 393–97; 7:310.

9. IMM, 328–37; GARF, 1467.1.709, 42–42ob; 102.316.1910.381, ch. 2, 109–109ob; *PZ*, 98.

10. GARF, 602.2.62, Rudnev, "Pravda"; Rassulin, *Vernaia Bogu*, 342.

11. GARF, 102.316.1910.381, ch. 2, 3–3ob.

12. PAAA, 15986, R.20996. Telegram of 15 June 1916 (NS) to Bethmann Hollweg.

13. Cook, *To Kill*, 232–39.

14. GARF, 1467.1.709, 21–22, 26, 32, 34, 36. On Nikitina: *Padenie*, 2:47–48, 3:390.

15. GARF, 102.253.188, 1–6ob; 1467.1.709, 16. Bernstein did publish portions of it in the newspaper *Der Tag*, before being sued by a rival publication. *New York Times*, 3 January 1917 (NS), p. 4; on the dispute, see 30, 31 December 1916.

16. *New York Times*, 24 October; 3 November; 30, 31 December 1916; GARF, 102.316.1910.381, ch. 2, 103–104.

17. *New York Times*, 27 December 1916; GARF, 102.314.36.

18. *New York Times*, 24 September; 24 November 1917.

19. FN, 13, 566–67.

20. RRR, 64.

56: With Us or With Them

1. *Petrogradskii listok*, 28 February 1916, p. 2.

2. Zhevakhov, *Vospominaniia*, 1:84–86; VR, 579–80; *Padenie*, 3.396–98.

3. NA, ГО 371/2/46, No. 212150. Russian original text in: CUL, Templewood Papers, II:1 (11).

4. WC, 292–93; FR, 174–77.

5. GARF, 613.1.40, 1–4.

6. WC, 562n339.

7. FR, 171–72; "Aleksandro-Nevskaia Lavra," 200–201.

8. VR, 583–85; Shavel'skii, *Vospominaniia*, 1:375–76, 383–85.

9. KVD, 286; WC, 292–93, 301. Note: the text incorrectly gives Pitirim's replacement as Aleksei, bishop of Pskov.

10. FR, 174.

11. GARF, 102.316.381, ch. 1, 214–17ob.

12. "Aleksandro-Nevskaia Lavra," 201–205; FR, 174; GARF, 1579.1.139, 1–17. Pitirim's homosexuality was generally known at the time. See Tikhomirov, *Dnevnik*, 203.

13. *Nov'*, 30 March 1914; *PK*, 29 March 1914, p. 2; GARF, 102.242.1912.297, ch. 1, 26. On Isidor: VR, 658, 701–702; FR, 173–74; WC, 617.

14. *TsM*, 2 June 1910, p. 2.

15. Shulgin, *Years*, 254.

16. Schelking, *Recollections*, 280; Buchanan, *Dissolution*, 142; Hoare, *Fourth Seal*, 344.

17. FR, 163.

18. WC, 352, 357n201.

19. GARF, 1467.1.13, 4.

20. FR, 357–58. Nickname: "Aleksandro-Nevskaia Lavra," 208.

21. Globachev, *Pravda*, 91–92.

22. WC, 413, 554n336, 561.

23. GARF, 640.1.323, 13ob.

24. FR, 178; OR/RNB, 1000.2.765, 301.

25. Shavel'skii, *Vospominaniia*, 2:212–21; WC, 421, 600, 628; VR, 610–13.

26. WC, 437–38.

27. Shavel'skii, *Vospominaniia*, 2:222; Lemke, *250 dnei*, 2:648.

28. KVD, 331, 335–36; GARF, 1467.1.479, 18ob–19.

29. The dates were recorded by the police in GARF, 111.1.2979a; Nicholas II, *Dnevniki*, 2(2): 225, 260.

30. Markow, *Wie*, 195.

31. RRR, 108.

32. Shishkin, *Rasputin*, 231–39; OR/RNB, 1000.1975.22, 35ob; GARF, 111.1.2981, 533, 535. The police gave his name as Semen Ivanovich Pkhakadze. On his service in the guards: GARF, 102.1916.246.357, 36–36ob.

33. RR, 385.

34. RRR, 109–10; HL/Sokolov, Vol. VII: testimony of M. Solovyova (Rasputina), undated. Oleg Shishkin thinks Pkhakadze had used Maria to get close to Rasputin as part of a plot to murder him. *Rasputin*, 231–39.

35. HL/Sokolov, Vol. VII: testimony of B. N. Solovyov, 31 December 1919. On Boris's parents: "Rasputin v osveshchenii," 272n6, 277–28.

36. RRR, 16–17, 111–12; HL/Sokolov, Vol. VII: testimony of M. Solovyova (Rasputina), undated.

37. RRR, 113–115; Steinberg, *Fall*, 390–91; Sokolov, *Ubiistvo*, 114–16; FN, 326.

38. WC, 392n225, 393, 406.

39. On the campaign, Dowling, *Brusilov*, esp. 67, 98, 167–76.

40. WC, 488, 546, 603, 608, 611, 611n372, 612.

41. The most authoritative study in English does not even mention Rasputin. Dowling, *Brusilov*. And see FR, 152–53; WC, 567n341.

57: Rasputin the Spy?

1. Paxman, "Strange Death."

2. Kolonitskii, *Tragicheskaia erotika*, 301, 311–13; Tikhomirov, *Dnevnik*, 211, 304, 307.

3. YLS, 202–203.

4. WC, 476n281a, 490.

5. *Rasputin*, 95–99. Andrew Cook made another unsuccesful attempt to prove

Rasputin was a spy in his 2005 *To Kill Rasputin*. See pp. 138–39. Shishkin does a good job debunking Cook's argument. See his *Rasputin*, 195–207. Nikolai Sokolov, the investigator of the murder of the Romanovs, believed Rasputin was a spy, as did Alexander Kerensky. See Sokolov, *Ubiistvo*, 109; VR, 672. Mikhail Komissarov, he of the "Troika," also claimed Rasputin and Voeikov were responsible. See his story in *New York Times*, 12 October 1924, p. 179.

6. Maud, *One Year*, 200.
7. Le Queux, *Rasputin*, v, 115–17, 123–24.
8. Omessa, *Rasputin*, 90–96.
9. PAAA, 3439, R.20366.
10. PAAA, R.10684; 5943.R.10740. On Lucius and his activities in Sweden: Nekludov, *Diplomatic Reminiscences*, 338–43.
11. PAAA, 15260 and 15986, R.20996. On Ropp and the league: Zetterberg, *Die Liga*.
12. PAAA, R.20467.
13. PAAA, A 35162, R.3079.
14. PAAA, 1001, R.20380.
15. PA, E/3/23/4, pp. 7–8.
16. *KVD*, 506.
17. Zhevakhov, *Vospominaniia*, 1:132, 170, 184.
18. BA, Vostokov Papers, "Tochnye dannye," pp. 4, 15–17; see also Maud, *One Year*, 191. And the words of Senin in *Iuzhnaia zaria*, 4 June 1910, p. 2.
19. Rodzianko, *Reign*, 30.
20. GARF, 102.316.1910.381, 49.
21. See Berger, "European Freemasonries"; idem, "Local—National—Transnational Heroes."
22. See, for example, PZ, 54–55, 62–63; VR, 171–72.
23. The most authoritative list of Russian Freemasons does not include Guchkov. See Serkov, *Russkoe masonstvo*. For more on Rasputin-Freemasons, see VR, 334–35.
24. GARF, 102.242.1912.297, ch. 1, 116.
25. GARF, 102.242.1912.297, ch. 2, 83–84, 204–206ob.
26. FN, 11; GARF, 612.1.42, 5ob.
27. Den, *Podlinnaia tsaritsa*, 60, 72–73, 81.
28. VR, 636–37.
29. FStr, 295–303.
30. YLS, 227, 231, 233. On the phantom "green" men, see Mel'gunov, *Legenda*, 379–89.
31. VR, 672–73; Bonch-Bruevich, *Vsia vlast'*, 73–74; Sokolov, *Ubiistvo*, 109; idem, "Predvaritel'noe sledstvie," 282–87.
32. FR, 145–46; Shishkin, *Rasputin*, 173–85; GARF, 102.1916.246.357, 36–36ob; 111.1.2979a, 291.

33. GARF, 102.1916.246.357, 37. Shishkin tries, with no credible evidence, to depict Gyulling as a spy. See his *Rasputin*, 173–85.

34. Shishkin, *Rasputin*, 184–85, 211–16; Bonch-Bruevich, *Vsia vlast'*, 73; Danilov, *Na puti*, 180–81; PA, LG/F/59/1/9; Nekludoff, *Diplomatic Reminiscences*, 458–59; *Padenie*, 2:24–25.

35. *Russia in Transition*, Phillips letter to Francis, 23 March 1916.

36. NA/US, RG165, Box 2040; NA2, M1194r161, MID, "Ivan Narodny," File 9140-2525/224, 21 January 1918; NA2, M1194r161, MID, "Ivan Narodny," File 274, 27 April 1918; NA/US, RG 165, Box 2073.

37. GARF, 1467.1.479, 32–32ob; Rudnev, *La vérité*; Fuller, *Foe*, 150–59; Pomeranz, "Provisional Government."

58: Rasputin and the Jews

1. OR/RNB, 1000.1975.22, 26ob.

2. Firsov, in Tereshchuk, *Grigorii Rasputin*, 484–86.

3. PZ, 196.

4. VR, 620; Globachev, *Pravda*, 72; Sliozberg, *Dela*, 3:349; HIA, Batyushin, "V chem byla sila;" FN, 30–31.

5. See FN, 30–32.

6. OR/RNB, 307.80, 10.

7. *PK*, 11 April 1914, p. 2; GARF, 102.242.1912.297, ch. 1, 34–45.

8. On Dobrovolsky: Globachev, *Pravda*, 72; RR, 276–77; FR, 137–38; FB, 381; VR, 455; *Padenie*, 5:238–39.

9. *GRS*, 1:370–71.

10. See, with enormous caution, the chapter "Rasputin i evrei" in Simanovich, *Rasputin*, 42–48.

11. Sliozberg, *Dela*, 3:347–48.

12. GARF, 102.316.1910.381, 152.

13. *GRS*, 2:347; VR, 614–18.

14. Sliozberg, *Dela*, 3:347–49.

15. Mel'gunov, *Vospominaniia*, 1:205.

16. RR, 279–80; Bokhanov, *Delovaia elita*, 217; *Padenie*, 7:412; VR, 629–30; PZ, 188–89.

17. GARF, 111.1.2980, 196–96ob.

18. VR, 631.

19. Globachev, *Pravda*, 72; RR, 280–81; Bokhanov, *Delovaia elita*, 178; *Padenie*, 1:178–80; Guchkov, *Guchkov*, 88–89.

20. HIA, Batyushin, "V chem byla sila Rasputina," 3, 26–35, 61–66, 69–71; VR, 623–26, 631; Batyushin, *Tainaia*, 219; Fuller, *Foe*, 150–59, 163–69.

21. GARF, 111.1.2980, 213.

22. GARF, 102.242.1912.297, ch. 2, 133; *Den'*, 21 December 1916, p. 72; FR, 137; Lemke, *250 dnei*, 2:346; *Za kulisami*, xiii, 31.
23. GARF, 713.1.9, 1–1ob.
24. VR, 620, 627–30; HIA, Batyushin, "V chem byla sila Rasputina," 61–66, 69–71.
25. *Padenie*, 6:390–91; Gessen, "Ignatii."
26. HIA, Batyushin, "V chem byla sila Rasputina," 3, 26–35.
27. VR, 633; Mel'gunov, *Legenda*, 398–403.
28. GARF, 102.314.35, 29; WC, 573–75; Lauchlan, *Hide*, 182; VR, 638–40; editors' commentary in Batyushin, *Tainaia*, 244–48.
29. GARF, 102.314.35, 29; *Gosudarstvennaia Duma*, 234–35.
30. On this interpretation, see editors' commentary in Batyushin, *Tainaia*, 246–48.
31. VR, 640–41; Simanovich, *Rasputin*, 108–109.
32. GARF, 1467.1.13, 26ob, 38.
33. Sokolov, "Predvaritel'noe sledstvie," 282–87.
34. WC, 607; VR, 632; Den, *Podlinnaia tsaritsa*, 74; Rassulin, *Vernaia Bogu*, 317–18.
35. VR, 632; *Padenie*, 2:326.
36. WC, 666–68. Incorrectly gives date of firing as 22 December. VR, 640.
37. Nekludoff, *Diplomatic Reminiscences*, 452.
38. WC, 677–68.
39. *Padenie*, 5:238–39.
40. SML, Spiridovich Papers, 359, Box 14, Folder 5, clipping.
41. *Odesskiia novosti*, 22 December 1916, p. 2.

59: "The sun will shine . . ."

1. WC, 498-99, 507; Ordovskii-Tanaevskii, *Vospominaniia*, 392–97; KVD, 331–32, 355.
2. GARF, 612.1.61, 79.
3. WC, 340–41, 496–98, 505, 508, 532, 541, 546; Pipes, *Russian Revolution*, 83.
4. Faleev, "Za chto," 173.
5. WC, 473–74.
6. RGIA, 1617.1.63, 53–54ob.
7. Shavel'skii, *Vospominaniia*, 2:67.
8. FR, 174–76; WC, 571.
9. WC, 562n339.
10. KVD, 360.
11. WC, 529.
12. CU, Bakhmeteff Archive, Tikhobrazov Papers, Box 3, Rasputin i stavka, pp. 5–11.
13. WC, 547, 655.

14. VR, 609–10.
15. *KVD*, 364-66; *WC*, 548, 550n30; RGIA, 878.2.186, 155; *Tsesarevich*, 62.
16. Vyrubova, *Stranitsy*, 121.
17. Den, *Podlinnaia tsaritsa*, 69–71; Vyrubova, *Stranitsy*, 121.
18. Smirnov, *Neizvestnoe*, 21–23.
19. *KVD*, 370.
20. VR, 642; Rassulin, *Vernaia Bogu*, 121.

60: Apotheosis

1. *KVD*, 371; *WC*, 554; GARF, 1467.1.479, 18ob–19.
2. *WC*, 571.
3. *KVD*, 372.
4. *WC*, 573–75.
5. *LP*, 472.
6. FR, 178–79; NIOR/RGB, 15.4.1, 68ob–70.
7. FR, 179–81; Sliozberg, *Dela*, 3:352–53; Savich, *Vospominaniia*, 172–73.
8. Blok, *Sobranie sochinenii*, 5:363–64.
9. Globachev, *Pravda*, 95.
10. Shulgin, *Years*, 270.
11. FR, 179–80; *Za kulisami*, x–xv; *WC*, 514n308.
12. GARF, 713.1.50, 1–3ob.
13. *Za kulisami*, 29–30.
14. GARF, 713.1.52, 2, 5–6.
15. VR, 661; and see Blok, *Sobranie sochinenii*, 5:363–64.
16. *WC*, 598.
17. Shishkin, *Rasputin*, 162.
18. AD, Correspondance politique et commerciale, Guerre, 1914–18: répertoires. Dossier Général, No. 644, No. 102.
19. Lyandres, "Progress Bloc," 451–55.
20. *WC*, 595, 610. Spelling and punctuation as in original. And *KVD*, 386.
21. Krarup, *42 Aar*, 128.
22. The best source is Fuller, *Foe*, 40–60, 80–83, 190, 203–205, 209. And: Shulgin, *Years*, 233–35; *WC*, 600, 634; Rasputin's telegram to Vyrubova in GARF, 612.1.61, 70.
23. *WC*, 373, 582–83, 610 and n371a, 634 and n387; Gatrell, *Russia's First*, 154–75.
24. RRR, 53–54.
25. FDNO, 276.
26. RGADA, 1412.3.1593.
27. *LP*, 473; *WC*, 631–32, 636, 638–39; Vasil'ev, *Ochrana*, 134–35; VR, 435.
28. *WC*, 584, 598, 612.

29. Coonrod, "Fourth Duma," 8, 22–24.
30. Gatrell, *Russia's First*, 169–72; Fuller, *Foe*, 229–30.
31. *WC*, 549, 573–75, 627.
32. *VR*, 435.

61: Stupidity or Treason

1. *WC*, 619.
2. *RR*, 386, 418, 448; *VR*, 649.
3. *RRR*, 117.
4. Buranov, "Strannik," 57; *FR*, 193–94; Paléologue, *Ambassador's Memoirs*, 2:240.
5. Rasputin, "Dnevnik," 526.
6. HIA, Nikolaevsky Papers, Series No. 74, 129–6.
7. Shulgin, *Years*, 270–77; Lyandres, "Progressive Bloc," 459–61. Also: Savich, *Vospominaniia*, 173.
8. *VR*, 662.
9. *RR*, 408, 411, 415; *Russkaia volia*, 20 December 1916 in OR/RNB, 1000.1975.22, 36; Chernow, *Warburgs*, 178–79; NA, FO 371/2746, Letter of E. Howard, 14 December 1916 (NS); Nekludoff, *Diplomatic Reminiscences*, 424–27, 452–55: he writes that Vasilev chose not to meet Warburg with the other two men, realizing the impression it might create. Also: *Padenie*, 1:138–39.
10. PAAA, AS 2929, R 20467.
11. AD, Correspondance politique et commerciale, Guerre, 1914–18: répertoires. Dossier Général, No. 644, pp. 243–44. Also: Dossier Général, No. 645, Nos. 677–79. And: PA, LG/E/3/23/2. George Buchanan to "Charlie", 20 October 1916.
12. *KVD*, 404; Hall, *Little Mother*, 271–72; *WC*, 632–33; CU, Bakhmeteff Archive, G. A. Tal Papers, Memoirs, Notebook 32, pp. 13–14.
13. *WC*, 642–43.
14. Kolonitskii, *Tragicheskaia erotika*, 222–24; YLS, 203, 230–31. On the congress: NIOR/RGB, 14.4.1, 74–75, 93.
15. *VR*, 674–75; Coonrod, "Fourth Duma," 16.
16. See Lyandres, "Progressive Bloc."
17. *VR*, 671; NIOR RGB, 140.7.8, 16; Tikhomirov, *Dnevnik*, 310–11.
18. *VR*, 674.
19. Lyandres, "Progressive Bloc," 454.
20. RGIA, 472.50.1619, 8, 10; Hoare, *Fourth Seal*, 115.
21. *VR*, 651–52.
22. *WC*, 640–41, including n296.
23. RGIA, 920.1.54, 440ob–41, 444–45; Mikhail, *Dnevnik*, 306–307.
24. Shavel'skii, *Vospominaniia*, 2:224–25.

25. Chebotaryova, "V dvortsovom lazarete," 181:240; FSA, 349; 817n244, 822n259, 822–23n260; Vyrubova, *Stranitsy*, 89; WC, 642–43; Purishkevich, *Murder*, 142; RR, 420–22; Raupakh, *Facies*, 169.
26. OR/RNB, 585.5696, 28ob.
27. Telegrams in: Bokhanov, *Rasputin*, 346.
28. WC, 649–51.
29. FR, 181–83.
30. VR, 664–66; FR, 181–83.

62: "Vanya has arrived."

1. Coonrod, "Fourth Duma," 18–19; GARF, 1467.1.567, 575a–78.
2. FR, 203.
3. Shulgin, *Years*, 45.
4. Purishkevich, *Murder*, 46–50, 99.
5. GARF, 102.242.1912.297, ch. 1, 80.
6. Purishkevich, *Murder*, 44, 62.
7. *PK*, 6 June 1914, p. 2; 7 July 1914, p. 1; GARF, 102.242.1912.297, ch. 1, 63, 83.
8. KVD, 424.
9. GARF, 1467.1.628, 15.
10. Purishkevich, *Murder*, 72–73, 73–78.
11. Radzinsky, with no evidence, writes it was Dmitry's idea. See RR, 429–30. Bokhanov, also unconvincingly, states it was Maklakov's: see his *Rasputin*, 353–59.
12. YLS, 217.
13. *Gosudarstvennaia Duma*, 357–59.
14. HIA, Vasily Maklakov Collection, 15-14, pp. 1–9; YLS, 234–35; Purishkevich, *Murder*, 124; Mel'gunov, *Legenda*, 369.
15. YLS, 217–18; FR, 203. Purishkevich writes that Sukhotin was in the Preobrazhensky Guards. *Murder*, 73–78. See also FDNO, 275.
16. Vulliamy, *Red Archives*, 108, 110, 113–14; Mel'gunov, *Legenda*, 369n3. For more on her commitment to killing Rasputin, see RR, 400; Voeikov, *S tsarem*, 149–50.
17. *Reka vremen*, 2:149.
18. Vulliamy, *Red Archives*, 115–16; Mel'gunov, *Legenda*, 369–70.
19. YLS, 234.
20. Purishkevich, *Murder*, 73–78; FR, 203.
21. YLS, 234–35; Purishkevich, *Murder*, 124.
22. Marie, *Education*, 280.
23. YLS, 234–35; Purishkevich, *Murder*, 58–59, 124; FR, 202, 212. In his 1920 testimony to investigator Nikolai Sokolov, Maklakov makes no mention of

where the poison came from. HIA, Vasily Maklakov Collection, 15-14, pp. 1–9.

24. Purishkevich, *Murder*, 81–83, 91–93. The bridge was also known as the Krestovsky.

25. Shulgin, *Years*, 267–68.

26. OR/RNB, 585.5696, 7.

27. SML, Spiridovich Papers, Box 6, Folder 3, pp. 366–67; Mel'gunov, *Legenda*, 371. Here the name is given as "Bener."

28. Hoare, *Fourth Seal*, 67–68; CUL, II:1 (34), p. 58. Grand Duke Dmitry gave subtle hints to his friends about the plot at the time. See Gavriil Konstantinovich, *Velikii kniaz'*, 287.

29. *Reka vremen*, 2:149–50. "Malanya" is not identified. Radzinsky dates the letter to 27 November and writes that Malanya refers to Marianna Derfelden. RR, 440–41, 477.

30. Dolgova, *Nakanune*, 174–76.

31. GARF, 102.314.35, 9–10.

32. OR/RNB, 307.80, 10.

33. GARF, 111.1.2981a.

34. YLS, 218–19, 227–29.

35. *Reka vremen*, 2:149; on nickname: GARF, 102.314.35, 9–10.

36. Purishkevich, *Murder*, 95, 122–23.

63: "My hour will soon strike."

1. Lincoln, *Passage*, 215–17; Gatrell, *Russia's First*, 70–71.

2. Bashkiroff, *Sickle*, 27.

3. Lobanov-Rostovsky, *Grinding Mill*, 193–94. And: Paléologue, *Ambassador's Memoirs*, 3:164.

4. Nekludoff, *Diplomatic Reminiscences*, 455–56.

5. Pokrovskii, ed. "Politicheskoe polozhenie," 4, 6, 11.

6. Nekludoff, *Diplomatic Reminiscences*, 455–56.

7. LP, 489; YLS, 202; KVD, 429, 431; VR, 649–50.

8. LP, 482; KVD, 433; Vyrubova, *Stranitsy*, 127–28.

9. *Novoe vremia*, 2 December 1916, pp. 6–7.

10. Tikhomirov, *Dnevnik*, 313–15.

11. FSA, 349–50, 823n261, 823–24n262; WC, 656n413. Alexandra received a second, similar letter that month from Nikolai Balashov, courtier and wealthy Petersburg aristocrat.

12. GARF, 97.4.118, 9–10; and 102.316.1910.381, ch. 2, 93–95; OR/RNB, 585.5696, 16ob; and 152.4.189, 7; WC, 660, 664.

13. LP, 486–87; WC, 658, 665, 672, 675, 678.

14. OR/RNB, 1000.2.551, 1–5; WC, 672; Zhevakhov, *Vospominaniia*, 1:187–88;

Petrogradskaia gazeta, 21 March 1917, p. 2. Stories that Rasputin accompanied them to Novgorod are false. Photo of icon: *KVD*, Insert before p. 418.

15. *WC*, 670–71n433; OR/RNB, 1000.2.551, 5.
16. *KVD*, 451–52.
17. *WC*, 659.
18. GARF, 650.1.19, 45–49.
19. Beletskii, *Vospominaniia*, 18.
20. Vyrubova, *Neizvestnye fragmenty*, 66. See also FDNO, 272.
21. Beletskii, *Vospominaniia*, 18. On Rasputin and Dobrovolsky: Sokolov, "Predvaritel'noe sledstvie," 284.
22. Krarup, *42 Aar*, 137–38.
23. Voeikov, *S tsarem*, 149–50.
24. *WC*, 678.
25. GARF, 111.1.2979a, 288–291.
26. Simanovich, *Rasputin*, 138–39. On this bogus testimony, VR, 692–93; Romanov, *Voennyi dnevnik*, 211.
27. RRR, 151–53. A photostat copy of the original is in: SML, Spiridovich Papers, Box 16, Folder 3. The original letter was purchased by the Chicago surgeon Max Thorek in 1956, having for many years belonged to André de Coppet of New York. Its subsequent fate is unknown. *New York Times*, 26 July 1956, p. 26.

64: The Last Day

1. *WC*, 679n447.
2. OR/RNB, 307.80, 10.
3. OR/RNB, 1000.1975.22, 35ob, and 307.80, 10; *Odesskie novosti*, 22 December 1916, 4.
4. Vyrubova, *Stranitsy*, 102–103; FDNO, 277–78. Golovina's memoir, written in the wake of that day's later tragic events, depicts Rasputin as committed to going through with his visit, although he sensed it would mean his death.
5. LP, 492–93.
6. RRR, 122–23; OR/RNB, 307.80, 10; GARF, 102.314.35, 11–11ob.
7. GARF, 102.314.35, 14–14ob.
8. GARF, 102.314.35, 19–20; OR/RNB, 307.80, 10.
9. YLS, 240-43. On Rasputin's sending home the agents that night: GARF, 650.1.19, 51–52; Shishkin, *Rasputin*, 291. On car: GARF, 102.314.35, 17–17ob; OR/RNB, 307.80, 10–11; Purishkevich, *Murder*, 125, 132–34; Romanov, *Voennyi dnevnik*, 226–27.

65: A Cowardly Crime

1. YLS, 239-54; GRS, 4:237.
2. The work appeared in three languages at the time: English, French, and Russian. See: FN, 29, 653n124. The Russian was titled "Kak my ubivali Rasputina" and "Konets Rasputina."
3. Mel'gunov, *Legenda*, 380note; VR, 687.
4. Compare "Kak my ubivali," No. 51, p. 14 with YLS, 250–51. See also the differing accounts of Yusupov attacking Rasputin with Maklakov's rubber club: No. 51, p. 14; YLS, 253, and Yusupov, *Murder*, 162–63; Purishkevich, *Murder*, 151.
5. Vorres, *Last Grand Duchess*, 142.
6. "Helped to Kill Rasputin," *New York Times*, 23 September 1918. A bogus treatment of the murder was published under Lazovert's name in 1923 as well. See FR, 209; FN, 28–29.
7. On the various editions, see Shishkin, *Rasputin*, 191; FN, 28–29.
8. Purishkevich, *Murder*, 56–57, 160–61. The palace, now known as the Beloselsky-Belozersky Palace, had previously belonged to Dmitry's uncle Grand Duke Sergei Alexandrovich.
9. RRR, 134.
10. Purishkevich, *Murder*, 60; Faleev, "Za chto," 161; RR, 442.
11. Shishkin, *Rasputin*, 187, 266–67, 295; Dobson, *Prince*, 93. Also: Vasil'ev, *Ochrana*, 158.
12. It was told soon after the killing that Yusupov claimed the poison did not work since it had been exposed to high temperature and become inert. See: RGIA, 948.1.180, 10–10ob. Humidity can also render cyanide crystals non-toxic. See: Moe, *Prelude*, 567–68.
13. RRR, 134.
14. See, for example, Groian, *Muchenik*, 174–85.

66: The Investigation

1. Purishkevich, *Murder*, 149–50.
2. GARF, 102.314.35, 4-5, 21–21ob, 23–24ob; "Kak my ubivali," No. 51, 14–15; Purishkevich, *Murder*, 165. Also: Savich, *Vospominaniia*, 188–90.
3. GRS, 4:231–36.
4. Romanov, *Voennyi dvornik*, 227–29; GARF, 650.1.19, 51.
5. OR/RNB, 307.80, 10–11; *Byloe*, No. 1 (23), July 1917, p. 70.
6. YLS, 254–56.
7. Shishkin, *Rasputin*, 36; OR/RNB, 1000.1975.22, 35ob; Lauchlan, *Russian Hide*, 150n10, 151, 182.

8. Romanov, *Voennyi dnevnik*, 227–29; YLS, 259–60; OR/RNB, 307.8, 10–11; GRS, 4:236.

9. [Gibbs,] *Russian Diary*, 76; Harmer, *Forgotten Hospital*, 117; Powell, *Women*, 304. A nurse from the Anglo-Russian Hospital in Dmitry's palace claimed Yusupov had been injured in the neck. If true, it could not have been serious, for he showed up at the palace in the afternoon.

10. Purishkevich, *Murder*, 127, 165–66; OR/RNB, 152.4.189, 13.

11. BV, 20 December 1916, p. 4; *Byloe*, No. 1 (23), July 1917, pp. 64, 74–75; OR/RNB, 307.80, 10; GARF, 102.314.35, 7. Krarup later wrote that the boot belonged to Simanovich, Rasputin having grabbed the wrong pair when he left with Yusupov. Maria, however, told the police the boot belonged to her father. Krarup, *42 Aar*, 139.

12. GARF, 102.1916g.246.357, 9–9ob.

13. GARF, 102.314.35, 25–27; OR/RNB, 307.80, 10–11. On drink: Vasil'ev, *Ochrana*, 177; YLS, 260.

14. Romanov, *Voennyi dnevnik*, 205–206.

67: The Body in the Water

1. Marie, *Education*, 258.

2. WC, 683.

3. FSA, 456–57.

4. WC, 684.

5. GARF, 640.2.50, 1–4ob. Vyrubova wrote that the letter was received at the palace on the seventeenth. *Stranitsy*, 103–104.

6. GARF, 102.314.35, 9–10, 19–20.

7. Vasil'ev, *Ochrana*, 174–75; Vyrubova, *Stranitsy*, 104.

8. Den, *Podlinnaia tsaritsa*, 75–76.

9. FR, 216–17; OR/RNB, 152.4.189, 8. Rumor of a fine: OR/RNB, 585.5696, 23–27. On the reporter for the newspaper and his actions on the seventeenth, Savich, *Vospominaniia*, 188–90.

10. CU, Bakhmeteff Archive, Tikhobrazov Papers, Box 3, Rasputin i stavka, pp. 21–28. Other sources concur with Tikhobrazov's assessment of the tsar's reaction. See, for example, the memoirs of Georgii Tal, also at Stavka that day: CU, Bakhmeteff Archive, Tal Papers, Memoirs, "Tragediia tsarskoi sem'i i vliianie Rasputina," pp. 30–31. General Voeikov, however, claims just the opposite, that he never saw any emotion from the tsar. See *S tsarem*, 147. See also the memoirs of General N. Danilov in *Na puti*, 171–72; Mordvinov, *Poslednii imperator*, 51.

11. FSA, 456-58; Vyrubova, *Stranitsy*, 104, 107; WC, 684–86.

12. WC, 686.

13. "Svidanie," 23.

14. FSA, 350–51, 825n264; *KVD*, 487–88; *WC*, 686.

15. Den, *Podlinnaia tsaritsa*, 77.

16. On the search and recovery: *BV*, 20 December 1916, p. 4; Koshko, *Ocherki*, 130–32; GARF, 670.1.410, 1; and 651.1.19, 49–50; OR/RNB, 307.80, 10; Romanov, *Voennyi dnevnik*, 229–30.

17. RRR, 146–47.

18. See, for example, Vyrubova, *Stranitsy*, 104.

19. OR/RNB, 1000.1975.22, 35ob–36, 50–50ob; *Russkaia volia*, 9 March 1917, p. 5; Koshko, *Ocherki*, 131–32.

20. Vyrubova, *Stranitsy*, 105.

21. FSA, 456–57; *KVD*, 487–88; Voeikov, *S tsarem*, 147.

22. OR/RNB, 152.4.189, 10, and 1000.1975.22, 30; *BV*, 19 December 1916, 4; *Rech'*, 19 December 1916, p. 2.

23. OR/RNB, 152.4.189, 11; and 1000.1975.22, 50ob; and 307.80, 16.

24. FR, 220.

25. Purishkevich, *Murder*, 155–56.

26. *GRS*, 4:240.

27. CUL, Templewood Papers, II:1 (34), p. 71.

28. *Originalakten*.

29. Roullier, *Raspoutine*, 515. For later works that cite Roullier as an authority, see Cook, *To Kill*, 70–71; Cullen, *Rasputin*, 150–52; Shishkin, *Rasputin*, 51–54.

30. Kulegin, *Kto ubil*, 16–17; *Russkaia volia*, 13 March 1917. Sereda's account, written down by Grand Duke Andrei Vladimirovich Romanov, is in GARF, 650.1.19, 49–50.

31. IIL/Sokolov, Vol. VII, Testimony of M. Solovyova (Rasputina), no date [26 December 1919?].

32. FR, 220–21, 226; GARF, 650.1.19, 49–50. Also see on the cause of death: *GRS*, 4:239. On how potassium cyanide, had it been ingested, might have failed to show up in the autopsy, see Cullen, *Rasputin*, 222–23.

33. *BV*, 21 December 1916, p. 4. Also: OR RNB, 1000.1975.22, 35.

34. Vyrubova, *Stranitsy*, 104–105; RRR, 146–47; Den, *Podlinnaia tsaritsa*, 77; Chebotaryova, "V dvortsovom lazarete," 182:207; PAAA, 4351, R.20382; *Temnye sily*; *Tainy Rasputnogo dvora*, 9–10; PA, LG/F/59/1/12; *Russkaia volia*, 9 March 1917, No. 6, p. 5.

35. See, for example, Roullier, *Raspoutine*, 515; PZ, 226; Smirnov, *Neizvestnoe*, 85; RR, 484; Fuller, *Foe*, 230. Among those who have tried to debunk the myth, see especially FR, 217–19. The documents sold by Hiersemann attest that Rasputin was dead when he hit the water and did not die of drowning. See *Originalakten*, 8–10.

36. FR, 222; OR/RNB, 307.80, 10; VR, 658, 705–706; Den, *Podlinnaia tsaritsa*, 79. On the coffin: GARF, 102.OO.1916.246.357, 109.

37. *GRS*, 4:238; GARF, 650.1.19, 36–37; OR/RNB, 307.80, 10. Krarup wrote that she and several dozen others visited the body there as well. See *42 Aar*, 140.

38. Voeikov, *S tsarem*, 147–48; SML, Spiridovich Papers 359, Box 16, Folder 2.
39. Den, *Podlinnaia tsaritsa*, 77–78.
40. FR, 222.
41. Den, *Podlinnaia tsaritsa*, 78–79; LP, 511; VR, 702–703; Voeikov, *S tsarem*, 150; FSA, 456–57, 817n244; RRR, 484–86. Other sources state that Bishop Isidor conducted the burial rites. See VR, 701.
42. Chebotaryova, "V dvortsovom lazarete," 182:207. And see ibid., 181:210–11. On the rumors: Romanov, *Voennyi dnevnik*, 210; RGIA, 948.1.180, 6ob; NIOR/RGB, 436.11.1, 72–73; GRS, 2:347; VR, 705–706. And, with caution, Alexei Khvostov's testimony: *Padenie*, 1:39–40.
43. LP, 511.
44. FSA, 456, 458.
45. OR/RNB, 585.5696, 33; and 307.80, 10–11; NIOR/RGB, 218.1325.2, 22–22ob; BV, 20 December 1916, p. 4; GARF, 102.1916.246.357, 83. Some had a quite accurate knowledge of the burial site. See: [Gibbs], *Russian Diary*, 90, 94.
46. FSA, 456–57.
47. PZ, 229.
48. Vyrubova, *Stranitsy*, 106–107.
49. RRR, 150–51.
50. KVD, 499; Nicholas II, *Dnevniki*, 2(2): 272.
51. GARF, 640.2.142, 1–1ob. My gratitude to Mariana Markova for her translation.
52. WC, 603, 702. The only Freemason with any connection to the killing was Vasily Maklakov. See Serkov, *Russkoe masonstvo*, 509–511. Nonetheless, contemporary nationalist historians have tried to depict the killing as part of a larger Jewish-Masonic plot against Orthodox Russia. See, for example, PZ, 224–25; Kulegin, *Kto ubil*, 19–21.

68: The Romanov Family Drama

1. HIA, Papers of Grand Duchess Ksenia Alexandrovna, Box 6, Folder 13, 21 December 1916.
2. Marie, *Education*, 250, 253–56.
3. LP, 505–506.
4. Vorres, *Last Grand Duchess*, 142; Trotsky, *History*, 1:56.
5. "Podrobnosti ubiistva," 97.
6. GARF, 102.1916g.246.357, 6. Telegram to Zenaida in French; to Dmitry in English. Published in *Byloe*, No. 1 (23), July 1917, pp. 81–82. "Darlings" in telegram to Dmitry.
7. Marie, *Education*, 280.

8. GARF, 651.1.19, 11; NA, FO 371/2994, No. 2804, 3 January 1917 (NS); Harmer, *Forgotten Hospital*, 116–19.

9. HL/DiaryDP, Book 5, 16 December 1917, p. 53; Marie, *Education*, 260–63. On the rumors of Dmitry's murder: OR/RNB, 585.5696, 36.

10. Romanov, *Voennyi dnevnik*, 202, 206.

11. RR, 460–61; "Kak my ubivali," No. 52, p. 16.

12. GARF, 651.1.19, 10; Romanov, *Voennyi dnevnik*, 205.

13. Marie, *Education*, 265–67.

14. "Podrobnosti ubiistva," 98; YLS, 264.

15. Marie, *Education*, 275–77.

16. GARF, 651.1.19, 11–13.

17. *LP*, 510; Romanov, *Voennyi dnevnik*, 206–207.

18. *LP*, 505–506, 515; GARF, 650.1.19, 25–26.

19. Mariia Fedorovna, *Dnevniki imperatritsy*, 164.

20. *LP*, 515–16.

21. GARF, 651.1.19, 11–13.

22. GARF, 102.1916g.246.357, 9–9ob; RGIA, 948.1.180, 5–9.

23. GARF, 650.1.19, 51. On 4 March 1917, Alexander Kerensky, minister of justice of the new Provisional Government, officially closed the investigation. OR/RNB, 307.80, 1; KVD, 513.

24. HL/DiaryDP, Book 5, 24 December 1917, pp. 71–78; "Svidanie," 24. And, with caution, Marie, *Education*, 265–69.

25. Marie, *Education*, 270–71; HL/DiaryDP, Book 5, 16 December 1917, 54–55; Steinberg, *Fall*, 71n8; *Collection du Prince*, 69, 71; RGIA, 948.1.180, 3–4; [Gibbs], *Russian Diary*, 88–89; Moe, *Prelude*, 574–75; "Podrobnosti ubiistva," 102; Powell, *War*, 353.

26. Marie, *Education*, 282.

27. RGIA, 948.1.180, 5; GARF, 650.1.19, 32; Stopford, *Russian Diary*, 93; HL/DiaryDP, Book 5, 24 December 1917, pp. 78–79.

28. Baratov Papers, HIA, Box 1, Folder 4, Diary: 31 December 1916.

29. "Podrobnosti ubiistva," 102.

30. Marie, *Education*, 277–78; FDNO, 274–75, including n40 and n41.

31. Gavriil Konstantinovich, *Velikii kniaz'*, 293–94; GARF, 601.1.2148, 6–7. This is the original of the final, clean draft sent to Nicholas, with his reply.

32. OR RNB, 585.5696, 33–33ob.

33. *LP*, 517.

34. "Podrobnosti ubiistva," 102.

35. *LP*, 530.

36. GARF, 102.OO.1916g.246.357a, 3, 6, 12, 16–17.

37. *Byloe*, No. 1 (23), July 1917, pp. 82–83.

38. VR, 691.

69: Orgies, Gay Love, and the Secret Hand of the British

1. Cockfield, *White Crow*, 75–76. On Rasputin's being told to kill himself, see also Francis, *Russia in Transition*, Francis letter, 11 February 1917 (NS); CUL, Templewood Papers, II:1 (16); OR/RNB, 585.5696, 23–27; GARF, 651.1.19, 4–5; Oreshnikov, *Dnevnik*, 97–98, 535n107; PAAA, R.10684; PAAA, 4351, R.20382; NA, FO 371/2994, No. 2804, 3 January 1917; NA, FO 395/105, No. 13794, 5 January 1917.
2. *Russkaia volia*, 10 March 1917, p. 3.
3. AD, Correspondance politique et commerciale, Guerre, 1914–18: répertoires. Dossier Général, No. 645, No. 1367. Samuel Hoare also reported back to London that Rasputin had been killed during an orgy. CUL, Templewood Papers, II(1): 16.
4. OR/RNB, 1000.1975.22, 50ob. Possibly Anna von Drenteln, daughter of Alexander von Drenteln.
5. GARF, 111.1.2981b, 12; GARF, 102.1916.246.357, 51–51ob.
6. OR/RNB, 307.80, 10.
7. HL/DiaryDP, Book 5, 16 December 1917, p. 53.
8. GARF, 102.1916.246.357, 52–56, 59–61, 73–75, 77–79.
9. RGIA, 948.1.180, 2.
10. OR/RNB, 307.80, 10; RGIA, 948.1.180, 5–5ob.
11. RGIA, 948.1.180, 5–9.
12. On Kroits: FDNO, 237; RGIA, 948.1.180, 2–2ob.
13. "Podrobnosti ubiistva," 104–105.
14. RR, 478–79; Etkind, *Khlyst*, 258–59, 628–29.
15. GARF, 102.314.35, 25–27.
16. Shishkin, *Rasputin*, 118, 214–15, 307–08; Kulegin, *Kto ubil*, 19.
17. FR, 204; Shishkin, *Rasputin*, 304; Kniaz'kin, *Bol'shaia kniga*, 8–12.
18. FR, 200–201; Kotsiubinskii, *Rasputin*, 225; Figes, *People's Tragedy*, 189; Nelipa, *Murder*, 102–206; Cockfield, *White Crow*, 175–77; YLS, 263–65. Also on the grand duke's not being involved in the plot: Mel'gunov, *Legenda*, 374–75.
19. Romanov, *Voennyi dnevnik*, 235; "Pozornoe vremia," 36–37.
20. HL/DiaryDP, Book 5, 16 December 1917, p. 54.
21. PAAA, 4351, R.20382. Report to the king: HIA, Papers of King Ferdinand I, Box 62, Folder 11 (Reel 81), "Bericht über eine Reise," p. 2. On Russian talk, see VR, 690.
22. GARF, 97.4.118, 20–21.
23. Vyrubova, *Stranitsy*, 96.
24. SML, Spiridovich Papers, Box 14, Folder 6; VVFR, 1:204–05. Margarita Nelipa (*Murder*, 197–99), following Jamie Cockfield (*White Crow*, 175), has also argued that Buchanan knew of the plot based on her misreading of the diary of Grand Duke Nikolai Mikhailovich for 17 December 1916. She asserts the

5:30 telephone call the grand duke received from Buchanan came in the morning, and so Buchanan could only have known of the murder that early if he had been involved. But it is clear from the diary that this refers to 5:30 p.m., by which time the entire city was talking about the crime. For the diary, see "Podrobnosti ubiistva," 97–98. That the call came at 5:30 p.m. is also confirmed in [Gibbs], *Russian Diary*, 74–75.

25. NA, FO 371/2994, No. 705, 31 December 1916 (NS).

26. NA, FO 395/105, No. 13794, 5 January 1917 (NS); Vogel-Jørgensen, *Rasputin*, 125–28. The story also appeared in *Odesskie novosti*, 23 December 1916, p. 76. On the commission: Hoare, *Fourth Seal*, 241.

27. CUL, Templewood Papers, II:1 (50).

28. CUL, Templewood Papers, II:1(34), 72; *Yorkshire Post*, 22 June 1933, p. 10. Zhevakhov, too, saw the British as responsible. *Vospominaniia*, 1:250–51.

29. NA, FO 371/3002, No. 11942, 14 January 1917 (NS).

30. See Vyrubova, *Stranitsy*, 133–34.

31. See Cook, *To Kill*, 76–84, 142, 155; Cullen, *Rasputin*, 16–17.

32. OPI/GIM, 411.66, 24–24ob.

33. NA, FO 371/2994, p. 11.

34. YLS, 262.

35. Cook, *To Kill*, 217.

36. See Cullen, *Rasputin*, 204–207. The letter apparently is in the possession of Alley's descendants. I have not been able to locate its whereabouts.

37. See, for example, Cook, *To Kill*, 220–21; Cullen, *Rasputin*, iv; VR., 687 88, 691.

38. FR, 221.

39. Cullen, *Rasputin*, 210–11; Cook, *To Kill*, 210–14. See also FR, 229.

40. *New York Times Current History*, 17:306–307.

41. GARF, 63.47.484(35), 98.

42. See Jeffrey, *Secret History*, 98–109. Professor Jeffrey had complete access to Britain's long-secret M16 archive and found nothing to suggest any English involvement in the killing. Email communication with author, 14 January 2014.

43. *Church Times*, 9 March 1934, p. 294; *Daily Express*, 3 March 1934, p. 7.

44. Romanov, *Voennyi dnevnik*, 235.

45. NIOR/RGB, 140.7.9, 6ob. And also: NIOR/RGB, 436.11.1, 72ob–73.

46. See James J. Kenney, Jr., "The Politics of Assassination" (esp. pp. 126–27, 137, 141) in Ragsdale, *Paul I*.

47. Kir'ianov, "Pravye," 221.

48. GARF, 97.4.118, 114.

70: The End of the Tobolsk Yoke

1. CUL, Templewood Papers, II:1 (16). And: VR, 695; Tikhomirov, *Dnevnik*, 321.
2. OR/RNB, 585.5696, 27–27ob.
3. Shulgin, *Years*, 269; NIOR/RGB, 218.1325.2, 22ob–23.
4. *The Times*, 9 January 1917 (NS), p. 6.
5. OR/RNB, 585.5696, 29ob; and 1000.1975.22, 50ob.
6. Kolonitskii, *Tragicheskaia erotika*, 235–36.
7. GARF, 651.1.19, 19.
8. GARF, 97.4.118, 8.
9. GARF, 102.196.246.357, 36–38ob.
10. OR/RNB, 1000.1975.22, 35.
11. *Russkoe slovo*, 21 December 1916, p. 68.
12. OR/RNB, 1000.1975.22, 35–35ob. And also: *Rech'*, 20 December 1916, p. 3; 21 December, p. 2; *BV*, 21 December 1916, p. 3; *Odesskie novosti*, 22 December 1916, p. 4.
13. OR/RNB, 1000.1975.22, 31ob.
14. *Kievlianin*, 23 December 1916, p. 202; Shulgin, *Years*, 269; idem, *Poslednii*, 125, 329.
15. Ordovskii-Tanaevskii, *Vospominaniia*, 396, 422–27.
16. Bulgakov, *Avtobiograficheskie zametki*, 85.
17. VR, 700.
18. Màrkov, *Pokinutaia*, 304–305.
19. Peregudova, *Okhranka*, 2:123–24.
20. VR, 699; Raupakh, *Facies*, 193–94; Miliukov, *Vospominaniia*, 447; NIOR/RGB, 436.11.1, 72ob–73.
21. Markow, *Wie*, 145.
22. RGIA, 948.1.180, 2–2ob.
23. Beletskii, *Vospominaniia*, 18–19.
24. Blok, *Poslednie dni*, 8.
25. GARF, 102.1916.246.357, 45–46ob, 80–83; Blok, *Zapisnye knizhki*, 363.
26. *Lettres des Grands-Ducs*, 207.
27. PA, LG/F/59/1/6, Buchanan to Charlie, 13 January 1917 (NS).
28. *LP*, 518.

71: A Time for Dominoes

1. PAAA, R.10684, Lucius to Bethmann Hollweg, 23 January 1917 (NS). A similar report reached Vienna. See HHStA, P.A. V, Karton 55, Bericht 15.

Others mentioned Pitirim and Varnava as also on the list of those to be killed. Tikhomirov, *Dnevnik*, 331.

2. GARF, 102.1916.246.357, 64.

3. NA, FO 371/2994, No. 1187, 1 January 1917 (NS); FO 371/3002, No. 8111, 9 January 1917 (NS).

4. NA, FO 371.2998, No. 3743. And: PA, LG/F/59/1/18. Letter dated 30 January 1917 (NS).

5. NA, FO 371/3002, No. 13484. The French embassy reported similar talk to Paris. See: AD, Correspondance politique et commerciale, Nouvelle série, 1896–1918, "Guerre, 1914–1918:" répertoires. Dossier Général, No. 647. Report of 5 March 1917 (NS).

6. NIOR/RGB, 140.7.9, 10ob–12.

7. PAAA, R.10684.

8. PAAA, AS 251, R.10694. The list refers to Tsar Paul I, murdered in a palace coup in 1801; Gaius Asinius Pollio, a Roman politician put to death on the order of Empress Valeria Messalina in the first century AD; Jean Jaurès, leading French socialist assassinated in 1914; and Roger Casement, Irish nationalist hanged as a traitor in London in August 1916.

9. PAAA, 3008, R.10741.

10. *LP*, 526–31.

11. Mel'gunov, *Legenda*, 378.

12. NA, FO 371/3002, No. 10744.

13. *Russia in Transition*, Francis letter, 11 February 1917 (NS); Cockfield, *Dollars*, 81 85.

14. AD, Correspondance politique et commerciale, Nouvelle série, 1896–1918, "Guerre, 1914–1918:" répertoires. Dossier Général, No. 647. Report of 5 March 1917 (NS); PA, LG/F/59/1/6, p. 3; NA, FO 395/107, No. 26862; PAAA, AS 339, R.10694; NIOR/RGB, 15.4.1, 93ob–94; Schelking, *Recollections*, 294; VR, 717; Romanov, *Voennyi dnevnik*, 222; Globachev, *Pravda*, 95.

15. PAAA, R.10684. Letter dated 1 March 1917 (NS).

16. Oreshnikov, *Dnevnik*, 102, 538n9; *Sibirskaia torgovaia gazeta*, 1 March 1917, p. 2.

17. Lemke, *250 dnei*, 2:371–72; SML, Spiridovich Papers 359, Box 14, Folder 1; PAAA, R.10684; PAAA, 4351, R.202382; GARF, 111.1.2091a, 12.

18. OR/RNB, 152.4.189, 12. Also: 1000.1975.22, 50ob.

19. Rodzianko, *Reign*, 158.

20. *Odesskie novosti*, 22 December 1916, p. 4.

21. GARF, 102.OO.1916g.246.357a, 44. See also: *Zemshchina*, 31 December 1916, p. 71.

22. Shavel'skii, *Vospominaniia*, 2:253.

23. *WC*, 686–87.

24. *KVD*, 510.

25. *WC*, 688n463, 689, 695.

26. *Poslednie dnevniki*, 16–17.
27. AD, Correspondance politique et commerciale, Nouvelle série, 1896–1918, "Guerre, 1914–1918:" répertoires. Dossier Général, No. 647. No. 303.
28. Lieven, *Nicholas II*, 232.
29. *WC*, 699.
30. Warth, *Nicholas II*, 247–48.
31. OR/RNB, 585.1.4402, 38.

72: Here Lies the Dog

1. Kulegin, *Zagrobnye prikliucheniia*, 5.
2. OR/RNB, 307.80, 10; *Den'*, 9 March 1917, No. 4, p. 3; *Russkaia volia*, 9 March 1917, No. 6, p. 5; FN, 155.
3. Kulegin, *Zagrobnye prikliucheniia*, 8.
4. Kupchinskii, "Kak ia szhigal," 1–4; Nelipa, *Murder*, 446. Colonel Yevgeny Kobylinsky, appointed commandant of Tsarskoe Selo in early March, offers a somewhat different version of events: HL/Sokolov, Vol. III, pp. 106–136.
5. VR, 707–708.
6. Kupchinskii, "Kak ia szhigal," 6–7.
7. VR, 704, 708–709; Kulegin, *Zagrobnye prikliucheniia*, 10.
8. Kulegin, *Zagrobnye prikliucheniia*, 11–13; Nelipa, *Murder*, 449–61.

73: The Myth

1. *Al'manakh "Svoboda,"* 1. The story about photographic passports appears also in *Zhivoe slovo*, 10 March 1917, p. 3. Note: Stories of a harem, women held against their will, control over great distances go back to 1910. *Iuzhnaia zaria*, 30 May 1910, pp. 2–3; *Rech'*, 28 May 1910, pp. 2–3.
2. *Al'manakh "Svoboda"* 2:8.
3. Kulikowskii, "Rethinking," 174.
4. *Petrogradskii listok*, 4 May 1917, p. 11.
5. OR/RNB, 152.4.189, 12; *Al'manakh "Svoboda,"* 1:7; Sokolov, *Temnye sily*, 4–6; BV, 9 March 1917, p. 4.
6. *Grishka Rasputin*, 4.
7. *The Times*, 23 April 1929, p. 14.
8. Le Queux, *Rasputin*, 4.
9. *Russia in Transition*, Francis letter, 11 February 1917 (NS).
10. *Daily Express*, 3 March 1934, p. 7.
11. Bostunich, *Otchego*, pp. 11–12; Kolonitskii, *Tragicheskaia erotika*, 352, 358–61.
12. Marsden, *Rasputin*, 23; and Mikhailov, *Temnye sily*.
13. *Petrogradskaia gazeta*, No. 68, 21 March 1917, p. 2.

14. Kovyl'-Bobyl', *Tsaritsa i Rasputin*.

15. Al'manakh "Svoboda," 2:7–8.

16. OR/RNB, 307.80, 16. Another story stated the snow atop his grave contained special curative powers. *Petrogradskaia gazeta*, No. 68, 21 March 1917, p. 2.

17. Tumanskii, "Zlobodnevnye p'esy."

18. Kolonitskii, *Tragicheskaia erotika*, 364–65.

19. OR/RNB, 307.80, 3; Vishnevskii, *Khudozhestvennye fil'my*, 132–41; FN, 17–19; Kolonitskii, *Tragicheskaia erotika*, 365–66; Grashchenkova, *Kino*, 135.

20. *Sibirskaia torgovaia gazeta*, No. 65, 22 March 1917, p. 2.

21. Kulikowskii, "Rethinking," 174–79; Kolonitskii, *Tragicheskaia erotika*, 362. For an example, see *Petrogradskii vesel'chak*, Nos. 14, 15, 17, 19 for April and May 1917.

22. Kolonitskii, *Tragicheskaia erotika*, 354; Chebotaryova, "V dvortsovom lazarete," 182:206.

23. RGIA, 919.2.1161, 1. For more anti-Rasputin verses and the like: NIOR/RGB, 439.33.10; NIOR/RGB, 140.9.16.

24. OR/RNB, 1000.2.1145, 3.

25. GARF, 102.1916.246.357, 101–102, 116; Kolonitskii, *Tragicheskaia erotika*, 323. Also: *Trepach*, No. 1, 1917, p. 14; Khersonskii, *Akafist*, 2–3.

26. Kolonitskii, *Tragicheskaia erotika*, 356.

27. *Sovremennyi mir*, Nos. 2–3, 1917, pp. 306–307.

74: Unsettled Business

1. *Novoe vremia*, 12 March 1917, p. 7; 14 March, p. 7; *Russkaia volia*, 13 March 1917, p. 3. Yusupov had a long conversation with Ambassador Buchanan about these purported drugs that spring. See PA, LG/F/59/1/14.

2. Marie, *Princess*, 102–103; RGIA, 948.1.180, 11ob.

3. YLS, 276–77.

4. Mel'nik, *Vospominaniia*, 48. See also Stopford, *Russian Diary*, 163; Bulgakov, *Avtobiograficheskie zametki*, 85–86.

5. YLS, 294–95.

6. GARF, 644.1.170, 11–26, 42–47, 49–50, 62ob–65; Steinberg, *Fall*, 135–36.

7. HL/DiaryDP, Book 5, 16 December 1917, pp. 2–3, 50–56.

8. Vyrubova, *Stranitsy*, 116–17, 160; RR, 499; GARF, 124.69.529, 1–5ob; Blok, *Zapisnye knizhki*, 352, 357.

9. Rassulin, *Vernaia Bogu*, 283–89.

10. GARF, 602.2.62, Rudnev, "Pravda."

11. Rassulin, *Vernaia Bogu*, 354–61.

12. FN, 141, 377–38.

13. VR, 709–13; *Petrogradskii listok*, 3 May 1917, p. 4.

14. *Petrogradskii listok*, 11 May 1917, p. 13.

15. *Petrogradskii listok*, 3 May 1917, p. 4; VR, 713–14.
16. VR, 714.
17. GARF, 1467.1.479, 85–88.
18. *KVD*, 517–18.
19. Steinberg, *Fall*, 166n3, 168; Yale University, Beinecke Library, Romanov Collection, GEN MSS 313, Box 1, Folder 2.
20. *KVD*, 519.
21. *Poslednie dnevniki*, 72.
22. Steinberg, *Fall*, 168–71.
23. *Petrogradskaia gazeta*, 21 March 1917, p. 3; *Sibirskaia torgovaia gazeta*, 22 March 1917, p. 2; RRR, 157–61, 175–83.
24. RRR, 182–83; Steinberg, *Fall*, 222; Buranov, "Strannik," 57; HL/Sokolov, Vol. VII: Testimony of M. Solovyova (Rasputina), undated. Here her name is given as "Shag."
25. GBUTO/GAGT, I-154.24.58, 7–10, 19ob.
26. GBUTO/GAGT, I-733.1.49, 5–5ob, 19–21. On money for Dmitry: HL/Sokolov, Vol. VII: testimony of B. N. Solovyov, 29 December 1919.
27. Rasputin, "Dnevnik," 541.
28. Details from the investigatory file: GBUTO/GAGT, I-774.1.1. Raevsky did both a large, full-body portrait, and a smaller drawing that the artist considered the better, more successful of the two works. For some reason the smaller work was not shown at the 1912 exhibition. Both works have been lost. See: OR/RNB, 1000.1975.22, 26ob.
29. HL/Sokolov, Vol. VII: testimony of M. Solovyova (Rasputina), undated; and of B. N. Solovyov, 29 and 31 December 1919; FN, 328–29.
30. Vyrubova, *Stranitsy*, 119; Alfer'ev, *Pis'ma*, 191.
31. *KVD*, 521–22; Alfer'ev, *Pis'ma*, 187–88.
32. RRR, 175–83.
33. Markow, *Wie*, 169; RRR, 185–94.
34. Alfer'ev, *Pis'ma*, 242–43, 253, 260–61, 263; M. Rasputin, "Dnevnik," 529n17, 531n20; *KVD*, 523; FN, 319; Markov, *Pokinutaia*, 314; *Poslednie dnevniki*, 135–40.
35. Warth, *Nicholas II*, 262.
36. Markov, *Pokinutaia*, 303.
37. Markow, *Wie*, 206–207. Solovyov returned to Tobolsk in early March: *Poslednie dnevniki*, 163.
38. M. Rasputin, "Dnevnik," 530–31. All dates in her diary are OS.
39. Alfer'ev, *Pis'ma*, 321; Markow, *Wie*, 159; *Poslednie dnevniki*, 177.
40. M. Rasputin, "Dnevnik," 537–39. Some of the dates here are contradicted by those in HL/Sokolov, Vol. VII, although the general outline of events is in agreement.
41. LP, 616; *KVD*, 527; *Poslednie dnevniki*, 195. NB: 27 April (NS).
42. *KVD*, 528. Maria's sketch in RRR, between pp. 64–65.
43. Warth, *Nicholas II*, 263. Dates here are now NS.

44. Steinberg, *Fall*, 305; M. Rasputin, "Dnevnik," 640.

45. Preston, *Before the Curtain*, 105.

46. KVD, 526, 529–32; PZ, 6; Sokolov, *Ubiistvo*, 346; Diterikhs, *Ubiistvo*, 1:32, 188.

47. Sokolov, *Ubiistvo*, 270–71; and photograph No. 119; Diterikhs, *Ubiistvo*, 1:212.

48. HL/Sokolov, Vol. I: Descriptions dated 11, 12, 14 August 1918; Vol. III: Protocol for 15–25 August 1919; Vol. IV: Protocols for 23 January 1919; 19 May 1919.

Epilogue

1. VR, 718–68; FN, 500–501; Izmozik, *Zhandarmy*, 455.

2. BA, Z. A. Rzhevskaia, Ms., 1965; Globachev, *Pravda*, 87–88; SML, Spiridovich Papers, No. 359, 14/5; Savchenko, *Avantiuristy*, 145–47; Faitel'berg-Blank, *Odessa*, 135–37.

3. Mramornov, *Deiatel'nost'*, 327–33; Alfer'ev, *Pis'ma*, 322; M. Rasputin, "Dnevnik," 548; VR, 741.

4. GATO, 198.1.7, 9, 34, 73; GATO, 198.1.87, 10ob–11; GBUTO/GAGT, R-1042.3.59, 275ob, 286ob; VR, 752–53; Smirnov, *Neizvestnoe*, 96–99. The sources on the final years of the Rasputin family are at times contradictory.

5. Smirnov, *Neizvestnoe*, 94–96. With caution also RRR, 201–22; FR, 235. Radzinsky makes the bizarre claim Varvara lived in Leningrad into the 1960s. See RR, 492.

6. For an overview of the controversy, see VR, 729–36. Those arguing he was an agent: Hall, *Little Mother*, 296–97; YLS, 297; Sokolov, *Ubiistvo*, 114–18, 133–34. And those against: Markov, *Pokinutaia*, 473–74, 477, 485; FN, 329–31; Steinberg, *Fall*, 181–82. The evidence gathered by Sokolov suggests the charges against Solovyov were baseless. See: HL/Sokolov, Vol. 1: S. Y. Sedov; Vol. III: S. G. Loginov; Vol. VII: E. K. Loginov; K. S. Melnik; V. S. Botkin; B. N. Solovyov; M. Y. Solovyova (Rasputina).

7. HL/Sokolov, documents in Vol. VII. On Sharaban: Bisher, *White Terror*, 152; RRR, 185–94.

8. SML, Spiridovich Papers, Box 16, Folder 2. Newspaper clipping; Krarup, *42 Aar*, 141.

9. *Daily Mirror*, 11 January 1933, p. 17; 15 December 1934, p. 1.

10. *New York Times*, 3 April 1936, p. 16; 1 June 1946, p. 4.

11. HIA, A. Tarsaidze, Box 16, Folder 16–18. Obituary clipping.

12. SML, Spiridovich Papers, Box 16, Folder 1; VR, 762–63.

13. Perry, *Flight*, 256–61, 299–305.

14. Marie, *Princess*, 20–21, 69, 102–103, 282.

15. *Collection du Prince*, 72.

16. Marie, *Princess*, 103–104.
17. SML, Spiridovich Papers, Box 14, folder 6. Clipping from *Dni*, 10, 11 January 1928; *New York Times*, 26 January 1928, p. 9; 18 October 1928, p. 16.
18. *The Times*, 29 February 1932, p. 11; 25, 28 November 1932, p. 19.
19. Napley, *Rasputin*, 196–97.
20. *The Times*, 9 November 1965, p. 12; *New York Times*, 21 October 1965, p. 12.
21. FR, 236.
22. NA, FO 371/3338, Nos. 136473, 140545, 144465, 14506, 145796.
23. *New York Times*, 23 September 1918, p. 3; *New York Times Current History*, 17:306–307; FR, 236.
24. *New York Times*, 5 February 1931, p. 10.
25. VR, 756–78.
26. VR, 765–66; "Russkii fashist," Radio Svoboda.
27. Iliodor, *Velikaia stalingradskaia*, 53, 69.
28. *New York Times*, 12 June 1922, p. 3; Iliodor, "Pis'mo"; idem, *Pamiatka*, 5–6; idem, *Velikaia stalingradskaia*, 75–77; idem, "The Mystery"; Dixon, "'Mad Monk',", 411; Shulgin, *Years*, 78n; VR, 759–60.
29. Iliodor, *Velikaia stalingradskaia*, 56–57, 75–77; *New York Times*, 12 December 1923, p. 10; 20 January 1924, p. 58.
30. *New York Times*, 19 June 1936, p. 23.
31. Iliodor, *Pamiatka*, 5–6.
32. Dixon, "'Mad Monk',", 413; press photograph of Serge Trufanoff with caption, Keystone View Co. of NY, author's collection.
33. VR, 412; Kulegin, *Kto ubil*, 9; FStr, 264–70.
34. GARF 124. 69. 529; RR, 499.
35. FDNO, 246 and n11.
36. VR, 760–61.
37. Krarup, *42 Aar*, 125–29.
38. Massie, *Romanovs*, 6–8; Steinberg, *Fall*, 354; Sokolov, *Ubiistvo*, 270–71; and photograph No. 119. On Four Brothers, Diterikhs, *Ubiistvo*, 1:212.

Index